Teacher's Wraparound Edition

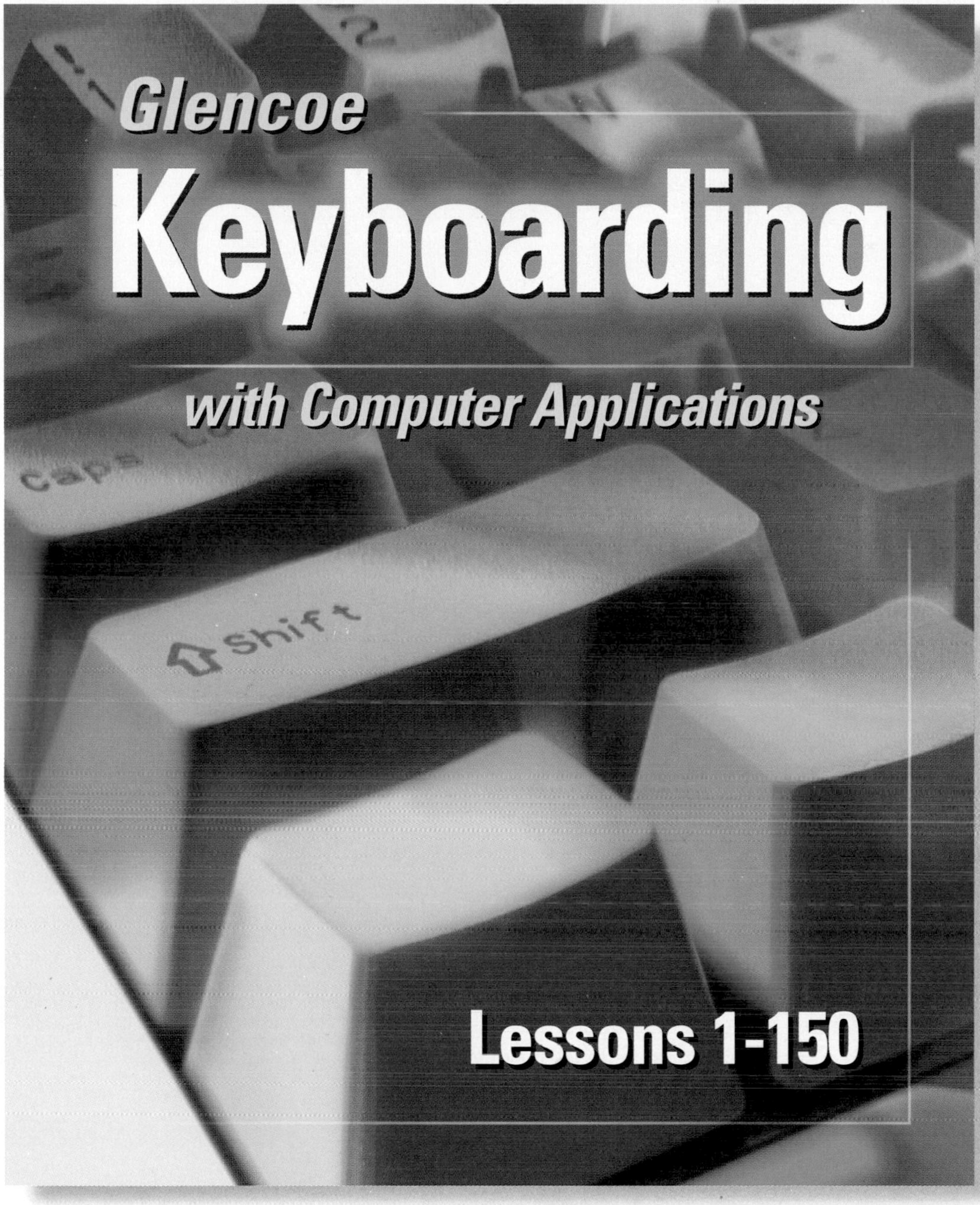

Glencoe

Keyboarding

with Computer Applications

Lessons 1-150

Jack E. Johnson, Ph.D.
Director of Business Education
Department of Management
and Business Systems
State University of West Georgia
Carrollton, Georgia

Judith Chiri-Mulkey
Adjunct Teacher
Department of Computer
Information Systems
Pikes Peak Community College
Colorado Springs, Colorado

Delores Sykes Cotton
Supervisor, Business Education
Detroit Public Schools
Detroit, Michigan

Carole G. Stanley, M.Ed.
Keyboarding/Technology Teacher
Pewitt Junior High School
Omaha, Texas

Glencoe
McGraw-Hill

New York, New York
Columbus, Ohio
Woodland Hills, California
Peoria, Illinois

Glencoe/McGraw-Hill

A Division of The McGraw-Hill Companies

Glencoe Keyboarding With Computer Applications
Teacher's Wraparound Edition

Send all inquiries to:

Glencoe/McGraw-Hill
936 Eastwind Drive
Westerville, OH 43081

ISBN 0-02-804171-2 (Student Edition, Lessons 1–150)
ISBN 0-02-804172-0 (Student Edition, Lessons 1–80)
ISBN 0-02-804184-4 (Teacher's Wraparound Edition)

2 3 4 5 6 7 8 9 0 083 05 04 03 02 01 00

REVIEWERS

Judy Senden
West High School
Anchorage, AK

Betty Gross Malone
Jackson-Olin High School
Birmingham, AL

Debra Scott
Arkansas High School
Texarkana, AR

Donna Green
Mingus Union High School
Cottonwood, AZ

Sue Julian
El Molino High School
Forestville, CA

Dr. Rita Schnittgrund
Denver West High School
Denver, CO

Janyce Wininger
Stafford High School
Stafford Spring, CT

Marjorie Stewart
Caesar Rodney High School
Camden Wyoming, DE

Patricia McCollough
Fort Walton Beach High School
Fort Walton Beach, FL

Barbara Williams-Mims
Columbus High School
Columbus, GA

Patricia J. Pierce
Linn-Mar High School
Marion, IA

Dan Petersen
State Division of Vocational Education
Business and Office Technology Education
Boise, ID

Gerrie L. Trossman
Good Counsel High School
Chicago, IL

Barbara Coleman
Salina High School South
Salina, KS

N. Jean Andrada
Pleasure Ridge High School
Louisville, KY

Terry Smith
Alcee Fortier High School
New Orleans, LA

Betsy Nilsen
Cape Elizabeth High School
Cape Elizabeth, ME

Kathy Jensen
Mankato West High School
Mankato, MN

Vera Mitchell
Forest Hill High School
Jackson, MS

Judy W. Cox
J. H. Rose High School
Greenville, NC

Nancy Stevens
Manteo High School
Manteo, NC

Mike Opdahl
Larimore High School
Larimore, ND

Betty Sup
Creighton Preparatory School
Omaha, NE

Maria Alvarez
Farmington High School
Farmington, NH

Sandra M. Richardson
Life Center Academy
Burlington, NJ

Bernadine Elmore
New Mexico Military Institution
Roswell, NM

Leesa Lyman
Roy Martin School
Las Vegas, NV

Lorraine Harrison
HS for Arts and Business
Corona, NY

Michael Prandy
John Marshall High School
Oklahoma City, OK

Sherri Sollars
Westview High School
Portland, OR

Susan Howe
Chariho Regional High School
Wood River Junction, RI

Patricia B. Hook
Airport High School
West Columbia, SC

Jane Bradfield
O'Gorman High School
Sioux Falls, SD

Edna Earle Bond
Central High School
Memphis, TN

Susan Shirey
Grand Prairie High School
Grand Prairie, TX

Patricia Kay Fordham
Central High School
Salt Lake City, UT

Patricia C. Smith
Kennewick High School
Kennewick, WA

Gail Springsteen
Waupaca High School
Waupaca, WI

Nancy Byrd
Morgantown High School
Morgantown, WV

CONTENTS

Course Overview

Introduction

Today's students have grown up using computers. They have played computer games, completed CD-ROM educational programs related to courses taken in earlier grades, and used electronic encyclopedias for preparing term papers. Many of them have seen their parents work with computers in home-based businesses or for personal uses such as maintaining the family mailing list for holiday greetings, keeping files of favorite recipes, tracking family financial records, and preparing personal correspondence.

With the popularity of the Internet and e-mail, families communicate inexpensively and frequently with relatives and friends all over the world. Pen pal takes on a whole new meaning in this day of e-mail messages. Individuals today have mastered the use of the Internet to perform banking transactions, file income tax returns, purchase items—from books and music to exercise equipment and, yes, even cars and homes. Families research and plan vacations, making all the arrangements on-line.

Today's students are even more computer savvy than many teachers because their because students were born into the computer age rather than having to adjust to it. The computer is second nature to many students. For that reason, learning to use the computer keyboard efficiently will be motivational and exciting to them.

Course Organization

The *Glencoe Keyboarding with Computer Applications* textbook is divided into eight units, the first seven of which contain 20 lessons each, with the last unit containing 10 lessons.

Unit 1 covers the alphabetic keyboard and the basic punctuation marks. Unit 2 covers the numeric and symbol keys, the numeric keypad, and an orientation to word processing. The 20 lessons in Unit 3 provides instruction and practice on documents such as reports, agendas, minutes of meetings, personal and business letters, envelopes, résumés, and application letters. Unit 4 covers letters with special features, tables, and reports with additional parts. These first 80 lessons provide students with

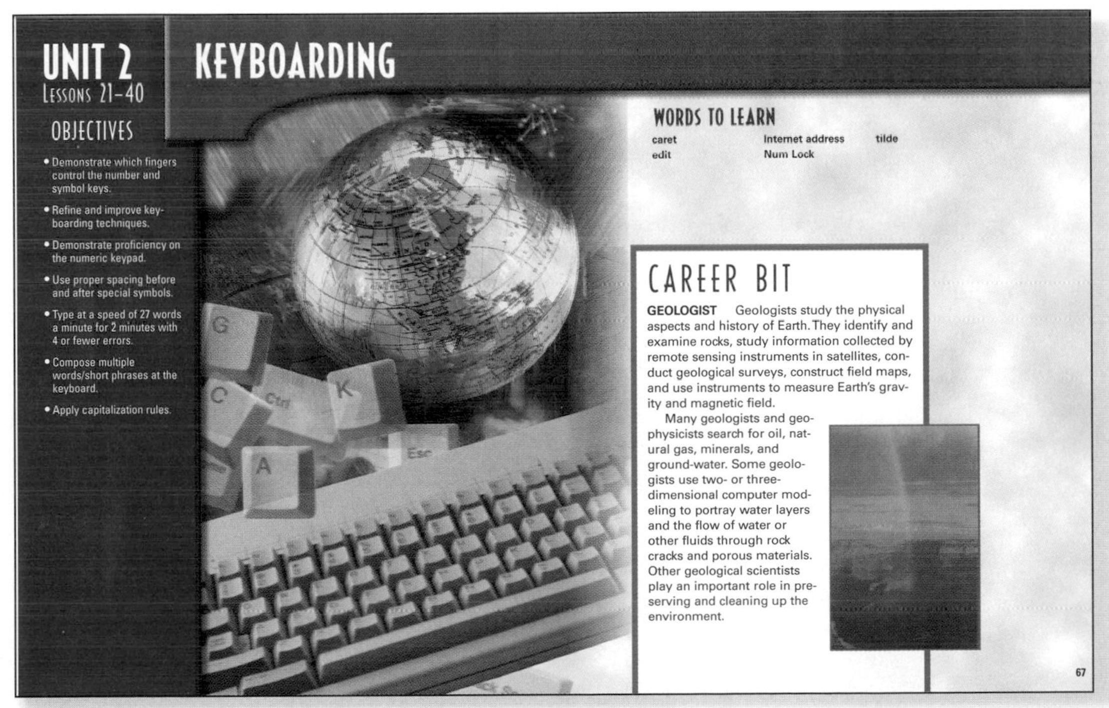

UNIT 2 KEYBOARDING

LESSONS 21–40

OBJECTIVES

- Demonstrate which fingers control the number and symbol keys.
- Refine and improve keyboarding techniques.
- Demonstrate proficiency on the numeric keypad.
- Use proper spacing before and after special symbols.
- Type at a speed of 27 words a minute for 2 minutes with 4 or fewer errors.
- Compose multiple words/short phrases at the keyboard.
- Apply capitalization rules.

WORDS TO LEARN

caret, edit, Internet address, Num Lock, tilde

CAREER BIT

GEOLOGIST Geologists study the physical aspects and history of Earth. They identify and examine rocks, study information collected by remote sensing instruments in satellites, conduct geological surveys, construct field maps, and use instruments to measure Earth's gravity and magnetic field.

Many geologists and geophysicists search for oil, natural gas, minerals, and ground-water. Some geologists use two- or three-dimensional computer modeling to portray water layers and the flow of water or other fluids through rock cracks and porous materials. Other geological scientists play an important role in preserving and cleaning up the environment.

67

an excellent coverage of most documents that they will need to prepare during the remainder of their formal education.

Unit 5 covers more advanced word processing documents—the merge feature, special table styles, calculations, international addresses, and other formats. The 20 lessons in Unit 6 cover desktop publishing tasks that enable the students to create promotional announcements, invitations, newsletters, letterhead stationery, text boxes, graphics, drawing, and other exciting documents.

Unit 7 deals with spreadsheets, covering such things as data entry, formatting values, formulas, calculations, sorting, charts and graphs, and special design features. Unit 8 contains 10 lessons dealing with database creation and maintenance.

Course Goals

The intent of *Glencoe Keyboarding with Computer Applications* is to give students keyboarding and computer skills that will serve them throughout their school years, in their personal lives, and in their careers. Even though computers and software programs will continue to improve, students will learn to use the computer keyboard more efficiently than if they use the "hunt and peck" system often used by people who have never had a keyboarding course.

Aaron Haupt

Specific student goals are provided at the beginning of each unit and each lesson. For average students, the goals at the end of the course are:

- To type at a rate of 40 words a minute for 5 minutes with no more than 5 errors.
- To apply basic language arts principles correctly while typing a variety of documents.
- To operate the computer and the software quickly and correctly.
- To type reports in a variety of formats.
- To type various kinds of business correspondence in a variety of formats.
- To prepare tables.
- To create desktop published documents.
- To learn how to navigate in and use a spreadsheet.
- To learn how to create and use a database.

As a result of this course—depending upon the units you cover in your course—your students will be able to use various software applications such as word processing, desktop publishing, spreadsheets, and databases. While learning these skills, your students will be applying them to documents, calculations, and communications that connect with their other curricular areas. This course will provide tools that will enable your students to perform better in their other courses.

Standards

The level of achievement in this course will depend upon the amount of time you have for the course and the number of units you are able to include in the course. Each unit opener and lesson opener provide suggested standards that you may use in evaluating your students. In addition, the booklet entitled *Grading and Evaluation,* which you will find in the Teacher's Classroom Resources package, will provide additional guidelines for evaluating your students. Timings are included throughout the Student Edition and in several Teacher's Classroom Resources package supplements. The timings in the Student Edition are scored by the courseware that is available for use in your keyboarding course. In addition, objective and production tests and their solutions are provided in the Teacher's Classroom Resources package.

Using the Teacher Management program, you may modify the grading standards for timings as well as for the production documents. You can determine the types of work you wish to evaluate and assign a weight or percentage to each type.

While the authors consider the speed and accuracy goals as realistic and achievable, you should consider these goals as suggestions. They may be modified as necessary based upon the amount of time you have in the course, the abilities of your students, and other factors that impact upon the students' achievement. Not only should your students be able to perform at the standards you establish for the course, they should acquire other valuable skills for their personal, academic, and career endeavors. They will learn to think more critically and creatively, evaluate the quality of their own work, recognize acceptable document formats, appreciate the relationships among the subjects they study, enjoy differences between them and their classmates, and communicate more effectively with the computer-literate population.

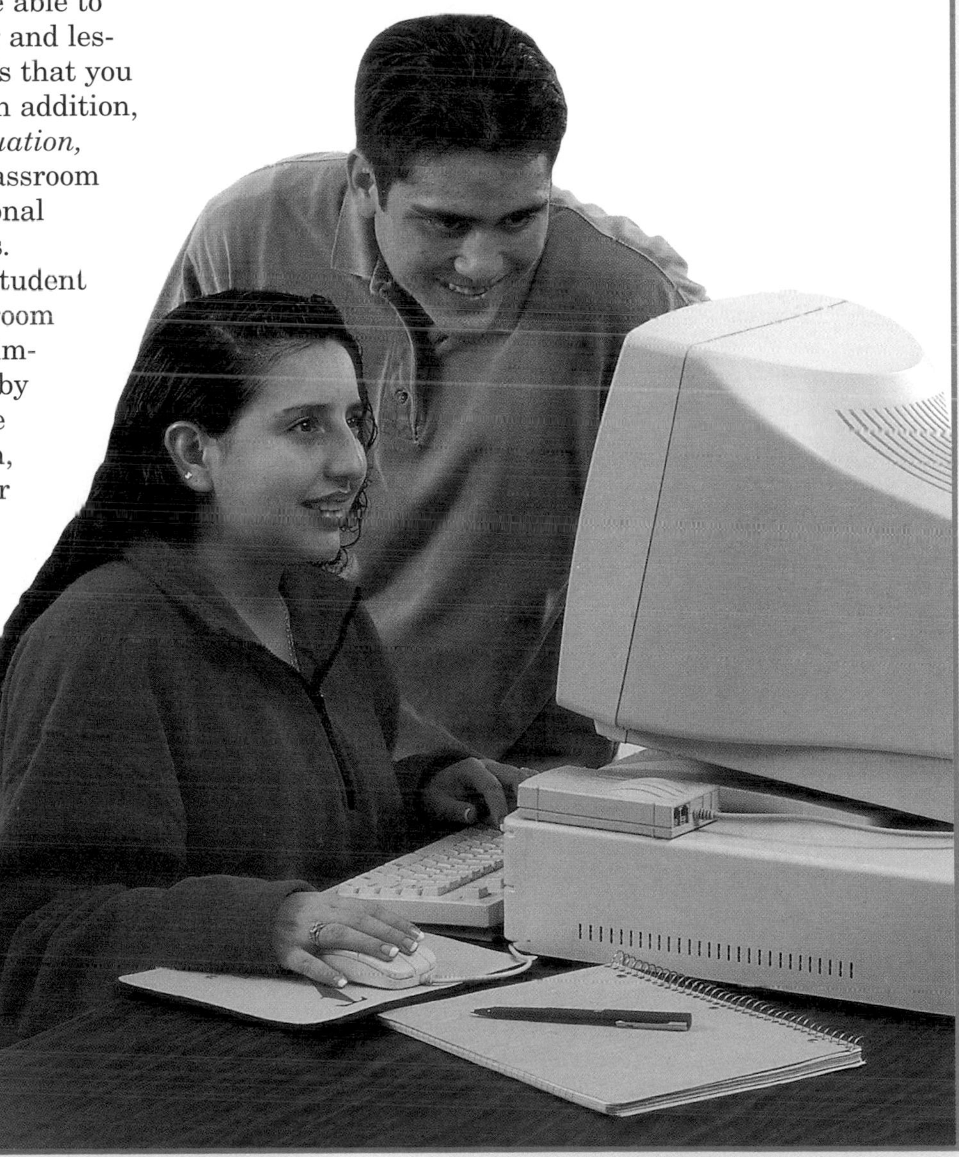

Geoff Butler

Features

The Teacher's Wraparound Edition (TWE) provides a wealth of teaching material to make your job easier. In addition to the four-step instructional plan discussed at the end of these TWE illustrations, the margins or wraparound part of the teacher's edition provides a companion for most of the special features in the Student Edition. For example, the *Journal Entry* feature in the Student Edition also has a *Journal Entry* feature in the TWE, which provides you with ideas for using the information for class discussion or for additional applications. This is true for all the Student Edition features. In addition, the TWE provides the following other instructional features:

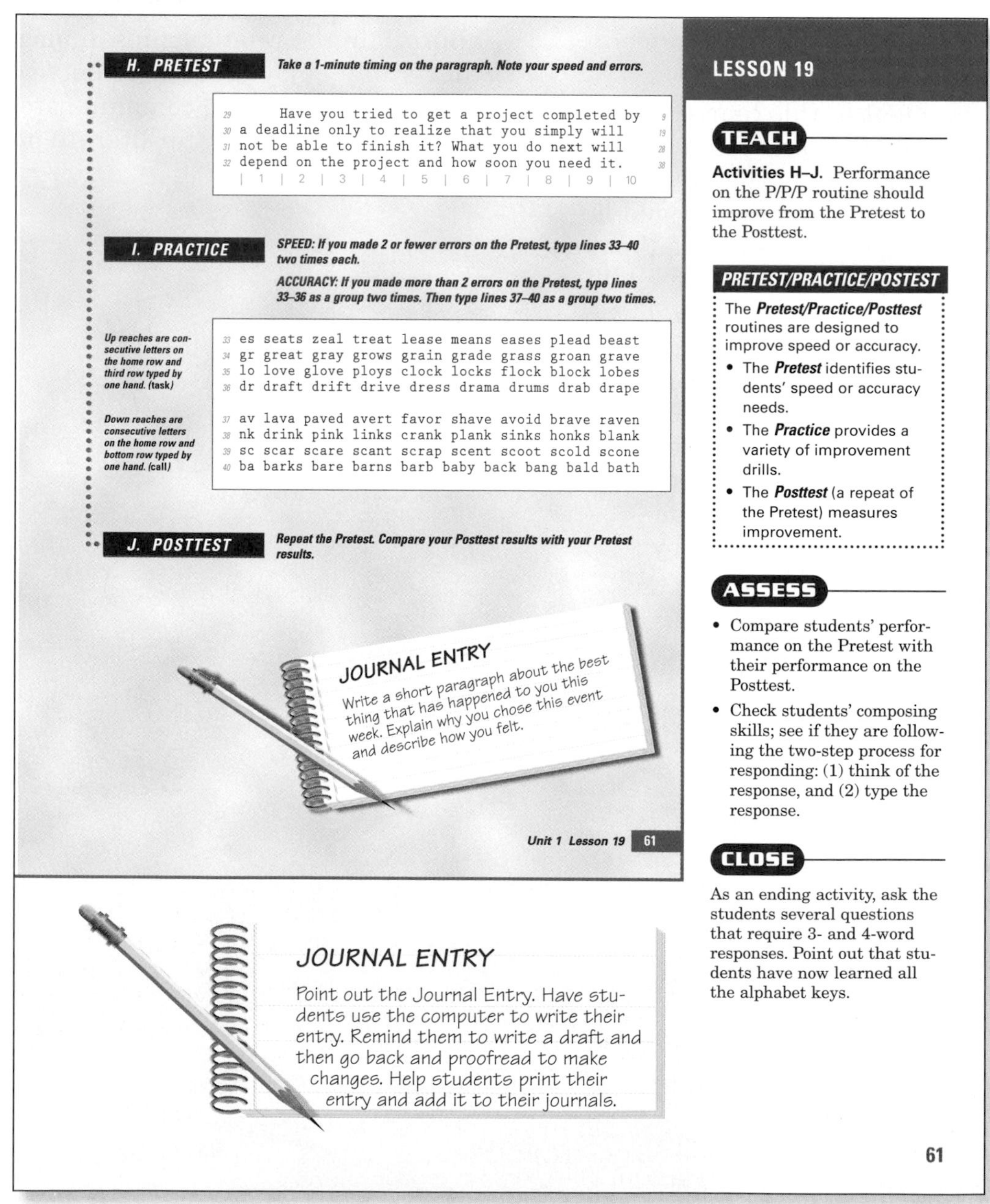

H. PRETEST *Take a 1-minute timing on the paragraph. Note your speed and errors.*

```
29      Have you tried to get a project completed by    9
30  a deadline only to realize that you simply will    19
31  not be able to finish it? What you do next will    28
32  depend on the project and how soon you need it.    38
    | 1 | 2 | 3 | 4 | 5 | 6 | 7 | 8 | 9 | 10
```

I. PRACTICE *SPEED: If you made 2 or fewer errors on the Pretest, type lines 33–40 two times each.*

ACCURACY: If you made more than 2 errors on the Pretest, type lines 33–36 as a group two times. Then type lines 37–40 as a group two times.

Up reaches are consecutive letters on the home row and third row typed by one hand. (task)

Down reaches are consecutive letters on the home row and bottom row typed by one hand. (call)

```
33 es seats zeal treat lease means eases plead beast
34 gr great gray grows grain grade grass groan grave
35 lo love glove ploys clock locks flock block lobes
36 dr draft drift drive dress drama drums drab drape

37 av lava paved avert favor shave avoid brave raven
38 nk drink pink links crank plank sinks honks blank
39 sc scar scare scant scrap scent scoot scold scone
40 ba barks bare barns barb baby back bang bald bath
```

J. POSTTEST *Repeat the Pretest. Compare your Posttest results with your Pretest results.*

JOURNAL ENTRY

Write a short paragraph about the best thing that has happened to you this week. Explain why you chose this event and describe how you felt.

Unit 1 Lesson 19 61

JOURNAL ENTRY

Point out the Journal Entry. Have students use the computer to write their entry. Remind them to write a draft and then go back and proofread to make changes. Help students print their entry and add it to their journals.

LESSON 19

TEACH

Activities H–J. Performance on the P/P/P routine should improve from the Pretest to the Posttest.

PRETEST/PRACTICE/POSTEST

The ***Pretest/Practice/Posttest*** routines are designed to improve speed or accuracy.

- The ***Pretest*** identifies students' speed or accuracy needs.
- The ***Practice*** provides a variety of improvement drills.
- The ***Posttest*** (a repeat of the Pretest) measures improvement.

ASSESS

- Compare students' performance on the Pretest with their performance on the Posttest.
- Check students' composing skills; see if they are following the two-step process for responding: (1) think of the response, and (2) type the response.

CLOSE

As an ending activity, ask the students several questions that require 3- and 4-word responses. Point out that students have now learned all the alphabet keys.

61

Bellringers are suggested activities for you to use to get students involved in the lesson at the very beginning of class while you take care of any classroom management activities such as taking attendance.

Extending the Content provides additional information that goes beyond the basics needed for completion of the course. This information will generally be of a "nice-to-know" nature that can be shared at your discretion and if time permits.

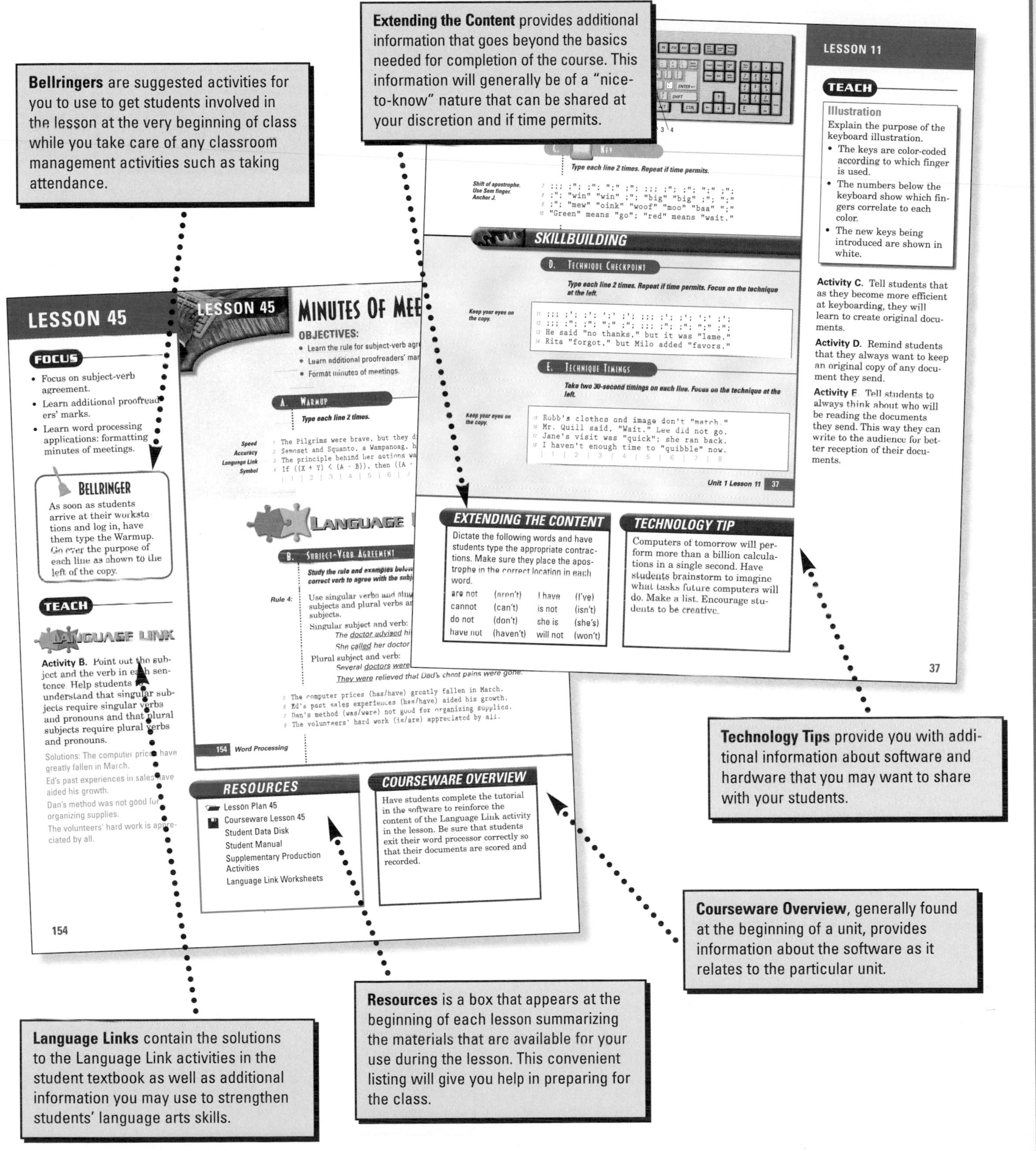

LESSON 45
FOCUS
• Focus on subject-verb agreement.
• Learn additional proofreaders' marks.
• Learn word processing applications: formatting minutes of meetings.
BELLRINGER
As soon as students arrive at their workstations and log in, have them type the Warmup. Go over the purpose of each line as shown to the left of the copy.
TEACH
LANGUAGE LINK
Activity B. Point out the subject and the verb in each sentence. Help students understand that singular subjects require singular verbs and pronouns and that plural subjects require plural verbs and pronouns.
Solutions: The computer prices have greatly fallen in March.
Ed's past experiences in sales have aided his growth.
Dan's method was not good for organizing supplies.
The volunteers' hard work is appreciated by all.
154
LESSON 45
MINUTES OF MEE
OBJECTIVES:
• Learn the rule for subject-verb agr
• Learn additional proofreaders' mar
• Format minutes of meetings.
A. WARMUP
Type each line 2 times.
B. SUBJECT-VERB AGREEMENT
154 Word Processing
RESOURCES
Lesson Plan 45
Courseware Lesson 45
Student Data Disk
Student Manual
Supplementary Production Activities
Language Link Worksheets
COURSEWARE OVERVIEW
Have students complete the tutorial in the software to reinforce the content of the Language Link activity in the lesson. Be sure that students exit their word processor correctly so that their documents are scored and recorded.
LESSON 11
TEACH
Illustration
Explain the purpose of the keyboard illustration.
• The keys are color-coded according to which finger is used.
• The numbers below the keyboard show which fingers correlate to each color.
• The new keys being introduced are shown in white.
Activity C. Tell students that as they become more efficient at keyboarding, they will learn to create original documents.
Activity D. Remind students that they always want to keep an original copy of any document they send.
Activity E. Tell students to always think about who will be reading the documents they send. This way they can write to the audience for better reception of their documents.
SKILLBUILDING
D. TECHNIQUE CHECKPOINT
E. TECHNIQUE TIMINGS
Unit 1 Lesson 11 37
EXTENDING THE CONTENT
Dictate the following words and have students type the appropriate contractions. Make sure they place the apostrophe in the correct location in each word.
are not (aren't) I have (I've)
cannot (can't) is not (isn't)
do not (don't) she is (she's)
have not (haven't) will not (won't)
TECHNOLOGY TIP
Computers of tomorrow will perform more than a billion calculations in a single second. Have students brainstorm to imagine what tasks future computers will do. Make a list. Encourage students to be creative.
37

Technology Tips provide you with additional information about software and hardware that you may want to share with your students.

Courseware Overview, generally found at the beginning of a unit, provides information about the software as it relates to the particular unit.

Language Links contain the solutions to the Language Link activities in the student textbook as well as additional information you may use to strengthen students' language arts skills.

Resources is a box that appears at the beginning of each lesson summarizing the materials that are available for your use during the lesson. This convenient listing will give you help in preparing for the class.

Features

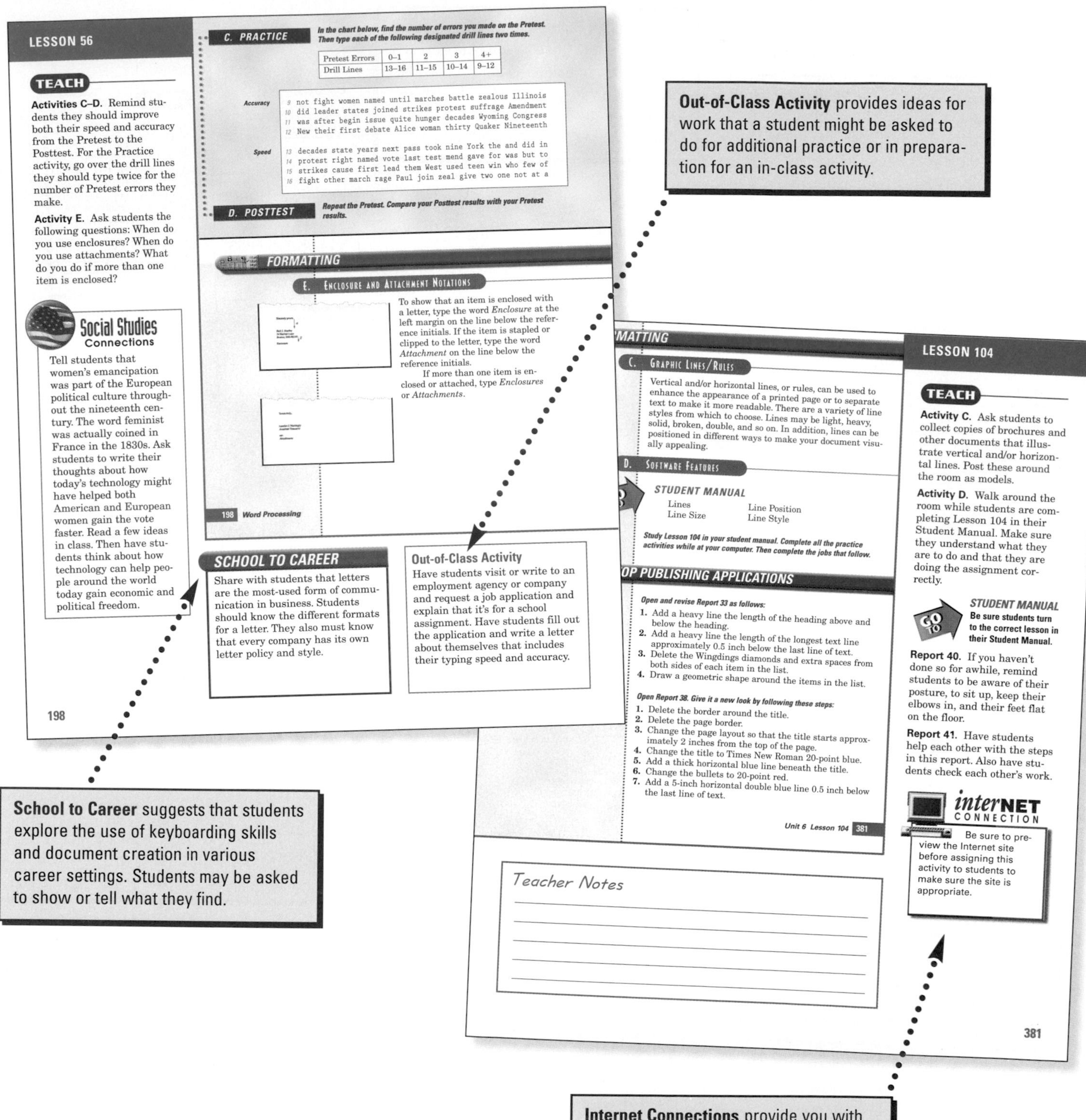

Out-of-Class Activity provides ideas for work that a student might be asked to do for additional practice or in preparation for an in-class activity.

School to Career suggests that students explore the use of keyboarding skills and document creation in various career settings. Students may be asked to show or tell what they find.

Internet Connections provide you with suggestions for using the Internet to supplement classroom activities and with URLs that you may want students to access for specific information relating to their daily lessons.

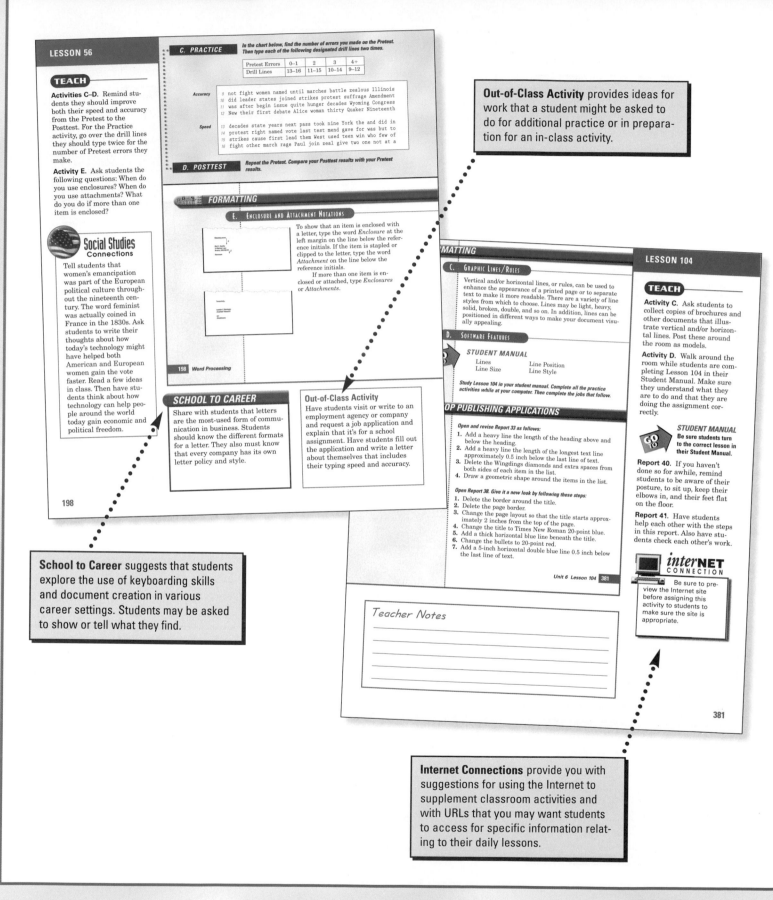

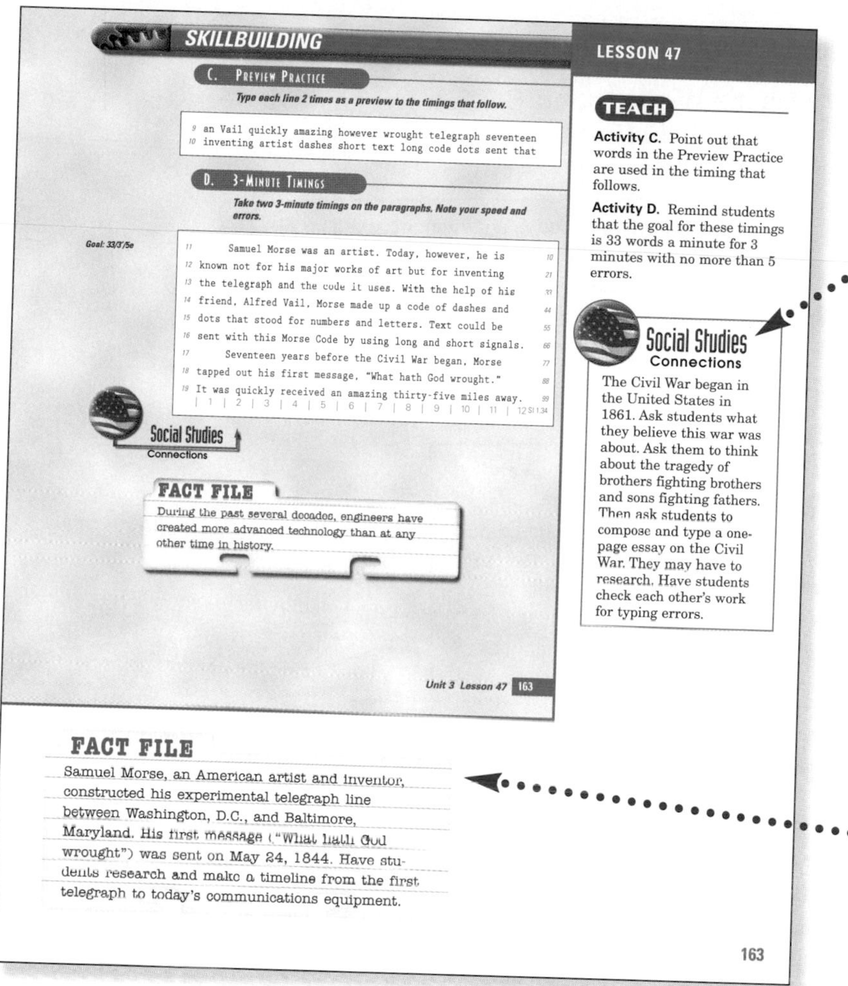

SKILLBUILDING

C. Preview Practice

Type each line 2 times as a preview to the timings that follow.

```
an Vail quickly amazing however wrought telegraph seventeen
inventing artist dashes short text long code dots sent that
```

D. 3-Minute Timings

Take two 3-minute timings on the paragraphs. Note your speed and errors.

Goal: 33/3'/5e

```
     Samuel Morse was an artist. Today, however, he is        10
known not for his major works of art but for inventing        21
the telegraph and the code it uses. With the help of his      33
friend, Alfred Vail, Morse made up a code of dashes and       44
dots that stood for numbers and letters. Text could be        55
sent with this Morse Code by using long and short signals.    66
     Seventeen years before the Civil War began, Morse        77
tapped out his first message, "What hath God wrought."        88
It was quickly received an amazing thirty-five miles away.    99
 | 1 | 2 | 3 | 4 | 5 | 6 | 7 | 8 | 9 | 10 | 11 | 12 SI 1.34
```

Social Studies Connections

FACT FILE

During the past several decades, engineers have created more advanced technology than at any other time in history.

Unit 3 Lesson 47 163

LESSON 47

TEACH

Activity C. Point out that words in the Preview Practice are used in the timing that follows.

Activity D. Remind students that the goal for these timings is 33 words a minute for 3 minutes with no more than 5 errors.

Social Studies Connections

The Civil War began in the United States in 1861. Ask students what they believe this war was about. Ask them to think about the tragedy of brothers fighting brothers and sons fighting fathers. Then ask students to compose and type a one-page essay on the Civil War. They may have to research. Have students check each other's work for typing errors.

FACT FILE

Samuel Morse, an American artist and inventor, constructed his experimental telegraph line between Washington, D.C., and Baltimore, Maryland. His first message ("What hath God wrought") was sent on May 24, 1844. Have students research and make a timeline from the first telegraph to today's communications equipment.

163

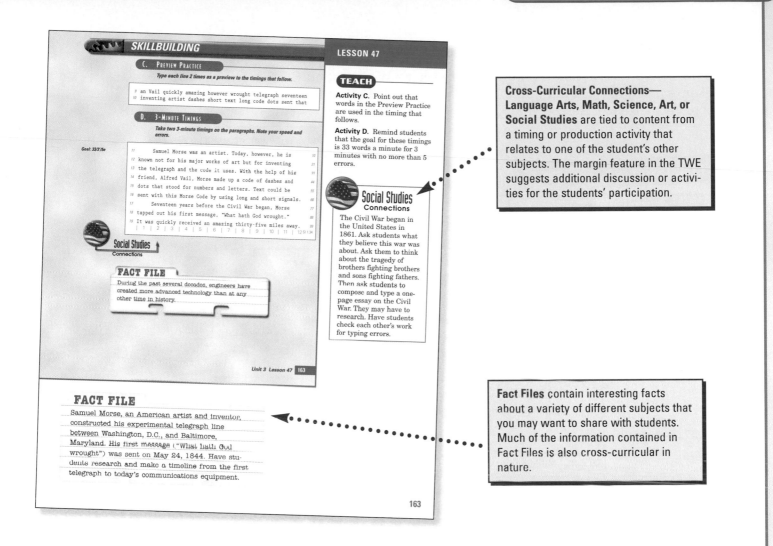

Cross-Curricular Connections—Language Arts, Math, Science, Art, or Social Studies are tied to content from a timing or production activity that relates to one of the student's other subjects. The margin feature in the TWE suggests additional discussion or activities for the students' participation.

Fact Files contain interesting facts about a variety of different subjects that you may want to share with students. Much of the information contained in Fact Files is also cross-curricular in nature.

Unit Organizer is a two-page spread that summarizes the content of the unit. The grid provides the focus for each lesson as well as a listing of the following items with their page numbers: special features, skillbuilding material, Pretest/Practice/Posttest exercises, Language Links, documents for each lesson, and GO TO activities. The Unit Resource Manager is a box listing all materials available for the unit, including courseware and Teacher Classroom Resources supplements. The Assessment and Evaluation box shows a list of all the materials available for assessing the students' progress, and the SCANS Competencies box relates the unit content to SCANS.

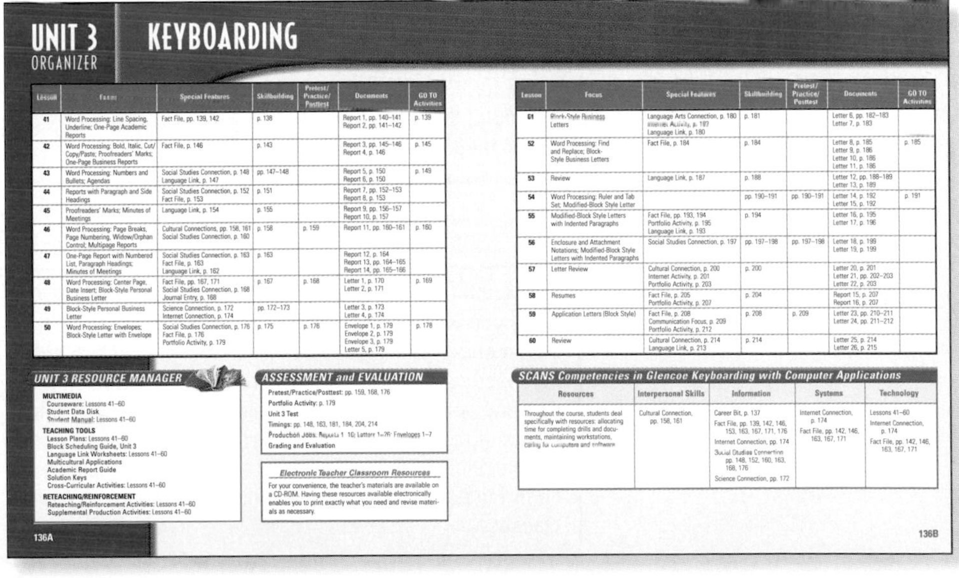

UNIT 3 ORGANIZER — KEYBOARDING

Lesson	Focus	Special Features	Skillbuilding	Pretest/ Practice/ Posttest	Documents	GO TO Activities
41	Word Processing: Line Spacing, Underline; One-Page Academic Reports	Fact File, pp. 139, 142	p. 138		Report 1, pp. 140–141 Report 2, pp. 141–142	p. 139
42	Word Processing: Bold, Italic, Cut/Copy/Paste; Proofreaders' Marks; One-Page Business Reports	Fact File, p. 146	p. 143		Report 3, pp. 145–146 Report 4, p. 146	p. 145
43	Word Processing: Numbers and Bullets; Agendas	Social Studies Connection, p. 148 Language Link, p. 147	pp. 147–148		Report 5, p. 150 Report 6, p. 150	p. 149
44	Reports with Paragraph and Side Headings	Social Studies Connection, p. 152 Fact File, p. 153	p. 151		Report 7, pp. 152–153 Report 8, p. 153	
45	Proofreaders' Marks; Minutes of Meetings	Language Link, p. 154	p. 155		Report 9, pp. 156–157 Report 10, p. 157	
46	Word Processing: Page Breaks, Page Numbering, Widow/Orphan Control; Multipage Reports	Cultural Connections, pp. 158, 161 Social Studies Connection, p. 160	p. 158	p. 159	Report 11, pp. 160–161	p. 160
47	One-Page Report with Numbered List, Paragraph Headings; Minutes of Meetings	Social Studies Connection, p. 163 Fact File, p. 163 Language Link, p. 162	p. 163		Report 12, p. 164 Report 13, pp. 164–165 Report 14, pp. 165–166	
48	Word Processing: Center Page, Date Insert; Block-Style Personal Business Letter	Fact File, pp. 167, 171 Social Studies Connection, p. 168 Journal Entry, p. 168	p. 167	p. 168	Letter 1, p. 170 Letter 2, p. 171	p. 169
49	Block-Style Personal Business Letter	Science Connection, p. 172 Internet Connection, p. 174	pp. 172–173		Letter 3, p. 173 Letter 4, p. 174	
50	Word Processing: Envelopes; Block-Style Letter with Envelope	Social Studies Connection, p. 176 Fact File, p. 176 Portfolio Activity, p. 179	p. 175	p. 176	Envelope 1, p. 179 Envelope 2, p. 179 Envelope 3, p. 179 Letter 5, p. 179	p. 178
51	Block-Style Business Letters	Language Arts Connection, p. 180 Internet Activity, p. 197 Language Link, p. 180	p. 181		Letter 6, pp. 182–183 Letter 7, p. 183	
52	Word Processing: Find and Replace; Block-Style Business Letters	Fact File, p. 184	p. 184		Letter 8, p. 185 Letter 9, p. 186 Letter 10, p. 186 Letter 11, p. 186	p. 185
53	Review	Language Link, p. 187	p. 188		Letter 12, pp. 188–189 Letter 13, p. 189	
54	Word Processing: Ruler and Tab Set; Modified-Block Style Letter		pp. 190–191	pp. 190–191	Letter 14, p. 192 Letter 15, p. 192	p. 191
55	Modified-Block Style Letters with Indented Paragraphs	Fact File, pp. 193, 194 Portfolio Activity, p. 195 Language Link, p. 193	p. 194		Letter 16, p. 195 Letter 17, p. 196	
56	Enclosure and Attachment Notations; Modified-Block Style Letters with Indented Paragraphs	Social Studies Connection, p. 197	pp. 197–198	pp. 197–198	Letter 18, p. 199 Letter 19, p. 199	
57	Letter Review	Cultural Connection, p. 200 Internet Activity, p. 201 Portfolio Activity, p. 203	p. 200		Letter 20, p. 201 Letter 21, pp. 202–203 Letter 22, p. 203	
58	Resumes	Fact File, p. 205 Portfolio Activity, p. 207	p. 204		Report 15, p. 207 Report 16, p. 207	
59	Application Letters (Block Style)	Fact File, p. 208 Communication Focus, p. 209 Portfolio Activity, p. 212	p. 208	p. 209	Letter 23, pp. 210–211 Letter 24, pp. 211–212	
60	Review	Cultural Connection, p. 214 Language Link, p. 213	p. 214		Letter 25, p. 214 Letter 26, p. 215	

UNIT 3 RESOURCE MANAGER

MULTIMEDIA
Courseware: Lessons 41–60
Student Data Disk
Student Manual: Lessons 41–60

TEACHING TOOLS
Lesson Plans: Lessons 41–60
Block Scheduling Guide, Unit 3
Language Link Worksheets: Lessons 41–60
Multicultural Applications
Academic Report Guide
Solution Keys
Cross-Curricular Activities: Lessons 41–60

RETEACHING/REINFORCEMENT
Reteaching/Reinforcement Activities: Lessons 41–60
Supplemental Production Activities: Lessons 41–60

ASSESSMENT and EVALUATION

Pretest/Practice/Posttest: pp. 159, 168, 176
Portfolio Activity: p. 179
Unit 3 Test
Timings: pp. 148, 163, 181, 184, 204, 214
Production Jobs: Reports 1–10; Letters 1–26; Envelopes 1–7
Grading and Evaluation

Electronic Teacher Classroom Resources

For your convenience, the teacher's materials are available on a CD-ROM. Having these resources available electronically enables you to print exactly what you need and revise materials as necessary.

SCANS Competencies in Glencoe Keyboarding with Computer Applications

Resources	Interpersonal Skills	Information	Systems	Technology
Throughout the course, students deal specifically with resources: allocating time for completing drills and documents, maintaining workstations, caring for computers and software	Cultural Connection, pp. 158, 161	Career Bit, p. 137 Fact File, pp. 139, 142, 146, 153, 163, 167, 171, 176 Internet Connection, pp. 174 Social Studies Connection pp. 148, 152, 160, 163, 168, 176 Science Connection, pp. 172	Internet Connection, p. 174 Fact File, pp. 142, 146, 163, 167, 171	Lessons 41–60 Internet Connection, p. 174 Fact File, pp. 142, 146, 163, 167, 171

136A 136B

Four-Step Instructional Plan

The four-step instructional plan in the Teacher's Wraparound Edition lessons presents a sound teaching guide for each lesson, including these four essential steps: Focus, Teach, Assess, and Close.

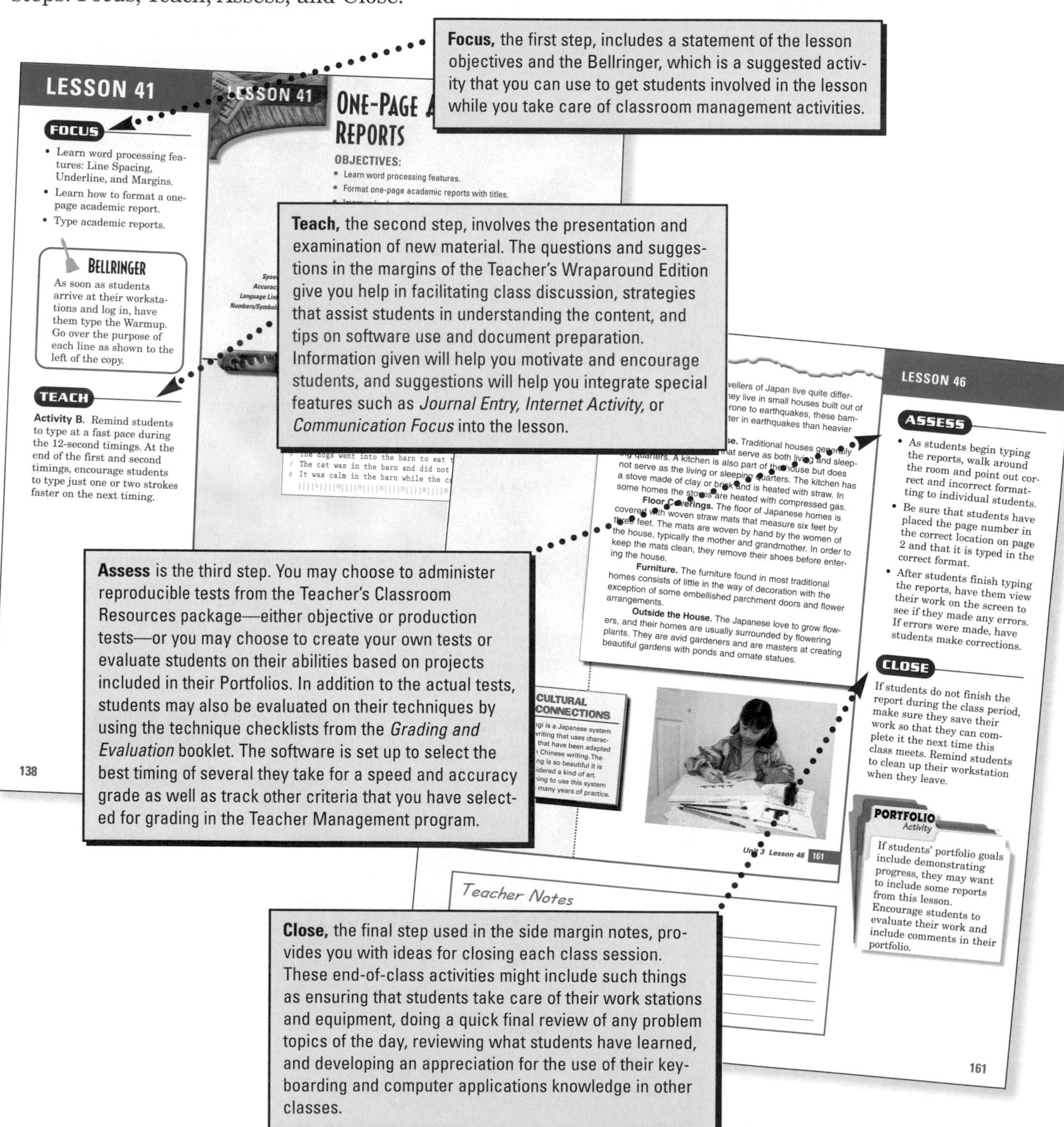

Focus, the first step, includes a statement of the lesson objectives and the Bellringer, which is a suggested activity that you can use to get students involved in the lesson while you take care of classroom management activities.

Teach, the second step, involves the presentation and examination of new material. The questions and suggestions in the margins of the Teacher's Wraparound Edition give you help in facilitating class discussion, strategies that assist students in understanding the content, and tips on software use and document preparation. Information given will help you motivate and encourage students, and suggestions will help you integrate special features such as *Journal Entry, Internet Activity,* or *Communication Focus* into the lesson.

Assess is the third step. You may choose to administer reproducible tests from the Teacher's Classroom Resources package—either objective or production tests—or you may choose to create your own tests or evaluate students on their abilities based on projects included in their Portfolios. In addition to the actual tests, students may also be evaluated on their techniques by using the technique checklists from the *Grading and Evaluation* booklet. The software is set up to select the best timing of several they take for a speed and accuracy grade as well as track other criteria that you have selected for grading in the Teacher Management program.

Close, the final step used in the side margin notes, provides you with ideas for closing each class session. These end-of-class activities might include such things as ensuring that students take care of their work stations and equipment, doing a quick final review of any problem topics of the day, reviewing what students have learned, and developing an appreciation for the use of their keyboarding and computer applications knowledge in other classes.

Program Resources

Student Textbooks

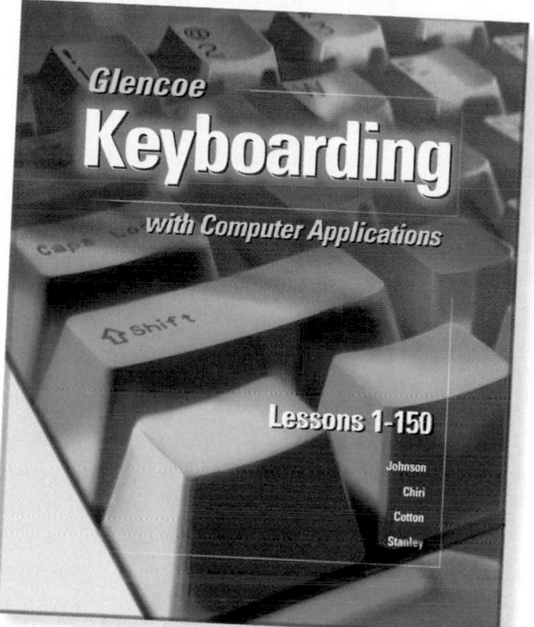

The Student Edition of the textbook is available in two versions: the Lessons 1–80 text for a one-semester course and the Lessons 1–150 text for a full-year course. Both versions are generic in that they do not depend upon a specific software package. Lessons 1–80 cover the basic keyboarding instruction, including number and symbol keys as well as the numeric keypad and all the basic word processing lessons. The additional 70 lessons in the complete book contain more advanced word processing production problems, desktop publishing, spreadsheets, and database instruction.

Student Manuals

Three versions of the student manuals have been developed for use with *Glencoe Keyboarding with Computer Applications.* Other student manuals may be added to the program as commercial soft-ware companies introduce new software versions. The current manuals are based upon the following software platforms:

- Microsoft Office Professional 97
- Corel WordPerfect 8 Professional Suite
- Microsoft Works 4.5

Each student manual provides step-by-step instructions for using the software features introduced in each lesson. Practice documents are provided to give the students clear understanding of the steps involved. The *GO TO* icon in the Student Edition of the textbook identifies points in each lesson where the student should refer to the student manual for software instruction. You will need to be sure that your students have the correct manual to use depending upon the software used in your classroom or lab.

If you are using software other than these three versions, your students will need to refer to the software manual that accompanies your software. You may also need to modify the names used to describe those functions in the Software Features activity to correlate to the names used in your specific software package.

Simulations

Two simulations are available for use with *Glencoe Keyboarding with Computer Applications.*

Desktop Publishing Simulation: Global Marketing Services This is a 15- to 20-hour simulation that provides students with an opportunity to demonstrate their keyboarding proficiency as well as their ability to use the desktop publishing features of their software. While working through this simulation, students will use their best judgment to create attractive, well-designed documents and at the same time learn what it means to be responsible, productive employees for this international company. They will use interpersonal skills, manage resources, process information, and apply thinking skills to perform effectively. The simulation is designed to be used after students complete Lesson 100 of *Glencoe Keyboarding with Computer Applications* or the equivalent instruction.

Integrated Office Simulation: Synchronized Sounds, Inc. This is a 15- to 20-hour capstone simulation based upon students' working in a music company. An introduction to the company, an explanation of the student's role, and a procedures manual will provide the orientation for completion of a variety of activities that require the use of word processing, desktop publishing, spreadsheet, and database skills. The skills will be integrated where possible; for example, the student may add a spreadsheet graph to a report and use a database to prepare labels for a mailing. Other skills required will be setting priorities, making decisions, organizing files, tracking time, and using good judgment. The simulation will provide "real" work experience for the student.

Courseware

The courseware that accompanies *Glencoe Keyboarding with Computer Applications* provides an exciting instructional strategy for learning the proper key reaches and manipulation of the computer keyboard. The software guides students through every activity in the textbook including learning new keys and completing production activities. New-key reaches are effectively demonstrated using "hand" animations to show proper keystroke techniques. Timing speed and accuracy are automatically computed. Most production work is scored.

Individual lessons may be accessed by selecting the lesson from a special menu that simulates a CD-ROM player. In addition to being able to access individual skillbuilding activities through the graphical lesson menu, students will also be able to access them from a separate Skillbuilding menu. This is also true of the Language Link activities, which may be accessed through an individual lesson or through the separate Language Link menu. A student's data files may be stored on the student data disk, on a local hard-disk drive, or on a network drive.

The software that accompanies *Glencoe Keyboarding with Computer Applications* practically eliminates the need to check papers in the traditional way. The software checks keystrokes, identifies errors, and counts them; this is true for both timings and word processing production work.

Link to Commercial Software For the production activities, the software for *Glencoe Keyboarding with Computer Applications* is designed to link to Microsoft Office 97 Professional or to Corel Professional Suite 8. This link will facilitate the students' completion of word processing, desktop publishing, spreadsheet, and database applications. Students will not need to change disks as they move from skill-building to production work. Student manuals are referenced by GO TO notations in the Student Edition to let students know what software features to study in the manuals. In addition to Microsoft Office 97 and the Corel Professional Suite, a manual is also available to instruct the students on the use of Microsoft Works 4.5.

Teacher Management Program The Teacher Management Program which is included in the software enables you to create new classes, add or delete students, transfer students from one class to another, view and print student reports, establish grading parameters, and set options. Some of the options that you can modify are whether or not

- students may edit drills and timings.
- the tennis game is enabled.
- one or two spaces will be used after end of sentence punctuation and after colons (one space is the default).

You will also be able to determine the grading criteria you will use and the percentage of the total grade each individual criterion will count. You may change the default selection in the program and identify other grades that will be assigned. The Teacher Management Program tracks each student's grades and allows you to print reports.

Teacher's Classroom Resources

This box of teacher resources is available to you as an adopter of *Glencoe Keyboarding with Computer Applications.* It contains a variety of materials designed to help you teach your course. Once you have adopted the Student Edition of the textbook, you may photocopy pages from the following to use with your students:

Cross-Curricular Applications and Solutions

A selection of applications that relate to other courses taken by your students provide additional practice for students who may be interested in a specific area of study or students who may need additional challenge. This booklet contains the applications and their solutions.

Multicultural Applications and Solutions

This booklet contains copy about multicultural topics that will increase students' awareness of different cultures around the world. The activities may be used for timings of three to five minutes. In addition to the timings, additional production activities of a multicultural nature are provided with suggested solutions.

Reteaching and Reinforcement Activities

This booklet provides ideas for using a different approach to presenting the Student Edition material in the eight units. These ideas will assist you in providing students needing additional instruction an alternative way of looking at the material.

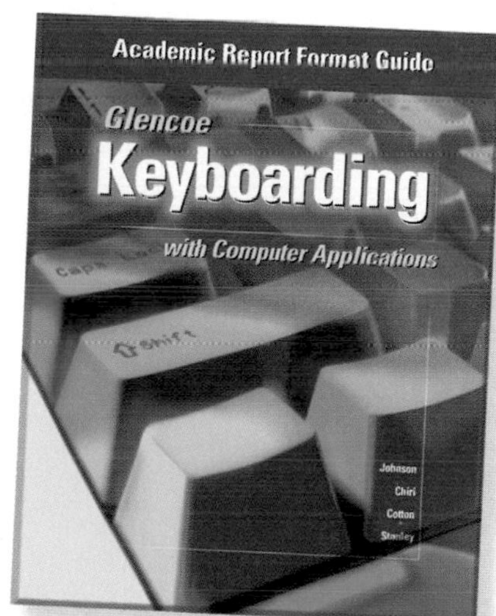

Academic Report Format Guide

This 16-page guide summarizes in a separate publication the instruction students will need to follow in preparing reports throughout their academic program. Guidelines are provided for spacing the body of the document as well as for title page, table of contents, notes and references, and other parts of a formal report.

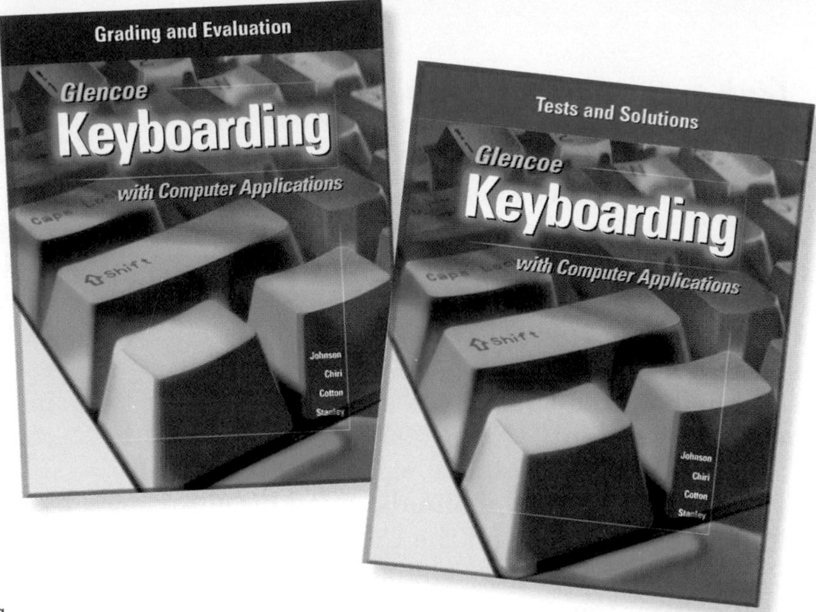

Grading and Evaluation

This booklet provides suggestions on evaluating your students on everything from techniques, timings, and production work of all types. Checklists are provided which you may photocopy to use for observing individual students' techniques at the keyboard.

Tests and Solutions

Objective test questions have been provided for each of the eight units within the Student Edition. In addition, performance or production tests are also provided. These tests give students the opportunity to demonstrate their ability to complete projects using unit instruction. Answers to the objective tests as well as suggested solutions for the production tests are provided at the end of this booklet.

Lesson Plans with Disk

These materials provide detailed plans for every lesson including supplementary activities. The disk will enable you to customize the plans for your class.

Block Scheduling Guide

This booklet contains suggestions for modifying lessons for shorter or longer class periods.

Language Link Worksheets and Solutions

This separate booklet reinforces the textbook activities and is ideal for out-of-class assignments to help strengthen students' language skills.

Supplementary Production Activities and Solutions

These are correlated to the textbook and provide additional production jobs for review, extra credit, or reinforcement.

Textbook Production Solutions

These are printed solutions to most production problems in the student text. Some problems are based upon original compositions by the students and will not have specific solutions. These printed solutions are ideal for checking the formats of word processed documents, which would not be checked by the software, and for checking the solutions to spreadsheet and database projects.

PowerPoint Slide Show

Use these illustrations of document formats as well as step-by-step instructional information for group presentations.

Wall Chart

The keyboard Wall Chart provides a poster-sized diagram of the keyboard for visual reinforcement of keyboard reaches and locational security.

Electronic Teacher's Classroom Resource

This is a single CD-ROM that contains all of the content from the Teacher's Classroom Resources package and provides you with easy access and storage of these materials.

Teacher Responsibilities

In *Glencoe Keyboarding with Computer Applications,* the students are involved in learning skills that will be valuable to them for the rest of their lives. Even though technology will continue to change rapidly, the basic skills will remain useful. You, as the teacher, have responsibilities that will make the difference in how well the students learn these skills. In meeting these responsibilities you need to

- Observe the students' keyboarding techniques to assure efficient operation of the keys.
- Be available to the students to clarify the instructions for document formats and software functions.
- Facilitate the students' self-evaluations of documents prepared so that they will have a sense of acceptable and outstanding quality.
- Encourage students to strive for increased speed and accuracy.
- Provide opportunities for students to work together whenever possible.
- Provide appropriate materials, software, equipment, and guidance.
- Evaluate student outcomes.

Student Responsibilities

Students also have responsibilities if they are going to develop skills that will serve them well throughout the rest of their lives. These responsibilities call for students to

- Use correct techniques to insure efficient operation of the keyboard and to avoid fatigue or wrist problems.
- Have the textbook, appropriate student manual, student data disk, and other required material for use at all times during class.
- When working with other students on desktop publishing or other types of projects, draw upon their own creativity and on the strengths of their teammates.
- Evaluate the appearance and accuracy of the documents they produce.
- Communicate with their teacher whenever they are having difficulties in order to avoid wasting time.

Cross-Curricular Focus

Cross-curricular focus refers to applying what is learned in one course to what is learned in other courses. Seeing this relationship emphasizes to the student that the concepts presented have meaning outside a particular course. Keyboarding and document preparation skill can readily be applied to any of the student's other courses.

Glencoe Keyboarding with Computer Applications provides a number of ways to integrate the academic subjects with the skills learned in the eight units. Many of the timings, activities, and production documents are related to other courses the students take. Students are asked to prepare reports, letters, databases, and spreadsheets using content related to other courses. The skills learned may help reinforce concepts from other courses; preparation of the documents for other courses provide practice of skills learned in the keyboarding course. All the activities will prove useful in the students' personal jobs and in future careers.

In addition to the projects in the Student Edition and the Teacher's Wraparound Edition, the Teacher's Classroom Resource package provides supplemental projects, most of which will be related to cross-curricular or multicultural topics. Students may also be encouraged to bring to class projects that they need to prepare for other courses. These projects might be an outline of a report, a letter requesting materials about a topic being researched for a science report, a flyer for a student organization that needs to be desktop published, or the content for a student organization newsletter.

Flexibility

Because there are so many educational variables—differing schools, students, curricula, and teachers—most textbooks are designed to meet the needs of the average school and the average student. For this reason teachers of classes that are not completely average—and most classes are not—must be able to adapt textual materials to fit the needs of their particular schools, classes, students, and curricula. Because such individualization is essential to the development of good keyboarding skills, the authors of *Glencoe Keyboarding with Computer Applications* have organized the textbook and designed supplementary materials for flexibility so that you can make the necessary adaptations easily.

Fast Keyboard Operators When modifying published lesson plans, you should include various activities to challenge the outstanding students in your classes. You may use the following methods to accommodate the fast keyboard operators:

- Use supplementary materials from the Teacher's Classroom Resources package, such as the Supplementary Production Activities or the Cross-Curricular Activities or use the two simulations: *Desktop Publishing Simulation* or *Integrated Office Simulation.*
- Have students repeat jobs, aiming for a faster production speed on the second try.
- Ask the students to use a format different from the one specified in the textbook lesson. Along with changing the format students could also be asked to change some of the content, or revise the document to improve it or make it more concise.
- Assign nontext activities such as some actual project needed by school administrators, other teachers, or a student organization.

Slow Keyboard Operators You must also make a special effort to select the most appropriate materials for slower keyboard operators. The following suggestions are worth considering:

- Eliminate selected jobs, being certain to eliminate jobs that do not contain new concepts, new formats, or general information that may be needed for future jobs. The idea is that students who are able to complete exercises will have better skills than those who are never able to complete them.
- Use skillbuilding techniques to help students eliminate hesitant reactions and move toward increasing production skills. One-minute drills on the opening and closing lines of letters may very well reduce the excess hesitations of students inadequately prepared to type letters.
- Use piecemeal practice to allow students to practice each individual part of the task before typing the entire job. Sometimes learning the individual parts of a job before attempting to type the entire job provides students with confidence.

A. Ramey/Stock Boston

- Delay production work until individual students have achieved a minimum straight-copy rate of possibly 22 to 25 words a minute. During this postponement, you should use the skillbuilding routines specifically designed for improving speed and accuracy scores: 12-second timings, 30-second timings, paced practices, selective practices, and OK timings.

Students with Disabilities You may have the opportunity to teach students with disabilities. This experience can be challenging if you have never worked with people who have learning disabilities, deafness, visual impairments, or physical disabilities such as missing fingers or arms. While you may wish to explore specific disabilities further, the following suggestions may offer some help to you:

- Students who have hearing impairment should be seated near the front of the room so that they may lipread the teacher's instructions. Classroom noise should be kept to a minimum so that these students will be able to use any residual hearing. You should remember to give clear and simple directions and should face the class when speaking. If needed, you may wish to investigate the availability of special equipment. In *Glencoe Keyboarding with Computer Applications,* PowerPoint slides may be projected on a screen and visuals within the software will benefit these students.
- Students who have visual impairments need to be oriented to their workstations and to the classroom in general. Any environmental changes should be communicated in advance. If large screen monitors are available, these may help students with visual impairments. Students should be seated where they can hear the teacher clearly. Print in early lessons is larger than that in some other keyboarding texts. If students need additional help, devices that magnify book pages, special large-type versions of the text, or audio recordings may be made available through organizations such as United Way, Recordings for the Blind, or other organizations.
- Students with physical disabilities may require the use of wheelchairs, special software like voice recognition technology, special furniture, or special materials. If a student is missing a finger, modifications may have to be made in the finger reaches and stroking techniques. Special emphasis must be given to the height of the computer keyboard and to adjustable features of chairs and desks.
- If a student has learning disabilities, the teacher's confidence, enthusiasm, and positive attitude toward the student's ability will help that student tremendously. Be very specific, and teach even the minor details of a task. Use a variety of visual aids and present information in a series of small steps. Check the student's progress frequently, and praise the student for accomplishing a task—no matter how insignificant that task might be. Students should find the key reach illustrations in the software motivational and helpful.

Students with Previous Keyboard Training When students enrolled in the beginning keyboarding class have had previous instruction in keyboarding, such as students coming from middle school, the teacher must take steps to ensure that the needs of the "beginners" and these "advanced beginners" are met. Advanced beginners should be seated close together since their speed may be intimidating to the true beginners. These students with previous training should be given a pretest consisting of straight-copy keyboarding and two or three production jobs of varying levels of difficulty. You should observe the students' techniques while they complete the pretest. Based on the test, you should determine any remedial work they may need to improve techniques, build speed, improve accuracy, or relearn formats and other production concepts.

Types of Assessment

Your students have many different learning styles and different means of expressing their knowledge and skills. The combination of learning styles and the need to evaluate the students' skills calls for alternative methods of assessment.

Objective Tests

If you wish to test the students on their understanding and recall of content, objective questions are provided for each of the eight units. Each unit test has a variety of test items, including such types as true/false, multiple choice, and short answer. These tests may be photocopied and given as they are, or you may use these tests as the basis for tests you construct. These questions will be available on the Electronic Teacher Classroom Resource CD-ROM so that you may download and customize them for your students.

Production Tests

In this course, students spend most of their time performing; thus, the best measure of their learning and skill acquisition is the production or performance tests. In the Teacher's Classroom Resource package and in the Electronic Teacher Classroom Resource CD-ROM, production test projects are given for all units except Units 1 and 2, which cover keyboarding basics. Suggested solutions are also provided in the test booklet.

Portfolio Activities

At various points during the course, students are asked to select some of their best work to be included in their portfolios. These projects incorporate all the instruction and content for certain types of documents and from the student's best timings to measure speed and accuracy. They serve as evidence of what the student has learned. Some of the student's *Journal Entry* compositions and *Language Link* compositions could also be included in the portfolio as evidence of acquired skill and knowledge.

Observation and Questioning

Observation of keyboarding techniques with checklists completed at various points during the course serve as evaluation of the student's performance. You as teacher should also observe operation of the computer, ability to follow instructions, use of the Student Manual for study of software functions, or ability to work as part of a team or within a whole-class setting will enable you to assess the student's progress.

Self-Evaluation

A student's ability to evaluate performance in a course like keyboarding and computer applications is invaluable. Such a skill will enable the student to be a better worker than someone who must rely on others to say "job well done" or "you could do better." Several features are provided in the Student Edition of the text to facilitate self-evaluation. Formatting instructions and model documents provide students with a way to compare their finished documents to the ideal. Portfolio Activities also provide questions that students may answer as they select some of their better work. Any additional practice you can provide students in identifying work done well and work that could be improved will be helpful in future careers.

SCANS Foundations and Competencies

In 1991, the U.S. Department of Labor released a report entitled, *What Work Requires of Schools: A SCANS Report for America 2000.* SCANS stands for the Secretary's Commission on the Achieving Necessary Skills. The report identified five competencies which, in conjunction with a three-part foundation of skills and personal qualities, lie at the heart of job performance and are needed by all workers in order to prosper in the emerging workplace. *Glencoe Keyboarding with Computer Applications* integrates these skills throughout and will provide your students an outstanding basis for future development of these skills and competencies in other aspects of their schooling.

SCANS FOUNDATIONS	LESSONS IN WHICH THESE ARE MET
Basic Skills—reads, writes, performs arithmetic and mathematical operations, listens, and speaks	*Reads*—Lessons 1-150 *Writes*—Lessons 4, 8, 12, 16, 17, 19, 20, 24, 28, 30, 31, 35, 38, 39, 42, 43, 45, 47, 49, 51, 53, 55, 58, 60, 63, 65, 67, 69, 71, 73, 75, 77, 79, 81, 84, 85, 88, 89, 93, 95, 98, 100, 103, 105, 107, 109, 111, 113, 115, 117, 119, 121, 123, 125, 127, 129, 131, 133, 135, 137, 143, 145, 147, 149 *Performs arithmetic and mathematical operations*—Lessons 6, 7, 40, 41, 54, 65, 66, 67, 68, 76, 94, 96, 100, 116, 121-140, 145, 149 *Listens*—Lessons 1-30, 76 *Speaks*—Lessons 24, 91
Thinking Skills—thinks creatively, makes decisions, solves problems, visualizes, knows how to learn, and reasons	*Thinks creatively*—Lessons 4, 8, 12, 16, 17, 19, 20, 24, 30, 31, 43, 51, 55, 58, 60, 62, 67, 73, 75, 79, 85, 93, 98, 103, 109, 110, 115, 121, 127, 133, 145 *Makes decisions*—Lessons 28, 30, 35, 45, 47, 53, 60, 63, 65, 69, 71, 75, 77, 79, 80, 81, 88, 95, 100, 105, 106, 107, 110, 111, 113, 117, 125, 129, 131, 135, 137, 139, 141, 143, 147 *Solves problems*—Lessons 96, 131, 132, 145, 147, 148, 149 *Visualizes*—Lessons 110, 137, 138, 150 *Knows how to learn*—Lessons 1-150 *Reasons*—Lessons 28, 31, 35, 38, 39, 45, 47-65, 67, 69, 71, 75, 77, 81, 83, 84, 88, 89, 95, 98, 100, 103, 105, 107, 111, 113, 117, 119, 123, 125, 129, 131, 135, 137, 143, 147, 149
Personal Qualities—Displays responsibility, self-esteem, sociability, self-management, and integrity and honesty	*Displays responsibility*—Lessons 1-150 *Self-esteem*—Lessons 16, 26, 51, 66, 68, 74, 75, 79, 80, 92 *Sociability*—Lessons 26, 67, 74, 98, 150 *Self-management*—Lessons 1-150 *Integrity and honesty*—Lesson 41

SCANS COMPETENCIES	LESSONS IN WHICH THESE ARE MET
Resources—identifies, organizes, plans, and allocates resources	*Identifies, organizes, plans, and allocates time*—Lessons 1-150 *Identifies, organizes, plans, and allocates money*—Lessons 73, 74, 79, 87 *Identifies, organizes, plans, and allocates materials and facilities*—Lessons 1-150 *Identifies, organizes, plans, and allocates human resources*—Lessons 83, 102, 103, 110, 150
Interpersonal Skills—works with others	*Participates as a member of a team*—Lesson 30 *Teaches others new skills*—Lesson 30 *Services clients/ customers*—Lesson 131 *Exercises leadership*—Lessons 28, 58, 75, 77, 107, 110 *Negotiates*—Lesson 3 *Works with diversity*—Lessons
Information—acquires and uses information	*Acquires and evaluates information*—Lessons 1-150 *Organizes and maintains information*—Lessons 62, 75, 102 *Interprets and communicates information*—Lessons 102, 103, 105, 127 *Uses computers to process information*—Lessons 1-150
Systems—understands complex interrelationships	*Understands systems*—Lessons 72, 73, 92, 102, 118, 127 *Monitors and corrects performance*—Lessons 80, 92 *Improves or designs systems*—Lessons 102, 131
Technology—works with a variety of technologies	*Selects technology*—Lesson 73 *Applies technology to task*—Lessons 1-150 *Maintains and troubleshoots equipment*—Lesson 51

Jack E. Johnson, Ph.D.
Director of Business Education
Department of Management and Business Systems
State University of West Georgia
Carrollton, Georgia

Judith Chiri-Mulkey
Adjunct Teacher
Department of Computer Information Systems
Pikes Peak Community College
Colorado Springs, Colorado

Delores Sykes Cotton
Supervisor, Business Education
Detroit Public Schools
Detroit, Michigan

Carole G. Stanley, M.Ed.
Keyboarding and Computer Literacy Teacher, Retired
Rains Junior High School
Emory, Texas

New York, New York
Columbus, Ohio
Woodland Hills, California
Peoria, Illinois

Glencoe/McGraw-Hill
A Division of The McGraw-Hill Companies

Glencoe Keyboarding With Computer Applications, Lessons 1-150

Send all inquiries to:

Glencoe/McGraw-Hill
936 Eastwind Drive
Westerville, OH 43081

ISBN 0-02-804171-2

2 3 4 5 6 7 8 9 027 05 04 03 02 01 00 99

ii

REVIEWERS

Judy Senden
West High School
Anchorage, AK

Betty Gross Malone
Jackson-Olin High School
Birmingham, AL

Debra Scott
Arkansas High School
Texarkana, AR

Donna Green
Mingus Union High School
Cottonwood, AZ

Sue Julian
El Molino High School
Forestville, CA

Dr. Rita Schnittgrund
Denver West High School
Denver, CO

Janyce Wininger
Stafford High School
Stafford Spring, CT

Marjorie Stewart
Caesar Rodney High School
Camden Wyoming, DE

Patricia McCollough
Fort Walton Beach High School
Fort Walton Beach, FL

Barbara Williams-Mims
Columbus High School
Columbus, GA

Patricia Pierce
Linn-Marr High School
Marion, IA

Dan Petersen
State Division of Vocational Education
Business and Office Technology Education
Boise, ID

Gerrie L. Trossman
Good Counsel High School
Chicago, IL

Barbara Coleman
Salina High School South
Salina, KS

N. Jean Andrada
Pleasure Ridge High School
Louisville, KY

Terry Smith
Alcee Fortier High School
New Orleans, LA

Betsy Nilsen
Cape Elizabeth High School
Cape Elizabeth, ME

Kathy Jensen
Mankato West High School
Mankato, MN

Judy Cox
J. H. Rose High School
Greenville, NC

Nancy Stevens
Manteo High School
Manteo, NC

Mike Opdahl
Larimore High School
Larimore, ND

Betty Sup
Creighton Preparatory School
Omaha, NE

Maria Alvarez
Farmington High School
Farmington, NH

Sandra M. Richardson
Life Center Academy
Burlington, NJ

Bernadine Elmore
New Mexico Military Institution
Roswell, NM

Leesa Lyman
Roy Martin School
Las Vegas, NV

Lorraine Harrison
HS for Arts and Business
Corona, NY

Michael Prandy
John Marshall High School
Oklahoma City, OK

Sherri Sollars
Westview High School
Portland, OR

Susan Howe
Chariho Regional High School
Wood River Junction, RI

Patricia B. Hook
Airport High School
West Columbia, SC

Jane Bradfield
O'Gorman High School
Sioux Falls, SD

Edna Earle Bond
Central High School
Memphis, TN

Susan Shirey
Grand Prairie High School
Grand Prairie, TX

Patricia Kay Fordham
Central High School
Salt Lake City, UT

Patricia Smith
Kennewick High School
Kennewick, WA

Gail Springsteen
Waupaca High School
Waupaca, WI

Nancy Byrd
Morgantown High School
Morgantown, WV

iii

TABLE OF CONTENTS

UNIT 4 WORD PROCESSING

TABLE OF CONTENTS *(continued)*

UNIT 5 WORD PROCESSING

UNIT 6 DESKTOP PUBLISHING

UNIT 7 SPREADSHEETS

TABLE OF CONTENTS *(continued)*

UNIT 8 DATABASES

ABOUT YOUR BOOK

STRUCTURE

Your book is divided into 8 units. **Note:** If you are using the book with Lessons 1–80, your book will have just 4 units. Each unit except the last one is further divided into 20 lessons. Unit 8, because of its complexity, contains only 10 lessons. Each unit opens with a two-page spread which provides a list of the unit objectives (what you will learn in the unit), *Words to Learn* (words that are introduced or used within the unit), and a *Career Bit* (a brief description of a career in which keyboarding skill is helpful).

UNITS

In Units 1 and 2 you will learn to operate the keyboard by touch with speed and accuracy—a skill you will be able to use throughout your education and career. In Unit 3, you will be introduced to the ten-key numeric keypad and some basic word processing features.

In Units 4 and 5 you will use your keyboarding skill to create documents and to format them correctly. In addition, you will continue to learn about more advanced word processing features as you progress.

Unit 6 includes desktop publishing lessons where you will continue to learn word processing features such as draw and text/word art and use them to create a variety of documents including some original designs. You will also learn about inserting, sizing, and positioning graphics.

In Unit 7, you will learn about spreadsheets: what they are, how to create them, how to use them for "what if" queries, and how to create pie and bar charts.

Finally, in Unit 8, you will learn about databases: what they are, how they can be used, how to create database tables, how to sort, and how to query databases.

LESSONS

Each lesson is divided into several sections. Every lesson (except the first) begins with a Warmup that you should begin typing as soon as you are settled at your keyboard. In the early lessons, *New-Key* sections introduce the new keys for that lesson and provide you with practice lines on these keys.

Every lesson contains a *Skillbuilding* section that is easy to identify because of its blue background. The skillbuilding sections contain a variety of different activities including Technique Timings, Diagnostic Practice, Paced Practice, and 1-, 3-, and 5-minute timings.

Many skillbuilding sections include a *Pretest, Practice, Posttest* routine. This routine is designed to help you improve either speed or accuracy through step-by-step procedures. The Pretest helps you identify your speed or accuracy needs. The Practice activities contain a variety of intensive improvement drills. Finally, the Posttest measures your improvement.

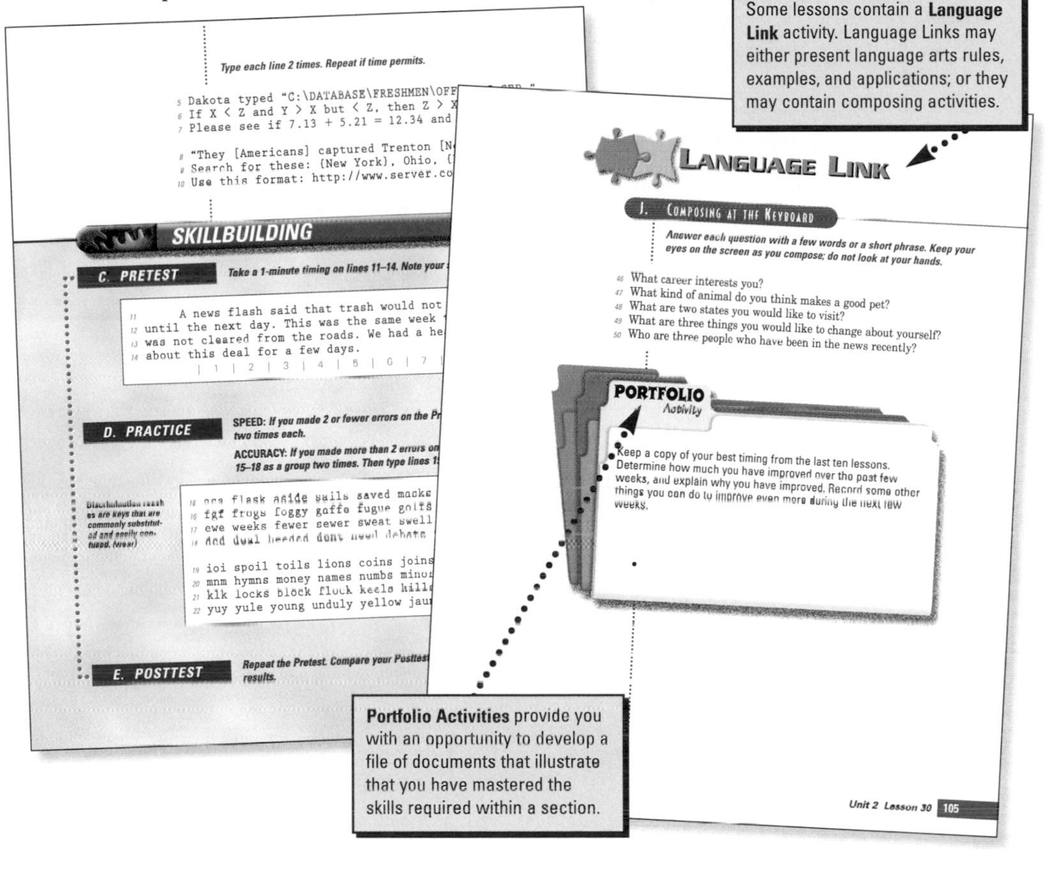

Some lessons contain a **Language Link** activity. Language Links may either present language arts rules, examples, and applications; or they may contain composing activities.

Portfolio Activities provide you with an opportunity to develop a file of documents that illustrate that you have mastered the skills required within a section.

LESSONS

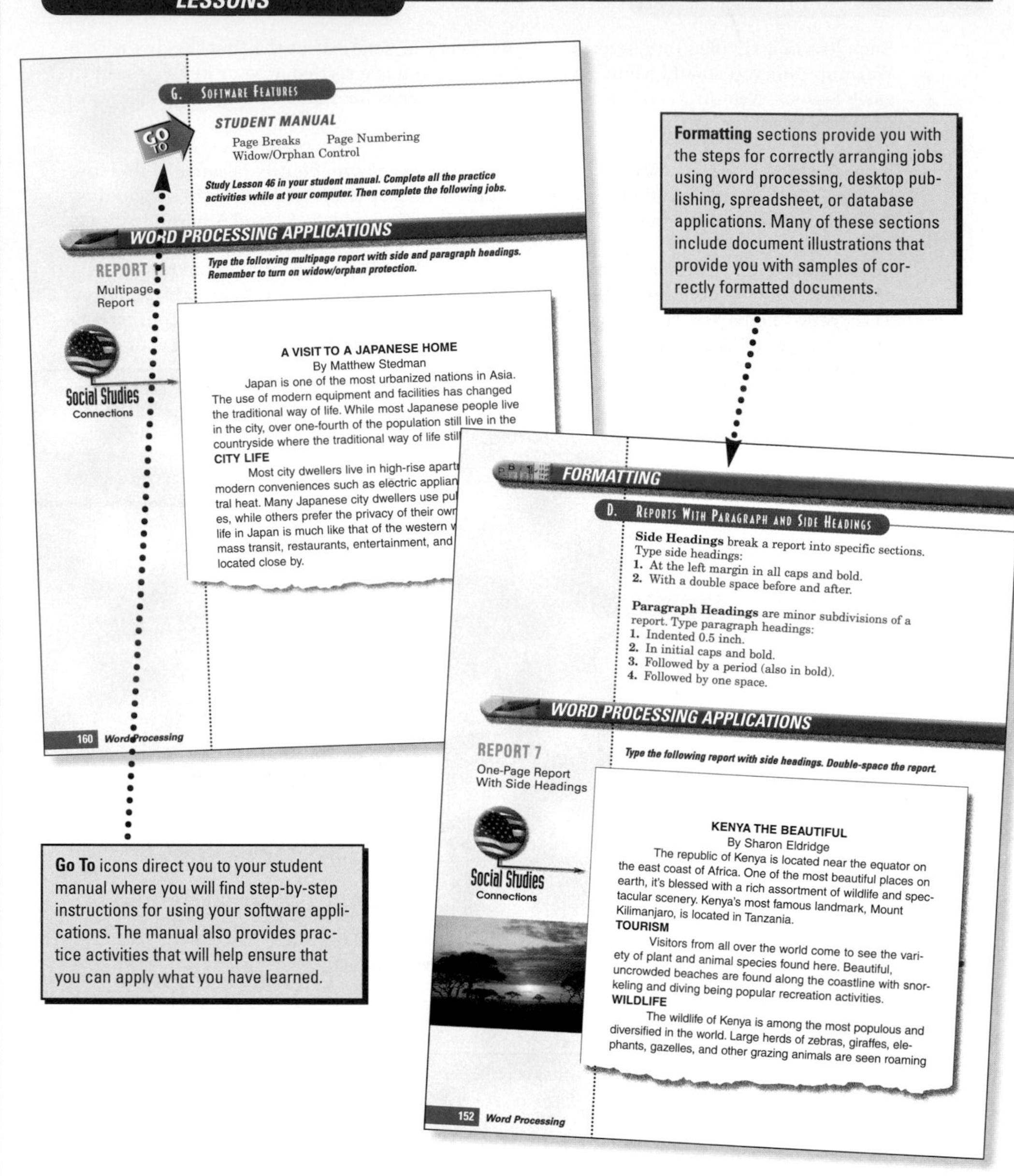

Formatting sections provide you with the steps for correctly arranging jobs using word processing, desktop publishing, spreadsheet, or database applications. Many of these sections include document illustrations that provide you with samples of correctly formatted documents.

Go To icons direct you to your student manual where you will find step-by-step instructions for using your software applications. The manual also provides practice activities that will help ensure that you can apply what you have learned.

SPECIAL FEATURES

In addition to regular keyboarding lesson content, the lessons include a variety of special features. The following pages show samples of these features.

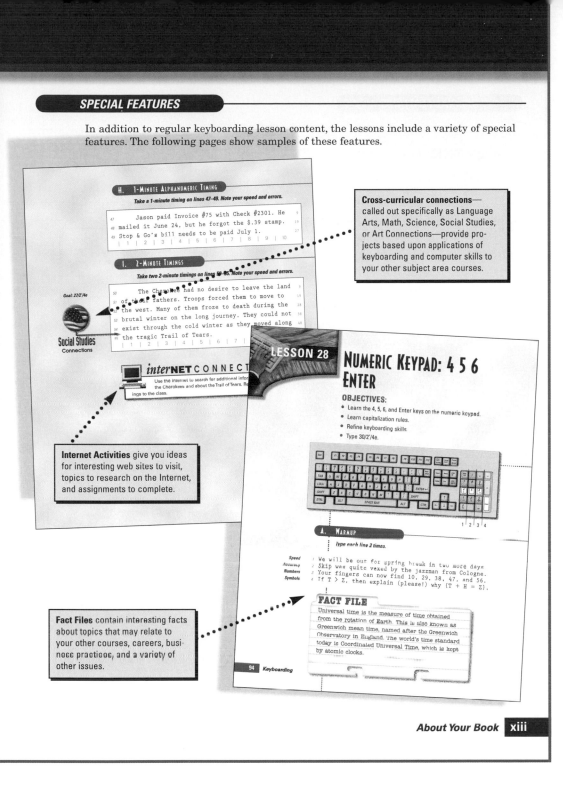

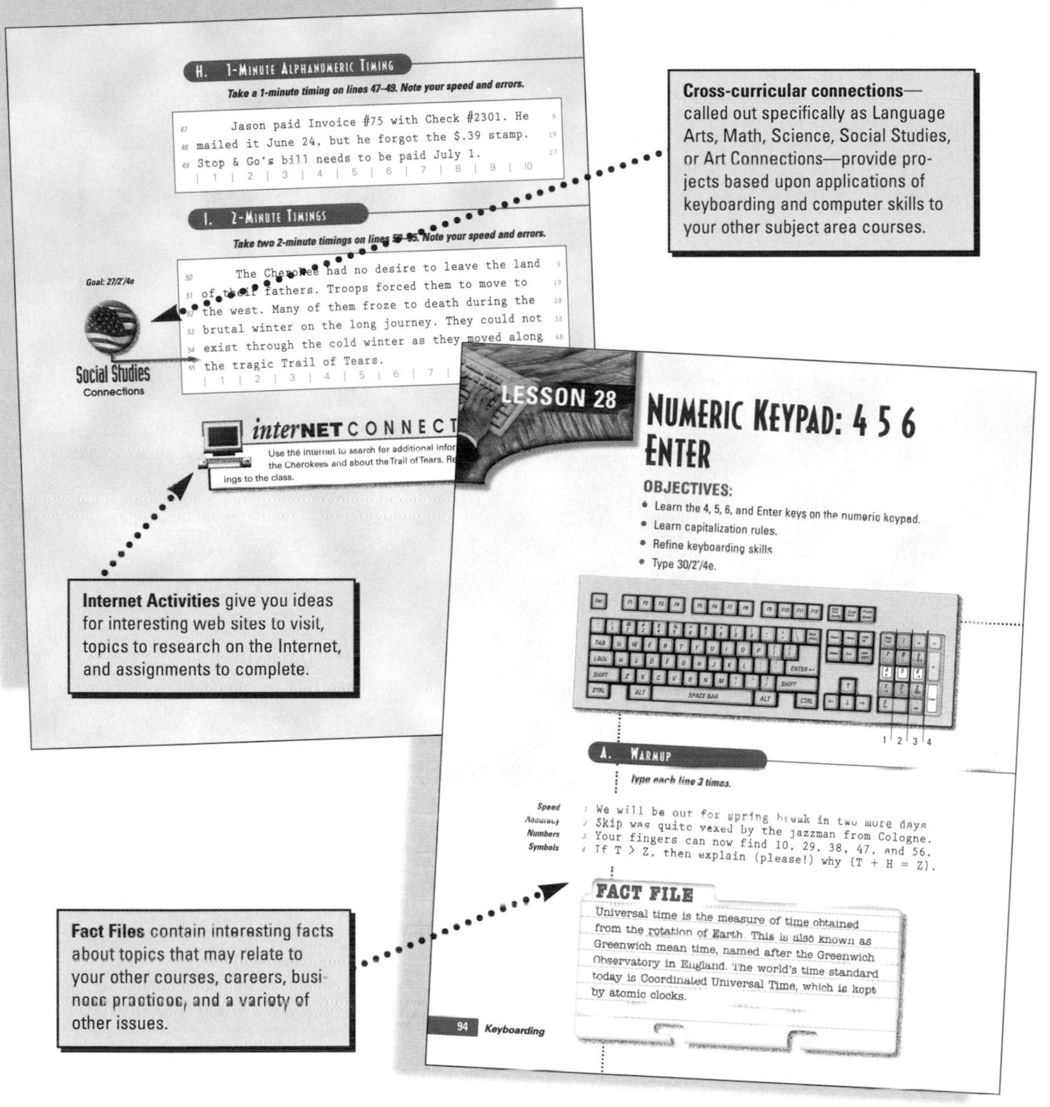

H. 1-Minute Alphanumeric Timing
Take a 1-minute timing on lines 47–49. Note your speed and errors.
Jason paid Invoice #75 with Check #2301. He
mailed it June 24, but he forgot the $.39 stamp.
Stop & Go's bill needs to be paid July 1.
I. 2-Minute Timings
Goal: 27/2'/4e
The Cherokee had no desire to leave the land
of their fathers. Troops forced them to move to
the west. Many of them froze to death during the
brutal winter on the long journey. They could not
exist through the cold winter as they moved along
the tragic Trail of Tears.
Social Studies
Connections
interNET CONNECT
Use the Internet to search for additional infor
the Cherokees and about the Trail of Tears. Re
ings to the class.
LESSON 28
NUMERIC KEYPAD: 4 5 6
ENTER
OBJECTIVES:
Learn the 4, 5, 6, and Enter keys on the numeric keypad.
Learn capitalization rules.
Refine keyboarding skills.
Type 30/2'/4e.
A. WARMUP
Type each line 2 times.
Speed
Accuracy
Numbers
Symbols
We will be out for spring break in two more days
Skip was quite vexed by the jazzman from Cologne.
Your fingers can now find 10, 29, 38, 47, and 56.
If T > Z, then explain (please!) why (T + H = Z).
FACT FILE
Universal time is the measure of time obtained
from the rotation of Earth. This is also known as
Greenwich mean time, named after the Greenwich
Observatory in England. The world's time standard
today is Coordinated Universal Time, which is kept
by atomic clocks.
94 Keyboarding

Cross-curricular connections—called out specifically as Language Arts, Math, Science, Social Studies, or Art Connections—provide projects based upon applications of keyboarding and computer skills to your other subject area courses.

Internet Activities give you ideas for interesting web sites to visit, topics to research on the Internet, and assignments to complete.

Fact Files contain interesting facts about topics that may relate to your other courses, careers, business practices, and a variety of other issues.

SPECIAL FEATURES

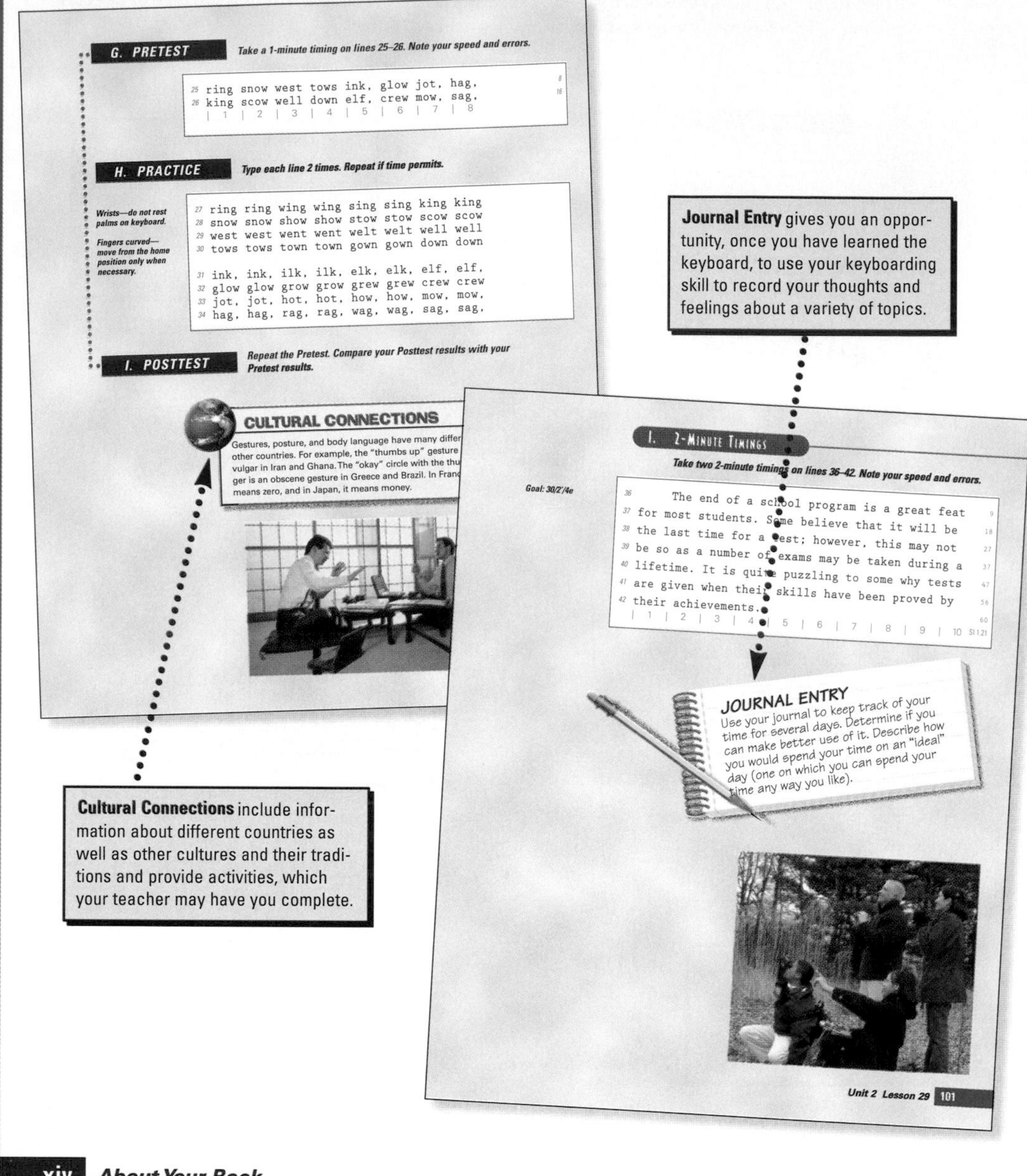

G. PRETEST
Take a 1-minute timing on lines 25–26. Note your speed and errors.
ring snow west tows ink, glow jot, hag,
king scow well down elf, crew mow, sag.
H. PRACTICE
Type each line 2 times. Repeat if time permits.
I. POSTTEST
Repeat the Pretest. Compare your Posttest results with your Pretest results.
CULTURAL CONNECTIONS
I. 2-MINUTE TIMINGS
Take two 2-minute timings on lines 36–42. Note your speed and errors.
JOURNAL ENTRY
Use your journal to keep track of your time for several days. Determine if you can make better use of it. Describe how you would spend your time on an "ideal" day (one on which you can spend your time any way you like).
Unit 2 Lesson 29 101

Journal Entry gives you an opportunity, once you have learned the keyboard, to use your keyboarding skill to record your thoughts and feelings about a variety of topics.

Cultural Connections include information about different countries as well as other cultures and their traditions and provide activities, which your teacher may have you complete.

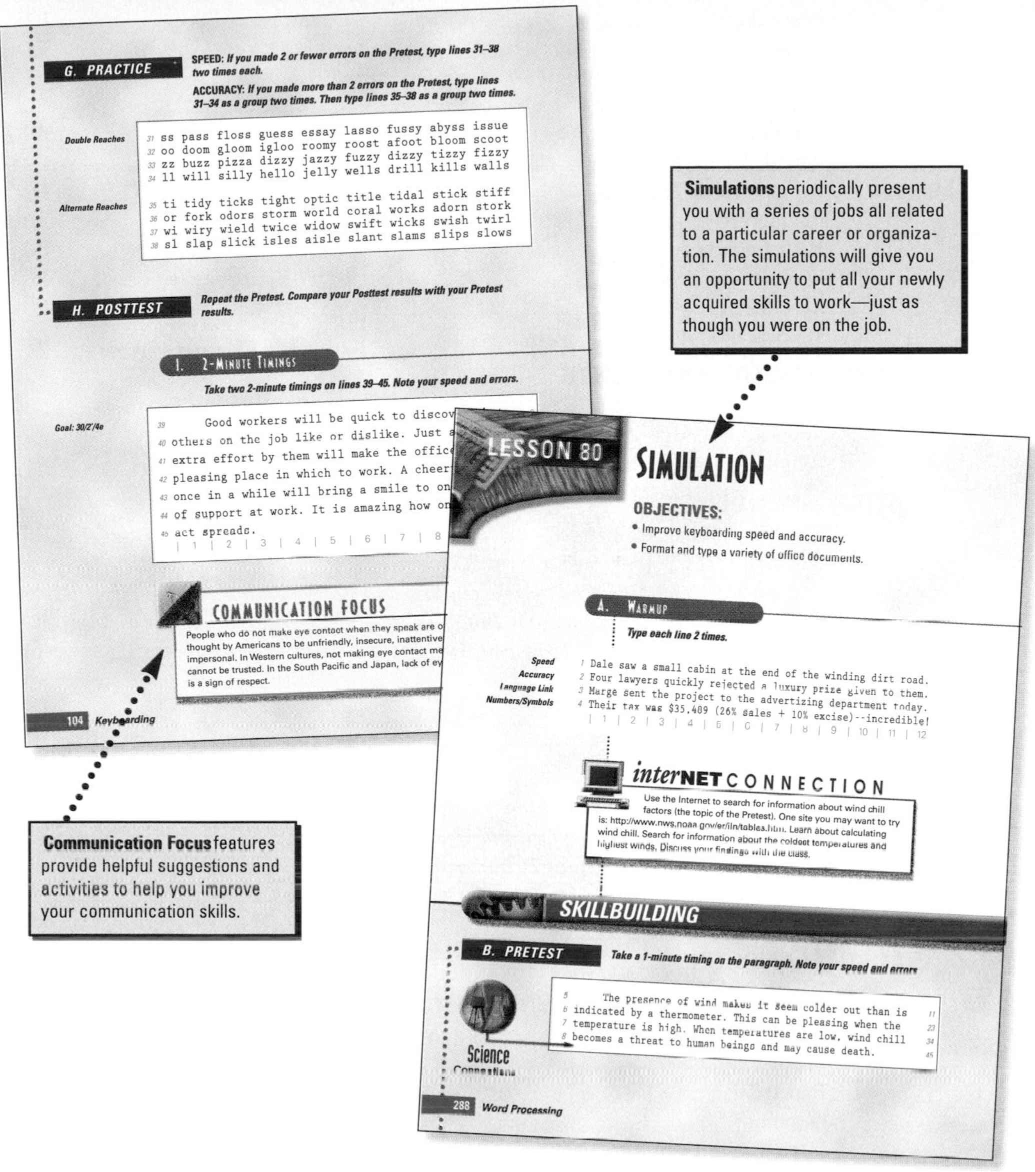

Simulations periodically present you with a series of jobs all related to a particular career or organization. The simulations will give you an opportunity to put all your newly acquired skills to work—just as though you were on the job.

Communication Focus features provide helpful suggestions and activities to help you improve your communication skills.

REFERENCE SECTION *Table of Contents*

REPORTS

EMPLOYMENT DOCUMENTS

CORRESPONDENCE

TABLES

MISCELLANEOUS

LANGUAGE LINKS

REPORT OUTLINE

↓6x

HOW TO MAKE DECISIONS ON THE JOB ↓2x

I. DETERMINE WHAT CHOICES YOU HAVE. ↓2x

   A. Make use of all available reference materials.
      1. Check company policy manuals.
      2. Go to the company library or files.
   B. Ask your co-workers and your supervisors questions.
   C. Be observant and pay close attention in meetings. ↓2x

II. DO NOT MAKE DECISIONS HASTILY.

   A. Postpone any doubtful decisions.
   B. Decisions based on emotions are usually not the best ones.
      1. If you are angry, allow enough time to consider things calmly.
      2. You will risk losing others' respect if you act impulsively.

III. EVALUATE YOUR DECISIONS OBJECTIVELY.

   A. Keep an open mind about the consequences of your decisions.
   B. Learn from past decisions you have made.
      1. Evaluate the results of each decision you make.
      2. Learn something good from a poor decision.

COVER PAGE

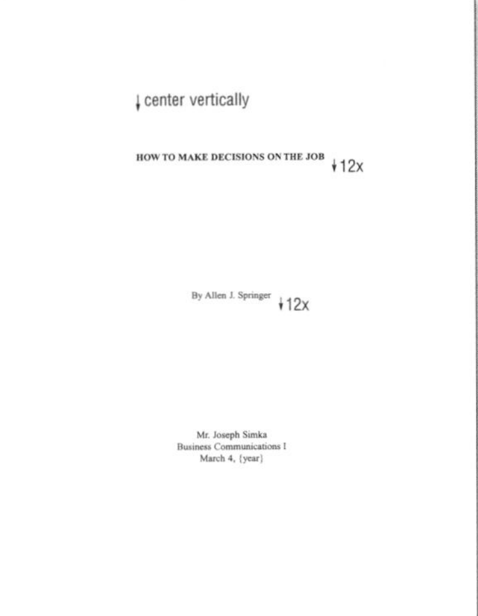

↓ center vertically

HOW TO MAKE DECISIONS ON THE JOB ↓12x

By Allen J. Springer ↓12x

Mr. Joseph Simka
Business Communications I
March 4, {year}

TABLE OF CONTENTS

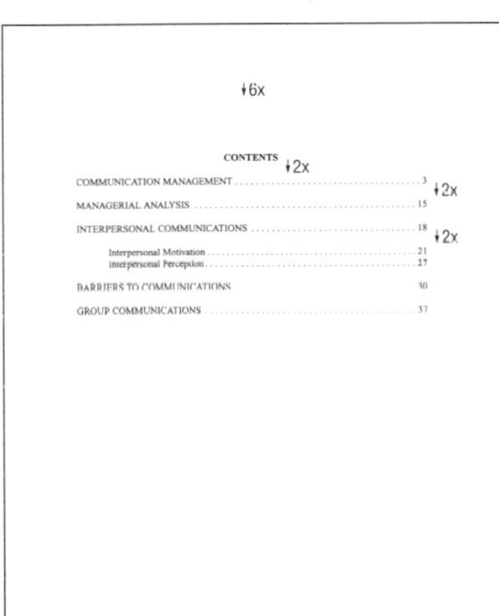

↓6x

CONTENTS ↓2x

COMMUNICATION MANAGEMENT . . . . 3 ↓2x

MANAGERIAL ANALYSIS 15

INTERPERSONAL COMMUNICATIONS . . . . 18 ↓2x

   Interpersonal Motivation 21
   Interpersonal Perception 27

BARRIERS TO COMMUNICATIONS 30

GROUP COMMUNICATIONS 37

UNBOUND REPORT, PAGE 1

(with side and paragraph headings)

↓3x

THE INFORMATION EXPLOSION ↓1x

By Ann A. Minichiello ↓1x

Whether you work as an executive or an administrative assistant, in today's business world you will find yourself at the center of an information explosion. Today's offices are equipped with modems, fax machines, electronic mail, and voice mail—all designed to make the flow of communication faster and more effective. As a result, you must have excellent information skills to succeed in the business world. ↓1x

KNOW YOUR PRODUCT ↓1x

Every worker should know the product he or she is responsible for. If you work in an office, your product is information. Your primary responsibility will be to handle information—to receive it and store it for future use, to research information and share it with others, or to evaluate the information and report on your evaluation.

COMMUNICATION

The role of communication is receiving a great deal of attention. The need to write and speak effectively is critical to success. Equally important to communication is the individual's ability to plan and organize information.

Planning. It is important to plan and organize information. Every office worker must plan ahead to determine information needs. The first step in communicating is to

REFERENCE SECTION *(continued)*

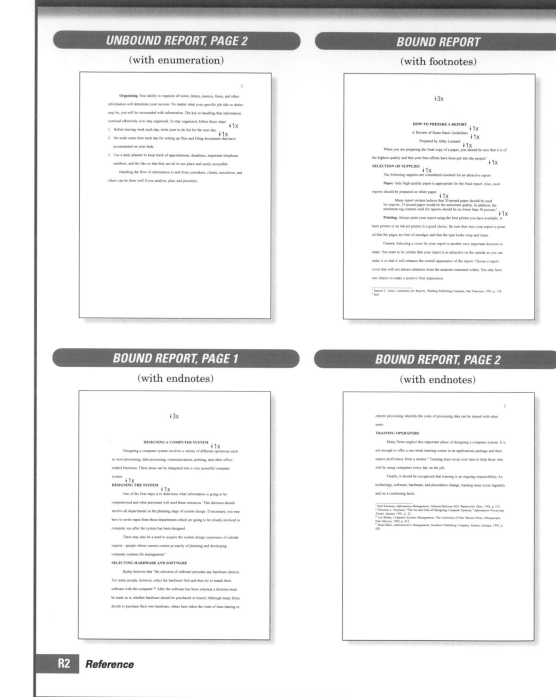

UNBOUND REPORT, PAGE 2

(with enumeration)

2

Organizing. Your ability to organize all notes, letters, memos, faxes, and other information will determine your success. No matter what your specific job title or duties may be, you will be surrounded with information. The key to handling that information overload effectively is to stay organized. To stay organized, follow these steps: ↓1x

1. Before leaving work each day, write your to-do list for the next day. ↓1x
2. Set aside some time each day for setting up files and filing documents that have accumulated on your desk.
3. Use a daily planner to keep track of appointments, deadlines, important telephone numbers, and the like so that they are all in one place and easily accessible.

Handling the flow of information to and from coworkers, clients, executives, and others can be done well if you analyze, plan, and prioritize.

BOUND REPORT

(with footnotes)

↓3x

HOW TO PREPARE A REPORT ↓1x

A Review of Some Basic Guidelines ↓1x

Prepared by Abby Leonard ↓1x

When you are preparing the final copy of a paper, you should be sure that it is of the highest quality and that your best efforts have been put into the project.[1] ↓1x

SELECTION OF SUPPLIES ↓1x

The following supplies are considered essential for an attractive report:

Paper. Only high-quality paper is appropriate for the final report. Also, most reports should be prepared on white paper. ↓1x

> Many report writers believe that 20-pound paper should be used for reports; 15-pound paper would be the minimum quality. In addition, the minimum rag content used for reports should be no lower than 50 percent.[2] ↓1x

Printing. Always print your report using the best printer you have available. A laser printer or an ink-jet printer is a good choice. Be sure that once your report is printed that the pages are free of smudges and that the type looks crisp and clean.

Covers. Selecting a cover for your report is another very important decision to make. You want to be certain that your report is as attractive on the outside as you can make it so that it will enhance the overall appearance of the report. Choose a report cover that will not detract attention from the material contained within. You only have one chance to make a positive first impression.

[1] Samuel C. Jones, *Guidelines for Reports,* Walding Publishing Company, San Francisco, 1993, p. 138.
[2] Ibid.

BOUND REPORT, PAGE 1

(with endnotes)

↓3x

DESIGNING A COMPUTER SYSTEM ↓1x

Designing a computer system involves a variety of different operations such as word processing, data processing, communications, printing, and other office-related functions. These areas can be integrated into a very powerful computer system. ↓1x

DESIGNING THE SYSTEM ↓1x

One of the first steps is to determine what information is going to be computerized and what personnel will need these resources.[i] This decision should involve all departments in the planning stage of system design. If necessary, you may have to invite input from those departments which are going to be closely involved in computer use after the system has been designed.

There may also be a need to acquire the system design experience of outside experts—people whose careers consist primarily of planning and developing computer systems for management.[ii]

SELECTING HARDWARE AND SOFTWARE

Bailey believes that "the selection of software precedes any hardware choices. Too many people, however, select the hardware first and then try to match their software with the computer."[iii] After the software has been selected, a decision must be made as to whether hardware should be purchased or leased. Although many firms decide to purchase their own hardware, others have taken the route of time-sharing or

BOUND REPORT, PAGE 2

(with endnotes)

2

remote processing whereby the costs of processing data can be shared with other users

TRAINING OPERATORS

Many firms neglect this important phase of designing a computer system. It is not enough to offer a one-week training course in an applications package and then expect proficiency from a worker.[iv] Training must occur over time to help those who will be using computers every day on the job.

Finally, it should be recognized that training is an ongoing responsibility. As technology, software, hardware, and procedures change, training must occur regularly and on a continuing basis.

[i] Neal Swanson, *Information Management,* Glencoe/McGraw-Hill, Westerville, Ohio, 1992, p. 372.
[ii] Christine L. Seymour, "The Ins and Outs of Designing Computer Systems," *Information Processing Trends,* January 1991, p. 23.
[iii] Lee Bailey, *Computer Systems Management,* The University of New Mexico Press, Albuquerque, New Mexico, 1992, p. 413.
[iv] Paula Blair, *Administrative Management,* Southern Publishing Company, Atlanta, Georgia, 1992, p. 420.

BIBLIOGRAPHY FOR A BOUND REPORT

3

↓6x

BIBLIOGRAPHY ↓2x

Blanchard, Christie, *Experience a Successful Interview,* Beringson Printing, New York, 1998. ↓2x

Dolfeld, Kyle B., and Lisa R. Simmons, *Using an Interview to Get the Job,* Masterson Books, Aptos, California, 1999. ↓2x

Johnson, Karen C., "What to Do After the Interview," *Journal of Communications,* Vol. XVII, No. 6, May 1995, pp. 17-20.

Lymanski, James T., et al., "The Secrets to Interviewing: Style and Organization," *HRD Journal,* Vol. LXVII, No. 5, October 1999, pp. 58-61.

"Preparing for the Interview," *Sales Marketing Journal,* Vol. XXVII, No. 2, August 21, 1997, pp. 103-105.

Secretarial Association, *The Job Interview and Your Success,* Georgia College Press, Carrollton, Georgia, 1996.

MLA REPORT

↓1 inch Finklestein 1

Cynthia Finklestein ↓1x

Professor Roberts ↓1x

Business Communication 300 ↓1x

2 February {year} ↓1x

Communication Skills Needed in International Business ↓1x

International business plays an increasingly important role in the U.S. economy, and U.S. companies recognize that to be competitive nationally, they must be competitive internationally. Reflecting this trend, direct investment by U.S. private enterprises in foreign countries increased from $409 billion in 1994 to $528 billion in 1999, an increase of 29 percent in four years (Connor 253). Today, more than 3,000 U.S. corporations have over 25,000 subsidiaries and affiliates in 125 foreign countries, and more than 25,000 American firms are engaged in international marketing (Newby 193, 205).

International business is highly dependent on communication. According to Arnold LePoole, chief executive officer of Amstrand Industries, an international supplier of automotive parts:

> If a company cannot communicate with its foreign subsidiaries, customers, suppliers, and governments, it cannot achieve success. The sad fact is that most American managers are not equipped to communicate with their international counterparts. (143-144)

Because excellent business communication skills are one of the most important components for success in international business affairs, a survey instrument was designed to explore the importance of, level of competence in, and methods of developing four types of international business speaking skills. The survey was sent to over 5,000 international companies with staff members located around the world. Each company was asked to share the survey with

WORKS CITED PAGE

↓1 inch Kyslowsky 17

Works Cited

Connor, Earl. "Exploring Body Language Cues." Management Today June 1994: 250-261, 273.

LePoole, Arnold. What American Business Can (and Must) Learn From the Japanese. New York: Management Press, 1990.

Newby, Corrine J. "Global Implications for American Business: the Numbers Don't Lie." Marketing Research Quarterly 50 (1994): 190-215.

Roncaro, Paul L., and Glenn D. Lance. "Losing Something in the Translation." Winston Salem Herald 2 June 1992: 1A+.

"Tell It Like It Is: Making Yourself Understood in the New Russia." International Times 19 October 1999: 38.

AGENDA

↓6x

INTERNET, INC. EXECUTIVE COMMITTEE ↓2x

Meeting Agenda ↓2x

August 7, {year}, 2 p.m. ↓2x

1. Call to order
2. Approval of minutes of July 8 meeting
3. Progress report on building addition and parking lot restrictions (Satbir Bedi and Janelle Graham)
4. May 15 draft of Five-Year Plan
5. Review of National Computer Technology annual convention
6. Employee grievance filed by Letitia Burrows (Johann Lundstrom)
7. New expense-report form (John Constantino)
8. Announcements
9. Adjournment

REFERENCE SECTION *(continued)*

MINUTES OF A MEETING

↓6x

RESOURCE COMMITTEE ↓2x

Minutes of the Meeting ↓2x

March 13, {year} ↓2x

ATTENDANCE ↓2x

The Resource Committee met on March 13, {year}, at the Airport Sheraton in Portland,Oregon, in conjunction with the western regional meeting. Members present were Michael Davis, Cynthia Giovanni, Don Madsen, and Edna Pointer. Michael Davis, chairperson, called the meeting to order at 2:30 p.m. ↓2x

OLD BUSINESS ↓2x

The members of the committee reviewed the sales brochure on electronic copyboards. They agreed to purchase an electronic copyboard for the conference room. Cynthia Giovanni will secure quotations from at least two vendors.

NEW BUSINESS

The committee reviewed a request from the Purchasing Department for three new computers. After extensive discussion regarding the appropriate use of the computers in the Purchasing Department and software to be purchased, the committee approved the request.

ADJOURNMENT

The meeting was adjourned at 4:45 p.m. The next meeting has been scheduled for May 4, in the headquarters conference room. Members are asked to bring with them copies of the latest resource planning document. ↓2x

Respectfully submitted, ↓4x

D. S. Madsen, Secretary

RESUME

↓center vertically

Terry M. Martina
250 Maxwell Avenue, Apt. 8
Boulder, CO 80304
303-555-9331
tmm@netex.com ↓2x

OBJECTIVE ↓2x

To obtain a position as a resort manager in Colorado. ↓2x

EDUCATION ↓2x

Edgewood Community College, Boulder, Colorado 80304
Associate of Arts degree to be awarded May 2000
Major: Hotel Administration
Overall grade point average of 3.1 (on 4.0 scale).
Received Board of Regents' tuition scholarship.

Durango High School, Durango, Colorado 81301
Graduated: May 1998

EXPERIENCE

Burger King, 4404 Foxhound Road, Boulder, Colorado 80305
Position: Assistant Manager

July 1997 to present (full-time during summers, part-time during school year)
Developed work schedules for 19 part-time employees.
Supervised employees and handled daily receipts.

Ski Valley Haven, Aspen, Colorado 81612
Position: Assistant to the Night Manager of a 200-room ski resort

September-December 1998
Gained practical experience in operating First-Guest management system.
Produced daily occupancy reports.

PERSONAL

Secretary of Hospitality Services Association
Special Olympics volunteer—summer 1998

REFERENCES

References available upon request.

APPLICATION LETTER

↓center page

March 2, {year} ↓4x

Ms. Lauren MacMillan, Director
Human Resources Department
Wilderness Lodge
P.O. Box 214
Denver, CO 80214 ↓2x

Dear Ms. MacMillan: ↓2x

Please consider me an applicant for the position of registration clerk for Wilderness Lodge as advertised in last Sunday's *Denver Times*. ↓2x

I will receive my A.A. degree in hotel administration from Edgewood Community College in May and will be available for full-time employment immediately. In addition to extensive coursework in hospitality services and business, I've had experience in working for a ski lodge in Aspen similar to Wilderness Lodge. As a lifelong resident of Colorado and an avid skier, I understand the needs of guests and how they should be treated. I would also be able to provide your guests with any information they request.

After you have reviewed my enclosed resume, I would appreciate having an opportunity to discuss with you in person why I believe I have the right qualifications and personality to serve as your registration clerk. I can be reached at 303-555-9311 after 4 p.m. daily. ↓2x

Sincerely, ↓4x

Chris L. Katroubis
250 Maxwell Avenue, Apt. 8
Boulder, CO 83035 ↓2x

Enclosure

FOLLOW-UP LETTER

↓center vertically

tab to centerpoint   May 10, {year} ↓4x

Mr. Herbert A. Juneau
Director of personnel
Apex Products Inc.
6532 Turtle Creek Boulevard
Dallas, TX 75205 ↓2x

Dear Mr. Juneau: ↓2x

Thank you for the time you spent telling me about the billing clerk position with Apex Products. The interview you gave me yesterday definitely reaffirmed my interest in working for your company.

I was especially impressed with the Payroll Department at Apex. The people and equipment in that department make this position very appealing to me.

The combination of my bookkeeping experience and the in-house training you provide for all new employees convinces me that this position is precisely the job that I have been seeking. When you have reached your decision, I will be most eager to hear from you. If you desire a second interview, I would be available after 12 noon any weekday. ↓2x

tab to centerpoint   Sincerely yours, ↓4x

Eleanor G. Corsi
672 Wesley Street
Greenville, TX 75401

BLOCK-STYLE PERSONAL BUSINESS LETTER

↓center page

January 3, {year} ↓4x

Mr. Luis Fernandez, Manager
Arvon Industries, Inc.
21 St. Claire Avenue East
Toronto, Ontario M4T 1L9
CANADA ↓2x

Dear Mr. Fernandez: ↓2x

As a former employee and present stockholder of Arvon Industries, I protest the planned sale of the Consumer Products Division to Browning Manufacturing Company. ↓2x

According to published reports, consumer products accounted for 19 percent of last year's corporate profits, and they are expected to account for at least as much this year. In addition, Dun & Bradstreet predicts that consumer products nationwide will outpace the general economy for the next five years.

I am concerned about the effect the planned sale of the division will have on overall corporate profits, on cash dividends for investors, and on the economics of Louisville and Paducah, where the two consumer-products plants are located.

Please ask your board of directors to reconsider this matter. ↓2x

Sincerely, ↓4x

Roger J. Michaelson
901 East Benson, Apt. 3
Ft. Lauderdale, FL 33310

MODIFIED-BLOCK STYLE LETTER

(with subject line, enclosure notation, and copy notation)

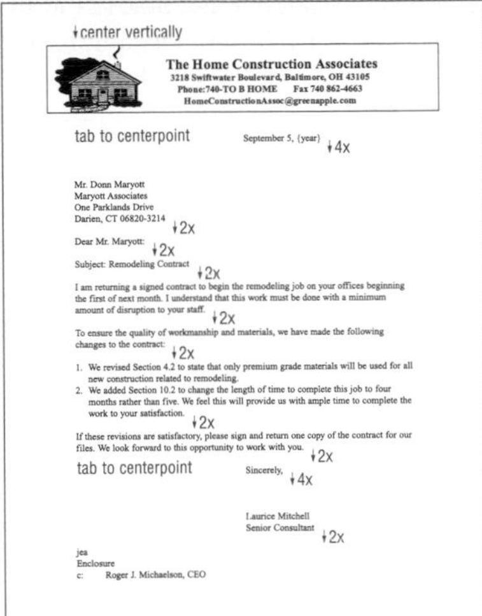

↓center vertically

The Home Construction Associates
3218 Swiftwater Boulevard, Baltimore, OH 43105
Phone:740-TO B HOME Fax 740 862-4663
HomeConstructionAssoc@greenapple.com

tab to centerpoint September 5, {year} ↓4x

Mr. Donn Maryott
Maryott Associates
One Parklands Drive
Darien, CT 06820-3214 ↓2x

Dear Mr. Maryott: ↓2x

Subject: Remodeling Contract ↓2x

I am returning a signed contract to begin the remodeling job on your offices beginning the first of next month. I understand that this work must be done with a minimum amount of disruption to your staff. ↓2x

To ensure the quality of workmanship and materials, we have made the following changes to the contract: ↓2x

1. We revised Section 4.2 to state that only premium grade materials will be used for all new construction related to remodeling.
2. We added Section 10.2 to change the length of time to complete this job to four months rather than five. We feel this will provide us with ample time to complete the work to your satisfaction. ↓2x

If these revisions are satisfactory, please sign and return one copy of the contract for our files. We look forward to this opportunity to work with you. ↓2x

tab to centerpoint Sincerely, ↓4x

Laurice Mitchell
Senior Consultant ↓2x

jea
Enclosure
c: Roger J. Michaelson, CEO

MODIFIED-BLOCK STYLE LETTER

(with open punctuation, table)

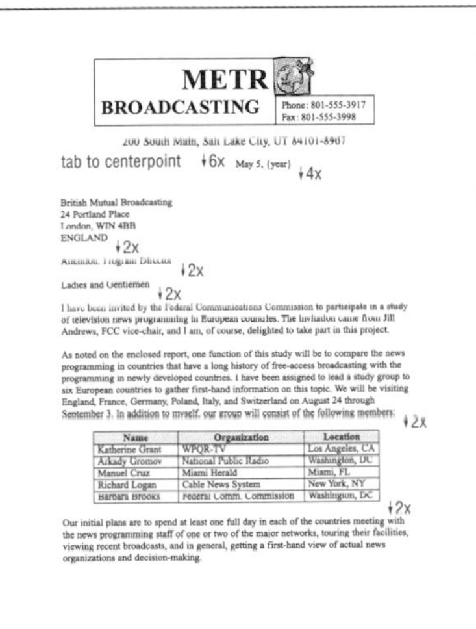

METR BROADCASTING
Phone: 801-555-3917
Fax: 801-555-3998
200 South Main, Salt Lake City, UT 84101-8987

tab to centerpoint ↓6x May 5, {year} ↓4x

British Mutual Broadcasting
24 Portland Place
London, WIN 4BB
ENGLAND ↓2x

Attention: Program Director ↓2x

Ladies and Gentlemen ↓2x

I have been invited by the Federal Communications Commission to participate in a study of television news programming in European countries. The invitation came from Jill Andrews, FCC vice-chair, and I am, of course, delighted to take part in this project.

As noted on the enclosed report, one function of this study will be to compare the news programming in countries that have a long history of free-access broadcasting with the programming in newly developed countries. I have been assigned to lead a study group to six European countries to gather first-hand information on this topic. We will be visiting England, France, Germany, Poland, Italy, and Switzerland on August 24 through September 3. In addition to myself, our group will consist of the following members: ↓2x

Name	Organization	Location
Katherine Grant	WPQR-TV	Los Angeles, CA
Arkady Gromov	National Public Radio	Washington, DC
Manuel Cruz	Miami Herald	Miami, FL
Richard Logan	Cable News System	New York, NY
Barbara Brooks	Federal Comm. Commission	Washington, DC

↓2x

Our initial plans are to spend at least one full day in each of the countries meeting with the news programming staff of one or two of the major networks, touring their facilities, viewing recent broadcasts, and in general, getting a first-hand view of actual news organizations and decision-making.

MODIFIED-BLOCK STYLE LETTER

(with enumeration, attachment, delivery notation, postscript)

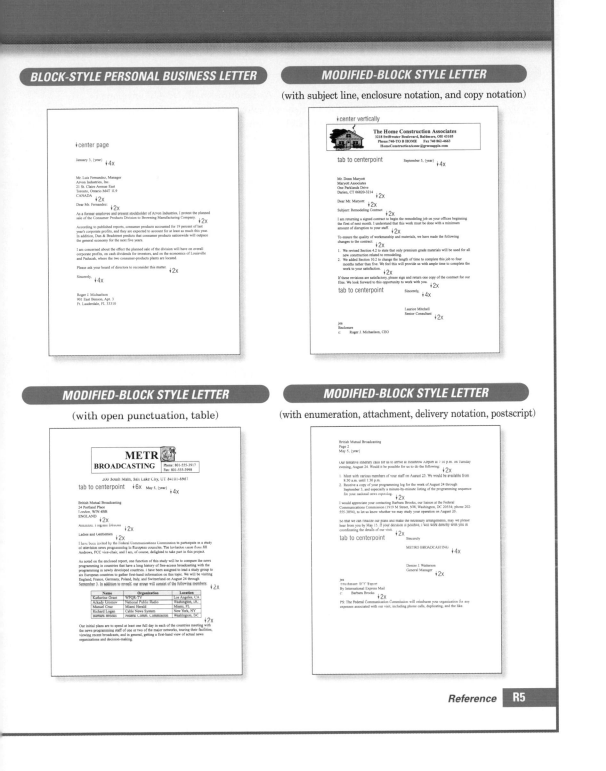

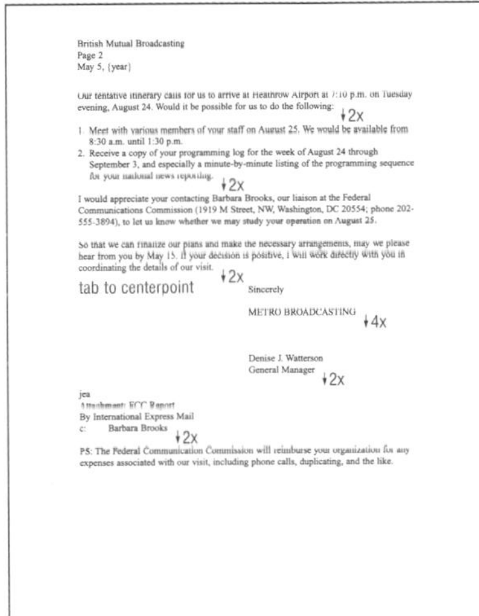

British Mutual Broadcasting
Page 2
May 5, {year}

Our tentative itinerary calls for us to arrive at Heathrow Airport at 7:10 p.m. on Tuesday evening, August 24. Would it be possible for us to do the following: ↓2x

1. Meet with various members of your staff on August 25. We would be available from 8:30 a.m. until 1:30 p.m.
2. Receive a copy of your programming log for the week of August 24 through September 3, and especially a minute-by-minute listing of the programming sequence for your national news reporting. ↓2x

I would appreciate your contacting Barbara Brooks, our liaison at the Federal Communications Commission (1919 M Street, NW, Washington, DC 20554; phone 202-555-3894), to let us know whether we may study your operation on August 25.

So that we can finalize our plans and make the necessary arrangements, may we please hear from you by May 15. If your decision is positive, I will work directly with you in coordinating the details of our visit. ↓2x

tab to centerpoint Sincerely

METRO BROADCASTING ↓4x

Denise J. Watterson
General Manager ↓2x

jea
Attachment: FCC Report
By International Express Mail
c: Barbara Brooks ↓2x

PS: The Federal Communication Commission will reimburse your organization for any expenses associated with our visit, including phone calls, duplicating, and the like.

FORMATTING ENVELOPES

A standard large (No. 10) envelope is 9½ by 4⅛ inches. A standard small (No. 6¾) envelope is 6½ by 3⅝ inches. Although either address format shown below is acceptable, the format shown for the large envelope (all capital letters and no punctuation) is recommended by the U.S. Postal Service for mail that will be sorted by an electronic scanning device.

George Ellis
1553 Oak Lane
Muncie, IN 47302
Ms. Louise Tye
P.O. Box 770
Shreveport, LA 71101
Cape Cod Resorts
1408 Oceanside
Sandwich, MA 02563
DR MIA JENNINGS
9019 LAYTON AVENUE
LUBBOCK TX 79041-9019

FOLDING LETTERS

To fold a letter for a small envelope:

1. Place the letter *face up* and fold up the bottom half to 0.5 inch from the top edge of the paper.
2. Fold the right third over to the left.
3. Fold the left third over to 0.5 inch from the right edge of the paper.
4. Insert the last crease into the envelope first, with the flap facing up.

To fold a letter for a large envelope:

1. Place the letter *face up* and fold up the bottom third.
2. Fold the top third down to 0.5 inch from the bottom edge of the paper.
3. Insert the last crease into the envelope first, with the flap facing up.

MEMO (TEMPLATE)

Memorandum

To: Elizabeth Barnett

From: Catherine Argetes

Date: Current

Re: Flexible Scheduling

Several of our employees who have certain family obligations have asked us to explore the possibility of flexible scheduling. These staff members feel that a flexible schedule will help to increase morale and productivity and reduce absenteeism and turnover.

We are now considering several options, which include flextime, job sharing, and compressed workweeks.

Flextime is the most popular option. Employees would work a set number of hours per day with flexible start and finish times. However, employees would be required to be on the job during particular hours of the day.

Job sharing involves two employees sharing the same job. The employees might have divided job responsibilities, or they might have totally unrelated responsibilities. The two employees involved in sharing a job would need to work out the hours that each would work so that we have full coverage of the position at all times.

Compressed workweeks are those in which employees work the same number of total hours, but they do so over a shorter number of days. Using a compressed workweek would enable us to extend our business hours and provide employees with an opportunity to handle their personal obligations during the week.

I have attached more complete descriptions for your review and will schedule a meeting before the end of the month to discuss all of these options with you.

urs
Attachment

CONFIDENTIAL 1

OPEN TABLE

(with blocked column heads)

↓center page

SALES ANALYSIS
Borden Manufacturing Company
June 30, {year}
↓1x

Salesperson	**Units**	**Gross Sales ($)**
Brazinski, Robert	10	427.70
Dawkins, Carol	18	769.86
Greene, Janice	20	855.40
Herrera, Jose	17	727.09
Kessler, Diane	15	641.55
Yeung, Joe	19	812.63

BOXED TABLE

(with centered column heads)

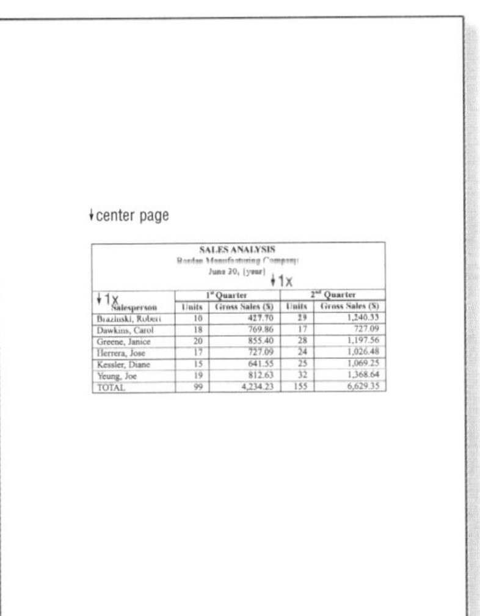

↓center page

SALES ANALYSIS
Borden Manufacturing Company
June 30, {year}
↓1x

↓1x **Salesperson**	**1st Quarter**		**2nd Quarter**	
	Units	**Gross Sales ($)**	**Units**	**Gross Sales ($)**
Brazinski, Robert	10	427.70	29	1,240.33
Dawkins, Carol	18	769.86	17	727.09
Greene, Janice	20	855.40	28	1,197.56
Herrera, Jose	17	727.09	24	1,026.48
Kessler, Diane	15	641.55	25	1,069.25
Yeung, Joe	19	812.63	32	1,368.64
TOTAL	99	4,234.23	155	6,629.35

BOXED TABLE

(with multi-line heads, footnote)

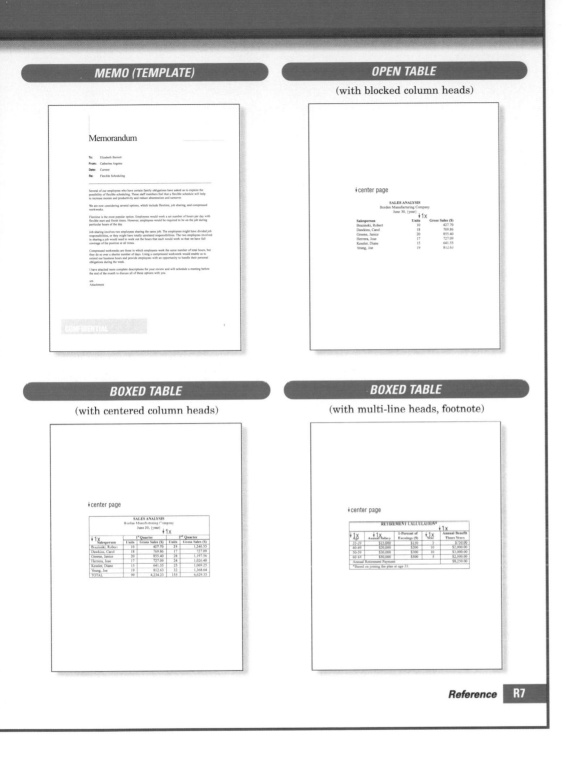

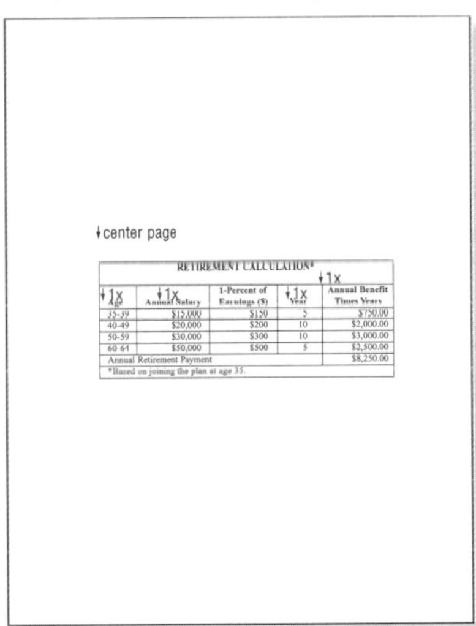

↓center page

RETIREMENT CALCULATION*
↓1x

↓1x **Age**	↓1x **Annual Salary**	**1-Percent of Earnings ($)**	↓1x **Year**	**Annual Benefit Times Years**
35-39	$15,000	$150	5	$750.00
40-49	$20,000	$200	10	$2,000.00
50-59	$30,000	$300	10	$3,000.00
60-64	$50,000	$500	5	$2,500.00
Annual Retirement Payment				$8,250.00

*Based on joining the plan at age 35.

BOXED TABLE

(with shading)

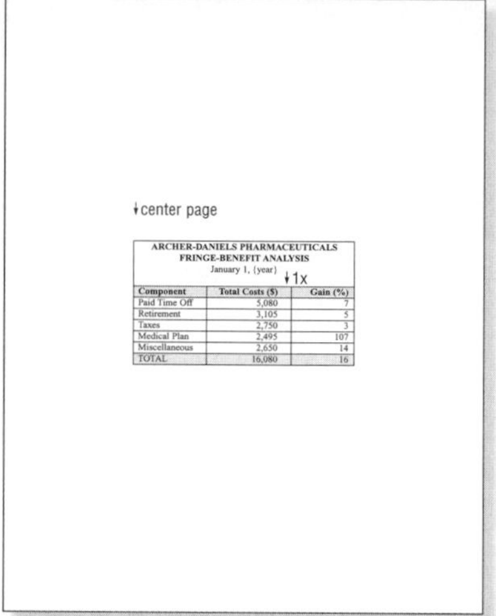

↓center page

ARCHER-DANIELS PHARMACEUTICALS FRINGE-BENEFIT ANALYSIS January 1, (year) ↓1x		
Component	**Total Costs ($)**	**Gain (%)**
Paid Time Off	5,080	7
Retirement	3,105	5
Taxes	2,750	3
Medical Plan	2,495	107
Miscellaneous	2,650	14
TOTAL	16,080	16

RULED TABLE

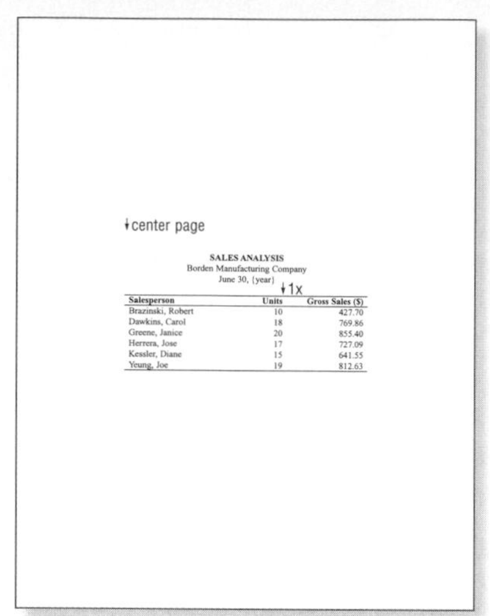

↓center page

SALES ANALYSIS
Borden Manufacturing Company
June 30, (year) ↓1x

Salesperson	Units	Gross Sales ($)
Brazinski, Robert	10	427.70
Dawkins, Carol	18	769.86
Greene, Janice	20	855.40
Herrera, Jose	17	727.09
Kessler, Diane	15	641.55
Yeung, Joe	19	812.63

PROOFREADERS' MARKS

Proofreaders' Marks	Draft	Final Copy
⁀ Omit space	data base	database
v or ∧ Insert	if he's going (not)	if he's not going,
≡ Capitalize	Maple street	Maple Street
Delete	a final draft	a draft
# Insert space	allready to	all ready to
when/if Change word	and if you (when)	and when you
/ Use lowercase letter	our President	our president
¶ Paragraph	¶ Most of the	Most of the
... Don't delete	a true story	a true story
○ Spell out	the only (1)	the only one
∽ Transpose	they all see	they see all
ss Single-space	ss [first line second line	first line second line
ds Double-space	ds [first line second line	first line second line
⊐ Move right	Please send	Please send
⊏ Move left	May I	May I
~~ Bold	Column Heading	**Column Heading**
ital Italic	ital Time magazine	*Time* magazine
u/l Underline	u/l Time magazine	Time magazine
Move as shown	readers will see	will see readers

LANGUAGE LINKS

ALWAYS SPACE ONCE...

- After a comma.
  We ordered two printers, one computer, and three monitors.
- After a semicolon.
  They flew to Dallas, Texas; Reno, Nevada; and Rome, New York.
- After a period following someone's initials.
  Mr. Henson, Ms. Hovey, and Mrs. Syzmanski will attend the meeting.
- After a period following the abbreviation of a single word.
  We will send the package by 7 p.m. next week. [Note: space once after the final period in the "p.m." abbreviation, but do not space after the first period between the two letters.]
- Before a ZIP code.
  Send the package to 892 Maple Street, Grand Forks, ND 58201.
- Before and after an ampersand.
  We were represented by the law firm of Argue & Johnson; they were represented by the law firm of Crandall & Humphries.
- After a period at the end of a sentence.
  Don't forget to vote. Vote for the candidate of your choice.
- After a question mark.
  When will you vote? Did you vote last year?
- After an exclamation point.
  Wow! What a performance! It was fantastic!
- After a colon.
  We will attend on the following days: Monday, Wednesday, and Friday.

PUNCTUATION

COMMAS:

1. Use a comma between independent clauses joined by a conjunction. (An independent clause is one that can stand alone as a complete sentence.)
   We requested Brown Industries to change the date, and they did so within five days.
2. Use a comma after an introductory expression (unless it is a short prepositional phrase).
   Before we can make a decision, we must have all the facts.
   In 1992 our nation elected a president.
3. Use a comma before and after the year in a complete date.
   We will arrive at the plant on June 2, 1995, for the conference.
4. Use a comma before and after a state or country that follows a city (but not before a ZIP Code).
   Joan moved to Vancouver, British Columbia, in September.
   Send the package to Douglasville, GA 30135, by express mail.
5. Use a comma between each item in a series of three or more.
   We need to order paper, toner, and font cartridges.
6. Use a comma before and after a transitional expression (such as *therefore* and *however*).
   It is critical, therefore, that we finish the project on time.
7. Use a comma before and after a direct quotation.
   When we left, James said, "Let us return to the same location next year."
8. Use a comma before and after a nonessential expression. (A nonessential expression is a word or group of words that may be omitted without changing the basic meaning of the sentence.)
   Let me say, to begin with, that the report has already been finalized.
9. Use a comma between two adjacent adjectives that modify the same noun.
   We need an intelligent, enthusiastic individual for this job.

SEMICOLONS

1. Use a semicolon to join two closely related independent clauses that are not connected by a conjunction (such as *and, but,* or *nor*).
   Management favored the vote; stockholders did not.
2. Use a semicolon to separate three or more items in a series if any of the items already contain commas.
   Region 1 sent their reports in March, April, and May; and Region 2 sent their reports in September, October, and November.

HYPHENS:

1. Hyphenate compound adjectives that come before a noun (unless the first word is an adverb ending in *-ly*).
   We reviewed an up-to-date report on Wednesday.
   We attended a highly rated session on multimedia software.

2. Hyphenate compound numbers (between twenty-one and ninety-nine) and fractions that are expressed as words.
   We observed twenty-nine infractions during the investigation.
   Bancroft Industries reduced their sales force by one-third.

3. Hyphenate words that are divided at the end of a line. Do not divide one-syllable words, contractions, or abbreviations; divide other words only between syllables.
   To appreciate the full significance of our actions, you must review the entire docu-
   ment that was sent to you.

APOSTROPHES:

1. Use *'s* to form the possessive of singular nouns.
   The hurricane caused major damage to Georgia's coastline.

2. Use only an apostrophe to form the possessive of plural nouns that end in *s*.
   The investors' goals were outlined in the annual report.

3. Use *'s* to form the possessive of indefinite pronouns (such as *someone's* or *anybody's*); do not use an apostrophe with personal pronouns (such as *hers, his, its, ours, theirs,* and *yours*).
   She was instructed to select anybody's paper for a sample.
   Each computer comes carefully packed in its own container.

COLONS:

1. Use a colon to introduce explanatory material that follows an independent clause. (An independent clause is one that can stand alone as a complete sentence.)
   The computer satisfies three criteria: speed, cost, and power.

DASHES:

1. Use a dash instead of a comma, semicolon, colon, or parenthesis when you want to convey a more forceful separation of words within a sentence. (If your keyboard has a special dash character, use it. Otherwise, form a dash by typing two hyphens, with no space before, between, or after.)
   At this year's meeting, the speakers—and topics—were superb.

PERIODS:

1. Use a period to end a sentence that is a polite request. (Consider a sentence a polite request if you expect the reader to respond by doing as you ask rather than by giving a yes-or-no answer.)
   Will you please call me if I can be of further assistance.

QUOTATION MARKS:

1. Use quotation marks around the titles of newspaper articles, magazine articles, chapters in a book, reports, conferences, and similar items.
   The best article I found in my research was entitled "Multimedia for Everyone."
2. Use quotation marks around a direct quotation.
   Harrison responded by saying, "This decision will not affect our merger."

ITALIC (OR UNDERLINE):

1. Italicize (or underline) the titles of books, magazines, newspapers, and other complete published works.
   I read The Pelican Brief last month.

GRAMMAR

AGREEMENT:

1. Use singular verbs and pronouns with singular subjects and plural verbs and pronouns with plural subjects.
   I was pleased with the performance of our team.
   Reno and Phoenix were selected as the sites for our next two meetings.
2. Some pronouns (*anybody, each, either, everybody, everyone, much, neither, no one, nobody,* and *one*) are always singular and take a singular verb. Other pronouns (*all, any, more, most, none,* and *some*) may be singular or plural, depending on the noun to which they refer.
   Each employee is responsible for summarizing the day's activities.
   Most of the workers are going to get a substantial pay raise.
3. Disregard any intervening words that come between the subject and verb when establishing agreement.
   The box containing the books and pencils has not been found.
4. If two subjects are joined by *or, either/or, nor, neither/nor,* or *not only/but also,* the verb should agree with the subject nearer to the verb.
   Neither the players nor the coach is in favor of the decision.
5. The subject *a number* takes a plural verb; *the number* takes a singular verb.
   A number of us will take the train to the game.
   The number of errors has increased in the last two attempts.
6. Subjects joined by *and* take a plural verb unless the compound subject is preceded by *each, every*, or *many a (an).*
   Every man, woman, and child is included in our survey.
7. Verbs that refer to conditions that are impossible or improbable (that is, verbs in the *subjunctive* mood) require the plural form.
   If the total eclipse were to occur tomorrow, it would be the second one this year.

PRONOUNS:

1. Use nominative pronouns (such as *I, he, she, we,* and *they*) as subjects of a sentence or clause.
   They traveled to Minnesota last week but will not return until next month.

2. Use objective pronouns (such as *me, him, her, us,* and *them*) as objects in a sentence or clause.
   The package has been sent to her.

ADJECTIVES AND ADVERBS:

1. Use comparative adjectives and adverbs (*-er, more,* and *less*) when referring to two nouns; use superlative adjectives and adverbs (*-est, most,* and *least*) when referring to more than two.
   Of the two movies you have selected, the shorter one is the more interesting.
   The highest of the three mountains is Mt. Everest.

WORD USAGE:

1. Do not confuse the following pairs of words:
   - *Accept* means "to agree to"; *except* means "to leave out."
     We ***accept*** *your offer for developing the new product.*
     Everyone ***except*** *Sam and Lisa attended the meeting.*
   - *Affect* is most often used as a verb meaning "to influence"; *effect* is most often used as a noun meaning "result."
     Mr. Smith's decision will not ***affect*** *our programming plans.*
     It will be weeks before we can assess the ***effect*** *of this action.*
   - *Farther* refers to distance; *further* refers to extent or degree.
     Did we travel ***farther*** *today than yesterday?*
     We need to discuss our plans ***further****.*
   - *Personal* means "private"; *personnel* means "employees."
     The letters were very ***personal*** *and should not have been read.*
     We hope that all ***personnel*** *will comply with the new regulations.*
   - *Principal* means "primary"; *principle* means "rule."
     The ***principal*** *means of research were interviewing and surveying.*
     They must not violate the ***principles*** *under which our company was established.*
   - *Passed* means "went by"; *past* means "before now."
     We ***passed*** *another car from our home state.*
     In the ***past****, we always took the same route.*
   - *Advice* means "to provide guidance"; *advise* means "help."
     My doctor ***advised*** *me to take it easy.*
     His ***advice*** *was to get plenty of sleep.*
   - *Council* is a group; *counsel* is a person who provides advice.
     The student ***council*** *met to discuss graduation.*
     The court asked that ***counsel*** *be present at the hearing.*

- *Then* means "at that time"; *than* is used for comparisons.
  He read for a while; ***then*** *he turned out the light.*
  She reads more books ***than*** *I do.*
- *Its* is the possessive form of it; *it's* is a contraction for it is.
  It's *not too late to finish the project.*
  We researched the country and ***its*** *people.*
- *Two* means "more than one"; *too* means "also"; *to* means "in a direction."
  There were ***two*** *people in the boat.*
  We wished we were on board, ***too.***
  The boat headed out ***to*** *sea.*
- *Stationery* means "paper"; *stationary* means "fixed position."
  Please buy some ***stationery*** *so that I can write letters.*
  The ***stationary*** *bike at the health club provides a good workout.*

MECHANICS

CAPITALIZATION:

1. Capitalize the first word of a sentence.
Please prepare a summary of your activities for our next meeting.

2. Capitalize proper nouns and adjectives derived from proper nouns. (A proper noun is the official name of a particular person, place, or thing.)
Judy Hendrix drove to Albuquerque in her new automobile, a Pontiac.

3. Capitalize the names of the days of the week, months, holidays, and religious days (but do not capitalize the names of the seasons).
On Thursday, November 25, we will celebrate Thanksgiving, the most popular fall holiday.

4. Capitalize nouns followed by a number or letter (except for the nouns *line, note, page, paragraph,* and *size*).
Please read Chapter 5, but not page 94.

5. Capitalize compass points (such as *north, south,* or *northeast*) only when they designate definite regions.
The Crenshaw's will vacation in the Northeast this summer.
We will have to drive north to reach the closest Canadian border.

6. Capitalize common organizational terms (such as *advertising department* and *finance committee*) when they are the actual names of the units in the writer's own organization and when they are preceded by the word *the*.
The quarterly report from the Advertising Department will be presented today.

7. Capitalize the names of specific course titles but not the names of subjects or areas of study.
I have enrolled in Accounting 201 and will also take a marketing course.

NUMBER EXPRESSION:

1. In general, spell out numbers 1 through 10, and use figures for numbers above 10.
   We have rented two movies for tonight.
   The decision was reached after 27 precincts had sent in their results.

2. Use figures for:
   - Dates (use *st, d,* or *th* only if the day precedes the month).
     We will drive to the camp on the 23d of May.
     The tax report is due on April 15.
   - All numbers if two or more related numbers both above and below ten are used in the same sentence.
     Mr. Carter sent in 7 receipts; Ms. Cantrell sent in 22 receipts.
   - Measurements (time, money, distance, weight, and percent).
     At 10 a.m. we delivered the $500 coin bank in a 17-pound container.
   - Mixed numbers.
     Our sales are up 9½ percent over last year.

3. Spell out:
   - Numbers used as the first word in a sentence.
     Seventy people attended the conference in San Diego last week.
   - The smaller of two adjacent numbers.
     We have ordered two 5-pound packages for the meeting.
   - The words *millions* and *billions* in even amounts (do not use decimals with even amounts).
     The lottery is worth 28 million this month.
   - Fractions.
     About one-half of the audience responded to questionnaire.

ABBREVIATIONS:

1. In nontechnical writing, do not abbreviate common nouns (such as *dept.* or *pkg.*), compass points, units of measure, or the names of months, days of the week, cities, or states (except in addresses).
   The Sales Department will meet on Tuesday, March 7, in Tempe, Arizona.

2. In lowercase abbreviations made up of single initials, use a period after each initial but no internal spaces.
   We will be including several states (e.g., Maine, New Hampshire, Vermont, Massachusetts, and Connecticut).

3. In all-capital abbreviations made up of single initials, do not use periods or internal spaces. (Exception: Keep the periods in most academic degrees and in abbreviations of geographic names other than two-letter state abbreviations.)
   You need to call the EEO office for clarification on that issue.

UNIT 1 ORGANIZER

KEYBOARDING

Lesson	Focus	Special Features	Skillbuilding	Pretest/Practice/Posttest
1	Home Keys Space Bar ENTER Key		pp. 5–6	p. 6
2	H, E, O	Fact File, p. 8	p. 9	p. 9
3	M, R, I	Internet Connection, p. 11	p. 12	p. 12
4	Review	Cultural Connection, p. 14 Journal Entry, p. 15	pp. 13–14	p. 15
5	T, N, C	Social Studies Connection, p. 17	p. 18	p. 18
6	V, Right Shift, Period	Fact File, p. 22	pp. 20–21	p. 22
7	W, Comma, G	Communication Focus, p. 24 Fact File, p. 26	pp. 25–26	p. 26
8	Review	Cultural Connection, p. 29	pp. 27–28	p. 29
9	B, U, Left Shift	Internet Connection, p. 32	p. 31	p. 32
10	Q, Slash	Fact File, p. 35	p. 34	p. 35

UNIT 1 RESOURCE MANAGER

MULTIMEDIA
Courseware: Lessons 1–20
Student Data Disk
Wall Charts

TEACHING TOOLS
Lesson Plans: Lessons 1–20
Block Scheduling Guide, Unit 1

RETEACHING/REINFORCEMENT
Reteaching and Reinforcement Activities: Lessons 1–20

ASSESSMENT and EVALUATION

Pretest/Practice/Posttest: pp. 6, 9, 12, 15, 18, 22, 26, 29, 32, 35, 38, 40, 43, 45, 49, 51–52, 55, 58, 61, 64
Portfolio Activity: p. 65
Unit 1 Test
Timings: pp. 52, 58, 65
Grading and Evaluation

Electronic Teacher Classroom Resources

For your convenience, the teacher's materials are available on a CD-ROM. Having these resources available electronically enables you to print exactly what you need and revise materials as necessary.

Lesson	Focus	Special Features	Skillbuilding	Pretest/Practice/Posttest
11	Quote, Apostrophe	Fact File, p. 38	pp. 37–38	p. 38
12	Review		pp. 39–40	p. 40
13	P, X	Cultural Connection, p. 42	pp. 42–43	p. 43
14	Y, Tab		p. 45	p. 45
15	Z, Colon	Internet Connection, p. 48	pp. 48–49	p. 49
16	Review	Language Link, p. 52	pp. 50–51	pp. 51–52
17	Question Mark, Caps Lock	Language Link, p. 55	p. 54	p. 55
18	Hyphen, Underscore		p. 57	p. 58
19	Skillbuilding	Journal Entry, p. 61	pp. 59–60	p. 61
20	Skillbuilding	Portfolio Activity, p. 65	pp. 62–64	p. 64

SCANS Competencies in Glencoe Keyboarding with Computer Applications

Resources	Interpersonal Skills	Information	Systems	Technology
Throughout the course, students deal specifically with resources: allocating time for completing drills and documents, maintaining workstations, caring for computers and software.	Communication Focus, p. 24 Cultural Connection, pp. 14, 29, 42	Career Bit, p. 1 Fact File, pp. 8, 22, 26, 35, 38 Internet Connection, pp. 11, 32, 48	Internet Connection, pp. 11, 32, 48	Lessons 1–20 Internet Connection, pp. 11, 32, 48

INTRODUCING THE UNIT

Ask students if they are experienced in using computers. For what have they used computers? Write a list of uses on the board. Ask students how they have operated the computer—by mouse or keyboard? Add to the list any other ways students may use a computer—to write e-mail messages, create reports for classes, write letters, resumes, and so forth.

Ask students why they think it is important to operate the keyboard by touch with speed and accuracy. Also ask them how they think they might use these skills in their future careers as well as in their personal lives.

FUN Facts

Cortez Peters, Jr., is recognized as the world's fastest typist. Cortez Peters began typing at the age of 12. He participated in—and won—12 typing contests. His best speed on a 1-minute timing was 225 net words a minute. Cortez Peters also developed a method for helping others to improve their typing skills.

UNIT 1 KEYBOARDING

Lessons 1–20

OBJECTIVES

- Demonstrate which fingers control each key on the keyboard.
- Use home key anchors to assist in developing location security.
- Develop and practice correct keyboarding techniques.
- Type at a speed of 25 words a minute for 1 minute with 2 or fewer errors.
- Use proper spacing after common marks of punctuation.
- Compose single word responses at the keyboard.

COURSEWARE OVERVIEW

Glencoe Keyboarding With Computer Applications courseware includes both textbook activities and a teacher management program for scoring, grading, and tracking students' progress. The user's guide explains available options and provides instructions for using the courseware.

WORDS TO LEARN

cursor
default
insertion point
technique
word scale
word count
word wrap

CAREER BIT

NURSING Many modern hospitals use computers to store medical records of their patients. Information from each patient's medical chart is entered into a computer file. Nurses update this file every time they give medications or check the patient's blood pressure, pulse rate, temperature, and overall progress.

When nurses change shifts, they need only to have a quick briefing because the essential information about the patient's care is already on the computer.

1

WORDS TO LEARN

The terms in Words to Learn are defined in the Glossary at the back of the book. Ask students if they are familiar with any of the terms. Have them define the terms they know. Compare their definitions with those in the Glossary.

CAREER BIT

After students read the information on nursing, have them brainstorm to create a list of other health occupations in which computers may be used. Write the titles of these occupations on the board. Ask students to interview someone who works in one of these fields to learn how computers are used on the job. Have students meet in small groups to discuss what they learned. Have the small groups prepare a short report, then have one representative from each group give the report to the class. Have students discuss as a class how they think computers will be used in medicine in the future.

COURSEWARE OVERVIEW

Before students begin Lesson 1, be sure that they are familiar with how to operate the equipment and that they have their textbook and data disk. Help students with the login procedure, explain the various menu options, and explain how the program will score their work

LESSON 1

FOCUS

- Learn proper technique for typing.
- Learn the home keys, ENTER key, and space bar.
- Understand the technique checkpoint feature.

BELLRINGER

As soon as students are seated, demonstrate the proper posture for sitting at the keyboard.

TEACH

Illustration

Explain the purpose of the keyboard illustration.

- The keys are color-coded according to which finger is used.
- The hands below the keyboard show which fingers correlate to each color.
- The new keys being introduced are shown in white.

Activity A. Demonstrate the placement of the fingers on the home keys. Point out that the raised marker or "dimple" on the F and J keys will help them to maintain correct home-key position.

NEW KEYS: A S D F J K L ; SPACE BAR ENTER

OBJECTIVE:

- Learn the home keys, the space bar, and the ENTER key.

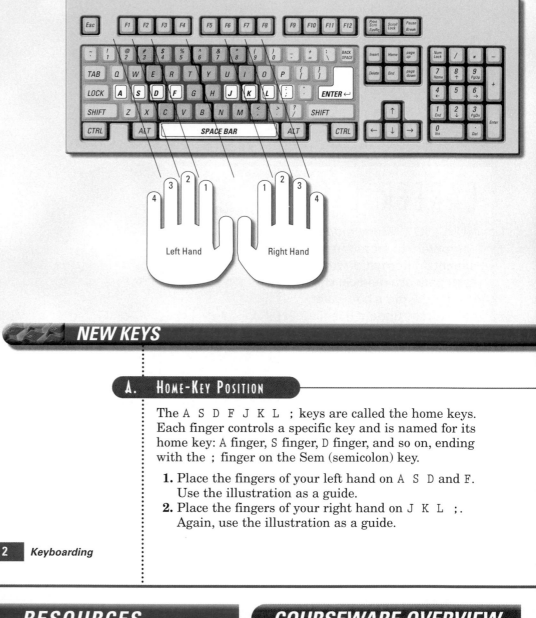

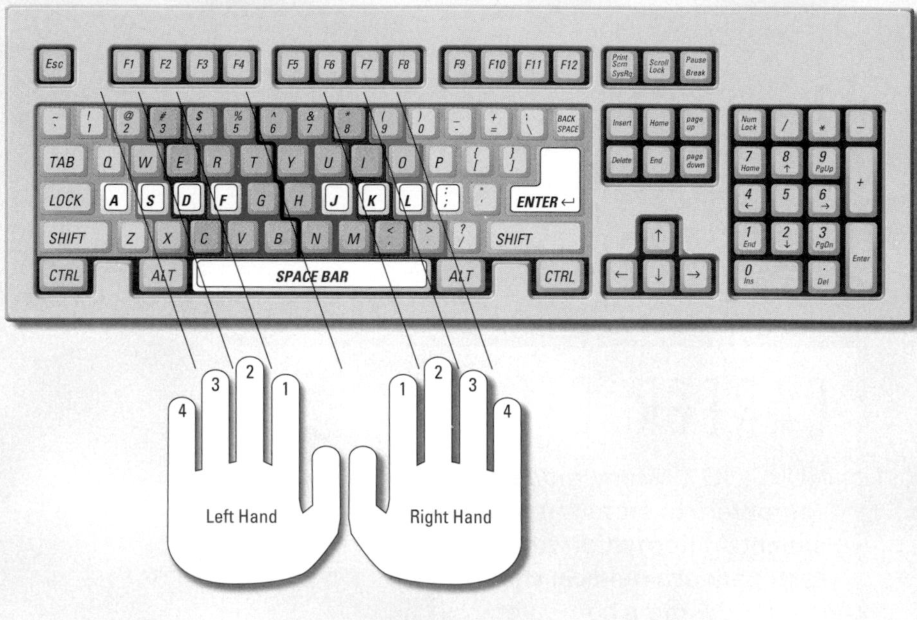

NEW KEYS

A. HOME-KEY POSITION

The A S D F J K L ; keys are called the home keys. Each finger controls a specific key and is named for its home key: A finger, S finger, D finger, and so on, ending with the ; finger on the Sem (semicolon) key.

1. Place the fingers of your left hand on A S D and F. Use the illustration as a guide.
2. Place the fingers of your right hand on J K L ;. Again, use the illustration as a guide.

RESOURCES

- Lesson Plan 1
- Courseware Lesson 1
- Student Data Disk
- Wallchart

COURSEWARE OVERVIEW

Before students begin Lesson 1, help them through the login and password process. Be sure that students are familiar with using a mouse and know how to access the keyboarding program (referred to as KCA); that they have their data disk in the drive; do not remove disks until the drive light is off; and that they read all instructional screens carefully.

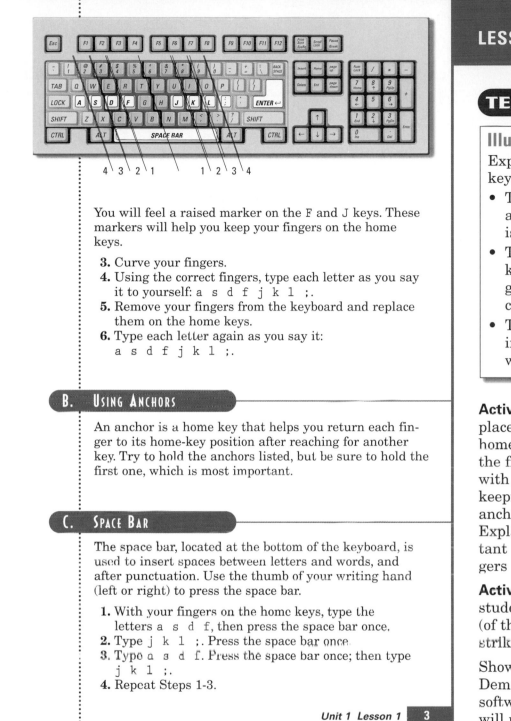

4 3 2 1 1 2 3 4

You will feel a raised marker on the F and J keys. These markers will help you keep your fingers on the home keys.

3. Curve your fingers.
4. Using the correct fingers, type each letter as you say it to yourself: `a s d f j k l ;`.
5. Remove your fingers from the keyboard and replace them on the home keys.
6. Type each letter again as you say it: `a s d f j k l ;`.

B. Using Anchors

An anchor is a home key that helps you return each finger to its home-key position after reaching for another key. Try to hold the anchors listed, but be sure to hold the first one, which is most important.

C. Space Bar

The space bar, located at the bottom of the keyboard, is used to insert spaces between letters and words, and after punctuation. Use the thumb of your writing hand (left or right) to press the space bar.

1. With your fingers on the home keys, type the letters `a s d f`, then press the space bar once.
2. Type `j k l ;`. Press the space bar once.
3. Type `a s d f`. Press the space bar once; then type `j k l ;`.
4. Repeat Steps 1-3.

TECHNOLOGY TIP

To avoid potential damage to equipment, keep food and drink away from the work area around the computer. A spilled beverage can damage files, disks, and even the hard drive of the computer. Food crumbs can get into the keyboard or greasy foods may leave spots on documents.

Out-of-Class Activity

Encourage students to practice the new keys at home. Have students who do not have a keyboard available to them make a simulated keyboard. Advise students to close their eyes when they practice. Also have students visualize where the home keys are located and how their fingers press each key.

TEACH

Illustration

Explain the purpose of the keyboard illustration.

- The keys are color-coded according to which finger is used.
- The numbers below the keyboard show which fingers correlate to each color.
- The new keys being introduced are shown in white.

Activity B. Have students place their fingers on the home keys. Ask them to tap the first anchor keys (F and J) with their index fingers while keeping their other fingers anchored on the home keys. Explain that it is very important to return their index fingers to the first anchor keys.

Activity C. Demonstrate to students the use of the thumb (of their writing hand) to strike the space bar.

Show students how to use the Demonstrate button in the software. Explain that they will use the Demonstrate button to view the correct reach for each key as it is introduced.

TEACH

Illustration

Explain the purpose of the keyboard illustration.

- The keys are color-coded according to which finger is used.
- The numbers below the keyboard show which fingers correlate to each color.
- The new keys being introduced are shown in white.

Activity D. Demonstrate the correct reach for the ENTER key. Point out that the cursor moves back to the left margin when the ENTER key is pressed. Have students use the Demonstrate button in the software to view the correct reaches for the ENTER key.

Activities E–H. Emphasize that drill lines are shown in two-line increments in the first lesson to illustrate the practice pattern for all succeeding lessons.

Make sure students are using the correct fingers to type each home key. Emphasize the importance of technique and its impact on speed and accuracy.

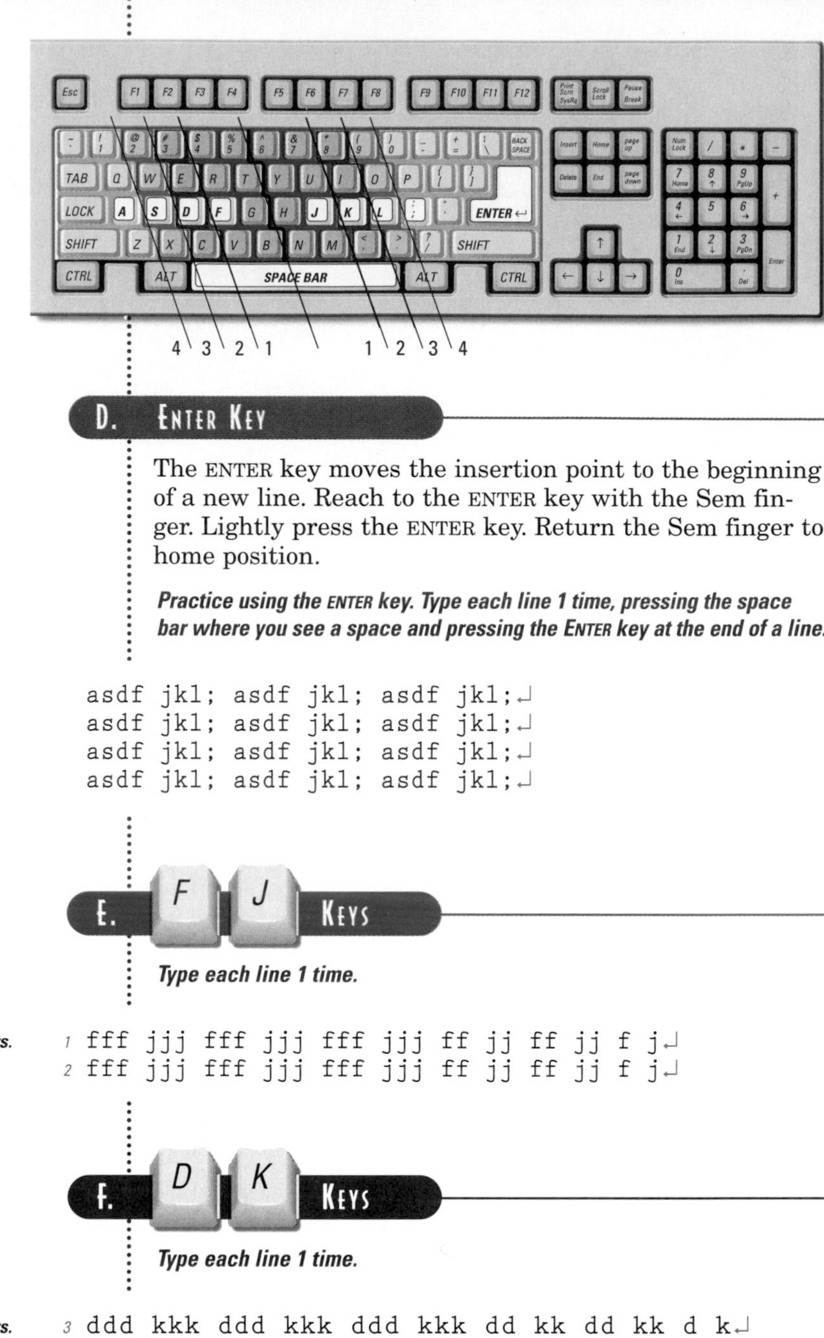

D. ENTER KEY

The ENTER key moves the insertion point to the beginning of a new line. Reach to the ENTER key with the Sem finger. Lightly press the ENTER key. Return the Sem finger to home position.

Practice using the ENTER key. Type each line 1 time, pressing the space bar where you see a space and pressing the ENTER key at the end of a line.

```
asdf jkl; asdf jkl; asdf jkl;↵
asdf jkl; asdf jkl; asdf jkl;↵
asdf jkl; asdf jkl; asdf jkl;↵
asdf jkl; asdf jkl; asdf jkl;↵
```

E. F J KEYS

Type each line 1 time.

Use F and J fingers.

```
1 fff jjj fff jjj fff jjj ff jj ff jj f j↵
2 fff jjj fff jjj fff jjj ff jj ff jj f j↵
```

F. D K KEYS

Type each line 1 time.

Use D and K fingers.

```
3 ddd kkk ddd kkk ddd kkk dd kk dd kk d k↵
4 ddd kkk ddd kkk ddd kkk dd kk dd kk d k↵
```

4 *Keyboarding*

FACT FILE

The first computer, the ENIAC, required 1,500 square feet of floor space. To compare this to today's computers, have students measure and chart your classroom, the ENIAC computer, and the computer they use today, using graph paper and colored markers. One square on the graph paper equals one foot.

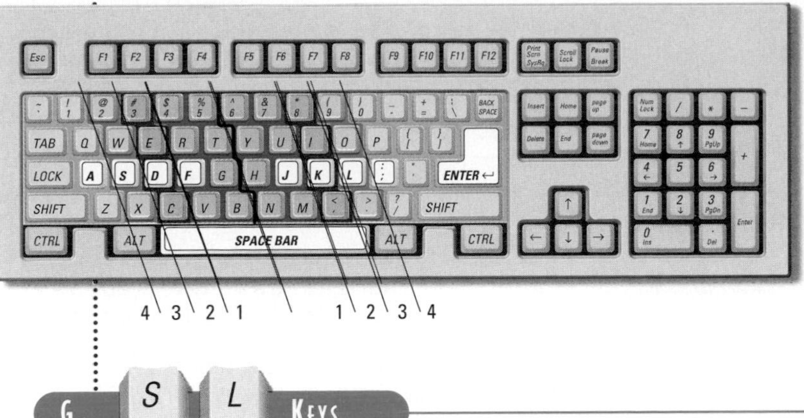

G. S L Keys

Type each line 1 time.

Use S and L fingers.

```
sss lll sss lll sss lll ss ll ss ll s l↵
sss lll sss lll sss lll ss ll ss ll s l↵
```

H. A ; Keys

Type each line 1 time.

Use A and ; fingers.

```
aaa ;;; aaa ;;; aaa ;;; aa ;; aa ;; a ;↵
aaa ;;; aaa ;;; aaa ;;; aa ;; aa ;; a ;↵
```

SKILLBUILDING

I. Technique Checkpoint

Technique Checkpoints enable you to practice new keys. They also give you and your teacher a chance to evaluate your keyboarding techniques. Focus on the techniques listed in the margin, such as:

- Use correct fingers.
- Keep eyes on copy.
- Press ENTER without pausing.
- Maintain correct posture.
- Maintain correct arm, hand, and finger position.

TEACH

Illustration

Explain the purpose of the keyboard illustration.

- The keys are color-coded according to which finger is used.
- The numbers below the keyboard show which fingers correlate to each color.
- The new keys being introduced are shown in white.

Activity I. Remind students to keep eyes on copy, fingers on home keys.

PORTFOLIO Activity

Explain to students that they will place some documents they create in a file folder, binder, or other cover. Have them decorate the folder to reflect their learning in this class.

Career Exploration

Have students work in groups of three or four to research types of careers available to them in the computer industry. Have them prepare an oral report for the class that describes three careers, the training that is needed, and how this class is helping to prepare them for these careers.

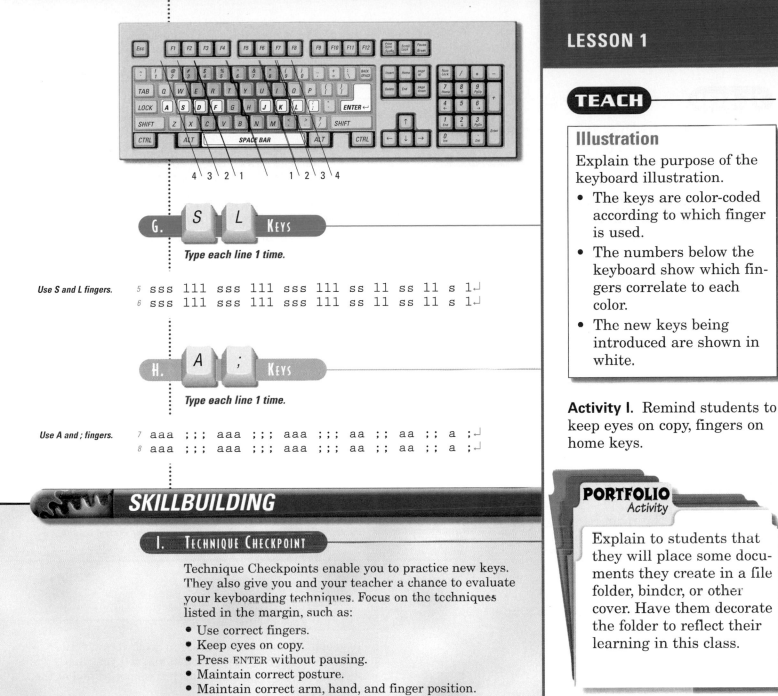

TEACH

Activities J–L. Introduce the Pretest, Practice, and Posttest to students.

PRETEST/PRACTICE/POSTEST

The ***Pretest/Practice/Posttest*** routines are designed to improve speed or accuracy.

- The ***Pretest*** identifies students' speed or accuracy needs.
- The ***Practice*** provides a variety of improvement drills.
- The ***Posttest*** (a repeat of the Pretest) measures improvement.

ASSESS

- Walk around the room to see if students enter and exit the program software correctly.
- Check students' position at the keyboard. Check to see if they are using their writing hand thumb to press the space bar. Check to see if they are striking the ENTER key by touch and are keeping their eyes on the copy (or on the screen).

CLOSE

Tell students what should be done at the end of every class period.

- Save their work to a disk.
- Exit the program.
- Remove the disk.
- Remove books and materials from the work space.

Type lines 9 and 10 one time.

Focus on these techniques:
- *Keep eyes on copy.*
- *Keep fingers on home keys.*

```
9  ff jj dd kk ss ll aa ;; f j d k s l a ;↵
10 ff jj dd kk ss ll aa ;; f j d k s l a ;↵
```

J. PRETEST

Type lines 11–12 for 1 minute. Repeat if time permits. Keep your eyes on the copy.

Hold Anchor Keys

```
11 sad sad fad fad ask ask lad lad dad dad↵
12 as; as; fall fall alas alas flask flask↵
```

K. PRACTICE

Type lines 13–24 one time. Repeat if time permits.

Leave a blank line after each set of lines (13–14, 15–16, and so on) by pressing ENTER 2 times.

```
13 aaa ddd sad sad aaa sss lll lll all all↵
14 aaa ddd sad sad aaa sss lll lll all all↵↵

15 aaa sss kkk ask ask fff aaa ddd fad fad↵
16 aaa sss kkk ask ask fff aaa ddd fad fad↵↵

17 aaa ddd ddd add add lll aaa ddd lad lad↵
18 aaa ddd ddd add add lll aaa ddd lad lad↵↵

19 aaa sss ;;; as; as; ddd aaa ddd dad dad↵
20 aaa sss ;;; as; as; ddd aaa ddd dad dad↵↵

21 f fl fla flas flask; l la las lass lass↵
22 f fl fla flas flask; l la las lass lass↵↵

23 f fa fal fall falls; a al ala alas alas↵
24 f fa fal fall falls; a al ala alas alas↵↵
```

L. POSTTEST

Type lines 11–12 for 1 minute. Repeat if time permits. Keep your eyes on the copy. Compare your Posttest results with your Pretest results.

M. End-of-Class Procedure

To keep hardware and software in good working order, treat them carefully. Your teacher will tell you what should be done at the end of each class period and at the end of the day.

Teacher Notes

New Keys: H E O

OBJECTIVE:

- Learn the H, E, and O keys.

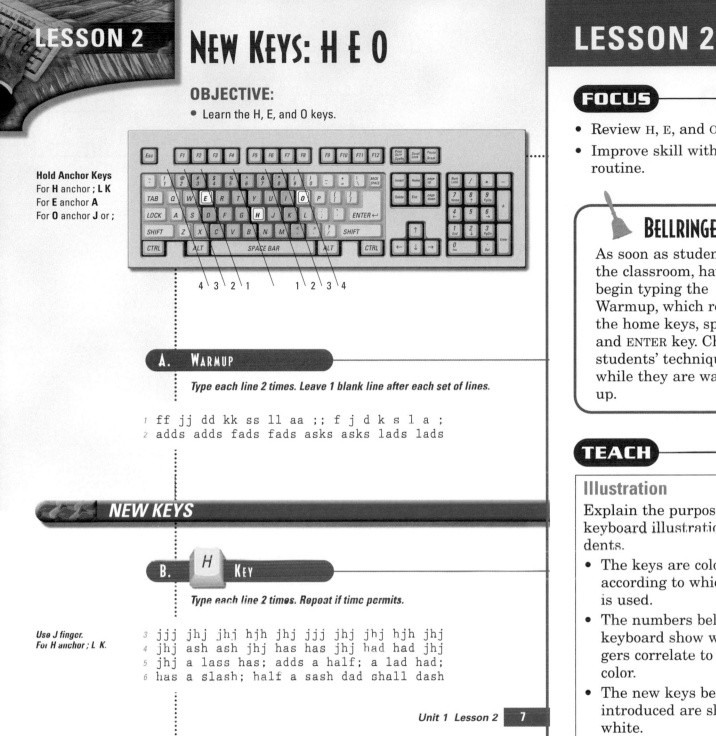

Hold Anchor Keys
For **H** anchor **; L K**
For **E** anchor **A**
For **O** anchor **J** or **;**

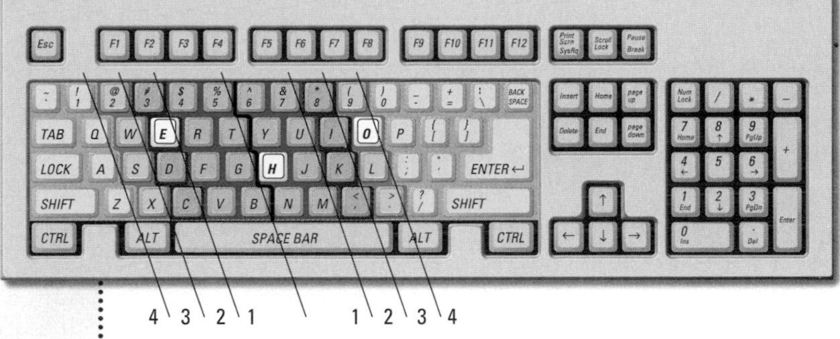

A. Warmup

Type each line 2 times. Leave 1 blank line after each set of lines.

```
1 ff jj dd kk ss ll aa ;; f j d k s l a ;
2 adds adds fads fads asks asks lads lads
```

NEW KEYS

B. H Key

Type each line 2 times. Repeat if time permits.

Use J finger.
For H anchor ; L K.

```
3 jjj jhj jhj hjh jhj jjj jhj jhj hjh jhj
4 jhj ash ash jhj has has jhj had had jhj
5 jhj a lass has; adds a half; a lad had;
6 has a slash; half a sash dad shall dash
```


RESOURCES

- Lesson Plan 2
- Courseware Lesson 2
- Student Data Disk
- Wallchart
- Grading and Evaluation, Technique Checklist

COURSEWARE OVERVIEW

Explain the menus to students and how they should proceed through each lesson. You may also want to point out the other options available at the top of their screen. Remind students to check the status bar and the information bar on their screens to be sure they are working on the correct activity.

LESSON 2

FOCUS

- Review H, E, and O keys.
- Improve skill with P/P/P routine.

BELLRINGER

As soon as students enter the classroom, have them begin typing the Warmup, which reviews the home keys, space bar, and ENTER key. Check students' techniques while they are warming up.

TEACH

Illustration

Explain the purpose of the keyboard illustration to students.

- The keys are color-coded according to which finger is used.
- The numbers below the keyboard show which fingers correlate to each color.
- The new keys being introduced are shown in white.

Activity B. Have students press the Demonstration button to view the correct reach for the H, E, and O keys.

Remind students to type lines 3–6 individually; i.e., type line 3 twice, then line 4 twice, and so forth. Also, remind students to leave a blank line after the second attempt of each of the Practice lines.

TEACH

Illustration

Explain the purpose of the keyboard illustration to students.

- The keys are color-coded according to which finger is used.
- The numbers below the keyboard show which fingers correlate to each color.
- The new keys being introduced are shown in white.

Activities C–D. Ask students what new letters they are going to learn. (E and O) Point out to students they are also going to be putting words together in these activities. Have students put their fingers on the home keys, then show them how to use the D finger to reach for the E key. Have them begin this practice, then show students how to use the L finger to reach for the O key.

FACT FILE

Point out the Fact File on this page to students. Ask them why they think developers of word processing programs add foreign language fonts to programs. Take a survey to see what fonts students would like to see in their word processing packages.

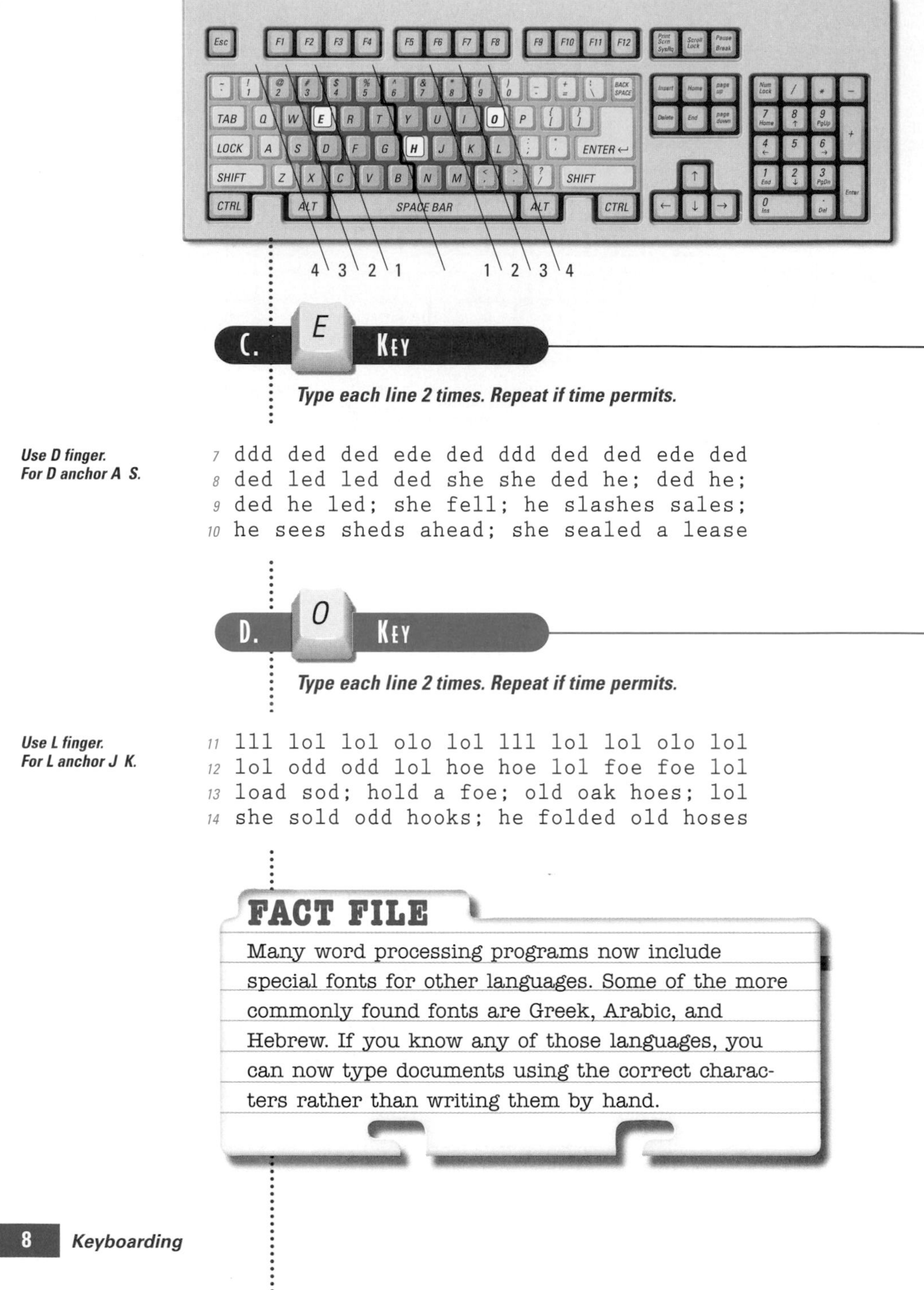

C. E KEY

Type each line 2 times. Repeat if time permits.

Use D finger. For D anchor A S.

```
7  ddd ded ded ede ded ddd ded ded ede ded
8  ded led led ded she she ded he; ded he;
9  ded he led; she fell; he slashes sales;
10 he sees sheds ahead; she sealed a lease
```

D. O KEY

Type each line 2 times. Repeat if time permits.

Use L finger. For L anchor J K.

```
11 lll lol lol olo lol lll lol lol olo lol
12 lol odd odd lol hoe hoe lol foe foe lol
13 load sod; hold a foe; old oak hoes; lol
14 she sold odd hooks; he folded old hoses
```

FACT FILE

Many word processing programs now include special fonts for other languages. Some of the more commonly found fonts are Greek, Arabic, and Hebrew. If you know any of those languages, you can now type documents using the correct characters rather than writing them by hand.

8 Keyboarding

TECHNOLOGY TIP

When using the software, students can access an activity within a lesson by (a) double-clicking on the activity in the lesson menu, or (b) clicking on the activity to highlight it and then pressing ENTER.

Out-of-Class Activity

Ask students to use the dictionary or thesaurus or other books to find three words that begin with H, E, and O. Have students write down their nine words with definitions. Have students write a one-page story that uses the words they just learned. Ask for volunteers to read their stories in class.

E. Technique Checkpoint

Type each line 2 times. Repeat if time permits. Focus on the technique at the left.

Focus on this technique: Press and release each key quickly.

```
15 ddd ded ded ede ded ddd ded ded ede ded
16 lll lol lol olo lol lll lol lol olo lol
17 jjj jhj jhj hjh jhj jjj jhj jhj hjh jhj
18 she has old jokes; he has half a salad;
```

F. PRETEST

Type lines 19–20 for 1 minute. Repeat if time permits. Keep your eyes on the copy.

Hold Anchor Keys

```
19 heed jade hoof elf; hash folk head hole
20 seed lake look jell sash hold dead half
```

G. PRACTICE

Type each line 2 times. Repeat if time permits.

When you repeat a line:
- ***Speed up as you type the line.***
- ***Type it more smoothly.***
- ***Leave a blank line after the second line (press ENTER 2 times).***

```
21 heed heed feed feed deed deed seed seed
22 jade jade fade fade fake fake lake lake
23 hoof hoof hood hood hook hook look look
24 elf; elf; self self sell sell jell jell

25 hash hash lash lash dash dash sash sash
26 folk folk fold fold sold sold hold hold
27 head head heal heal deal deal dead dead
28 hole hole hale hale hall hall half half
```

H. POSTTEST

Type lines 19–20 for 1 minute. Repeat if time permits. Keep your eyes on the copy. Compare your Posttest results with your Pretest results.

Teacher Notes

TEACH

Activity E. Point out to students that they should press and release each key quickly. Have them hold down a key to demonstrate what happens if they don't release a key.

Activities F–H. Point out the Pretest, Practice, and Posttest Activities for this lesson. Have students complete these activities.

PRETEST/PRACTICE/POSTEST

The ***Pretest/Practice/Posttest*** routines are designed to improve speed or accuracy.

- The ***Pretest*** identifies students' speed or accuracy needs.
- The ***Practice*** provides a variety of improvement drills.
- The ***Posttest*** (a repeat of the Pretest) measures improvement.

ASSESS

- Check technique as students reach for the H, E, and O keys.
- Check to see if students make progress from the Pretest to the Posttest.

CLOSE

Review with students how to properly close and exit the software. Remind students that if they did not finish a lesson, the software will open that lesson the next time they log on for the start of class.

LESSON 3

FOCUS

- Use proper technique for typing.
- Learn the M, R, and I keys.

BELLRINGER

As soon as students arrive at their workstations and log in, have them type the Warmup that reviews letters they have learned.

TEACH

Illustration

Explain the purpose of the keyboard illustration to students.

- The keys are color-coded according to which finger is used.
- The numbers below the keyboard show which fingers correlate to each color.
- The new keys being introduced are shown in white.

Activity B. Have students press the Demonstration button to view the correct reach for the M, R, and I keys. Be sure students type each drill line two times.

Explain that the M key is reached with the J finger and anchored with the L and ; fingers.

LESSON 3 NEW KEYS: M R I

OBJECTIVE:

- Learn the M, R, and I keys.

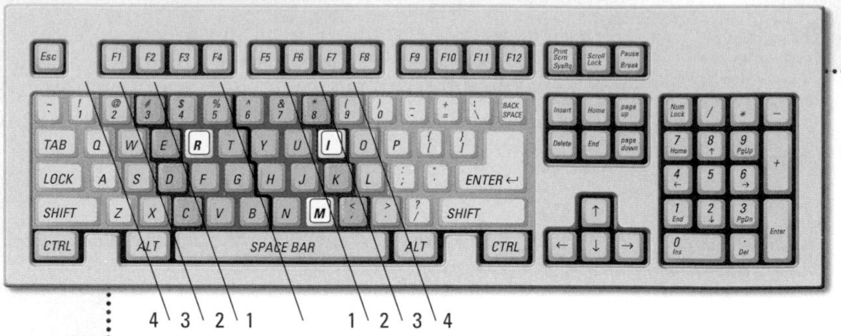

A. WARMUP

Type each line 2 times. Leave 1 blank line after each set of lines.

```
1 asdf jkl; heo; asdf jkl; heo; asdf jkl;
2 jade jade fake fake held held lose lose
```

NEW KEYS

B. M KEY

Type each line 2 times. Repeat if time permits.

Use J finger.
For M anchor ; L K.

```
3 jjj jmj jmj mjm jmj jjj jmj jmj mjm jmj
4 jmj mom mom jmj mad mad jmj ham ham jmj
5 jmj make a jam; fold a hem; less flame;
6 messes make some moms mad; half a dome;
```


RESOURCES

- Lesson Plan 3
- Courseware Lesson 3
- Student Data Disk
- Wallchart
- Grading and Evaluation, Technique Checklists

COURSEWARE OVERVIEW

Point out that once students complete a lesson, a marker appears on the lesson menu. You may also want to explain to students how the software scores their exercises.

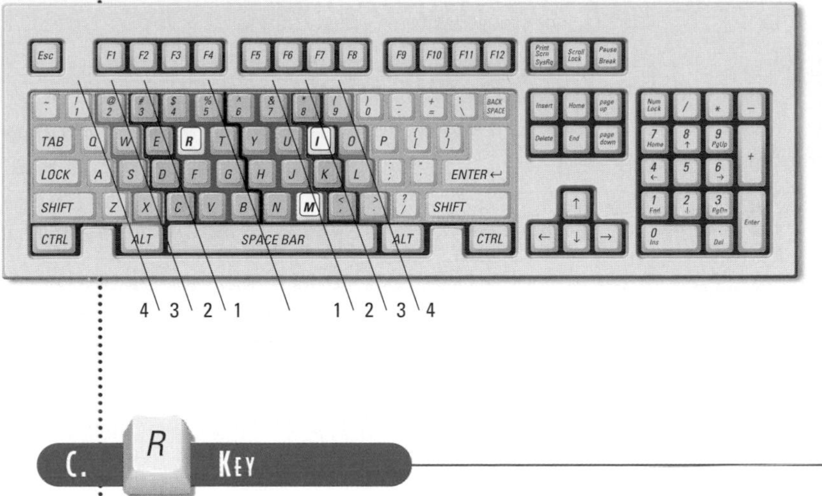

C. R KEY

Type each line 2 times. Repeat if time permits.

Use F finger.
For R anchor A S D.

```
7  fff frf frf rfr frf fff frf frf rfr frf
8  frf far far frf for for frf err err frf
9  frf more rooms; for her marks; from me;
10 he reads ahead; more doors are far ajar
```

D. I KEY

Type each line 2 times. Repeat if time permits.

Use K finger.
For I anchor ;.

```
11 kkk kik kik iki kik kkk kik kik iki kik
12 kik dim dim kik lid lid kik rim rim kik
13 kik if she did; for his risk; old mill;
14 more mirrors; his middle silo is filled
```

interNET CONNECTION

Whatis.com is an easy-to-use, searchable technology dictionary that alphabetically lists hundreds of terms. The site also has resources for computer novices.

interNET ACTIVITY

Have students access *Whatis.com* and find three new words and three new facts about computers. Have students print out or write down these new words with their definitions and the new facts about computers.

Multiple Learning Styles

To help students who are primarily visual learners, provide them with colored markers, paint, brushes, scissors, glue, and old magazines. Attach a large sheet of butcher paper to the classroom wall. Ask students to draw a large keyboard in the center. Remind students to color-code the keys.

TEACH

Illustration

Explain the purpose of the keyboard illustration to students.

- The keys are color-coded according to which finger is used.
- The numbers below the keyboard show which fingers correlate to each color.
- The new keys being introduced are shown in white.

Activities C–D. Point out the new letters to students—R and M and I. Explain to students the F finger reaches for the R key while the ASD fingers stay anchored. After students practice the R key, point out the I key. Explain that the I key is reached with the K finger and anchored with the L and ; fingers.

FACT FILE

The Internet is a world-wide network of computers that are connected. In 1969, the U.S. Defense Department created a network to allow researchers to exchange information. The first network consisted of only four computers.

TEACH

Activity E. Remind students to keep their fingertips on the home keys and to keep their wrists off the keyboard.

Activities F–H. Have students perform the Pretest, Practice, and Posttest activities for this lesson.

PRETEST/PRACTICE/POSTEST

The ***Pretest/Practice/Posttest*** routines are designed to improve speed or accuracy.

- The ***Pretest*** identifies students' speed or accuracy needs.
- The ***Practice*** provides a variety of improvement drills.
- The ***Posttest*** (a repeat of the Pretest) measures improvement.

ASSESS

- Check technique as students reach for the M, R, and I keys.
- Using the P/P/P routine, check on students' progress.
- Check the Summary Report in Reporting for completion of the drill work.

CLOSE

Point out to students that they have now learned half the alphabet on their keyboards. Explain that they will not learn any new keys in Lesson 4. They will have an opportunity to build their skill on keys they have already learned.

SKILLBUILDING

E. Technique Checkpoint

Type each line 2 times. Repeat if time permits. Focus on the techniques at the left.

Focus on these techniques:
- ***Fingertips touching home keys.***
- ***Wrists up, off keyboard.***

```
15 jjj jmj jmj mjm jmj jjj jmj jmj mjm jmj
16 fff frf frf rfr frf fff frf frf rfr frf
17 kkk kik kik iki kik kkk kik kik iki kik
18 he did; his firm red desk lid is a joke
```

F. PRETEST

Type lines 19–20 for 1 minute. Repeat if time permits. Keep your eyes on the copy.

```
19 joke ride sale same roam aims sire more
20 jars aide dark lame foal elms hire mare
```

G. PRACTICE

Type each line 2 times. Repeat if time permits.

Eyes on copy. It will be easier to keep your eyes on the copy if you:
- ***Review the charts for key positions and anchors.***
- ***Maintain an even pace.***
- ***Resist looking up from your copy.***

```
21 joke joke jade jade jams jams jars jars
22 ride ride hide hide side side aide aide
23 sale sale dale dale dare dare dark dark
24 same same fame fame dame dame lame lame

25 roam roam loam loam foam foam foal foal
26 aims aims arms arms alms alms elms elms
27 sire sire dire dire fire fire hire hire
28 more more mire mire mere mere mare mare
```

H. POSTTEST

Type lines 19–20 for 1 minute. Repeat if time permits. Keep your eyes on the copy. Compare your Posttest results with your Pretest results.

Teacher Notes

LESSON 4

REVIEW

OBJECTIVE:

- Improve keyboarding skill.

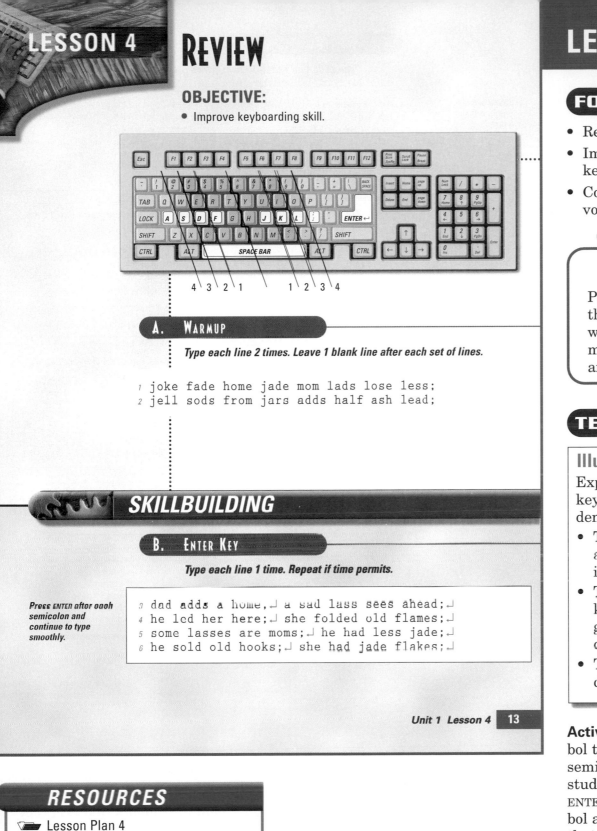

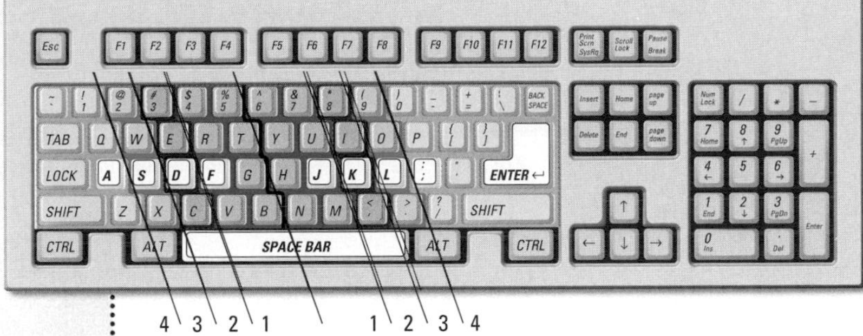

A. WARMUP

Type each line 2 times. Leave 1 blank line after each set of lines.

```
1 joke fade home jade mom lads lose less;
2 jell sods from jars adds half ash lead;
```

SKILLBUILDING

B. ENTER KEY

Type each line 1 time. Repeat if time permits.

Press ENTER after each semicolon and continue to type smoothly.

```
3 dad adds a home;↵ a sad lass sees ahead;↵
4 he led her here;↵ she folded old flames;↵
5 some lasses are moms;↵ he had less jade;↵
6 he sold old hooks;↵ she had jade flakes;↵
```


RESOURCES

- Lesson Plan 4
- Courseware Lesson 4
  Student Data Disk
- Wallchart
  Grading and Evaluation, Technique Checklists

LESSON 4

FOCUS

- Review the keyboard.
- Improve use of the ENTER key.
- Concentrate on missing vowels.

BELLRINGER

Pair students and ask them to help each other with posture, feet placement, hand and arm angle, and finger position.

TEACH

Illustration

Explain the purpose of the keyboard illustration to students.

- The keys are color-coded according to which finger is used.
- The numbers below the keyboard show which fingers correlate to each color.
- The new keys being introduced are shown in white.

Activity B. Point out the symbol that appears after each semicolon and explain that students are to press the ENTER key each time the symbol appears. Remind students that no new keys are learned in this lesson. Therefore, they have an opportunity to build speed and accuracy.

TEACH

Activity C. Remind students to use the thumb of their writing hand to press the space bar.

Activity D. This lesson presents a Concentration drill for the first time. Explain that the students are to fill in the missing vowels as they type. Point out that the missing vowel occurs to the left of each line.

Activity E. Remind students to keep their fingertips on the home keys and to keep their wrists off the keyboard.

CULTURAL CONNECTIONS

Have students work in groups of three or four. Each group is to choose a country of interest and a computer career. Have groups use the Internet or library or write to the country's embassy to research the computer-related job in that country. Have them find out how to apply for the job, salary, and other related facts.

C. Space Bar

Type each line 1 time. Repeat if time permits.

Space between words without pausing.

```
7  as a sad lass; ask a lad; as a sad dad;
8  he had old sod; she made me mad; a door
9  mom hems; dad marked rare oak; mash ash
10 see her; make me; a sad lad; ash doors;
```

D. Concentration

Fill in the missing vowels shown at the left as you type each line 1 time.

Keep eyes on copy.

```
E  11 h- s--s s-al-d l-as-s; sh- h-ars a r--d
A  12 al-s - s-d l-d h-d - lo-d of f-ke smoke
O  13 ask her f-r a l-ad -f s-me -ld -ak m-ld
I  14 she sa-d d-m m-rrors make h-m look sl-m
```

E. Technique Checkpoint

Type each line 2 times. Repeat if time permits. Focus on the techniques at the left.

Focus on:
- *Fingertips touching home keys.*
- *Wrists up.*

```
15 his dark oak desk lid is a joke; he did
16 make a firm door from some rare red ash
17 a lad made a shed; he slashed odd sales
18 foals roam a farm; she sees a small elm
```

CULTURAL CONNECTIONS

Education is very different in European countries. For example, in Great Britain, education is divided into three stages. Primary education is for pupils ranging in age from 5 through 11. Secondary is for pupils from ages 11 or 12 through 16 (the age at which compulsory education ends) or older. Some students continue on to what is known as sixth form to gain additional education that will enable them to attend universities or other schools of higher education.

TECHNOLOGY TIP

Students who have trouble double-clicking can click once and then press ENTER until they have mastered the double-click technique. Have students practice both techniques to see which feels more natural to them.

School to Career

Explain to students that accuracy and speed are key factors in job placements. The proper techniques they are learning now will help them develop accuracy and speed as they progress through this course. Have students find out the typing speed expected for job placement.

F. PRETEST

Type lines 19–20 for 1 minute. Repeat if time permits. Keep your eyes on the copy.

```
19 more sire aims roam same sale ride joke
20 mare hire elms foal lame dark aide jars
```

G. PRACTICE

Type each line 2 times. Repeat if time permits. Keep your eyes on the copy.

***Eyes on copy.* It will be easier to keep your eyes on the copy if you:**
- ***Review the charts for key positions and anchors.***
- ***Maintain an even pace.***
- ***Resist looking up from the copy.***

```
21 more more mire mire mere mere mare mare
22 sire sire dire dire fire fire hire hire
23 aims aims arms arms alms alms elms elms
24 roam roam loam loam foam foam foal foal

25 same same fame fame dame dame lame lame
26 sale sale dale dale dare dare dark dark
27 ride ride hide hide side side aide aide
28 jade jade made made mode mode mole mole
```

H. POSTTEST

Type lines 19–20 for 1 minute. Repeat if time permits. Keep your eyes on the copy. Compare your Posttest results with your Pretest results.

JOURNAL ENTRY
Write about your reasons for taking a keyboarding class. Include something about what you hope to accomplish by the end of the course and how this skill will help you in the future.

TEACH

Activities F–H. For the P/P/P routine, tell students that the first word of each line in Practice lines 21–26 appears in line 19 in the Pretest and the last word of each line of 21–26 appears in line 20. Typing these words in the Pretest will help them in the Practice lines. Remind students that only one character in every two words changes in the Practice lines.

PRETEST/PRACTICE/POSTEST

The ***Pretest/Practice/Posttest*** routines are designed to improve speed or accuracy.

- The ***Pretest*** identifies students' speed or accuracy needs.
- The ***Practice*** provides a variety of improvement drills.
- The ***Posttest*** (a repeat of the Pretest) measures improvement.

ASSESS

- Check to see that students are typing the practice lines in an even rhythm.
- Compare students' total words typed in the Pretest with the total words typed in the Posttest.

CLOSE

Remind students that the only way to improve speed and accuracy is by practicing the keys routinely. Emphasize technique, not the final product.

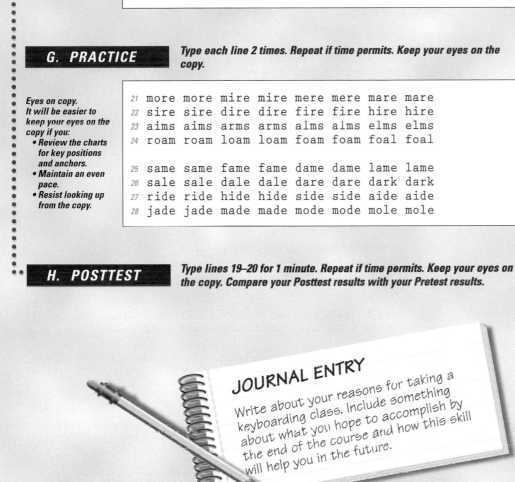

JOURNAL ENTRY

Have students obtain a notebook as their journal. Explain that throughout this course, they will have the opportunity to record their thoughts in this journal.

LESSON 5

FOCUS

- Use proper technique for typing.
- Learn the T, N, and C keys.

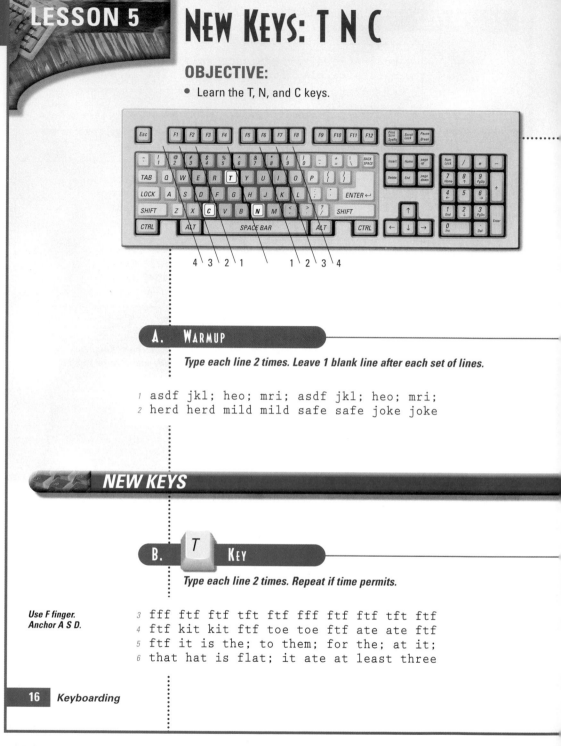

BELLRINGER

As soon as students are at their workstations and logged in, have them type the Warmup that reviews letters they have learned.

TEACH

Illustration

Explain the purpose of the keyboard illustration to students.

- The keys are color-coded according to which finger is used.
- The numbers below the keyboard show which fingers correlate to each color.
- The new keys being introduced are shown in white.

Activity B. Have students press the Demonstration button to view the correct reach for the T, N, and C keys.

LESSON 5 NEW KEYS: T N C

OBJECTIVE:

- Learn the T, N, and C keys.

A. WARMUP

Type each line 2 times. Leave 1 blank line after each set of lines.

```
1 asdf jkl; heo; mri; asdf jkl; heo; mri;
2 herd herd mild mild safe safe joke joke
```

NEW KEYS

B. T KEY

Type each line 2 times. Repeat if time permits.

Use F finger.
Anchor A S D.

```
3 fff ftf ftf tft ftf fff ftf ftf tft ftf
4 ftf kit kit ftf toe toe ftf ate ate ftf
5 ftf it is the; to them; for the; at it;
6 that hat is flat; it ate at least three
```


RESOURCES

- Lesson Plan 5
- Courseware Lesson 5
- Student Data Disk
- Wallchart
- Grading and Evaluation, Technique Checklists

C. N Key

Type each line 2 times. Repeat if time permits.

Use J finger. Anchor ; L K.

```
7  jjj jnj jnj njn jnj jjj jnj jnj njn jnj
8  jnj ten ten jnj not not jnj and and jnj
9  jnj nine tones; none inside; on and on;
10 nine kind lines; ten done in an instant
```

D. C Key

Type each line 2 times. Repeat if time permits.

Use D finger. Anchor A.

```
11 ddd dcd dcd cdc dcd ddd dcd dcd cdc dcd
12 dcd ace ace dcd can can dcd arc arc dcd
13 dcd on a deck; in each car; cannot act;
14 act at once; call to cancel the tickets
```

SOCIAL STUDIES CONNECTION

Apollo flights (named after Apollo, the Greek god of learning) had the goal of landing a human on the moon. Apollo 11 achieved the first lunar landing by humans on July 20, 1969, when Neil Armstrong set foot on the moon.

Unit 1 Lesson 5 17

TEACH

Illustration

Explain the purpose of the keyboard illustration to students.

- The keys are color-coded according to which finger is used.
- The numbers below the keyboard show which fingers correlate to each color.
- The new keys being introduced are shown in white.

Activities C–D. Point out to students that if they are too close to the keyboard, they will have difficulty with the bottom-row keys in this lesson (N and C).

Social Studies Connections

Explain to students that Apollo was one of the 12 main gods in Greek mythology. Usually he is depicted as a beardless youth with long hair. He had a twin sister, Artemis. Have students work in pairs and use the Internet or library to research Apollo to find an additional three facts about Apollo and report these to the class.

TECHNOLOGY TIP

Remind students that they can press the F6 key to advance to the next screen.

Multiple Learning Styles

To help students whose learning style is auditory, suggest that they speak the keys out loud as they press them. Explain that some people learn more easily when their ears hear the letters. Also explain that by listening to the sound of their typing, they can improve concentration.

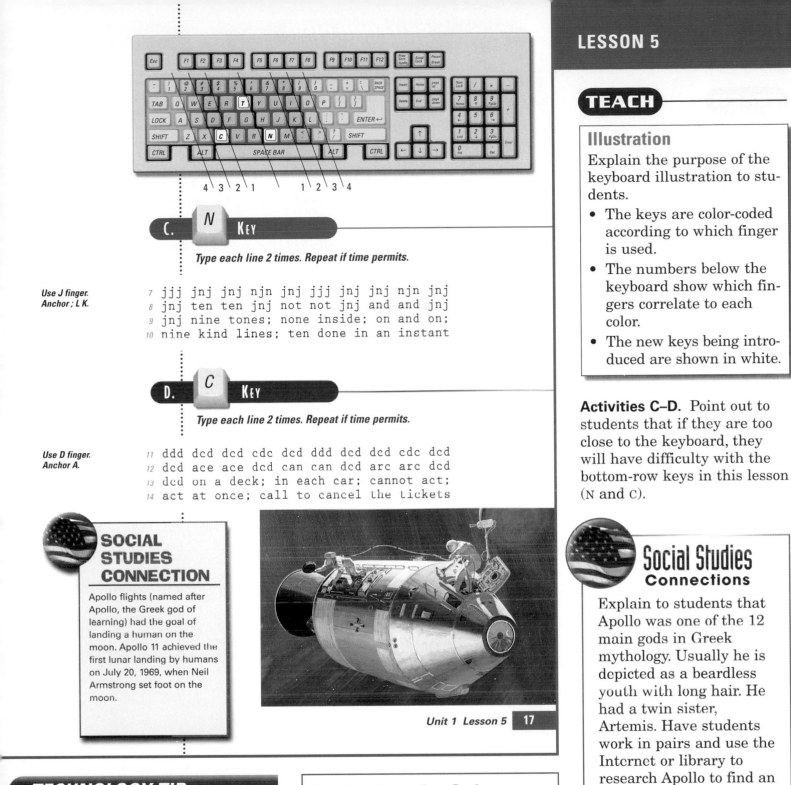

TEACH

Activity E. Remind students to hold the anchor keys and to keep their eyes on the copy, not the keyboard.

Activities F–H. Use the P/P/P routine to build skill. Have students speed up slightly on the second typing of each of the Practice lines.

PRETEST/PRACTICE/POSTTEST

The ***Pretest/Practice/Posttest*** routines are designed to improve speed or accuracy.

- The ***Pretest*** identifies students' speed or accuracy needs.
- The ***Practice*** provides a variety of improvement drills.
- The ***Posttest*** (a repeat of the Pretest) measures improvement.

ASSESS

- Check technique as students reach for the T, N, and C keys.
- Make sure students return to the home row keys after they press the T, N, or C keys.
- Using the P/P/P routine, check to see what progress students are making.
- Check the Summary Report in Reporting for completion of the drill work.

CLOSE

Remind students that accuracy is the result of good technique.

SKILLBUILDING

E. Technique Checkpoint

Type each line 2 times. Repeat if time permits. Focus on the techniques at the left.

Hold Anchor Keys
Eyes on copy.

```
15 fff ftf ftf tft ftf fff ftf ftf tft ftf
16 jjj jnj jnj njn jnj jjj jnj jnj njn jnj
17 ddd dcd dcd cdc dcd ddd dcd dcd cdc dcd
18 the carton of jam is here on this dock;
```

F. PRETEST

Type lines 19–20 for 1 minute. Repeat if time permits. Keep your eyes on the copy.

```
19 sail farm jets kick this none care ink;
20 rain hand jots tick then tone came sink
```

G. PRACTICE

Type each line 2 times. Repeat if time permits.

To increase skill:
- ***Keep eyes on copy.***
- ***Maintain good posture.***
- ***Speed up on the second typing.***

```
21 sail sail said said raid raid rain rain
22 farm farm harm harm hard hard hand hand
23 jets jets lets lets lots lots jots jots
24 kick kick sick sick lick lick tick tick

25 this this thin thin than than then then
26 none none lone lone done done tone tone
27 care care cake cake cane cane came came
28 ink; ink; link link rink rink sink sink
```

H. POSTTEST

Type lines 19–20 for 1 minute. Repeat if time permits. Compare your Posttest results with your Pretest results.

Teacher Notes

NEW KEYS: V RIGHT SHIFT PERIOD (.)

OBJECTIVES:

- Learn the V, right shift, and period keys.
- Learn spacing with the period.
- Figure speed (typing rate in words a minute).

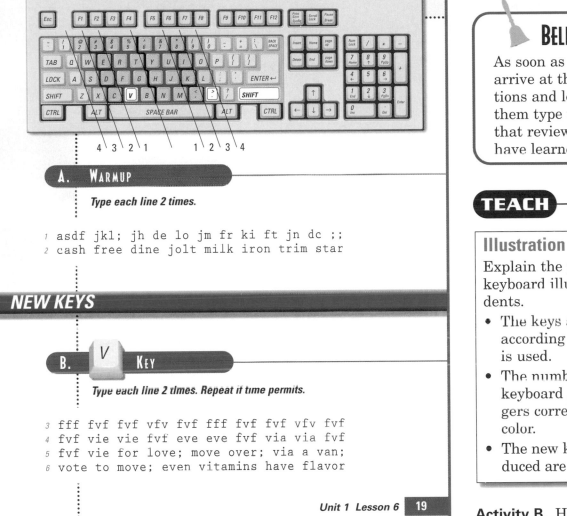

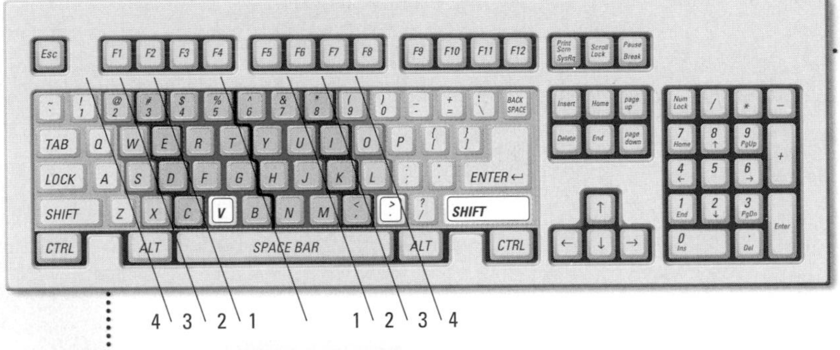

4 3 2 1 1 2 3 4

A. WARMUP

Type each line 2 times.

```
1 asdf jkl; jh de lo jm fr ki ft jn dc ;;
2 cash free dine jolt milk iron trim star
```

NEW KEYS

B. V KEY

Type each line 2 times. Repeat if time permits.

Use F finger. Anchor A S D.

```
3 fff fvf fvf vfv fvf fff fvf fvf vfv fvf
4 fvf vie vie fvf eve eve fvf via via fvf
5 fvf vie for love; move over; via a van;
6 vote to move; even vitamins have flavor
```


RESOURCES

- Lesson Plan 6
- Courseware Lesson 6
- Student Data Disk
- Wallchart
- Grading and Evaluation, Technique Checklists

COURSEWARE OVERVIEW

Explain how to determine speed manually. Remind students that the software computes their speed automatically.

FOCUS

- Learn the V, period, and right shift keys.
- Learn correct spacing after the period.

BELLRINGER

As soon as students arrive at their workstations and log in, have them type the Warmup that reviews letters they have learned.

TEACH

Illustration

Explain the purpose of the keyboard illustration to students.

- The keys are color-coded according to which finger is used.
- The numbers below the keyboard show which fingers correlate to each color.
- The new keys being introduced are shown in white.

Activity B. Have students press the Demonstration button to view the correct reach for the V, period, and right shift keys.

TEACH

Illustration

Explain the purpose of the keyboard illustration to students.

- The keys are color-coded according to which finger is used.
- The numbers below the keyboard show which fingers correlate to each color.
- The new keys being introduced are shown in white.

Activity C. Remind students that the right shift key is used to capitalize letters typed with the left hand.

Activity D. Remind students it is often helpful to speak the letters aloud when practicing. This way their ears hear what their eyes see and fingers feel. Engaging more physical senses accelerates learning.

Activity E. Remind students to space once only after a period at the end of a sentence and after a period at the end of an abbreviation.

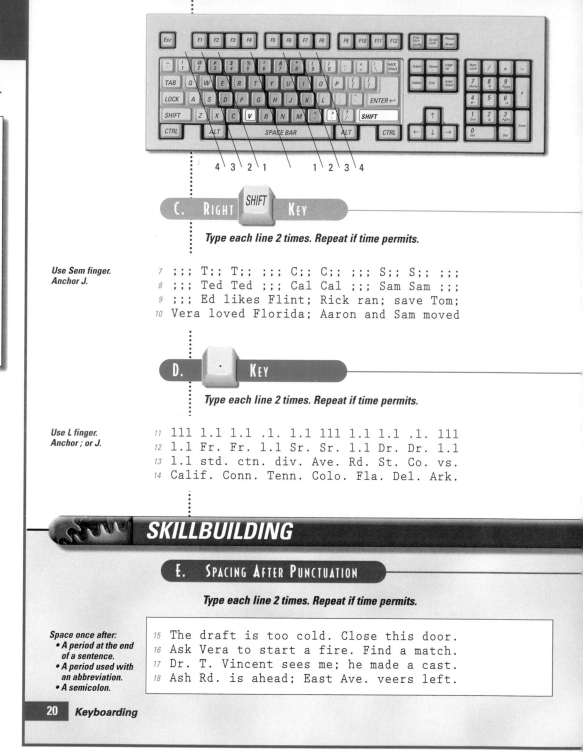

4 3 2 1 1 2 3 4

C. Right SHIFT Key

Type each line 2 times. Repeat if time permits.

Use Sem finger. Anchor J.

```
7  ;;; T;; T;; ;;; C;; C;; ;;; S;; S;; ;;;
8  ;;; Ted Ted ;;; Cal Cal ;;; Sam Sam ;;;
9  ;;; Ed likes Flint; Rick ran; save Tom;
10 Vera loved Florida; Aaron and Sam moved
```

D. . Key

Type each line 2 times. Repeat if time permits.

Use L finger. Anchor ; or J.

```
11 111 1.1 1.1 .1. 1.1 111 1.1 1.1 .1. 111
12 1.1 Fr. Fr. 1.1 Sr. Sr. 1.1 Dr. Dr. 1.1
13 1.1 std. ctn. div. Ave. Rd. St. Co. vs.
14 Calif. Conn. Tenn. Colo. Fla. Del. Ark.
```

SKILLBUILDING

E. Spacing After Punctuation

Type each line 2 times. Repeat if time permits.

Space once after:
- ***A period at the end of a sentence.***
- ***A period used with an abbreviation.***
- ***A semicolon.***

```
15 The draft is too cold. Close this door.
16 Ask Vera to start a fire. Find a match.
17 Dr. T. Vincent sees me; he made a cast.
18 Ash Rd. is ahead; East Ave. veers left.
```


Career Exploration

Have students write about their dream job. Give them the prompt, "If I could be whatever I wanted, I would...." Then have students connect how they would use typing in their dream job. For example, "I wish to be a financier. I would use typing to connect me to the Internet and the world market."

Social Studies Connections

Refer students to Activity D. Point out that line 14 lists state abbreviations. Have students locate each state on a map. Ask students which states they would like to visit and why?

F. Technique Checkpoint

Type each line 2 times. Focus on the technique at the left.

Hold Anchor Keys
Eyes on copy.

```
19 fff fvf fvf vfv fvf fff fvf fvf vfv fvf
20 ;;; T;; T;; ;;; C;; C;; ;;; S;; S;; ;;;
21 111 1.1 1.1 .1. 1.1 111 1.1 1.1 .1. 111
22 Dee voted for vivid vases on her visit.
```

G. Figuring Speed

Typing speed is measured in words a minute (wam). To determine your typing speed:

- Type for 1 minute.
- Determine the number of words you typed. Every 5 strokes (characters and spaces) count as 1 word. Therefore, a 40-stroke line equals 8 words. Two 40-stroke lines equal 16 words.
- Use the cumulative word count at the end of lines to determine the number of words in a complete line.

To determine the number of words in an incomplete line:

- Use the word scale below the last line (below line 24 on this page).
- The number over which you stopped typing is the number of words for that line. For example, if you typed line 23 and completed up to the word *vice* in line 24, you have typed 14 words a minute (8 + 6 = 14).

```
23 fold hide fast came hold ride mast fame    8
24 hone rice mask fade none vice task jade   16
   | 1 | 2 | 3 | 4 | 5 | 6 | 7 | 8
```


TEACH

Activity F. Have students hold the anchor keys. Remind them to keep their eyes on the copy and not the keyboard.

Activity G. Review the concept of an "average typing word." Introduce the word count scale.

Math Connections

Have students calculate their typing speed by following the information in Activity G. Have students type the information in Activity E and F while you time them for 1 minute. Then have them count the number of words they typed. Remind students that accuracy is as important as speed. Pair students who have trouble figuring out the number of words they typed with a peer tutor.

Teacher Notes

TEACH

Activities H–J. Point out to students the Pretest, Practice, and Posttest for this lesson. Have students complete these activities.

PRETEST/PRACTICE/POSTTEST

The ***Pretest/Practice/Posttest*** routines are designed to improve speed or accuracy.

- The ***Pretest*** identifies students' speed or accuracy needs.
- The ***Practice*** provides a variety of improvement drills.
- The ***Posttest*** (a repeat of the Pretest) measures improvement.

ASSESS

- Observe students to see if they are using the little finger on the right hand to capitalize letters typed with the left hand.
- Compare students' performance on the Pretest with their performance on the Posttest.

CLOSE

Review word counts and the word scale introduced in this lesson

H. PRETEST

Type lines 23–24 for 1 minute. Repeat if time permits. Note your speed. Keep your eyes on the copy.

23 fold hide fast came hold ride mast fame 8
24 hone rice mask fade none vice task jade 16
| 1 | 2 | 3 | 4 | 5 | 6 | 7 | 8

I. PRACTICE

Type each line 2 times. Repeat if time permits.

Build speed on repeated word patterns.

25 fold fold hold hold sold sold told told
26 hide hide ride ride rice rice vice vice
27 fast fast mast mast mask mask task task
28 came came fame fame fade fade jade jade

29 last last vast vast cast cast case case
30 mats mats mars mars cars cars jars jars
31 fell fell jell jell sell sell seal seal
32 dive dive five five live live love love

J. POSTTEST

Repeat the Pretest. Compare your Posttest results with your Pretest results.

FACT FILE

The modern computer is a descendant of the abacus—one of the world's first calculators. The abacus used units of ones, tens, hundreds, and thousands. Today, we still use the base ten, or decimal, number system.

FACT FILE

Have someone demonstrate how an abacus is used. Explain the abacus was used in ancient times by the Hindus, Egyptians, Greeks, and Chinese. Originally it was a wooden board covered with sand, upon which numerals were written. A modern abacus is still used in China today.

NEW KEYS: W COMMA (,) G

OBJECTIVES:

- Learn the W, comma, and G keys.
- Learn the spacing with a comma.

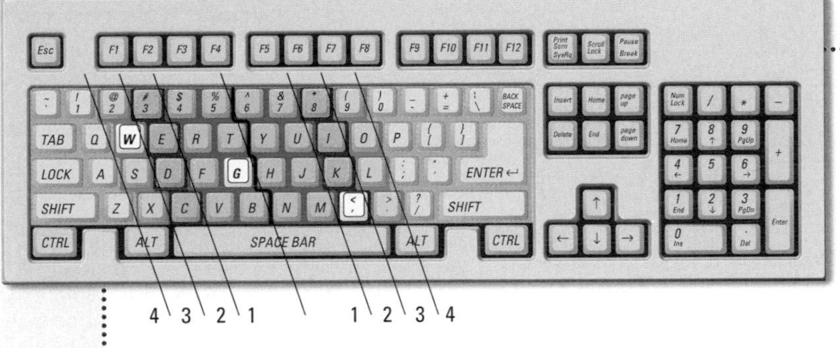

A. WARMUP

Type each line 2 times.

```
1 fail not; jest mist chin Rev. card sake
2 Rick did not join; Val loves that fame.
```

NEW KEYS

B. W KEY

Type each line 2 times. Repeat if time permits.

Use S finger. Anchor F.

```
3 sss sws sws wsw sws sss sws sws wsw sws
4 sws was was sws own own sws saw saw sws
5 sws white swans swim; sow winter wheat;
6 We watched some whales while we walked.
```


RESOURCES

- Lesson Plan 7
- Courseware Lesson 7
- Student Data Disk
- Wallchart
- Grading and Evaluation, Technique Checklist
- Power Point

COURSEWARE OVERVIEW

Using information provided in your Teacher's Courseware Manual, explain to students how the software marks errors. There is also information about the color coding of errors available through the Help menu in the software.

LESSON 7

FOCUS

- Learn the W, comma, and G keys.
- Learn how to count errors.

BELLRINGER

As soon as students arrive at their workstations and log in, have them type the Warmup that reviews letters they have learned. If time permits, have them retype line 1 with all words capitalized.

TEACH

Illustration

Explain the purpose of the keyboard illustration to students.

- The keys are color-coded according to which finger is used.
- The numbers below the keyboard show which fingers correlate to each color.
- The new keys being introduced are shown in white.

Activity B. Have students press the Demonstration button to view the correct reach for the W, comma, and G keys.

TEACH

Illustration

Explain the purpose of the keyboard illustration to students.

- The keys are color-coded according to which finger is used.
- The numbers below the keyboard show which fingers correlate to each color.
- The new keys being introduced are shown in white.

Activity C. Tell students to space once after a comma. Point out there are two types of punctuation in this activity—commas and a period. Ask students where the period in line 10 is. (after Alaska)

Activity D. Remind students when they practice to visualize the keys as their fingers press them. This will help them learn faster.

C. , KEY

Type each line 2 times. Repeat if time permits.

Use K finger. Anchor ;. Space once after a comma.

```
7  kkk k,k k,k ,k, k,k kkk k,k k,k ,k, k,k
8  k,k it, it, k,k or, or, k,k an, an, k,k
9  k,k if it is, two, or three, as soon as
10 Vic, his friend, lives in Rich, Alaska.
```

D. G KEY

Type each line 2 times. Repeat if time permits.

Use F finger. Anchor A S D.

```
11 fff fgf fgf gfg fgf fff fgf fgf gfg fgf
12 fgf leg leg fgf egg egg fgf get get fgf
13 fgf give a dog, saw a log, sing a song,
14 Gen gets a large sagging gift of games.
```

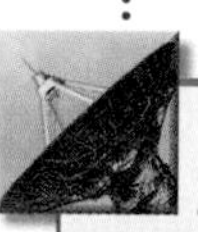

COMMUNICATION FOCUS

An *emoticon* or *smiley* is a symbol used to compensate for the absence of nonverbal clues when communicating on the Internet. For example, <g> signifies a "grin," :) or :-) signifies a "smile" when inserted into the text of an e-mail message. These symbols alert the reader not to take the message seriously.

FACT FILE

In Native American tradition, Spider gave human beings their first alphabet. She wove letters into her web in geometric patterns and angles so the children of Earth could make a record of their lives. This way future generations could understand what life was like for their ancestors.

SKILLBUILDING

E. Technique Checkpoint

Type each line 2 times. Repeat if time permits. Focus on the techniques at the left.

Hold Anchor Keys
Keep elbows in.

```
15 sss sws sws wsw sws sss sws sws wsw sws
16 kkk k,k k,k ,k, k,k kkk k,k k,k ,k, k,k
17 fff fgf fgf gfg fgf fff fgf fgf gfg fgf
18 Wanda watched the team jog to the glen.
```

F. Counting Errors

Count 1 error for each word, even if it contains several errors. Count as an error:

1. A word with an incorrect character.
2. A word with incorrect spacing after it.
3. A word with incorrect punctuation after it.
4. Each mistake in following directions for spacing or indenting.
5. A word with a space.
6. An omitted word.
7. A repeated word.
8. Transposed (switched in order) words.

Compare these incorrect lines with the correct lines (19–21). Each error is highlighted in color.

```
Frank sold sold Dave old an washing mshcone .
     Carl joked with Al ice, Fran, Edith.
Wamda wore redsocks; Sadie wore green,
```

Type each line 2 times. Proofread carefully and note your errors.

```
19 Frank sold Dave an old washing machine.
20 Carl joked with Alice, Fran, and Edith.
21 Wanda wore red socks; Sadie wore green.
```


TEACH

Activity E. Remind students when they type to keep their shoulders relaxed, elbows in, backs straight, and feet on the floor. Good posture is necessary for improved typing skill and for the health of their backs and bodies.

Activity F. Review and discuss the criteria for counting errors in typing. Remind students that only one error is counted per word, regardless of how many errors they may have made in typing that word. Also remind them that keeping their eyes on their copy will minimize the number of errors they make when they type.

interNET ACTIVITY

Ask students if anyone has sent or received e-mail. Tell students they can correspond with people all over the world through the Internet. Have students write (an e-mail message) to another person in the class. Have students give each other their messages.

TECHNOLOGY TIP

Explain to students that software catches many spelling errors; however, students must still proofread their documents to make sure the correct word is used. For example, the words *to, too,* and *two* are all correctly spelled but have entirely different meanings. Ask students for other examples.

TEACH

Activities G–I. Point out to students the Pretest, Practice, and Posttest for this lesson. Have students complete these activities.

PRETEST/PRACTICE/POSTEST

The ***Pretest/Practice/Posttest*** routines are designed to improve speed or accuracy.

- The ***Pretest*** identifies students' speed or accuracy needs.
- The ***Practice*** provides a variety of improvement drills.
- The ***Posttest*** (a repeat of the Pretest) measures improvement.

ASSESS

- Use the P/P/P routine to check progress students make from the Pretest to the Posttest.
- In lines 22–23, students should finish each line of type before proofreading their copy. They should not be correcting errors as they type the individual words.

CLOSE

Emphasize to students the importance of proofreading their copy to find any errors they may have made.

G. PRETEST

Take a 1-minute timing on lines 22–23. Note your speed and errors. Keep your eyes on the copy.

```
22 sag, mow, crew elf, down well scow king     8
23 hag, jot, glow ink, tows west snow ring    16
   | 1 | 2 | 3 | 4 | 5 | 6 | 7 | 8
```

H. PRACTICE

Type each line 2 times. Repeat if time permits.

Focus on:
- ***Wrists up; do not rest palms on keyboard.***
- ***Fingers curved; move from home position only when necessary.***

```
24 sag, sag, wag, wag, rag, rag, hag, hag,
25 mow, mow, how, how, hot, hot, jot, jot,
26 crew crew grew grew grow grow glow glow
27 elf, elf, elk, elk, ilk, ilk, ink, ink,

28 down down gown gown town town tows tows
29 well well welt welt went went west west
30 scow scow stow stow show show snow snow
31 king king sing sing wing wing ring ring
```

I. POSTTEST

Repeat the Pretest. Compare your Posttest results with your Pretest results.

Science Connections

FACT FILE

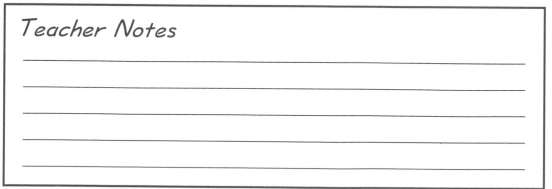

Did you know that wood could turn to stone? For wood to become stone (petrified), it must be quickly covered by some material that prevents the wood from receiving any oxygen. This prevents the wood from decaying naturally. If conditions are right, the organic portion of the wood dissolves slowly and any organic matter is replaced by minerals. These minerals may be silica, calcite, pyrite, or marcasite.

26 ***Keyboarding***

Teacher Notes

LESSON 8 REVIEW

OBJECTIVES:

- Improve keyboarding skill.
- Improve speed and accuracy.
- Strengthen reaches to third, home, and bottom rows.

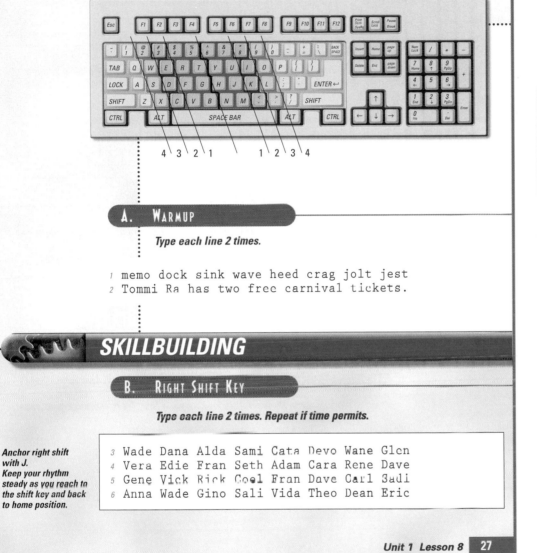

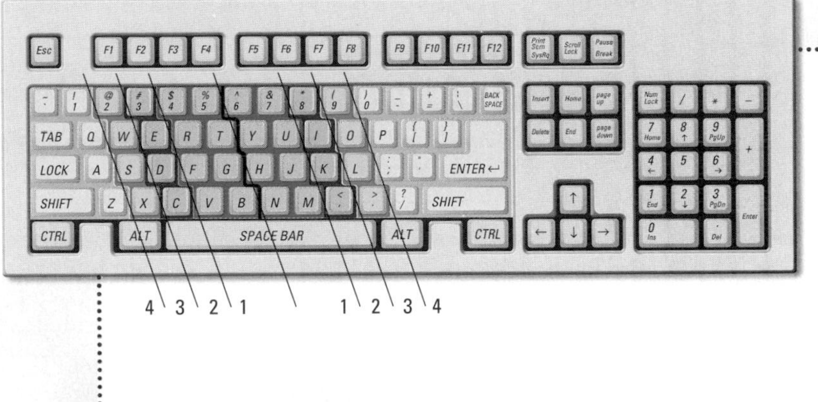

A. WARMUP

Type each line 2 times.

1 memo dock sink wave heed crag jolt jest
2 Tommi Ra has two free carnival tickets.

SKILLBUILDING

B. RIGHT SHIFT KEY

Type each line 2 times. Repeat if time permits.

Anchor right shift with J.
Keep your rhythm steady as you reach to the shift key and back to home position.

3 Wade Dana Alda Sami Cata Devo Wane Glen
4 Vera Edie Fran Seth Adam Cara Rene Dave
5 Gene Vick Rick Cool Fran Dave Carl Sadi
6 Anna Wade Gino Sali Vida Theo Dean Eric

RESOURCES

- Lesson Plan 8
- Courseware Lesson 8
- Student Data Disk
- Wallchart
- Grading and Evaluation, Technique Checklist

LESSON 8

FOCUS

- Review the right shift key.
- Concentrate on providing missing characters.
- Improve speed and accuracy.

BELLRINGER

When students are seated at their workstations, have them pair off and check each other's position at the keyboard.

TEACH

Illustration

Explain the purpose of the keyboard illustration to students.

- The keys are color-coded according to which finger is used.
- The numbers below the keyboard show which fingers correlate to each color.
- The new keys being introduced are shown in white.

Activity B. The J finger anchor should be maintained when the right shift key is pressed. Make sure students maintain a steady rhythm.

TEACH

Activity C. Remind students that the missing letters for lines 7–12 are provided in the margin.

Activity D. Check students' technique as they press the right shift key. Watch for students moving their whole hand to strike the right shift key.

Activity E. Teach students the correct procedure for taking a 30-second timing—one timing is taken on each pair of lines.

Activity F. Time students in three 12-second timings, encouraging them to increase their speed with each timing. Tell students to push themselves just a little past their comfort zone with each practice to improve their speed.

C. Concentration

Fill in the missing letters shown at the left as you type each line 1 time.

Keep eyes on copy.

O	7	S-me w-rk s- we make the w-rld cleaner.
E	8	W- hav- th-m saf-; V-ra l-ft to s-- it.
R	9	See, the -ive-s and st-eams a-e -ising.
H	10	A damaging c-emical mig-t -arm t-e men.
M	11	Their -o- -akes ja- and so-e sew ite-s.
I	12	W-ll-am -s -ll and w-ll l-ve -n Alaska.

D. Technique Checkpoint

Type lines 13–16 one time. Remember to space once after a comma. Focus on the technique at the left.

Right Shift Key *Keep your rhythm steady as you reach to the shift key and back to home position.*

13 Deloris sold red, tan, and orchid ties.
14 Dana had dogs, cats, and a tan hamster.
15 Todd ate mangoes, kiwis, and an orange.
16 Alicia worked on math, French, and law.

E. Technique Timings

Take two 30-second timings on each line. Focus on the techniques at the left.

Sit up straight and keep both feet flat on the floor.

17 Edie Victor saw the Alo Reed dress too.
18 Tom Salt and Arti Wiggs saw Sam and Di.
19 Rick saw Chris at three Eastmoor games.
20 Donna wrote to Anna, Ellen, and Rachel.
| 1 | 2 | 3 | 4 | 5 | 6 | 7 | 8

F. 12-Second Sprints

Take three 12-second timings on each line. Try to increase your speed on each timing.

Each stroke in a 12-second timing is counted as 1 word. If you complete a line, your speed is 40 words a minute.

21 Al had one good mark and told me later.
22 We want to go west to work in the rain.
23 The snow fell one dark night last fall.
24 Watch the river flow over the dark dam.
| | | | 5 | | | | 10 | | | | 15 | | | | 20 | | | | 25 | | | | 30 | | | | 35 | | | | 40

Teacher Notes

G. PRETEST

Take a 1-minute timing on lines 25–26. Note your speed and errors.

```
25 ring snow west tows ink, glow jot, hag,    8
26 king scow well down elf, crew mow, sag,   16
   | 1 | 2 | 3 | 4 | 5 | 6 | 7 | 8
```

H. PRACTICE

Type each line 2 times. Repeat if time permits.

Wrists—do not rest palms on keyboard.

Fingers curved—move from the home position only when necessary.

```
27 ring ring wing wing sing sing king king
28 snow snow show show stow stow scow scow
29 west west went went welt welt well well
30 tows tows town town gown gown down down

31 ink, ink, ilk, ilk, elk, elk, elf, elf,
32 glow glow grow grow grew grew crew crew
33 jot, jot, hot, hot, how, how, mow, mow,
34 hag, hag, rag, rag, wag, wag, sag, sag,
```

I. POSTTEST

Repeat the Pretest. Compare your Posttest results with your Pretest results.

CULTURAL CONNECTIONS

Gestures, posture, and body language have many different meanings in other countries. For example, the "thumbs up" gesture is considered vulgar in Iran and Ghana. The "okay" circle with the thumb and forefinger is an obscene gesture in Greece and Brazil. In France, this gesture means zero, and in Japan, it means money.

TEACH

Activities G–I. Point out to students the Pretest, Practice, and Posttest for this lesson. Have students complete these activities. Performance on the P/P/P should improve from the Pretest to the Posttest.

PRETEST/PRACTICE/POSTEST

The ***Pretest/Practice/Posttest*** routines are designed to improve speed or accuracy.

- The ***Pretest*** identifies students' speed or accuracy needs.
- The ***Practice*** provides a variety of improvement drills.
- The ***Posttest*** (a repeat of the Pretest) measures improvement.

ASSESS

- Check technique as students use the right shift key.
- Compare students' performance on the Pretest with their performance on the Posttest.

CLOSE

Review the correct procedure for pressing the right shift key. Dictate lines 4 and 5 (on page 27) to students, having them type the words as you watch their technique in pressing the right shift key.

CULTURAL CONNECTIONS

Provide students with colored markers, old magazines, scissors, glue and poster board. Form groups of four or five students and have each group create a bulletin board illustrating that gestures, posture, and body language have different meanings in different cultures. Display posters in the room.

Multiple Learning Styles

Explain to students that connecting movement to what they are trying to learn helps their learning. Form groups of four or five. Invite groups to create a song about the keyboard and placement of fingers. Then have students create a dance to go with the song. Provide class time for students to perform their creations.

LESSON 9

FOCUS

- Learn the B, U, and left shift keys.

BELLRINGER

As soon as students arrive at their workstations and log in, have them type the Warmup that reviews letters they have learned.

TEACH

Illustration

Explain the purpose of the keyboard illustration to students.

- The keys are color-coded according to which finger is used.
- The numbers below the keyboard show which fingers correlate to each color.
- The new keys being introduced are shown in white.

Activity B. Have students press the Demonstration button to view the correct reach for the B, U, and left shift keys.

NEW KEYS: B U LEFT SHIFT

OBJECTIVE:

- Learn the B, U, and left shift keys.

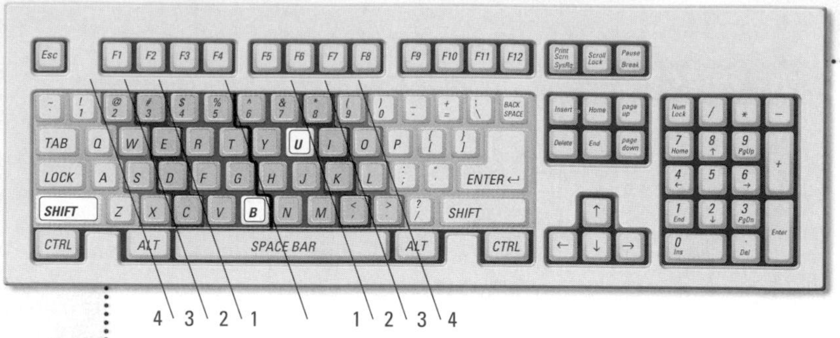

A. WARMUP

Type each line 2 times.

```
1 dim logo wags jive foal corn them wags,
2 Wanda mailed the jewels that Carl made.
```

NEW KEYS

B. B KEY

Type each line 2 times. Repeat if time permits.

Use F finger. Anchor A and S.

```
3 fff fbf fbf bfb fbf fff fbf fbf bfb fbf
4 fbf rob rob fbf ebb ebb fbf bag bag fbf
5 fbf a bent bin, a back bend, a big bag,
6 That boat had been in a babbling brook.
```


RESOURCES

- Lesson Plan 9
- Courseware Lesson 9
- Student Data Disk
- Wallchart
- Grading and Evaluation, Technique Checklist

C. U Key

Type each line 2 times. Repeat if time permits.

Use J finger. Anchor ; L and K.

```
7  jjj juj juj uju juj jjj juj juj uju juj
8  juj jug jug juj urn urn juj flu flu juj
9  juj jungle bugs, just a job, jumbo jets
10 Students show unusual business success.
```

D. Left SHIFT Key

Type each line 2 times. Repeat if time permits.

Use A finger. Anchor F.

```
11 aaa Kaa Kaa aaa Jaa Jaa aaa Laa Laa aaa
12 aaa Kim Kim aaa Lee Lee aaa Joe Joe aaa
13 aaa Jan left; Nora ran; Uncle Lee fell;
14 Mari and Ula went to Kansas in October.
```

SKILLBUILDING

E. Technique Checkpoint

Type each line 2 times. Repeat if time permits. Focus on the technique at the left.

Keep F or J anchored when shifting.

```
15 fff fbf fbf bfb fbf fff fbf fbf bfb fbf
16 jjj juj juj uju juj jjj juj juj uju juj
17 aaa Kaa Kaa aaa Jaa Jaa aaa Laa Laa aaa
18 Jo told Mike and Nel that she would go.
```

Unit 1 Lesson 9 31

Teacher Notes

TEACH

Illustration

Explain the purpose of the keyboard illustration to students.

- The keys are color-coded according to which finger is used.
- The numbers below the keyboard show which fingers correlate to each color.
- The new keys being introduced are shown in white.

Activity C. Remind students that a space goes after a comma. Make sure they are using the correct thumb for the space bar.

Activity D. Remind students that the left shift key is used to capitalize letters typed with the right hand.

Activity E. Now that both shift keys have been introduced, make sure students are using the correct shift key for capitalizing letters.

FACT FILE

When CD-ROM disks first appeared on the market, they were "read-only." Today's technology, however, makes it possible to save data on a CD and to reuse the disk repeatedly if you have a read/write CD-ROM drive.

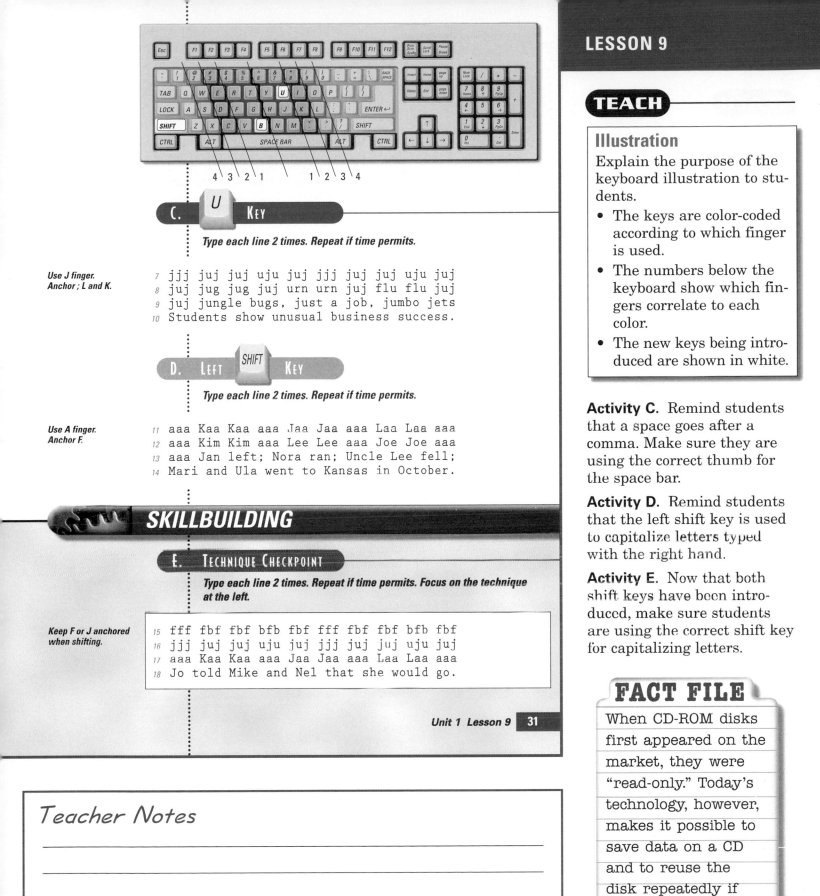

TEACH

Activities F–H. Point out to students the Pretest, Practice, and Posttest for this lesson. Have students complete these activities.

PRETEST/PRACTICE/POSTEST

The ***Pretest/Practice/Posttest*** routines are designed to improve speed or accuracy.

- The ***Pretest*** identifies students' speed or accuracy needs.
- The ***Practice*** provides a variety of improvement drills.
- The ***Posttest*** (a repeat of the Pretest) measures improvement.

ASSESS

- Visually check for proper hand movement when students reach for the shift keys.
- Compare students' performance on the Pretest with their performance on the Posttest.

CLOSE

Remind students to clean up their workstation when they leave. An organized work area will promote better performance in class.

F. PRETEST

Take a 1-minute timing on lines 19–20. Note your speed and errors.

```
19 bran gist vast blot sun, bout just beef    8
20 craw just rest bran sum, dole hunk bear   16
   | 1 | 2 | 3 | 4 | 5 | 6 | 7 | 8
```

G. PRACTICE

Type each line 2 times. Repeat if time permits.

Place your feet:
- ***In front of the chair.***
- ***Firmly on the floor, square, flat.***
- ***Apart, with 6 or 7 inches between the ankles.***
- ***One foot a little ahead of the other***

```
21 bran brad bred brew brow crow crew craw
22 gist list mist must gust dust rust just
23 vast vest jest lest best west nest rest
24 blot blob blow blew bled bred brad bran

25 sun, nun, run, bun, gun, gum, hum, sum,
26 bout boat boot blot bold boll doll dole
27 just dust dusk dunk bunk bulk hulk hunk
28 beef been bean bead beak beam beat bear
```

H. POSTTEST

Repeat the Pretest. Compare your Posttest results with your Pretest results.

*inter*NET CONNECTION

Did you know that one of the largest "bookstores" is available through the Internet? Locate *amazon.com* on the Internet, and search that site for a book you would like to read. Determine the price of the book and any shipping costs involved.

*inter*NET ACTIVITY

Have students make a list of ten items they would like to buy. Items may by anything, such as a car, clothes, or books. Then have students use a search engine and find places to buy these items on the Internet. Have students research the cost of their items.

Career Exploration

Divide the class into pairs of students. Assign each group five letters that have been learned through Lesson 9. Have the students list a business occupation requiring typing skills that begins with each of the letters they have been assigned. Discuss the occupations.

LESSON 10

NEW KEYS: Q /

OBJECTIVE:

- Learn the Q and / (slash or diagonal) keys.

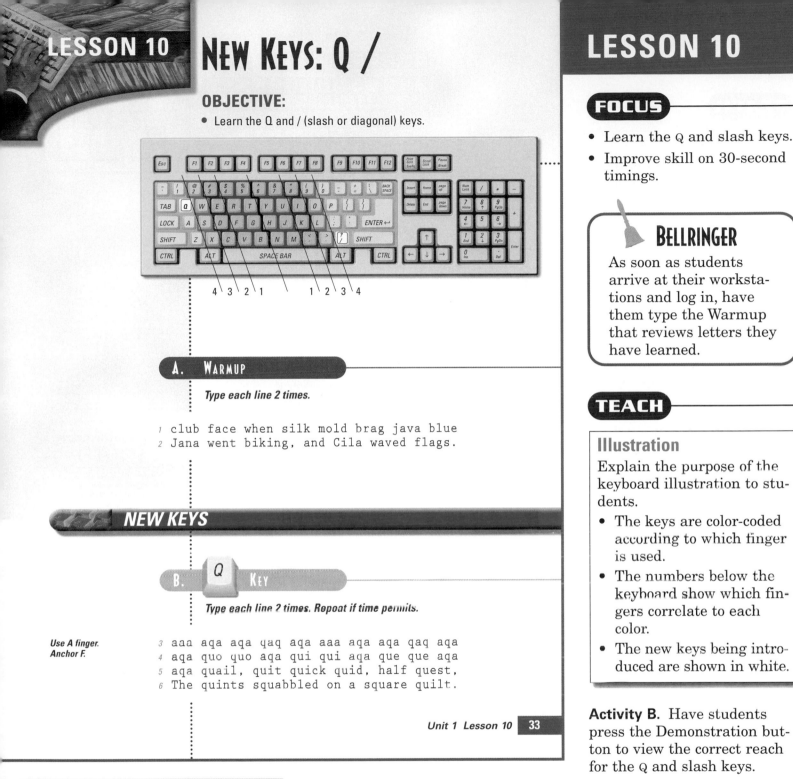

A. WARMUP

Type each line 2 times.

```
1 club face when silk mold brag java blue
2 Jana went biking, and Cila waved flags.
```

NEW KEYS

B. Q KEY

Type each line 2 times. Repeat if time permits.

Use A finger. Anchor F.

```
3 aaa aqa aqa qaq aqa aaa aqa aqa qaq aqa
4 aqa quo quo aqa qui qui aqa que que aqa
5 aqa quail, quit quick quid, half quest,
6 The quints squabbled on a square quilt.
```


RESOURCES

Lesson Plan 10

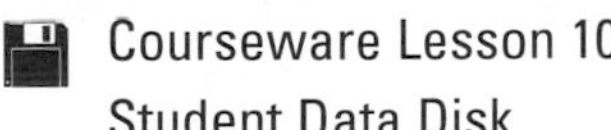

Courseware Lesson 10

Student Data Disk

Wallchart

Grading and Evaluation, Technique Checklist

FOCUS

- Learn the Q and slash keys.
- Improve skill on 30-second timings.

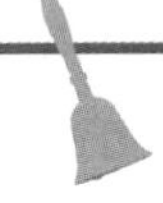

BELLRINGER

As soon as students arrive at their workstations and log in, have them type the Warmup that reviews letters they have learned.

TEACH

Illustration

Explain the purpose of the keyboard illustration to students.

- The keys are color-coded according to which finger is used.
- The numbers below the keyboard show which fingers correlate to each color.
- The new keys being introduced are shown in white.

Activity B. Have students press the Demonstration button to view the correct reach for the Q and slash keys.

TEACH

Illustration

Explain the purpose of the keyboard illustration to students.

- The keys are color-coded according to which finger is used.
- The numbers below the keyboard show which fingers correlate to each color.
- The new keys being introduced are shown in white.

Activity C. Remind students not to space before or after typing a slash.

Activity D. Remind students to keep their backs straight and their feet flat on the floor. Check students to make sure their wrists are level and their fingers, curved.

Activity E. Make sure students keep their eyes on the copy when typing the 30-second timings.

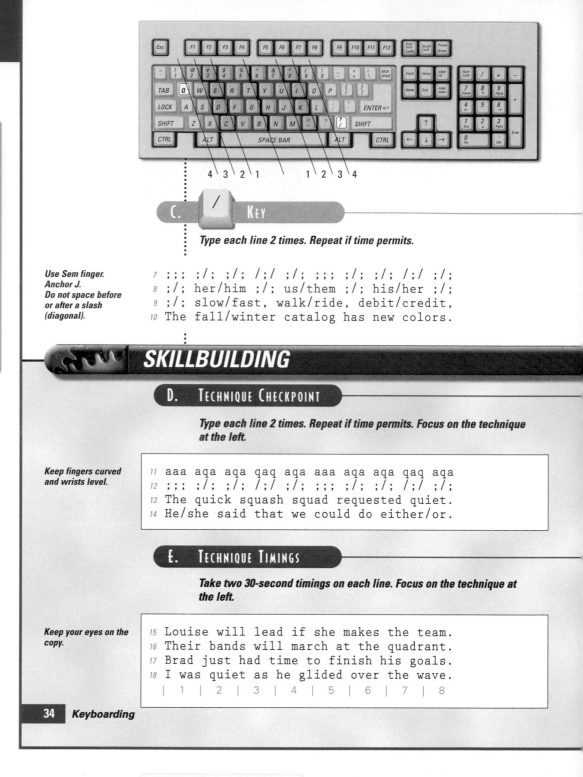

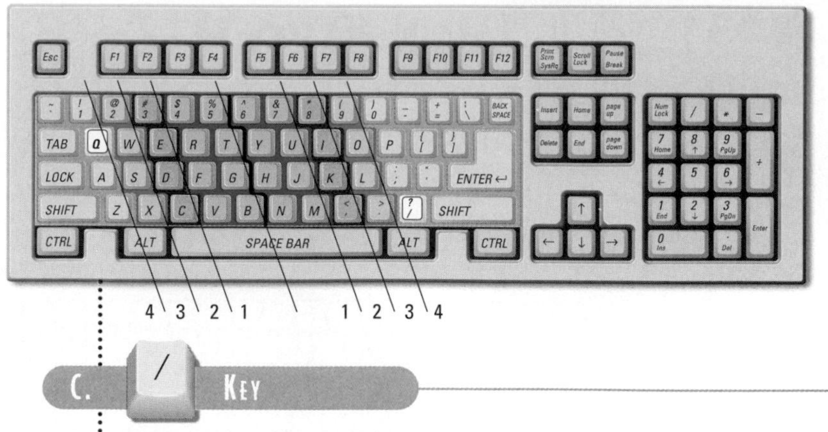

C. / KEY

Type each line 2 times. Repeat if time permits.

Use Sem finger. Anchor J. Do not space before or after a slash (diagonal).

```
7  ;;; ;/; ;/; /;/ ;/; ;;; ;/; ;/; /;/ ;/;
8  ;/; her/him ;/; us/them ;/; his/her ;/;
9  ;/; slow/fast, walk/ride, debit/credit,
10 The fall/winter catalog has new colors.
```

SKILLBUILDING

D. TECHNIQUE CHECKPOINT

Type each line 2 times. Repeat if time permits. Focus on the technique at the left.

Keep fingers curved and wrists level.

```
11 aaa aqa aqa qaq aqa aaa aqa aqa qaq aqa
12 ;;; ;/; ;/; /;/ ;/; ;;; ;/; ;/; /;/ ;/;
13 The quick squash squad requested quiet.
14 He/she said that we could do either/or.
```

E. TECHNIQUE TIMINGS

Take two 30-second timings on each line. Focus on the technique at the left.

Keep your eyes on the copy.

```
15 Louise will lead if she makes the team.
16 Their bands will march at the quadrant.
17 Brad just had time to finish his goals.
18 I was quiet as he glided over the wave.
   | 1 | 2 | 3 | 4 | 5 | 6 | 7 | 8
```


FACT FILE

Have a student bring a mini CD player to class to demonstrate how to download music from the Internet. Have students then use their personal listening devices to listen to the music. If no CD player is available, have students research the cost and availability of them on the Internet.

F. PRETEST

Take a 1-minute timing on lines 19–20. Note your speed and errors.

Hold those anchors.

```
19 find/seek boat fate jail cube brad swat    8
20 walk shut quid mile vane aqua slot quit   16
   | 1 | 2 | 3 | 4 | 5 | 6 | 7 | 8
```

G. PRACTICE

Type each line 2 times. Repeat if time permits.

To build skill:
- *Type each line two times.*
- *Speed up the second time you type the line.*

```
21 find/lose cats/dogs hike/bike walk/ride
22 seek/hide soft/hard mice/rats shut/ajar
23 boat goat moat mode rode rude ruin quid
24 fate face race rice nice Nile vile mile

25 jail fail fall gall mall male vale vane
26 cube Cuba tuba tube lube luau quad aqua
27 brad brat brag quag flag flat slat slot
28 swat swam swim slim slid slit suit quit
```

H. POSTTEST

Repeat the Pretest. Compare your Posttest results with your Pretest results.

FACT FILE

The compact disc was first available for consumer purchase in 1983. In that year, only 100,000 CDs were sold. By 1988, sales of CDs topped sales of LPs. By 1992, CD sales exceeded cassette tape sales. Today, approximately two-thirds of all music sold is produced on CDs.

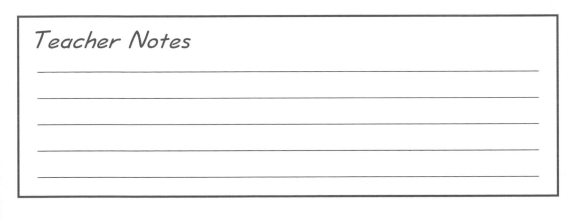

Teacher Notes

TEACH

Activities F–H. Point out to students the Pretest, Practice, and Posttest for this lesson. Have students complete these activities.

PRETEST/PRACTICE/POSTTEST

The ***Pretest/Practice/Posttest*** routines are designed to improve speed or accuracy.

- The ***Pretest*** identifies students' speed or accuracy needs.
- The ***Practice*** provides a variety of improvement drills.
- The ***Posttest*** (a repeat of the Pretest) measures improvement.

ASSESS

- Compare students' performance on the Pretest with their performance on the Posttest.
- Compare students' performance on the two 30-second timings.

CLOSE

Remind students to keep their elbows in and hold the home key position while typing. Students should concentrate on using the shift keys for capitalization.

FOCUS

- Learn the apostrophe and quotation mark keys.
- Improve speed and accuracy.

BELLRINGER

As soon as students arrive at their workstations and log in, have them type the Warmup that reviews keys they have learned.

TEACH

Illustration

Explain the purpose of the keyboard illustration.

- The keys are color-coded according to which finger is used.
- The numbers below the keyboard show which fingers correlate to each color.
- The new keys being introduced are shown in white.

Activity B. Have students press the Demonstration button to view the correct reach for the apostrophe and quotation mark keys.

LESSON 11

NEW KEYS: ' "

OBJECTIVES:

- Learn the apostrophe (') and the quotation mark (") keys.
- Improve speed and accuracy.

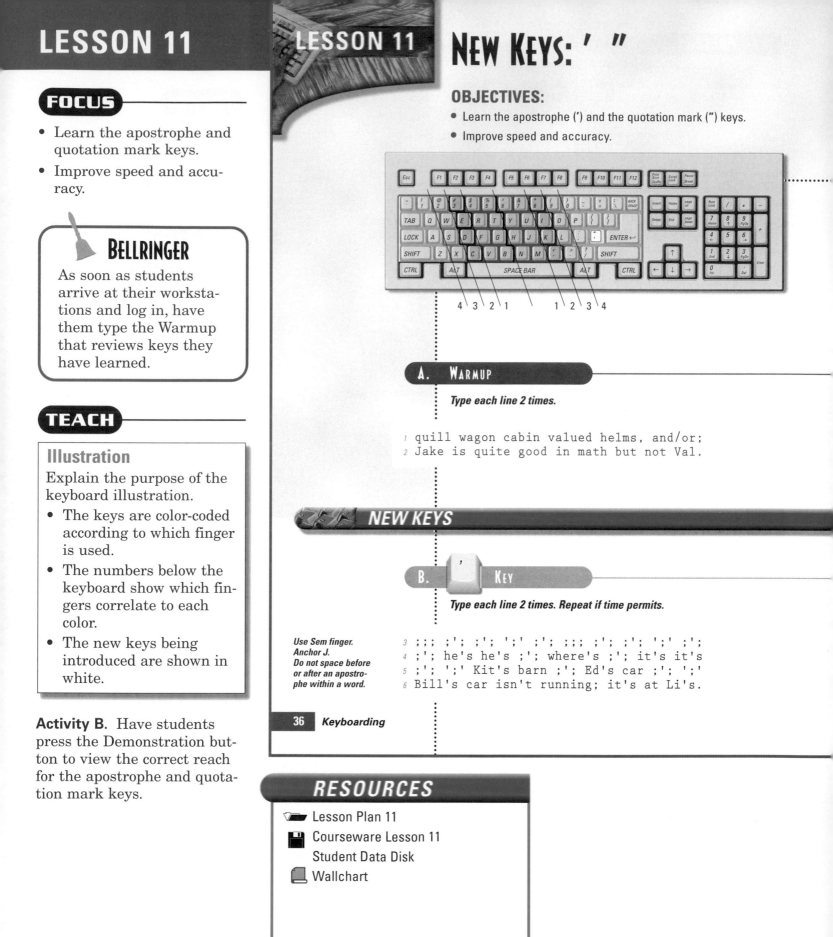

A. WARMUP

Type each line 2 times.

```
1 quill wagon cabin valued helms, and/or;
2 Jake is quite good in math but not Val.
```

NEW KEYS

B. ' KEY

Type each line 2 times. Repeat if time permits.

Use Sem finger. Anchor J. Do not space before or after an apostrophe within a word.

```
3 ;;; ;'; ;'; ';' ;'; ;;; ;'; ;'; ';' ;';
4 ;'; he's he's ;'; where's ;'; it's it's
5 ;'; ';' Kit's barn ;'; Ed's car ;'; ';'
6 Bill's car isn't running; it's at Li's.
```


RESOURCES

- Lesson Plan 11
- Courseware Lesson 11 Student Data Disk
- Wallchart

C. " Key

Type each line 2 times. Repeat if time permits.

Shift of apostrophe. Use Sem finger. Anchor J.

```
7  ;;; ;"; ;"; ";" ;"; ;;; ;"; ;"; ";" ;";
8  ;"; "win" "win" ;"; "big" "big" ;"; ";"
9  ;"; "mew" "oink" "woof" "moo" "baa" ";"
10 "Green" means "go"; "red" means "wait."
```

SKILLBUILDING

D. Technique Checkpoint

Type each line 2 times. Repeat if time permits. Focus on the technique at the left.

Keep your eyes on the copy.

```
11 ;;; ;'; ;'; ';' ;'; ;;; ;'; ;'; ';' ;';
12 ;;; ;"; ;"; ";" ;"; ;;; ;"; ;"; ";" ;";
13 He said "no thanks," but it was "lame."
14 Rita "forgot," but Milo added "favors."
```

E. Technique Timings

Take two 30-second timings on each line. Focus on the technique at the left.

Keep your eyes on the copy.

```
15 Robb's clothes and image don't "match."
16 Mr. Quill said, "Wait." Lee did not go.
17 Jane's visit was "quick"; she ran back.
18 I haven't enough time to "quibble" now.
   | 1 | 2 | 3 | 4 | 5 | 6 | 7 | 8
```


TEACH

Illustration

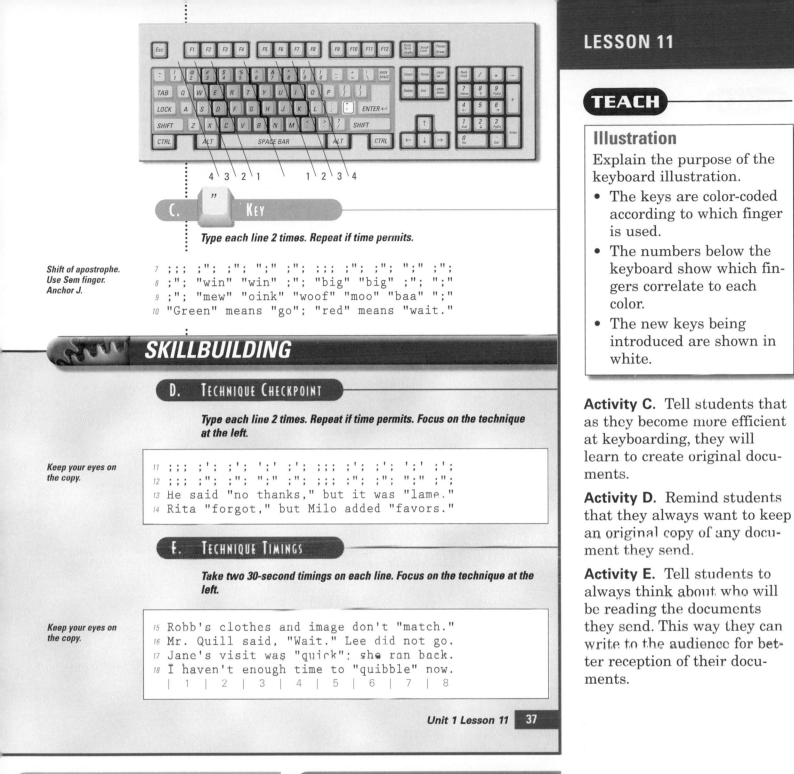

Explain the purpose of the keyboard illustration.

- The keys are color-coded according to which finger is used.
- The numbers below the keyboard show which fingers correlate to each color.
- The new keys being introduced are shown in white.

Activity C. Tell students that as they become more efficient at keyboarding, they will learn to create original documents.

Activity D. Remind students that they always want to keep an original copy of any document they send.

Activity E. Tell students to always think about who will be reading the documents they send. This way they can write to the audience for better reception of their documents.

EXTENDING THE CONTENT

Dictate the following words and have students type the appropriate contractions. Make sure they place the apostrophe in the correct location in each word.

are not	(aren't)	I have	(I've)
cannot	(can't)	is not	(isn't)
do not	(don't)	she is	(she's)
have not	(haven't)	will not	(won't)

TECHNOLOGY TIP

Computers of tomorrow will perform more than a billion calculations in a single second. Have students brainstorm to imagine what tasks future computers will do. Make a list. Encourage students to be creative.

TEACH

Activity F. Review the procedure for taking a 12-second timing. This routine is designed for building speed; therefore, students should place an emphasis on speed, not accuracy.

Activities G–I. Point out to students the Practice and Posttest for this lesson. Have them complete these activities.

PRETEST/PRACTICE/POSTTEST

The ***Pretest/Practice/Posttest*** routines are designed to improve speed or accuracy.

- The ***Pretest*** identifies students' speed or accuracy needs.
- The ***Practice*** provides a variety of improvement drills.
- The ***Posttest*** (a repeat of the Pretest) measures improvement.

ASSESS

- Compare students' performance on the Pretest with their performance on the Posttest.

CLOSE

Remind students that they will not learn any new keys in Lesson 12. They will have an opportunity to build skill on keys they have already learned.

F. 12-SECOND SPRINTS

Take three 12-second timings on each line. Try to increase your speed on each timing.

```
19 Go to the cabin and get us the dog now.
20 Now is the time to call all men for me.
21 She made a face when she lost the race.
22 Ask them if the vase is safe with them.
   | | | | 5 | | | | 10 | | | | 15 | | | | 20 | | | | 25 | | | | 30 | | | | 35 | | | | 40
```

G. PRETEST

Take a 1-minute timing on lines 23–24. Note your speed and errors.

```
23 We can't "remember" how Bo got bruised.      8
24 Burt's dad "asked" Kurt to assist Ross.     16
   |  1  |  2  |  3  |  4  |  5  |  6  |  7  |  8
```

H. PRACTICE

Type each line 2 times.

```
25 made fade face race lace lice nice mice
26 Burt Nora Will Mame Ross Kurt Olaf Elle
27 he's I've don't can't won't we've she's
28 Bo's dogs Lu's cows Mo's cats Di's rats

29 "mat" "bat" "west" "east" "gone" "tone"
30 He "quit"; she "tried." I hit a "wall."
31 sand/land vane/cane robe/lobe quit/suit
32 asks bask base vase case cast mast last
```

I. POSTTEST

Repeat the Pretest. Compare your Posttest results with your Pretest results.

FACT FILE

A computer *bug* is a programming error that causes a program or a computer system to malfunction, produce incorrect results, or crash.

FACT FILE

Have students use the Internet or computer stores to research anti-virus software. Provide students with colored markers and poster board. Then have students create a matrix with information about the cost, availability, updates, compatibility, and features.

LESSON 12 REVIEW

OBJECTIVE:

- Improve keyboarding skills.

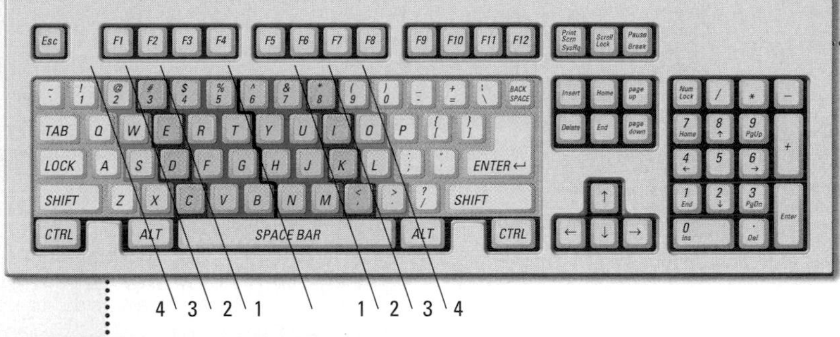

A. WARMUP

Type each line 2 times.

```
1 java blue club face when brag silk mold
2 Geof went sailing, but Lin was at home.
```

SKILLBUILDING

B. SHIFT KEYS

Type each line 2 times. Repeat if time permits.

Keep your rhythm steady as you reach to the shift keys. Anchor left shift with F. Anchor right shift with J.

```
3 Seth Kebo Otis Fran Iris Edie Jose Dave
4 Hans Cara Nita Rene Uris Vera Mark Adam
5 Theo Jean Saul Hugh Eric Noel Vida Ivan
6 Gino Leah Burt Olla Anna Kris Wade Mike
```

C. CONCENTRATION

Fill in the missing letters shown at the left as you type each line 1 time.

```
R   7 Ou- -ivers and oceans a-e being -uined.
EO  8 W- must w-rk t- mak- -ur w-rld cl-an-r.
H   9 -armful c-emicals fill muc- of t-e air.
ES 10 W- hav- lo-t u-ag- of -om- of our -oil.
```


RESOURCES

- Lesson Plan 12
- Courseware Lesson 12
- Student Data Disk
- Wallchart

LESSON 12

FOCUS

- Review the shift keys.
- Concentrate on providing missing characters.
- Improve speed and accuracy.

BELLRINGER

As soon as students arrive at their workstations and log in, have them type the Warmup that reviews keys they have learned.

TEACH

Illustration

Explain the purpose of the keyboard illustration.

- The keys are color-coded according to which finger is used.
- The numbers below the keyboard show which fingers correlate to each color.
- The new keys being introduced are shown in white.

Activity B. Remind students to keep their rhythm steady as they reach to the shift key.

Activity C. Remind students that the missing letters for lines 7–10 are provided in the margin.

TEACH

Activity D. Inform students that to succeed in business good grammar and proper punctuation are essential. If they are weak in these areas, they may want to take another course in English grammar.

Activity E. Inform students that according to ancient Chinese beliefs people are better able to concentrate if they sit up straight. There is a physiological basis for this, as the body's energy runs up the spine. If the spine is crooked, the energy gets stuck and slows down learning.

Activities F–H. Performance on the P/P/P routine should improve from the Pretest to the Posttest.

PRETEST/PRACTICE/POSTTEST

The ***Pretest/Practice/Posttest*** routines are designed to improve speed or accuracy.

ASSESS

- Check technique as students use the shift keys.
- Compare students' performance on the Pretest with their performance on the Posttest.

CLOSE

Emphasize the importance of proofreading typed copy to find any errors made.

D. Technique Checkpoint

Type each line 2 times. Repeat if time permits. Focus on the techniques at the left.

Sit up straight and keep your feet on the floor.

```
11 The cook went to work with cork boards.
12 Four foul jugs were left at the stream.
13 Toil in the weeds to get the seeds now.
14 Tell a joke, then gather other jesters.
```

E. Technique Timings

Take two 30-second timings on each line. Focus on the techniques at the left.

Keep your feet on the floor and sit up straight.

```
15 Ulan told Brian she would be glad to go.
16 In Boston one can see vast fish markets.
17 Bruce had this I/O switch changed again.
18 Treena saw quite a flock of "odd" birds.
   | 1 | 2 | 3 | 4 | 5 | 6 | 7 | 8
```

F. PRETEST

Take a 1-minute timing on lines 19–20. Note your speed and errors.

```
19 Walter took a ride to the quiet street.     8
20 Quakes threw her around the trick door.    16
   | 1 | 2 | 3 | 4 | 5 | 6 | 7 | 8
```

G. PRACTICE

SPEED: If you made 2 or fewer errors on the Pretest, type lines 21–28 two times each.
ACCURACY: If you made more than 2 errors on the Pretest, type lines 21–24 as a group two times; then type lines 25–28 as a group two times.

Third Row Keys
Check hands:
- *Curve fingers*
- *Hold home-key anchors.*

```
21 rook took cook cork work word ford fold
22 full fill file fire fore four foul fowl
23 jolt joke jets jerk jest just jugs jute
24 wire were went west jest quit quid quad

25 weed reed seed seat seal soil toil foil
26 dour sour sort tort tore wore sore lore
27 told hold sold sole hole role real teal
28 tire fire sire site suit quit whit with
```

H. POSTTEST

Repeat the Pretest. Compare your Posttest results with your Pretest results.

Teacher Notes

LESSON 13 NEW KEYS: P X

OBJECTIVE:

- Learn the P and X keys.

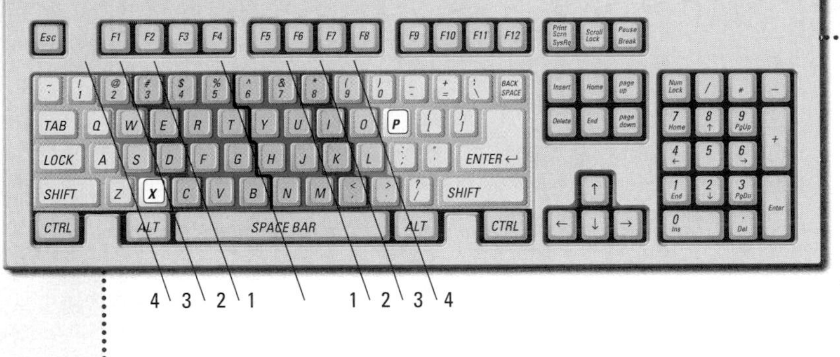

A. WARMUP

Type each line 2 times.

```
1 fade cave what swim quad blot king jars
2 Black liquids vanish from the jug I saw.
```

NEW KEYS

B. P KEY

Type each line 2 times. Repeat if time permits.

Use Sem finger. Anchor J and K.

```
3 ;;; ;p; ;p; p;p ;p; ;;; ;p; ;p; p;p ;p;
4 ;p; nap nap ;p; pen pen ;p; ape ape ;p;
5 ;p; perfect plot, a pale page, pen pal,
6 Pam pulled a pouting pup past a puddle.
```


RESOURCES

- Lesson Plan 13
- Courseware Lesson 13
- Student Data Disk
- Wallchart

LESSON 13

FOCUS

- Learn the P and X keys.
- Improve speed and accuracy on a P/P/P routine.

BELLRINGER

As soon as students arrive at their workstations and log in, have them type the Warmup that reviews keys they have learned.

TEACH

Illustration

Explain the purpose of the keyboard illustration.

- The keys are color-coded according to which finger is used.
- The numbers below the keyboard show which fingers correlate to each color.
- The new keys being introduced are shown in white.

Activity B. Have students press the Demonstration button to view the correct reach for the P and X keys.

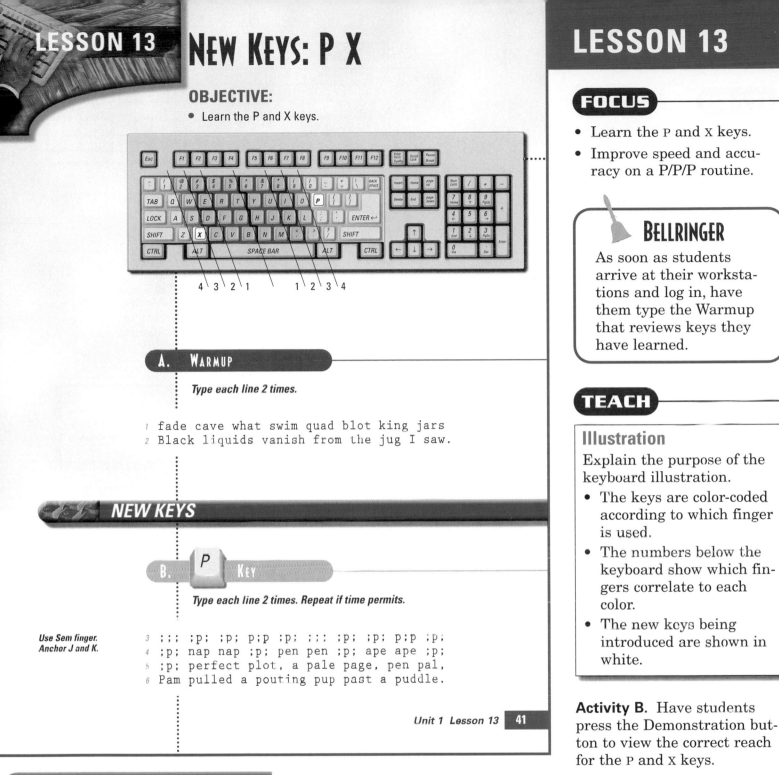

TEACH

Illustration

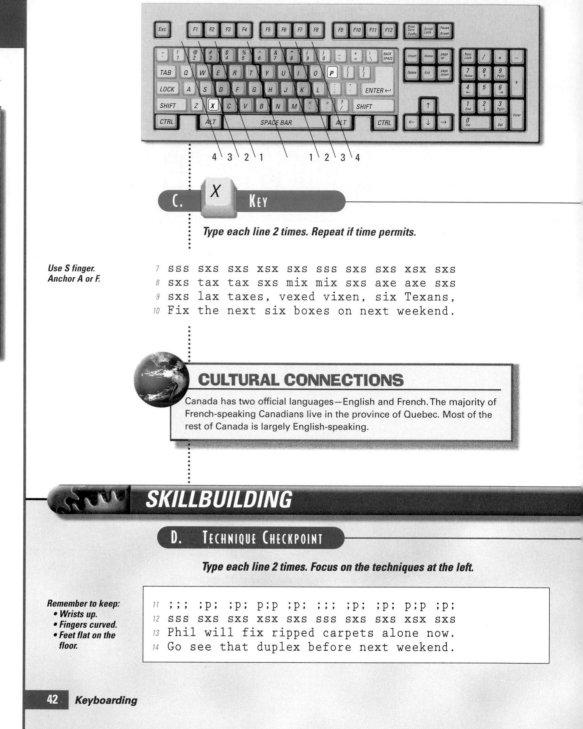

Explain the purpose of the keyboard illustration.

- The keys are color-coded according to which finger is used.
- The numbers below the keyboard show which fingers correlate to each color.
- The new keys being introduced are shown in white.

Activity C. Inform students that the letter X is used to represent many things. It may be used to indicate the signature of an illiterate person. An X also is used to represent an unknown factor. It is used as a delete sign when marked over other letters. Finally, it is used to indicate a motion picture that students are too young to see.

Activity D. Remind students to keep their wrists up, their fingers curved, and their feet flat on the floor.

CULTURAL CONNECTIONS

Inform students that Canada is the world's second largest country. It stretches across five time zones and has a population of 28.2 million. Have students use the Internet, CD-ROM, or library to find more information about Canada. Ask students to find five additional facts and bring them to class.

C.  X KEY

Type each line 2 times. Repeat if time permits.

Use S finger. Anchor A or F.

```
7  sss sxs sxs xsx sxs sss sxs sxs xsx sxs
8  sxs tax tax sxs mix mix sxs axe axe sxs
9  sxs lax taxes, vexed vixen, six Texans,
10 Fix the next six boxes on next weekend.
```

CULTURAL CONNECTIONS

Canada has two official languages—English and French. The majority of French-speaking Canadians live in the province of Quebec. Most of the rest of Canada is largely English-speaking.

SKILLBUILDING

D. TECHNIQUE CHECKPOINT

Type each line 2 times. Focus on the techniques at the left.

Remember to keep:
- *Wrists up.*
- *Fingers curved.*
- *Feet flat on the floor.*

```
11 ;;; ;p; ;p; p;p ;p; ;;; ;p; ;p; p;p ;p;
12 sss sxs sxs xsx sxs sss sxs sxs xsx sxs
13 Phil will fix ripped carpets alone now.
14 Go see that duplex before next weekend.
```


FACT FILE

Each generation of computer technology used different types of processors:

1st Generation (1946–58): vacuum tubes.

2nd Generation (1959–64): transistors.

3rd Generation (1965–70): integrated circuits.

4th Generation (1971–present): microprocessor.

E. Technique Timings

Take two 30-second timings on each line. Press Enter at the end of each sentence. Focus on the technique at the left.

Keep your rhythm steady as you reach to the Enter key and back to home position.

```
15 Pull on the tabs.↵ The box will open.↵
16 Speed is good.↵ Errors are not good.↵
17 Glue the picture.↵ The book is done.↵
18 Get the clothes.↵ Bring me their caps.↵
   | 1 | 2 | 3 | 4 | 5 | 6 | 7 | 8
```

F. PRETEST

Take a 1-minute timing on lines 19–20. Note your speed and errors.

```
19 slag chop gate plop tops bows veal dart    8
20 apex slab gave quit fix, hoax text jell   16
   | 1 | 2 | 3 | 4 | 5 | 6 | 7 | 8
```

G. PRACTICE

Type each line 2 times.

To type faster:
- *Read copy before typing.*
- *Type with smooth strokes.*

```
21 slag flag flap flax flux flex Alex apex
22 chop clop clap clan claw slaw slap slab
23 gate gale pale page pave have cave gave
24 plop flop flip slip ship whip quip quit

25 tops tips sips sits sit, six, mix, fix,
26 bows bowl jowl howl cowl coal coax hoax
27 veal real seal meal meat neat next text
28 dart part park bark balk ball bell jell
```

H. POSTTEST

Repeat the Pretest. Compare your Posttest results with your Pretest results.

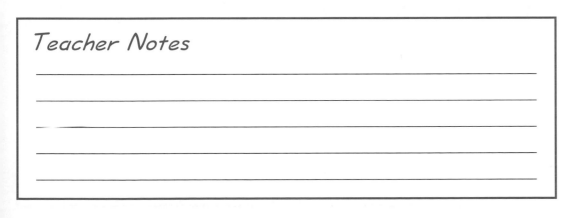

Teacher Notes

TEACH

Activity E. Remind students to press Enter after each sentence in this activity. Also point out that there are two sentences on each line.

Activities F–H. Tell students that if they value their education for what it will give them rather than what it will make out of them, they will gain more out of their education and life. Have them take the Pretest and then the Practice and Posttest.

PRETEST/PRACTICE/POSTEST

The ***Pretest/Practice/Posttest*** routines are designed to improve speed or accuracy.

- The ***Pretest*** identifies students' speed or accuracy needs.
- The ***Practice*** provides a variety of improvement drills.
- The ***Posttest*** (a repeat of the Pretest) measures improvement.

ASSESS

- Compare students' performance on the Pretest with their performance on the Posttest.

CLOSE

Remind students to clean up their workstation when they leave. An organized work area will promote better performance in class.

FOCUS

- Learn the Y and Tab keys.
- Build skill on 30-second timings.
- Improve speed and accuracy on a P/P/P routine.

BELLRINGER

As soon as students arrive at their workstations and log in, have them type the Warmup that reviews keys they have learned.

TEACH

Illustration

Explain the purpose of the keyboard illustration.

- The keys are color-coded according to which finger is used.
- The numbers below the keyboard show which fingers correlate to each color.
- The new keys being introduced are shown in white.

Activity B. Have students press the Demonstration button to view the correct reach for the Y and Tab keys.

LESSON 14

NEW KEYS: Y TAB

OBJECTIVE:

- Learn the Y and the tab keys.

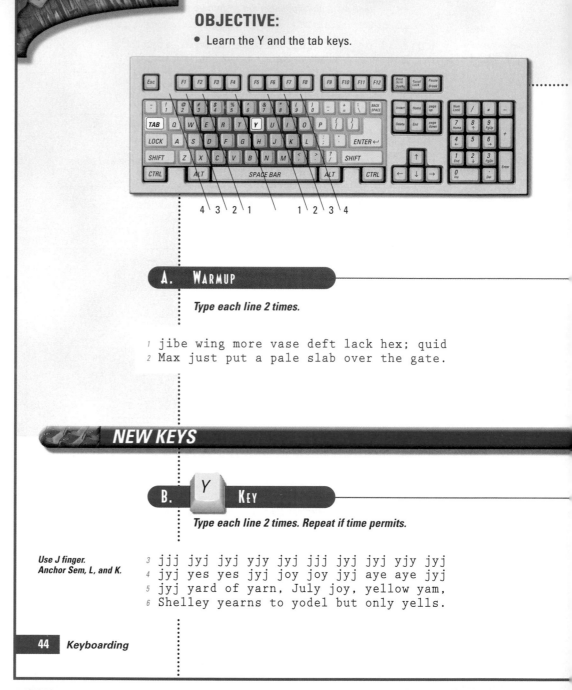

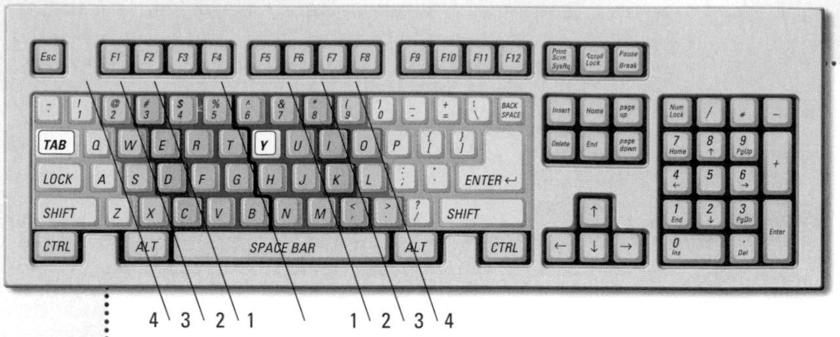

A. WARMUP

Type each line 2 times.

```
1 jibe wing more vase deft lack hex; quid
2 Max just put a pale slab over the gate.
```

NEW KEYS

B. Y KEY

Type each line 2 times. Repeat if time permits.

Use J finger. Anchor Sem, L, and K.

```
3 jjj jyj jyj yjy jyj jjj jyj jyj yjy jyj
4 jyj yes yes jyj joy joy jyj aye aye jyj
5 jyj yard of yarn, July joy, yellow yam,
6 Shelley yearns to yodel but only yells.
```


RESOURCES

- Lesson Plan 14
- Courseware Lesson 14
- Student Data Disk
- Wallchart

COURSEWARE OVERVIEW

This is the first time students will encounter word wrap. Explain word wrap to students and point out the symbol on their screens indicating whether they should have word wrap on or off.

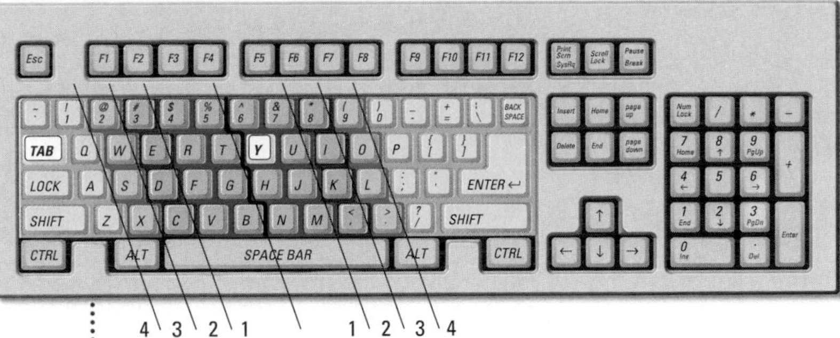

C. Tab Key

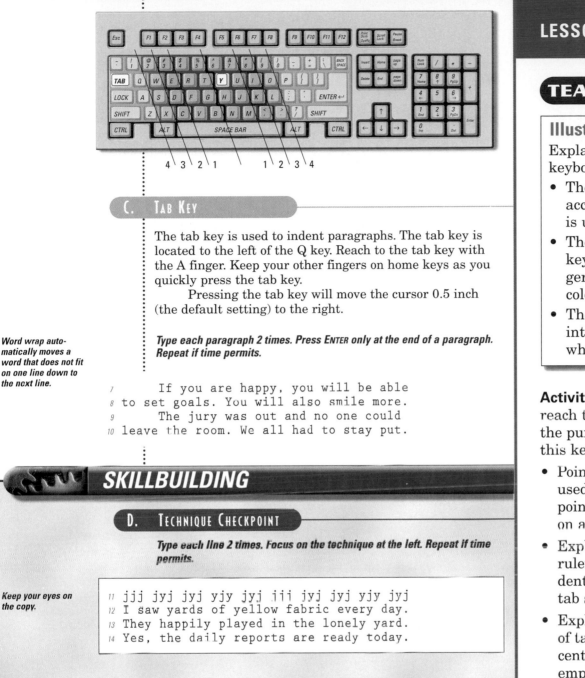

The tab key is used to indent paragraphs. The tab key is located to the left of the Q key. Reach to the tab key with the A finger. Keep your other fingers on home keys as you quickly press the tab key.

Pressing the tab key will move the cursor 0.5 inch (the default setting) to the right.

Word wrap automatically moves a word that does not fit on one line down to the next line.

Type each paragraph 2 times. Press Enter only at the end of a paragraph. Repeat if time permits.

```
7       If you are happy, you will be able
8  to set goals. You will also smile more.
9       The jury was out and no one could
10 leave the room. We all had to stay put.
```

SKILLBUILDING

D. Technique Checkpoint

Type each line 2 times. Focus on the technique at the left. Repeat if time permits.

Keep your eyes on the copy.

```
11 jjj jyj jyj yjy jyj jjj jyj jyj yjy jyj
12 I saw yards of yellow fabric every day.
13 They happily played in the lonely yard.
14 Yes, the daily reports are ready today.
```


TEACH

Illustration

Explain the purpose of the keyboard illustration.

- The keys are color-coded according to which finger is used.
- The numbers below the keyboard show which fingers correlate to each color.
- The new keys being introduced are shown in white.

Activity C. Demonstrate the reach to the Tab key. Explain the purpose and function of this key.

- Point out that this key is used to move the insertion point to preselected points on a line of writing.
- Explain how to display the ruler on the screen so students can view the default tab settings.
- Explain the different types of tab settings (left, right, center, and decimal), but emphasize the left (default) tab that is used in this lesson.

Activity D. Remind students to keep their eyes on the copy while typing. Make sure they type each line two times.

TECHNOLOGY TIP

Printing on a network may take a minute or so longer due to the process involved with sending information through the network and to the printer. Tell students to be patient and avoid sending a print command twice in succession when the job doesn't print immediately.

SCHOOL TO CAREER

Provide students with colored markers, tape, and butcher paper. Have them create a wall-size chart of careers related to this course. Along the left side, write the name of the career. Across the top create categories, such as education needed, salary range, etc. Add to chart throughout course.

TEACH

Activity E. Make sure students keep their eyes on the copy when typing the 30-second timing.

Activities F–H. Performance on the P/P/P routine should improve from the Pretest to the Posttest.

PRETEST/PRACTICE/POSTEST

The ***Pretest/Practice/Posttest*** routines are designed to improve speed or accuracy.

- The ***Pretest*** identifies students' speed or accuracy needs.
- The ***Practice*** provides a variety of improvement drills.
- The ***Posttest*** (a repeat of the Pretest) measures improvement.

ASSESS

- Compare students' performance on the two 30-second timings.
- Compare students' performance on the Pretest with their performance on the Posttest.

CLOSE

Emphasize the importance of proofreading typed copy to find any errors made.

E. Technique Timings

Take two 30-second timings on each line. Focus on the technique at the left.

Keep your eyes on the copy as you take each timing.

```
15 Push your fingers to find the keys now.
16 You will see your typing speed improve.
17 Have a goal to type faster than before.
18 Try every day to achieve that new goal.
   | 1 | 2 | 3 | 4 | 5 | 6 | 7 | 8
```

F. PRETEST

Take a 1-minute timing on lines 19–22. Note your speed and errors.

Remember: Press Enter only at the end of the paragraph (line 22).

```
19      A jury will meet next January to      7
20 get a verdict. People stole costly fuel   15
21 from the boys. We found bags of cards     22
22 next to the mops in the broom closet.     30
   | 1 | 2 | 3 | 4 | 5 | 6 | 7 | 8
```

G. PRACTICE

Type each line 2 times.

```
23 fuel duel duet suet suit quit quip quid
24 gape nape cape cave wave wage wags bags
25 mops pops maps hops tops toys joys boys
26 rope lope lops laps lips lids kids kiss

27 card cart curt hurt hurl furl fury jury
28 cost most lost lest best test text next
29 slab flab flap flaw flay slay clay play
30 pan, fan, tan, man, can, ran, Dan, Jan,
```

H. POSTTEST

Repeat the Pretest. Compare your Posttest results with your Pretest results.

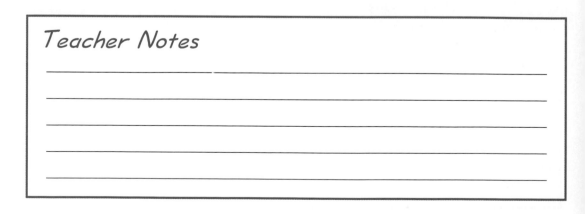

Teacher Notes

NEW KEYS: Z COLON (:)

OBJECTIVE:

- Learn the Z and colon keys.

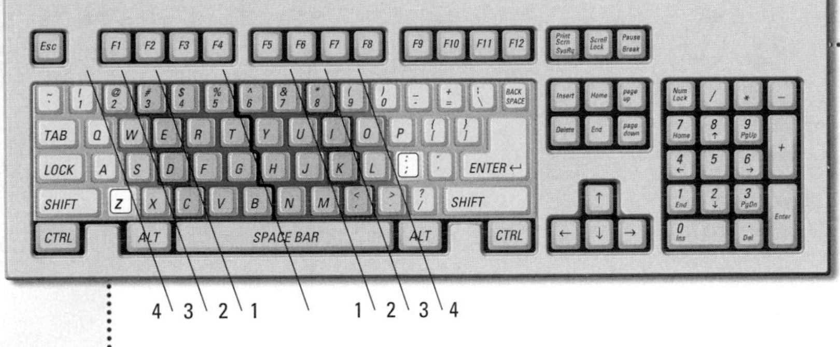

A. WARMUP

Type each line 2 times.

```
1 bake chin jogs wave quip dome onyx left
2 His soft big lynx quickly jumped waves.
```

NEW KEYS

B. Z KEY

Type each line 2 times. Repeat if time permits.

Use A finger. Anchor F.

```
3 aaa aza aza zaz aza aaa aza aza zaz aza
4 aza zip zip aza zoo zoo aza zap zap aza
5 aza dozing zebu, he zags, dazed zebras,
6 Zachary ate frozen pizza in the gazebo.
```


RESOURCES

- Lesson Plan 15
- Courseware Lesson 15
- Student Data Disk
- Wallchart

LESSON 15

FOCUS

- Learn the Z and colon keys.
- Build skill on 2-minute timings.

BELLRINGER

As soon as students arrive at their workstations and log in, have them type the Warmup that reviews keys they have learned.

TEACH

Illustration

Explain the purpose of the keyboard illustration.

- The keys are color-coded according to which finger is used.
- The numbers below the keyboard show which fingers correlate to each color.
- The new keys being introduced are shown in white.

Activity B. Have students press the Demonstration button to view the correct reach for the Z and colon keys.

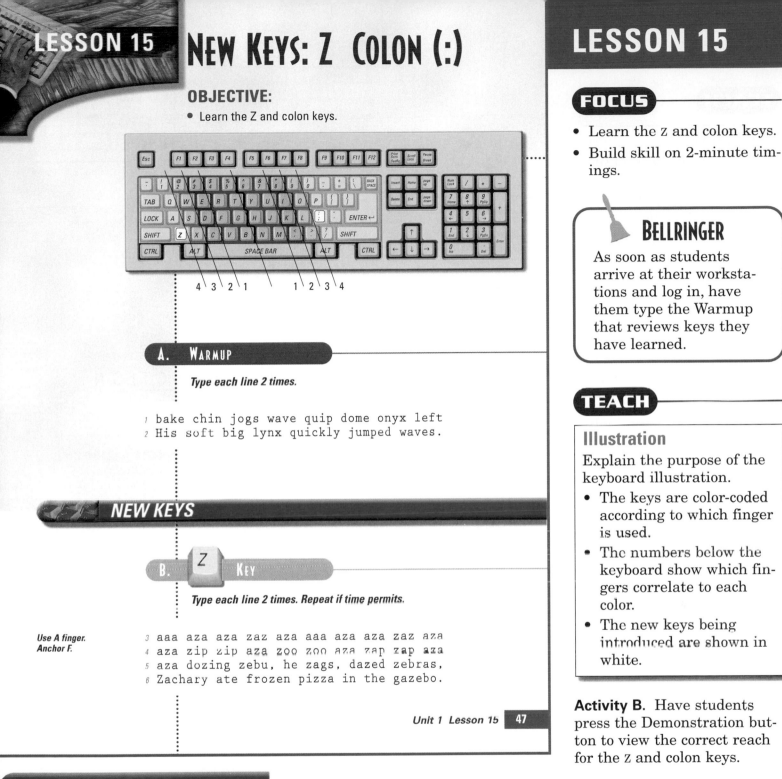

TEACH

Illustration

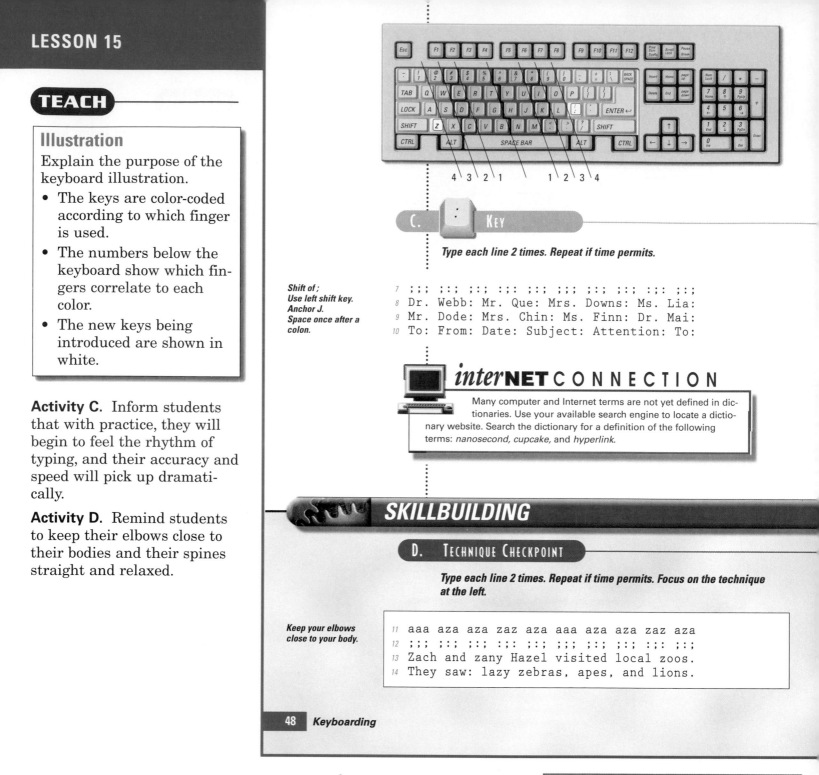

Explain the purpose of the keyboard illustration.

- The keys are color-coded according to which finger is used.
- The numbers below the keyboard show which fingers correlate to each color.
- The new keys being introduced are shown in white.

Activity C. Inform students that with practice, they will begin to feel the rhythm of typing, and their accuracy and speed will pick up dramatically.

Activity D. Remind students to keep their elbows close to their bodies and their spines straight and relaxed.

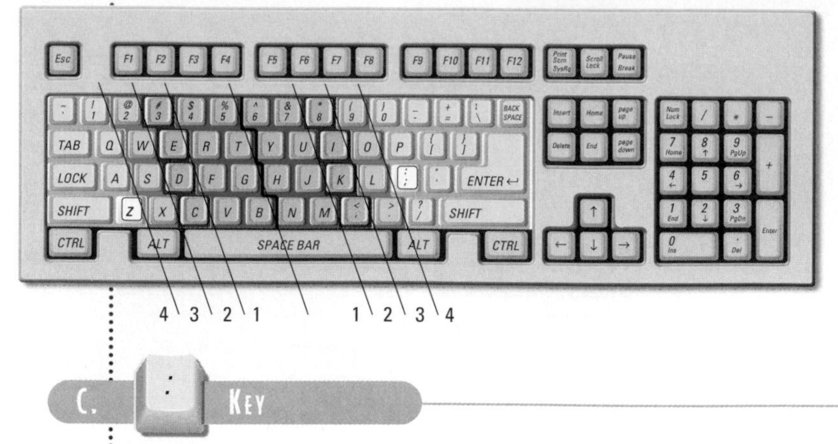

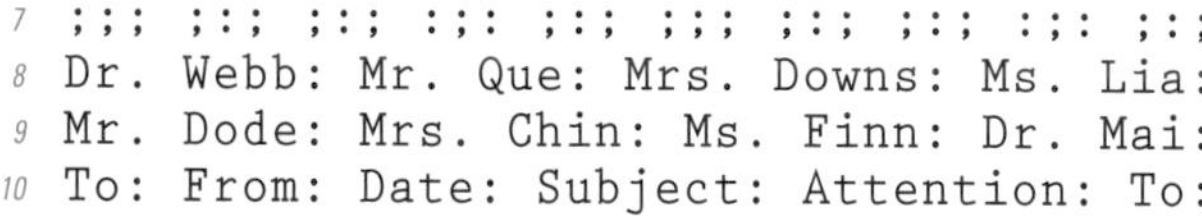

C. : KEY

Type each line 2 times. Repeat if time permits.

Shift of ;
Use left shift key.
Anchor J.
Space once after a colon.

```
7  ;;; ;;; ;;; ;;; ;;; ;;; ;;; ;;; ;;; ;;;
8  Dr. Webb: Mr. Que: Mrs. Downs: Ms. Lia:
9  Mr. Dode: Mrs. Chin: Ms. Finn: Dr. Mai:
10 To: From: Date: Subject: Attention: To:
```

interNET CONNECTION

Many computer and Internet terms are not yet defined in dictionaries. Use your available search engine to locate a dictionary website. Search the dictionary for a definition of the following terms: *nanosecond, cupcake,* and *hyperlink*.

SKILLBUILDING

D. TECHNIQUE CHECKPOINT

Type each line 2 times. Repeat if time permits. Focus on the technique at the left.

Keep your elbows close to your body.

```
11 aaa aza aza zaz aza aaa aza aza zaz aza
12 ;;; ;;; ;;; ;;; ;;; ;;; ;;; ;;; ;;; ;;;
13 Zach and zany Hazel visited local zoos.
14 They saw: lazy zebras, apes, and lions.
```


interNET ACTIVITY

Have each student begin an Internet dictionary. They can use a binder or spiral notebook. Along the left side, have students write computer terms they come across in class and on the Internet. Beside each term, students should write a definition.

Out-of-Class Activity

Have students log onto the Website of your school, community, or state to find out about special events that are to take place. Have students print out this information and bring it to class. Then have students create a bulletin board of postings about these special events.

E. Technique Timings

Take two 30-second timings on each line. Focus on the technique at the left.

Keep your elbows in by your sides.

15 Type fast to reach the end of the line.
16 Keep your eyes on the copy as you type.
17 Tests are easy if you know the answers.
18 If they go to the zoo, invite them too.
| 1 | 2 | 3 | 4 | 5 | 6 | 7 | 8

F. PRETEST

Take a 1-minute timing on the paragraph. Note your speed and errors.

Remember to press Enter only at the end of the paragraph.

19 As Inez roamed the ship, she told 7
20 fond tales. She slipped on that waxy 14
21 rung and fell to the deck. She hurt her 22
22 face and was dazed, but felt no pain. 30
| 1 | 2 | 3 | 4 | 5 | 6 | 7 | 8

G. PRACTICE

Type each line 2 times.

Check your posture.

23 waxy wavy wave save rave raze razz jazz
24 ship whip whop shop stop atop atoms At:
25 rung rang sang sing ring ping zing zinc
26 cure pure sure lure lyre byre bytes By:

27 tale kale Kate mate late lace face faze
28 fond pond bond binds bins inns Inez In:
29 gaze game fame same sale dale daze haze
30 roam loam loom zoom boom books took To:

H. POSTTEST

Repeat the Pretest. Compare your Posttest results with your Pretest results.

Teacher Notes

TEACH

Activity E. Tell students that when they feel stressed while practicing, they may stop and smile, then return to typing. Smiling is a quick and easy way to relieve stress.

Activities F–H. Point out to students the Pretest, Practice, and Posttest for this lesson. Remind students to press Enter only at the end of the paragraph.

PRETEST/PRACTICE/POSTTEST

The ***Pretest/Practice/Posttest*** routines are designed to improve speed or accuracy.

- The ***Pretest*** identifies students' speed or accuracy needs.
- The ***Practice*** provides a variety of improvement drills.
- The ***Posttest*** (a repeat of the Pretest) measures improvement.

ASSESS

- Compare students' performance on the Pretest with their performance on the Posttest.
- Compare performance on the 30-second timings with performance on a 1-minute timing.

CLOSE

Remind students that they have now learned all 26 letters on the keyboard. Tell them that future lessons will be used to build speed and accuracy in typing these keys.

LESSON 16

FOCUS

- Review third row keys.
- Review spacing used with punctuation.
- Introduce composing at the keyboard.

BELLRINGER

As soon as students arrive at their workstations and log in, have them type the Warmup that reviews keys they have learned.

TEACH

Illustration

Explain the purpose of the keyboard illustration.

- The keys are color-coded according to which finger is used.
- The numbers below the keyboard show which fingers correlate to each color.
- The new keys being introduced are shown in white.

Activity B. Point out that in this lesson the line length changes from a 40-character line to a 50-character line.

LESSON 16

REVIEW

OBJECTIVES:

- Refine keyboarding skills.
- Type 25/1'/2e (25 words a minute for 1 minute with 2 errors).
- Learn to compose at the keyboard.

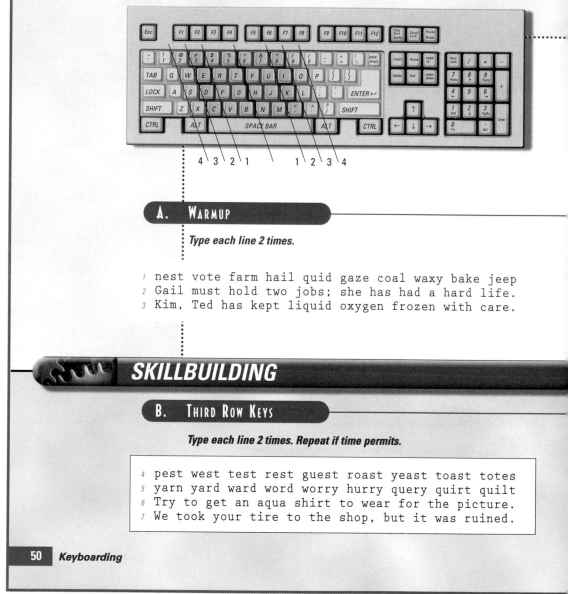

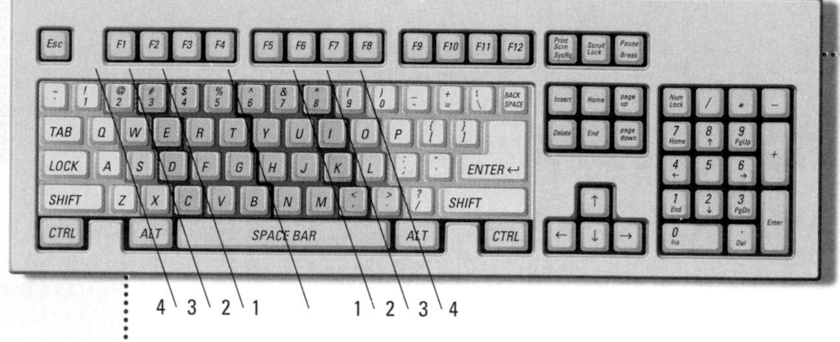

A. WARMUP

Type each line 2 times.

```
1 nest vote farm hail quid gaze coal waxy bake jeep
2 Gail must hold two jobs; she has had a hard life.
3 Kim, Ted has kept liquid oxygen frozen with care.
```

SKILLBUILDING

B. THIRD ROW KEYS

Type each line 2 times. Repeat if time permits.

```
4 pest west test rest guest roast yeast toast totes
5 yarn yard ward word worry hurry query quirt quilt
6 Try to get an aqua shirt to wear for the picture.
7 We took your tire to the shop, but it was ruined.
```


RESOURCES

- Lesson Plan 16
- Courseware Lesson 16
- Student Data Disk
- Wallchart

C. Punctuation Spacing

Space once after a colon, a semicolon, a period at the end of a sentence, and a period used with initials and titles.
Do not space after a period used within a.m. or p.m., geographic abbreviations, or academic degrees.

Type lines 8–12 one time. Note the spacing before and after each punctuation mark. Repeat if time permits.

```
8  Robb passed the test; he studied about two hours.
9  These courses are open: marketing, band, and art.
10 Karel wishes to type. Her cat is on the computer.
11 Dr. E. O. Anton was given the award in the U.S.A.
12 Gretchen received her B.S. and M.B.A. in the a.m.
```

D. Technique Timings

Take two 30-second timings on each line. Focus on the technique at the left.

Press Enter at the end of each line and continue typing smoothly.

```
13 Ask Brenda about the summer sale. It's in Tucson.
14 Wil could buy socks there. The price was minimal.
15 Today, stationery is half off. Help me buy paper.
16 Even the books are reduced. We want to read more.
   | 1 | 2 | 3 | 4 | 5 | 6 | 7 | 8 | 9 | 10
```

E. PRETEST

Take a 1-minute timing on the paragraph. Note your speed and errors.

```
17      My cousin, Vera, has been exercising for at     8
18 least seven weeks. I did my best to keep up with    16
19 her for at least one hour today, but it was much    24
20 too difficult. She is very strong and very quick.   32
   | 1 | 2 | 3 | 4 | 5 | 6 | 7 | 8 | 9 | 10
```

F. PRACTICE

***SPEED:** If you made 2 or fewer errors on the Pretest, type lines 21–28 two times each.*

***ACCURACY:** If you made more than 2 errors on the Pretest, type lines 21–24 as a group two times. Then type lines 25–28 as a group two times.*

Adjacent reaches are consecutive letters that are next to each other on the same row. (weld)
Jump reaches are consecutive letters on the top and bottom rows typed with one hand. (exam)

```
21 as base vases lasts haste taste fasts waste paste
22 po pole polar poems point poker polka spore spots
23 tr trade trips trace strut treat trend stray tray
24 re read real ream reel reeds breeds freed decreed

25 br bran brush brute broth bring break bread brain
26 mu must munch murky mushy musty music mumps mulch
27 ze amaze gauze dozen prize blaze craze glaze size
28 cr crate crater create crack crab crib crow croak
```

Unit 1 Lesson 16 51

JOURNAL ENTRY

Have students keep a journal to describe their problems and successes. Have them praise their successes. Have students write about why they are having problems and suggest possible solutions.

LESSON 16

TEACH

Activity C. Emphasize the spacing before and after punctuation marks. Give additional examples if necessary.

Activity D. Remind students to sit straight with their elbows to their sides and their feet flat on the floor.

Activity E. Suggest to students who need extra practice that they visualize the keyboard and placement of their fingers during class.

Activity F. Explain how each group of Practice lines contains a different type of reach: adjacent or jump reaches. Review the routine students should follow when typing for either speed or accuracy emphasis.

Activity G. Check students' speed and accuracy. Both should improve from the Pretest to the Posttest.

PRETEST/PRACTICE/POSTTEST

The ***Pretest/Practice/Posttest*** routines are designed to improve speed or accuracy.

- The ***Pretest*** identifies students' speed or accuracy needs.
- The ***Practice*** provides a variety of improvement drills.
- The ***Posttest*** (a repeat of the Pretest) measures improvement.

TEACH

Activity H. Remind students that their goal for these 1-minute timings is to type 25 words a minute for 1 minute with no more than 2 errors.

Activity I. Have students compose a journal entry on the keyboard. Students can choose any of the topics from the questions and write a paragraph about that topic. Remind students to keep their eyes on the screen and to not worry about errors.

Solutions: Answers will vary. Check to make sure that students have written 3 or more complete sentences and that they have checked their work to correct errors.

ASSESS

- Observe whether or not students are spacing correctly after punctuation marks in lines 8–12 (page 51).
- Compare students' Pretest performance with their Posttest performance on the P/P/P routine.

CLOSE

Remind students to clean up their workstation when they leave. An organized work area will promote better performance in class.

G. POSTTEST

Repeat the Pretest. Compare your Posttest results with your Pretest results.

H. 1-Minute Timings

Take two 1-minute timings on the paragraph. Note your speed and errors.

Goal: 25/1′/2e

```
29      It is good that you have learned all of the      9
30 alphabet keys. With just some extra practice, you    19
31 will zip through work quickly.                       25
   | 1 | 2 | 3 | 4 | 5 | 6 | 7 | 8 | 9 | 10   SI 1.22
```

I. Composing at the Keyboard

Keep your eyes on the screen as you type; do not worry about errors.

Composing at the keyboard enables you to create documents without having to write them by hand. As you compose at the keyboard, type at a comfortable pace. Do not look at your hands, and do not worry about errors. Get your thoughts recorded.

Answer each question with a single word.

32 Do you have a best friend?
33 What is your favorite sport?
34 Do you have a pet?
35 Have you ever ridden a horse?
36 What is your favorite color?

Teacher Notes

LESSON 17 NEW KEYS: ? CAPS LOCK

OBJECTIVES:

- Learn the ? key.
- Use the caps lock key to type all-capital letters.
- Compose at the keyboard.

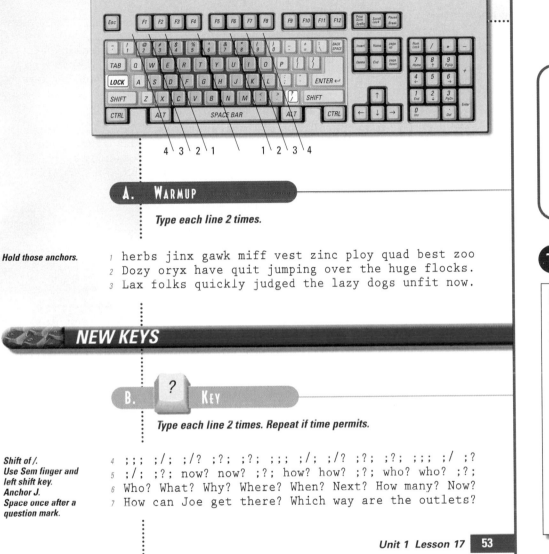

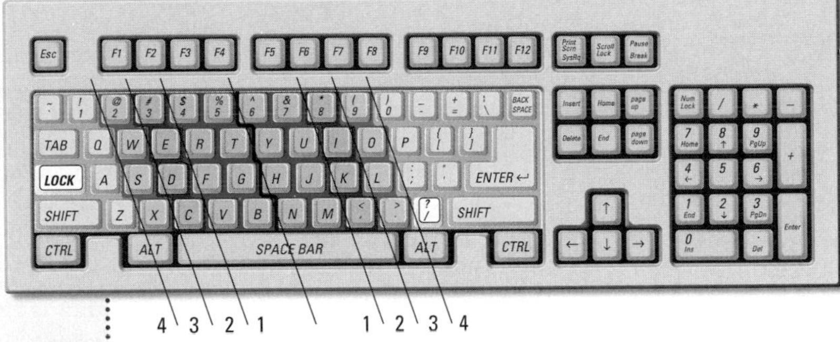

A. WARMUP

Type each line 2 times.

Hold those anchors.

```
1 herbs jinx gawk miff vest zinc ploy quad best zoo
2 Dozy oryx have quit jumping over the huge flocks.
3 Lax folks quickly judged the lazy dogs unfit now.
```

NEW KEYS

B. ? KEY

Type each line 2 times. Repeat if time permits.

Shift of /. Use Sem finger and left shift key. Anchor J. Space once after a question mark.

```
4 ;;; ;/; ;/? ;?; ;?; ;;; ;/; ;/? ;?; ;?; ;;; ;/ ;?
5 ;/; ;?; now? now? ;?; how? how? ;?; who? who? ;?;
6 Who? What? Why? Where? When? Next? How many? Now?
7 How can Joe get there? Which way are the outlets?
```


RESOURCES

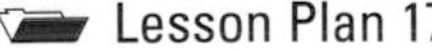

- Lesson Plan 17
- Courseware Lesson 17
- Student Data Disk
- Wallchart
- Grading and Evaluation

LESSON 17

FOCUS

- Learn the question mark and Caps Lock keys.
- Build skill on 30-second timings and on a P/P/P routine.

BELLRINGER

As soon as students arrive at their workstations and log in, have them type the Warmup that reviews keys they have learned.

TEACH

Illustration

Explain the purpose of the keyboard illustration.

- The keys are color-coded according to which finger is used.
- The numbers below the keyboard show which fingers correlate to each color.
- The new keys being introduced are shown in white.

Activity B. Have students press the Demonstration button to view the correct reach to the question mark key.

TEACH

Illustration

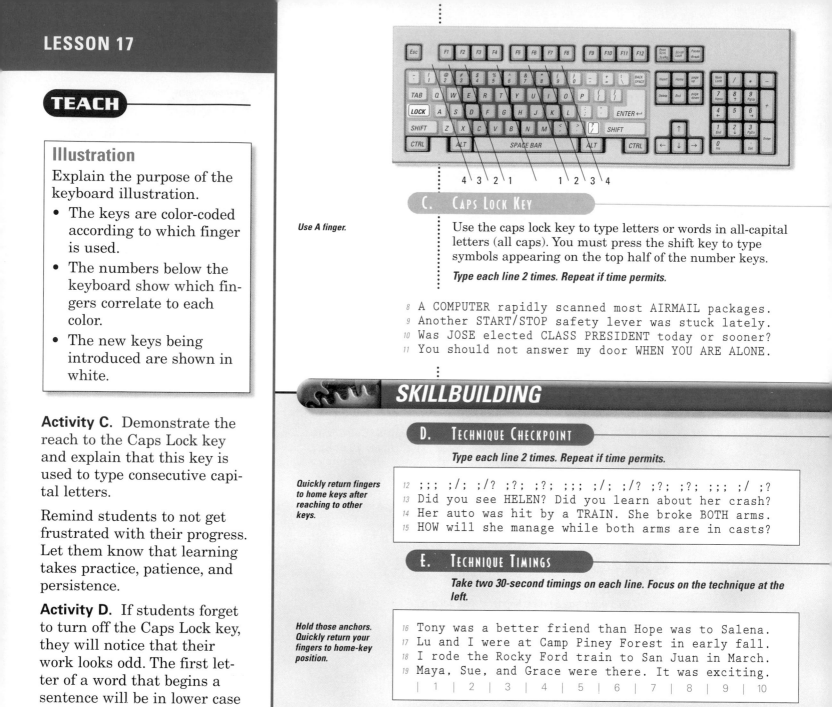

Explain the purpose of the keyboard illustration.

- The keys are color-coded according to which finger is used.
- The numbers below the keyboard show which fingers correlate to each color.
- The new keys being introduced are shown in white.

Activity C. Demonstrate the reach to the Caps Lock key and explain that this key is used to type consecutive capital letters.

Remind students to not get frustrated with their progress. Let them know that learning takes practice, patience, and persistence.

Activity D. If students forget to turn off the Caps Lock key, they will notice that their work looks odd. The first letter of a word that begins a sentence will be in lower case and the remaining letters in that word will be in all caps.

Activity E. Use the 30-second timing to build skill.

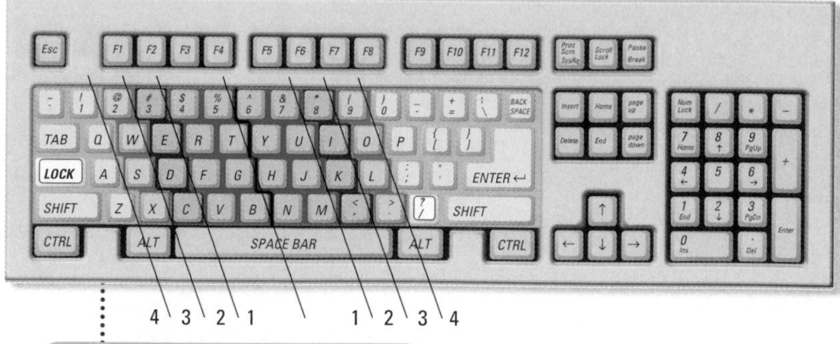

C. Caps Lock Key

Use A finger.

Use the caps lock key to type letters or words in all-capital letters (all caps). You must press the shift key to type symbols appearing on the top half of the number keys.

Type each line 2 times. Repeat if time permits.

```
8  A COMPUTER rapidly scanned most AIRMAIL packages.
9  Another START/STOP safety lever was stuck lately.
10 Was JOSE elected CLASS PRESIDENT today or sooner?
11 You should not answer my door WHEN YOU ARE ALONE.
```

SKILLBUILDING

D. Technique Checkpoint

Type each line 2 times. Repeat if time permits.

Quickly return fingers to home keys after reaching to other keys.

```
12 ;;; ;/; ;/? ;?; ;?; ;;; ;/; ;/? ;?; ;?; ;;; ;/ ;?
13 Did you see HELEN? Did you learn about her crash?
14 Her auto was hit by a TRAIN. She broke BOTH arms.
15 HOW will she manage while both arms are in casts?
```

E. Technique Timings

Take two 30-second timings on each line. Focus on the technique at the left.

Hold those anchors. Quickly return your fingers to home-key position.

```
16 Tony was a better friend than Hope was to Salena.
17 Lu and I were at Camp Piney Forest in early fall.
18 I rode the Rocky Ford train to San Juan in March.
19 Maya, Sue, and Grace were there. It was exciting.
   |  1  |  2  |  3  |  4  |  5  |  6  |  7  |  8  |  9  |  10
```


FACT FILE

In May, 1997, the Russian chess Grandmaster Garry Kasparov was beaten in a six-game match, marking the first time a chess champion lost to a computer in a traditional match. The computer, designed at IBM, was named Deep Blue. Ask students how they feel about the computer winning.

F. PRETEST

Take a 1-minute timing on the paragraph. Note your speed and errors.

```
20      The blind slats are broken. Can you fix the     9
21 broken ones? My WILY dog jumped out of the window   19
22 which is how this happened. There should be some    29
23 way to stop him. For a young dog, he is AMAZING.    38
   | 1 | 2 | 3 | 4 | 5 | 6 | 7 | 8 | 9 | 10
```

G. PRACTICE

Type each line 2 times.

```
24 slat slit skit suit quit quid quip quiz whiz fizz
25 LASS bass BASE bake CAKE cage PAGE sage SAGA sags
26 maze mare more move wove cove core cure pure pore
27 mix; fix; fin; kin; kind wind wild wily will well

28 cape cane vane sane same sale pale pals pats bats
29 jump pump bump lump limp limb lamb jamb jams hams
30 slow BLOW blot SLOT plot PLOP flop FLIP blip BLOB
31 mite more wire tire hire hide hive jive give five
```

H. POSTTEST

Repeat the Pretest. Compare your Posttest results with your Pretest results.

I. Composing at the Keyboard

Answer the following questions with a single word.

Keep your eyes on the screen as you type.

32 What day of the week is today?
33 What is your favorite animal?
34 What is your favorite food?
35 What is your favorite ice cream flavor?
36 What month is your birthday?

Teacher Notes

LESSON 17

TEACH

Activities F–H. Check students' speed and accuracy. Both should improve from the Pretest to the Posttest.

PRETEST/PRACTICE/POSTTEST

The ***Pretest/Practice/Posttest*** routines are designed to improve speed or accuracy.

ASSESS

- Check to see if students are using the Caps Lock key to type consecutive capital letters in lines 8–11, 13–15, 21, 23, 25, and 30.
- Compare students' performance on the two 30-second timings.
- Compare students' performance on the Pretest with their performance on the Posttest.

LANGUAGE LINK

Activity I. After students have answered the questions, have them choose one of the topics and write a short paragraph about any one topic. Call for volunteers to read their paragraphs to the class.

Solutions: Answers will vary.

CLOSE

Have students retype lines 22, 24, 26, and 29. As the lines are typed, have students capitalize the first word and every other word in each line.

LESSON 18

FOCUS

- Learn the hyphen key.
- Build skill on 30-second and 1-minute timings.

BELLRINGER

As soon as students arrive at their workstations and log in, have them type the Warmup that reviews keys they have learned.

TEACH

Illustration

Explain the purpose of the keyboard illustration.

- The keys are color-coded according to which finger is used.
- The numbers below the keyboard show which fingers correlate to each color.
- The new keys being introduced are shown in white.

Activity B. Have students press the Demonstration button to view the correct reach for the hyphen key. This is a difficult reach. Often it is confused with the reach for the 0 key on the top row. Place extra emphasis on the drill lines for this reach.

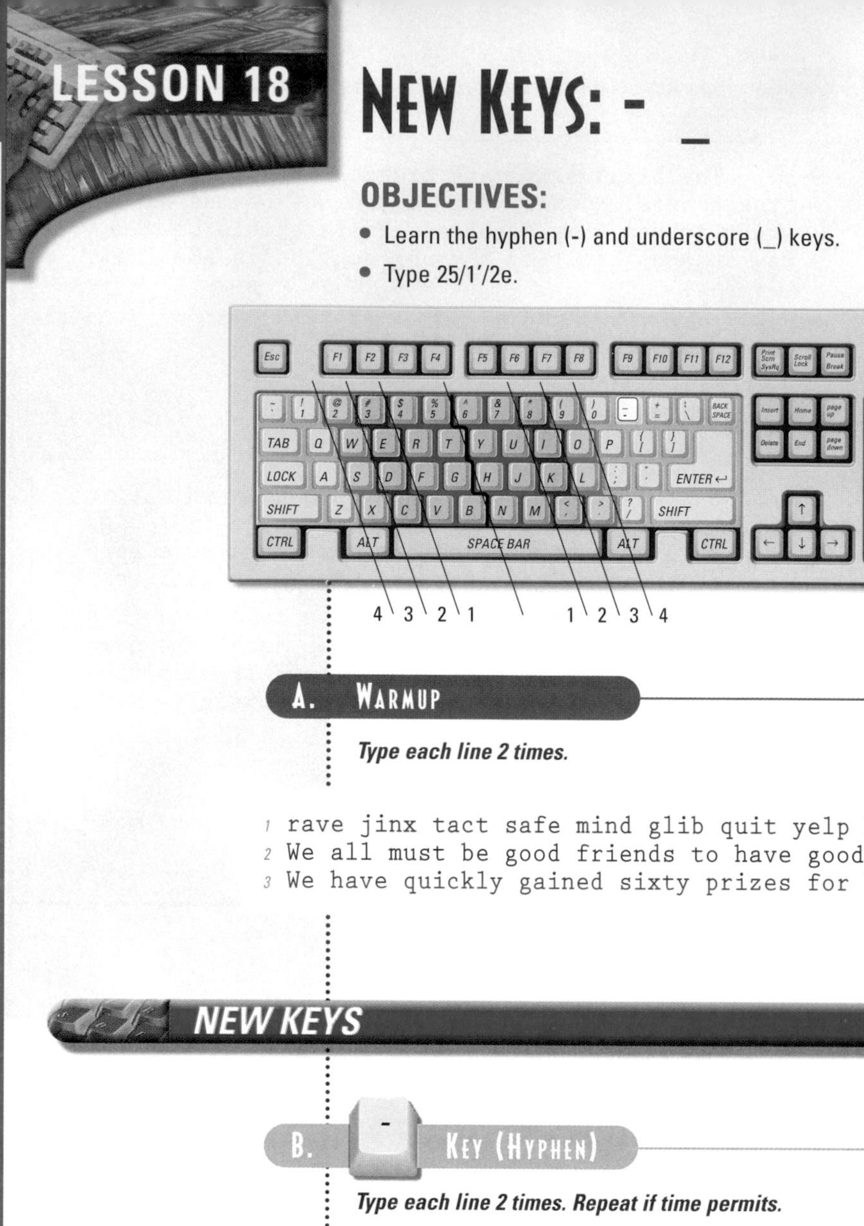

LESSON 18

NEW KEYS: - _

OBJECTIVES:

- Learn the hyphen (-) and underscore (_) keys.
- Type 25/1'/2e.

A. WARMUP

Type each line 2 times.

```
1 rave jinx tact safe mind glib quit yelp hawk doze
2 We all must be good friends to have good friends.
3 We have quickly gained sixty prizes for best jam.
```

NEW KEYS

B. - KEY (HYPHEN)

Type each line 2 times. Repeat if time permits.

Use Sem finger. Anchor J. Do not space before or after hyphens.

```
4 ;;; ;p; ;p-; ;-; -;- ;;; ;p; ;p-; ;-; -;- ;;; ;-;
5 ;p- ;-; self-made ;-; one-third ;p- one-sixth ;-;
6 ;p- ;-; part-time ;-; one-tenth ;p- two-party ;-;
7 Self-made Jim stopped at an out-of-the-way place.
```


RESOURCES

- Lesson Plan 18
- Courseware Lesson 18
- Student Data Disk
- Wallchart

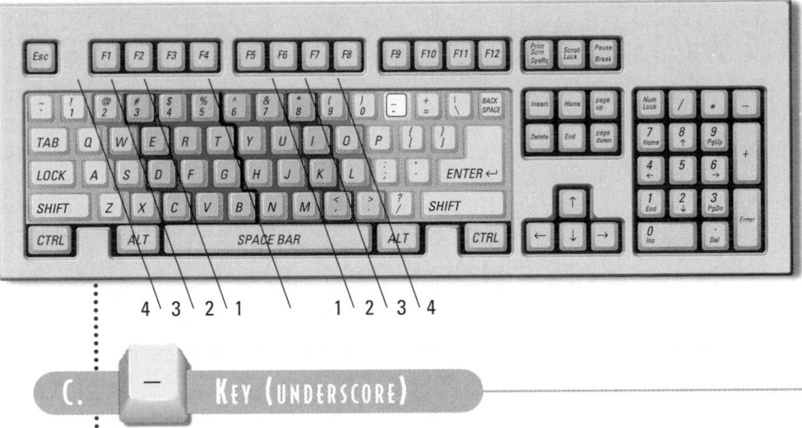

C. _ Key (Underscore)

Type each line 2 times. Repeat if time permits.

Use the Sem finger and the right shift key. Anchor J.

```
8  ;p; ;p- ;-; ;-_; ;-_; ;p-_ _;_ ;p-_ ;-_; ;_; ;p-_
9  ;;; ;p; ;p_; ;_; _;_ ;;; ;p; ;p_; ;_; _;_ ;;; ;_;
10 Quick, create this seven-character line: _______.
11 Be sure to use her e-mail name, jennifer_cochran.
```

SKILLBUILDING

D. Technique Checkpoint

Type each line 2 times. Repeat if time permits. Focus on the techniques at the left.

Keep your feet on the floor, back straight, elbows in.

```
12 ;;; ;p; ;p-; ;-; -;- ;;; ;p; ;p-; ;-; -;- ;;; ;-;
13 ;;; ;p; ;p_; ;_; _;_ ;;; ;p; ;p_; ;_; _;_ ;;; ;_;
14 Are you an easy-going person who gets along well?
15 The new name he now uses for e-mail is jute_rope.
```

E. Technique Timings

Take two 30-second timings on each line. Focus on the techniques at the left.

Sit up straight, keep your elbows in, and keep your feet flat on the floor.

```
16 Steward and Phon drove a car down to the shelter.
17 Ten people helped serve meals to thirty children.
18 They said it was hard work. Jung felt happy then.
19 This might help solve these problems in our city.
   | 1 | 2 | 3 | 4 | 5 | 6 | 7 | 8 | 9 | 10
```


TEACH

Illustration

Explain the purpose of the keyboard illustration.

- The keys are color-coded according to which finger is used.
- The numbers below the keyboard show which fingers correlate to each color.
- The new keys being introduced are shown in white.

Activity C. Remind students to keep their index fingers on the J anchor key when typing lines 8–11.

Activity D. Remind students to use proper posture when typing, keeping their feet on the floor, backs straight, and elbows in.

Activity E. Make sure students keep their eyes on the copy when typing the 30-second timing.

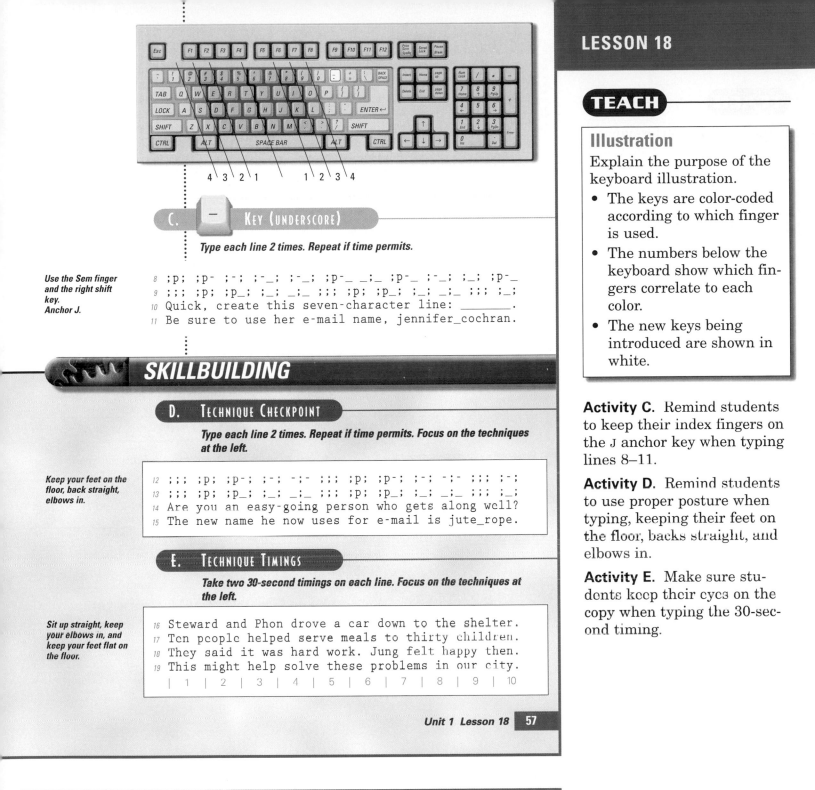

Teacher Notes

TEACH

Activities F–H. Performance on the P/P/P routine should improve from the Pretest to the Posttest.

PRETEST/PRACTICE/POSTTEST

The ***Pretest/Practice/Posttest*** routines are designed to improve speed or accuracy.

- The ***Pretest*** identifies students' speed or accuracy needs.
- The ***Practice*** provides a variety of improvement drills.
- The ***Posttest*** (a repeat of the Pretest) measures improvement.

TEACH

Activity I. Remind students that their goal is to type 25 words a minute for 1 minute with 2 errors or less.

ASSESS

- Compare students' performance on the two 30-second timings in Activity E.
- Compare students' performance on the Pretest with their performance on the Posttest.

CLOSE

As an ending activity, ask the students several questions that require one-word responses such as "What color are your eyes?" and have them type their responses.

F. PRETEST

Take a 1-minute timing on the paragraph. Note your speed and errors.

```
20      Look up in the western sky and see how it is      9
21 filled with magnificent pinks and reds as the sun     19
22 begins to set. As the sun sinks below the clouds,     29
23 you will see an amazing display of great colors.      39
   | 1 | 2 | 3 | 4 | 5 | 6 | 7 | 8 | 9 | 10
```

G. PRACTICE

***SPEED:** If you made 2 or fewer errors on the Pretest, type lines 24–31 two times each.*

***ACCURACY:** If you made more than 2 errors on the Pretest, type lines 24–27 as a group two times. Then, type lines 28–31 as a group two times.*

Left and right reaches are a sequence of at least three letters typed by fingers on either the left or the right hand. (lease, think)

```
24 was raged wheat serve force carts bears cages age
25 tag exact vases rests crank enter greet moves ear
26 was raged wheat serve force carts bears cages age
27 tag exact vases rests crank enter greet moves ear

28 get table stage hired diets gears wages warts rat
29 hop mouth union input polka alone moors tunic joy
30 him looms pumps nouns joked pound allow pours hip
31 lip mopes loose equip moods unite fills alike mop
```

H. POSTTEST

Repeat the Pretest. Compare your Posttest results with your Pretest results.

I. 1-Minute Timings

Take two 1-minute timings on the paragraph. Note your speed and errors.

Goal: 25/1′/2e

```
32      We saw where gray lava flowed down a path.       9
33 At the exit, Justin saw trees with no bark and a     19
34 quiet, fuzzy duck looking at me.                     25
   | 1 | 2 | 3 | 4 | 5 | 6 | 7 | 8 | 9 | 10        SI 1.23
```


EXTENDING THE CONTENT

Discuss composing at the keyboard. Emphasize that students should (1) think of the response they are going to make, and then (2) type the response while keeping their eyes on the screen.

Emphasize that composing at the keyboard is a "draft" process—not a "final copy" process. The important point in composing is to get the idea on the screen; the words they compose can be edited later.

LESSON 19 SKILLBUILDING

OBJECTIVES:

- Refine keyboarding skills.
- Use correct spacing before and after punctuation.

A. WARMUP

Type each line 2 times.

Words	1	fuzz busy flat apex gash avow junk quad czar mink
Speed	2	A good first impression must be made immediately.
Accuracy	3	Rob moved a psychology quiz to next week for Jay.

SKILLBUILDING

B. SPACE BAR

Type each line 2 times. Repeat if time permits.

Space between words without pausing.

```
4 up by rod hub cue dry mow zip elk jaw van era ark
5 do we fad wet tab boy hid lug mug zap box kid fog
6 in my car zoo tug pop vat jar lid yam fix war qua
7 so to add fun joy run sew lad man did nip was hop
```

C. SHIFT KEYS

Type each line 2 times. Repeat if time permits.

Type smoothly as you use the shift keys.

```
8 Quinton Robert Farris Cheryl Eunice Xavier George
9 Juliet Noelle Ulysses Ingmar Hunter Yasmin Melvin
10 Tamara Zachary Quenna Aurora Bryant Dawson Salome
11 Mignon Jeffrey Yvette Olinda Harold Joanna Lionel
```


RESOURCES

- Lesson Plan 19
- Courseware Lesson 19
- Student Data Disk
- Wallchart

COURSEWARE OVERVIEW

Now that students have completed the alphabetic portion of the keyboard, they can use the Skillbuilding activities for additional practice. Explain to them how to access these additional activities and when to access them.

FOCUS

- Improve speed and accuracy.
- Improve speed and accuracy on a P/P/P routine.

BELLRINGER

As soon as students arrive at their workstations and log in, have them type the Warmup that reviews keys they have learned.

TEACH

Activity B. Remind students that like music, there is a rhythm to typing. Encourage students to find their own rhythm.

Activity C. Tell students that they want to think about the messages they are sending via e-mail before they send them. Computers make sending messages to other people quick and easy, but we always want to stop and ask how we would feel if we received this message.

TEACH

Activity D. Tell students that in business writing, as with all writing, their best friends include a good dictionary, a thesaurus, and an English grammar book. A dictionary will help them with the meaning of words and spelling; a thesaurus will help them choose the best word to convey their meaning; and an English grammar book will help them with punctuation and grammar.

Activity E. Ask students why they think it is necessary to proofread a document even if they have used the spell check feature. Have them cite examples of errors that could occur.

Activity F. Tell students to write with simple, easy-to-understand words. The purpose of writing messages is to communicate with someone, not to try to impress them.

Activity G. Remind students to concentrate on smooth operation of the Shift keys.

FACT FILE

Facsimile (fax) machines have become quite popular, but they are not new. The first fax machine was used in Paris at the turn of the century to transmit newspaper photos. By 1959, a Japanese newspaper was faxing pages to a printer hundreds of kilometers away.

D. Tab Key

Type each paragraph 2 times. Press the tab key to indent the first line; press Enter only at the end of lines 13 and 15.

```
12      We read the daily newspaper to learn what is
13 going on in other countries. Do you also read it?

14      Do you read or watch the news? If you don't,
15 you should. How will you learn what is happening?
```

E. Concentration

Fill in the missing vowels as you type each line 1 time. Repeat if time permits.

```
16 E-ch d-y thos- fing-rs w-ll m-ve a l-ttl- f-st-r.
17 Y-u m-st le-rn to th-nk wh-re all thos- k-ys ar-.
18 D- y-u ke-p yo-r ey-s on th- c-py y-u ar- typ-ng?
19 On- d-y so-n yo-r f-ng-rs w-ll fly ov-r th- k-ys.
```

F. Punctuation Spacing

Type lines 20–24 one time. Note the spacing before and after each punctuation mark. Repeat if time permits.

```
20 Accounting is a good course. I am taking it soon.
21 Dr. Tim Bellio, Ph.D., is in the U.S. or the U.K.
22 Please turn on the TV; my favorite program is on.
23 Mr. C. L. Brickmann and his son, T. J., are home.
24 We must talk to two people: Anthony and Consuela.
```

G. Technique Timings

Take two 30-second timings on each line. Focus on the techniques at the left.

Lines 25 and 26: Concentrate on efficient, smooth operation of the shift keys.
Lines 27 and 28: Space quickly without pausing.

```
25 Jay and Ed were on time. Iva liked doing Tai Chi.
26 Alberto, set the clock. It is good to be on time.
27 Both Y. O. Fox and T. C. Ole had a Ph.D. in math.
28 Mr. Vasquez and Mr. Mayer were not in the office.
   | 1 | 2 | 3 | 4 | 5 | 6 | 7 | 8 | 9 | 10
```


Teacher Notes

H. PRETEST

Take a 1-minute timing on the paragraph. Note your speed and errors.

```
29      Have you tried to get a project completed by      9
30  a deadline only to realize that you simply will      19
31  not be able to finish it? What you do next will      28
32  depend on the project and how soon you need it.      38
    | 1 | 2 | 3 | 4 | 5 | 6 | 7 | 8 | 9 | 10
```

I. PRACTICE

***SPEED:** If you made 2 or fewer errors on the Pretest, type lines 33–40 two times each.*

***ACCURACY:** If you made more than 2 errors on the Pretest, type lines 33–36 as a group two times. Then type lines 37–40 as a group two times.*

Up reaches are consecutive letters on the home row and third row typed by one hand. (task)

```
33 es seats zeal treat lease means eases plead beast
34 gr great gray grows grain grade grass groan grave
35 lo love glove ploys clock locks flock block lobes
36 dr draft drift drive dress drama drums drab drape
```

Down reaches are consecutive letters on the home row and bottom row typed by one hand. (call)

```
37 av lava paved avert favor shave avoid brave raven
38 nk drink pink links crank plank sinks honks blank
39 sc scar scare scant scrap scent scoot scold scone
40 ba barks bare barns barb baby back bang bald bath
```

J. POSTTEST

Repeat the Pretest. Compare your Posttest results with your Pretest results.

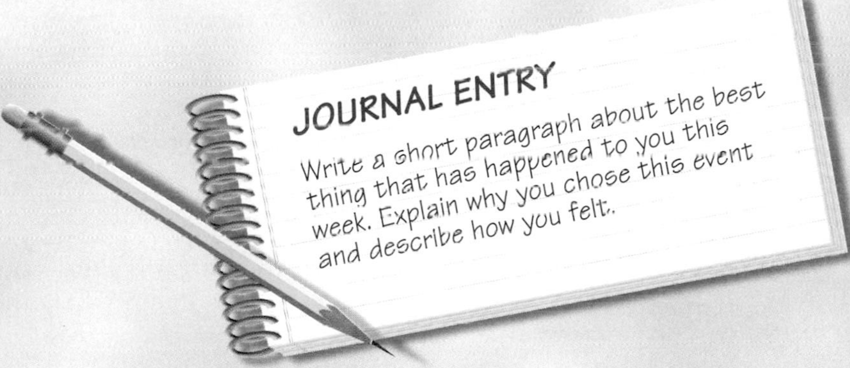
JOURNAL ENTRY
Write a short paragraph about the best thing that has happened to you this week. Explain why you chose this event and describe how you felt.

TEACH

Activities H–J. Performance on the P/P/P routine should improve from the Pretest to the Posttest.

PRETEST/PRACTICE/POSTTEST

The ***Pretest/Practice/Posttest*** routines are designed to improve speed or accuracy.

- The ***Pretest*** identifies students' speed or accuracy needs.
- The ***Practice*** provides a variety of improvement drills.
- The ***Posttest*** (a repeat of the Pretest) measures improvement.

ASSESS

- Compare students' performance on the Pretest with their performance on the Posttest.
- Check students' composing skills; see if they are following the two-step process for responding: (1) think of the response, and (2) type the response.

CLOSE

As an ending activity, ask the students several questions that require 3- and 4-word responses. Point out that students have now learned all the alphabet keys.

JOURNAL ENTRY

Point out the Journal Entry. Have students use the computer to write their entry. Remind them to write a draft and then go back and proofread to make changes. Help students print their entry and add it to their journals.

LESSON 20

FOCUS

- Review the letter keys, Shift key, and Tab key.
- Concentrate on providing missing vowels.
- Improve speed and accuracy through the P/P/P routine.

BELLRINGER

As soon as students arrive at their workstations and log in, have them type the Warmup that reviews keys they have learned.

TEACH

Activity B. Be sure students type lines 4–7 at least once. These lines provide an excellent alphabetic review.

Activity C. Students should type smoothly as they operate the Shift keys.

LESSON 20 SKILLBUILDING

OBJECTIVES:

- Refine keyboarding skills.
- Use correct spacing before and after punctuation.
- Type 25/1'/2e.

A. WARMUP

Type each line 2 times.

```
Words     1 itch plum jilt waxy fizz next clod quad brag skit
Speed     2 It is good to meet new people as soon as you can.
Accuracy  3 Cover the cozy liquid wax before Jack mops again.
```

SKILLBUILDING

B. ALPHABET REVIEW

Type each line 2 times. Repeat if time permits.

```
4 baffle quartz toxic veins major whack gaudy equip
5 banjo wizard rhyme heaven steep affix laugh quack
6 matrix shady squaw venom jacket spill zebra fudge
7 Be quick to move them up/down; jinx lazy fingers.
```

C. SHIFT KEYS

Type each line 2 times. Repeat if time permits.

Type smoothly as you use the shift keys.

```
8 Querida Arthur Donata Regina Gwynne Warden Samuel
9 Leilani Ursula Javier Margot Phoebe Irving Oliver
10 Timothy Carlos Elliot Felice Zenina Vernon Winona
11 Nokomis Isabel Hayley Pascal Justin Latham Kameko
```


RESOURCES

- Lesson Plan 20
- Courseware Lesson 20
- Student Data Disk
- Wallchart
- Grading and Evaluation

COURSEWARE OVERVIEW

The production portion of the unit tests is included within the software. The objective portion is not included. Provide students with instructions for taking unit tests.

D. Tab Key

Type each line 1 time. Repeat if time permits.

Press the tab key to begin each sentence, and press ENTER at the end of each sentence.

```
12 Did you meet your goals? I did not. They all did.
13 My car is stuck. I need it towed. Will you do it?
14 Let's see a movie. What's playing? I do not know.
15 Look at that. It is quite amazing. I am thrilled.
```

E. Concentration

Fill in the missing vowels as you type each line 1 time. Repeat if time permits.

```
16 K--p all f-ng-rs curv-d -nd y--r wr-sts up a b-t.
17 Ke-p yo-r b-ck er-ct, b-t le-n yo-r b-dy forw-rd.
18 Ke-p y-ur elb-ws r-lax-d and cl-se to y-ur s-des.
19 K-ep y-ur h-ad up -nd t-rned tow-rd th- textb--k.
20 K-ep b-th fe-t on th- flo-r, on- aft-r th- oth-r.
```

F. Punctuation Spacing

Type lines 21–25 one time. Note the spacing before and after each punctuation mark. Repeat if time permits.

```
21 Tom's flowers--especially the tulips--are lovely.
22 Have you seen her gloves? Are they in the drawer?
23 If Leilani can go tomorrow, we will go then also.
24 Estes Park has roads as well as hike/bike trails.
25 That fly-by-night business was selling old disks.
```


TEACH

Activity D. Be sure students are using the Tab key and not the Space Bar in the Technique Timing.

Activity E. Ask students to read aloud sentences 16 through 20 to be sure they know what vowels are missing before they start typing the lines.

FACT FILE

The Internet functions because of a common set of protocols and standards. Computer protocols known as TCP/IP (Transmission Control Protocol/Internet Protocol) form the base of the Internet. Every computer directly linked to the Net has a unique IP address.

SCHOOL TO CAREER

On the board write the following career titles across the top: *Industry*, *Farming*, and *Crafts*. Have students brainstorm how computer skills are used in each. Under each career title, write students' ideas. Have each student choose a career and write a paragraph about it.

TECHNOLOGY TIP

To sign on to the Internet, you need a password. A password is private and keeps anyone else from logging on and looking at your messages. A good password is one that includes letters and numbers. Never share your password with anyone.

TEACH

Activity F. Tell students that if they believe in what they are doing and their ability to do it well, it will happen. Their own doubt that they can do a good job may be standing in their way.

Activity G. Continue to encourage students. Have slower students work with peer tutors after class.

Activity H. Students should recognize the troublesome letter pairs that are emphasized in the Pretest (*as*, *fg*, *we*, *kl*, *nm*, and *oi*). These reaches are called discrimination reaches.

Activity I. Be sure students realize the correct procedure for the Practice routine. If they made 2 or fewer errors, they type each line twice (i.e., line 37 twice, line 38 twice, etc.); if they made more than 2 errors, they type lines 37–39 twice as a group; then they type lines 40–42 twice as a group.

Activity J. Performance on the P/P/P routine should improve from the Pretest to the Posttest.

PRETEST/PRACTICE/POSTEST

The ***Pretest/Practice/Posttest*** routines are designed to improve speed or accuracy.

- The ***Pretest*** identifies students' speed or accuracy needs.
- The ***Practice*** provides a variety of improvement drills
- The ***Posttest*** (a repeat of the Pretest) measures improvement.

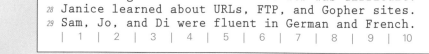

G. Technique Timings

Take two 30-second timings on each line. Focus on the technique at the left.

Try to type smoothly as you operate the shift keys.

26 Oliver let Margo answer the Gopher Internet quiz.
27 Connecting with the World Wide Web was difficult.
28 Janice learned about URLs, FTP, and Gopher sites.
29 Sam, Jo, and Di were fluent in German and French.
| 1 | 2 | 3 | 4 | 5 | 6 | 7 | 8 | 9 | 10

H. PRETEST

Take a 1-minute timing on the paragraph. Note your speed and errors.

30 There are fewer golf courses in Clark County 9
31 than in Milton County. One reason is the need for 19
32 rich soil to grow grass. Clark County has mostly 29
33 clay soil, which does not absorb water well. 38
| 1 | 2 | 3 | 4 | 5 | 6 | 7 | 8 | 9 | 10

I. PRACTICE

SPEED: If you made 2 or fewer errors on the Pretest, type lines 34–41 two times.

ACCURACY: If you made more than 2 errors on the Pretest, type lines 34–37 as a group two times. Then type lines 38–41 as a group two times.

Discrimination reaches are keys that are commonly substituted and easily confused. (wear)

34 asa aside sadly flask sails saved trash masks sas
35 fgf fight goofs golfs fugue gaffe foggy frogs gfg
36 wew weans sweet swell sweat sewer fewer weeks ewe
37 rtr art part port sort fort worth trade title rtr

38 klk kilns kilts kills keels flock block locks lkl
39 nmn means lemon minor numbs names money hymns mnm
40 oio boils soils joins coins lions toils spoil ioi
41 jhj joy jewels judge huge hugs jugs just jury jhj

J. POSTTEST

Repeat the Pretest. Compare your Posttest results with your Pretest results.

Teacher Notes

K. 1-Minute Timings

Take two 1-minute timings on the paragraph. Note your speed and errors.

Goal: 25/1'/2e

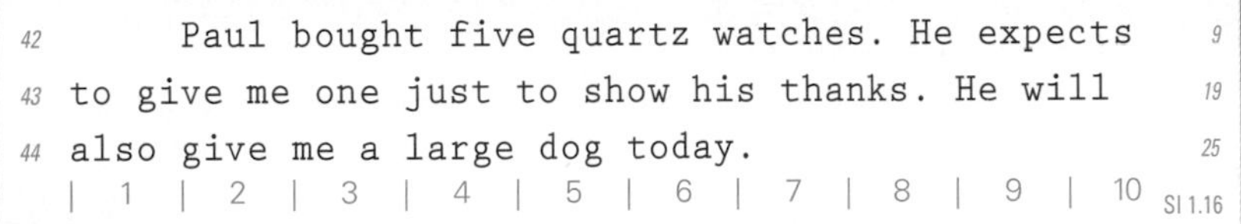

Paul bought five quartz watches. He expects 9
to give me one just to show his thanks. He will 19
also give me a large dog today. 25

| 1 | 2 | 3 | 4 | 5 | 6 | 7 | 8 | 9 | 10 SI 1.16

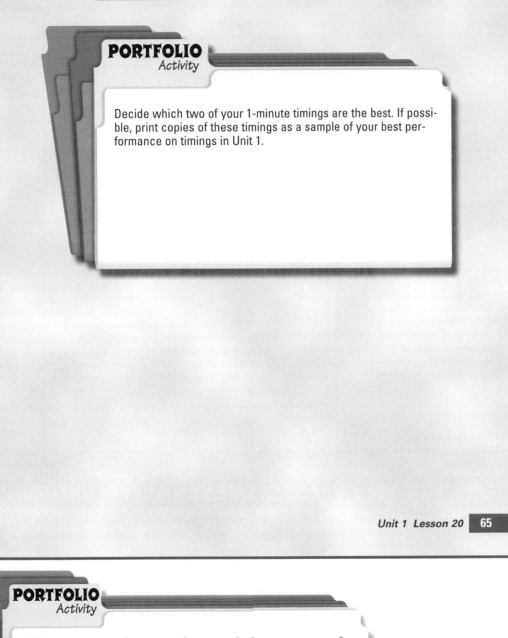

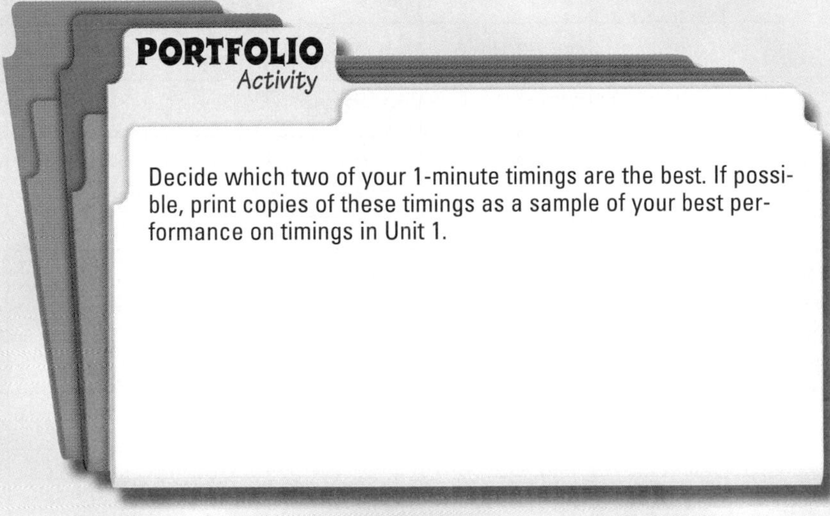

PORTFOLIO *Activity*

Decide which two of your 1-minute timings are the best. If possible, print copies of these timings as a sample of your best performance on timings in Unit 1.

LESSON 20

TEACH

Activity K. Remind students that the goal for these 1-minute timings is to type 25 words a minute for 1 minute with no more than 2 errors.

ASSESS

- Check students' accuracy in filling in the missing vowels in lines 16–20.
- Compare student's performance on the Pretest with their performance on the Posttest.

CLOSE

As an ending activity, ask the students several questions that require complete sentence responses.

PORTFOLIO *Activity*

Make sure students understand the purpose of their portfolio. Remind them of how the portfolio will be used as part of this course and how they can use it in the future.

UNIT 2 ORGANIZER

KEYBOARDING

Lesson	Focus	Special Features	Skillbuilding	Pretest/ Practice/ Posttest	Documents	GO TO Activities
21	4, $, 7, &	Fact File, p. 71	p. 69	p. 70		
22	3, #, 8, *		pp. 73–74	pp. 73–74		
23	2, @, 9, (		p. 77	pp. 77–78		
24	Review	Language Link, p. 81	pp. 79–80	p. 80		
25	1, !, 0,)		p. 83	pp. 83–84		
26	5, %, 6, ^	Fact File, p. 88	p. 86	p. 87		
27	Special Symbols	Internet Connection, p. 93 Social Studies Connections, p. 93	p. 91	p. 91		
28	Numeric Keypad: 4, 5, 6, ENTER	Fact File, p. 94 Language Link, p. 95	pp. 96–97			
29	Numeric Keypad: 7, 8, 9	Fact File, p. 98 Journal Entry, p. 101	pp. 99–100	p. 100		
30	Review	Communication Focus, p. 104 Portfolio Activity, p. 105 Language Link, p. 105	pp. 102–103	pp. 103–104		
31	Numeric Keypad: 1, 2, 3	Internet Connection, p. 106 Language Link, p. 109	pp. 107–108	p. 108		
32	Numeric Keypad: 0, Period (.)	Fact File, p. 110 Science Connections, p. 113	p. 112	pp. 112–113		

UNIT 2 RESOURCE MANAGER

MULTIMEDIA
- Courseware: Lessons 21–40
- Student Data Disk
- Wall Charts

TEACHING TOOLS
- Lesson Plans: Lessons 21–40
- Block Scheduling Guide, Unit 2

RETEACHING/REINFORCEMENT
- Reteaching and Reinforcement Activities: Lessons 21–40

ASSESSMENT and EVALUATION

Pretest/Practice/Posttest: pp. 70, 73–74, 77–78, 80, 83–84, 87, 91, 100, 103–104, 108, 112–113, 115, 121, 124, 133
Portfolio Activity: p. 105
Unit 2 Test
Timings: pp. 71, 75, 78, 81, 84, 88, 93, 97, 101, 104, 109, 113, 116, 119, 122, 127, 135
Grading and Evaluation

Electronic Teacher Classroom Resources

For your convenience, the teacher's materials are available on a CD-ROM. Having these resources available electronically enables you to print exactly what you need and revise materials as necessary.

Lesson	Focus	Special Features	Skillbuilding	Pretest/ Practice/ Posttest	Documents	GO TO Activities
33	Review	Social Studies Connections, p. 116 Science Connections, p. 116	pp. 114–115	p. 115		
34	Skillbuilding	Fact File, p. 117 Science Connections, p. 119	pp. 117–118			
35	Skillbuilding	Fact File, p. 120 Social Studies Connections, pp. 120, 122 Language Link, p. 120	p. 121	p. 121		
36	Word Processing: New File, Open File, Close File, Quit		p. 123	p. 124		p. 124
37	Word Processing: Moving Around in Document, Spelling Check, Correcting Errors, Backspacing, Saving File	Fact File, p. 126 Internet Connection, p. 127	pp. 125–126			p. 127
38	Word Processing: Font Styles, Font Sizes, Print/Page Preview, Print	Internet Connection, p. 128	pp. 129–130			p. 129
39	Word Processing: Alignment, Show/Hide, Reveal Codes, Selecting Text	Communication Focus, p. 131	p. 132	p. 133		p. 133
40	Word Processing: Center Page, Help	Social Studies Connection, pp. 134–135	pp. 134–135			p. 135

SCANS Competencies in Glencoe Keyboarding with Computer Applications

Resources	Interpersonal Skills	Information	Systems	Technology
Throughout the course, students deal specifically with resources: allocating time for completing drills and documents, maintaining workstations, caring for computers and software.	Communication Focus, pp. 104, 131	Career Bit, p. 67 Fact File, pp. 71, 88, 94, 98, 110, 117, 120, 126 Internet Connection, pp. 93, 106, 127, 128 Social Studies Connection, pp. 93, 116, 120, 122, 134, 135 Science Connection, pp. 113, 116, 119	Internet Connection, pp. 93, 106, 127, 128	Lessons 21–40 Internet Connection, pp. 93, 106, 127, 128

UNIT 2

Lessons 21–40

KEYBOARDING

OBJECTIVES

- Demonstrate which fingers control the number and symbol keys.
- Refine and improve keyboarding techniques.
- Demonstrate proficiency on the numeric keypad.
- Use proper spacing before and after special symbols.
- Type at a speed of 27 words a minute for 2 minutes with 4 or fewer errors.
- Compose multiple words/short phrases at the keyboard.
- Apply capitalization rules.

INTRODUCING THE UNIT

Ask students why they will need to know the number keys and the symbol keys. Ask students what refining means. What do they think improving typing technique means? Ask: What is the difference between the keypad and the keyboard?

Explain that the goal in this unit is to learn to type at a speed of 27 words a minute for 2 minutes with 4 or fewer errors. Remind them that this is an achievable goal—that only a short while ago they didn't even know the keyboard. Also tell them that they will be learning how to compose and type multiple words and short phrases.

FUN Facts

Desktop computers are vulnerable to more than 13,000 known computer viruses. This number grows by about six new virus programs per day! A computer virus is a segment of program code. It gives directions to change the computer's programs or destroy data in the computer. Installing an antivirus program is the best protection you can have against computer viruses.

COURSEWARE OVERVIEW

Beginning with Lesson 36, students will need to have their student manuals in addition to their textbooks and data disks. Lesson 36 introduces students to word processing features. The student manuals provide software-specific instructions for accessing and using each feature. In addition, the manual contains practice activities to reinforce students' learning.

WORDS TO LEARN

caret
edit
Internet address
Num Lock
tilde

CAREER BIT

GEOLOGIST Geologists study the physical aspects and history of Earth. They identify and examine rocks, study information collected by remote sensing instruments in satellites, conduct geological surveys, construct field maps, and use instruments to measure Earth's gravity and magnetic field.

Many geologists and geophysicists search for oil, natural gas, minerals, and ground-water. Some geologists use two- or three-dimensional computer modeling to portray water layers and the flow of water or other fluids through rock cracks and porous materials. Other geological scientists play an important role in preserving and cleaning up the environment.

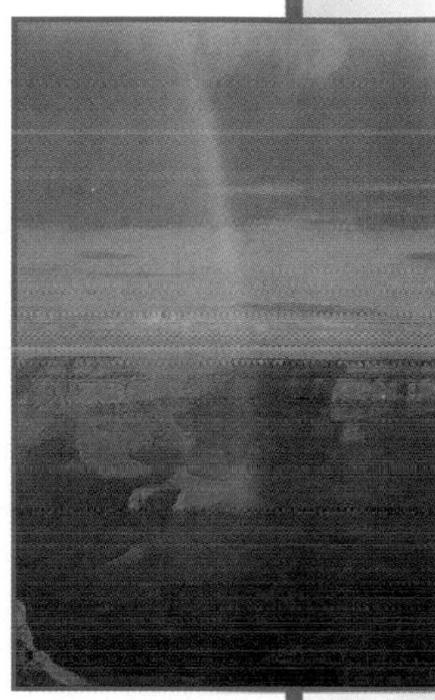

67

COURSEWARE OVERVIEW

Typically, students will complete activities sequentially. However, the courseware provides separate Skillbuilding and Language Link menus. The Skillbuilding menu includes the various skillbuilding activities arranged by type. The Language Link menu includes the textbook Language Link activities and the interactive Language Link tutorials.

WORDS TO LEARN

The terms in Words to Learn are defined in the Glossary at the back of the book. Ask students if they are familiar with any of the terms. Have them define the terms they know. Compare their definitions with those in the Glossary.

Provide students with an example of an Internet address. Consider using the address for your school or school district, your local or state government, the public library, or a business that is located in or near your community. (The components for an Internet address are as follows: @domainname)

CAREER BIT

Have students explore other activities in which geologists are involved. These may include things such as analyzing seismic activity, searching for gas and minerals, designing and monitoring waste disposal sites, preserving water supplies, and reclaiming contaminated land and water to comply with Federal environmental regulations, and helping to locate safe sites for hazardous waste facilities and landfills. You may also want to mention their involvement in engineering problems in constructing large buildings, dams, tunnels, and highways.

FOCUS

- Learn the 4, $, 7, and & keys.
- Improve skill on a P/P/P routine.
- Complete 1- and 2-minute timings.

BELLRINGER

As soon as students arrive at their workstations and log in, have them type the Warmup that reviews keys they have learned.

TEACH

Illustration

Explain the purpose of the keyboard illustration.

- The keys are color-coded according to which finger is used.
- The numbers below the keyboard show which fingers correlate to each color.
- The new keys being introduced are shown in white.

Activity B. Have students press the Demonstration button to view the correct reach for the 4, $, 7, and & keys.

To help students with the correct reach to the number keys, try using the interceding character technique described in Extending the Content at the bottom of page 69.

LESSON 21

NEW KEYS: 4 $ 7 &

OBJECTIVES:

- Learn the 4, $, 7, and & keys.
- Refine keyboarding techniques.
- Type 27/2'/4e.

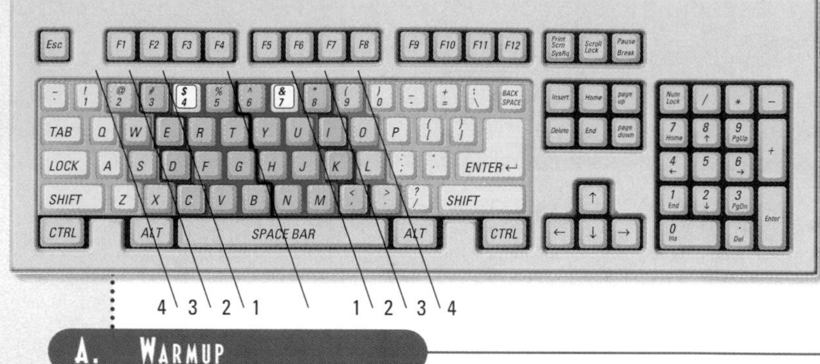

A. WARMUP

Type each line 2 times.

Words	1 shot idea jobs corn quip give flex whey maze elks
Speed	2 It is not a good idea to play ball in the street.
Accuracy	3 My joke expert amazed five huge clowns in Quebec.

NEW KEYS

B. 4 AND $ KEY

Type each line 2 times. Repeat if time permits.

Use F finger. Anchor A.

4 frf fr4f f4f 444 f4f 4/44 f4f 44.4 f4f 44,444 f4f
5 44 films, 44 foes, 44 flukes, 44 folders, or 4.44
6 I saw 44 ducks, 4 geese, and 4 swans on the lake.
7 Today, our team had 4 runs, 4 hits, and 4 errors.

Use F finger and right shift. Anchor A. Do not space between the $ and the number.

8 frf fr4 f4f f4$f f$f f$f $4 $44 $444 f$f f4f $444
9 $444, 44 fish, 4 fans, $44, 444 fellows, $4, $444
10 Jo paid $44 for the oranges and $4 for the pears.
11 They had $444 and spent $44 of it for 4 presents.

RESOURCES

- Lesson Plan 21
- Courseware Lesson 21
- Student Data Disk
- Wallchart
- Grading and Evaluation

COURSEWARE OVERVIEW

Before beginning a new unit, you may want to delete older files from students data disks.

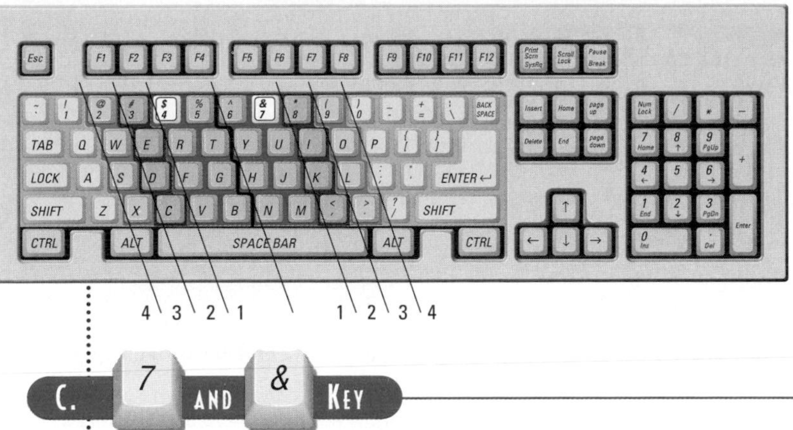

C. 7 AND & KEY

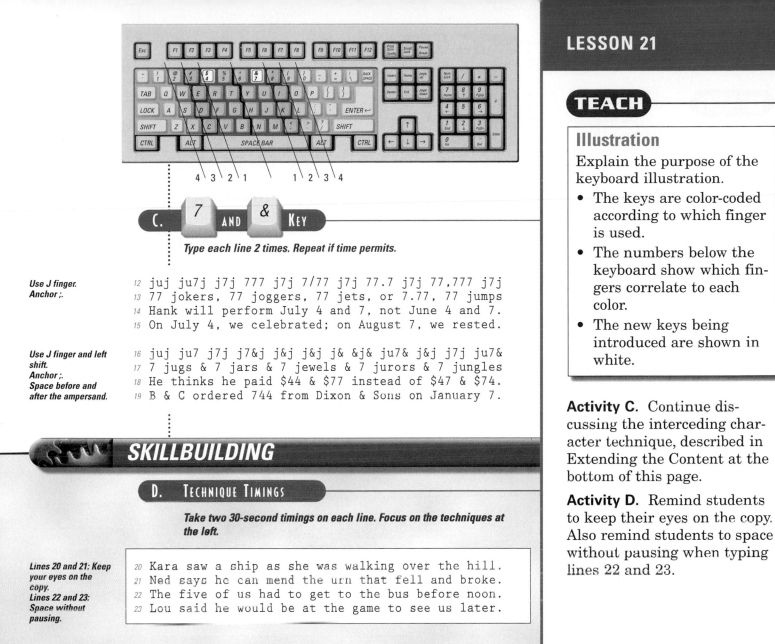

Type each line 2 times. Repeat if time permits.

Use J finger. Anchor ;.

```
12 juj ju7j j7j 777 j7j 7/77 j7j 77.7 j7j 77,777 j7j
13 77 jokers, 77 joggers, 77 jets, or 7.77, 77 jumps
14 Hank will perform July 4 and 7, not June 4 and 7.
15 On July 4, we celebrated; on August 7, we rested.
```

Use J finger and left shift. Anchor ;. Space before and after the ampersand.

```
16 juj ju7 j7j j7&j j&j j&j j& &j& ju7& j&j j7j ju7&
17 7 jugs & 7 jars & 7 jewels & 7 jurors & 7 jungles
18 He thinks he paid $44 & $77 instead of $47 & $74.
19 B & C ordered 744 from Dixon & Sons on January 7.
```

SKILLBUILDING

D. TECHNIQUE TIMINGS

Take two 30-second timings on each line. Focus on the techniques at the left.

Lines 20 and 21: Keep your eyes on the copy. Lines 22 and 23: Space without pausing.

```
20 Kara saw a ship as she was walking over the hill.
21 Ned says he can mend the urn that fell and broke.
22 The five of us had to get to the bus before noon.
23 Lou said he would be at the game to see us later.
```


TEACH

Illustration

Explain the purpose of the keyboard illustration.

- The keys are color-coded according to which finger is used.
- The numbers below the keyboard show which fingers correlate to each color.
- The new keys being introduced are shown in white.

Activity C. Continue discussing the interceding character technique, described in Extending the Content at the bottom of this page.

Activity D. Remind students to keep their eyes on the copy. Also remind students to space without pausing when typing lines 22 and 23.

EXTENDING THE CONTENT

Interceding Character Technique. Dictate **fr4f space** and have students strike the keys and the space bar as they watch their keyboard. (Note: **r** is the interceding character.) Repeat this sequence three or four times. Make sure students keep the A anchor as they reach for the 4 key. With students watching you, not their keyboards, dictate **fr4f space**. Repeat this sequence three or four times.

Repeat the dictation described above without the interceding character. Dictate **f4f space** and have students strike the keys and the space bar as they watch their keyboards. Repeat this sequence three or four times. With students watching you, not their keyboards, dictate **f4f space**. Repeat this sequence three or four times. Have students type the textbook drill lines in Activity B on page 68.

Repeat this procedure for the 7, with U as the interceding key. Have students type the textbook drill lines in Activity C on this page.

TEACH

Activities E–G. Go over the adjacent and jump reaches in the P/P/P routine. Adjacent reaches involve keys that are next to each other on the keyboard, such as **tr**, **op**, and **er**. Jump reaches are those reaches that require students to jump from the top row to the bottom row (or vice versa) when striking two consecutive keys, such as **on**, **ex**, and **ve**.

PRETEST/PRACTICE/POSTEST

The ***Pretest/Practice/Posttest*** routines are designed to improve speed or accuracy.

- The ***Pretest*** identifies students' speed or accuracy needs.
- The ***Practice*** provides a variety of improvement drills.
- The ***Posttest*** (a repeat of the Pretest) measures improvement.

Activity H. Students' results on 1-minute timings on the alphanumeric copy may be slower because of the addition of numbers and symbols. Assure them that their speed on alphanumeric timings will improve with practice.

E. PRETEST

Take a 1-minute timing on the paragraph. Note your speed and errors.

```
     Each of us should try to eat healthful food,    9
get proper rest, and exercise moderately. All of    19
these things will help each of us face life with    29
more enthusiasm and more energy.                    35
|  1  |  2  |  3  |  4  |  5  |  6  |  7  |  8  |  9  |  10
```

F. PRACTICE

SPEED: *If you made 2 or fewer errors on the Pretest, type lines 28–35 two times.*

ACCURACY: *If you made more than 2 errors on the Pretest, type lines 28–31 as a group two times. Then type lines 32–35 as a group two times.*

Adjacent Reaches

```
tr train tree tried truth troop strum strip stray
op open slope opera sloop moped scoop hoped opine
er were loner every steer error veers sewer verge
po port porter pole pods potter potion pound pout
```

Jump Reaches

```
on onion ozone upon honor front spoon phone wrong
ex exams exist exact flex exits exalt vexed Texas
ve even veers vests verbs leave every verge heave
ni nine ninth night nimble nifty nice nickel nigh
```

G. POSTTEST

Repeat the Pretest. Compare your Posttest results with your Pretest results.

H. 1-Minute Alphanumeric Timing

Take a 1-minute timing on the paragraph. Note your speed and errors.

```
     Luke sent a $47 check to Computers & Such to    9
get a disk with 44 games & 4 special programs for   19
7 friends. He saw 47 of his friends at 4 p.m.       28
|  1  |  2  |  3  |  4  |  5  |  6  |  7  |  8  |  9  |  10
```

70 *Keyboarding*

PORTFOLIO *Activity*

Tell students to keep a copy of their best timings in Lessons 21 through 30. In Lesson 30 they will be asked to determine how much they have improved and explain why they have improved.

I. 2-Minute Timings

Take two 2-minute timings on lines 39–44. Note your speed and errors.

Goal: 27/2'/4e

```
39      Have you been to our zoo? This is a great         9
40 thing to do in the summer. Bring your lunch to        18
41 eat in the park by the lake. You can watch a bear     28
42 cub perform or just view the zebras. Then explore     38
43 this spot and see the many quail and ducks. Take      48
44 some photos to capture the day.                       54
   | 1 | 2 | 3 | 4 | 5 | 6 | 7 | 8 | 9 | 10          SI 1.12
```

FACT FILE

In 1947, photographer Edwin Land demonstrated a new invention. He developed a camera that could take a picture, develop it, and print it in about a minute. His invention became known as the Polaroid camera.

LESSON 21

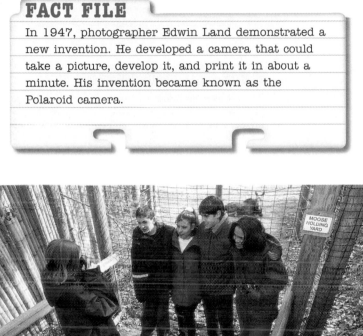

Activity I. Tell students that the goal for 2-minute timings is to type 27 words a minute for 2 minutes with no more than 4 errors.

ASSESS

- Check students' ability to type the number and symbol keys by touch.
- Compare students' performance on the Pretest with their performance on the Posttest.

CLOSE

Remind students they want to practice for both speed and accuracy. Have them pair with another student to proofread each other's Posttest for accuracy.

FACT FILE

When George Eastman introduced roll film in 1889, he paved the way for amateur photographers. Today, digital cameras and scanners allow computer users to add photographic images to documents and presentations as an integral part of the message or for visual appeal.

LESSON 22

FOCUS

- Learn the 3, #, 8, and * keys.
- Improve skill on 30-second timings.
- Improve skill on a P/P/P routine.
- Complete 1- and 2-minute timings.

BELLRINGER

As soon as students arrive at their workstations and log in, have them type the Warmup that reviews keys they have learned.

TEACH

Illustration

Explain the purpose of the keyboard illustration.

- The keys are color-coded according to which finger is used.
- The numbers below the keyboard show which fingers correlate to each color.
- The new keys being introduced are shown in white.

Activity B. Have students press the Demonstration button to view the correct reach for the 3, #, 8, and * keys. To help students with the correct reach to the number keys, try using the interceding character technique described in Extending the Content at the bottom of page 73.

LESSON 22 NEW KEYS: 3 # 8 *

OBJECTIVES:

- Learn the 3, #, 8, and * keys.
- Refine keyboarding skills.
- Type 27/2′/4e.

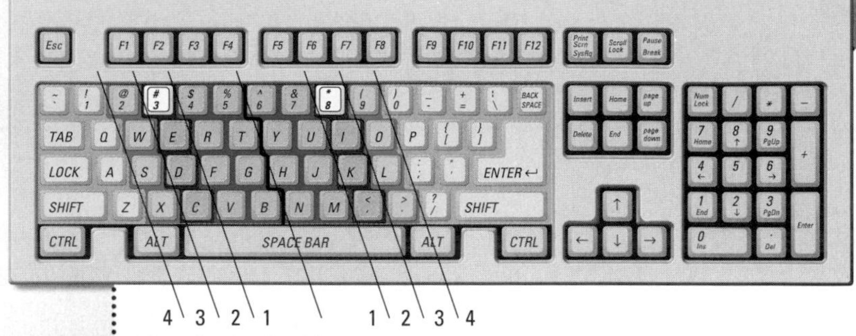

A. WARMUP

Type each line 2 times.

Speed	1	The time for Andrew to stop is when the sun sets.
Accuracy	2	Ten foxes quickly jumped high over twelve zebras.
Numbers	3	Lines 47, 77, and 44 were right; line 74 was not.
Symbols	4	Bakes & Deli pays $4, $4.77, and $7.44 for dimes.

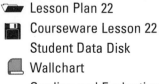

NEW KEYS

B. 3 AND # KEY

Type each line 2 times. Repeat if time permits.

Use D finger. Anchor A or F.

5 ded de3d d3d 333 d3d 3/33 d3d 33.3 d3d 33,333 d3d
6 33 dimes, 33 dishes, 33 dots, 33 daisies, or 3.33
7 Draw 33 squares, 3,333 rectangles, and 3 circles.
8 They had 333 dogs in 33 kennels for over 3 weeks.

The # (number or pound sign) is the shift of 3. Anchor A or F. Do not space between the number and #.

9 ded de3 d3d d3#d d#d d#d #3 #33 #333 d#d d3d #333
10 #3, 3 dots, #33, 33 dogs, #333, 333 ditches, #333
11 Is Invoice #373 for 344#, 433#, or 343# of fruit?
12 The group used 43# of grade #3 potatoes at lunch.

RESOURCES

- Lesson Plan 22
- Courseware Lesson 22
- Student Data Disk
- Wallchart
- Grading and Evaluation

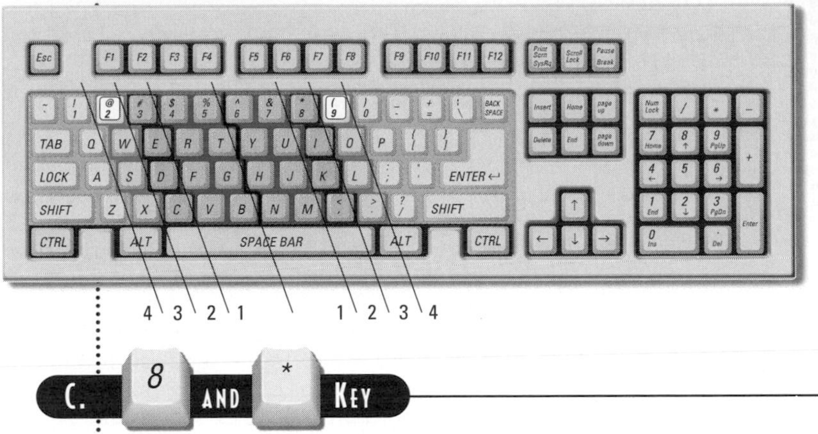

C. 8 AND * KEY

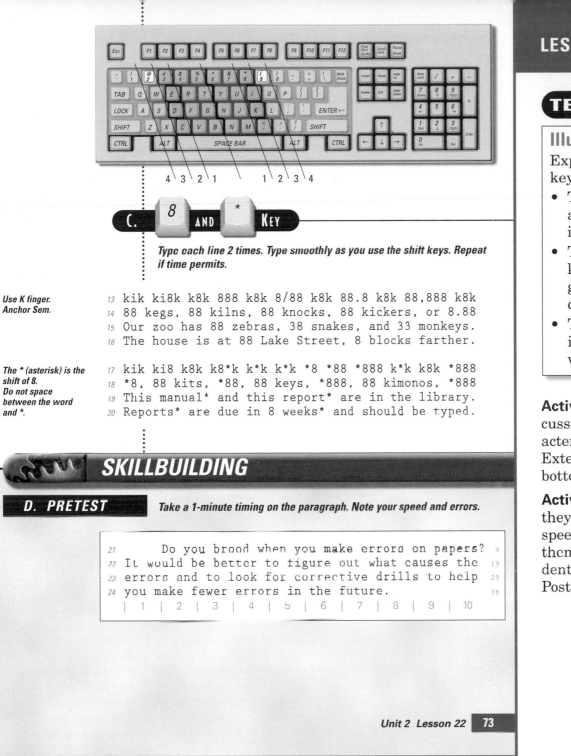

Type each line 2 times. Type smoothly as you use the shift keys. Repeat if time permits.

Use K finger. Anchor Sem.

```
13 kik ki8k k8k 888 k8k 8/88 k8k 88.8 k8k 88,888 k8k
14 88 kegs, 88 kilns, 88 knocks, 88 kickers, or 8.88
15 Our zoo has 88 zebras, 38 snakes, and 33 monkeys.
16 The house is at 88 Lake Street, 8 blocks farther.
```

*The * (asterisk) is the shift of 8. Do not space between the word and *.*

```
17 kik ki8 k8k k8*k k*k k*k *8 *88 *888 k*k k8k *888
18 *8, 88 kits, *88, 88 keys, *888, 88 kimonos, *888
19 This manual* and this report* are in the library.
20 Reports* are due in 8 weeks* and should be typed.
```

SKILLBUILDING

D. PRETEST

Take a 1-minute timing on the paragraph. Note your speed and errors.

```
21       Do you brood when you make errors on papers?   9
22 It would be better to figure out what causes the   19
23 errors and to look for corrective drills to help   29
24 you make fewer errors in the future.               36
   | 1 | 2 | 3 | 4 | 5 | 6 | 7 | 8 | 9 | 10
```


TEACH

Illustration

Explain the purpose of the keyboard illustration.

- The keys are color-coded according to which finger is used.
- The numbers below the keyboard show which fingers correlate to each color.
- The new keys being introduced are shown in white.

Activity C. Continue discussing the interceding character technique described in Extending the Content at the bottom of this page.

Activity D. Remind students they want to practice for both speed and accuracy. Have them pair with another student to proofread each other's Posttest for accuracy.

EXTENDING THE CONTENT

Interceding Character Technique. Dictate **de3d space** and have students strike the keys and the space bar as they watch their keyboard. (Note: **e** is the interceding character.) Repeat this sequence three or four times. Make sure students keep the D anchor as they reach for the 3 key. With students watching you, not their keyboards, dictate **de3d space**. Repeat this sequence three or four times.

Repeat the dictation described above without the interceding character. Dictate **d3d space** and have students strike the keys and the space bar as they watch their keyboard. Repeat this sequence three or four times. Make sure students keep the D anchor as they reach for the 3 key. With students watching you, dictate **d3d space**. Repeat sequence three or four times. Have students type textbook drill lines in Activity C on page 73.

Repeat this procedure for the 8 and * key, with U as the interceding key.

TEACH

Activity E. Explain that words with double letters are easy for beginners to type because the same letter is struck in succession. Point out the double letters in lines 25–28. For the advanced typist, words with alternate letters are easier to type because both hands are used to strike the two-letter combination. Point out the alternate letters in lines 29–32.

Activity F. Have students compare their Posttest with the Pretest. If they are not pleased with their improvement, have them type Practice and then retake the Posttest.

PRETEST/PRACTICE/POSTEST

The ***Pretest/Practice/Posttest*** routines are designed to improve speed or accuracy.

- The ***Pretest*** identifies students' speed or accuracy needs.
- The ***Practice*** provides a variety of improvement drills.
- The ***Posttest*** (a repeat of the Pretest) measures improvement.

Activity G. Continue to offer encouragement to students as they work with numbers. Remind them to be patient. Numbers may be more difficult for them to learn than letters were. Remind them that greater speed and accuracy comes with practice.

E. PRACTICE

SPEED: *If you made 2 or fewer errors on the Pretest, type lines 25–32 two times.*

ACCURACY: *If you made more than 2 errors on the Pretest, type lines 25–28 as a group two times. Then type lines 29–32 as a group two times.*

Double Reaches

```
25 rr errs hurry error furry berry worry terry carry
26 ll bill allay hills chill stall small shell smell
27 tt attar jetty otter utter putty witty butte Otto
28 ff stuff stiff cliff sniff offer scuff fluff buff
```

Alternate Reaches

```
29 is this list fist wish visit whist island raisins
30 so sons some soap sort soles sound bosses costume
31 go gone goat pogo logo bogus agora pagoda doggone
32 fu fun fume fund full fuel fuss furor furry fuzzy
```

F. POSTTEST

Repeat the Pretest. Compare your Posttest results with your Pretest results.

G. Number and Symbol Practice

Type each line 1 time. Repeat if time permits.

```
33 83 doubts, 38 cubs, 37 shrubs, 33 clubs, 34 stubs
34 87 aims, 83 maids, 88 brains, 73 braids, 84 raids

35 78 drinks, 48 brinks, 43 inks, 83 minks, 33 links
36 88 canes, 78 planes, 73 manes, 34 cans, 84 cranes

37 #7 blue, 4# roast, $3 paint, 77 books,* 3 & 4 & 8
38 7# boxes, 38 lists, $4 horse, #8 tree,* 7 & 3 & 4

39 Seek & Find Research sells this book* for $37.84.
40 The geometry test grades were 88, 87, 84, and 83.
```


FACT FILE

The asterisk (*) has multiple uses. In word processing it can be used for footnote references. It is the multiplication key in spreadsheets and computer calculators. It also is used as a wild card character in some software applications.

H. 1-Minute Alphanumeric Timing

Take a 1-minute timing on the paragraph. Note your speed and errors.

```
     B. Warmsly & J. Barnett paid the $847 charges    9
for the closing costs of their home at 3487 Cliff    19
Road; claim #47* shows the charge.                    26
 | 1 | 2 | 3 | 4 | 5 | 6 | 7 | 8 | 9 | 10
```

I. 2-Minute Timings

Take two 2-minute timings on lines 44–49. Note your speed and errors.

Goal: 27/2'/4e

```
     We just want to stay all day in the store to     9
see the very new shoe styles. Sue quickly saw the    19
mix of zany colors. Jo put on a yellow and green     29
pair and looked in a mirror. The shoes had wide      39
strips on the soles. We were certain of the good     48
brand, so I bought two pair.                          54
 | 1 | 2 | 3 | 4 | 5 | 6 | 7 | 8 | 9 | 10   SI 1.12
```

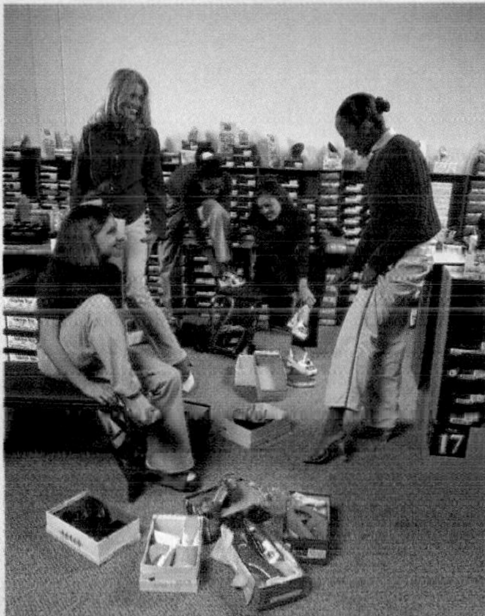

LESSON 22

Activity H. Students may see their 1-minute speed decrease in the alphanumeric timing because of the addition of numbers and symbols to the timed writing copy. Have students compare their times to the Posttest in Activity F.

Activity I. Remind students that the goal for these 2-minute timings is to type 27 words a minute for 2 minutes with no more than 4 errors.

ASSESS

- Check students' ability to type the number and symbol keys by touch.
- Review students' performance on the 1-minute timings.
- Compare students' performance on the Pretest with their performance on the Posttest.

CLOSE

For number and symbol practice, have students use the Posttest on page 74. Pair students who are having trouble with peer tutors for coaching.

Teacher Notes

LESSON 23

FOCUS

- Learn the 2, @, 9, and (keys.
- Improve skill on a P/P/P routine.
- Complete 1- and 2-minute timings.

BELLRINGER

As soon as students arrive at their workstations and log in, have them type the Warmup that reviews keys they have learned.

TEACH

Illustration

Explain the purpose of the keyboard illustration.

- The keys are color-coded according to which finger is used.
- The numbers below the keyboard show which fingers correlate to each color.
- The new keys being introduced are shown in white.

Activity B. Have students press the Demonstration button to view the correct reach for the 2, @, 9, and (keys. To help students with the correct reach to the number keys, try using the interceding character technique described in Extending the Content at the bottom of page 77.

LESSON 23 NEW KEYS: 2 @ 9 (

OBJECTIVES:

- Learn the 2, @, 9, and (keys.
- Refine keyboarding skills.
- Type 27/2'/4e.

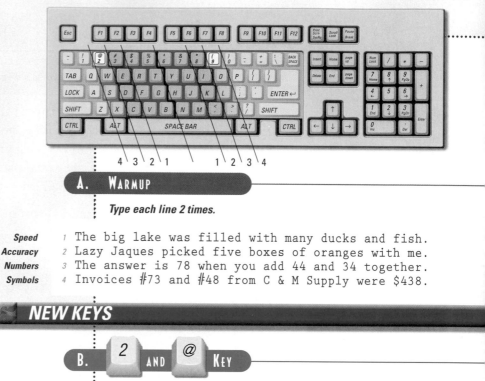

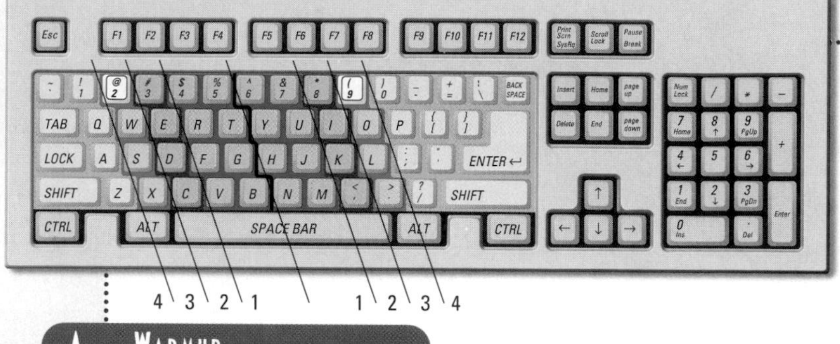

A. WARMUP

Type each line 2 times.

Speed	1 The big lake was filled with many ducks and fish.
Accuracy	2 Lazy Jaques picked five boxes of oranges with me.
Numbers	3 The answer is 78 when you add 44 and 34 together.
Symbols	4 Invoices #73 and #48 from C & M Supply were $438.

NEW KEYS

B. 2 AND @ KEY

Type each line 2 times. Repeat if time permits.

Use S finger. For 2 and @, anchor F.

```
5  sws sw2s s2s 222 s2s 22.2 s2s 2/22 s2s 22,222 s2s
6  22 sips, 22 swings, 22 signals, 22 sites, or 2.22
7  Our class used 22 pens, 23 disks, and 24 ribbons.
8  There were 22 people waiting for Bus 22 on May 2.
```

@ (at) is the shift of 2. Space once before and after @ except when it is used in an e-mail address.

```
9  sws sw2 s2s s2@s s@s s@s @2 @22 @222 s@s s2s @222
10 @2, 2 sons, @22, 22 sets, @222, 222 sensors, @222
11 Paul said his e-mail address was smith@acc.co.us.
12 She bought 2 @ 22 and sold 22 @ 223 before 2 p.m.
```


RESOURCES

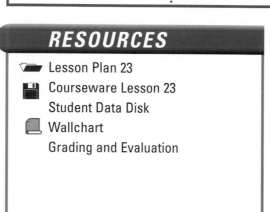

- Lesson Plan 23
- Courseware Lesson 23
- Student Data Disk
- Wallchart
- Grading and Evaluation

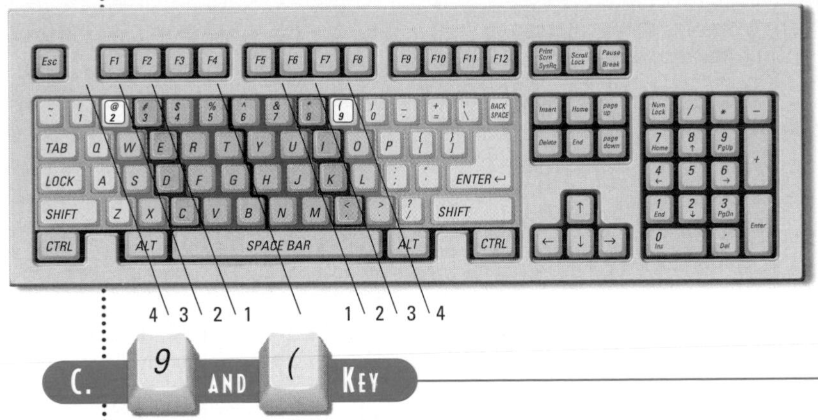

LESSON 23

C. 9 AND (KEY

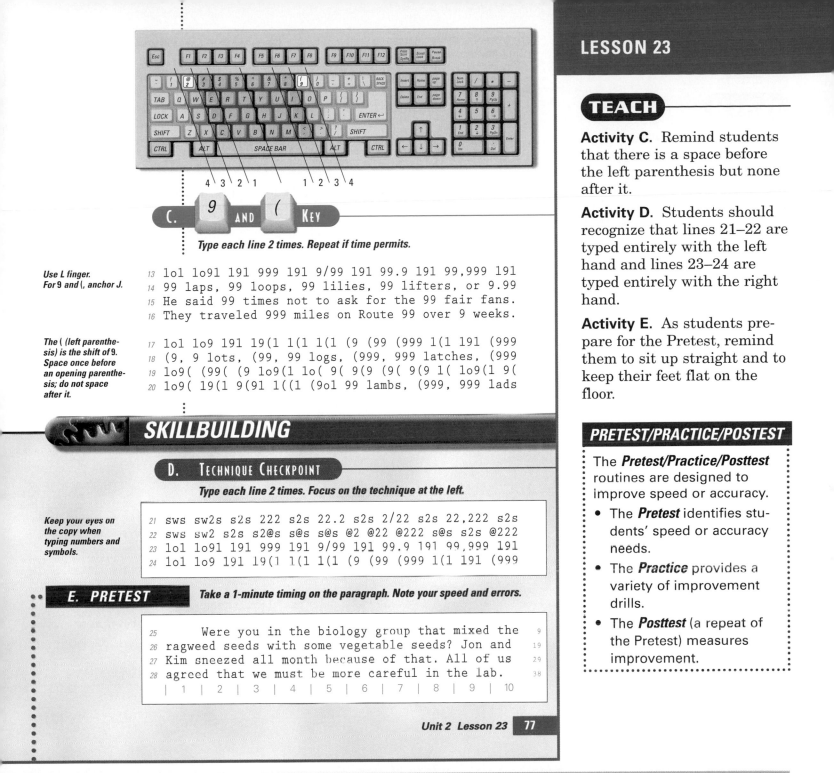

Type each line 2 times. Repeat if time permits.

Use L finger. For 9 and (, anchor J.

```
13 lol lo91 191 999 191 9/99 191 99.9 191 99,999 191
14 99 laps, 99 loops, 99 lilies, 99 lifters, or 9.99
15 He said 99 times not to ask for the 99 fair fans.
16 They traveled 999 miles on Route 99 over 9 weeks.
```

The ((left parenthesis) is the shift of 9. Space once before an opening parenthesis; do not space after it.

```
17 lol lo9 191 19(1 1(1 1(1 (9 (99 (999 1(1 191 (999
18 (9, 9 lots, (99, 99 logs, (999, 999 latches, (999
19 lo9( (99( (9 lo9(1 lo( 9( 9(9 (9( 9(9 1( lo9(1 9(
20 lo9( 19(1 9(91 1((1 (9ol 99 lambs, (999, 999 lads
```

SKILLBUILDING

D. TECHNIQUE CHECKPOINT

Type each line 2 times. Focus on the technique at the left.

Keep your eyes on the copy when typing numbers and symbols.

```
21 sws sw2s s2s 222 s2s 22.2 s2s 2/22 s2s 22,222 s2s
22 sws sw2 s2s s2@s s@s s@s @2 @22 @222 s@s s2s @222
23 lol lo91 191 999 191 9/99 191 99.9 191 99,999 191
24 lol lo9 191 19(1 1(1 1(1 (9 (99 (999 1(1 191 (999
```

E. PRETEST

Take a 1-minute timing on the paragraph. Note your speed and errors.

```
25      Were you in the biology group that mixed the     9
26 ragweed seeds with some vegetable seeds? Jon and     19
27 Kim sneezed all month because of that. All of us     29
28 agreed that we must be more careful in the lab.      38
   | 1 | 2 | 3 | 4 | 5 | 6 | 7 | 8 | 9 | 10
```


TEACH

Activity C. Remind students that there is a space before the left parenthesis but none after it.

Activity D. Students should recognize that lines 21–22 are typed entirely with the left hand and lines 23–24 are typed entirely with the right hand.

Activity E. As students prepare for the Pretest, remind them to sit up straight and to keep their feet flat on the floor.

PRETEST/PRACTICE/POSTTEST

The ***Pretest/Practice/Posttest*** routines are designed to improve speed or accuracy.

- The ***Pretest*** identifies students' speed or accuracy needs.
- The ***Practice*** provides a variety of improvement drills.
- The ***Posttest*** (a repeat of the Pretest) measures improvement.

EXTENDING THE CONTENT

Interceding Character Technique. Dictate **sw2s space** and have students strike the keys and the space bar as they watch their keyboard. (Note: **w** is the interceding character.) Repeat this sequence three or four times. Make sure students keep the s anchor as they reach for the 2 key. With students watching you, not their keyboards, dictate **sw2s space**. Repeat this sequence three or four times.

Repeat the dictation described above without the interceding character. Dictate **s2s space** and have students strike the keys and the space bar as they watch their keyboard. Repeat sequence three or four times. Make sure students keep the s anchor as they reach for the 2 key. With students watching you, dictate **s2s space**. Repeat sequence three or four times. Have students type the textbook drill lines in Activity C on page 77.

Repeat this procedure for the 9 key, with o as the interceding key.

TEACH

Activity F. Point out to students that they are to type lines 29–36 two times each only if they made fewer than 2 errors on the Pretest. If they made more than 2 errors, they should type lines 29–32 as a group, and then type lines 33–36 as a group.

Activity G. Have students compare their Posttest results with their Pretest. Have them note their scores for speed and accuracy.

Activity H. Have students compare this alphanumeric 1-minute timing with the alphanumeric timing in the Pretest. Students' alphanumeric timing scores should be improving.

Activity I. Remind students that their goal for this timing is to type 27 words a minute for 2 minutes with no more than 4 errors.

ASSESS

- Check students' ability to type the number and symbol keys by touch.
- Compare students' performance on the Pretest with their performance on the Posttest.

CLOSE

Have students practice Activity I. Have them push themselves each time for greater speed.

F. PRACTICE

SPEED: *If you made 2 or fewer errors on the Pretest, type lines 29–36 two times each.*

ACCURACY: *If you made more than 2 errors on the Pretest, type lines 29–32 as a group two times. Then type lines 33–36 as a group two times.*

Left Reaches

```
29 tab wards grace serve wears farce beast crate car
30 far weeds tests seeds tread graze vexed vests saw
31 bar crest feast refer cease dated verge bread gas
32 car career grasses bread creases faded vested tad
```

Right Reaches

```
33 you Yukon mummy ninon jolly union minim pylon hum
34 mom nylon milky lumpy puppy holly pulpy plink oil
35 pop oomph jumpy unpin nippy imply hippo pupil nip
36 you union bumpy upon silly hill moon pink ill mop
```

G. POSTTEST

Repeat the Pretest. Compare your Posttest results with your Pretest results.

H. 1-Minute Alphanumeric Timing

Take a 1-minute timing on the paragraph. Note your speed and errors.

```
37      The planned ski tour #4 begins at 2:43 p.m.,    9
38 and tour #3 begins at noon. Every tour costs $43,   19
39 and everyone will end at 7:38 p.m.                  26
   | 1 | 2 | 3 | 4 | 5 | 6 | 7 | 8 | 9 | 10
```

I. 2-Minute Timings

Take two 2-minute timings on lines 40–45. Note your speed and errors.

Goal: 27/2'/4e

```
40      It is a joy to end a term with good grades.      9
41 Fall term could be very nice if it were not for     19
42 exams and quizzes. Jan, though, likes to study to   29
43 show how much she has learned. She places great     38
44 value in having high marks. She knows her peers     48
45 admire the grades she achieved.                     54
   | 1 | 2 | 3 | 4 | 5 | 6 | 7 | 8 | 9 | 10  SI 1.15
```


TECHNOLOGY TIP

Tell students that the within the next few years, the Internet will connect 80 percent of the world's computers. With instant worldwide access at their fingertips, they can learn about and even interact with people all over the world.

interNET ACTIVITY

Explain to students that they can use the Internet to keep in touch with friends via e-mail. Have students type a short e-mail message that they would send to a friend who lives in another town.

LESSON 24 REVIEW

OBJECTIVES:

- Improve keyboarding skill.
- Type 27/2'/2e.
- Compose at the keyboard.

A. WARMUP

Type each line 2 times.

Speed	1	The first time Alf drove a car, he hit a pothole.
Accuracy	2	Zigzag through the zebu with zip to avoid injury.
Numbers	3	Room 43 holds 87 people, but only 29 are present.
Symbols	4	Buy 78 gross* of #2 pencils @ $3.94 at the store.

SKILLBUILDING

B. TAB KEY

Type each paragraph 2 times. Press the tab to indent the first line; press ENTER only at the end of lines 6 and 8. Repeat if time permits.

```
5      We found 99 gnats, 44 flies, 33 fleas, and
6 77 seals beside the 33 trees at the 2-acre beach.

7      Bo & Son bought 88 axles @ $42.98. They said
8 Rule #37 on page 88 was now Rule #42 on page 93.
```

C. ENTER KEY

Type each line 2 times. Press ENTER at the end of every sentence. Continue typing smoothly. Repeat if time permits.

Remember to press ENTER at the end of every sentence.

```
9  Study all of Chapter 29. It covers pages 234-249.
10 Chelsea lives at 778 Cherokee. That's in Paducah.
11 Write Jo at pets@coyote.com. Jo's address is new.
12 That text* is at B & B Printing. It is makeready.
```


RESOURCES

 Lesson Plan 24
- Courseware Lesson 24
- Student Data Disk
- Wallchart
- Grading and Evaluation

LESSON 24

FOCUS

- Review the Tab and ENTER keys.
- Review spacing with punctuation.
- Use a P/P/P routine to build speed and improve accuracy.
- Take a 1-minute alphanumeric timing.
- Take 2-minute timings.

BELLRINGER

As soon as students arrive at their workstations and log in, have them type the Warmup that reviews keys they have learned.

TEACH

Activity B. Remind students to use the Tab key to indent the first line of each paragraph.

Activity C. Have students press the Demonstration button to review the correct reach for the ENTER keys. Remind students to press the ENTER key at the end of each sentence.

TEACH

Activity D. Be sure students are using proper posture when taking these 30-second timings. They should be sitting up straight, with feet on the floor, and holding elbows in.

Activities E–G. Remind students their speed and accuracy should improve between the Pretest and Posttest.

PRETEST/PRACTICE/POSTEST

The ***Pretest/Practice/Posttest*** routines are designed to improve speed or accuracy.

- The ***Pretest*** identifies students' speed or accuracy needs.
- The ***Practice*** provides a variety of improvement drills.
- The ***Posttest*** (a repeat of the Pretest) measures improvement.

D. Technique Timings

Take two 30-second timings on each line. Focus on the technique at the left.

Keep elbows in.

```
13 She works for Mr. D. N. Logan at Logan Locksmith.
14 Is the May/June issue late? My copy has not come.
15 Find these colors: pink, blue, green, and purple.
16 My hoity-toity behavior was rude, extremely rude.
   | 1 | 2 | 3 | 4 | 5 | 6 | 7 | 8 | 9 | 10
```

E. PRETEST

Take a 1-minute timing on the paragraph. Note your speed and errors.

```
17      Ed's prize-winning ewe stays on Mario's farm    9
18 until the petting zoo opens. Every day Skip takes   19
19 that ewe and her lamb to the fair. It's amazing     29
20 to see how much time is spent caring for animals.   39
   | 1 | 2 | 3 | 4 | 5 | 6 | 7 | 8 | 9 | 10
```

F. PRACTICE

SPEED: ***If you made 2 or fewer errors on the Pretest, type lines 21–28 two times each.***

ACCURACY: ***If you made more than 2 errors on the Pretest, type lines 21–24 as a group two times. Then type lines 25–28 as a group two times.***

Adjacent Reaches	21 io trio riot pious Mario ew ewes mews sewer views
Jump Reaches	22 un tune dune under bound ze zeal zest prize seize
Double Reaches	23 ss hiss boss dress gloss ll fall tall small jolly
Up Reaches	24 dr drip drive dream drab ho hope hole hold hollow
Alternate Reaches	25 ro rode rote crows throw do doze judo kudos docks
Left Reaches	26 fa farm fast favor fazed er errs were erase terms
Right Reaches	27 ki kiln skip skill skimp pl plot plum plows plugs
Down Reaches	28 ca call caps cards caper ni niece nine nick night

G. POSTTEST

Repeat the Pretest. Compare your Posttest results with your Pretest results.

FACT FILE

The first home personal computer was sold in 1977. In 1983, there were approximately 2 million personal computers in use in the United States. In 1993, that number jumped to more than 90 million. Today, there are more than 100 million personal home computers in use.

H. 1-Minute Alphanumeric Timing

Take a 1-minute timing on lines 29–31. Note your speed and errors.

```
29      Our black cat, Beauty, weighed 9#. She had a    9
30 checkup at Paws & Claws on June 23. Her shots and   19
31 exam cost $48, but she's worth it all.              27
   | 1 | 2 | 3 | 4 | 5 | 6 | 7 | 8 | 9 | 10
```

I. 2-Minute Timings

Take two 2-minute timings on lines 32–37. Note your speed and errors.

Goal: 27/2'/4e

```
32      Why use proper grammar when you speak? One      9
33 of the best reasons is that others judge you        19
34 by your speech. Fair or not, people examine the     28
35 words you use and how you use them. You have to     38
36 speak well each day. Avoid buzzwords and slang.     48
37 People will be quick to judge you.                  54
   | 1 | 2 | 3 | 4 | 5 | 6 | 7 | 8 | 9 | 10  SI 1.19
```

J. Composing at the Keyboard

Answer each question with a few words or a short phrase.

38 Who is your best friend?
39 Who are two people who have been in the news this week?
40 Are you a licensed driver?
41 What is your favorite type of music?
42 What is your favorite song?

Teacher Notes

LESSON 24

TEACH

Activity H. Have students take the 1-minute alphanumeric timing. They should concentrate on improving both speed and accuracy.

Activity I. Remind students that the goal for these timings is to type 27 words a minute for 2 minutes with no more than 4 errors.

Activity J. Remind students to use a two-step process when responding to these questions: (1) think of the response, and (2) type the response.

Solutions: Answers will vary.

ASSESS

- Check students' ability to type the number and symbol keys by touch.
- Compare students' performance on the Pretest with their performance on the Posttest.

CLOSE

Have students practice Activity I. Remind them that their goal is to type 27 words a minute for 2 minutes with no more than 4 errors. Have them push themselves each time for greater speed.

LESSON 25

FOCUS

- Learn the 1, !, 0, and) keys.
- Improve skill on a P/P/P routine.
- Complete 1- and 2-minute timings.

BELLRINGER

As soon as students arrive at their workstations and log in, have them type the Warmup that reviews keys they have learned.

TEACH

Illustration

Explain the purpose of the keyboard illustration.

- The keys are color-coded according to which finger is used.
- The numbers below the keyboard show which fingers correlate to each color.
- The new keys being introduced are shown in white.

Activity B. Have students press the Demonstration button to view the correct reach for the 1, !, 0, and) keys. To help students with the correct reach to the number keys, try using the interceding character technique described in Extending the Content at the bottom of page 83.

LESSON 25

NEW KEYS: 1 ! 0)

OBJECTIVES:

- Learn the 1, !, 0, and) keys.
- Refine keyboarding skills.
- Type 27/2'/4e.

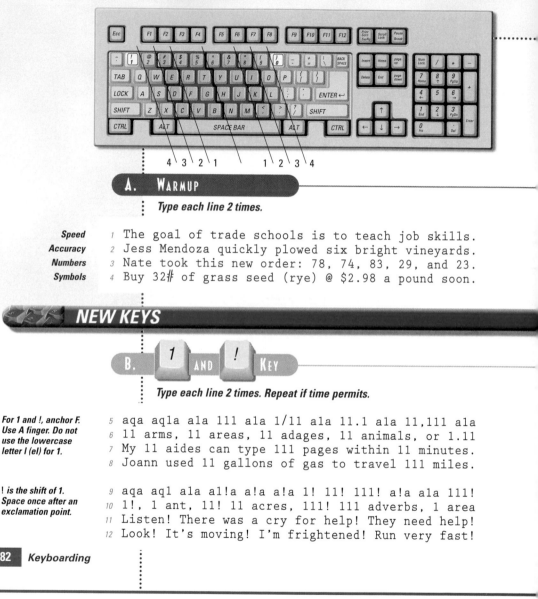

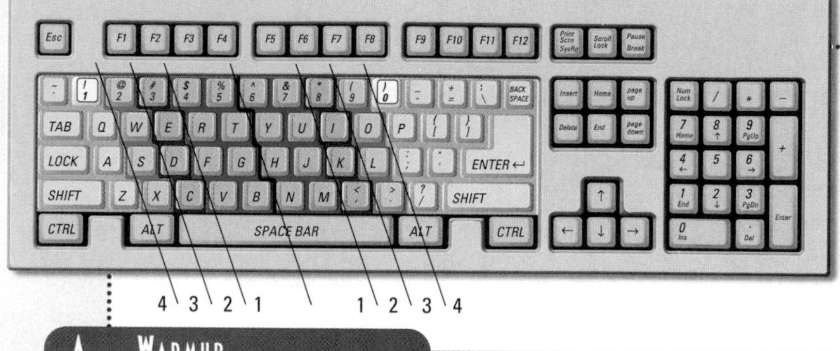

A. WARMUP

Type each line 2 times.

Speed	1	The goal of trade schools is to teach job skills.
Accuracy	2	Jess Mendoza quickly plowed six bright vineyards.
Numbers	3	Nate took this new order: 78, 74, 83, 29, and 23.
Symbols	4	Buy 32# of grass seed (rye) @ $2.98 a pound soon.

NEW KEYS

B. 1 AND ! KEY

Type each line 2 times. Repeat if time permits.

For 1 and !, anchor F. Use A finger. Do not use the lowercase letter l (el) for 1.

5 aqa aq1a a1a 111 a1a 1/11 a1a 11.1 a1a 11,111 a1a
6 11 arms, 11 areas, 11 adages, 11 animals, or 1.11
7 My 11 aides can type 111 pages within 11 minutes.
8 Joann used 11 gallons of gas to travel 111 miles.

! is the shift of 1. Space once after an exclamation point.

9 aqa aq1 a1a a1!a a!a a!a 1! 11! 111! a!a a1a 111!
10 1!, 1 ant, 11! 11 acres, 111! 111 adverbs, 1 area
11 Listen! There was a cry for help! They need help!
12 Look! It's moving! I'm frightened! Run very fast!

RESOURCES

- Lesson Plan 25
- Courseware Lesson 25
- Student Data Disk
- Wallchart
- Grading and Evaluation

LESSON 25

C. 0 AND) KEY

Type each line 2 times. Repeat if time permits.

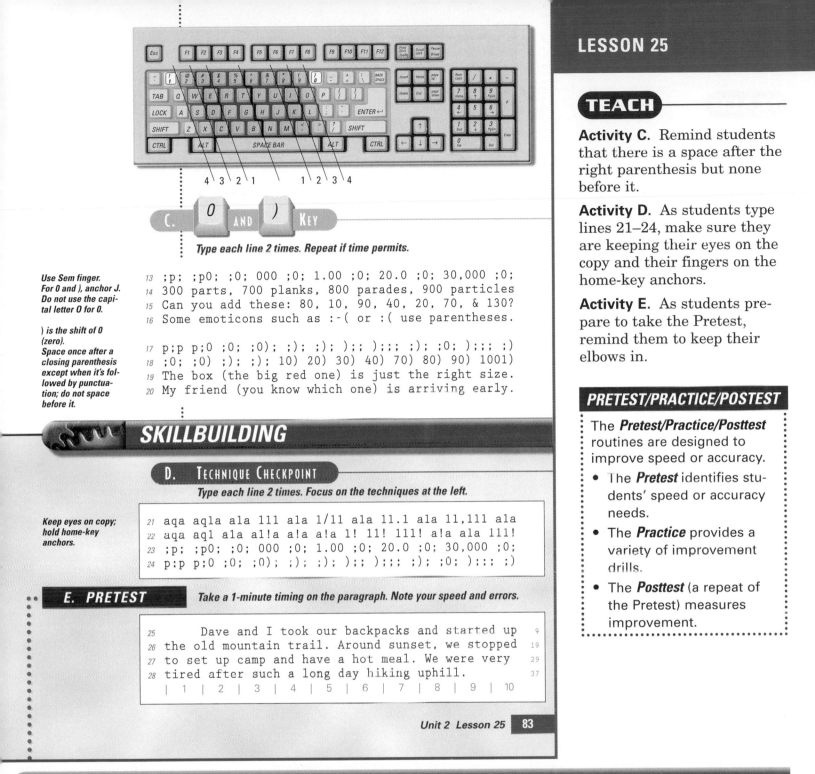

Use Sem finger. For 0 and), anchor J. Do not use the capital letter O for 0.

) is the shift of 0 (zero). Space once after a closing parenthesis except when it's followed by punctuation; do not space before it.

```
13 ;p; ;p0; ;0; 000 ;0; 1.00 ;0; 20.0 ;0; 30,000 ;0;
14 300 parts, 700 planks, 800 parades, 900 particles
15 Can you add these: 80, 10, 90, 40, 20, 70, & 130?
16 Some emoticons such as :-( or :( use parentheses.

17 p;p p;0 ;0; ;0); ;); ;); );; );;; ;); ;0; );;; ;)
18 ;0; ;0) ;); ;); 10) 20) 30) 40) 70) 80) 90) 1001)
19 The box (the big red one) is just the right size.
20 My friend (you know which one) is arriving early.
```

SKILLBUILDING

D. TECHNIQUE CHECKPOINT

Type each line 2 times. Focus on the techniques at the left.

Keep eyes on copy; hold home-key anchors.

```
21 aqa aqla ala 111 ala 1/11 ala 11.1 ala 11,111 ala
22 aqa aql ala a!a a!a a!a l! 11! 111! a!a ala 111!
23 ;p; ;p0; ;0; 000 ;0; 1.00 ;0; 20.0 ;0; 30,000 ;0;
24 p;p p;0 ;0; ;0); ;); ;); );; );;; ;); ;0; );;; ;)
```

E. PRETEST

Take a 1-minute timing on the paragraph. Note your speed and errors.

```
25      Dave and I took our backpacks and started up   9
26 the old mountain trail. Around sunset, we stopped  19
27 to set up camp and have a hot meal. We were very   29
28 tired after such a long day hiking uphill.         37
   | 1 | 2 | 3 | 4 | 5 | 6 | 7 | 8 | 9 | 10
```


TEACH

Activity C. Remind students that there is a space after the right parenthesis but none before it.

Activity D. As students type lines 21–24, make sure they are keeping their eyes on the copy and their fingers on the home-key anchors.

Activity E. As students prepare to take the Pretest, remind them to keep their elbows in.

PRETEST/PRACTICE/POSTTEST

The ***Pretest/Practice/Posttest*** routines are designed to improve speed or accuracy.

- The ***Pretest*** identifies students' speed or accuracy needs.
- The ***Practice*** provides a variety of improvement drills.
- The ***Posttest*** (a repeat of the Pretest) measures improvement.

EXTENDING THE CONTENT

Interceding Character Technique. Dictate **aq1a space** and have students strike the keys and the space bar as they watch their keyboard. (Note: **q** is the interceding character.) Repeat this sequence three or four times. Make sure students keep the A anchor as they reach for the 1 key. With students watching you, not their keyboards, dictate **aq1a space**. Repeat this sequence three or four times.

Repeat the dictation described above without the interceding character. Dictate **a1a space** and have students strike the keys and the space bar as they watch their keyboard. Repeat this sequence three or four times. Make sure students keep the A anchor as they reach for the 1 key. With students watching you, not their keyboards, dictate **a1a space**. Repeat this sequence three or four times.

Have students type the textbook drill lines in Activity C on page 83. Repeat the dictation procedure for the 0 key, with P as the interceding key.

TEACH

Activity F. Students concentrate on up reaches and down reaches in this activity. Point out that they are to type lines 29–36 two times each only if they made fewer than 2 errors on the Pretest. If they made more than 2 errors, they should type lines 29–32 as a group, and then type lines 33–36 as a group.

Activity G. Remind students to compare their Posttest with their Pretest.

Activity H. Have students take the 1-minute alphanumeric timing. Their speed on the alphanumeric timings should be improving.

Activity I. Remind students that their goal is to type 27 words a minute for 2 minutes with no more than 4 errors.

ASSESS

- Check students' ability to type the number and symbol keys by touch.
- Compare students' performance on the Pretest with their performance on the Posttest.

CLOSE

Remind students to clean up their workstation when they leave. An organized work area will promote better performance in class.

F. PRACTICE

SPEED: *If you made 2 or fewer errors on the Pretest, type lines 29–36 two times each.*

ACCURACY: *If you made more than 2 errors on the Pretest, type lines 29–32 as a group two times. Then type lines 33–36 as a group two times.*

Up Reaches

```
29 ho shock chose phone shove hover holly homes shot
30 st stair guest stone blast nasty start casts step
31 il lilac filed drill build spill child trail pail
32 de dear redeem warden tide render chide rode dead
```

Down Reaches

```
33 ab squab labor habit cabin cable abate about able
34 ca pecan recap catch carve cable scale scamp camp
35 av ravel gavel avert knave waved paved shave have
36 in ruin invent winner bring shin chin shrink pine
```

G. POSTTEST

Repeat the Pretest. Compare your Posttest results with your Pretest results.

H. 1-Minute Alphanumeric Timing

Take a 1-minute timing on lines 37–39. Note your speed and errors.

```
37      Joy wanted to get a dozen (12) baseball bats     9
38 @ $4.29 from the sports store at 718 Miner Place.    19
39 When I went, only 10 bats were left.                 26
   | 1 | 2 | 3 | 4 | 5 | 6 | 7 | 8 | 9 | 10
```

I. 2-Minute Timings

Take two 2-minute timings on lines 40–45. Note your speed and errors.

Goal: 27/2'/4e

```
40      In the fall of the year, I find pleasure in      9
41 zipping up to the hills to quietly view the trees    19
42 changing colors. Most all aspens turn to shades      29
43 of gold. Oak trees exude tones of red and orange.    39
44 The plants change colors each fall, but all these    49
45 changes are an amazing sight.                        54
   | 1 | 2 | 3 | 4 | 5 | 6 | 7 | 8 | 9 | 10   SI 1.25
```


Teacher Notes

LESSON 26 New Keys: 5 % 6 ^

OBJECTIVES:

- Learn the 5, %, 6, and ^ keys.
- Refine keyboarding skills.
- Type 27/2'/4e.

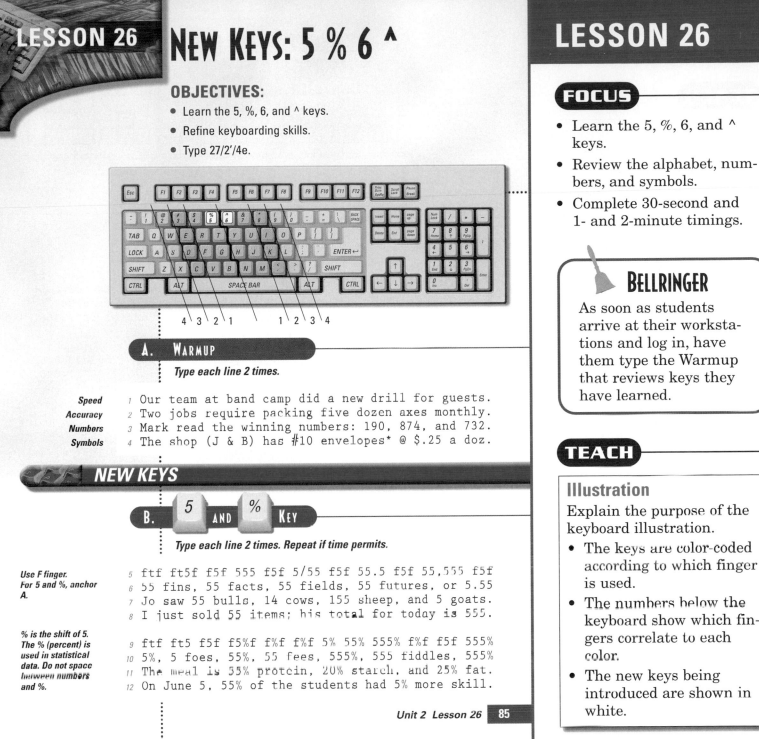

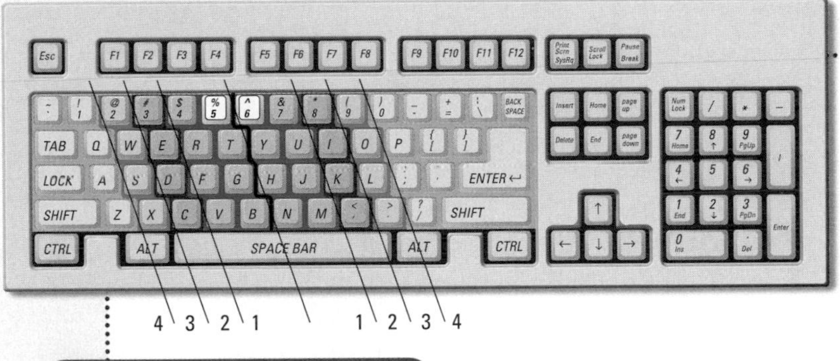

A. Warmup

Type each line 2 times.

```
Speed     1 Our team at band camp did a new drill for guests.
Accuracy  2 Two jobs require packing five dozen axes monthly.
Numbers   3 Mark read the winning numbers: 190, 874, and 732.
Symbols   4 The shop (J & B) has #10 envelopes* @ $.25 a doz.
```

NEW KEYS

B. 5 and % Key

Type each line 2 times. Repeat if time permits.

Use F finger. For 5 and %, anchor A.

```
5 ftf ft5f f5f 555 f5f 5/55 f5f 55.5 f5f 55,555 f5f
6 55 fins, 55 facts, 55 fields, 55 futures, or 5.55
7 Jo saw 55 bulls, 14 cows, 155 sheep, and 5 goats.
8 I just sold 55 items; his total for today is 555.
```

% is the shift of 5. The % (percent) is used in statistical data. Do not space between numbers and %.

```
9  ftf ft5 f5f f5%f f%f f%f 5% 55% 555% f%f f5f 555%
10 5%, 5 foes, 55%, 55 fees, 555%, 555 fiddles, 555%
11 The meal is 55% protein, 20% starch, and 25% fat.
12 On June 5, 55% of the students had 5% more skill.
```


RESOURCES

- Lesson Plan 26
- Courseware Lesson 26
- Student Data Disk
- Wallchart
- Grading and Evaluation

LESSON 26

FOCUS

- Learn the 5, %, 6, and ^ keys.
- Review the alphabet, numbers, and symbols.
- Complete 30-second and 1- and 2-minute timings.

BELLRINGER

As soon as students arrive at their workstations and log in, have them type the Warmup that reviews keys they have learned.

TEACH

Illustration

Explain the purpose of the keyboard illustration.

- The keys are color-coded according to which finger is used.
- The numbers below the keyboard show which fingers correlate to each color.
- The new keys being introduced are shown in white.

Activity B. Have students press the Demonstration button to view the correct reach for the 5, %, 6, and ^ keys. Try using the interceding character technique described in Extending the Content at the bottom of page 86. This procedure is especially important for learning the 6 key, because it is the furthest reach on the alphanumeric keyboard.

TEACH

Illustration

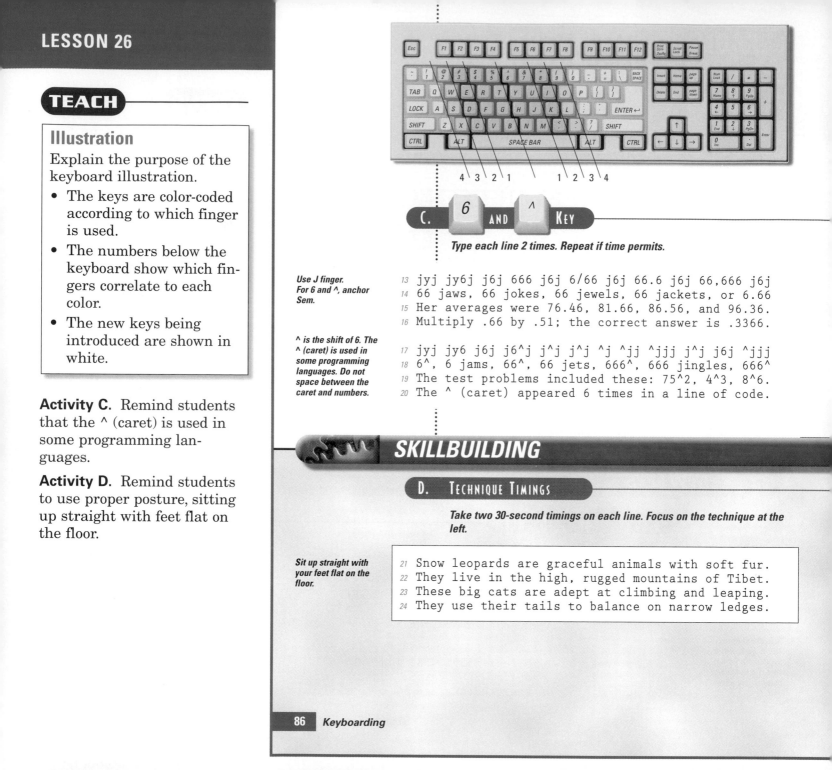

Explain the purpose of the keyboard illustration.

- The keys are color-coded according to which finger is used.
- The numbers below the keyboard show which fingers correlate to each color.
- The new keys being introduced are shown in white.

Activity C. Remind students that the ^ (caret) is used in some programming languages.

Activity D. Remind students to use proper posture, sitting up straight with feet flat on the floor.

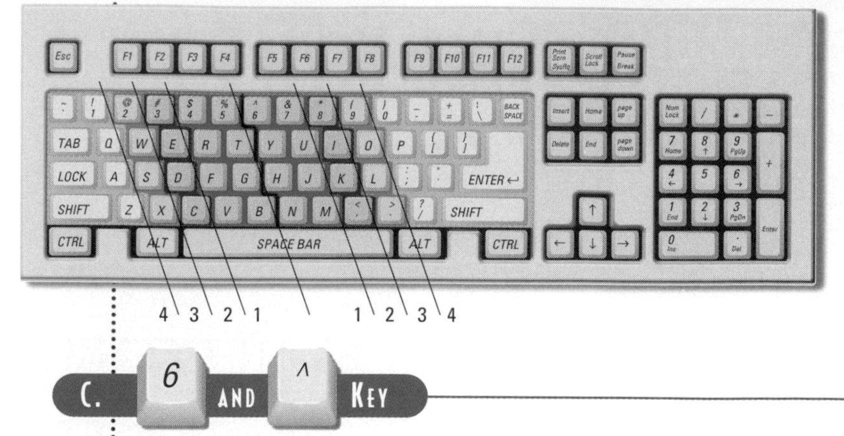

C. 6 AND ^ KEY

Type each line 2 times. Repeat if time permits.

Use J finger. For 6 and ^, anchor Sem.

13 jyj jy6j j6j 666 j6j 6/66 j6j 66.6 j6j 66,666 j6j
14 66 jaws, 66 jokes, 66 jewels, 66 jackets, or 6.66
15 Her averages were 76.46, 81.66, 86.56, and 96.36.
16 Multiply .66 by .51; the correct answer is .3366.

^ is the shift of 6. The ^ (caret) is used in some programming languages. Do not space between the caret and numbers.

17 jyj jy6 j6j j6^j j^j j^j ^j ^jj ^jjj j^j j6j ^jjj
18 6^, 6 jams, 66^, 66 jets, 666^, 666 jingles, 666^
19 The test problems included these: 75^2, 4^3, 8^6.
20 The ^ (caret) appeared 6 times in a line of code.

SKILLBUILDING

D. TECHNIQUE TIMINGS

Take two 30-second timings on each line. Focus on the technique at the left.

Sit up straight with your feet flat on the floor.

21 Snow leopards are graceful animals with soft fur.
22 They live in the high, rugged mountains of Tibet.
23 These big cats are adept at climbing and leaping.
24 They use their tails to balance on narrow ledges.

EXTENDING THE CONTENT

Interceding Character Technique. Dictate **hy6y space** and have students strike the keys and the space bar as they watch their keyboard. (Note: Y is the interceding character.) Repeat this sequence three or four times. Make sure students keep the H anchor as they reach for the 6 key. With students watching you, not their keyboards, dictate **hy6y space**. Repeat this sequence three or four times.

Repeat the dictation described above without the interceding character. Dictate **h6h space** and have students strike the keys and the space bar as they watch their keyboard. Repeat this sequence three or four times. Make sure students keep the H anchor as they reach for the 6 key. With students watching you, not their keyboards, dictate **h6h space**. Repeat this sequence three or four times.

Repeat this procedure for the ^ key, with 6 as the interceding key.

E. PRETEST

Take a 1-minute timing on lines 25–28. Note your speed and errors.

```
25      As a flock, the crows flew to some clumps of    9
26 stalks near the eddy. They seemed to eat the pods   19
27 joyfully as they fed in the field. We like to       28
28 watch them, especially in the morning.              36
   | 1 | 2 | 3 | 4 | 5 | 6 | 7 | 8 | 9 | 10
```

F. PRACTICE

SPEED: *If you made 2 or fewer errors on the Pretest, type lines 29–36 two times each.*

ACCURACY: *If you made more than 2 errors on the Pretest, type lines 29–32 as a group two times. Then type lines 33–36 as a group two times.*

```
Adjacent     29 po pods poem point poise lk hulk silk polka stalk
Jump         30 mp jump pump trump clump cr cram crow crawl creed
Double       31 dd odds eddy daddy caddy tt mitt mutt utter ditto
Consecutive  32 un unit punk funny bunch gr grab agree angry grip

Alternate    33 iv give dive drive wives gl glad glee ogled gland
Left/Right   34 fe fear feat ferns fetal jo joys join joker jolly
Up/Down      35 sw swan sway sweat swift k, ark, ask, tick, wick,
In/Out       36 lu luck blunt fluid lush da dash date sedan panda
```

G. POSTTEST

Repeat the Pretest. Then compare your Posttest results with your Pretest results.

H. 1-Minute Alphanumeric Timing

Take a 1-minute timing on lines 37–39. Note your speed and errors.

```
37      Kim ran the 7.96-mile race last week. Yanni    9
38 ran 14.80 miles. Zeke said the next 5K run will    19
39 be held on August 14 or August 23.                 25
   | 1 | 2 | 3 | 4 | 5 | 6 | 7 | 8 | 9 | 10
```


TEACH

Activity E. Students should concentrate on both speed and accuracy on the Pretest 1-minute timing, noting scores for both.

Activity F. Point out to students that they are to type lines 29–36 two times each only if they made fewer than 2 errors on the Pretest. If they made more than 2 errors, they should type lines 29–32 as a group, and then type lines 33–36 as a group.

Activity G. Remind students they should improve both speed and accuracy from the Pretest to the Posttest.

PRETEST/PRACTICE/POSTEST

The ***Pretest/Practice/Posttest*** routines are designed to improve speed or accuracy.

- The ***Pretest*** identifies students' speed or accuracy needs.
- The ***Practice*** provides a variety of improvement drills.
- The ***Posttest*** (a repeat of the Pretest) measures improvement.

Activity H. This activity uses all of the number keys and most of the alphabet keys.

Out-of-Class Activity

Now that students have learned all of the alphanumeric keys, encourage them to practice typing outside of class. If students don't have access to a keyboard at home, offer suggestions of school and community locations where you know they can practice their new skills.

SCHOOL TO CAREER

Have students work in groups of four. Provide each group with the name of an industry, such as manufacturing or food service. Have students use the telephone book and other resources to make a list of companies in your community that are part of their group's industry. Have them type the list.

TEACH

Activity I. This activity uses all of the alphabet keys. Remind students that their goal is to type 27 words a minute for 2 minutes with 4 or fewer errors.

ASSESS

- Check students' ability to type the number and symbol keys by touch.
- Compare students' performance on the Pretest with their performance on the Posttest.
- Check students' performance on the 1- and 2-minute timings.

CLOSE

Review proper technique and reach for the numbers and symbols introduced in this lesson.

FACT FILE

On the Internet, etiquette is known as Netiquette. A few rules of Netiquette include the following: keep messages brief and use proper grammar and spelling; be polite; do not use offensive language; use capital letters only when appropriate.

I. 2-Minute Timings

Take two 2-minute timings on lines 40–45. Note your speed and errors.

Goal: 27/2'/4e

```
40      As you look for jobs, be quite sure that          9
41 the way you dress depicts the position that you       18
42 want. If you hope to obtain an office job, zippy      28
43 fashions are not for you. Expect to arrive in a       38
44 clean, pressed business suit. Your clothes should     48
45 match the job you are trying for.                     54
   | 1 | 2 | 3 | 4 | 5 | 6 | 7 | 8 | 9 | 10  SI 1.21
```

FACT FILE

E-mail acronyms are commonly used instead of phrases that you would otherwise type in full. Some of the most popular ones are these: IMHO (in my humble opinion), BTW (by the way), RTM (read the manual), LOL (laughing out loud), FWIW (for what it's worth), and ROFL (rolling on the floor laughing).

Teacher Notes

LESSON 27 SPECIAL SYMBOLS

OBJECTIVES:

- Learn the <, >, \, +, =, {, }, [,], and ~keys.
- Refine keyboarding skills.
- Type 27/2'/4e.

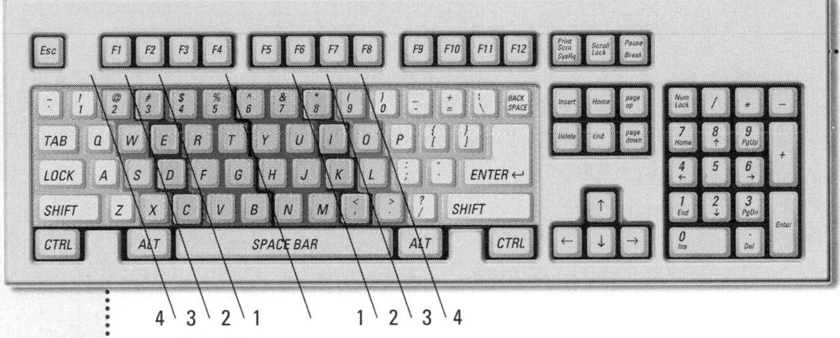

A. WARMUP

Type each line 2 times.

Speed	1	Brent hurt his arm today and is in a lot of pain.
Accuracy	2	The tax is zero on these dozen tax-exempt pizzas.
Numbers	3	The population of Cooper is 216,974, not 326,815.
Symbols	4	Stop & Shop has 25% off reams of 24# paper @ $13.

NEW KEYS

B. SPECIAL SYMBOLS

You have learned to type many frequently used symbols by touch. Other less frequently used symbols also appear on the keyboard. Although it is not necessary to learn these symbols by touch, you should know what they are, how they are used, where they are located, and what fingers to use.

RESOURCES

- Lesson Plan 27
- Courseware Lesson 27
- Student Data Disk
- Wallchart
- Grading and Evaluation
- PowerPoint

LESSON 27

FOCUS

- Learn special symbols keys: \ < > = + [ ] { } ~
- Review the alphabetic, number, and symbol keys.
- Take a 1-minute alphanumeric timing.
- Take 2-minute timings.

BELLRINGER

As soon as students arrive at their workstations and log in, have them type the Warmup that reviews keys they have learned.

TEACH

Illustration

Explain the purpose of the keyboard illustration.

- The keys are color-coded according to which finger is used.
- The numbers below the keyboard show which fingers correlate to each color.
- The new keys being introduced are shown in white.

Activity B. Have students press the Demonstration button to view the special symbol keys.

TEACH

Illustration

Explain the purpose of the keyboard illustration.

- The keys are color-coded according to which finger is used.
- The numbers below the keyboard show which fingers correlate to each color.
- The new keys being introduced are shown in white.

Refer students to the table on this page. Point out the different features including the key, name of the symbol, its use, the finger used, spacing, and the example.

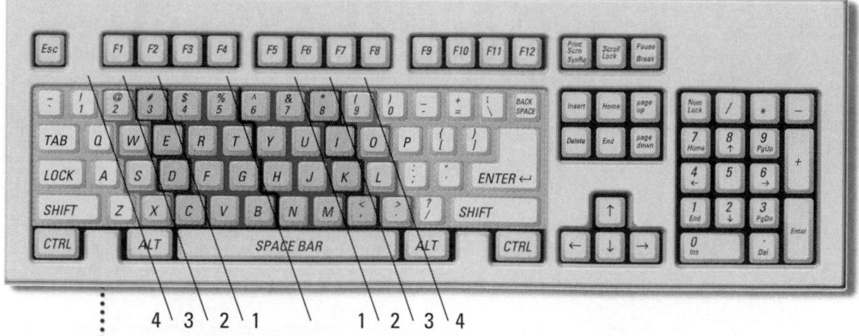

Find each of the symbols shown below on your keyboard. Note which finger controls each key and the spacing used with the symbol. In the example column, study how the symbol is used.

Key	Name	Use	Finger	Spacing	Example
\	Back Slash	Naming files/ directories	Sem	No space before and after.	`a:\Medical\ Doctor.cgs`
<	Less Than	Math	K	One space before and after.	`15 < 25`
>	Greater Than	Math	L	One space before and after.	`31 < 19`
=	Equal	Math	Sem	One space before and after.	`A = 27`
+	Plus	Math	Sem	One space before and after.	`3 + 3 = 6`
[ ]	Left and Right Brackets	Enclose special text	Sem	No space after [or before].	`"He [Twain] wrote . . . "`
{ }	Left and Right Curly Braces	Math and Internet searches	Sem	No space after { or before }.	`{{4, 2, 6}}`
~	Tilde	Internet addresses	A	No space before and after.	`www.isp.com/~jon`

FACT FILE

A byte refers to memory in a computer. In computer terminology, a KB (kilobyte) is approximately 1,000 bytes; a MB (megabyte) is approximately 1,000,000 bytes; a GB (gigabyte) is approximately a billion bytes.

Type each line 2 times. Repeat if time permits.

```
5  Dakota typed "C:\DATABASE\FRESHMEN\OFFICERS.SEP."
6  If X < Z and Y > X but < Z, then Z > X and Z > Y.
7  Please see if 7.13 + 5.21 = 12.34 and 9 + 2 = 11.

8  "They [Americans] captured Trenton [New Jersey]."
9  Search for these: {New York}, Ohio, {New Mexico}.
10 Use this format: http://www.server.com/~username.
```

LESSON 27

TEACH

Activities C–E. Remind students they should improve both speed and accuracy from the Pretest to the Posttest.

SKILLBUILDING

C. PRETEST

Take a 1-minute timing on lines 11–14. Note your speed and errors.

```
11      A news flash said that trash would not be picked up   11
12 until the next day. This was the same week that the snow   22
13 was not cleared from the roads. We had a heated debate     33
14 about this deal for a few days.                            39
        | 1 | 2 | 3 | 4 | 5 | 6 | 7 | 8 | 9 | 10
```

D. PRACTICE

SPEED: *If you made 2 or fewer errors on the Pretest, type lines 15–22 two times each.*

ACCURACY: *If you made more than 2 errors on the Pretest, type lines 15–18 as a group two times. Then type lines 19–22 as a group two times.*

Discrimination reaches *are keys that are commonly substituted and easily confused. (wear)*

```
15 asa flask aside sails saved masks sadly trash sas
16 fgf frogs foggy gaffe fugue golfs goofs fight gfg
17 ewe weeks fewer sewer sweat swell sweet weans wew
18 ded deal heeded dent need debate feed student ede

19 ioi spoil toils lions coins joins soils boils oio
20 mnm hymns money names numbs minor lemon means nmn
21 klk locks block flock keels kills kilts kilns lkl
22 yuy yule young unduly yellow jaunt aunt jumpy uyu
```

E. POSTTEST

Repeat the Pretest. Compare your Posttest results with your Pretest results.

PRETEST/PRACTICE/POSTTEST

The ***Pretest/Practice/Posttest*** routines are designed to improve speed or accuracy.

- The ***Pretest*** identifies students' speed or accuracy needs.
- The ***Practice*** provides a variety of improvement drills.
- The ***Posttest*** (a repeat of the Pretest) measures improvement.

FACT FILE

Many text files are less than a kilobyte in size. Adding graphics can dramatically increase file size. A graphic may take up a megabyte or more of disk space. While computer hard drives can store several gigabytes, a 3½-inch disk can only hold 1.44MB of data.

TEACH

Activities F–G. Remind students that the purpose of the alphabet review lines and the number/symbol review lines is to build skill in typing both alphabetic characters as well as number/symbol characters. This skill will be tested in the 1-minute alphanumeric timing in Activity H.

Social Studies Connections

Cherokee, once one of the largest Indian nations in the Southeast, lived in permanent villages in the southern Appalachian region until forced to relocate to Oklahoma by the U.S. government in the winter of 1838–1839. The winter was harsh and about one-fourth of the Cherokee died from disease, starvation, exposure, or exhaustion along the way. Some Cherokee refused to leave their homeland when the U.S. Army came. Descendants of these Cherokee still live in the mountains of western North Carolina.

F. Alphabet Review

Type each line 1 time. Repeat if time permits.

```
23 aa alas also again after bb bake blow begin black
24 cc came coat charm clear dd drop door dream dated

25 ee ever each eager enemy ff five foal frame flute
26 gg game give grate guard hh hope hall heavy human

27 ii iced into ideal ionic jj jail joke jewel juice
28 kk keep kick knife knock ll long lace lower lever

29 mm mope mail merit music nn name none never night
30 oo over open order occur pp pure pain piece plump

31 qq quit quad quest quote rr roar rain rhyme rural
32 ss sing soap saber sense tt time talk tooth trait

33 uu us urge upon vv via vase vine ww wag west warm
34 xx ox axis exit yy yen year yank zz zoo zany zinc
```

G. Number And Symbol Review

Type each line 1 time. Repeat if time permits.

```
35 46 maps, 69 snaps, 65 traps, 15 drapes, 63 grapes
36 57 lots, 85 plots, 16 slots, 50 floats, 86 clocks

37 53 hams, 46 trams, 95 slams, 62 flames, 67 blames
38 58 ails, 60 sails, 96 nails, 45 snails, 47 trails

39 (1) 32% of $17, (2) 2^9, (3) 15 @ $.81, (4) Wait!
40 (5) the key,* (6) A & W, (7) 56 @ $.10, (8) 40^3*

41 Tony said 3^2 and 20% of 40 have the same answer.
42 He rented 56 vases, 239 tables, and 4,078 chairs.

43 A & Z billed us for 79 pens @ $.23 on Invoice #8.
44 Dan collected 98 flowers, 39 bugs, and 47 leaves.

45 Nice & Clean (formerly #1 Laundry) is in Memphis.
46 The 743 people were served 980 rolls by 12 girls.
```

interNET ACTIVITY

Have students type a short report on their findings on the Cherokee and the Trail of Tears. At the bottom of their report, have students create a chart that shows the search engine they used and path of their Internet search. Post the reports and charts around the room.

CULTURAL CONNECTIONS

On index cards, write the name of a Native North American nation, which may include Shawnee, Iroquois, Miami, Natchez, Winnebago, Iroquois, or other. Have students work in groups of three and research their group's nation on the Internet.

H. 1-Minute Alphanumeric Timing

Take a 1-minute timing on lines 47–49. Note your speed and errors.

```
47      Jason paid Invoice #75 with Check #2301. He       9
48 mailed it June 24, but he forgot the $.39 stamp.      19
49 Stop & Go's bill needs to be paid July 1.             27
   | 1 | 2 | 3 | 4 | 5 | 6 | 7 | 8 | 9 | 10
```

I. 2-Minute Timings

Take two 2-minute timings on lines 50–55. Note your speed and errors.

Goal: 27/2'/4e

Social Studies Connections

```
50      The Cherokee had no desire to leave the land       9
51 of their fathers. Troops forced them to move to        19
52 the west. Many of them froze to death during the       28
53 brutal winter on the long journey. They could not      38
54 exist through the cold winter as they moved along      48
55 the tragic Trail of Tears.                             54
   | 1 | 2 | 3 | 4 | 5 | 6 | 7 | 8 | 9 | 10        SI 1.21
```

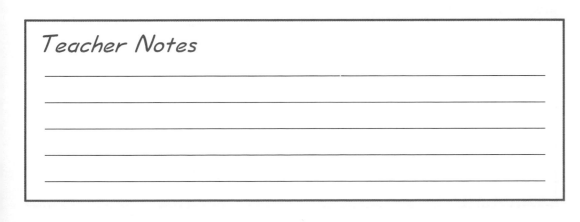

*inter*NET CONNECTION

Use the Internet to search for additional information about the Cherokees and about the Trail of Tears. Report your findings to the class.

Teacher Notes

TEACH

Activity H. Remind students that their speed in the 1-minute alphanumeric timing might not be as fast as what they will achieve on the 2-minute straight alphabetic timing. This is because they have had more practice in typing alphabetic characters.

Activity I. Remind students that the goal for this timing is typing 27 words a minute for 2 minutes with 4 errors.

ASSESS

- Check students' ability to create the special symbols. Be sure they have used correct spacing before and after the symbols.
- Ask students if any of them achieved a word-a-minute rate on the alphanumeric timing that is close to or equals their straight-copy rate.
- Watch students as they type the alphanumeric copy. Be sure they keep their eyes on the copy when typing the paragraph.

CLOSE

Remind students to follow end-of-class procedures: Quit and save all their work. Exit from the software. Log off the network (if necessary). Leave their workstation neat and clean. Push in their chair when leaving the area. Take all their materials with them.

LESSON 28

FOCUS

- Learn how to activate the numeric keypad.
- Learn the home keys and ENTER keys on a numeric keypad.
- Learn a capitalization rule.
- Take a technique timing and a 2-minute timing.

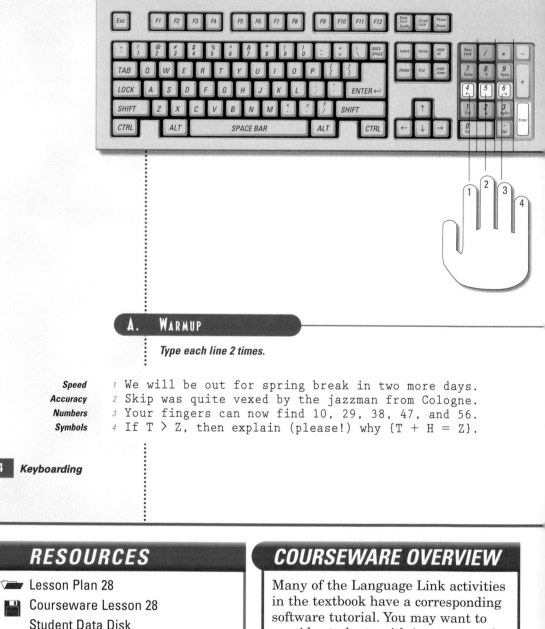

BELLRINGER

As soon as students arrive at their workstations and log in, have them type the Warmup that reviews keys they have learned.

FACT FILE

Point out the Fact File to students. Ask students what time zone they live in. Have them check a time zone map to find out how many hours different this is than the time on the East Coast or the West Coast.

NUMERIC KEYPAD: 4 5 6 ENTER

OBJECTIVES:

- Learn the 4, 5, 6, and Enter keys on the numeric keypad.
- Learn capitalization rules.
- Refine keyboarding skills.
- Type 30/2′/4e.

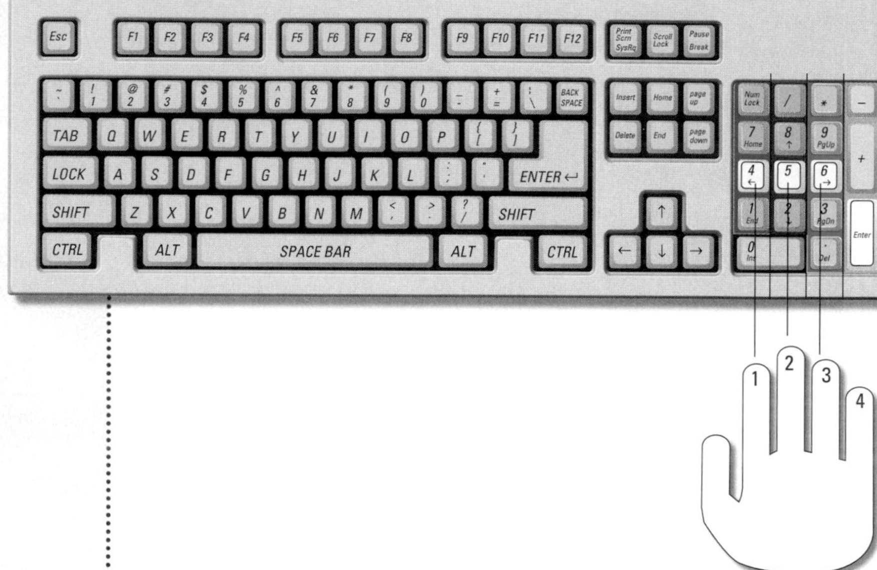

A. WARMUP

Type each line 2 times.

Speed	1	We will be out for spring break in two more days.
Accuracy	2	Skip was quite vexed by the jazzman from Cologne.
Numbers	3	Your fingers can now find 10, 29, 38, 47, and 56.
Symbols	4	If T > Z, then explain (please!) why {T + H = Z}.

RESOURCES

- Lesson Plan 28
- Courseware Lesson 28
- Student Data Disk
- Wallchart
- Grading and Evaluation
- Language Link Worksheets

COURSEWARE OVERVIEW

Many of the Language Link activities in the textbook have a corresponding software tutorial. You may want to provide students with instructions for when, or if, they should complete the tutorials.

B. Capitalization

Study the rules and the examples below. Then edit lines 5–8 to correct any errors in capitalization.

Rule 1: Capitalize the first word of a sentence.

The weather bureau predicted a winter storm. It was severe.

Rule 2: Capitalize the names of the days of the week, months, holidays, and religious days. Do not capitalize the names of the seasons.

In the fall, we celebrate Thanksgiving on Thursday, November 24.

Edit the lines to correct any errors in capitalization.

```
5 memorial day this year will fall on monday, may 27.
6 why wait until wednesday? we can leave later today.
7 during the Winter, they skied and skated every day.
8 Offices are closed on memorial day and on thursday.
```

NEW KEYS

C. Keypad Home-Key Position

The Num Lock key must be active before you can enter numbers on the keypad. If the Num Lock light is not on, press the Num Lock key.

The 4, 5, and 6 are the home keys for the numeric keypad.

1. Place your J, K, and L fingers on 4, 5, and 6 on the numeric keypad. You will feel a raised marker on the 5 key. This marker will help you keep your fingers on the home keys.
2. Place your Sem finger over the ENTER key. The ENTER key on the numeric keypad functions just like the ENTER key on the alphabetic keyboard.

EXTENDING THE CONTENT

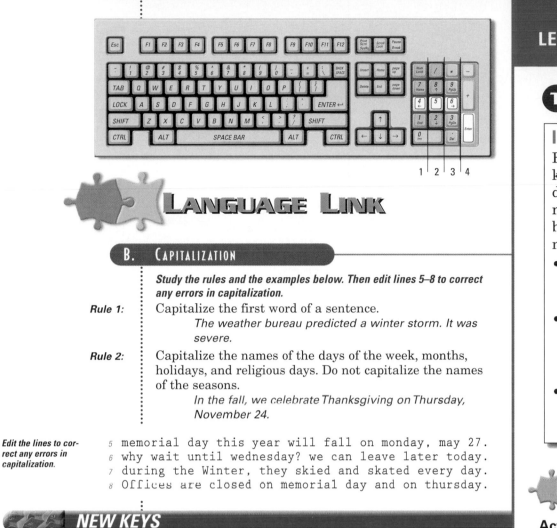

Show students how to access the Language Link tutorial for learning the first rule of capitalization. Demonstrate how to progress from screen to screen when using the Language Link tutorial. Emphasize to students that they should complete the Language Link tutorial if they are not familiar with the rule being presented or if they need additional reinforcement on the rule. Remind students that each Language Link rule that is presented has several application screens in the tutorial and that after the final screen has been satisfactorily completed, the software will move them to the next rule in the lesson or to the next activity in that lesson.

TEACH

Illustration

Explain the purpose of the keyboard illustration to students. Point out that the numbers below the keyboard are pointing to the numeric keyboard.

- The keys are color-coded according to which finger is used.
- The numbers below the numeric keypad show which fingers correlate to each color.
- The new keys being introduced are shown in white.

Activity B. Have students edit lines 5–8 on screen.

Solutions: Memorial Day this year will fall on Monday, May 27.

Why wait until Wednesday? We can leave later today.

During the winter, they skied and skated every day.

Offices are closed on Memorial Day and on Thursday.

Activity C. Show students where the numeric keypad is located on their keyboard. Explain that the numeric keypad is designed to be used primarily when entering only numbers—not numbers and text.

Show students how to activate the numeric keypad by depressing the Num Lock key. Demonstrate the correct finger location (home keys) on a numeric keypad.

TEACH

Illustration

Explain the purpose of the keyboard illustration to students. Point out that the numbers below the keyboard are pointing to the numeric keyboard.

- The keys are color-coded according to which finger is used.
- The numbers below the numeric keypad show which fingers correlate to each color.
- The new keys being introduced are shown in white.

Activity D. Point out that the 5 key has a raised dot on it to aid students in locating the correct home-key position.

Activity E. Reinforce the home-key position on a numeric keypad and compare it to the home keys on the alphabetic keyboard.

D. 4 5 6 Keys

Enter the following numbers column by column. Use the proper finger for each key. Press ENTER after the final digit of each number. Repeat if time permits.

Use J, K, and L fingers.

Keep your eyes on the copy.

Accuracy is very important when entering numbers.

444	456	454
555	654	464
666	445	546
455	446	564
466	554	654
544	556	645
566	664	666
644	665	555
655	456	444
456	654	456

SKILLBUILDING

E. Keypad Practice

Enter the following numbers column by column. Press ENTER after the final digit of each number. Keep your eyes on the copy. Repeat if time permits.

Use J, K, and L fingers.

Keep your eyes on the copy.

Accuracy is very important when entering numbers.

444	455	464	555	466	646	666	544	456	445	644
546	554	556	454	645	664	545	654	665	565	465
445	446	455	466	456	454	465	464	554	556	544
644	655	645	646	654	656	666	464	555	665	456
654	456	564	465	646	656	464	456	546	564	465

TECHNOLOGY TIP

You can input information into a computer using a variety of devices. Some of the more common input devices are the keyboard, mouse, trackball, touch pad, touch screen, pen, joy stick, scanner, bar code reader, video camera, digital camera, and microphone.

Career Exploration

Challenge students to make a list of at least 10 computer-related careers. Brainstorm in class to help students get started. For example, students might name graphic designers for billboards, computer-generated graphics for television, or cashiers in checkout lanes in stores.

F. Technique Timings

Take two 30-second timings on each line. Focus on the techniques at the left.

Lines 24 and 25: Efficient and smooth operation of the shift keys.
Lines 26 and 27: Efficient and smooth operation of the ENTER key.

24 Will Zeb and Vern work Zone Two with Cam and Nic?
25 Miriam and Dolores saw Broadway and Main Streets.
26 Did Ben Milo fix that off/on switch? Did it work?
27 Ivan is grateful that it is ready for the winter.

G. Diagnostic Practice: Alphabet

Turn to the Diagnostic Practice: Alphabet routine on page SB1. Type one of the Pretest/Posttest paragraphs and identify any errors. Then type the corresponding drill lines two times for each letter on which you made 2 or more errors and one time for each letter on which you made only 1 error. Finally, repeat the same Pretest paragraph and compare your performance.

H. 12-Second Sprints

Take three 12-second timings on each line. Try to increase your speed on each timing.

28 Walking can pick you up if you are feeling tired.
29 Your heart and lungs can work harder as you walk.
30 It may be that a walk is often better than a nap.
31 You will keep fit if you walk each and every day.
| | | | 5 | | | | 10 | | | | 15 | | | | 20 | | | | 25 | | | | 30 | | | | 35 | | | | 40 | | | | 45 | | | | 50

I. 2-Minute Timings

Take two 2-minute timings on lines 32–38. Note your speed and errors.

Goal: 30/2'/4e

32 Some senior students realize that once they 9
33 leave school, they must plan for more education. 19
34 Most will not know exactly what their first job 28
35 will be or what skills will equip them to move 38
36 ahead in a job or to change to another job. You 47
37 should make plans for your future now while you 57
38 have the time. 60
| 1 | 2 | 3 | 4 | 5 | 6 | 7 | 8 | 9 | 10 SI 1.25

Teacher Notes

LESSON 28

TEACH

Activity F. Remind students that typing has a smooth rhythm. When reaching for the shift keys and enter key, they'll want to keep the rhythm smooth.

Activity G. Point out the diagnostic practice to students. Explain to them that this is an alphabet practice.

Activity H. Remind students they want to increase their speed each time they take the 12-second timings.

Activity I. Remind students that their goal in these timings is to type 30 words a minute for 2 minutes with no more than 4 errors.

ASSESS

- Watch students' hands as they reach for the number keys on the home keys of the keypad.
- Check the students' screens as they complete the tutorial on the keypad.
- Check students' scores on the 2-minute timing.

CLOSE

Remind students to close down their computers and clean up their workstations at the end of the class.

LESSON 29

FOCUS

- Learn the 7, 8, and 9 keys on a numeric keypad.
- Introduce students to the Paced Practice routine.
- Take 30-second OK timings and 2-minute timings.

BELLRINGER

As soon as students arrive at their workstations and log in, have them type the Warmup that reviews keys they have learned.

FACT FILE

Have students use a search engine to look up a leap second on the Internet. Have them then go to one related link and find three facts about this new information. Have students type a short report about the information they found. Post these reports around the room.

LESSON 29

NUMERIC KEYPAD: 7 8 9

OBJECTIVES:

- Learn the 7, 8, 9 keys on the numeric keypad.
- Refine keyboarding skills.
- Type 30/2'/4e.

A. WARMUP

Type each line 2 times.

Speed	1	No one can say that he is not giving full effort.
Accuracy	2	Alex was puzzled by the czar's quip about oxygen.
Language Link	3	He and Molly traveled to Iowa on Saturday by bus.
Numbers	4	Without looking I can type 67, 89, 23, 14, and 5.

FACT FILE

A leap second is inserted into the year (usually on New Year's Eve) to make up for the fact that Earth's rotation is slowing down. Scientists know when to insert a leap second by comparing Earth's rotation to an atomic clock.

RESOURCES

- Lesson Plan 29
- Courseware Lesson 29
- Student Data Disk
- Wallchart
- Grading and Evaluation

NEW KEYS

B. 7 8 9 Keys

Enter the following numbers column by column. Use the proper finger for each key. Press Enter after the final digit of each number. Keep your eyes on the copy. Repeat if time permits.

Use J, K, and L fingers.

Be sure Num Lock is on.

Concentrate on accuracy as you enter the numbers.

474	585	696
747	858	969
774	885	996
447	558	669
744	855	966
477	588	699
444	555	666
747	858	969
774	885	996
747	858	969

SKILLBUILDING

C. Keypad Practice

Enter the following numbers column by column. Press Enter after the final digit of each number. Keep your eyes on the copy. Repeat if time permits.

Keep eyes on copy. Use proper fingers. Concentrate on accuracy.

456	556	474	699	477	577	677	748	847	947
654	664	585	747	488	588	688	749	849	948
445	665	696	858	499	599	699	758	857	957
446	456	477	969	478	578	678	759	859	958
554	654	588	789	489	589	689	767	868	969

TEACH

Illustration

Explain the purpose of the keyboard illustration to students. Point out that the numbers below the keyboard are pointing to the numeric keyboard.

- The keys are color-coded according to which finger is used.
- The numbers below the numeric keypad show which fingers correlate to each color.
- The new keys being introduced are shown in white.

Activity B. Remind students to press Enter after each number. Also remind them that thay are entering the numbers column by column.

Activity C. Make sure that students are keeping their eyes on the copy and using the proper fingers on the keypad.

interNET ACTIVITY

Have students use a search engine to find a news headline, a current movie, and an electronic library. Remind students to use the proper fingers on the keys even when searching the Internet. Have students track their search.

SCHOOL TO CAREER

Explain to students that we live in an international world. Ask them to think about their clothes or things. Did anything come from another country? Explain that it is helpful in business to understand the cultures of other countries. Have students research one country on the Internet.

TEACH

Activity D. Introduce students to the Paced Practice routine:

- Take a 1-minute timing to establish a base rate.
- Select a passage from Skillbuilding, page SB7, that has a rate that is 2 words a minute faster than the rate established in the previous step.
- Take a 2-minute timing on this passage until the speed goal of the passage is achieved.
- Drop back 2 words a minute to the previous passage and type it until it is finished in 2 minutes with no more than 2 errors.

Activity E. Remind students they are working toward refining their typing skills. They want to keep practicing for accuracy and speed.

Activities F–H. Remind students they should improve both their speed and accuracy from the Pretest to the Posttest.

PRETEST/PRACTICE/POSTEST

The ***Pretest/Practice/Posttest*** routines are designed to improve speed or accuracy.

- The ***Pretest*** identifies students' speed or accuracy needs.
- The ***Practice*** provides a variety of improvement drills.
- The ***Posttest*** (a repeat of the Pretest) measures improvement.

D. Paced Practice

Turn to the Paced Practice routine beginning on page SB7. Take a 1-minute timing on the Entry Timing paragraph. Then follow the directions at the top of page SB-7 for completing the activity.

E. 30-Second OK Timings

Take two 30-second OK timings on lines 20–21. Then take two 30 second OK timings on lines 22–23. Goal: no errors.

```
20      He wants to work for a company that provides
21 benefits to workers. Jay's benefits are terrific.

22      Flat computer screen means that I can set up
23 my computer on my desk because the parts all fit.
```

F. PRETEST

Take a 1-minute timing on the paragraph. Note your speed and errors.

```
24      Jenny loved most all of the opera music that   9
25 the kids sang. No one could deny how funny they     19
26 looked in muffs and emu feathers. Everyone had a    28
27 blast that afternoon.                               33
   | 1 | 2 | 3 | 4 | 5 | 6 | 7 | 8 | 9 | 10
```

G. PRACTICE

SPEED: ***If you made 2 or fewer errors on the Pretest, type lines 28–35 two times each.***

ACCURACY: ***If you made more than 2 errors on the Pretest, type lines 28–31 as a group two times. Then type lines 32–35 as a group two times.***

Adjacent Reaches

```
28 as mast blast phase clash ashes atlas brash hasty
29 op crop opera flops opens poppy drops opals mopes
30 ds kids spuds grids bonds birds brads leads holds
31 lk milk talks walks balks milky silky bulky sulky
```

Jump Reaches

```
32 mu mute music muffs munch murky mulls musty muddy
33 ve cove verse serve curve verve wives chive sieve
34 ny deny funny phony shiny sunny irony corny agony
35 in sink blink slink whine shine winds pines inlet
```

H. POSTTEST

Repeat the Pretest. Compare your Posttest results with your Pretest results.

Teacher Notes

I. 2-Minute Timings

Take two 2-minute timings on lines 36–42. Note your speed and errors.

Goal: 30/2'/4e

```
36      The end of a school program is a great feat    9
37 for most students. Some believe that it will be    18
38 the last time for a test; however, this may not    27
39 be so as a number of exams may be taken during a   37
40 lifetime. It is quite puzzling to some why tests   47
41 are given when their skills have been proved by    56
42 their achievements.                                60
   | 1 | 2 | 3 | 4 | 5 | 6 | 7 | 8 | 9 | 10       SI 1.21
```

JOURNAL ENTRY
Use your journal to keep track of your time for several days. Determine if you can make better use of it. Describe how you would spend your time on an "ideal" day (one on which you can spend your time any way you like).

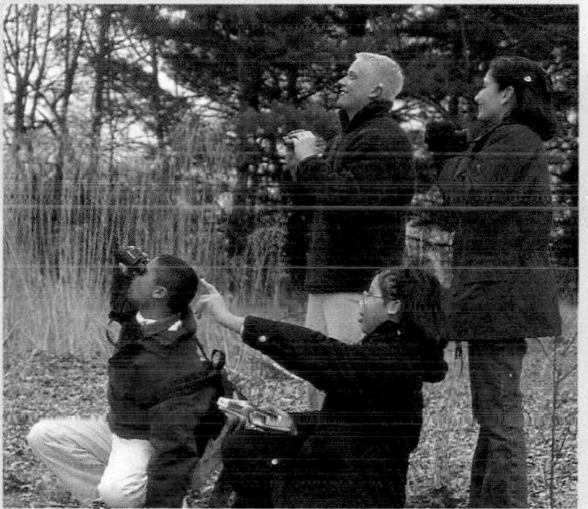

LESSON 29

TEACH

Activity I. Remind students that their goal for these 2-minute timings is to type 30 words a minute for 2 minutes with no more than 4 errors.

ASSESS

- Watch students' hands as they reach for the number keys on the home keys of the keypad.
- Check the students' screens as they complete the tutorial on the keypad.
- Check students' scores on the 2-minute timing.

CLOSE

Have students check their workstations to make sure they are neat and clear of debris.

JOURNAL ENTRY

Have students pair up to read the journal entries on how to make better use of time. Have the pairs discuss their ideas with each other and add thoughts about how their partners might achieve their goals.

LESSON 30

FOCUS

- Review the numeric key-pad.
- Review the alphabet and shift key.
- Use a P/P/P routine to build speed and improve accuracy.
- Compose short-phrase responses at the keyboard.

BELLRINGER

As soon as students arrive at their workstations and log in, have them type the Warmup that reviews keys they have learned.

TEACH

Activity B. Remind students to use the correct fingers as they enter each set of numbers.

Activity C. Have students focus on operating the left and right shift keys smoothly.

LESSON 30 REVIEW

OBJECTIVES:

- Refine numeric keypad skills.
- Refine keyboarding skills.
- Type 30/2'/4e.
- Compose at the keyboard.

A. WARMUP

Type each line 2 times.

Speed	1	Tish dances with grace and seems to float on air.
Accuracy	2	Zudora and Javan are amazed by the tranquil pool.
Language Link	3	we took ms. verhetsel to the airport on thursday.
Numbers/Symbols	4	Movies 7 (on Highway 59) charges $2 on Thursdays.

SKILLBUILDING

B. KEYPAD REVIEW

Enter the following numbers column by column. Press ENTER after the final digit of each number. Keep your eyes on the copy. Repeat if time permits.

Use the correct fingers as you enter each set of numbers. Operate the numeric keypad smoothly.

5	444	999	657	547	557	985	968	897	766	687
6	555	489	658	548	558	986	969	898	768	697
7	666	589	659	549	559	964	894	899	769	567
8	777	689	654	554	987	965	895	764	684	459
9	888	789	655	556	984	967	896	765	685	648

C. TECHNIQUE CHECKPOINT

Type each line 2 times. Focus on the technique at the left.

Concentrate on smooth operation of the shift keys.

10 Benji typed a report on New Guinea and Australia.
11 Kodi said that all of us should meet after class.
12 I bought yards of flannel at Sew Easy this month.
13 Oren donated his profit to the Find-a-Child Fund.

RESOURCES

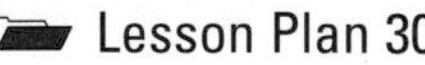

Lesson Plan 30

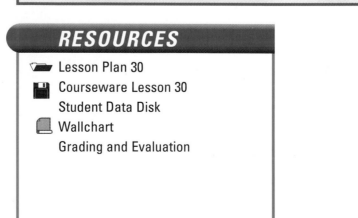

Courseware Lesson 30
Student Data Disk
Wallchart
Grading and Evaluation

D. Alphabet Review

Type each line 1 time. Concentrate on efficient and smooth operation of the shift keys. Repeat if time permits.

14 A Anna Aram Alan B Bel Bern Beth C Curt Chan Cleo
15 D Desi Dino Dona E Ean Erin Egan F Fifi Finn Faye
16 G Gaby Gian Gena H Ham Hank Hedy I Ilse Ilya Iris

17 J Jess Jori Jojo K Kia Kern Kwan L Luke Lars Lyda
18 M Miki Marc Mara N Noe Niki Noel O Olin Otto Olga
19 P Pace Pita Powa Q Qam Quin Quan R Rani Reid Rory

20 S Suni Saul Shan T Tov Taio Tobi U Ulma Urie Ushi
21 V Vera Vick Vala W Web Wren Wilt X Xann Xela Xuxa
22 Y Yoki York Ynez Yusif Z Zizi Zane Zena Zeke Zara

E. Technique Timings

Take two 30-second timings on each line. Focus on the technique at the left.

Concentrate on smooth operation of the shift keys.

23 David and Ian still work at B. K. Dry Goods, Inc.
24 Mrs. R. K. Dunn taught Spanish at Jefferson High.
25 Rory, Anna, and Han ran the Mile-High Race today.
26 She is at the top in her new job at the car wash.
| 1 | 2 | 3 | 4 | 5 | 6 | 7 | 8 | 9 | 10

F. PRETEST

Take a 1-minute timing on the paragraph. Note your speed and errors.

27 Buzz did research about the history of tidal 9
28 waves. The doom and gloom of his essay threw our 19
29 class into a tizzy. The wild storm outside didn't 29
30 help matters. We were all upset that day. 37
| 1 | 2 | 3 | 4 | 5 | 6 | 7 | 8 | 9 | 10

TEACH

Activity D. Remind students to concentrate on the efficient and smooth operation of the shift keys.

Activity E. Remind students to use correct posture for typing and keep their elbows in.

Activity F. Be sure that students complete all of the review segments in the text before starting the P/P/P routine.

FACT FILE

More than 500 years ago, Johannes Gutenberg invented the printing press, which revolutionized the world by making the printed word accessible to the public. Have students research Gutenberg on the Internet.

TEACH

Activities G–H. Remind students they should improve both their speed and accuracy from the Pretest to the Posttest.

PRETEST/PRACTICE/POSTEST

The ***Pretest/Practice/Posttest*** routines are designed to improve speed or accuracy.

- The ***Pretest*** identifies students' speed or accuracy needs.
- The ***Practice*** provides a variety of improvement drills.
- The ***Posttest*** (a repeat of the Pretest) measures improvement.

Activity I. Remind students to keep their eyes on the screen as they take the 2-minute timings. The goal for these 2-minute timings is to type 30 words a minute, for 2 minutes, with no more than 4 errors.

COMMUNICATION ACTIVITY

Body language, like eye contact, is different in other cultures. In Egypt people stand very close. Try this: (1) Have students stand a normal distance apart and then move close. (2) Have students use eye contact while speaking; then have them speak without eye contact. Discuss students' reactions.

G. PRACTICE

SPEED: ***If you made 2 or fewer errors on the Pretest, type lines 31–38 two times each.***

ACCURACY: ***If you made more than 2 errors on the Pretest, type lines 31–34 as a group two times. Then type lines 35–38 as a group two times.***

Double Reaches

```
31 ss pass floss guess essay lasso fussy abyss issue
32 oo doom gloom igloo roomy roost afoot bloom scoot
33 zz buzz pizza dizzy jazzy fuzzy dizzy tizzy fizzy
34 ll will silly hello jelly wells drill kills walls
```

Alternate Reaches

```
35 ti tidy ticks tight optic title tidal stick stiff
36 or fork odors storm world coral works adorn stork
37 wi wiry wield twice widow swift wicks swish twirl
38 sl slap slick isles aisle slant slams slips slows
```

H. POSTTEST

Repeat the Pretest. Compare your Posttest results with your Pretest results.

I. 2-MINUTE TIMINGS

Take two 2-minute timings on lines 39–45. Note your speed and errors.

Goal: 30/2'/4e

```
39      Good workers will be quick to discover what      9
40 others on the job like or dislike. Just a bit of     19
41 extra effort by them will make the office a more     29
42 pleasing place in which to work. A cheerful card     38
43 once in a while will bring a smile to one in need    48
44 of support at work. It is amazing how one kind       58
45 act spreads.                                         60
   | 1 | 2 | 3 | 4 | 5 | 6 | 7 | 8 | 9 | 10  SI 1.21
```

COMMUNICATION FOCUS

People who do not make eye contact when they speak are often thought by Americans to be unfriendly, insecure, inattentive, and impersonal. In Western cultures, not making eye contact means you cannot be trusted. In the South Pacific and Japan, lack of eye contact is a sign of respect.

J. Composing at the Keyboard

Answer each question with a few words or a short phrase. Keep your eyes on the screen as you compose; do not look at your hands.

46 What career interests you?
47 What kind of animal do you think makes a good pet?
48 What are two states you would like to visit?
49 What are three things you would like to change about yourself?
50 Who are three people who have been in the news recently?

PORTFOLIO *Activity*

Keep a copy of your best timing from the last ten lessons. Determine how much you have improved over the past few weeks, and explain why you have improved. Record some other things you can do to improve even more during the next few weeks.

TEACH

Activity J. Remind students to keep their eyes on the screen as they compose. Also remind them to get their thoughts down and then go back and proofread.

Solutions: Answers will vary

ASSESS

- Check to see that students complete each of the review sections before moving on to the next activity.
- Check students' screens when they compose responses at the keyboard; be sure that they have created short phrases in their responses.
- Check to see if the students show signs of improvement from the Pretest to the Posttest.
- Check students' scores on the 2-minute timings.

CLOSE

Have students check their Portfolio to see if all lesson activities have been completed.

PORTFOLIO *Activity*

Have students choose one idea to work on this week from their list of ways they can improve. Break the class into groups of three or four. Have each student in the group name his/her goal for this week. Then have students brainstorm with each other on ways to accomplish their goals. Have groups check in with each other and set new goals every week.

LESSON 31

FOCUS

- Learn the 1, 2, and 3 keys on a numeric keypad.
- Use a P/P/P routine to build speed and improve accuracy.
- Take 30-second and 2-minute timings.
- Compose short phrases at the keyboard in response to questions.

BELLRINGER

As soon as students arrive at their workstations and log in, have them type the Warmup that reviews keys they have learned. Point out the purpose of each line as shown to the left of the copy.

LESSON 31

NUMERIC KEYPAD: 1 2 3

OBJECTIVES:

- Learn the 1, 2, and 3 keys on the numeric keypad.
- Refine numeric keypad skills.
- Refine keyboarding skills.
- Type 30/2'/4e.
- Compose at the keyboard.

interNET CONNECTION

Rain, sunshine, and earthquakes are physical phenomena present in our environmental system. We have virtually no control over their existence or non-existence in our environment. Search the Internet for definitions of these terms. Write a brief description of each term and what causes each to happen. Are these terms common throughout the world?

A. WARMUP

Type each line 2 times.

Speed	1	The rain will stop soon; then the sun will shine.
Accuracy	2	Zeke exhibits exuberance on quizzes about quakes.
Language Link	3	Shalena will meet us Saturday at Happy Rock Park.
Numbers/Symbols	4	Paige added 7 + 1 + 24 + 13 + 22 + 11 and got 78.

RESOURCES

Lesson Plan 31

Courseware Lesson 31

Student Data Disk

Wallchart

interNET ACTIVITY

Provide students with a world map. Divide the world into four parts. Assign each part to a student group. Have groups use the Internet to research world weather conditions. Then have them identify the countries.

NEW KEYS

Enter the following numbers column by column. Use the proper finger for each key. Press* ENTER *after the final digit of each number. Keep your eyes on the copy. Repeat if time permits.

Use J, K, and L fingers. Keep your eyes on the copy. Concentrate on accuracy.

```
444   555   666
111   222   333
144   225   336
441   552   663
144   255   366
411   522   633
444   555   666
414   525   636
141   252   363
411   525   636
```

SKILLBUILDING

C. Keypad Practice

Enter the following numbers column by column. Press* ENTER *after the final digit of each number. Keep your eyes on the copy. Repeat if time permits.

Keep your eyes on the copy.

```
476   167   754   531   746   334   568   829   957   146
372   426   193   942   853   712   149   637   486   329
551   789   592   726   962   365   438   218   582   381
983   238   812   861   147   819   129   341   673   247
421   945   638   397   285   654   247   759   149   655
```


FACT FILE

Chat is a real-time conversation on the Internet. A chat room is the communications channel that allows users to converse with one another. People with similar interests "talk" live to others in the chat room by sending and receiving messages instantly.

TEACH

Illustration

Point out the illustration of the keyboard to the students. Remind them of the following:

- The keys are color-coded according to which finger is used.
- The numbers below the numeric keypad show which fingers correlate to each color.
- The new keys being introduced are shown in white.

Activity B. Have students press the Demonstration button to review the correct reach for the 1, 2, and 3 keys. Show students how to reach for the 1, 2, and 3 keys on the numeric keypad while maintaining the home-key position.

Activity C. Remind students to keep their eyes on the copy even though they may be tempted to look at the keypad.

TEACH

Activity D. Remind students to sit up straight while typing.

Activity E. Use the P/P/P routine to build skill. Have students speed up slightly the second time they type each Pretest line.

Activity F. Point out to students that they are to type lines 28–35 two times each only if they made fewer than 2 errors on the Pretest. If they made more than 2 errors, they should type lines 28–31 as a group, and then type lines 32–35 as a group.

Activity G. Remind students that their Posttest should show greater accuracy and speed after the Practice.

PRETEST/PRACTICE/POSTTEST

The ***Pretest/Practice/Posttest*** routines are designed to improve speed or accuracy.

- The ***Pretest*** identifies students' speed or accuracy needs.
- The ***Practice*** provides a variety of improvement drills.
- The ***Posttest*** (a repeat of the Pretest) measures improvement.

SKILLBUILDING

D. Technique Timings

Take two 30-second timings on each line. Focus on the technique at the left.

Keep your eyes on the copy.

```
20 The high school students will visit other places.
21 I toured an art museum that was west of the city.
22 Twenty letters were addressed to the three of us.
23 My car (the blue convertible) is hard to keep up.
   | 1 | 2 | 3 | 4 | 5 | 6 | 7 | 8 | 9 | 10
```

E. PRETEST

Take a 1-minute timing on the paragraph. Note your speed and errors.

```
24      Molly and Abe took water to the barn for the    9
25 horses to drink. Half an hour later, Ralph filled   19
26 the hay racks. It was he who discovered Star, our   29
27 very best horse, was ill.                           30
   | 1 | 2 | 3 | 4 | 5 | 6 | 7 | 8 | 9 | 10
```

F. PRACTICE

SPEED: ***If you made 2 or fewer errors on the Pretest, type lines 28–35 two times each.***

ACCURACY: ***If you made more than 2 errors on the Pretest, type lines 28–31 as a group two times. Then type lines 32–35 as a group two times.***

Left Reaches

```
28 Abe purse bases debts large match ocean nurse Tad
29 red urban water yearn Jerry trays racks horse set
30 war rated tubes upset verbs Xerox quart image cad
31 car fears raven carts froze graze exact grave sad
```

Right Reaches

```
32 Lon pilot linen Molly hours Louis zooms films Jim
33 mop jumps knows plugs Naomi quill flint drink hum
34 nip human flood Ralph mound joins yolks co-op poi
35 mop polka plums homey plump mound limps money Lou
```

G. POSTTEST

Repeat the Pretest. Compare your Posttest results with your Pretest results.

*inter*NET ACTIVITY

Have students go online and enter a chat room appropriate for your class. Have them read the FAQ if available and observe the conversation. Once the thread of the conversation is clear, have them post messages to the chat room.

SCHOOL TO CAREER

Explain that computers have opened up new learning resources and opportunities. Students can even take college courses over the Internet. Have students choose a college or university and then go online to find a list of courses available there. Have students bring the list to school.

H. 2-Minute Timings

Goal: 30/2'/4e

Take two 2-minute timings on lines 36–42. Note your speed and errors.

```
36      A good way to earn extra money is by taking    9
37 care of children. It is not a job for the lazy.    19
38 Being in charge of a small child requires hard     28
39 work and savvy. You can take workshops to learn    38
40 the basics of child care, and you should take a    47
41 course in first aid so you are prepared for any    57
42 medical crisis.                                    60
   | 1 | 2 | 3 | 4 | 5 | 6 | 7 | 8 | 9 | 10      SI 1.22
```

I. Composing at the Keyboard

Answer each question with a short phrase. Keep your eyes on the screen as you compose.

43 What are three things you should know before you agree to baby-sit?

44 Why should you keep your eyes on the copy when you type?

45 What three things do you admire most about your best friend?

FACT FILE

The Roman Empire has a 1,000-year history. Julius Caesar and an army of men conquered most of Western Europe for the Roman Empire. Have students research one Roman person—an emperor, philosopher, or citizen—and type a short report.

TEACH

Activity H. Remind students to note their speed and errors on the timing. The goal is to type 30 words a minute for 2 minutes with no more than 4 errors.

Language Link

Activity I. Ask students what the difference is between a phrase and a complete sentence. Tell them that their answers for the Language Link should be in short phrases. Once students have answered the questions by typing short phrases, have them choose one topic and write three complete sentences about it.

Solutions: Answers will vary.

ASSESS

- Watch students' hands as they reach for the number keys on the keypad.
- Check to see if students show signs of improvement from the Pretest to the Posttest.

CLOSE

Remind students to clean up their workstation when they leave. An organized work area will promote better performance in class.

LESSON 32

FOCUS

- Learn the 0 and decimal key on a numeric keypad.
- Use a P/P/P routine to build speed and improve accuracy.
- Take 12-second sprints and 2-minute timings.

BELLRINGER

As soon as students arrive at their workstations and log in, have them type the Warmup that reviews keys they have learned. Go over the purpose of each line as shown to the left of the copy.

FACT FILE

The human hand contains 38 bones. Ten metacarpal bones make up the palm and 28 phalanx make up the fingers and thumb. There are two phalanx in the thumb and three in each of the four fingers.

LESSON 32

NUMERIC KEYPAD: 0 .

OBJECTIVES:

- Learn the 0 and decimal keys on the numeric keypad.
- Refine numeric keypad skills.
- Refine keyboarding skills.
- Type 30/2'/4e.

A. WARMUP

Type each line 2 times.

Speed	1	To have more pep, walk one or two miles each day.
Accuracy	2	Zorba has cichlids imported from Lake Tanganyika.
Language Link	3	She watches while I write it out and he signs it.
Numbers/Symbols	4	S & A closed at 3 7/16, up 5/8, a +14.71% change.

FACT FILE

The hand is the most versatile part of the skeleton. The hand enables people to grasp and manipulate objects. The intricate hand movements are achieved by using small muscles that are contained entirely within the hand and the much larger forearm muscles.

RESOURCES

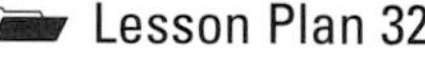
Lesson Plan 32

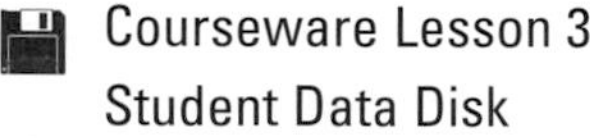
Courseware Lesson 32
Student Data Disk

Wallchart
Grading and Evaluation

NEW KEYS

B. 0 KEY

Enter the following numbers column by column. Press ENTER after the final digit of each number. Keep your eyes on the copy. Repeat if time permits.

Use the right thumb. Keep your eyes on the copy. Concentrate on accuracy.

404	470	502
505	500	603
606	690	140
707	410	250
808	520	360
909	630	701
101	407	802
202	508	903
303	609	405
505	401	506

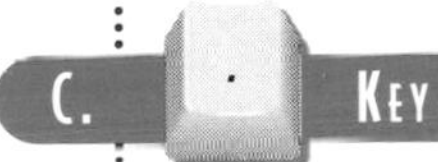

C. . KEY

Enter the following numbers column by column. Press ENTER after the final digit of each number. Keep your eyes on the copy. Repeat if time permits.

Use L finger. Keep K finger anchored on the 5 key as you reach down to the decimal.

4.5	7.8	1.2
6.5	9.8	3.2
4.4	7.7	1.1
4.4	7.7	1.1
5.5	8.8	2.2
5.5	8.8	2.2
6.6	9.9	3.3
6.5	9.9	3.3
4.5	7.8	1.2
6.5	8.9	1.3

TEACH

Illustration

Point out the illustration of the keyboard to the students. Remind them of the following:

- The keys are color-coded according to which finger is used.
- The numbers below the numeric keypad show which fingers correlate to each color.
- The new keys being introduced are shown in white.

Activity B. Have students press the Demonstration button to review the correct reach for the 0 and decimal keys. Show students how to reach for the 0 and decimal keys on the numeric keypad while maintaining the home-key position.

Activity C. Remind students to keep the K finger anchored on the 5 key as they reach down to the decimal.

FACT FILE

The earliest writings come from the Sumerians. The Sumerians developed a script in 3500 B.C. known as "cuneiform," or pictures that represent words or sounds. Cuneiform was scratched onto clay tablets with reed pens by specially trained scribes. The Sumerians lived in western Asia.

TEACH

Activity D. Remind students to keep their eyes on the copy. If they find themselves having trouble with this, suggest they practice typing blindfolded.

Activity E. Remind students their goal is to increase their speed on each 12-second timing.

Activity F. Use the P/P/P routine to build skill. Have students speed up slightly on the second typing of each of the Pretest lines.

PRETEST/PRACTICE/POSTTEST

The ***Pretest/Practice/Posttest*** routines are designed to improve speed or accuracy.

- The ***Pretest*** identifies students' speed or accuracy needs.
- The ***Practice*** provides a variety of improvement drills.
- The ***Posttest*** (a repeat of the Pretest) measures improvement.

SKILLBUILDING

D. Keypad Practice

Enter the following numbers column by column. Press Enter after the final digit of each number. Keep your eyes on the copy. Repeat if time permits.

25	1.7	7.5	7.6	5.0	6.2	6.0	6.7	4.5	3.0	6.4
26	5.8	2.4	2.3	2.8	3.5	9.1	5.1	3.0	7.6	2.8
27	1.6	8.3	1.7	9.9	5.0	2.7	1.6	9.3	1.3	5.9
28	3.0	4.2	3.4	8.1	7.4	1.8	2.8	8.0	8.2	5.1
29	6.9	9.0	6.5	4.0	4.6	8.9	7.2	4.9	4.7	9.0

E. 12-Second Sprints

Take three 12-second timings on each line. Try to increase your speed on each timing.

```
30 If nothing nice can be said, do not say anything.
31 Be kind if you want others to be kind toward you.
32 You won't smell like roses if you play with pigs.
33 Keep the dog away from the cats to avoid a fight.
   |  |  |  |5 |  |  |  |10|  |  |  |15|  |  |  |20|  |  |  |25|  |  |  |30|  |  |  |35|  |  |  |40|  |  |  |45|  |  |  |50
```

F. PRETEST

Take a 1-minute timing on lines 34–37. Note your speed and errors.

```
34      Unless they are crazy, most humans prefer to    9
35 be free, not in jail. That is why laws that take    19
36 away our freedom for illegal acts we perform are    29
37 created and are effective.                          34
   | 1 | 2 | 3 | 4 | 5 | 6 | 7 | 8 | 9 | 10
```

CULTURAL CONNECTIONS

Native Americans believe that all life is sacred. When an animal is sacrificed, a ceremony takes place to bless and thank the animal for the gifts it provides to human beings. Have students research other cultures' beliefs about animals.

Career Exploration

Ask students what types of careers require use of a numeric keypad. Have students write their answers on the board. When 10 careers are mentioned, ask students if any of these sound interesting. Ask students to explain why a career does or does not interest them.

G. PRACTICE

SPEED: ***If you made 2 or fewer errors on the Pretest, type lines 38–45 two times each.***

ACCURACY: ***If you made more than 2 errors on the Pretest, type lines 38–41 as a group two times. Then type lines 42–45 as a group two times.***

Up Reaches

```
38 hu hunt shuts churn hunch human husky huffs hulls
39 de deck bride depth order wader adept video decay
40 fr free frock frame frost fryer fruit frail fresh
41 li line flies blind click slick limes light flier
```

Down Reaches

```
42 ac acre poach whack acrid actor tract slack enact
43 l. pal. hill. jail. nail. yowl. dial. peel. till.
44 az raze graze craze glaze dazed blaze gazed jazzy
45 on once ponds fonts stone clone alone don't front
```

H. POSTTEST

Repeat the Pretest. Compare your Posttest results with your Pretest results.

I. 2-Minute Timings

Take two 2-minute timings on lines 46–52. Note your speed and errors.

Goal: 30/2′/4e

```
46      Poachers hunt and kill game against the law.    9
47 Many species such as big cats, caimans, quetzal     19
48 birds, and whales may become extinct from being     28
49 killed for their fur, hides, or feathers. Laws      38
50 have been passed to help save wildlife. Parks are   48
51 jointly set up in all parts of the world to be      57
52 havens for game.                                    60
   | 1 | 2 | 3 | 4 | 5 | 6 | 7 | 8 | 9 | 10  SI 1.24
```

Science Connections

Teacher Notes

TEACH

Activity G. Point out to students that they are to type lines 38–45 two times each only if they made fewer than 2 errors on the Pretest. If they made more than 2 errors, they should type lines 38–41 as a group, and then type lines 42–45 as a group.

Activity H. Remind students that their Posttest should show greater accuracy and speed than the Pretest because they have completed the Practice.

Activity I. Remind students to note their speed and errors with the 2-minute timings. The goal is to type 30 words a minute for 2 minutes with no more than 4 errors.

ASSESS

- Watch students' hands as they reach for the number keys on the keypad.
- Check to see if students show signs of improvement from the Pretest to the Posttest.

CLOSE

Remind students to clean up their workstation when they leave. An organized work area will promote better performance in class.

LESSON 33

FOCUS

- Review the numeric keypad.
- Take timings to improve technique.
- Review numbers and symbols.
- Use a P/P/P routine to build speed and improve accuracy.

BELLRINGER

As soon as students arrive at their workstations and log in, have them type the Warmup that reviews keys they have learned. Go over the purpose of each line as shown to the left of the copy.

TEACH

Activity B. Remind students that in the numeric keypad review they are typing consecutive numbers with no text; therefore, they should use the keypad rather than the top row for typing the numbers.

Activity C. Remind students to enter numbers smoothly and to maintain their rhythm.

LESSON 33 REVIEW

OBJECTIVES:

- Refine keyboarding skills.
- Type 30/2′/4e

A. WARMUP

Type each line 2 times.

Speed	1	Think about this: If it is to be, it is up to me.
Accuracy	2	Vladimir Kosma Zworykin made the television tube.
Language Link	3	Syd catches a plane at O'Hare Airport in Chicago.
Numbers/Symbols	4	Nashville has *985,026 people; Miami, *1,192,582.

SKILLBUILDING

B. KEYPAD PRACTICE—3-DIGIT NUMBERS

Enter the following numbers column by column. Press ENTER after the final digit of each number. Keep your eyes on the copy, and use the proper finger for each key. Repeat if time permits.

Enter numbers smoothly. Use correct fingers. Keep eyes on copy.

5	136	964	806	295	597	628	728	627	959	172
6	940	250	275	407	426	519	546	341	241	859
7	852	173	394	718	618	537	639	730	862	931
8	710	982	180	363	304	405	410	859	730	604
9	788	829	903	120	311	441	349	555	668	776

C. KEYPAD PRACTICE—DECIMAL NUMBERS

Enter the following numbers column by column. Press ENTER after the final digit of each number. Keep your eyes on the copy, and use the proper finger for each key. Repeat if time permits.

Enter numbers smoothly. Use correct fingers. Keep eyes on copy.

10	1.97	5.08	6.19	3.52	4.33	17.44	52.28	68.61
11	3.85	6.44	9.37	8.10	2.19	14.20	23.85	60.97
12	6.55	6.65	7.87	9.00	3.10	20.49	88.47	19.39
13	2.10	2.81	2.33	7.06	7.68	67.99	44.53	45.54
14	8.83	7.90	4.16	8.20	1.49	55.20	15.62	37.39

RESOURCES

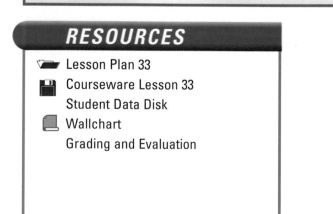

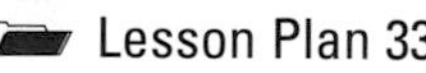 Lesson Plan 33

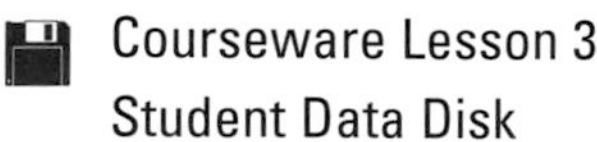 Courseware Lesson 33

Student Data Disk

Wallchart

Grading and Evaluation

D. Technique Timings

Take two 30-second timings on each line. Focus on the techniques at the left.

Lines 15–16: Type without pauses.

Lines 17–18: Type end-of-sentence punctuation smoothly.

```
15 Roy and Bob did their best to study for the test.
16 My two cats are eager to sit in my lap as I work.
17 If you are to make friends, you must be friendly.
18 Who me? Oh no! I can. What time? Look out! Did I?
   | 1 | 2 | 3 | 4 | 5 | 6 | 7 | 8 | 9 | 10
```

E. Pretest

Take a 1-minute timing on lines 19–22. Note your speed and errors.

```
19      Joy's niece darted in front of a car, but        8
20 the driver was able to stop quickly. She was only    18
21 dazed. She did not want us to cheer or make a        27
22 fuss over her.                                       30
   | 1 | 2 | 3 | 4 | 5 | 6 | 7 | 8 | 9 | 10
```

F. Practice

SPEED: *If you made 2 or fewer errors on the Pretest, type lines 23–30 two times each.*

ACCURACY: *If you made more than 2 errors on the Pretest, type lines 23–26 as a group two times. Then type lines 27–30 as a group two times.*

```
Adjacent Reaches    23 rt sort part heart start ui quit suit quiet quick
Jump Reaches        24 mo most move among money ce aced race cease niece
Double Reaches      25 ee glee weed keeps cheer ss sass fuss grass cross
In Reaches          26 st stay stop stray state pi pint pile pines spine

Alternate Reaches   27 to tofu torn storm torso pa paid pals pause pants
Left/Right Reaches  28 da dart dabs dazed dates jo joys join enjoy jolly
Up/Down Reaches     29 st star stop first coast h? ash? huh? Noah? dish?
Out Reaches         30 fa fall sofa loofa farms ho hose hone hoist phone
```

G. Posttest

Repeat the Pretest. Compare your Posttest results with your Pretest results.

TEACH

Activity D. Remind students to sit up straight and to keep their feet flat on the floor and elbows in.

Activities E–G. Remind students that they want to show improvement from the Pretest to the Posttest.

PRETEST/PRACTICE/POSTTEST

The ***Pretest/Practice/Posttest*** routines are designed to improve speed or accuracy.

- The ***Pretest*** identifies students' speed or accuracy needs.
- The ***Practice*** provides a variety of improvement drills.
- The ***Posttest*** (a repeat of the Pretest) measures improvement.

TECHNOLOGY TIP

Tell students that when they finish working, they should leave the power on and shut down the computer by clicking on the Start button and selecting the shut down feature.

Multiple Learning Styles

To help kinetic learners, have students create a simulation of a keyboard out of cardboard or paper. Have students leave off the letters and numbers. Select lively instrumental music to play while students watch their fingers "dancing" on the simulated keyboard.

TEACH

Activity H. Remind students that they are typing a mix of numbers and alphabetic characters in the alphanumeric timings; therefore, they are using the top row for numbers.

Activity I. Remind students to note their speed and errors when taking the timing. The goal is to type 30 words a minute for 2 minutes with no more than 4 errors.

ASSESS

- Watch students' hands as they reach for the number keys on the keypad.
- Check to see if students show signs of improvement from the Pretest to the Posttest.
- Check students' scores in the Performance Chart. Have students view the progress they have made in the past few lessons when taking 2-minute timings.

CLOSE

Remind students to clean up their workstation when they leave. An organized work area promotes better performance.

Social Studies Connections

H. 1-Minute Alphanumeric Timing

Take a 1-minute timing on lines 31–34. Note your speed and errors.

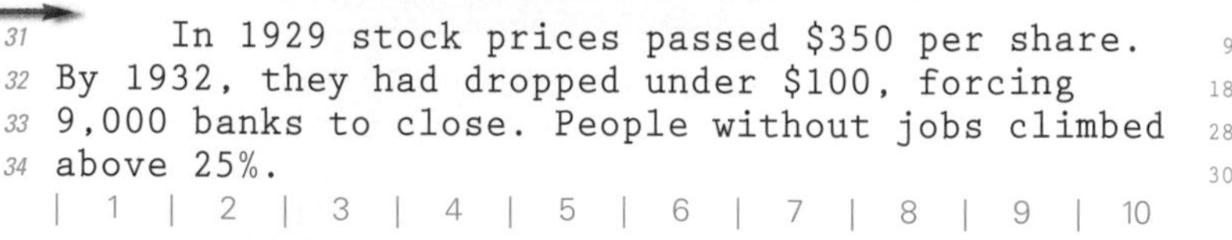

```
     In 1929 stock prices passed $350 per share.      9
By 1932, they had dropped under $100, forcing        18
9,000 banks to close. People without jobs climbed    28
above 25%.                                           30
 | 1 | 2 | 3 | 4 | 5 | 6 | 7 | 8 | 9 | 10
```

I. 2-Minute Timings

Take two 2-minute timings on lines 35–41. Note your speed and errors.

Goal: 30/2'/4e

```
     Zebras are members of the horse family and       9
are well known for their unique stripes. They        18
enjoy life on the plains and mountains of Africa     28
where they feed on grass and shrubs. Attempts to     38
use them for work and to ride have failed. The       47
quagga, which is now extinct due to hunting, was     57
kin to the zebra.                                    60
 | 1 | 2 | 3 | 4 | 5 | 6 | 7 | 8 | 9 | 10   SI 1.25
```

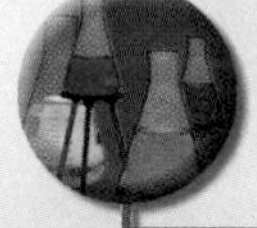

Science Connections

Social Studies Connections

On index cards, write the names of major stocks that can easily be found on the stock exchange. Pass out one card to each student. Have students use the Internet or newspaper to learn the current price of the stock on their index card.

LESSON 34 SKILLBUILDING

OBJECTIVES:

- Refine numeric keypad skills.
- Refine keyboarding skills.
- Type 31/3'/5e.

A. WARMUP

Type each line 2 times.

```
Speed             1 All of us have bad days now and then, but they do not last.
Accuracy          2 The quetzal, a superb green and gold bird, lives in Mexico.
Language Link     3 The exchange students arrived in winter and left in spring.
Numbers/Symbols   4 When Tip & Toe has a sale, buy 24 pairs of socks @ 25% off.
```

FACT FILE

One of the best-known birds of the desert is the roadrunner. This bird spends almost its entire life on the ground running, attaining speeds up to 40 kilometers (over 25 miles per hour). How does this speed compare with that of the best athletes today?

SKILLBUILDING

B. KEYPAD PRACTICE—4-DIGIT NUMBERS

Enter the following numbers column by column. Press ENTER after the final digit of each number. Keep your eyes on the copy, and use the proper finger for each key. Repeat if time permits.

Use correct fingers. Keep eyes on copy. Input accurately.

5	8964	8073	6182	8090	2401	3159	5361	6047
6	3103	2619	5079	9324	5561	8252	6873	7984
7	5295	5302	6416	7451	8564	2785	9790	1021
8	7206	6195	2840	5327	4963	7548	2080	1976
9	1847	8443	3594	1686	1378	9029	4303	4267

RESOURCES

- Lesson Plan 34
- Courseware Lesson 34
- Student Data Disk
- Wallchart
- Grading and Evaluation

LESSON 34

FOCUS

- Review the numeric keypad.
- Take timings to improve technique.
- Review the alphabetic keys.
- Take 3-minute timings.

BELLRINGER

As soon as students arrive at their workstations and log in, have them type the Warmup that reviews keys they have learned. Go over the purpose of each line as shown to the left of the copy.

TEACH

Activity B. Remind students that in the numeric keypad review they are typing consecutive numbers with no text; therefore, they should use the keypad rather than the top row for number typing.

FACT FILE

Have students interview someone they know who is involved in athletics. Brainstorm with students for questions to ask. Have them type a list of 10.

TEACH

Activity C. Remind students to press ENTER after the final digit of each number. Also point out that there is a decimal point in each number.

Activity D. Encourage students to try to increase speed with each 12-second timing. Also remind students to keep their elbows in when they are typing.

Activity E. Remind students to keep their eyes on the copy.

Activity F. Remind students that the alphabetic review will help them in the 3-minute timings that they will take in this lesson.

C. Keypad Practice—Decimal Numbers

Enter the following numbers column by column. Press ENTER after the final digit of each number. Keep your eyes on the copy, and use the proper finger for each key. Repeat if time permits.

80.5	9.72	67.04	4387.90	98.10	86.17
724.16	15.39	904.32	128.50	6524.01	349.05
7512.41	4607.09	583.55	95.63	141.16	2508.96
1204.78	672.80	808.23	379.94	6.39	677.28
339.45	453.92	1.62	4.63	7813.25	1.96

D. 12-Second Sprints

Take three 12-second timings on each line. Try to increase your speed on each timing.

You must repress your fears, or you will not be in control.
Our failures can teach us good lessons if we will let them.
When you have a dream, you must never, never give up on it.
You should give your best effort to everything that you do.
| | | | 5 | | | | 10 | | | | 15 | | | | 20 | | | | 25 | | | | 30 | | | | 35 | | | | 40 | | | | 45 | | | | 50 | | | | 55 | | | | 60

E. Technique Timings

Take two 30-second timings on each line. Focus on the technique at the left.

Keep your eyes on the copy.

Lau went to the cafe in the city to have a good dinner out.
She and Travis left the band and saw the parade in Detroit.
Isau moved the desk over to my right side during our class.
People who work at the desk like to keep paper on the left.
| 1 | 2 | 3 | 4 | 5 | 6 | 7 | 8 | 9 | 10 | 11 | 12

Teacher Notes

F. Alphabet Review

Type each line 1 time. Repeat if time permits.

```
23 Alf is able to add; Bill bikes by Beth; Cal can call Carli.
24 Darla's dad is Dale; Evi eats eggs; Flo's farm is far away.
25 Gary's grass is green; Hans has his hats; Ilse is innocent.

26 Just jump, Jeff; Kylie knows knives; Lyle loves Louisville.
27 Marta manages a mall; Nona noted nothing; Orion owns opals.
28 Pat pinches pennies; Quinn quietly quit; Rez reads rapidly.

29 Suni serves sushi; Tara tells tall tales; Uriah uses umber.
30 Val visits Vermont; Wilma washes windows; Xan x-rays Xylia.
31 Yvonne yearns for a yellow yo-yo; Zachariah's zest is zero.
```

G. Paced Practice

Turn to the Paced Practice routine beginning on page SB7. Take three 2-minute timings, starting at the point where you left off the last time.

H. 3-Minute Timings

Take two 3-minute timings on lines 32–40. Note your speed and errors.

Goal: 31/3'/5e

```
32      A rain forest and a jungle are not quite the same.      10
33 A rain forest has very lofty trees that form a canopy for   22
34 shorter trees as well as vines and other plants that grow   34
35 in the shade. The floor is more or less open. A jungle, on  45
36 the other hand, is the dense, scrubby brush that exists     57
37 on the floor after a rain forest has been cut.              66
38      Large rain forests can be found in the Amazon basin.    77
39 Rain forests give us timber and sites for crops like tea    88
40 and house many species.                                     93
   | 1 | 2 | 3 | 4 | 5 | 6 | 7 | 8 | 9 | 10 | 11 | 12  SI 1.26
```

Science Connections

TEACH

Activity G. Introduce students to the Paced Practice routine:

- Take a 1-minute timing to establish a base rate.
- Select a passage from Skillbuilding, page SB7, that is 2 words a minute faster than the rate set in the previous step.
- Take a 2-minute timing on this passage until the speed goal is achieved.
- Drop back 2 words a minute to the previous passage and type it until it is finished in 2 minutes with no more than 2 errors.

Activity H. Remind students that they will be typing for an additional minute in this timing; therefore, they may see their speed drop by a word or two until they get accustomed to this longer time.

ASSESS

- Have students check the Portfolio to view their accuracy in typing the keypad drills.
- Check students' scores in the Performance Chart. Compare their performance on 2-minute timings with their scores on the 3-minute timings.

CLOSE

Remind students to clean up their workstation when they leave.

Science Connections

Tell students that many rain forests are being destroyed by air pollution and over cutting for timber products. Have students compose an e-mail message to a friend that states how they feel about this destruction.

TECHNOLOGY TIP

To keep disks from being damaged, store them away from extreme heat or cold and liquids or food.

Disks also need to be stored away from strong magnetic fields, such as those found in stereo speakers.

LESSON 35

FOCUS

- Learn a capitalization rule.
- Review the numeric keypad.
- Use a P/P/P routine to build speed and improve accuracy.
- Take 3-minute timings.

BELLRINGER

As soon as students arrive at their workstations and log in, have them type the Warmup that reviews keys they have learned. Go over the purpose of each line as shown to the left of the copy.

TEACH

Activity B. Remind students to capitalize proper nouns, such as Thanksgiving, and the adjectives from proper nouns, such as the word Day if used with Thanksgiving or another holiday as an adjective.

Solutions:

Lou and Darian saw Chicago from the top of the Sears Tower.

We saw the American flag flying at our embassy in Scotland.

Mr. and Mrs. Haber wrote that they had visited San Antonio.

President Abraham Lincoln did write the Gettysburg Address.

LESSON 35

SKILLBUILDING

OBJECTIVES:

- Refine numeric keypad skills.
- Refine keyboarding skills.
- Learn capitalization rules.
- Type 31/3′/5e.

A. WARMUP

Type each line 2 times.

Speed	1	Set your goals, and then make plans to achieve those goals.
Accuracy	2	The bombastic flibbertigibbit was bedizened in a bombazine.
Language Link	3	We plan to travel on Tuesday to Baltimore for Thanksgiving.
Numbers/Symbols	4	Try this: 1 1/3 cup milk, 4/5 cup bananas, 1/8 cup raisins.

B. CAPITALIZATION

Study the rule and the examples below. Then edit lines 5–8 to correct any errors in capitalization.

Rule 3: Capitalize proper nouns and adjectives derived from proper nouns.

Tara and I always watch the Thanksgiving Day parade in Chicago.

Our supervisor, Mrs. Jazarian, is going to Tibet next year.

```
5 lou and darian saw chicago from the top of the sears tower.
6 we saw the american flag flying at our embassy in scotland.
7 mr. and mrs. haber wrote that they had visited san antonio.
8 president abraham lincoln did write the gettysburg address.
```


RESOURCES

- Lesson Plan 35
- Courseware Lesson 35
- Student Data Disk
- Wallchart
- Grading and Evaluation
- Language Link Worksheets

SKILLBUILDING

C. Keypad Review

Enter the following numbers column by column. Press Enter after the final digit of each number. Keep your eyes on the copy, and use the proper finger for each key. Repeat if time permits.

Use correct fingers. Keep eyes on copy. Be accurate.

9	3221	8997	5446	7114	2558	9336	5991	3775	4665	79.13
10	7987	6465	1323	4065	3120	9078	4005	7009	2003	10.05
11	5217	8469	1356	2007	3062	9940	1517	1492	1943	99.49
12	1541	1556	1603	1632	1689	1714	1763	1774	1775	18.04
13	6.59	2.58	37.4	20.0	9.48	7.11	30.6	51.2	8.83	25.67

D. PRETEST

Take a 1-minute timing on lines 14–17. Note your speed and errors.

```
14      The meadow is covered with sweet vetch and daisies. I     11
15 saw a covey of quail popping in and out of the shade and      22
16 a herd of cows foraging lazily among the bees. Soon it        38
17 will be too cold to walk in the meadow.                       41
   | 1 | 2 | 3 | 4 | 5 | 6 | 7 | 8 | 9 | 10 | 11 | 12
```

E. PRACTICE

SPEED: ***If you made 2 or fewer errors on the Pretest, type lines 18–25 two times each.***

ACCURACY: ***If you made more than 2 errors on the Pretest, type lines 18–21 as a group two times. Then type lines 22–25 as a group two times.***

***Discrimination reaches** are keys that are commonly substituted and easily confused. (wear)*

```
18 dsd sides dense shade dress daisy squad sedan dispel sedate
19 pop poise opens poach optic power piano opals proper option
20 wew wedge sweet weave tweed wreck vowel elbow twelve wealth
21 klk klutz bulky milky kilns slick click block plucky molusk

22 yuy ducky yours bumpy juicy murky truly query purify luxury
23 fgf gifts feign graft fling foggy fight grief forage fringe
24 vcv civil cover vicar covey havoc evict vetch vacate victor
25 mnm mania money numbs mines woman mints gnome sampan nomads
```

F. POSTTEST

Repeat the Pretest. Compare your Posttest results with your Pretest results.

LESSON 35

TEACH

Activity C. Remind students that in the numeric keypad review they are typing consecutive numbers with no text; therefore, they should use the keypad rather than the top row for number typing.

Activity D. Use the P/P/P routine to build skill. Have students speed up slightly the second time they type each Pretest line.

Activity E. Point out that the Practice lines focus on *discrimination reaches.* These reaches are easily confused.

Activity F. Remind students they should improve their speed and accuracy from the Pretest to the Posttest.

PRETEST/PRACTICE/POSTTEST

The ***Pretest/Practice/Posttest*** routines are designed to improve speed or accuracy.

- The ***Pretest*** identifies students' speed or accuracy needs.
- The ***Practice*** provides a variety of improvement drills.
- The ***Posttest*** (a repeat of the Pretest) measures improvement.

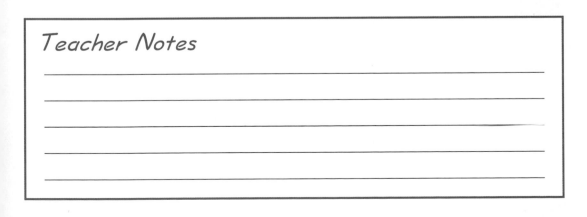

Teacher Notes

TEACH

Activity G. Remind students to pay attention to the spacing before and after punctuation marks.

Activity H. Again remind students that they will be typing for an additional minute. Therefore, they may see their speed drop by a word or two until they get used to this longer time. The goal is to type 31 words a minute for 3 minutes with no more than 4 errors.

ASSESS

- Watch students' hands as they reach for the number keys on the keypad.
- Have students check their Portfolio to view their accuracy in typing the keypad drills.
- Check students' scores in the Performance Chart. Have students view their progress they have made in the past few lessons when taking 2-minute timings. Compare their performance with their scores on the 3-minute timings.

CLOSE

Remind students to clean up their workstation when they leave. An organized work area will promote better performance in class.

G. Punctuation Spacing

Type each line 2 times. Note the spacing before and after each punctuation mark. Repeat if time permits.

Keep your eyes on the copy.

```
26 The shift of number 9 is (; be sure to hold anchor fingers.
27 Joy shops at Mann & Sons; she spent $72.33 today on slacks.
28 Add these numbers: 22, 33, 44, 77, 88, and 99. Answer: 363.

29 Paula owes Kim these amounts: $2.78, $3.47, $19.82, $21.42.
30 Sonja bought 44# of seed from Mrs. R. G. Herrera yesterday.
31 Look up Route #9 on the U.S.A. map for Ms. Lucky instantly.

32 Have you seen Perry? I think he went to 738 Mainard Street.
33 I need some #2 pencils. Will you get them for me at Paul's?
34 Belle and/or Jay will go to the airport tomorrow afternoon.
```

H. 3-Minute Timings

Take two 3-minute timings on lines 35–43. Note your speed and errors.

Goal: 31/3'/4e

```
35      Life on the Oregon Trail was not easy. The pioneers     10
36 had to leave in the spring and arrive before the winter      21
37 freeze blocked the passes. They packed their wagons with     32
38 all they owned and then walked beside them. Only those who   44
39 were sick or old or young rode on the journey. The plains    55
40 seemed endless, and the rivers that had to be crossed were   67
41 swift and raging. If a wagon fell behind, it might have to   79
42 be lightened quickly by taking off excess goods and leaving  91
43 them there.                                                  93
   | 1 | 2 | 3 | 4 | 5 | 6 | 7 | 8 | 9 | 10 | 11 | 12   SI 1.25
```

Social Studies Connections

Social Studies Connections

Have a class discussion about what students think life might have been like on the Oregon Trail. Ask students what items they would take if traveling on the Oregon Trail today. Why did they choose those items?

Out-of-Class Activity

Explain that Web pages contain links to other related Web pages or documents. By clicking on a link, students can learn information in a nonlinear way. Have students find five links from one source for a computer-related career. Have students record the path and bring this to class.

LESSON 36

ORIENTATION TO WORD PROCESSING

OBJECTIVES:

- Refine keyboarding skill.
- Refine techniques on adjacent and jump reaches.
- Learn word processing features.

A. WARMUP

Type each line 2 times.

Speed	1	Tom and Shelley may wish to sell this house if they own it.
Accuracy	2	While Sylvie waited, Jacques quickly fixed a dozen zippers.
Language Link	3	Winifred will accept delivery of paper from Brown Paper Co.
Numbers/Symbols	4	Joel Paxon got a 15% discount on the 24# of bread at B & B.

SKILLBUILDING

B. KEYPAD PRACTICE

Enter the following numbers column by column. Press ENTER after the final digit of each number. Keep your eyes on the copy, and use the proper finger for each key. Do not type the commas.

Numbers with 4 or more digits often contain commas to make the numbers easier to read. When entering numbers using the keypad, do not type the commas.

5	45.12	56.89	8,505	1,303	.89	404	975	488	312	38
6	36.78	74.04	9,606	5,238	.24	101	606	577	250	56
7	56.23	52.38	1,404	2,953	.72	232	491	186	598	71
8	90.46	58.52	2,505	1,404	.94	494	638	904	756	32
9	69.63	87.42	3,606	2,505	.62	456	240	496	387	97

LESSON 36

FOCUS

- Review typing on the keypad.
- Use a P/P/P routine to build speed and improve accuracy.
- Learn word processing features: New File, Open File, Close File, and Quit word processor.

BELLRINGER

As soon as students arrive at their workstations and log in, have them type the Warmup that reviews keys they have learned. Go over the purpose of each line as shown to the left of the copy.

TEACH

Activity B. Remind students to leave out the commas when using the keypad. Also remind students to press ENTER after the final digit of each number.

RESOURCES

Lesson Plan 36

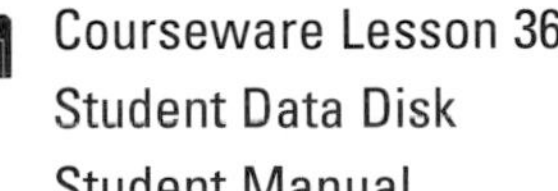
Courseware Lesson 36

Student Data Disk

Student Manual

COURSEWARE OVERVIEW

The KCA program will automatically "launch" the word processor when necessary. Be sure students know how to correctly exit the word processor so their documents are scored, and how to return to KCA.

Activities C–É. Remind students they should improve their speed and accuracy from the Pretest to the Posttest.

STUDENT MANUAL
Be sure students turn to the correct lesson in their Student Manual.

Activity F. Introduce students to the software manual. Explain how it will be used together with their textbook and computer software.

- Demonstrate how to start the word processing software.
- Use the pages in the manual to explain the parts of the computer screen.
- Show students how to open files to access the Practice activities.
- Show students how to close the files and exit the word processing program.

ASSESS

- Check to see if students show signs of improvement from the Pretest to the Posttest.
- Check the steps students use to start and close the word processing software.
- Watch to see if students can open and close files correctly.

CLOSE

Remind students to clean up their workstation when they leave.

C. PRETEST

Take a 1-minute timing on lines 10–13. Note your speed and errors.

```
10      If they have any extra fruit and milk, can you please    11
11 deliver them to the annex? I must buy twenty stamps before    23
12 tomorrow to mail my food-drive flyers. If I don't get these   35
13 in the mail quickly, we will not meet our goal.               44
   | 1 | 2 | 3 | 4 | 5 | 6 | 7 | 8 | 9 | 10 | 11 | 12
```

D. PRACTICE

SPEED: ***If you made 2 or fewer errors on the Pretest, type lines 14–21 two times each.***

ACCURACY: ***If you made more than 2 errors on the Pretest, type lines 14–17 as a group two times. Then type lines 18–21 as a group two times.***

Adjacent Reaches

```
14 ui suits fruit guilt quilt quint squid fluid guide build ui
15 we weigh swept tweed tower power dowel jewel fewer vowel we
16 lk caulk yolks talks hulks sulks stalk balky silky chalk lk
17 as vases masts tasks lasts pasta gases aspen cases bases as
```

Jump Reaches

```
18 ex excel exact exert exile exist extra annex vexed index ex
19 mp skimp mumps stamp plump imply champ ample swamp crimp mp
20 mo lemon month money movie mouse emote smoke among model mo
21 ce cents mince paces cease piece slice fence place faces ce
```

E. POSTTEST

Repeat the Pretest. Compare your Posttest results with your Pretest results.

FORMATTING

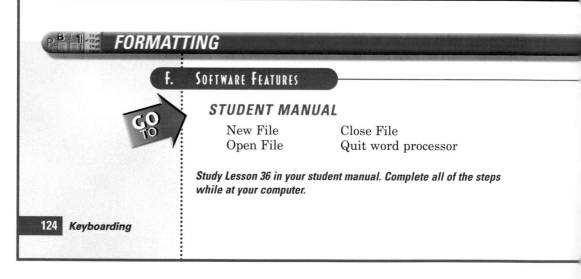

F. SOFTWARE FEATURES

STUDENT MANUAL

New File	Close File
Open File	Quit word processor

Study Lesson 36 in your student manual. Complete all of the steps while at your computer.

Teacher Notes

LESSON 37 ORIENTATION TO WORD PROCESSING

OBJECTIVES:

- Learn about special symbols.
- Learn word processing features.
- Type 31/3'/5e.

A. WARMUP

Type each line 2 times.

Speed	1	`We may make a nice profit if all of the work is done right.`
Accuracy	2	`From the tower Dave saw six big jet planes quickly zoom by.`
Language Link	3	`May saw her uncle at the Ohio State football game Saturday.`
Numbers	4	`Please buy 50 paper clips, 9 pencils, 7 pens, and 4 stamps.`

SKILLBUILDING

B. SPECIAL SYMBOLS

Many keys on the keyboard can be used to represent special symbols. The most common of these special symbols are shown below.

Symbols	Keystrokes	Examples
Roman numerals	Capital letters: I, V, X, L, C, D, and M	Chapters VII-XV
Feet and inches	Apostrophe, feet; quotation mark, inches	Marion is 5′ 2″.
Minutes and seconds	Apostrophe, minutes; quotation mark, seconds	My time: 3′ 15″
Multiply	Small letter x with a space before and after	What is 58 x 12?
Subtract	Single hyphen with a space before and after	240 - 106 = 134
Ellipsis	Three periods (space before, between and after); four periods if words are omitted at the end of the sentence.	He . . . and no

FOCUS

- Review special symbols.
- Learn to use a Preview Practice.
- Take 3-minute timings.
- Learn word processing features: Moving Around in a Document, Spelling Check, Correcting Errors, Backspacing, and Saving Files.

BELLRINGER

As soon as students arrive at their workstations and log in, have them type the Warmup that reviews keys they have learned. Go over the purpose of each line as shown to the left of the copy.

TEACH

Activity B. Explain to students the special symbols presented here. Demonstrate where these symbols are found on the keyboard.

RESOURCES

Lesson Plan 37
Courseware Lesson 37
Student Data Disk
Student Manual
Grading and Evaluation
PowerPoint

COURSEWARE OVERVIEW

As students learn to use the spell checker, remind them that they still must proofread their documents. Explain that the software automatically supplies file names for textbook activities.

TEACH

Activity C. Remind students to be aware of the spacing with the symbols.

Activity D. Remind students to work toward increasing their speed with each 12-second timing.

Activity E. Tell students that the purpose of the Preview Practice is to warm up for the 3-minute timings. Remind them to type each line 2 times.

FACT FILE

Have students use the Internet, library, or CD-ROM to research Kenya. Have them find three facts and bring these facts to class. Put a large world map up in the classroom. Have students type the facts they found and add these to Kenya on the map.

Activity F. Remind students that their goal is to type 31 words a minute for 3 minutes with no more than 5 errors.

C. Symbol Practice

Type each line 1 time. Notice the spacing with the symbols and how the symbols are used.

```
5  Dr. Karl told us to read Chapters II and IV from Volume XX.
6  At 6' 3", Mike was able to beat the record time of 10' 32".
7  Does Satbir know the answer to this: 480 x 120 – 150 x 307?
8  During a long, hot summer . . . water was extremely scarce.
```

D. 12- Second Sprints

Take three 12-second timings on each line. Try to increase your speed on each timing.

```
9  As you read a map, bear in mind that the top part is north.
10 If the top of a map is north, then the right of it is east.
11 Maps have legends that tell what the symbols and codes are.
12 When you can read maps, you possess a skill of great value.
   ||||5||||10||||15||||20||||25||||30||||35||||40||||45||||50||||55||||60
```

E. Preview Practice

Type each line 2 times as a preview to the 3-minute timings that follow.

```
13 zips expect Quaker January conference excitement basketball
14 finals their shown eight they this goal when ends the to if
```


Teacher Notes

F. 3-Minute Timings

Take two 3-minute timings on lines 15–23. Note your speed and errors.

Goal: 31/3'/5e

```
     Those five members of the basketball team hope to be       11
chosen as part of the main team. They will need a lot of        22
practice to attain this goal. However, they know what the       34
excitement will be if they are chosen for the finals.           45
     They expect that their team will be in first place in      56
its conference when the season ends. The team has shown a       67
lot more zip since February. Only eight more away games         78
have yet to be played. They must not lose the last game to      90
Quaker State.                                                   93
| 1 | 2 | 3 | 4 | 5 | 6 | 7 | 8 | 9 | 10 | 11 | 12          SI 1.23
```

FORMATTING

G. Software Features

STUDENT MANUAL

Moving Around in a Document
Spelling Check
Correcting Errors
Backspacing
Saving Files

Study Lesson 37 in your student manual. Complete all the practice activities while at your computor.

interNET CONNECTION

A Website dictionary is often an excellent place to start to locate the spelling of obscure words or new words that may not be in a standard printed dictionary yet. Use the Internet site http://www.onelook.com and look up various words such as *spam*, *netiquette*, and *smiley*.

interNET ACTIVITY

A resource for definitions of computer technology words is the Webopedia site. This online encyclopedia features a word of the day. Have students visit the site and check the word of the day for several days. The address is http://www.webopedia.com.

TEACH

STUDENT MANUAL

Be sure students turn to the correct lesson in their Student Manual.

Activity G. Continue orientation to word processing.

- Show students how to move around in a document using the mouse, the arrow keys, and special function keys.
- Show students how to activate and use the Spell Check feature.
- Teach students the difference between Save and Save As when saving a file.

ASSESS

- Watch students' hands as they type the special symbols.
- Walk around the room as students practice moving the insertion point within a document.
- Watch to see if students are able to activate and close the Spell Check dialog box.
- Be sure students are completing the Practice exercises in the manual correctly.
- Be sure students save their files correctly.

CLOSE

Remind students to clean up their workstation when they leave.

LESSON 38

FOCUS

- Review easily confused words.
- Review typing special symbols.
- Learn word processing features: Font Styles, Font Sizes, Print/Page Preview, Print.

BELLRINGER

As soon as students arrive at their workstations and log in, have them type the Warmup that reviews keys they have learned. Go over the purpose of each line as shown to the left of the copy.

CULTURAL CONNECTIONS

Emphasize to students that in our culture it is necessary to always be on time for business appointments. It also is important to be punctual when doing business abroad, despite local customs. Ask students why they think our culture values promptness.

LESSON 38

ORIENTATION TO WORD PROCESSING

OBJECTIVES:

- Learn about confusing words.
- Refine techniques on typing symbols.
- Learn word processing features.

A. WARMUP

Type each line 2 times.

Speed	1	Tom kept his bank records for both last year and this year.
Accuracy	2	Braxton's wacky quip amazed but vexed his girlfriend, Thuy.
Language Link	3	Svetlana will change planes at Kennedy Airport in New York.
Symbols	4	He saw Jan's new car. It's not "up" but "down"! (I'm sure.)

interNET CONNECTION

Some cultures consider being on time important. Other cultures are more flexible about time. For example, in Central and South America, it is common to arrive 30 minutes late for an appointment.

Search the Internet for other examples of time-related cultural diversity. How do businesspeople in the United States value time when appointments are made?

Use the following URL to research the protocol for meetings in Russia, which are very different from meetings in other countries. http://www.businesseurope.com/russia/meet.htm

RESOURCES

- Lesson Plan 38
- Courseware Lesson 38
- Student Data Disk
- Student Manual
- PowerPoint

COURSEWARE OVERVIEW

Tell students how, when, and where you want them to print their documents. Formatted documents also can be printed from within the KCA program.

B. Confusing Words

Easily confused words include* homonyms *(words spelled and pronounced alike) and* homophones *(words pronounced alike but spelled differently). Study the confusing words and their meanings shown below. Read each sentence carefully and determine which word should be used. Then edit lines 5–8 by choosing the correct word.

accept (v.) — to take willingly
except (prep.) — other than

stationary (adj.) — fixed, immovable
stationery (n.) — paper, writing materials

I will accept the award. Everyone attended except Jo.

The boat remained stationary while I wrote my letter on nautical stationery.

5 Why did she (except/accept) all of the programs (except/accept) the one entry?
6 Our motto will be, "We will (except/accept) nothing (except/accept) the best."
7 A (stationary/stationery) wall unit is used to store our new (stationary/stationery).
8 While he designed our new (stationary/stationery), he remained (stationary/stationery).

SKILLBUILDING

C. Technique Timings

Take two 30-second timings on each line. Focus on the techniques at the left.

Keep your fingers curved and your elbows in.

```
 9 You should know how you would use a computer before buying.
10 Decide what kinds of programs you will be using most often.
11 Will you be using database or spreadsheet programs with it?
12 Choose a computer that will meet all of your current needs.
  | 1 | 2 | 3 | 4 | 5 | 6 | 7 | 8 | 9 | 10 | 11 | 12
```


LESSON 38

TEACH

Activity B. Have students compose and type four sentences. Use each one of the words correctly in a separate sentence.

Solutions: Why did she accept all of the programs except the one entry?

Our motto will be, "We will accept nothing except the best."

A stationary wall unit is used to store our new stationery.

While he designed our new stationery, he remained stationary.

Activity C. Remind students to keep their fingers curved and their elbows in.

JOURNAL ENTRY

Have students write a journal entry about word pairs that give them trouble. Ask students to also write about the tricks they use to help them keep the words straight. Call on a few volunteers to read their entries to the class.

TEACH

Activity D. Ask students what types of jobs might use the symbols in this activity. Do any of these careers sound interesting to them?

STUDENT MANUAL

Be sure students turn to the correct lesson in their Student Manual.

Activity E. Continue orientation to word processing.

- Show students how to change fonts and font sizes.
- Demonstrate how to preview a document before printing it.
- Explain how to print a document. Emphasize the importance of saving the file before printing.

ASSESS

- See how many students applied the Language Link rule correctly by asking for a show of hands.
- Be sure students understand how to change fonts and font sizes.
- Watch students as they preview and print their documents. Be sure they all save their files before printing.

CLOSE

Remind students to clean up their workstation when they leave.

D. Symbol Review

Type each line 1 time. Repeat if time permits.

```
$   13 Buy 11 blue @ $.79, 43 purple @ $.85, and 17 green @ $1.19.
@   14 Our e-mail addresses are david@xyz.com or larry@netnow.com.

#   15 Carpet remnants #3, #16, and #37 sell for 25% and 35% less.
%   16 Their #7, #8, and #9 sizes are from 36% to 46% higher here.

&   17 Pair them as follows: 10 & 29, 38 & 47, 56 & 65, 135 & 780.
:   18 What is the correct date: 1919* or 1943* or 1955* or 2002*?

*   19 S & L* left at 10:30 and arrived at 11:45. Peter* was late.
=   20 The answers are: 91 + 82 = 173; 14 + 76 = 90; 24 + 36 = 60.

+   21 Lisa, did you know that (3 + 4)(2 + 6)(5 + 7) = 7 x 8 x 12?
()  22 Bella labeled items (10), (21), (65), (74), (83), and (92).

[]  23 Their [Aztec] houses were [very] old and expensive [$400K].
{}  24 Mrs. Gibson assigned this: ({7^2} {4^3}) + ({17^4} {13^5}).
<>  25 In ASCII, G < H and J < K. Are T > S and W > V and Z > A-Y?
```

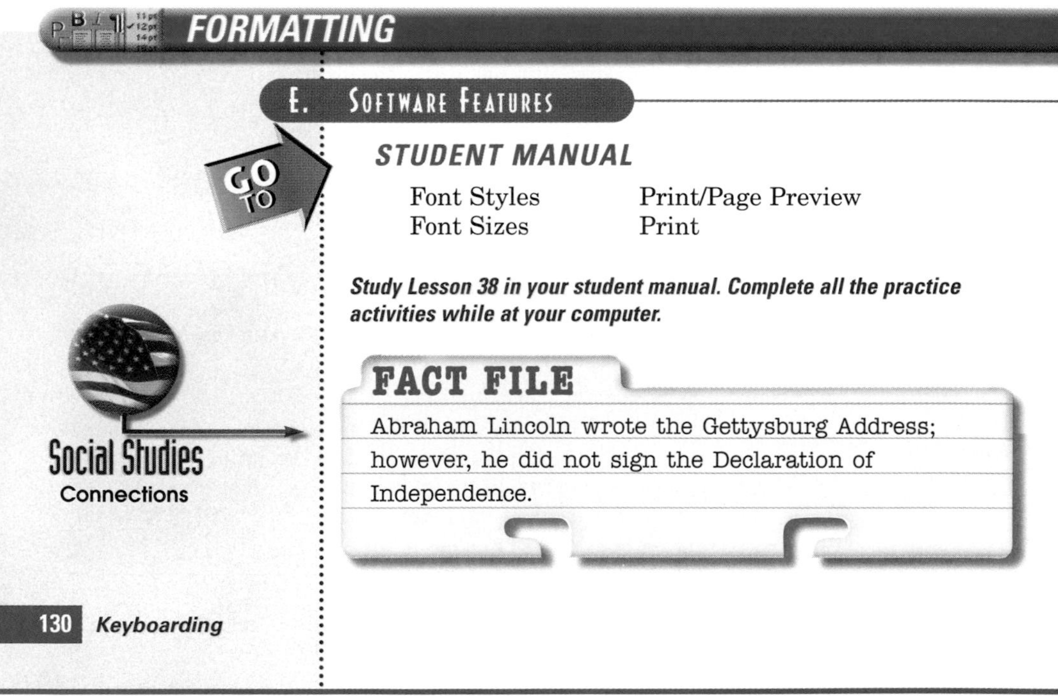

FORMATTING

E. Software Features

STUDENT MANUAL

Font Styles	Print/Page Preview
Font Sizes	Print

Study Lesson 38 in your student manual. Complete all the practice activities while at your computer.

Social Studies Connections

FACT FILE

Abraham Lincoln wrote the Gettysburg Address; however, he did not sign the Declaration of Independence.

Teacher Notes

Orientation to Word Processing

OBJECTIVES:

- Learn about confusing words.
- Refine skills on double letters and alternate reaches.
- Learn word processing features.

A. Warmup

Type each line 2 times.

Speed	1	I did not see her take the pencil, but I know that she did.
Accuracy	2	Taxi drivers are quick to zip by the huge jumble of wagons.
Language Link	3	It's the secretary who accepted the stationery on Thursday.
Numbers/Symbols	4	Lee cut the pieces of twine 9 1/2, 7 3/4, and 6 5/8 inches.

COMMUNICATION FOCUS

To avoid confusing people, choose your words carefully. Some words are often misunderstood and misused. Which of the following words give you difficulty?

accept—except access—excess than—then cite—sight—site

Look up the definitions of these words in a dictionary or thesaurus. Use each of them in a sentence. You may want to start a list of confusing words to review regularly.

LESSON 39

FOCUS

- Review easily confused words.
- Take 30-second OK timings.
- Use a P/P/P routine to build speed and improve accuracy.
- Learn word processing features: Alignment, Show/Hide, Reveal Codes, and Selecting Text.

BELLRINGER

As soon as students arrive at their workstations and log in, have them type the Warmup that reviews keys they have learned. Go over the purpose of each line as shown to the left of the copy.

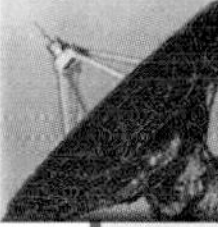

COMMUNICATION ACTIVITY

Have students compose a short story or essay that uses each of the confusing words. Remind students to write what comes to mind, then to go back and edit and proofread. Form groups and have students read their pieces within their groups.

RESOURCES

 Lesson Plan 39

Courseware Lesson 39

Student Data Disk

Student Manual

PowerPoint

TEACH

Activity B. Tell students these easy tricks to remember the correct usage of these words: the principal who is my pal is spelled *principal*; *it's* is really two words coming together—*it* and *is*. Have students use each of the four words correctly in a short paragraph they compose and type.

Solutions: The principle upon which this principal was hired is clear.

Does the principal know what principle affected the choice?

It's good to see that the firm is improving its poor image.

Its quiet movement is a sign that it's operating very well.

Activity C. Remind students that the purpose of the 30-second OK timing is to improve accuracy. The goal is to type without errors.

B. Confusing Words

Study the confusing words and their meanings shown below. Read each sentence carefully to determine which word should be used. Then edit lines 5–8 by choosing the correct word.

principle (n.)	rule, code of conduct
principal (adj.)	chief, leading
(n.)	a person in a leading position
it's	contraction meaning "it is"
its	possessive pronoun, belonging to it

The students consider the coach a man of principle.
The school principal treats all students fairly.
It's a challenge to hold a job after school and study.
The coach praised the team for its leadership.

```
5 The (principle/principal) upon which this (principle/principal)
  was hired is clear.
6 Does the (principle/principal) know what (principle/principal)
  affected the choice?
7 (It's/Its) good to see that the firm is improving (it's/its)
  poor image.
8 (It's/Its) quiet movement is a sign that (it's/its) operating
  very well.
```

SKILLBUILDING

C. 30-Second OK Timings

Take two 30-second OK (errorless) timings on lines 9–10. Then take two 30-second OK timings on lines 11–12. Goal: No errors.

```
 9 The students begin to excel when they have peace and quiet.
10 Analyze your study habits and learn to be successful daily.
11 When you type, try moving your fingers quickly to the keys.
12 I think I have answered all of your questions at this time.
   | 1 | 2 | 3 | 4 | 5 | 6 | 7 | 8 | 9 | 10 | 11 | 12
```


JOURNAL ENTRY

Have students write about any problems they have with these two confusing word pairs (*principle/principal* and *it's/its*) and any tricks they use to help them remember the correct usage. Call on a few volunteers to share their tricks.

D. PRETEST

Take a 1-minute timing on lines 13–16. Note your speed and errors.

```
13      When the food fight began, we all laughed. But Coach   11
14 Parr took one look and ushered all eight guilty students    22
15 to the office for mops and scrubbing supplies. All of them  31
16 were very quiet as they cleaned up the mess.
   | 1 | 2 | 3 | 4 | 5 | 6 | 7 | 8 | 9 | 10 | 11 | 12
```

E. PRACTICE

SPEED: ***If you made 2 or fewer errors on the Pretest, type lines 17–24 two times each.***

ACCURACY: ***If you made more than 2 errors on the Pretest, type lines 17–20 as a group two times. Then type lines 21–24 as a group two times.***

Double Reaches

```
17 ff offer cliff stuff bluff affix scuff cliff sniff whiff ff
18 oo goose looks shoot loose noose scoop boost swoop roost oo
19 rr error carry tarry berry merry worry sorry furry hurry rr
20 ee cheer jeers trees sleep keeps weeps breed creek deeds ee
```

Alternate Reaches

```
21 tight fight hairy eight sight bland rigid girls laugh Blair
22 chair girls chant clams flame worms their maybe prowl Chris
23 signs usher heist other growl light gowns proxy prism Diana
24 vigor field anvil bugle dozen quake names right soaps Jamel
```

F. POSTTEST

Repeat the Pretest. Compare your Posttest results with your Pretest results.

FORMATTING

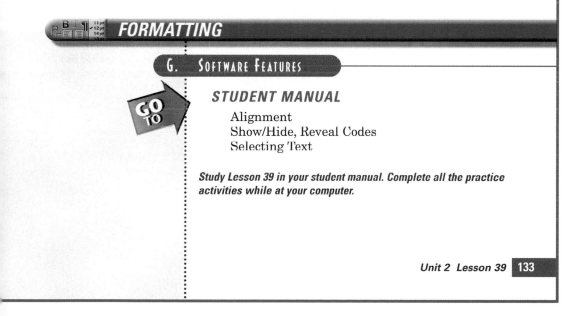

G. SOFTWARE FEATURES

STUDENT MANUAL

Alignment
Show/Hide, Reveal Codes
Selecting Text

Study Lesson 39 in your student manual. Complete all the practice activities while at your computer.

Teacher Notes

LESSON 39

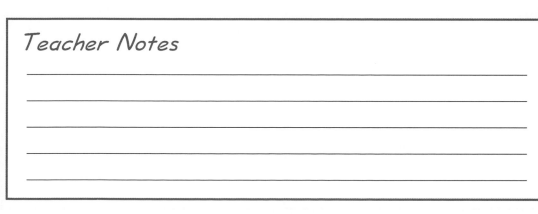

Activities D–F. Remind students their goal is to improve their speed and accuracy from the Pretest to the Posttest.

TEACH

STUDENT MANUAL

Be sure students turn to the correct lesson in their Student Manual.

Activity G. Continue orientation to word processing.

- Show students how to align copy using toolbar commands or keyboard shortcuts.
- Show students how to display codes in their word processing software.
- Show students how to select text by dragging the mouse over the text, clicking the mouse on the text, or using the shortcut keys.

ASSESS

- Check students' screens as they select text using one of the three techniques.

CLOSE

Remind students to save their files correctly before exiting the software. Also remind them to clean up their workstation when they leave.

LESSON 40

FOCUS

- Use a Diagnostic Practice.
- Use a Preview Practice.
- Take 3-minute timings.
- Learn a word processing feature: Help

BELLRINGER

As soon as students arrive at their workstations and log in, have them type the Warmup. Go over the purpose of each line as shown to the left of the copy.

Social Studies Connections

Explain to students that the story of Lewis and Clark has been called America's epic of exploration. Have students research on the Internet to learn why. Have each student find four facts about Lewis and Clark.

TEACH

Activity B. Tell students they should use the Diagnostic Practice: Numbers routine on page SB4 for this practice. Their goal is to type without errors.

Activity C. Remind students to sit up straight when typing.

LESSON 40

ORIENTATION TO WORD PROCESSING

OBJECTIVES:

- Learn word processing features.
- Type 32/3'/5e.

A. WARMUP

Type each line 2 times.

Speed	1 I like to read about Lewis and Clark as they traveled west.
Accuracy	2 Sacagawea was the Shoshone who helped navigate the terrain.
Language Link	3 The expedition included gunsmiths and carpenters in winter.
Numbers/Symbols	4 After 18 months and 4,000 miles, the journey ended in 1805.

SKILLBUILDING

B. DIAGNOSTIC PRACTICE: NUMBERS

Turn to the Diagnostic Practice: Numbers routine on page SB-4. Type one of the Pretest/Posttest paragraphs and identify any errors made. Then type the corresponding drill lines 2 times for each number on which you made 2 or more errors and 1 time for each number on which you made only 1 error. Finally, repeat the Pretest and compare your performance.

C. PREVIEW PRACTICE

Type each line 2 times as a preview to the 3-minute timings that follow.

```
5 in Civil maize Quapaw Arkansas smallpox Oklahoma eighteenth
6 migrate topped homes beans tribe clay went East and War the
```

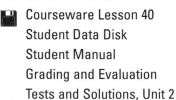

RESOURCES

 Lesson Plan 40

 Courseware Lesson 40

Student Data Disk

Student Manual

Grading and Evaluation

Tests and Solutions, Unit 2

COURSEWARE OVERVIEW

The KCA reference manual can be accessed from within the word processing programs. Remind students about this feature.

D. 3-Minute Timings

Take two 3-minute timings on lines 7–15. Note your speed and errors.

Goal: 32/3'/5e

Social Studies Connections

7 The Quapaw Indians first lived on the East Coast. They 11
8 moved to the prairies of the Midwest and later went to the 23
9 Arkansas River where they built and lived in homes of earth 35
10 topped with tree bark. They grew maize and beans and were 47
11 noted for their red and white clay jars. 55
12 In the eighteenth century, much of the tribe was wiped 66
13 out by smallpox. Floods and the Civil War caused the Quapaw 78
14 to migrate many times. Today, although the tribe has few 89
15 members, they live in Oklahoma. 96
| 1 | 2 | 3 | 4 | 5 | 6 | 7 | 8 | 9 | 10 | 11 | 12 SI 1.27

FORMATTING

E. Software Features

STUDENT MANUAL

Help

Study Lesson 40 in your student manual. Complete all the practice activities while at your computer.

TEACH

Activity D. Remind students that the goal on this timing is to type 32 words a minute for 3 minutes with no more than 5 errors.

CULTURAL CONNECTIONS

Tell students that during World War II, Navajo Indian soldiers wrote the secret codes for the United States in the Navajo language. It was the only code that was not broken during the war. Have students research these Navajo war heroes and their language and bring a few facts to class.

TEACH

STUDENT MANUAL

Be sure students turn to the correct lesson in their Student Manual.

Activity E. Show students how to access the Help Topics dialog box and to view the Help topics in their word processing software.

ASSESS

- Walk around the room to see if students are able to find a specific Help topic.

CLOSE

Remind students to save their files correctly before exiting the software.

Teacher Notes

UNIT 3 ORGANIZER

KEYBOARDING

Lesson	Focus	Special Features	Skillbuilding	Pretest/ Practice/ Posttest	Documents	GO TO Activities
41	Word Processing: Line Spacing, Underline; One-Page Academic Reports	Fact File, pp. 139, 142	p. 138		Report 1, pp. 140–141 Report 2, pp. 141–142	p. 139
42	Word Processing: Bold, Italic, Cut/ Copy/Paste; Proofreaders' Marks; One-Page Business Reports	Fact File, p. 146	p. 143		Report 3, pp. 145–146 Report 4, p. 146	p. 145
43	Word Processing: Numbers and Bullets; Agendas	Social Studies Connection, p. 148 Language Link, p. 147	pp. 147–148		Report 5, p. 150 Report 6, p. 150	p. 149
44	Reports with Paragraph and Side Headings	Social Studies Connection, p. 152 Fact File, p. 153	p. 151		Report 7, pp. 152–153 Report 8, p. 153	
45	Proofreaders' Marks; Minutes of Meetings	Language Link, p. 154	p. 155		Report 9, pp. 156–157 Report 10, p. 157	
46	Word Processing: Page Breaks, Page Numbering, Widow/Orphan Control; Multipage Reports	Cultural Connections, pp. 158, 161 Social Studies Connection, p. 160	p. 158	p. 159	Report 11, pp. 160–161	p. 160
47	One-Page Report with Numbered List, Paragraph Headings; Minutes of Meetings	Social Studies Connection, p. 163 Fact File, p. 163 Language Link, p. 162	p. 163		Report 12, p. 164 Report 13, pp. 164–165 Report 14, pp. 165–166	
48	Word Processing: Center Page, Date Insert; Block-Style Personal Business Letter	Fact File, pp. 167, 171 Social Studies Connection, p. 168 Journal Entry, p. 168	p. 167	p. 168	Letter 1, p. 170 Letter 2, p. 171	p. 169
49	Block-Style Personal Business Letter	Science Connection, p. 172 Internet Connection, p. 174	pp. 172–173		Letter 3, p. 173 Letter 4, p. 174	
50	Word Processing: Envelopes; Block-Style Letter with Envelope	Social Studies Connection, p. 176 Fact File, p. 176 Portfolio Activity, p. 179	p. 175	p. 176	Envelope 1, p. 179 Envelope 2, p. 179 Envelope 3, p. 179 Letter 5, p. 179	p. 178

UNIT 3 RESOURCE MANAGER

MULTIMEDIA
- Courseware: Lessons 41–60
- Student Data Disk
- Student Manual: Lessons 41–60

TEACHING TOOLS
- Lesson Plans: Lessons 41–60
- Block Scheduling Guide, Unit 3
- Language Link Worksheets: Lessons 41–60
- Multicultural Applications
- Academic Report Guide
- Solution Keys
- Cross-Curricular Activities: Lessons 41–60

RETEACHING/REINFORCEMENT
- Reteaching/Reinforcement Activities: Lessons 41–60
- Supplemental Production Activities: Lessons 41–60

ASSESSMENT and EVALUATION

Pretest/Practice/Posttest: pp. 159, 168, 176

Portfolio Activity: p. 179

Unit 3 Test

Timings: pp. 148, 163, 181, 184, 204, 214

Production Jobs: Reports 1–16; Letters 1–26; Envelopes 1–7

Grading and Evaluation

Electronic Teacher Classroom Resources

For your convenience, the teacher's materials are available on a CD-ROM. Having these resources available electronically enables you to print exactly what you need and revise materials as necessary.

Lesson	Focus	Special Features	Skillbuilding	Pretest/ Practice/ Posttest	Documents	GO TO Activities
51	Block-Style Business Letters	Language Arts Connection, p. 180 Internet Activity, p. 183 Language Link, p. 180	p. 181		Letter 6, pp. 182–183 Letter 7, p. 183	
52	Word Processing: Find and Replace; Block-Style Business Letters	Fact File, p. 184	p. 184		Letter 8, p. 185 Letter 9, p. 186 Letter 10, p. 186 Letter 11, p. 186	p. 185
53	Review	Language Link, p. 187	p. 188		Letter 12, pp. 188–189 Letter 13, p. 189	
54	Word Processing: Ruler and Tab Set; Modified-Block Style Letter		pp. 190–191	pp. 190–191	Letter 14, p. 192 Letter 15, p. 192	p. 191
55	Modified-Block Style Letters with Indented Paragraphs	Fact File, pp. 193, 194 Portfolio Activity, p. 195 Language Link, p. 193	p. 194		Letter 16, p. 195 Letter 17, p. 196	
56	Enclosure and Attachment Notations; Modified-Block Style Letters with Indented Paragraphs	Social Studies Connection, p. 197	pp. 197–198	pp. 197–198	Letter 18, p. 199 Letter 19, p. 199	
57	Letter Review	Cultural Connection, p. 200 Internet Activity, p. 201 Portfolio Activity, p. 203	p. 200		Letter 20, p. 201 Letter 21, pp. 202–203 Letter 22, p. 203	
58	Resumes	Fact File, p. 205 Portfolio Activity, p. 207	p. 204		Report 15, p. 207 Report 16, p. 207	
59	Application Letters (Block Style)	Fact File, p. 208 Communication Focus, p. 209 Portfolio Activity, p. 212	p. 208	p. 209	Letter 23, pp. 210–211 Letter 24, pp. 211–212	
60	Review	Cultural Connection, p. 214 Language Link, p. 213	p. 214		Letter 25, p. 214 Letter 26, p. 215	

SCANS Competencies in Glencoe Keyboarding with Computer Applications

Resources	Interpersonal Skills	Information	Systems	Technology
Throughout the course, students deal specifically with resources: allocating time for completing drills and documents, maintaining workstations, caring for computers and software.	Cultural Connection, pp. 158, 161	Career Bit, p. 137 Fact File, pp. 139, 142, 146, 153, 163, 167, 171, 176 Internet Connection, pp. 174 Social Studies Connection, pp. 148, 152, 160, 163, 168, 176 Science Connection, pp. 172	Internet Connection, p. 174 Fact File, pp. 142, 146, 163, 167, 171	Lessons 41–60 Internet Connection, p. 174 Fact File, pp. 142, 146, 163, 167, 171

UNIT 3 WORD PROCESSING

LESSONS 41–60

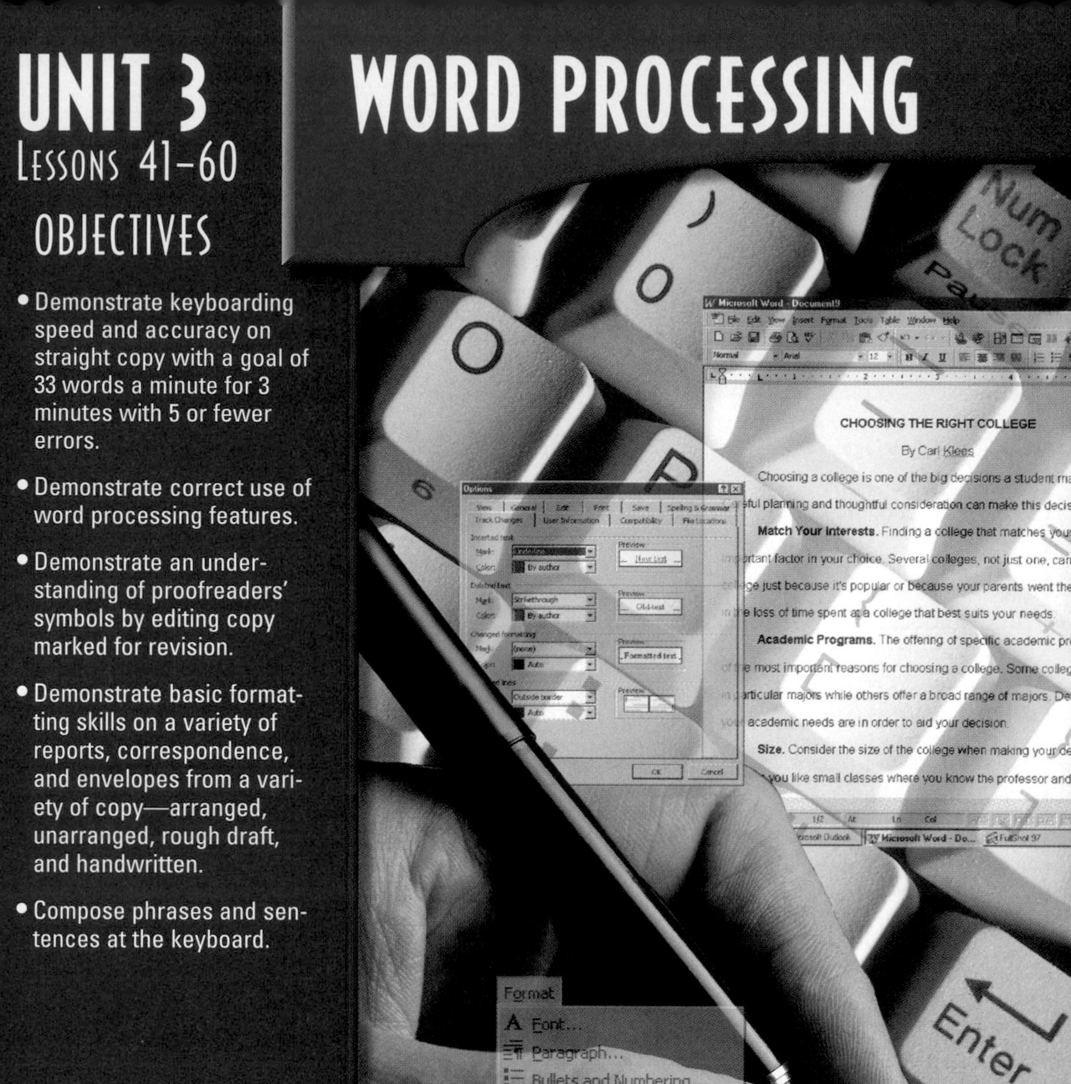

OBJECTIVES

- Demonstrate keyboarding speed and accuracy on straight copy with a goal of 33 words a minute for 3 minutes with 5 or fewer errors.
- Demonstrate correct use of word processing features.
- Demonstrate an understanding of proofreaders' symbols by editing copy marked for revision.
- Demonstrate basic formatting skills on a variety of reports, correspondence, and envelopes from a variety of copy—arranged, unarranged, rough draft, and handwritten.
- Compose phrases and sentences at the keyboard.

INTRODUCING THE UNIT

Tell students that they will learn the correct use of word processing features in this unit. Word processing allows them to compose letters, reports, and other documents. They will also learn proofreaders' marks and how to edit copy.

Explain to students that the goal in this unit is to reach a typing speed of 33 words a minute for 3 minutes with 5 or fewer errors. Encourage students to believe that this is an achievable goal.

Ask students if they have questions about what they are going to learn in this unit.

FUN Facts

Castles were built in Europe from the 8th century until around 1600. Fortified residents for kings and nobles, castles were small cities within stone walls. Most castles had a church, a prison, and a comfortable chamber for the lady of the castle. Dogs were kept as pets and pigs were kept as food. Outside the walls were villages of farmers who would take refuge inside the castle.

COURSEWARE OVERVIEW

The courseware automatically links to the specified word processor when students begin the applications. A KCA menu for exiting the word processor appears on the menu bar. Have students use the KCA menu to ensure that their documents are scored (keystrokes only) and saved to their data disks. Use the Teacher Manager program to view students' documents in the word processor (you will need their data disks) or have students print documents for you to check formats.

WORDS TO LEARN

bold
center page
cut/copy/paste
date insert
envelopes
italic
line spacing
numbering command
page break
page numbering
underline
widow/orphan control

CAREER BIT

RESERVATION AGENT

Reservation agents help people plan trips and make reservations. They answer telephone inquiries and offer suggestions on travel arrangements such as routes, time schedules, rates, and types of accommodation. They quote fares and room rates, make and confirm transportation and hotel reservations, and sell tickets. Agents use computerized systems to quickly obtain information needed to make, change, or cancel reservations for customers.

WORDS TO LEARN

The terms in Words to Learn are defined in the Glossary at the back of the book. Ask students if they are familiar with any of the terms. Have them define the terms they know. Compare their definitions with those in the Glossary.

CAREER BIT

After students read the information on reservation agents, invite a reservation agent or travel agent to class to speak. Have students write a letter of invitation. The letter should request the guest to bring along tickets, brochures, or other materials to help show students what the job is like. Students should type a list of questions to ask the guest and a thank-you letter after the guest has spoken.

COURSEWARE OVERVIEW

The courseware names all textbook documents. File names follow these conventions: a letter code for the type of document followed by the number of the document followed by a period and the software extension. The file name for Letter 15 is *L15.doc* (Word) and *L15.wpd* (WordPerfect).

FOCUS

- Learn word processing features: Line Spacing, Underline, and Margins.
- Learn how to format a one-page academic report.
- Type academic reports.

BELLRINGER

As soon as students arrive at their workstations and log in, have them type the Warmup. Go over the purpose of each line as shown to the left of the copy.

TEACH

Activity B. Remind students to type at a fast pace during the 12-second timings. At the end of the first and second timings, encourage students to type just one or two strokes faster on the next timing.

ONE-PAGE ACADEMIC REPORTS

OBJECTIVES:

- Learn word processing features.
- Format one-page academic reports with titles.
- Improve keyboarding skill.

A. WARMUP

Type each line 2 times.

Speed	1	Nancy came into the room knowing that we were hiding there.
Accuracy	2	Voltaire wrote about Zadig, a Babylonian forced into exile.
Language Link	3	Please buy oranges, apples, and bananas when you have time.
Numbers/Symbols	4	Go to the store (M & W Feed) and buy 9# of #7 corn* @ $.43.
		| 1 | 2 | 3 | 4 | 5 | 6 | 7 | 8 | 9 | 10 | 11 | 12

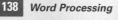

SKILLBUILDING

B. 12-SECOND SPRINTS

Take three 12-second timings on each line. Try to increase your speed on each timing.

5 He did see my two dogs walk along the road to the red barn.
6 The dogs went into the barn to eat their meals and to rest.
7 The cat was in the barn and did not want the dogs in there.
8 It was calm in the barn while the cat hid in the dark silo.
|||5|||10|||15|||20|||25|||30|||35|||40|||45|||50|||55|||60

RESOURCES

 Lesson Plan 41
 Courseware Lesson 41
Student Data Disk
Student Manual
Academic Report Guide
Supplementary Production Activities
Cross-Curricular Activities

COURSEWARE OVERVIEW

Documents have file names assigned by the software. This is to ensure that they are scored accurately. Documents done in the word processor are scored for keystrokes only.

FACT FILE

A ballet is a story acted out through the art of dancing. The French did much to develop the classical type of ballet we know today.

TEACH

Illustration

Use the illustration to point out the various parts of one academic report.

Activity C. Refer students to the Reference Manual in the textbook to study the various parts of an MLA report.

STUDENT MANUAL

Be sure students turn to the correct lesson in their Student Manual.

Activity D. Explain the software features presented in this activity.

- Demonstrate how to change line spacing.
- Demonstrate how to underline text.
- Demonstrate how to set margins.

FORMATTING

C. One-Page Academic Reports

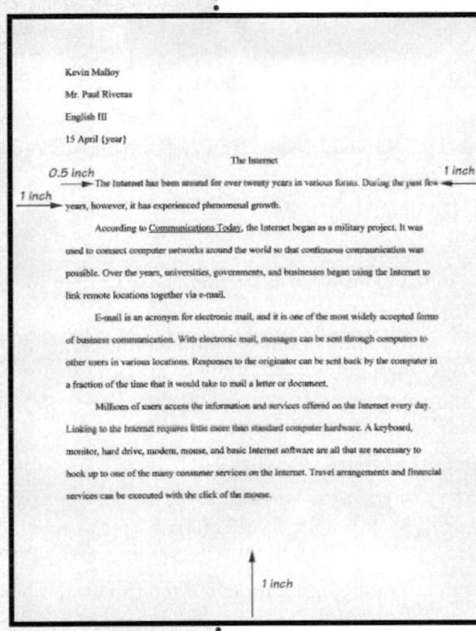

Kevin Malloy

Mr. Paul Riveras

English III

15 April {year}

The Internet

The Internet has been around for over twenty years in various forms. During the past few years, however, it has experienced phenomenal growth.

According to Communications Today, the Internet began as a military project. It was used to connect computer networks around the world so that continuous communication was possible. Over the years, universities, governments, and businesses began using the Internet to link remote locations together via e-mail.

E-mail is an acronym for electronic mail, and it is one of the most widely accepted forms of business communication. With electronic mail, messages can be sent through computers to other users in various locations. Responses to the originator can be sent back by the computer in a fraction of the time that it would take to mail a letter or document.

Millions of users access the information and services offered on the Internet every day. Linking to the Internet requires little more than standard computer hardware. A keyboard, monitor, hard drive, modem, mouse, and basic Internet software are all that are necessary to hook up to one of the many consumer services on the Internet. Travel arrangements and financial services can be executed with the click of the mouse.

There are many different formats for reports. Academic reports, however, are usually formatted in the MLA (Modern Language Association) style. To format a report in MLA style:

1. Use 1-inch top, bottom, and side margins.
2. Double-space the entire report, including the heading information.
3. Type the heading information (your name, your teacher's name, the class name, and the date) at the left margin.
4. Type the date in military style: 15 April {year}.
5. Center and type the title with initial capital letters for each important word.
6. Indent paragraphs 0.5 inch.

D. Software Features

STUDENT MANUAL

Line Spacing   Underline   Margins

Study Lesson 41 in your student manual. Complete all the practice activities while at your computer. Then complete the jobs that follow.

FACT FILE

Have students research to find other forms of dance performed throughout the world. Then hold a class discussion about dance. Write the names of the different dance forms students have learned about on the board. Ask students what the benefits of dance are. (artistic expression, good form of exercise, entertainment value, etc.)

TEACH

Report 1. Introduce one-page academic reports.

- Remind students to set line spacing for double-spacing before they begin typing a one-page report.
- Remind students that word wrap is used when typing the report. When typing the body of the report, the ENTER key is pressed only at the end of a paragraph.

PORTFOLIO *Activity*

If students' portfolio goals include demonstrating progress, they may want to include a report from this lesson. Encourage students to evaluate their work and include comments in their portfolio.

WORD PROCESSING

REPORT 1
One-Page MLA Format

Type this report in MLA format. Underline the magazine title in the second paragraph.

Kevin Malloy

Mr. Paul Riveras

English III

15 April {year}

The Internet

The Internet has been around for over twenty years in various forms. During the past few years, however, it has experienced phenomenal growth.

According to Communications Today, the Internet began as a military project. It was used to connect computer networks around the world so that continuous communication was possible. Over the years, universities, governments, and businesses began using the Internet to link remote locations together via e-mail.

E-mail is an acronym for electronic mail, and it is one of the most widely accepted forms of business communication. With electronic mail, messages can be sent through computers to other users in various locations. Responses to the originator can be sent back by the computer in a fraction of the time that it would take to mail a letter or document.

TECHNOLOGY TIP

You can tell a lot by looking at an Internet address. A **.com** extension means a commercial site; **.mil** is a military address; **.gov** is a government site; **.edu** is an educational address; **.net** is an Internet administration site; **.org** is a professional or non-profit organization site.

Out-of-Class Activity

Have students type a one-page report on the topic of their choice. Encourage them to use a topic that relates to one of the other courses they are currently taking. To help students get started, brainstorm with them about possible topics.

Millions of users access the information and services offered on the Internet every day. Linking to the Internet requires little more than standard computer hardware. A keyboard, monitor, hard drive, modem, mouse, and basic Internet software are all that are necessary to hook up to one of the many consumer services on the Internet. Travel arrangements and financial services can be executed with the click of the mouse.

REPORT 2

One-Page MLA Format

Type this report in MLA format. Underline the book title in the last paragraph.

Lindy Alvarez

Mrs. Karen Schmidt

Computer Literacy II

13 November {year}

Software Ethics

Everyone who owns a computer uses software for various activities such as word processing, spreadsheets, and games.

That neat game your friend has would be great to add to your collection of games. Of course, you would also allow your friend to make a copy of one of your games. Before you copy software, be aware that you and your friend would be breaking the law.

TEACH

Report 2. Introduce one-page academic reports.

- Remind students to set line spacing for double-spacing before they begin typing a one-page report.
- Remind students that word wrap is used when typing the report. When typing the body of the report, the ENTER key is pressed only at the end of a paragraph.

FACT FILE

Tell students why it is both unethical and illegal to copy software. (Unethical because it hurts someone—the author. Illegal because it violates copyright laws.) Ask what they would do if they worked for a company that is copying software illegally. What if a friend is doing the same?

*inter*NET ACTIVITY

Have students access the MLA home page: <http: //www.mla.org_homepage.htm.> Explain that the Modern Language Association (MLA) sets the style for academic reports. Have students find three facts about MLA style.

Language Arts Connection

Introduce students to *The Chicago Manual of Style,* the reference book used by writers for books. Journalists use *The Associated Press Stylebook and Libel Manual* as their reference. Have students research other style guides.

ASSESS

- Walk around the room as students are completing the Line Spacing, Underline, and Margin Practice activities on pages 140–142.
- As students begin typing the reports, walk around the room and point out correct and incorrect formatting to individual students.
- After students finish typing Reports 1 and 2, have them view their work on the screen to see if they made any errors. If errors were made, have students make corrections.
- Check to see if students have underlined the title of the magazine in Report 1 and the title of the book in Report 2.

CLOSE

If students do not finish both reports during the class period, make sure they save their work so that they can complete it the next time this class meets. Remind students to clean up their workstation when they leave.

Illegal copying of software is called piracy. When you purchase software, you have the right to use the software only on your computer. New methods of preventing software piracy are being implemented every year. Soon every computer will have a "fingerprint" that will prevent a person from installing software on another person's computer.

The creators and writers of the software that you purchase in stores own what is called a copyright on their programs. A copyright is a legal right to exclusive publication, distribution, sale, or use of the copyrighted work. Musicians and authors own the same right for songs and books they write. The ease of copying software, even though it is illegal and unethical, has caused a real problem for the owners of software copyrights. Jane Ellis writes in her book, <u>Don't Share That Software!</u>, that what seems like a harmless thing to do is costing businesses and consumers millions, perhaps billions, of dollars.

FACT FILE

Microprocessors (computer chips) are the brains for personal computers. They are also used in many common items including microwave ovens, VCRs, and TV remote controls. Before the invention of microprocessors, machines could be programmed to do only one task at a time.

Teacher Notes

LESSON 42 ONE-PAGE BUSINESS REPORTS

OBJECTIVES:

- Improve keyboarding skill.
- Learn proofreaders' marks.
- Learn word processing features.
- Format a one-page business report with a title and by-line.

A. WARMUP

Type each line 2 times.

Speed	1 Have you been to the new cafe that is down on Marsh Street?
Accuracy	2 Egyptians carved the Sphinx to guard King Khafre's pyramid.
Language Link	3 Please accept the stationery that Principal White gave you.
Numbers/Symbols	4 Bill paid $85 for 3 shirts and $197.50 for 2 pair of pants.

| 1 | 2 | 3 | 4 | 5 | 6 | 7 | 8 | 9 | 10 | 11 | 12

SKILLBUILDING

B. CONCENTRATION DRILLS

Type each line 1 time. Concentrate on keeping your eyes on the copy. Repeat if time permits.

5 accommodation lackadaisical weatherproofed environmentalist
6 objectionable bougainvillea characteristic hyperventilation
7 philosophical discombobulate identification thoughtlessness
8 filibustering noninvolvement reconnaissance departmentalize

C. TECHNIQUE CHECKPOINT

Type each line 2 times. Repeat if time permits. Focus on the technique at the left.

Do not hesitate before or after pressing the space bar.

9 I will not go to Joe Yen's home if he has gone to the mall.
10 You are the one to be at the home when all of us have gone.
11 It is a good idea to have me save all of my pay that I can.
12 Go get the cat and the dog so we can get to the park early.

RESOURCES

 Lesson Plan 42

 Courseware Lesson 42

Student Data Disk

Student Manual

Supplementary Production Activities

COURSEWARE OVERVIEW

You may want to explain the Undo and Redo buttons at this time so that if students make a mistake they can easily correct it.

LESSON 42

FOCUS

- Learn word processing features: Bold, Italic, and Cut/Copy/Paste.
- Learn proofreaders' marks.
- Learn how to format a one-page business report.
- Type business reports.

BELLRINGER

As soon as students arrive at their workstations and log in, have them type the Warmup. Go over the purpose of each line as shown to the left of the copy.

TEACH

Activity B. Concentration Drills require students to focus their attention and keep their eyes on the copy. Most of the words in the Concentration Drill have multiple syllables. Many are words that students do not use everyday.

Activity C. Remind students that proper technique is a building block for speed and accuracy.

TEACH

Activity D. Stress the importance of using standardized proofreaders' marks. Tell students proofreaders' marks allow revisions in copy to be made quickly. They also allow one person to indicate the revisions for another person to type.

Activity E. Refer students to the Reference Manual in the textbook to study the various parts of a business report.

FORMATTING

D. Proofreaders' Marks

Proofreaders' marks are used to indicate changes and corrections in a document (called a rough draft) that is being revised for final copy. Study the proofreaders' marks and examples that follow, and learn what each mark means.

Proofreaders' Marks	Draft	Final Copy
Omit space	data base	database
Insert	if hes going not	if he's not going,
Capitalize	Maple street	Maple Street
Delete	a final draft	a draft
Insert space	allready to #	all ready to
Change word	and if you when	and when you
Use lowercase letter	our President	our president
Paragraph	¶ Most of the	Most of the
Bold	He did say	He **did** say

E. One-Page Business Report

The format of a business report is different from an academic report. To format a business report:

1. Use default side and bottom margins.
2. Double-space the entire report. Change the line spacing before you begin the report.
3. Leave an approximate 2-inch top margin (press ENTER 3 times).
4. Center and type the report title in all caps and bold.
5. Center and type the subtitle (a further description of the title) or the byline (the author's name) in initial caps.

Language Arts Connections

Have students use the Internet or the library to research proofreaders' marks. Remind students of the different style books you discussed in Lesson 41. This is where they can find proofreaders' marks. Using poster board and markers, have students make a chart of proofreaders' marks.

SCHOOL TO CAREER

Brainstorm with students how proofreaders' marks are used in different careers. Encourage them to think of careers other than writing and editing. Have them write the careers on the board then research one career, and give a short report to the class.

F. Software Features

STUDENT MANUAL

Bold Cut/Copy/Paste
Italic

Study Lesson 42 in your student manual. Complete all the practice activities while at your computer. Then complete the jobs that follow.

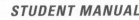

WORD PROCESSING APPLICATIONS

REPORT 3

One-Page Business Report

Type the following one-page report. Make the corrections indicated by the proofreaders' marks.

THE AMAZING COMPUTER

by Gayle Todd

The computer is and amazing electronic device. It can compute complex calculations, store vast amounts of data, and process information with the stroke of a key. All this can take place within amatter of ~~minutes~~ seconds.

Computers are a significant part of our lives, and new and exciting uses are continually being developed. soft-ware is the fastest changing component ofthe computer. new and improved versions of Software are frequently introduced that improve the capability and functions ofthe computer.

according to one of the monthly computer magazines, ~~Education Software~~, what and how we learn has also been affected by the computer. Interactive Software ~~allows~~ enables students and

TEACH

STUDENT MANUAL

Be sure students turn to the correct lesson in their Student Manual.

Activity F. Explain the software features presented in this activity.

- Demonstrate how to bold and italicize text as you type.
- Demonstrate how to bold and italicize exisiting text.
- Demonstrate cutting, copying, and pasting text.

Report 3. Introduce one-page business reports.

- Caution students to read Report 3 carefully before typing the text to be sure they know what changes to make.
- Remind students to set line spacing for double-spacing before they begin typing a one-page report.
- Instruct students to press ENTER three times before typing the title.
- Provide examples of academic and business reports to illustrate differences.
- Remind students to press ENTER only at the end of a paragraph.

FACT FILE

Explain that Internet addresses begin with "http," which stands for hypertext transfer protocol. Hypertext is text that can be connected to other documents; protocols are instructions that tell computers how to send hypertext documents. Have students open a Web address.

TEACH

Report 4. Advise students to check the formatting when they cut and paste.

ASSESS

- Walk around the room as students are completing the Bold, Italic, and Cut/Copy/Paste Practice activities on pages 145–146.
- As students begin typing Report 3, walk around the room and point out correct and incorrect formatting to individual students.
- After students finish typing Report 3, have them view their work on the screen to see if they made any errors. If errors were made, have students make corrections.

CLOSE

If students do not finish the report during the class period, make sure they save their work so that they can complete it the next time this class meets. Remind students to clean up their workstation when they leave.

PORTFOLIO *Activity*

If students' portfolio goals include demonstrating progress, they may want to include some of the reports from this lesson. Encourage students to evaluate their work and add comments to their portfolio.

teachers to explore subject areas previously limited to textbooks. Math and Science classes utilizes the computer to teach complex concepts using a hands-on approach. Language Arts and Literature classes write reports and creative assignments using computers. Business classes teach students to use the latest software currently being used in businesses and colleges. Computers continue to become an integrated part of our lives. It would be ~~hard~~ difficult, if not impossible, to name an area of our ~~life~~ lives that has not been affected by this amazing device.

REPORT 4
One-Page Business Report

Open Report 3 and revise it by moving the second paragraph to the beginning of the report. Move the last paragraph to before the third paragraph.

FACT FILE

To prevent damage to your computer screen, use a screen saver. A screen saver displays constantly moving images. These moving images prevent your screen from being etched by an image that does not change for a period of time. You can set the amount of time your computer is idle before the screen saver automatically appears. There are many different kinds of screen savers including graphics, photos, or animated characters.

Teacher Notes

LESSON 43 LISTS AND AGENDAS

OBJECTIVES:

- Learn word processing features.
- Compose at the keyboard.
- Format enumerations in agendas.
- Type 33/3'/5e.

A. WARMUP

Type each line 2 times.

Speed	1	After the cats ate lunch, they bathed their paws and faces.
Accuracy	2	Quentin and Ynez Zbleski moved to Phoenix, Arizona, in May.
Language Link	3	It's just weird how the kitten lost its red leather collar.
Numbers/Symbols	4	On August 23-25, A.D. 79, 19-23 feet of ash buried Pompeii.

| 1 | 2 | 3 | 4 | 5 | 6 | 7 | 8 | 9 | 10 | 11 | 12

B. COMPOSING AT THE KEYBOARD

Answer each question with a few words or short phrases.

5 Which season is your favorite?
6 What is the most recent movie you have seen?
7 Where would you like to go on summer vacation?
8 Who is your favorite recording artist?

SKILLBUILDING

C. DIAGNOSTIC PRACTICE: ALPHABET

Turn to the Diagnostic Practice: Alphabet routine on page SB1. Type one of the Pretest/Posttest paragraphs and identify any errors made. Then type the corresponding drill lines 2 times for each letter on which you made 2 or more errors and 1 time for each letter on which you made only 1 error. Finally, repeat the Pretest and compare your performance.

Unit 3 Lesson 43 **147**

RESOURCES

- Lesson Plan 43
- Courseware Lesson 43
- Student Data Disk
- Student Manual
- Supplementary Production Activities
- Grading and Evaluation

COURSEWARE OVERVIEW

Mention to students that different software packages have different defaults for features such as bullets and numbers. Throughout the program, we encourage you to use defaults.

LESSON 43

FOCUS

- Compose short answers.
- Take 30-second OK timings and 3-minute timings.
- Type agendas and enumerations in reports.
- Learn the word processing feature for page numbering.

BELLRINGER

As soon as students arrive at their workstations and log in, have them type the Warmup. Go over the purpose of each line as shown to the left of the copy.

TEACH

Activity B. After students complete the composing activity, have them choose one of the topics and write three short paragraphs about the subject. Then have students move the third paragraph to the beginning of the report and move the original first paragraph to the end of the report.

Solutions: Answers will vary.

Activity C. Make sure students understand that Diagnostic Practice is designed to help identify areas that need improvement and provide needed practice.

TEACH

Activity D. Point out that 30-second OK timings are designed to encourage accuracy.

Activity E. Point out that the words in the Preview Practice are used in the timing that follows.

Activity F. Remind students to be aware of their posture, to sit up, keep their elbows in, and their feet flat on the floor. The goal is to type 33 words a minute for 3 minutes with no more than 5 errors.

FACT FILE

For more than 1,500 years, Pompeii, an ancient city of Italy, lay beneath the ashes of an earthquake that completely destroyed it in A.D. 79. The discovery of Pompeii taught us about life in that ancient city. Have students research facts about Pompeii.

D. 30-Second OK Timings

Take two 30-second OK (error-free) timings on lines 9–10. Then take two 30-second OK timings on lines 11–12. Goal: no errors.

```
 9      Exercise your fingers on these drill lines every day,   11
10  and watch them zip and bound over all of the keys quickly.  23

11      Exercise such as walking gives your body the zest it    11
12  needs to adjust to the pace needed to maintain good health. 23
    | 1 | 2 | 3 | 4 | 5 | 6 | 7 | 8 | 9 | 10 | 11 | 12
```

E. Preview Practice

Type each line 2 times as a preview to the timings that follow.

```
13  worship weather freedom journey equipped Pilgrims craftsmen
14  disease friends native their north knew farm fish hunt guns
```

F. 3-Minute Timings

Take two 3-minute timings on the paragraphs. Note your speed and errors.

Goal: 33/3'/5e

```
15      The Pilgrims were a mix of people who wanted freedom    11
16  to worship and poor farmers and craftsmen who hoped for a   22
17  better life. They had guns but knew little about hunting.   34
18  They planned to fish but knew nothing about fishing.        44
19      When their journey took them north of their target,     55
20  it was winter, and they found they were not equipped for    66
21  the harsh weather. Almost half of the Pilgrims froze or     77
22  died of hunger and diseases. In the early spring, four      89
23  native friends taught them to farm, hunt, and fish.         99
    | 1 | 2 | 3 | 4 | 5 | 6 | 7 | 8 | 9 | 10 | 11 | 12 SI 1.28
```

Social Studies Connections

148 *Word Processing*

Social Studies Connections

Direct students to the Disney film *Squanto: A Warrior's Tale.* This movie gives the Native American perspective of the Pilgrim's arrival. Have students type a short report in MLA style about the Pilgrims and Native Americans.

Multiple Learning Styles

To help auditory learners, read aloud (or have a student read aloud) directions for activities and timings. Also suggest that students make an audio tape of the information they want to learn. They can play the tape while they are doing other things such as traveling to school.

G. Numbered and Bulleted Lists

Use numbers or bullets to display items in a list. Numbers and bullets are automatically positioned at the left margin, and carryover lines are automatically indented to align with the text in the line above.

1. If the order of the items is important, use numbers; otherwise, use bullets.
2. If the list is part of a single-spaced document, single-space the list, press ENTER 2 times before and after the list.
3. If the list is part of a double-spaced document, double-space the list (press ENTER only 1 time before and after the list).

H. Agendas

An agenda may be a list of topics to be discussed at a meeting, or it may be a formal program of a meeting. To format an agenda:

1. Use default side and bottom margins.
2. Leave an approximate 2-inch top margin (press ENTER 6 times).
3. Center and type the name of the committee or the company in all caps and bold.
4. Press ENTER 2 times; then center and type *Meeting Agenda* in initial caps.
5. Press ENTER 2 times; then center and type the date in initial caps.
6. Press ENTER 2 times; then turn on the numbering command and type each item.

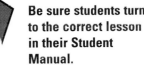

I. Software Features

STUDENT MANUAL

Numbers and Bullets

Study Lesson 43 in your student manual. Complete all the practice activities while at your computer. Then complete the jobs that follow.

TEACH

Activity G. Review the information for using the bullets and numbering feature.

Activity H. Explain that automatic numbering for lists makes numbering lists easy. If you make changes in a list, use automatic numbering and the item numbers are changed automatically. You can also choose different kinds of numbers including Arabic numbers, roman numerals, or letters.

STUDENT MANUAL

Be sure students turn to the correct lesson in their Student Manual.

Activity I. Explain the software features presented in this activity.

- Demonstrate how to add bullets and numbers as you type.
- Demonstrate how to add bullets and numbers to existing text.

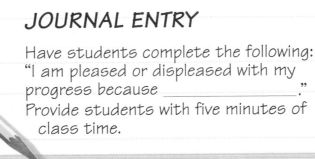

JOURNAL ENTRY

Have students complete the following: "I am pleased or displeased with my progress because ."
Provide students with five minutes of class time.

TEACH

Report 5. Remind students to use the numbering feature and to not space before or after the diagonal.

Report 6. Explain to students the need for making corrections indicated by the proofreaders' marks.

ASSESS

- Walk around the room as students are completing the practice activities on page 149.
- As students begin typing Report 5, walk around the room and point out correct and incorrect formatting.

CLOSE

If students do not finish Report 6 during the class period, make sure they save their work so that they can complete it the next time this class meets. Remind students to clean up their workstation when they leave.

PORTFOLIO *Activity*

If students' portfolio goals include demonstrating progress, they may want to include some reports from this lesson. Encourage students to evaluate their work and include comments in their portfolio.

REPORT 5
Agenda

Type the following agenda using the bullets and numbering feature for the numbered items. Do not space before or after the diagonal.

ASSOCIATION OF COMPUTER USERS

Meeting Agenda

January 6, {year}

1. Access the World via the Internet, Christine Melrose/Alexander Room
2. Break/President's Foyer
3. Technology in the Workplace, Willard Gallagher/Saturn Room
4. Virtual Reality: A Training Tool, Michael Laney/Franklin Room
5. Lunch/Ballroom A
6. Teleconference Roundtables, Steven Pulliam and Karen Klein/Ballroom B

REPORT 6
List

Type this report using the bullets and numbering feature. Double-space the entire report.

ANNUAL CRAFT FAIR

November 30, {year}

Our annual craft fair is fast approaching. As you know, we rely heavily on donations from staff, students, and local businesses to make this a success. Following is a list of items that are still needed. Please share this list with as many people as possible.

- White or other light colored poster board
- Plywood sheets that are approximately 8 ft by 4 ft
- Any kind of folding chairs
- Large rolls of white craft paper that will be used to cover tables
- Any kind of plastic or wire display racks
- Large, recyclable trash bags

Teacher Notes

LESSON 44 REPORTS WITH HEADINGS

OBJECTIVES:

- Improve keyboarding skill.
- Format reports with side headings and paragraph headings.

A. WARMUP

Type each line 2 times.

Speed	1	I am quite sure that we have had rain every day this month.
Accuracy	2	Zanzibar, a part of Tanzania, exports cassava and coconuts.
Language Link	3	Except for one, all students wanted to take a French class.
Numbers/Symbols	4	Pets & Paws will groom my dog for $45 (that's a lot) today.

| 1 | 2 | 3 | 4 | 5 | 6 | 7 | 8 | 9 | 10 | 11 | 12

SKILLBUILDING

B. 12-SECOND SPRINTS

Take three 12-second timings on each line. Try to increase your speed on each timing.

5 We all like to be able to have fun and get the chores done.
6 While we work, we may find more work that needs to be done.
7 As we work at a job, we know what to do and it gets easier.
8 The more you do the same task, the better you become at it.

| | | | 5 | | | | 10 | | | | 15 | | | | 20 | | | | 25 | | | | 30 | | | | 35 | | | | 40 | | | | 45 | | | | 50 | | | | 55 | | | | 60

C. PACED PRACTICE

Turn to the Paced Practice routine beginning on page SB7. Take three 2-minute timings, starting at the point where you left off the last time.

LESSON 44

FOCUS

- Learn how to format a report with side headings.
- Learn how to format a report with paragraph headings.
- Type a report with side headings.
- Type a report with paragraph headings

BELLRINGER

As soon as students arrive at their workstations and log in, have them type the Warmup. Go over the purpose of each line as shown to the left of the copy.

TEACH

Activity B. Remind students to type at a fast pace during the 12-second timing. At the end of the first and second timings, encourage students to type just one or two strokes faster on the next timing.

Activity C. Review with students the procedure for the Paced Practice activity. (See Lesson 34, page 119.)

RESOURCES

 Lesson Plan 44

 Courseware Lesson 44

Student Data Disk

Student Manual

Supplementary Production Activities

Grading and Evaluation

TEACH

Activity D. Refer students to the Reference Manual in the textbook to study the format for typing paragraph and side headings in a report.

Report 7. Point out that side headings are typed in bold and all caps.

Social Studies Connections

Have students research Kenya on the Internet and write a short report on one aspect of the republic. Have students make a copy of their report and give it to two other students to proofread. Have students use proofreaders' marks to correct any errors.

FORMATTING

D. Reports With Paragraph and Side Headings

Side Headings break a report into specific sections. Type side headings:
1. At the left margin in all caps and bold.
2. With a double space before and after.

Paragraph Headings are minor subdivisions of a report. Type paragraph headings:
1. Indented 0.5 inch.
2. In initial caps and bold.
3. Followed by a period (also in bold).
4. Followed by one space.

WORD PROCESSING APPLICATIONS

REPORT 7

One-Page Report With Side Headings

Social Studies Connections

Type the following report with side headings. Double-space the report.

KENYA THE BEAUTIFUL
By Sharon Eldridge

The republic of Kenya is located near the equator on the east coast of Africa. One of the most beautiful places on earth, it's blessed with a rich assortment of wildlife and spectacular scenery. Kenya's most famous landmark, Mount Kilimanjaro, is located in Tanzania.

TOURISM

Visitors from all over the world come to see the variety of plant and animal species found here. Beautiful, uncrowded beaches are found along the coastline with snorkeling and diving being popular recreation activities.

WILDLIFE

The wildlife of Kenya is among the most populous and diversified in the world. Large herds of zebras, giraffes, elephants, gazelles, and other grazing animals are seen roaming

Out-of-Class Activity

Have students type a one-page report about an activity in which they have recently participated. Suggest topics related to sports, hobbies, and academics. The report should include side or paragraph headings. Have students check each other's reports.

Science Connections

Have students research wildlife in Kenya. Choose four or five wildlife categories and write these on the board. Have students add information they learned about Kenya's wildlife beneath each category.

the landscape in search of food. There is also an abundance of predator animals such as the leopard, the wild dog, and the cheetah.

LANDSCAPE

Both the deserts and highlands can be found in Kenya. The forests that once covered the highlands have been decreasing due to clearing the land for crops. The desert area has little in the way of trees, but grazing grasses cover the desert floor.

REPORT 8

One-Page Report With Paragraph Headings

Type the following report with paragraph headings. Double-space the report, and remember to turn off bold after typing the period in the paragraph heading.

Science Connections

FACT FILE

The crested caracara is also known as the Mexican eagle. The crested caracara is often seen in the Sonoran Desert perched on giant saguaro or organ pipe cactus. This bird typically does not hunt for food; rather it eats carrion instead.

BIRD WATCHING IS FUN

By Thomas Chastain

Bird watching is the most popular and fastest growing outdoor activity for people of all ages. Both young and old delight in observing all kinds of birds from the common backyard bird to the majestic eagle. No special equipment is needed for bird watching; it is easily the most inexpensive outdoor activity today.

Birds are identified in two ways, either by sight or by sound. Learning to identify birds is challenging, educational, and fun. There is also a sense of accomplishment when the identification is correct.

Identification by Sight. When a bird is perched in a tree, it can be identified by its silhouette, by its movement, or by its flight pattern. The color and special markings of a bird also help to identify it.

Identification by Sound. Identifying birds by sound is an additional aid to identification and also adds fun to bird watching. Sound is also a way for the blind to participate in this fun activity. Birds sing for two reasons: to find a mate and to mark their territory. Many birds look alike making positive identification difficult. Sound is one way to distinguish between look-alikes. Birds that look alike generally have very different songs. Knowing the song of a particular bird can aid in positive identification.

LESSON 44

TEACH

Report 8. Point out that the basic difference between side headings and paragraph headings is capitalization: side headings are typed in all caps and paragraph headings are typed with initial caps only.

PORTFOLIO *Activity*

If students' portfolio goals include demonstrating progress, they may want to include reports from this lesson. Encourage students to evaluate their work and include comments in their portfolio.

ASSESS

- Check to see if students are increasing their speed as they complete the 12-second timings.
- As students begin typing the reports, walk around the room and point out correct and incorrect formatting for individual students. Check to be sure that the headings are formatted correctly.

CLOSE

If students do not finish Report 8, make sure they save their work so that they can complete it the next time this class meets.

***interNET* ACTIVITY**

Have students use the Internet to research birds, then draw or paste pictures of the birds on a poster. Have them type the name and a few facts about each bird to create a collage.

LESSON 45

FOCUS

- Focus on subject-verb agreement.
- Learn additional proofreaders' marks.
- Learn word processing applications: formatting minutes of meetings.

BELLRINGER

As soon as students arrive at their workstations and log in, have them type the Warmup. Go over the purpose of each line as shown to the left of the copy.

TEACH

Activity B. Point out the subject and the verb in each sentence. Help students to understand that singular subjects require singular verbs and pronouns and that plural subjects require plural verbs and pronouns.

Solutions: The computer prices have greatly fallen in March.

Ed's past experiences in sales have aided his growth.

Dan's method was not good for organizing supplies.

The volunteers' hard work is appreciated by all.

MINUTES OF MEETINGS

OBJECTIVES:

- Learn the rule for subject-verb agreement.
- Learn additional proofreaders' marks.
- Format minutes of meetings.

A. WARMUP

Type each line 2 times.

```
Speed          1 The Pilgrims were brave, but they did not know how to live.
Accuracy       2 Samoset and Squanto, a Wampanoag, helped the Pilgrims farm.
Language Link  3 The principle behind her actions was accepted; she was not.
Symbol         4 If ({X + Y} < {A - B}), then ({A - B} > {X + Y}), isn't it?
                 | 1 | 2 | 3 | 4 | 5 | 6 | 7 | 8 | 9 | 10 | 11 | 12
```

B. SUBJECT-VERB AGREEMENT

Study the rule and examples below. Then edit lines 5–8 by choosing the correct verb to agree with the subject in each sentence.

Rule 4: Use singular verbs and singular pronouns with singular subjects and plural verbs and plural pronouns with plural subjects.

Singular subject and verb:

The doctor advised his patients to stay in bed.

She called her doctor to see if she should get a flu shot.

Plural subject and verb:

Several doctors were able to agree on the prognosis.

They were relieved that Dad's chest pains were gone.

```
5 The computer prices (has/have) greatly fallen in March.
6 Ed's past sales experiences (has/have) aided his growth.
7 Dan's method (was/were) not good for organizing supplies.
8 The volunteers' hard work (is/are) appreciated by all.
```


RESOURCES

 Lesson Plan 45

 Courseware Lesson 45

Student Data Disk

Student Manual

Supplementary Production Activities

Language Link Worksheets

SKILLBUILDING

C. Diagnostic Practice: Alphabet

Turn to the Diagnostic Practice: Alphabet routine on page SB-1. Type one of the Pretest/Posttest paragraphs and identify any errors made. Then type the corresponding drill lines 2 times for each letter on which you made 2 or more errors and 1 time for each letter on which you made only 1 error. Finally, repeat the Pretest and compare your performance.

FORMATTING

D. Proofreaders' Marks

More proofreaders' marks are illustrated below. Study these proofreaders' marks and learn what each mark means.

Proofreaders' Marks	Draft	Final Copy
Transpose	how you can	how can you
Single-space	ss first line second line	first line second line
Double-space	ds first line second line	first line second line
Spell out	keep 1 copy	keep one copy
Don't delete	our two copies	our two copies
Move left	She fell	She fell
Move right	The final	The final
Move as shown	The two pages extra	The extra two pages
Italic	ital Vogue magazine	*Vogue* magazine
underline	u/l Vogue magazine	Vogue magazine

TEACH

Activity C. Make sure that students understand that this Diagnostic Practice activity is designed to help identify areas that need improvement and provide needed practice.

Activity D. Review the proofreaders' marks students learned in Lesson 42, then introduce the new proofreaders' marks. Ask students why it is important to learn these symbols.

Language Arts Connection

Type a section from a piece of literature and add several errors. Have students correct the errors using proofreaders' marks. As homework, have students search newspapers and other printed material for errors and mark with proofreaders' marks.

SCHOOL TO CAREER

Explain that students will use proofreaders' marks regardless of their career. Have students type a phrase or two to explain how proofreaders' marks could be used in the following careers: administrative assistant, college professor, retail clerk, waitress, and medical transcriber.

TEACH

Activity E. Explain to students that minutes of meetings provide a permanent record of what happened at the meeting. Minutes should be distributed to all meeting participants as soon after the meeting as possible. If the participants find any errors in the minutes, they should contact the secretary immediately.

Report 9. Remind students to leave a blank line before and after each side heading, and to use today's date.

E. Minutes of Meetings

The secretary of an organization is responsible for taking and keeping minutes of meetings. Minutes are the official record of what happened at a meeting. To format minutes:

1. Use default side and bottom margins and single spacing.
2. Leave an approximate 2-inch top margin (press Enter 6 times).
3. Center and type the name of the committee or the company in all caps and bold.
4. Press Enter 2 times, then center and type *Minutes of the Meeting* in initial caps 2 lines below the title.
5. Press Enter 2 times, then center and type the date in initial caps.
6. Type the side headings in all caps and bold at the left margin. Leave a blank line above and below the side headings.
7. After the last section, press Enter 2 times and begin the closing at the left margin.
8. Then press Enter 4 times and type the secretary's name and title at the left margin.

WORD PROCESSING APPLICATIONS

REPORT 9
Minutes of Meeting

Type these minutes. Remember to leave a blank line before and after the side headings.

LINCOLN HIGH PARENT ORGANIZATION

Minutes of the Meeting

(Current Date)

ATTENDANCE

The monthly meeting of the Lincoln High School Parent Organization was held in the school library with Mario Palazollo presiding. The meeting was called to order at 7 p.m. Forty-seven parents attended. All officers were present.

APPROVAL OF MINUTES

The secretary read the minutes of the last meeting. They were approved as read. The treasurer reported that there was $790 in the treasury as of the end of the month.

JOURNAL ENTRY

Have students write in their journals about any meetings they have attended. Were minutes taken? If so, did they receive a copy afterwards? If not, would receiving a copy have been helpful? Why or why not?

ADJOURNMENT

There being no new business, the meeting was adjourned at 9 p.m.

Respectfully submitted,

Mary Upchurch, Secretary

REPORT 10

Minutes of Meeting

Type these minutes. Remember to leave a blank line above and below the side headings.

THE CHILDREN'S FOUNDATION
Minutes of the Meeting
November 16, {year}

CALL TO ORDER
The meeting was called to order by Elsie Russell at 11:30 a.m. in the Conference Room of the Foundation Building. The meeting was adjourned at 1 p.m. All members of the Board were present except Anne Laster.
UNFINISHED BUSINESS
The minutes of the October meeting were read and approved. The Treasurer's report was reviewed an accepted as submitted. The proposed budget was presented and discussed. There was agreement that the amount listed in the budget from from grants ~~the budget~~ as income should be ~~should be~~ decreased from $40,000 to $20,000. The proposed budget was approved as revised.

The Executive Director's report was read and accepted. Ms. Russell shared that we need to expend our Big Brother/Big Sister outreach program. Suggestions for accomplishing this were discussed.
NEW BUSINESS
Mrs. Costa suggested that there is a need to establish a publicity Plan for the work being done by the foundation. This would help with fund-raising ~~efforts~~.

Motion carried to accept ④ new prospective members as members of the Board of Directors--Richard Bates, Wanda Rudd, Florence Loucks and Melvin Hearns.
Respectfully submitted,
Arlene Porter, Secretary

Unit 3 Lesson 45 **157**

TEACH

Report 10. Remind students to keep their eyes on the copy when typing Report 10. Ask them what they need to remember about blank lines and side headings.

PORTFOLIO *Activity*

If students' portfolio goals include demonstrating progress, they may want to include some reports from this lesson. Encourage students to evaluate their work and include comments in their portfolio.

ASSESS

- As students begin typing the reports, walk around the room and point out correct and incorrect formatting to individual students.
- After students finish typing the reports, have them view their work on the screen to see if they made any errors. If errors were made, have students make corrections.

CLOSE

If students do not finish Report 10 during the class period, make sure they save their work so that they can complete it the next time this class meets. Remind students to clean up their workstation when they leave.

Out-of-Class Activity

Ask students what organizations they belong to. Suggest they volunteer to record and type the minutes of the organization's meetings. If they do not belong to any organizations, have them visit a meeting and unofficially record the minutes.

TECHNOLOGY TIP

In business today, people from different parts of the world can meet through teleconferencing. Participants speak to one another on the phone while their image is shown on a television screen. Minutes are e-mailed to participants within hours.

LESSON 46

FOCUS

- Take 30-second timings.
- Use a P/P/P routine to build speed and improve accuracy.
- Learn word processing features: Page Breaks, Page Numbering, and Widow/Orphan Control.
- Learn how to format and type a multipage report.

BELLRINGER

As soon as students arrive at their workstations and log in, have them type the Warmup. Go over the purpose of each line as shown to the left of the copy.

TEACH

Activity B. Remind students that their goal for 30-second timings is to improve speed with each of the timings.

LESSON 46 MULTIPAGE REPORTS

OBJECTIVES:

- Practice the top-row number keys.
- Learn word processing features.
- Format multipage reports.

A. WARMUP

Type each line 2 times.

```
Speed              1 Check our lists to be sure that we are ready for this trip.
Accuracy           2 Zachariah analyzed the situation and queried the witnesses.
Language Link      3 One box of staplers and tape dispensers was shipped Monday.
Numbers/Symbols    4 Our seat assignments are 30-41, 56-72, 88-109, and 111-114.
                     | 1 | 2 | 3 | 4 | 5 | 6 | 7 | 8 | 9 | 10 | 11 | 12
```

CULTURAL CONNECTIONS

A chemical engineer, Mae Jemison, became the first African American woman to go into space in 1992.

SKILLBUILDING

B. 30-SECOND TIMINGS

Take two 30-second timings on lines 5–6. Then take two 30-second timings on lines 7–8. Try to increase your speed on each timing.

```
5      Before you drive a car, adjust your seat and mirrors.   11
6 Lock the doors and buckle your seat belt. Drive with care.   23

7      Eating like a bird could mean drilling trees for ants   11
8 or diving in water for fish or probing mud for marine life.  23
  | 1 | 2 | 3 | 4 | 5 | 6 | 7 | 8 | 9 | 10 | 11 | 12
```


RESOURCES

 Lesson Plan 46

 Courseware Lesson 46

Student Data Disk

Student Manual

Supplementary Production Activities

C. PRETEST

Take a 1-minute timing on lines 9–12. Note your speed and errors.

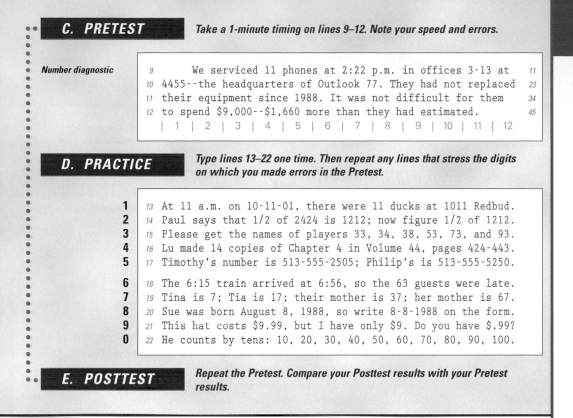

Number diagnostic

9 We serviced 11 phones at 2:22 p.m. in offices 3-13 at 11
10 4455--the headquarters of Outlook 77. They had not replaced 23
11 their equipment since 1988. It was not difficult for them 34
12 to spend $9,000--$1,660 more than they had estimated. 45
| 1 | 2 | 3 | 4 | 5 | 6 | 7 | 8 | 9 | 10 | 11 | 12

D. PRACTICE

Type lines 13–22 one time. Then repeat any lines that stress the digits on which you made errors in the Pretest.

1 13 At 11 a.m. on 10-11-01, there were 11 ducks at 1011 Redbud.
2 14 Paul says that 1/2 of 2424 is 1212; now figure 1/2 of 1212.
3 15 Please get the names of players 33, 34, 38, 53, 73, and 93.
4 16 Lu made 14 copies of Chapter 4 in Volume 44, pages 424-443.
5 17 Timothy's number is 513-555-2505; Philip's is 513-555-5250.

6 18 The 6:15 train arrived at 6:56, so the 63 guests were late.
7 19 Tina is 7; Tia is 17; their mother is 37; her mother is 67.
8 20 Sue was born August 8, 1988, so write 8-8-1988 on the form.
9 21 This hat costs $9.99, but I have only $9. Do you have $.99?
0 22 He counts by tens: 10, 20, 30, 40, 50, 60, 70, 80, 90, 100.

E. POSTTEST

Repeat the Pretest. Compare your Posttest results with your Pretest results.

FORMATTING

F. MULTIPAGE REPORTS

To format a multipage report:

1. Use default side margins for all pages of the report.
2. Leave an approximate 2-inch top margin on page 1; leave a 1-inch top margin on continuing pages.
3. Leave an approximate 1-inch bottom margin on all pages. A soft page break will be inserted automatically at the bottom of each page as you type the report.
4. Turn on widow/orphan protection.
5. Do not number the first page. However, number all continuing pages at the top right.

TEACH

Activity C. Be sure students are using proper fingers for numbers as they take the 1-minute timing. They should focus on both speed and accuracy.

Activity D. Have students note the numbers they had trouble with in the Pretest. Then have them note which lines in the Practice contain those numbers. They should type those lines twice.

Activity E. Remind students they should improve both their speed and accuracy from the Pretest to the Posttest.

PRETEST/PRACTICE/POSTTEST

The ***Pretest/Practice/Posttest*** routines are designed to improve speed or accuracy.

- The ***Pretest*** identifies students' speed or accuracy needs.
- The ***Practice*** provides a variety of improvement drills.
- The ***Posttest*** (a repeat of the Pretest) measures improvement.

Activity F. Refer students to the Reference Manual in the textbook to study the format for typing a multipage report.

TEACH

STUDENT MANUAL

Be sure students turn to the correct lesson in their Student Manual.

Activity G. Explain the software features presented in this activity.

- Demonstrate how to insert a page break.
- Demonstrate how to insert page numbers.
- Demonstrate how to use widow/orphan control.

Report 11. Remind students that when they reach the bottom of the first page in the multipage report:

- A page break will automatically appear to move them to the second page.
- The widow/orphan protect feature will prevent single lines in a paragraph from appearing at the bottom of the page.
- The page 2 heading will automatically be placed at the top of page 2.

Art Connections

Explain to students that in Japan things of beauty are highly regarded. Have students find pictures in magazines, books, or on the Internet of Japanese art forms and bring these to class to display.

G. Software Features

STUDENT MANUAL

Page Breaks Page Numbering
Widow/Orphan Control

Study Lesson 46 in your student manual. Complete all the practice activities while at your computer. Then complete the following jobs.

WORD PROCESSING APPLICATIONS

REPORT 11
Multipage Report

Type the following multipage report with side and paragraph headings. Remember to turn on widow/orphan protection.

Social Studies Connections

A VISIT TO A JAPANESE HOME
By Matthew Stedman

Japan is one of the most urbanized nations in Asia. The use of modern equipment and facilities has changed the traditional way of life. While most Japanese people live in the city, over one-fourth of the population still live in the countryside where the traditional way of life still prevails.

CITY LIFE

Most city dwellers live in high-rise apartments with modern conveniences such as electric appliances and central heat. Many Japanese city dwellers use public bath houses, while others prefer the privacy of their own baths. City life in Japan is much like that of the western world with mass transit, restaurants, entertainment, and shopping located close by.

FACT FILE

A widow is the last line of a paragraph printed by itself at the top of a page. An orphan is the first line of a paragraph printed by itself at the bottom of a page. The default setting in many word processing programs prevents widows and orphans.

COUNTRY LIFE

The countryside dwellers of Japan live quite differently than city dwellers. They live in small houses built out of bamboo. Since Japan is prone to earthquakes, these bamboo structures hold up better in earthquakes than heavier structures.

Rooms in the House. Traditional houses generally have three to four rooms that serve as both living and sleeping quarters. A kitchen is also part of the house but does not serve as the living or sleeping quarters. The kitchen has a stove made of clay or brick and is heated with straw. In some homes the stoves are heated with compressed gas.

Floor Coverings. The floor of Japanese homes is covered with woven straw mats that measure six feet by three feet. The mats are woven by hand by the women of the house, typically the mother and grandmother. In order to keep the mats clean, they remove their shoes before entering the house.

Furniture. The furniture found in most traditional homes consists of little in the way of decoration with the exception of some embellished parchment doors and flower arrangements.

Outside the House. The Japanese love to grow flowers, and their homes are usually surrounded by flowering plants. They are avid gardeners and are masters at creating beautiful gardens with ponds and ornate statues.

CULTURAL CONNECTIONS

Kangi is a Japanese system of writing that uses characters that have been adapted from Chinese writing. The writing is so beautiful it is considered a kind of art. Learning to use this system takes many years of practice.

Teacher Notes

ASSESS

- As students begin typing the reports, walk around the room and point out correct and incorrect formatting to individual students.
- Be sure that students have placed the page number in the correct location on page 2 and that it is typed in the correct format.
- After students finish typing the reports, have them view their work on the screen to see if they made any errors. If errors were made, have students make corrections.

CLOSE

If students do not finish the report during the class period, make sure they save their work so that they can complete it the next time this class meets. Remind students to clean up their workstation when they leave.

PORTFOLIO *Activity*

If students' portfolio goals include demonstrating progress, they may want to include some reports from this lesson. Encourage students to evaluate their work and include comments in their portfolio.

TEACH

- Learn a subject/verb agreement rule.
- Type a Preview Practice for a timing.
- Take 3-minute timings.
- Review and type reports and minutes of meetings.

BELLRINGER

As soon as students arrive at their workstations and log in, have them type the Warmup. Go over the purpose of each line as shown to the left of the copy.

TEACH

Activity B. Remind students that *the number* takes a singular verb and that *a number* takes a plural verb. Have students check each other's work for accuracy. Have students correctly type any sentences they missed.

Solutions: A number of students in the class are working on a project.

The number of men attending the convention was greater than expected.

The number of cars to be parked exceeds the number of spaces available.

A number of workers were waiting for word about that.

LESSON 47 REVIEW

OBJECTIVES:

- Learn the rules for correct subject-verb agreement.
- Review reports and minutes of meetings.
- Type 33/3'/5e.

A. WARMUP

Type each line 2 times.

Speed	1	The Sun is center of our solar system and our closest star.
Accuracy	2	The Aztecs built Tenochtitlan on an island in Lake Texcoco.
Language Link	3	The seas of Australia include the Tasman Sea and Coral Sea.
Technique	4	Ada Bob Cam Don Evi Fay Gil Hal Ian Joy Kay Lon Mya Nan Ola
		| 1 | 2 | 3 | 4 | 5 | 6 | 7 | 8 | 9 | 10 | 11 | 12

B. SUBJECT/VERB AGREEMENT

Study the rule and examples below. Then edit lines 5–8 by choosing the correct verb for subject/verb agreement.

Rule 5: The subject *the number* takes a singular verb; *a number* takes a plural verb.

The number of children riding in the bus was minimal.
The number of dogs and cats is astronomical.
A number of pages were missing from the file.
A number of women were to meet for lunch.

5 A number of students in the class (is/are) working on a project.
6 The number of men attending the convention (was/were) greater than expected.
7 The number of cars to be parked (exceeds/exceed) the number of spaces available.
8 A number of workers (was/were) waiting for word about that.

RESOURCES

 Lesson Plan 47
 Courseware Lesson 47
Student Data Disk
Student Manual
Reteaching and Reinforcement
Grading and Evaluation
Language Link Worksheets

SKILLBUILDING

C. Preview Practice

Type each line 2 times as a preview to the timings that follow.

```
an Vail quickly amazing however wrought telegraph seventeen
inventing artist dashes short text long code dots sent that
```

D. 3-Minute Timings

Take two 3-minute timings on the paragraphs. Note your speed and errors.

Goal: 33/3'/5e

```
     Samuel Morse was an artist. Today, however, he is        10
known not for his major works of art but for inventing        21
the telegraph and the code it uses. With the help of his      33
friend, Alfred Vail, Morse made up a code of dashes and       44
dots that stood for numbers and letters. Text could be        55
sent with this Morse Code by using long and short signals.    66
     Seventeen years before the Civil War began, Morse        77
tapped out his first message, "What hath God wrought."        88
It was quickly received an amazing thirty-five miles away.    99
 | 1 | 2 | 3 | 4 | 5 | 6 | 7 | 8 | 9 | 10 | 11 | 12 SI 1.34
```

Social Studies Connections

FACT FILE

During the past several decades, engineers have created more advanced technology than at any other time in history.

TEACH

Activity C. Point out that words in the Preview Practice are used in the timing that follows.

Activity D. Remind students that the goal for these timings is 33 words a minute for 3 minutes with no more than 5 errors.

Social Studies Connections

The Civil War began in the United States in 1861. Ask students what they believe this war was about. Ask them to think about the tragedy of brothers fighting brothers and sons fighting fathers. Then ask students to compose and type a one-page essay on the Civil War. They may have to research. Have students check each other's work for typing errors.

FACT FILE

Samuel Morse, an American artist and inventor, constructed his experimental telegraph line between Washington, D.C., and Baltimore, Maryland. His first message ("What hath God wrought") was sent on May 24, 1844. Have students research and make a timeline from the first telegraph to today's communications equipment.

TEACH

Report 12. Refer students to the Reference Manual in the software to review the format for typing a report with a numbered list.

Report 13. Refer students to the Reference Manual in the textbook to review the format for typing minutes.

COMMUNICATION ACTIVITY

Have students study the information in Report 12, then have each student choose a partner. Students then count off 1, 2, 1, 2, 1, 2. Partner 1 is the caller; partner 2, the person answering the company phone. Have students make up a business scenario and role-play a phone call keeping in mind telephone techniques for the job. Have partners reverse roles.

WORD PROCESSING APPLICATIONS

REPORT 12

One-Page Report With Numbered List

Remember to double space the report.

TELEPHONE TECHNIQUES FOR THE JOB

When you answer the telephone, remember that you represent the company. Make the first impression of your business a good one by following these techniques:

1. Greet the caller by identifying your company and yourself. Ask how you may assist or direct the call.
2. Use a friendly tone, speak clearly and distinctly, and avoid slang or mumbling.
3. Listen carefully to be sure you understand everything the caller is saying.
4. Be professional if you have to place a caller on hold while you get files or if you need to transfer the call to someone else.
5. If you place a caller on hold, periodically return to the caller and ask if he or she wishes to continue holding, prefer to speak with someone else, or leave a message.
6. Offer to take a message or have someone return the phone call.
7. Record messages accurately. Include the caller's name and telephone number and any other important information such as when they called and why. Repeat the telephone number to be sure you wrote it correctly.
8. Close the call by expressing appreciation to the caller. Be sure you and the caller agree on what action is to be taken. Then say goodbye.

REPORT 13

Minutes of Meeting

the **PLANNING COMMITTEE**
Minutes of Meeting
November 13, {year}
ATTENDENCE
n
The Plaing Committee met on Nov. 13, {year}, at the Board Room of the Douglas County Courthouse. Members present were Ronald Horton, Lakisha Lopez, Tonnetta McCoy, Chris Ngyen, Martha Ristau, and Steve Vanderhoff. Ronald Horton, chairperson, called the meeting to order at 7:15 p.m.

JOURNAL ENTRY

Ask students to imagine they own a business. What would they expect from the person who answered the phone? Took minutes of meetings? Wrote reports? Will they give the same to their employer? Read a few entries in class.

UNFINISHED BUSINESS
Arbor Mall Station construction began on Nov. 10. Martha Ristau moved that land parcels on the east side of the construction site be auctioned to prospective new businesses, since those parcels are zoned E-5. Chris Ngyen seconded the motion. After a lengthy discussion, the motion was passed unanimously.
NEW BUSINESS
Kendall Construction Company presented a blue print for developing the land parcels across Douglas boulevard from Arbor Station Mall. Mr. Kevin O'Rourke from Kendall Construction Company proposed the building of several "big box" stores in those parcels. After several questions arose concerning the environment impact of developing these parcels, a motion was made to table a vote until the corps of Engineers could conduct land impact studies on the area. This item will be discussed at the December meeting.
ADJOURNMENT
The meeting was adjourned at 9:30 p.m. The next meeting for December 10, is scheduled {year}, in the Conference Room at Douglas County High School. Respectfully submitted, / J. D. Harper, Secretary

REPORT 14

Two-Page Report With Paragraph Headings

CHOOSING THE RIGHT COLLEGE
By Carl Klees

Choosing a college is one of the big decisions a student makes in life. Careful planning and thoughtful consideration can make this decision easier for you.

Match Your Interests. Finding a college that matches your interests is an important factor in your choice. Several colleges, not just one, can offer you an opportunity to match your interests with those of other students. Choosing a college just because it's popular or because your parents went there could result in the loss of time spent at a college that best suits your needs.

TEACH

Report 14. Refer students to the Reference Manual in the textbook to review the format for typing a one-page report with paragraph headings.

SCHOOL TO CAREER

Brainstorm with students about what their career expectations are. Provide students with colored markers and poster board, and have them make a map that shows where they are and where they want to be. Have them fill in the steps along the way to take them to their goal.

Career Exploration

Discuss students' plans for after high school. Explain that in today's world, additional education is important. Ask students to call or write for catalogs for business schools, colleges, technical schools, or other places of higher learning. Begin a career exploration library.

ASSESS

- Watch students as they complete the tutorial for subject/verb agreement to see if they are able to apply the rules correctly.
- As students begin typing the reports, walk around the room and point out correct and incorrect formatting to individual students.
- After students finish typing the reports, have them view their work on the screen to see if they made any errors. If errors were made, have students make corrections.

CLOSE

If students do not finish Report 14 during the class period, make sure they save their work so that they can complete it the next time this class meets. Remind students to clean up their workstation when they leave.

PORTFOLIO *Activity*

If students' portfolio goals include demonstrating progress, they may want to include some reports from this lesson. Encourage students to evaluate their work and include comments in their portfolio.

Academic Programs. The offering of specific academic programs is one of the most important reasons for choosing a college. Some colleges specialize in particular majors while others offer a broad range of majors. Determine what your academic needs are in order to aid your decision.

Size. Consider the size of the college when making your decision. Perhaps you like small classes where you know the professor and other classmates rather than classes held in lecture hall situations with hundreds of other students. Many people do better in small situations as opposed to large ones.

Extracurricular Activities. The extracurricular offerings of a college deserve a special look. Consider whether the college offers activities that you enjoy and whether these activities are available to people of your skill level. Also determine whether these activities will interfere with your class and study obligations. The activities offered outside the college in the surrounding community should also be considered.

Financial Considerations. Cost, of course, is an important consideration in college choice. Public versus private school will impact cost as will attending school in state or out of state. Tuition for out-of-state students is double or triple the cost of in-state students.

Plan a Visit. Once you have narrowed the choice down to a few colleges, plan to visit the campus. A visit to the campus can give you a better picture of the college, the students, the community, and whether the overall picture suits you. The earlier you begin considering colleges, the more time you will have to visit them.

Teacher Notes

LESSON 48 PERSONAL BUSINESS LETTERS

OBJECTIVES:

- Practice the top-row number keys.
- Learn word processing features.
- Format personal-business letters.

A. WARMUP

Type each line 2 times.

Speed	1	Check our lists to be sure that we are ready for this trip.
Accuracy	2	Zachariah analyzed the situation and queried the witnesses.
Language Link	3	A number of students were excused from their science class.
Numbers/Symbols	4	Buy 2# of pears (#1 Bartlett*) @ $1.98 at the Fruit & More.

FACT FILE

Engineers John Pierce and Harold Rosen designed successful communication satellites in the 1960s. Because of their developments, we can talk on the phone and watch television beamed up to satellites from places far away.

SKILLBUILDING

B. 30-SECOND OK TIMINGS

Take two 30-second OK (error-free) timings on lines 5–6. Then take two 30-second OK timings on lines 7–8. Goal: no errors.

```
5      Extend a burst of energy to your fingers as you force    11
6  them to zoom over the keys. Enjoy the rush of rapid typing.  23
7      People who routinely succeed squeeze value out of each   11
8  minute. They judge the best way to do a task and act on it.  23
```


LESSON 48

FOCUS

- Take 30-second OK timings.
- Use a P/P/P routine to build speed and improve accuracy.
- Learn word processing features: Center Page and Date Insert
- Learn how to format a personal business letter.
- Type personal business letters.

BELLRINGER

As soon as students arrive at their workstations and log in, have them type the Warmup. Go over the purpose of each line as shown to the left of the copy.

TEACH

Activity B. Remind students that their goal for 30-second OK timings is improved speed with each of the timings and no errors.

RESOURCES

 Lesson Plan 48

 Courseware Lesson 48

Student Data Disk

Student Manual

Supplementary Production Activities

Cross-Curricular Activities

TEACH

Activity C. Make sure students note speed and errors on this 1-minute timing.

Activity D. Point out that only one letter changes with each successive word typed in this Practice. Students should use this exercise to build speed.

Activity E. Remind students they should improve both their speed and accuracy from the Pretest to the Posttest.

PRETEST/PRACTICE/POSTEST

The ***Pretest/Practice/Posttest*** routines are designed to improve speed or accuracy.

- The ***Pretest*** identifies students' speed or accuracy needs.
- The ***Practice*** provides a variety of improvement drills.
- The ***Posttest*** (a repeat of the Pretest) measures improvement.

Social Studies Connections

Have students create a timeline on women's suffrage. Include information such as the date Wyoming gave women the right to vote and the date the Nineteenth Amendment was ratified. Students may have different events on their timelines.

C. PRETEST

Take a 1-minute timing on lines 9–12. Note your speed and errors.

Social Studies Connections

```
 9      Wyoming was the first state to give women the right to   11
10  vote. The other states in the West joined the cause in the   23
11  next two decades. After New York and Illinois gave women     34
12  the right to vote, Congress began to debate the issue.       45
    | 1 | 2 | 3 | 4 | 5 | 6 | 7 | 8 | 9 | 10 | 11 | 12
```

D. PRACTICE

Type each line 2 times.

Build speed on repeated word patterns.

```
13  road toad load loam loan moan moat goat coat coal cowl cows
14  vows bows rows tows tons tone zone cone come comb tomb bomb

15  quip quit suit suet sued sues cues cued coed toed toes does
16  dogs bogs cogs logs lots loss boss moss most cost lost post

17  noon soon loon boon boot soot spot spat scat swat swam swim
18  swum scum scup scud stud stun shun shin chin thin then them

19  Tex. text test rest west lest lost last mast past fast cast
20  case vase base bask back tack pack hack hark mark dark dart

21  gaze haze faze daze raze race pace pate gate bate bade wade
22  ware hare mare more mode rode rote vote tote tope rope hope

23  Dora Lora Lara Mara Myra Myla Nyla Nola Nona Rona Rena Zena
24  Bill Will Wilt Walt Dalt Dale Kale Kole Cole Colt Cort Cory
```

E. POSTTEST

Repeat the Pretest. Compare your Posttest results with your Pretest results.

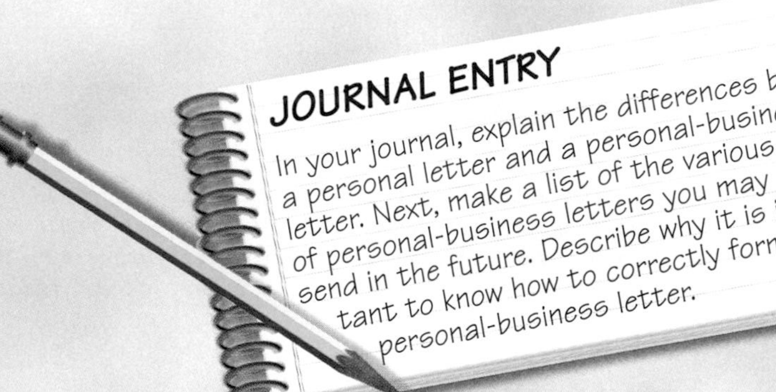

JOURNAL ENTRY
In your journal, explain the differences between a personal letter and a personal-business letter. Next, make a list of the various kinds of personal-business letters you may need to send in the future. Describe why it is important to know how to correctly format a personal-business letter.

TECHNOLOGY TIP

Following the manufacturer's instructions, demonstrate to students the proper cleaning procedure for their mouse. Explain to students the mouse must be kept clean in order for it to smoothly move the insertion point on the screen. A dirty mouse causes the insertion point to malfunction.

F. Personal-Business Letters

A letter from an individual to a business is called a personal-business letter. A personal-business letter should contain these parts:

Date Line. The month, day, and year the letter is typed.
Inside Address. The name and address of the person to whom the letter is being sent.
Salutation. An opening greeting such as *Dear Ms. Jones.*
Body. The text of the letter.
Complimentary Closing. A closing to the letter such as *Sincerely* or *Yours truly.*
Signature. The writer's signature.
Writer's Identification. The writer's typed name and address.

To format a personal-business letter in block style:

1. Type all lines beginning at the left margin.
2. Center the letter vertically, then type the date.
3. After the date, press ENTER 4 times and type the inside address. Leave 1 space between the state and the ZIP code.
4. After the inside address, press ENTER 2 times and type the salutation.
5. Press ENTER 2 times and begin the body of the letter. Single-space the body, but press ENTER 2 times between paragraphs.
6. After the last paragraph, press ENTER 2 times and type the complimentary closing.
7. Press ENTER 4 times and type the writer's name and address.

G. Software Features

STUDENT MANUAL

Center Page Date Insert

Study Lesson 48 in your student manual. Complete all the practice activities while at your computer. Then complete the following jobs.

TEACH

Activity F. Refer students to the Reference Manual in the textbook to study the format for typing a personal business letter.

Activity G. Explain the software features presented in this activity.

- Demonstrate how to center a document vertically.
- Demonstrate how to insert the current date.

STUDENT MANUAL

Be sure students turn to the correct lesson in their Student Manual.

Illustration

Use the illustration to point out the placement of the writer's name and address. Explain that the address could also precede the date.

JOURNAL ENTRY

Brainstorm with students about letters they have written. Have them write a journal entry about three reasons an individual would write a personal-business letter. Ask for volunteers to read entries aloud.

TEACH

Letter 1. Demonstrate the Date Insert feature. Show students how to access the command in their software.

Remind students that the writer's address is included in the closing lines of a personal business letter.

Social Studies Connections

Ask the class if they could take a class trip to anywhere in the country where would that be. Write students' suggestions on the board; then take a vote and choose one destination. Have the class research the destination, including writing for information. Post pictures and brochures in the room.

WORD PROCESSING APPLICATIONS

LETTER 1

Block Style
Personal-Business

Type the following letter in block style. Vertically center the letter, and insert the current date. Use standard punctuation: a colon after the salutation and a comma after the complimentary closing.

(Current Date)

Mrs. Joan L. Locke
2356 North Central Avenue
Phoenix, AZ 85004

Dear Mrs. Locke:

Thank you for helping our sponsor by assisting on our trip to Flagstaff last week. It was a pleasure to meet you and hear about the various trips you have made in southwestern United States. As you know, we just moved to Arizona. It's my intention to learn about and see more of my new state.

I was particularly interested in Flagstaff and its importance as a vacation area. The presentation by the Chamber of Commerce was very worthwhile. It surprised me to learn that skiing is one of Flagstaff's top winter tourist attractions. No one would think that skiers would come from such states as California, New Mexico, or Texas to ski in Arizona. I would have thought it was too warm in Arizona for such a winter sport.

My parents and I plan to go to the Grand Canyon this coming summer; I told them that Flagstaff was the gateway to the Canyon. They indicated to me that my grandparents had taken a train to Flagstaff and then, taken a bus to the Canyon. I hope I can do something similar.

Thanks again for helping us on our trip.

Sincerely yours,

Ms. Alice L. L'Huillier
2314 Oak Street
Scottsdale, AZ 85257

interNET ACTIVITY

Have students use the Internet to locate maps of your community and the destination of their imaginary class trip. Ask students to chart the routes between locations, and to use the Internet to check air, train, and bus fares.

LETTER 2

Block Style
Personal-Business

Type the following letter in block style. The slash marks in the inside address and closing lines indicate line endings. Do not type the slashes.

The ¶ symbol indicates the start of a new paragraph. Do not indent a new paragraph. However, leave one blank line before beginning a new paragraph.

Current Date / Ms. Caroline Davis / 5200 Roselawn Avenue / Topeka, KS 67218 / Dear Ms. Davis: /
¶Your presentation at the Kentwood Business Club was one of the most enjoyable our club has ever had.
¶It is always a pleasure to have a professional like you speak on ways a graduate can seek a job. The follow-up question-and-answer period as well as your handouts were well received.
¶On the advice of our teacher, our accounting class has decided that one way we can follow up your presentation is to bring to class employment ads, and then write letters of application. Already the class has prepared twelve letters, which were sent to our teacher as the employer; thirteen more are all ready to be signed.
¶I believe this is one of the most interesting projects I have ever been assigned. Members of the class have learned to critique the letters without feeling self-conscious about their work.
¶Would you consider reviewing some of our letters and advise us which you think are the best? We hope you will say, "yes!" I will call you next Monday to discuss the details.
Sincerely yours, / Brian K. Long / 347 Main Street / Topeka, KS 67209

FACT FILE

Virtual reality is the creation of images and tactile sensations by means of a computer, producing the illusion of reality. Images are often projected onto special goggles to strengthen the illusion.

LESSON 48

TEACH

Letter 2. Tell students that in academic papers, they are to indent new paragraphs. However, in business writing they are to leave a blank line before beginning a new paragraph.

ASSESS

- Check to see if students show signs of improvement from the Pretest to the Posttest.
- As students begin typing the letters, walk around the room and point out correct and incorrect formatting to individual students.

CLOSE

If students do not finish Letter 2 during the class period, make sure they save their work so that they can complete it the next time this class meets. Remind students to clean up their workstation when they leave.

PORTFOLIO Activity

If students' portfolio goals include demonstrating progress, they may want to include one or both of the letters from this lesson. Encourage students to evaluate their work and include comments in their portfolio.

Career Exploration

Brainstorm with students about their different interests. Write these on the board. Have students with like interests meet in groups. If groups get too large, divide them. Have each group brainstorm careers that match their interests. Have groups come up with five careers and then research them.

Out-of-Class Activity

Have students work alone and in the groups they formed for Career Exploration. Have them search newspapers, check with employment agencies, or use other means to collect employment ads related to their careers. Have groups make a collage of their ads.

LESSON 49

FOCUS

- Build skill with 30-second timings.
- Type a Concentration Drill.
- Take 2-minute Paced Practice timings.
- Learn to format and type a block-style personal business letter.

BELLRINGER

As soon as students arrive at their workstations and log in, have them type the Warmup. Go over the purpose of each line as shown to the left of the copy.

TEACH

Activity B. Remind students that proper technique is a building block for speed and accuracy.

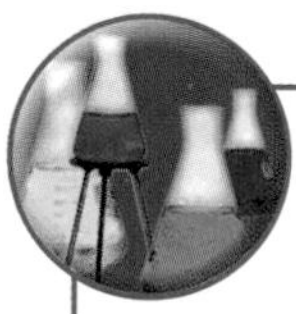

Science Connections

Have students locate a newspaper or magazine article related to trees and write a one-paragraph summary of the article. Divide the class into small groups for discussion.

LESSON 49 REINFORCEMENT

OBJECTIVES:

- Practice typing with continuity.
- Strengthen skill in formatting personal-business letters.

A. WARMUP

Type each line 2 times.

Speed	1 If you want to be the best typist, then practice correctly.
Accuracy	2 Xavier is amazed by the two jazz artists' expert qualities.
Language Link	3 The number of students involved in intramural sports is up.
Numbers	4 We are scheduled for April 29, May 14, June 30, and July 7.
	| 1 | 2 | 3 | 4 | 5 | 6 | 7 | 8 | 9 | 10 | 11 | 12

SKILLBUILDING

B. TECHNIQUE TIMINGS

Take two 30-second timings on each line. Focus on the technique at the left.

Type with continuity.

```
5 We would find life very different in a world without trees.
6 Trees provide us food, fuel, fibers, lumber, and chemicals.
7 Trees keep our soil from eroding and provide us windbreaks.
8 Even dead trees are useful by providing homes for wildlife.
  | 1 | 2 | 3 | 4 | 5 | 6 | 7 | 8 | 9 | 10 | 11 | 12
```

Science Connections

RESOURCES

 Lesson Plan 49

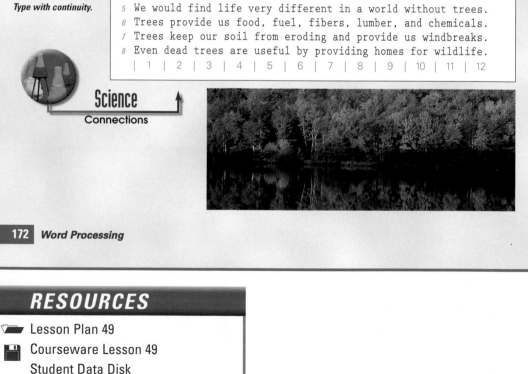

 Courseware Lesson 49

Student Data Disk

Student Manual

Reteaching and Reinforcement

Grading and Evaluation

C. Concentration Drills

Type each line 2 times. Concentrate on keeping your eyes on the copy.

9 A proficient secretary manipulates microcomputers expertly.
10 Authorized institutions substitute experimental techniques.
11 The Mississippi and Missouri Rivers provide transportation.
12 Agricultural goods surpass manufactured industrial gadgets.

D. Paced Practice

Turn to the Paced Practice routine beginning on page SB7. Take three 2-minute timings, starting at the point where you left off the last time.

WORD PROCESSING APPLICATIONS

LETTER 3

Block Style
Personal-Business

Type this letter in block style with standard punctuation. Insert the current date.

(Current Date) / Ms. Louise Feigleson / Personnel Director / Smith and Kovacs Agency / 7858 High Street / Columbus, OH 43216 / Dear Ms. Feigleson: /
¶I was told there were job opportunities in your agency this summer, and I would like to apply for a job in your accounting department.
¶I am completing my junior year as an accounting major at Ohio State University. I have completed basic, intermediate, and advanced accounting. I will be available for employment from May 15 through August 1. During the year, I have been employed as a part-time bookkeeper at the Buckeye Lodge in Westerville. Mr. John Forte, manager of the lodge, has indicated that he would send you a letter of recommendation. My academic advisor, Dr. Josephine Craig, will be happy to make a recommendation if you wish.
¶You may, at your convenience, call me at my dorm telephone number, 555-0677, after 3:30 p.m. Monday through Friday. If you would like for me to come in for an interview, please let me know.
Yours truly, / May Kent / 234B Hayes Hall / Ohio State University / Columbus, OH 43210

TEACH

Activity C. Concentration Drills require students to focus their attention and keep their eyes on the copy. Most of the words in the Concentration Drill have multiple syllables. Many are words that students do not use everyday.

Activity D. Review with students the procedure for the Paced Practice activity. (See Lesson 34, page 119.)

TEACH

Letter 3. Refer students to the Reference Manual in the textbook to review the format for typing a block-style personal-business letter.

CULTURAL CONNECTIONS

Have students compose and type a letter to a student who will be visiting from a foreign country. The letter's purpose is to introduce the visiting student to the community where he or she will be staying. Include information about location, population, and climate.

interNET ACTIVITY

Ask students to search the Internet for information about careers of interest. Suggest they begin with the name of the career and then use links to other documents and sites. Have students print the information they find and bring it to class.

TEACH

Letter 4. Refer students to the Reference Manual in the textbook to review the format for typing a block-style personal-business letter.

ASSESS

- As students begin typing the letters, walk around the room and point out correct and incorrect formatting to individual students.
- After students finish typing the letters, have them view their work on the screen to see if they made any errors. If errors were made, have students make corrections.

CLOSE

If students do not finish the letters during the class period, make sure they save their work so that they can complete them the next time this class meets.

Remind students to clean up their workstation when they leave.

PORTFOLIO *Activity*

If students' portfolio goals include demonstrating progress, they may want to include one or both letters from this lesson. Encourage students to evaluate their work and include comments in their portfolio.

LETTER 4

Block Style
Personal-Business

Type this letter in block style with standard punctuation. Make the corrections indicated by the proofreaders' marks.

(Current Date)

Mr. Jacob Ries, Manager
Longhorn Department Store
1366 South State St.
Chicago, IL 60616

Dear Mr. Reis:

Thank you for sending me an application for the position of a part-time clerk in your store.

I am currently working part time as a clerk at the One-A Supermarket. My cooperative education teacher assisted me in obtaining this position and I have been on this job for 2 years.

As is requested on the form, I am asking that the letters of recomendation be sent to you. You will receive letters from my coöperative teacher, current employer, and scout leader within the next few days. The high school office administration will send you a transcript of my grades.

As I indicated in my letter of application, I will be completeing high school in June, and will enroll at Northern Illinois University in September. I am pleased with the position you are offering me, and I know the position will assist me in financing my college education.

I look forward to meeting you, my fellow employees, and our customers in ~~July~~ June.

Sincerely yours,

Kyle Long
4578 Chicago Road
Evanston, IL 62242

interNET CONNECTION

Use the Internet to explore sites that provide career and job information. Some sites you may want to try are:

http://www.careermosaic.com/
http://www.stats.bls.gov.ocohome.htm
http://www.dbm.com/jobguide/

Teacher Notes

LESSON 50 ENVELOPES

OBJECTIVES:

- Improve keyboarding skills.
- Learn word processing features.
- Format envelopes.

A. WARMUP

Type each line 2 times.

```
Speed           1 The true beauty of that diamond was brought out by its cut.
Accuracy        2 Aquilla told Bix the difference in a xylophone and marimba.
Language Link   3 A number of fields of cotton and milo haven't been planted.
Technique       4 Paul Quan Rand Stan Trev Ulan Vern Ward Xerxes Yohann Zared
                  | 1 | 2 | 3 | 4 | 5 | 6 | 7 | 8 | 9 | 10 | 11 | 12
```

SKILLBUILDING

B. 30-SECOND OK TIMINGS

Take two 30-second OK (error-free) timings on lines 5–6. Then take two 30-second OK timings on lines 7–8. Goal: no errors.

```
5      Each of the students decided what he wanted to eat for   11
6 breakfast. Amazingly, just six bravely asked for ham quiche.  23

7      Both the dog and the fox were fat and lazy. They never   11
8 ran or jumped quickly. All they ever did was eat and sleep.   23
  | 1 | 2 | 3 | 4 | 5 | 6 | 7 | 8 | 9 | 10 | 11 | 12
```


LESSON 50

FOCUS

- Take 30-second OK timings.
- Fold letters for envelopes.
- Format and type a letter and envelopes.
- Learn word processing features: Envelopes.

BELLRINGER

As soon as students arrive at their workstations and log in, have them type the Warmup. Go over the purpose of each line as shown to the left of the copy.

TEACH

Activity B. Remind students that the goal for 30-second OK timings is improved accuracy with each timing.

RESOURCES

 Lesson Plan 50

Courseware Lesson 50

Student Data Disk

Student Manual

TEACH

Activities C–E. Remind students they should improve both their speed and accuracy from the Pretest to the Posttest. For the Practice activity, go over the drill lines they should type twice for the number of Pretest errors they make.

PRETEST/PRACTICE/POSTEST

The ***Pretest/Practice/Posttest*** routines are designed to improve speed or accuracy.

- The ***Pretest*** identifies students' speed or accuracy needs.
- The ***Practice*** provides a variety of improvement drills.
- The ***Posttest*** (a repeat of the Pretest) measures improvement.

C. PRETEST

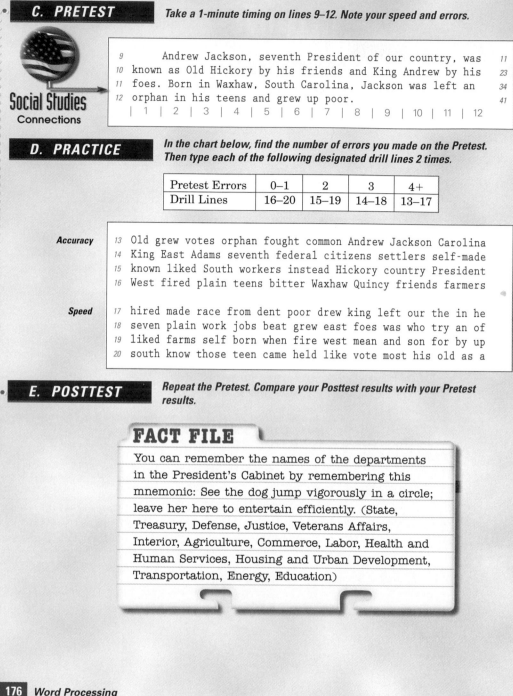

Take a 1-minute timing on lines 9–12. Note your speed and errors.

Social Studies Connections

```
9       Andrew Jackson, seventh President of our country, was    11
10  known as Old Hickory by his friends and King Andrew by his   23
11  foes. Born in Waxhaw, South Carolina, Jackson was left an    34
12  orphan in his teens and grew up poor.                        41
    | 1 | 2 | 3 | 4 | 5 | 6 | 7 | 8 | 9 | 10 | 11 | 12
```

D. PRACTICE

In the chart below, find the number of errors you made on the Pretest. Then type each of the following designated drill lines 2 times.

Pretest Errors	0–1	2	3	4+
Drill Lines	16–20	15–19	14–18	13–17

Accuracy

```
13  Old grew votes orphan fought common Andrew Jackson Carolina
14  King East Adams seventh federal citizens settlers self-made
15  known liked South workers instead Hickory country President
16  West fired plain teens bitter Waxhaw Quincy friends farmers
```

Speed

```
17  hired made race from dent poor drew king left our the in he
18  seven plain work jobs beat grew east foes was who try an of
19  liked farms self born when fire west mean and son for by up
20  south know those teen came held like vote most his old as a
```

E. POSTTEST

Repeat the Pretest. Compare your Posttest results with your Pretest results.

FACT FILE

You can remember the names of the departments in the President's Cabinet by remembering this mnemonic: See the dog jump vigorously in a circle; leave her here to entertain efficiently. (State, Treasury, Defense, Justice, Veterans Affairs, Interior, Agriculture, Commerce, Labor, Health and Human Services, Housing and Urban Development, Transportation, Energy, Education)

Social Studies Connections

Andrew Jackson obtained his nickname Old Hickory when, in 1813, he was stranded he was stranded without supplies with his soldiers. He led his troops home to Tennessee. His men said Jackson was as tough as hickory.

F. Envelopes

There are two commonly used envelope sizes: a No. 10 (large envelope) and a No. 6: (small envelope). The No. 10, which is the standard size for business letters, is 9 ½ by 4 ⅛ inches. A correctly addressed envelope should be typed as follows:

1. **Return Address.** The writer's name and address typed or printed in the upper left corner of the envelope (see the illustration that follows).
2. **Mailing Address.** The recipient's name and address beginning at least 2 inches from the top edge and 4 inches from the left edge of the envelope. The mailing address may be typed either in initial caps with punctuation (see the small envelope), or in all caps with no punctuation (see the large envelope).

MS JOAN R HUNTER
BOLWATER ASSOCIATES
ONE PARKLANDS DRIVE
DARIEN CT 06820-3214

Roger J. Michaelson
901 East Benson, Apt. 3
Ft. Lauderdale, FL 33301

Mr. Joseph G. Jenshak
17032 Stewart Avenue
Augusta, GA 30904

TEACH

Activity F. Refer students to the Reference Manual in the textbook to study the format for typing envelopes.

Illustration

Refer students to the illustrations of large and small envelopes. Note the formats of the return address and mailing address on both.

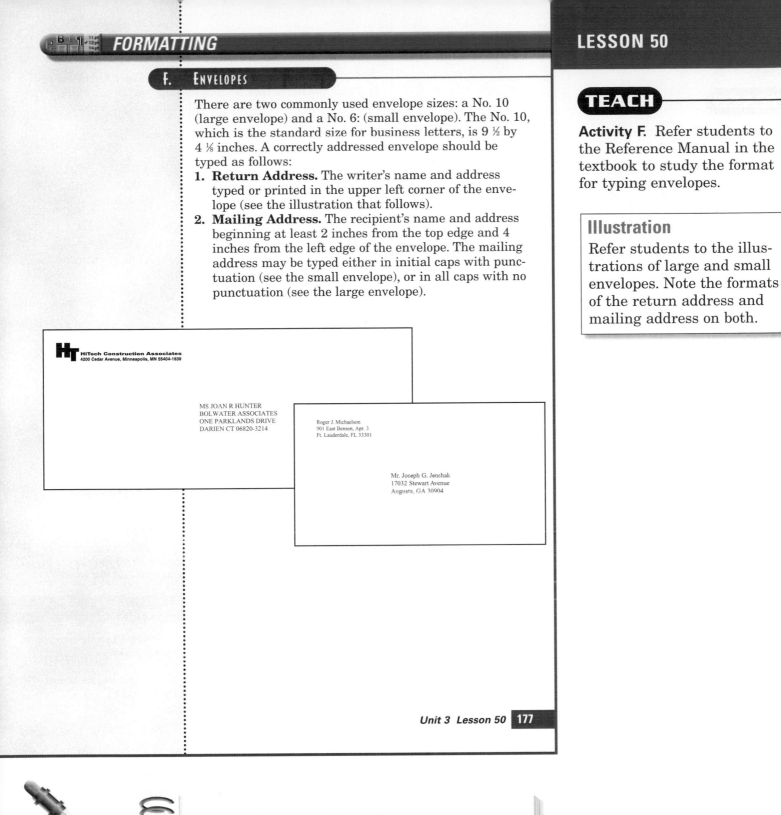

JOURNAL ENTRY

Have students write about a letter they wish they had written or one they wish they had not written. Have them reflect on why they wish they had or had not written the letter. What does this teach them?

TEACH

Activity G. Demonstrate the steps for folding a letter to be inserted into an envelope. Have students practice the steps.

STUDENT MANUAL

Be sure students turn to the correct lesson in their Student Manual.

Activity H. Explain the software features presented in this activity.

- Demonstrate how to format and print an envelope.
- Demonstrate how to omit the return address when printing an envelope.

Envelopes 1, 2, and 3. Review with students how to fold a letter for a large envelope.

G. Folding Letters

To fold a letter for a large envelope: (see the illustration)

1. Place the letter face up and fold up the bottom third.
2. Fold the top third down to approximately 0.5 inch from the bottom edge.
3. Insert the last crease into the envelope first with the flap facing up.

To fold a letter for a small envelope: (see the illustration)

1. Place the letter face up and fold up the bottom half to 0.5 inch from the top.
2. Fold the right third over to the left.
3. Fold the left third over to 0.5 inch from the right edge.
4. Insert the last crease into the envelope first with the flap facing up.

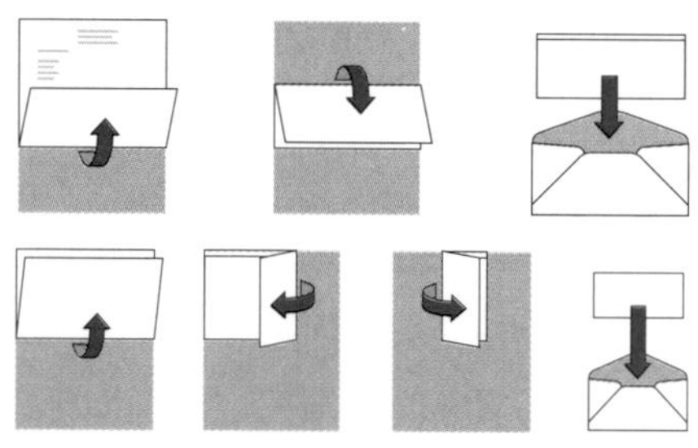

H. Software Features

STUDENT MANUAL

Envelopes

Study Lesson 50 in your student manual. Complete all the practice activities while at your computer. Then complete the jobs that follow.

WORD PROCESSING APPLICATIONS

ENVELOPE 1

Open the file for Letter 2, and prepare a No. 10 envelope. Use the correct return address and add/append the envelope to the letter.

ENVELOPE 2

Open the file for Letter 3, and prepare a No. 10 envelope. Use the correct return address and add/append the envelope to the letter.

Out-of-Class Activity

Ask students to collect envelopes and letters from different businesses and bring them to class. Hold a class discussion about the different formats used by different businesses. Ask students why the varying sizes of envelopes are used.

Multiple Learning Styles

Have students place in front of them several of the different size letters and envelopes they collected. Ask them to pick up one of the envelopes and then to close their eyes and concentrate on how this size feels in their hands. Repeat this exercise with different sizes.

ENVELOPE 3

Open the file for Letter 4, and prepare a No. 10 envelope. Use the correct return address and add/append the envelope to the letter.

LETTER 5

Block Style With Envelope

Type the following letter in block style, and prepare a large envelope for the letter.

(Current Date) / Ms. Kaye Lincoln / Waldo Travel Bureau / 8900 Longwood Avenue / Suite 1304 / Boston, MA 02115 / Dear Ms. Lincoln:
¶I am interested in a trip to England, Holland, France, and Germany this coming summer. Do you have special packaged tours for students?
¶My financial resources are limited. I am looking for a trip that would take less than a month and cost less than $2,000. Currently, I am working as a waiter in a local restaurant; and I hope to save additional money for the trip.
¶What is the round trip airfare from Boston to London? Can I use trains from London to Amsterdam, Paris, and Frankfort? Can you recommend a hostel in each city and give me some idea of the daily costs? I would appreciate your sending me brochures on airlines, railroads, and hostels you recommend. I plan to apply for my passport, and I am aware that it takes more than a week for processing.
¶If you have further questions concerning my proposed trip, please let me know. You may call me at 781-555-2535. I can get released time from work to see you, and I can see you at your convenience.
Sincerely yours, / William Stoneman / 678 Main Street / Milton, MA 02186

PORTFOLIO *Activity*

Decide which of the letters in this unit is your best one. Retype the letter using your name and address in the closing lines. Correct any errors, then print a copy and save the letter as an example of your work.

LESSON 50

TEACH

Letter 5. Remind students that the word processing software will automatically insert and position the return address and mailing address on an envelope after they have finished typing the letter.

ASSESS

- As students begin typing the envelopes, walk around the room and point out correct and incorrect formatting to individual students.
- After students finish typing the letter and envelopes, have them view their work on the screen to see if they made any errors. If errors were made, have students make corrections.

CLOSE

If students do not finish typing the letter and envelope during the class period, make sure they save their work so that they can complete it the next time this class meets.

PORTFOLIO *Activity*

If students' portfolio goals include demonstrating progress, they may want to include Letter 5 and its envelope. Encourage students to evaluate their work and include comments in their portfolio.

Teacher Notes

LESSON 51

FOCUS

- Compose at the keyboard.
- Take 12-second and 3-minute timings.
- Learn how to format and type block-style business letters.

BELLRINGER

As soon as students arrive at their workstations and log in, have them type the Warmup. Go over the purpose of each line as shown to the left of the copy.

TEACH

Activity B. After students have answered each question with a complete sentence, have them choose one of the topics and write a paragraph about it. Have students check each other's work for accuracy.

Answers will vary

LESSON 51

BUSINESS LETTERS

OBJECTIVES:

- Compose at the keyboard.
- Format business letters.
- Type 33/3′/5e.

A. WARMUP

Type each line 2 times.

Speed	1	We will be happy to see the sun after so many days of rain.
Accuracy	2	Janita and six friends quickly zipped by the two villagers.
Language Link	3	The number of farmers helping their sick neighbor was huge.
Numbers/Symbols	4	Our 9 cakes, 45 pies, 60 doughnuts, and 72 cookies arrived.

| 1 | 2 | 3 | 4 | 5 | 6 | 7 | 8 | 9 | 10 | 11 | 12

B. COMPOSING AT THE KEYBOARD

Answer each of the following questions with complete sentences.

5 Why is it important to have friends?
6 Why are hurricanes dangerous?
7 What historical person would you most like to meet? Why?
8 Do you prefer team or individual sports?
9 Why is music important to you?

LANGUAGE ARTS CONNECTIONS

The word *skate* comes from the German word meaning bone. People first began skating more than 2,000 years ago. They would tie animal bones to their feet so that they could move or slide quickly across the ice.

RESOURCES

 Lesson Plan 51

 Courseware Lesson 51

Student Data Disk

Student Manual

Supplementary Production Activities

Grading and Evaluation

COURSEWARE OVERVIEW

Be sure students add their reference initials to the personal information box so that their documents will score correctly.

SKILLBUILDING

C. 12-Second Sprints

Take three 12-second timings on each line. Try to increase your speed on each timing.

Ray looks nice in his new jacket, but he does not think so.
He finds it hard to accept nice words being said about him.
He should smile and thank the one who said the nice things.
Do you find you are ill at ease when a nice remark is made?
| | | | 5 | | | | 10 | | | | 15 | | | | 20 | | | | 25 | | | | 30 | | | | 35 | | | | 40 | | | | 45 | | | | 50 | | | | 55 | | | | 60

D. Preview Practice

Type each line 2 times as a preview to the timings that follow.

skills fixing machines produce equipped analyzing computers
every that free high have work data sure help you job it is

E. 3-Minute Timings

Take two 3-minute timings on the paragraphs. Note your speed and errors.

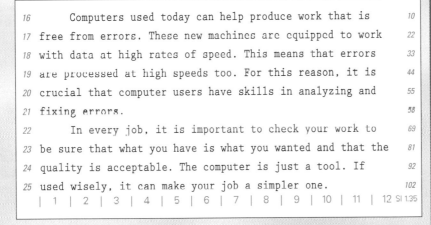

Computers used today can help produce work that is 10
free from errors. These new machines are equipped to work 22
with data at high rates of speed. This means that errors 33
are processed at high speeds too. For this reason, it is 44
crucial that computer users have skills in analyzing and 55
fixing errors. 58
In every job, it is important to check your work to 69
be sure that what you have is what you wanted and that the 81
quality is acceptable. The computer is just a tool. If 92
used wisely, it can make your job a simpler one. 102
| 1 | 2 | 3 | 4 | 5 | 6 | 7 | 8 | 9 | 10 | 11 | 12 SI 1.35

TEACH

Activity C. Remind students that the goal for 12-second sprints is improved speed.

Activity D. Point out that the words in the Preview Practice are used in the 3-minute timing that follows.

Activity E. Remind students to be aware of their posture—to sit up, keep their elbows in, and their feet flat on the floor.

SCHOOL TO CAREER

Explain to students that many writing projects require input from more than one person. Have students work in teams of four to write a collaborative letter of inquiry to an employment agency to learn about requirements to become a computer programmer.

Out-of-Class Activity

Have students research a career of interest to them by interviewing a person who works in that career field. The interview can be done either in person or by letter. Students should learn what education or training this person has, what working in the career is like, and other information of interest.

TEACH

Activity F. Refer students to the Reference Manual in the textbook to study the format for typing business letters. Introduce each of the numbered hot spots on the business letter as each letter part is discussed.

Illustration

Call students attention to the illustration. Explain that many companies choose their own style, and it may be very different from the format shown here.

Letter 6. Point out the differences between a business letter and a personal business letter. Go over the format for a block-style business letter.

FORMATTING

F. Business Letters

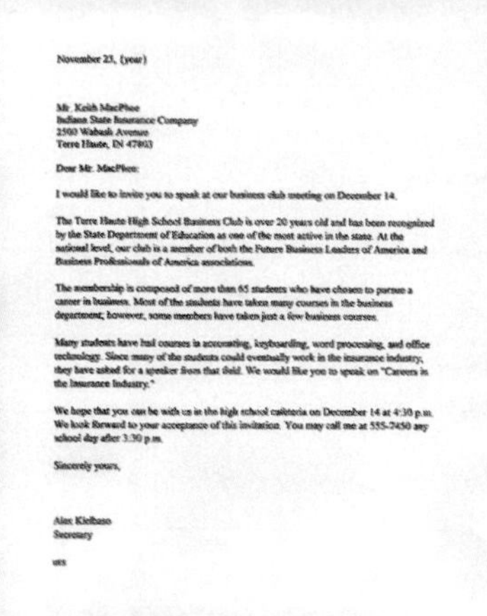

November 23, {year}

Mr. Keith MacPhee
Indiana State Insurance Company
2500 Wabash Avenue
Terre Haute, IN 47803

Dear Mr. MacPhee:

I would like to invite you to speak at our business club meeting on December 14.

The Terre Haute High School Business Club is over 20 years old and has been recognized by the State Department of Education as one of the most active in the state. At the national level, our club is a member of both the Future Business Leaders of America and Business Professionals of America associations.

The membership is composed of more than 65 students who have chosen to pursue a career in business. Most of the students have taken many courses in the business department; however, some members have taken just a few business courses.

Many students have had courses in accounting, keyboarding, word processing, and office technology. Since many of the students could eventually work in the insurance industry, they have asked for a speaker from that field. We would like you to speak on "Careers in the Insurance Industry."

We hope that you can be with us in the high school cafeteria on December 14 at 4:30 p.m. We look forward to your acceptance of this invitation. You may call me at 555-7450 any school day after 3:30 p.m.

Sincerely yours,

Alex Kielbaso
Secretary

urs

A business letter represents a company, not an individual. Business letters are usually printed on company stationery called letterhead. The letterhead usually includes the company's name, address, and telephone number. The differences between a business letter and a personal-business letter are these:

1. The writer's company name and address appear in the letterhead; therefore, they are not typed in the closing lines.
2. The writer's business title is typed below the name. A short title may be placed on the same line as the name, separated by a comma. The name and title are called the **writer's identification**.
3. The initials of the typist (called **reference initials**) are typed a double space below the writer's identification.

WORD PROCESSING APPLICATIONS

Type the following letter in block style. Use your own initials for the reference initials. Address a No. 10 envelope. Do not include a return address. Add/append the envelope to the letter.

LETTER 6
Block-Style Business

November 23, {year} / Mr. Keith MacPhee / Indiana State Insurance Company / 2500 Wabash Avenue / Terre Haute, IN 47803 / Dear Mr. MacPhee:
¶I would like to invite you to speak at our business club meeting on December 14.
¶The Terre Haute High School Business Club is over 20 years old and has been recognized by the State Department of Education as one of the most active in the state. At the national level, our club is a member of both the Future Business Leaders of America and Business Professionals of America associations.

interNET ACTIVITY

Have students open the Website for FBLA at www.fbla-plb.org/ or use a search engine and type Future Business Leaders of America. First check the FAQs, then have students look at Competitive Events, What's New, and other resources on the site.

Career Exploration

Have students use the FBLA Website to explore new thoughts about careers in business. Have them search for information on careers that sound interesting and write a short article that explains what the career is about and why they are interested in this career.

¶The membership is composed of more than 65 students who have chosen to pursue a career in business. Most of the students have taken many courses in the business department; however, some members have taken just a few business courses.
¶Many students have had courses in accounting, keyboarding, word processing, and office technology. Since many of the students could eventually work in the insurance industry, they have asked for a speaker from that field. We would like you to speak on "Careers in the Insurance Industry."
¶We hope that you can be with us in the high school cafeteria on December 14 at 4:30 p.m. We look forward to your acceptance of this invitation. You may call me at 555-7450 any school day after 3:30 p.m.
Sincerely yours, / Alex Kielbaso / Secretary / urs

Type the following letter in block style. Use your initials for the reference initials. Use the current date.

LETTER 7
Block-Style Business

(Current Date) / Ms. Elyse Demers / 2101 Market Street / York, PA 17404 / Dear Ms. Demers:
¶You have been scheduled for surgery next month by the Orthopedic Unit of St. Ann's Hospital. Within the next few days, you will receive a form that authorizes your physician to provide us with information on your medical history. This information is vital to us. It will help us to eliminate repeat tests and take into consideration any additional health problems you may have.
¶Please provide the name of your physician and your date of birth on the form. Then, sign and date the form and give it to your physician so that your medical history will be forwarded to us before your surgery.
¶If you have more than one physician from whom we need records or if you have any questions or concerns, please call us at 717-555-9000 and request additional forms.
Sincerely, / Marsha Cunningham / Administrator / urs

interNET CONNECTION

Use the Internet to learn more about the Future Business Leaders of America and the Business Professionals of America. Explore information about other members of these organizations.

LESSON 51

TEACH

Letter 7. Remind students to use today's date and to add their initials as reference initials.

ASSESS

- Check to see if students are increasing their word a minute speeds as they complete each 12-second timing.
- As students begin typing the letters, walk around the room and point out correct and incorrect formatting to individual students.
- After students finish typing the letters, have them view their work on the screen to see if they made any errors. If errors were made, have students edit their work and make corrections.

CLOSE

If students do not finish Letter 7 during the class period, make sure they save their work so that they can complete it the next time this class meets.

Remind students to clean up their workstation when they leave.

Teacher Notes

FOCUS

- Use Diagnostic Practice and Paced Practice to improve skills.
- Learn word processing features: Find and Replace.
- Practice typing and formatting block-style business letters.

BELLRINGER

As soon as students arrive at their workstations and log in, have them type the Warmup. Go over the purpose of each line as shown to the left of the copy.

TEACH

Activity B. Make sure that students understand that this Diagnostic Practice activity is designed to help identify areas that need improvement and provide needed practice.

Activity C. Review with students the procedure for the Paced Practice activity. (See Lesson 34, page 119.)

LESSON 52

BUSINESS LETTERS

OBJECTIVES:

- Improve keyboarding skill.
- Learn word processing features.
- Reinforce the skill of formatting business letters.

A. WARMUP

Type each line 2 times.

Speed	1	It will help to put away worry and doubt about your skills.
Accuracy	2	The dozen extra blue jugs were quickly moved from the pool.
Language Link	3	The number of items to remember to pick up is overwhelming.
Numbers/Symbols	4	(it is) [to the] {of a} 5 < 9 (in at) [by it] {be on} 7 > 1
		| 1 | 2 | 3 | 4 | 5 | 6 | 7 | 8 | 9 | 10 | 11 | 12

SKILLBUILDING

B. DIAGNOSTIC PRACTICE: ALPHABET

Turn to the Diagnostic Practice: Alphabet routine on page SB-1 Type one of the Pretest/Posttest paragraphs and identify any errors made. Then type the corresponding drill lines 2 times for each letter on which you made 2 or more errors and 1 time for each letter on which you made only 1 error. Finally, repeat the Pretest and compare your performance.

C. PACED PRACTICE

Turn to the Paced Practice routine beginning on page SB-7. Take three 2-minute timings starting at the point where you left off the last time.

FACT FILE

Silicon is a nonmetallic element from which semiconductors are made. Next to oxygen, it is the most abundant element found in nature. Silicon, which is found in rocks and sand, is also used in the manufacture of glass, concrete, brick, and pottery.

RESOURCES

 Lesson Plan 52

 Courseware Lesson 52

Student Data Disk

Student Manual

Supplementary Production Activities

FORMATTING

D. Software Features

STUDENT MANUAL

Find and Replace

Study Lesson 52 in your student manual. Complete all the practice activities while at your computer. Then complete the jobs that follow.

WORD PROCESSING APPLICATIONS

Type the following letter in block style. Use your own initials for the reference initials. Address a No. 10 envelope. Do not include a return address, and add/append the envelope to the letter.

LETTER 8

Block-Style Business

(Current Date) / Mrs. Alma Louise Yeu / President / Yeu & Yeu Associates / 4500 Elk Grove Avenue / Arlington Heights, IL 60004 / Dear Mrs. Yeu:

¶It is a pleasure to accept the task of chairperson for the United Fund campaign this fall.

¶As you are aware, I have been on the local United Fund board for the past eight years. I have had a great eight years; I look forward to at least four more years with the fund. Will I, as the new chairperson, have the responsibility of selecting the campaign committee? Jason Lewis, last year's chairperson, told me that it would be best if I could. He selected a committee composed of representatives from the business, industrial, educational, and lay communities. Last year's drive was the best yet; I think the results were due in large part to the committee.

¶Jason Lewis, Marsha Hunt, and Alex Garcia were on the committee last year; they were outstanding members. I plan to retain them if they are willing to serve again.

¶If you have questions about the proposed committee, please call me.

Sincerely yours, / Louise K. Fletcher / Production Engineer / urs

TEACH

STUDENT MANUAL

Be sure students turn to the correct lesson in their Student Manual.

Activity D. Explain the find and replace feature presented in this activity.

Letter 8. Refer students to the Reference Manual in the software to review the formats for typing block-style business letters.

CULTURAL CONNECTIONS

Explain to students that in 1863, the International Red Cross and Red Crescent Movement were created in Switzerland to provide nonpartisan care to the wounded and sick in times of war. Invite a local Red Cross worker to speak to your class about the organization today.

interNET ACTIVITY

Ask students if they have ever worked as a volunteer. Have them tell a little about their experience. Have students search the Internet to explore volunteering opportunities in your area. Students should document their search.

TEACH

Letter 9. Remind students to address an envelope for the letter.

Letter 10. Review all the options in the Find and Replace dialog box with the students.

Letter 11. Tell students that when they write letters, they should always be courteous and positive.

ASSESS

- After students finish typing the letters, have them view their work on the screen to see if they made any errors. If errors were made, have students edit their work and make corrections.

CLOSE

If students do not finish the letters during the class period, make sure they save their work so that they can complete it the next time this class meets.

Remind students to clean up their workstation when they leave.

PORTFOLIO *Activity*

If students' portfolio goals include demonstrating progress, they may want to include one or more letters from this lesson. Encourage students to evaluate their work and include comments in their portfolio.

Type the following letter in block style. Use your own initials for the reference initials. Address a No. 10 envelope. Do not include a return address, and add/append the envelope to the letter.

LETTER 9

Block-Style Business

(Current Date) / Mrs. Lottie Alexander / Personnel Director / Minneapolis Manufacturing Co. / 1700 University Avenue / Minneapolis, MN 55104-3020 / Dear Mrs. Alexander:
¶It is a pleasure to write a recommendation for John Saum for the position of word processor specialist with your company. John was in my accounting, computer, and multimedia classes; he was an outstanding student. He has an excellent background in grammar and spelling. He consistently received high grades in his production work on the computer.
¶Our advisory committee recommended him as the top student in the cooperative education program his senior year. John worked for the Miller Manufacturing Company as a word processor trainee in the mornings and attended afternoon classes. His supervisor consistently gave him exceptional ratings.
¶I am sure that John has asked the school to send you a copy of his transcript; it is outstanding. He indicates that he would like to attend a university once he has a job. I know that John Saum will be an excellent employee.
Sincerely yours, / Jose Sauceda / Business Instructor / urs

LETTER 10

Block-Style Business

Open Letter 8 and make these revisions: Use find and replace to change Yeu to Yeun and Jason Lewis to Leonard Whilhite.

LETTER 11

Block-Style Business

Open Letter 9 and make the following changes:

1. ***Use find and replace to change John Saum to Maria Suma.***
2. ***Use find and replace to change all the masculine pronouns to feminine pronouns (he, his, him to she, her).***
3. ***Be sure to change all instances of John's given name with Maria's name.***

Teacher Notes

LESSON 53 REVIEW

OBJECTIVES:

- Improve skill in formatting personal-business letters, envelopes, and business letters.
- Learn to use commas in a series and with transitional expressions.

A. WARMUP

Type each line 2 times.

Speed	1	`Emi would like to buy the dress if it comes in green denim.`
Accuracy	2	`Karl may sign up with five or six dozen clubs for jonquils.`
Language Link	3	`When our order arrived, a number of lightbulbs were broken.`
Symbols	4	`My brother-in-law gave Trev that you-know-what-I-mean look.`
		| 1 | 2 | 3 | 4 | 5 | 6 | 7 | 8 | 9 | 10 | 11 | 12

B. LANGUAGE LINK

Study the rules and examples below. Then edit lines 5–8 to correct any errors in comma usage.

Rule 6: Use a comma between each item in a series of three or more.

I walked the beach, read novels, and ate well while on vacation.

Rule 7: Use a comma before and after a transitional expression (such as *therefore* or *however*).

Our account, therefore, is current.

```
5 The ball bat and glove were in the garage beside the car.
6 Meg told about big cities tall buildings and busy people.
7 My yard is full of leaves and therefore needs to be raked.
8 Lowering gas prices however does not affect costs of cars.
```


RESOURCES

 Lesson Plan 53

 Courseware Lesson 53

Student Data Disk

Student Manual

Language Link Worksheets

Grading and Evaluation

Cross-Curricular Activities

LESSON 53

FOCUS

- Use 30-second timings to build speed.
- Apply Language Link rules for commas.
- Practice formatting and typing block-style business letters.

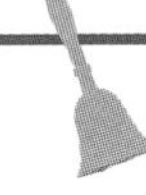

BELLRINGER

As soon as students arrive at their workstations and log in, have them type the Warmup. Go over the purpose of each line as shown to the left of the copy.

TEACH

Activity B. After students have edited and corrected any errors in comma usage, have them choose one of the sentences and write a letter to a friend about the topic. Have students exchange letters to check for typing accuracy.

Solutions: The ball, bat, and glove were in the garage beside the car.

Meg told about big cities, tall buildings, and busy people.

My yard is full of leaves and, therefore, needs to be raked.

Lowering gas prices, however, does not affect costs of cars.

TEACH

Activity C. Remind students that the goal for 30-second timings is improved speed.

Letter 12. Refer students to the Reference Manual in the textbook to review the formats for typing block-style business letters, if necessary.

SKILLBUILDING

C. 30-SECOND TIMINGS

Take two 30-second timings on lines 9–10. Then take two 30-second timings on lines 11–12. Try to increase your speed on each timing.

```
9       When you talk to customers on the phone, here are some   12
10  tips. Answer on the first ring, and identify the company.    24

11      Speak courteously. If you wear a smile, it will help     11
12  you have a friendly tone of voice. Try to be friendly.       22
    | 1 | 2 | 3 | 4 | 5 | 6 | 7 | 8 | 9 | 10 | 11 | 12
```

WORD PROCESSING APPLICATIONS

LETTER 12
Block-Style Business

Type the following rough-draft business letter. Make the corrections indicated by the proofreaders' marks. Use your initials as the typist.

(Current Date)

Mrs. Stephany Ackerman [ie]

3257 Lake Side Drive

Lake Oswago, OR 97053 [e]

Dear Mrs. Ackerman:

Thank you for asking for Pleasure Isalnd Tavel to plan your overseas trip. While we finalize you itenerary, you may want to apply for your passport. Often it takes weeks before you receive it in the mail.

A passport application can be otained from you post office or form any federal or state court. There is a required fee, and two current, identical photos of you are needed to help prove who you

FACT FILE

Ask students why they would need a passport or a visa. Tell them that not every country they visit requires a visa. What two bordering countries do not require a visa for visiting Americans? (Canada and Mexico) Have students choose a country and write a letter to the embassy asking about visa requirements for visitors.

are. You will also need a document, such as a certificate birth, to prove that you are a U.s. citizen. Instructions on the application detail the types of proof of citizenship that are accpetable. once your passport is issued, it will remain valid for five or ten years, depending on your age.

We would like to have your itinerary finalized in about two weeks. If there is any thing else we can do during that time to assist you, please give us a call.

Sincerely

Margret Sagan

Agent
urs

LETTER 13
Block-Style Business

Type the following business letter in block style.

(Current Date) / Ms. Alexia Wilcox / 956 Second Avenue /Seattle, WA 98101 / Dear Ms. Wilcox:

¶Thank you for your telephone call requesting information about the clothing we carry at Easygoing Wear. Under separate cover we have sent you a catalog which contains all of our clothing lines.

¶Our sales representative, Ms. Nelda Gomez, has received your name and address; she will be calling on you within the next few days. Ms. Gomez will answer any questions you have concerning purchases, credit, and deliveries. In addition, she will have an array of products we are featuring this year.

¶This week's ad for Jacobson's, a store that carries our line and advertises in *The Seattle Inquirer,* features clothing that could be worn this fall; the ad displays clothing for football games and hiking. Jacobson's tell us that our fall line is one of their best selling lines.

¶We hope that you will be impressed with our line and that you will consider purchasing some of our clothing. We believe that you will be pleased with the quality, the styling, and the price.

Sincerely yours, / Mr. Alexander Long / Sales Manager / urs

LESSON 53

TEACH

Letter 13. Remind students that in block style they do not indent at the beginning of a paragraph.

ASSESS

- Check to see if students are increasing their word a minute speeds as they complete each of the 30-second timings.
- Watch students as they complete the Language Link activity to see if they are able to apply the rules for comma usage correctly.
- As students begin typing the letters, walk around the room and point out correct and incorrect formatting to individual students.
- After students finish typing the letters, have them view their work on the screen to see if they made any errors. If errors were made, have students edit their work and make corrections.

CLOSE

If students do not finish the letters during the class period, make sure they save their work so that they can complete it the next time this class meets.

Remind students to clean up their workstation when they leave.

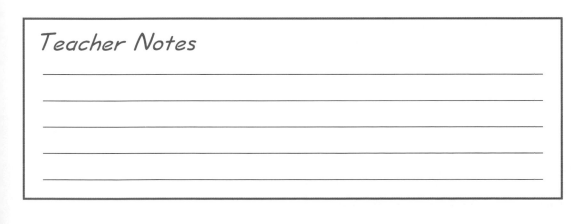

Teacher Notes

LESSON 54

FOCUS

- Use the Pretest/Practice/Posttest routine to build speed and accuracy
- Learn word processing features: Tab Set and Ruler.
- Learn how to format and type a modified-block style letter.

BELLRINGER

As soon as students arrive at their workstations and log in, have them type the Warmup. Go over the purpose of each line as shown to the left of the copy.

TEACH

Activities B and C. Remind students they should improve both their speed and accuracy from the Pretest to the Posttest.

PRETEST/PRACTICE/POSTEST

The ***Pretest/Practice/Posttest*** routines are designed to improve speed or accuracy.

- The ***Pretest*** identifies students' speed or accuracy needs.
- The ***Practice*** provides a variety of improvement drills.
- The ***Posttest*** (a repeat of the Pretest) measures improvement.

LESSON 54 MODIFIED-BLOCK LETTERS

OBJECTIVES:

- Strengthen reaches.
- Learn word processing features.
- Format modified-block letters.

A. WARMUP

Type each line 2 times.

Speed	1 The boys will miss swim class for the first time this term.
Accuracy	2 The lazy judge was quick to pay my taxes on the five barns.
Language Link	3 As soon as the facts are known, Hale will write the report.
Numbers/Symbols	4 $76.01 $13.02 $83.03 $92.04 $62.05 $30.06 $65.07 $82.08 $10

| 1 | 2 | 3 | 4 | 5 | 6 | 7 | 8 | 9 | 10 | 11 | 12

SKILLBUILDING

B. PRETEST

Take a 1-minute timing on the paragraph. Note your speed and errors.

5 The blazing paint gave off toxic odors which gagged 11
6 the nearby runners and joggers. Quickly the sunny sky grew 22
7 dimmer as it filled with the acrid smoke. Everyone ran 33
8 even faster to get away from the spreading flames. 43

| 1 | 2 | 3 | 4 | 5 | 6 | 7 | 8 | 9 | 10 | 11 | 12

C. PRACTICE

SPEED: If you made 2 or fewer errors on the Pretest, type lines 9–16 two times each.
ACCURACY: If you made more than 2 errors on the Pretest, type lines 9–12 as a group two times. Then type lines 13–16 as a group two times.

Double Reaches

9 mm comma gamma gummy mummy dummy yummy jimmy tummy hammy mm
10 gg baggy leggy foggy soggy doggy muggy piggy buggy jaggy gg
11 nn inner annoy sunny funny bunny bonny gunny nanny runny nn
12 tt kitty ditty bitty catty nutty witty vitta patty motto tt

RESOURCES

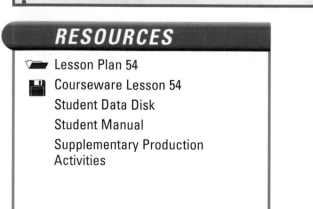

Lesson Plan 54

Courseware Lesson 54

Student Data Disk

Student Manual

Supplementary Production Activities

Alternate Reaches

```
13 toxic blame paint their towns bland panda theme tucks blend
14 panel throb turns flame pause throw tusks bogus proxy title
15 tutor boric prism tithe ticks bowls prowl tight bugle psych
16 rigor slept vigor quake chant flair shame snake right thigh
```

D. POSTTEST

Repeat the Pretest. Compare your Posttest results with your Pretest results.

E. 12-Second Sprints

Take three 12-second timings on each line. Try to increase your speed on each timing.

```
17 He bought the buns at the store for my friends in the park.
18 We went to the park to have a good time and play some ball.
19 The ball got lost in the water, and we had to find another.
20 None of us wanted to leave when it got dark, but we had to.
   |||| 5 |||| 10 |||| 15 |||| 20 |||| 25 |||| 30 |||| 35 |||| 40 |||| 45 |||| 50 |||| 55 |||| 60
```

FORMATTING

F. Modified-Block Style Letters

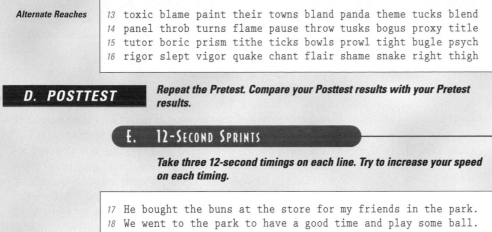

In the modified-block style letter, the date and closing lines (complimentary closing, writer's name, and title) begin at the center point of the writing line. Paragraphs in a modified-block style letter may be blocked at the left margin (the preferred style) or indented 0.5 inch.

G. Software Features

STUDENT MANUAL

Ruler and Tab Set

Study Lesson 54 in your student manual. Complete all the practice activities while at your computer. Then complete the jobs that follow.

LESSON 54

TEACH

Activity D. Remind students they should improve both their speed and accuracy from the Pretest to the Posttest.

Activity E. Remind students that the goal for 12-second sprints is improved speed with each timing.

Activity F. Explain to students that unlike block style, in modified-block style letters the beginning of paragraphs may be blocked at the left margin (preferred) or indented 0.5 inch.

STUDENT MANUAL

Be sure students turn to the correct page in their Student Manual.

Activity G. Explain the software feature presented in this activity.

- Demonstrate the use of the ruler.
- Demonstrate the tab set feature.

CULTURAL CONNECTIONS

In many ancient cultures, words held their own power. Words can make us laugh or cry; they can hurt or help others. Remind students to choose the words they use carefully and to be aware of the power of the words they use.

TEACH

Letter 14. Point out that the default setting for tabs is every ½ inch. Remind students how to activate the Ruler and how to set and clear tabs using the Ruler and the Format menu.

Letter 15. Remind students that the date and closing lines always begin at the center point of the writing line in a modified-block style letter.

ASSESS

- Check to see if students show signs of improvement from the Pretest to the Posttest.
- Make sure students are able to use the software features introduced in this lesson: Ruler and Tab Set.
- As students begin typing the letters, walk around the room and point out correct and incorrect formatting to individual students.
- After students finish typing the letters, have them view their work on the screen to see if they made any errors. If errors were made, have students edit their work and make corrections.

CLOSE

If students do not finish Letter 15 during the class period, make sure they save their work so that they can complete it the next time this class meets.

WORD PROCESSING APPLICATIONS

LETTER 14
Modified-Block

Type the following letter in modified-block style. Use your initials.

(Current Date) / Mr. Weijun Zhao, President / All-Star Appliances / 2200 South Maybelle Avenue / Tulsa, OK 74107-2000 / Dear Mr. Zhao: / Welcome to the select group of Apex television dealers. ¶Your application has been approved and we look forward to many years of successful business for both your firm and ours. ¶We take pride in the fact that we have never rescinded a dealership agreement in our 40 years of manufacturing quality television sets. Every dealer will tell you that we are a family working together to improve the industry —both the manufacturing and servicing industry. ¶We are aware of the fine reputation of your company for service and sales in the greater Tulsa area; therefore, it would be a pleasure to have you visit our offices and plant at our expense as soon as you have an opportunity to do so. / Sincerely yours, / Amos Morgan / President / urs

LETTER 15
Modified-Block

Type the following letter in modified-block style. Use your initials.

(Current Date) / Mr. William J. Gross, President / National Training and Development Association / 3500 Collingwood Boulevard / Toledo, OH 43624 / Dear Mr. Gross: / It is a pleasure to accept your invitation to speak at the National Training and Development Association's Annual Convention in Cleveland next April. I will be glad to speak either on the current status of word processing or the skills needed by a beginning word processor. ¶As you know, I have spent considerable time in advising various firms on how a quality word processing center affects the total communication system of the firm. The effects of a good center bring increased revenues and result in a better image of the firm. ¶If you wish, I would be most happy to discuss with your members the importance of hiring well-trained word processors. I have taught technology administration at the local university as well as developed in-house training programs for firms. I could include in the speech the need for highly developed technical, human relations, and personal skills. ¶You or your members may desire another topic in the area of word processing or its personnel; if so, please let me know. ¶Again, thank you for an invitation to speak at your annual meeting. / Sincerely yours, / David G. Morgan / Consultant / urs

Teacher Notes

LESSON 55 LETTERS WITH INDENTED PARAGRAPHS

OBJECTIVES:
- Compose at the keyboard.
- Improve keyboarding skill.
- Format letters with indented paragraphs.

A. WARMUP

Type each line 2 times.

Speed	1 I could not read the small print on the map she sent to me.
Accuracy	2 A dozen jumpy zebras quickly zipped over the six big gates.
Language Link	3 Because I had good grades, my scholarship has been renewed.
Symbols	4 it's hasn't we'll aren't they'll couldn't you've don't I've
	| 1 | 2 | 3 | 4 | 5 | 6 | 7 | 8 | 9 | 10 | 11 | 12

LANGUAGE LINK

B. COMPOSING AT THE KEYBOARD

Answer each of the following questions with complete sentences.

5 If you could invent something to improve the quality of our lives, what would it be?
6 Why did you choose to invent what you did?
7 What can pets teach us?
8 If you could travel anywhere in the world, where would you go? Why?

FACT FILE

On March 16, 1926, Robert H. Goddard became the first man to build a liquid-fueled rocket and to fire the rocket.

LESSON 55

FOCUS

- Use 30-second OK timings to improve accuracy.
- Compose Language Link answers using complete sentences.
- Learn how to format and type modified-block style letters with indented paragraphs.

BELLRINGER

As soon as students arrive at their workstations and log in, have them type the Warmup. Go over the purpose of each line as shown to the left of the copy.

TEACH

Activity B. After students have answered each question with one sentence, have them choose one topic and free write about the topic for five to ten minutes. Provide additional time for proofreading. Have students read their writing to another student.

Solutions: Answers will vary

RESOURCES

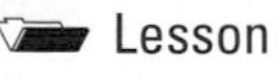

- Lesson Plan 55
- Courseware Lesson 55
- Student Data Disk
- Student Manual
- Supplementary Production Activities
- Multicultural Activities

COURSEWARE OVERVIEW

TEACH

Activity C. Remind students that the goal for 30-second OK timings is improved accuracy.

Activity D. Refer students to the Reference Manual in the textbook to study the format for typing letters with indented paragraphs.

Illustration

Point out that if an indented style is used, the date and closing lines must begin at the center point of the writing line.

SKILLBUILDING

C. 30-Second OK Timings

Take two 30-second OK (error-free) timings on lines 9–10. Then take two 30-second OK timings on lines 11–12. Goal: no errors.

```
 9      Bea majored in zoology after she qualified for a large   12
10  research grant. She must speak with her adviser, Dr. Haver.  24

11      I am anxious because I have a dozen errands and cannot   12
12  be late for class. Have Paula adjourn this meeting quickly.  24
   | 1 | 2 | 3 | 4 | 5 | 6 | 7 | 8 | 9 | 10 | 11 | 12
```

FACT FILE

One of the greatest problems for humans in space is weightlessness. On long missions, astronauts often come back in weakened physical state. Russian cosmonauts, who have spent the most time in space—up to a year, are sometimes so weak that they need help to get out of their space capsule.

FORMATTING

D. Letters With Indented Paragraphs

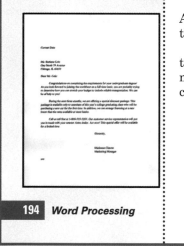

A variation of the modified-block style letter is to indent the first line of each paragraph, usually 0.5 inch.

When using the indented paragraph style, set two tabs—one for the paragraph (at 0.5 inch from the left margin) and one for the date and closing lines (at the center point of the line).

JOURNAL ENTRY

Have students write a journal entry with the following prompt: "Computers open up a whole new world for me by __________________." Have students write for five to ten minutes. Provide time for proofreading.

LETTER 16

Modified-Block With Indented Paragraphs

Type the following letter in modified-block style with indented paragraphs. Remember to set 2 tabs.

(Current Date) / Ms. Barbara Cole / One North 79 Avenue / Chicago, IL 60635 / Dear Ms. Cole:
¶Congratulations on completing the requirements for your undergraduate degree! As you look forward to joining the workforce on a full-time basis, you are probably trying to determine how you can stretch your budget to include reliable transportation. We can be of help to you!
¶ During the next three months, we are offering a special discount package. This package is available only to members of this year's college graduating class who will be purchasing a new car for the first time. In addition, we can arrange financing at a rate lower than the rates available at most banks.
¶Call us toll free at 1-800-555-5295. Our customer service representative will put you in touch with your nearest Astra dealer. Act now! This special offer will be available for a limited time.
Sincerely, / Madonna Chavez / Marketing Manager / urs

PORTFOLIO *Activity*

If you made any errors in Letter 16, correct them. Then print a copy of the letter and add it to your portfolio. In addition to the letter, write a short paragraph about the importance of proofreading all documents carefully and the need to learn a variety of formats.

TEACH

Letter 16. Remind students that in modified-block style they can either indent paragraphs or keep the paragraphs flush left. In this letter, they are to indent paragraphs.

PORTFOLIO *Activity*

If students' portfolio goals include demonstrating progress, they may want to include one or both letters from this lesson. Encourage students to evaluate their work and include comments in their portfolio.

Multiple Learning Styles

Suggest that students create learning cards to help them with new material. To create learning cards, have them type information on index cards. Then put these cards in different places. When they see a card, they are to read the material and then close their eyes and recall the information.

*inter*NET ACTIVITY

Have student use the Internet to research banks and financial institutions. Have them learn about the banks in your community. How large are they? Are they national? International? What services do they offer?

LESSON 55

TEACH

Letter 17. Remind students they are to indent paragraphs in this letter.

ASSESS

- Check to see if students are completing 30-second OK timings without any errors.
- Review the accuracy of students' responses to questions in the Language Link composing activity.
- As students begin typing the letters, walk around the room and point out correct and incorrect formatting to individual students.
- After students finish typing the letters, have them view their work on the screen to see if they made any errors. If errors were made, have students edit their work and make corrections.

CLOSE

If students do not finish Letter 17 during the class period, make sure they save their work so that they can complete it the next time the class meets.

Remind students to clean up their workstation when they leave.

LETTER 17

Modified-Block With Indented Paragraphs

Type the following letter in modified-block style with indented paragraphs, making the corrections indicated by the proofreaders' marks. Use your initials for reference.

(Current Date) ↓4

Mr. Marvin Estawick
Lawton Industries
5492 warren Avenue
Detroit, MI 48207-9602

Dear Mr. Estawick:

Mrs. Barbara Cole, who was an employee by your company as a summer intern, has applied for credit. Since Ms. Cole does not have a credit record, we will need a data sheet to be completed by her most recent employer.

Will you please fill out and return the form that was sent to you so we that we may process Ms. Cole's request for an automobile loan. A release statment has been signed giving you permision to disclose the requested information.

If you have any questions regarding this form can be answered by calling me at 312-555-9672, Ext. 40. Please FAX the form to me at 312-555-9677.

Sincerely,

Ms. Madonna Chavez
Marketing Manager

urs

Teacher Notes

LESSON 56

LETTERS WITH ENCLOSURES AND ATTACHMENTS

OBJECTIVES:

- Improve keyboarding skill.
- Format modified-block letters with enclosures and attachments.
- Type 33/3'/5e.

A. WARMUP

Type each line 2 times.

Speed	James was not here when all of us signed the card for Rita.
Accuracy	Jacqueline was glad her family took five or six big prizes.
Language Link	The picnic is always Labor Day (first Monday in September).
Technique	Will students use the SHIFT LOCK to type in SOLID CAPITALS?

| 1 | 2 | 3 | 4 | 5 | 6 | 7 | 8 | 9 | 10 | 11 | 12

SKILLBUILDING

B. PRETEST

Take a 1-minute timing on the paragraph. Note your speed and errors.

Social Studies Connections

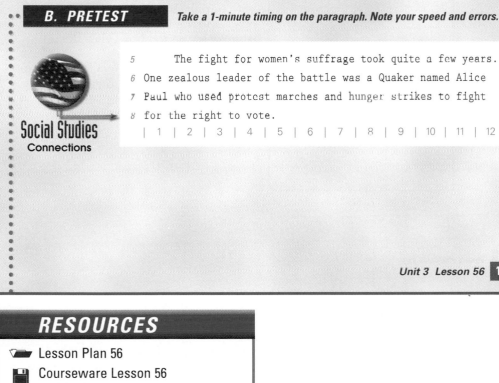

The fight for women's suffrage took quite a few years. 11
One zealous leader of the battle was a Quaker named Alice 22
Paul who used protest marches and hunger strikes to fight 33
for the right to vote. 37

| 1 | 2 | 3 | 4 | 5 | 6 | 7 | 8 | 9 | 10 | 11 | 12

RESOURCES

- Lesson Plan 56
- Courseware Lesson 56
- Student Data Disk
- Student Manual
- Supplementary Production Activities

LESSON 56

FOCUS

- Use the Pretest/Practice/Posttest routine to build speed and accuracy.
- Learn how to format and type modified-block style letters with indented paragraphs.
- Learn how to format enclosure and attachment notations on letters.

BELLRINGER

As soon as students arrive at their workstations and log in, have them type the Warmup. Go over the purpose of each line as shown to the left of the copy.

TEACH

Activity B. Remind students they should improve both their speed and accuracy from the Pretest to the Posttest.

PRETEST/PRACTICE/POSTEST

The ***Pretest/Practice/Posttest*** routines are designed to improve speed or accuracy.

- The ***Pretest*** identifies students' speed or accuracy needs.
- The ***Practice*** provides a variety of improvement drills.
- The ***Posttest*** (a repeat of the Pretest) measures improvement.

TEACH

Activities C–D. Remind students they should improve both their speed and accuracy from the Pretest to the Posttest. For the Practice activity, go over the drill lines they should type twice for the number of Pretest errors they make.

Activity E. Ask students the following questions: When do you use enclosures? When do you use attachments? What do you do if more than one item is enclosed?

Social Studies Connections

Tell students that women's emancipation was part of the European political culture throughout the nineteenth century. The word feminist was actually coined in France in the 1830s. Ask students to write their thoughts about how today's technology might have helped both American and European women gain the vote faster. Read a few ideas in class. Then have students think about how technology can help people around the world today gain economic and political freedom.

C. PRACTICE

In the chart below, find the number of errors you made on the Pretest. Then type each of the following designated drill lines two times.

Pretest Errors	0–1	2	3	4+
Drill Lines	13–16	11–15	10–14	9–12

Accuracy

```
 9 not fight women named until marches battle zealous Illinois
10 did leader states joined strikes protest suffrage Amendment
11 was after begin issue quite hunger decades Wyoming Congress
12 New their first debate Alice woman thirty Quaker Nineteenth
```

Speed

```
13 decades state years next pass took nine York the and did in
14 protest right named vote last test mend gave for was but to
15 strikes cause first lead them West used teen win who few of
16 fight other march rage Paul join zeal give two one not at a
```

D. POSTTEST

Repeat the Pretest. Compare your Posttest results with your Pretest results.

FORMATTING

E. Enclosure and Attachment Notations

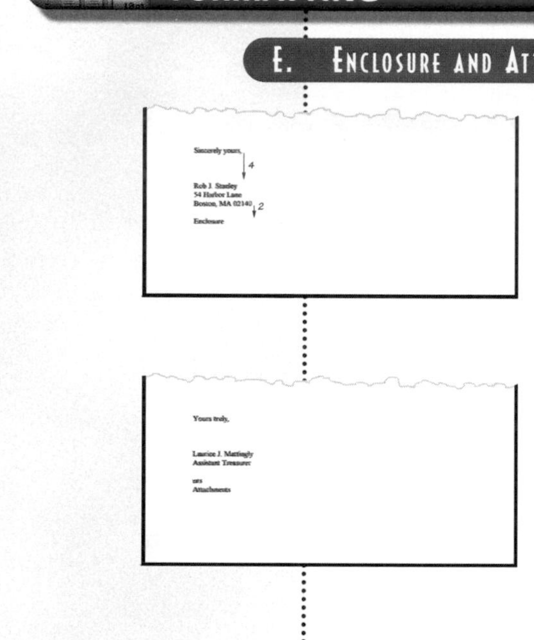

To show that an item is enclosed with a letter, type the word *Enclosure* at the left margin on the line below the reference initials. If the item is stapled or clipped to the letter, type the word *Attachment* on the line below the reference initials.

If more than one item is enclosed or attached, type *Enclosures* or *Attachments*.

SCHOOL TO CAREER

Share with students that letters are the most-used form of communication in business. Students should know the different formats for a letter. They also must know that every company has its own letter policy and style.

Out-of-Class Activity

Have students visit or write to an employment agency or company and request a job application and explain that it's for a school assignment. Have students fill out the application and write a letter about themselves that includes their typing speed and accuracy.

LETTER 18
Modified-Block With Indented Paragraphs

Type this letter in modified-block style with indented paragraphs. Be sure to include an enclosure notation.

(Current Date) / Mr. and Mrs. Marvin Carson / Circle Route, Box 318 / Elk City, OK 73644 / Dear Mr. and Mrs. Carson: ¶Congratulations on becoming the owner of a Model L350 dishwasher! The TurboKleen name on your dishwasher identifies it as a top-quality kitchen appliance.
¶For the past 25 years, we have produced appliances that are reliable—products that will help America's busy families better manage their limited time. Because we are so certain of the reliability of our appliances, every TurboKleen appliance comes with a ten-year warranty. Your warranty is enclosed with this letter. If your dishwasher should need servicing before that time, a call to our dealer will bring a service technician to your door within 24 hours.
¶Welcome to our family of satisfied customers. When we can be of any assistance to you, please let us know. /Cordially yours, / William Clifford / President / urs

LETTER 19
Modified-Block With Indented Paragraphs

Type this letter in modified-block style with indented paragraphs. Remember to type your reference initials and an enclosure notation.

May 17, (year)
Mrs. Rosa Ortez
39 McFarland Lane
Madison, WI 53714
Dear Mrs. Ortez:

We are pleased to answer the question of your science students about allergy testing. The test takes two days. This includes food allergy tests as well as the usual tests for plants, animals, and old spores, etc. Technicians in our labs must be able to conduct these tests.

You were interested in having your class visit our labs. This would be a good time to plan to have your students visit. I would be willing to come in early on the Thursday morning you specify to work with your students and you. When you have decided upon a date, please give me a call. Use the enclosed form to select the best time for your students to visit our labs.

Sincerely,
Hans Rosen
Clinic Manager

TEACH

Letter 18. Refer students to the Reference Manual in the textbook to study the format for typing letters with enclosures and/or attachments.

Letter 19. Tell students that when they write letters, they should choose simple, conversational language.

ASSESS

- Check to see if students show signs of improvement from the Pretest to the Posttest.
- As students begin typing the letters, walk around the room and point out correct and incorrect formatting to individual students.
- After students finish typing the letters, have them view their work on the screen to see if they made any errors. If errors were made, have students edit their work and make corrections.

CLOSE

If students do not finish Letter 19 during the class period, make sure they save their work so that they can complete it the next time this class meets.

Remind students to clean up their workstation when they leave.

Teacher Notes

LESSON 57

FOCUS

- Use technique timings to improve technique.
- Use the Paced Practice routine to improve skill.
- Practice formatting and typing different style business letters.
- Prepare envelopes for letters.

BELLRINGER

As soon as students arrive at their workstations and log in, have them type the Warmup. Go over the purpose of each line as shown to the left of the copy.

TEACH

Activity B. Remind students that proper technique is a building block for speed and accuracy.

Activity C. Review with students the procedure for the Paced Practice activity. (See Lesson 34, page 119.)

LESSON 57

LETTER REINFORCEMENT

OBJECTIVES:

- Improve keyboarding skill.
- Strengthen skill in formatting business letters.

A. WARMUP

Type each line 2 times.

Speed	1 It was a good idea to start to write your report this week.
Accuracy	2 My ax just zipped through the fine black wood quite evenly.
Language Link	3 The accident was distressing; however, no one was impaired.
Symbols	4 What a sight! Good luck! Watch out! At last! No way! Never!
	| 1 | 2 | 3 | 4 | 5 | 6 | 7 | 8 | 9 | 10 | 11 | 12

SKILLBUILDING

B. TECHNIQUE TIMINGS

Take two 30-second timings on each line. Focus on the techniques at the left.

Use the correct shift keys.
Type without pausing.

```
5 Dr. and Mrs. Wynans won tickets to the Hula Bowl in Hawaii.
6 The Gas & Go was first named Your Place and then Shop Stop.
7 Mr. Ulan is taking us to the Museum of Fine Arts in Boston.
8 I turned right on Lemon, left on Davis, and left on Fuller.
  | 1 | 2 | 3 | 4 | 5 | 6 | 7 | 8 | 9 | 10 | 11 | 12
```

C. PACED PRACTICE

Turn to the Paced Practice routine beginning on page SB-7. Take three 2-minute timings, starting at the point where you left off the last time.

CULTURAL CONNECTIONS

Did you know that students in Japan go to school five or six days a week? The school day usually begins about 8:30 a.m. and ends about 3:30 p.m. Saturday classes are usually over by noon. Most students begin studying English in the seventh grade and continue until they finish school.

RESOURCES

 Lesson Plan 57

 Courseware Lesson 57

Student Data Disk

Student Manual

Reteaching and Reinforcement

Grading and Evaluation

LETTER 20

Block-Style Personal-Business

Format the personal-business letter below in block style; prepare a No. 10 envelope. Use the writer's name and address for the return address on the envelope. Add/append the envelope to the letter.

(Current Date) / Ms. Zoe Albright / Merkel Realtors, Inc. / 150 E. Ponce De Leon / Decatur, GA 30032 / Dear Ms. Albright:
¶My family and I are moving to Decatur from Indianapolis in October, and I would like your help in finding our new home. Friends in Decatur have told me that you know which homes best suit your clients; no one can do better. I am employed by the Albertson Corporation as an accountant, and I would like to drive less than 10 miles to work.
¶We are interested in a four-bedroom home with three and a half baths, a family room, a double-car garage, and a pool, if possible. We would like either a brick ranch or two-story colonial home. My wife prefers the ranch style, and I prefer the colonial style. I have attached some pictures of similar homes that appeal to us.
¶As we have two children, a boy and a girl, two of the four bedrooms would be for their use. One bedroom and bath would be for guests. We would like a large master bedroom overlooking the rear of the property.
¶Please send me any available information on such a home including the location, price, taxes, closing costs, and other such fees. As soon as we hear from you, we will make an appointment to visit you and see the homes you suggest.
¶You may call me at work at 317-555-2900 or my wife at home at 317-555-8957.
Sincerely yours, / Lewis K. Lincoln / 3350 Carson Avenue / Indianapolis, IN 46227/Attachments

interNET CONNECTION

Use the Internet to search for sites that provide information about available properties for sale, information about a particular area, and financial information such as selling prices and mortgage rates.

Letter 20. Remind students that in block style, they do not indent paragraphs.

interNET CONNECTION

A great source of information about real estate is the Multiple Listings Service. Find the MLS Website address for your area and provide it to students.

JOURNAL ENTRY

Have students describe what attributes they have that would make them a good employee. Ask what they believe they need to improve about themselves in order to be a good employee.

TEACH

Letter 21. Remind students that with modified-block style they can have either blocked or indented paragraphs. In this letter they want blocked paragraphs.

LETTER 21

Modified-Block Style Business

Format the business letter below in modified-block style with blocked paragraphs. Make the corrections indicated by the proofreaders' marks, and prepare a large envelope. Append/add the envelope to the document.

(Current Date)

Mr. William J. Gross, President

National Word Processing Association

3500 Collingwood Boulevard

Toledo, OH 43624

Dear Mr. Gross:

Thank you for your letter of last week telling me that you believe a talk on the skills needed by a word processor would be of great interest to your association members. I have taken the liberty of developing a talk and have entitled it, "The Well-Trained Word Processor." The talk will take approximately one hour. I will need an overhead projector, a screen, and a microphone. It is my intent to have members involved during the talk, and I will need assistance in distributing handouts to the audience. Would it be possible for you to have two assistants available to help me?

Enclosed is an outline of my talk. I have also enclosed a synopsis of the talk. I thought you might be interested in what I was planning to discuss. If you have any suggestions for other points which should be included, please let me know.

interNET ACTIVITY

Have students work in groups and search for a major airline to obtain airline schedules for flights between your local airport and Toledo, OH; Decatur, GA; or Indianapolis, IN. Have groups share their information.

Multiple Learning Styles

To help auditory and kinetic learners, have students work in groups to create a song or rap about typing and letter styles. If possible, provide time for students to work together during class. Students can use musical instruments, taped music, or sing without accompaniment.

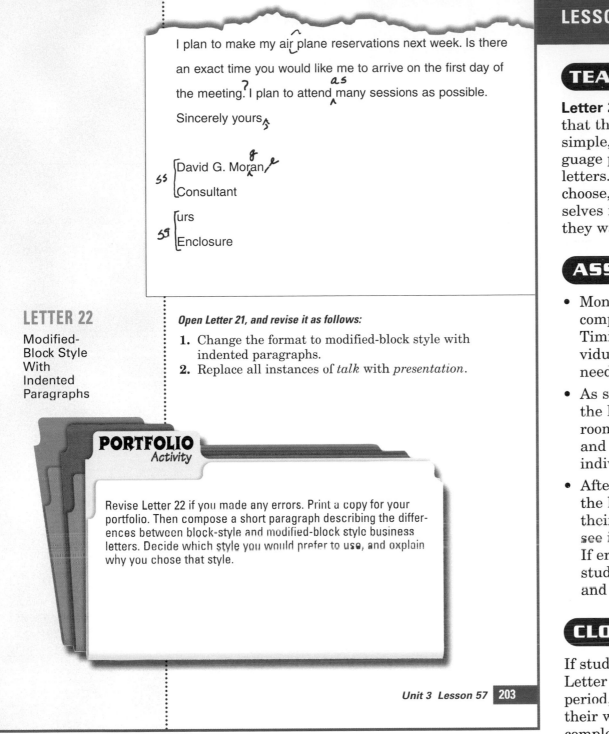

I plan to make my air plane reservations next week. Is there an exact time you would like me to arrive on the first day of the meeting. I plan to attend many sessions as possible.

Sincerely yours

David G. Moran
Consultant

urs
Enclosure

LETTER 22

Modified-Block Style With Indented Paragraphs

Open Letter 21, and revise it as follows:

1. Change the format to modified-block style with indented paragraphs.
2. Replace all instances of *talk* with *presentation*.

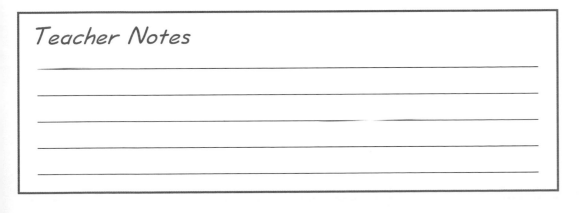

Revise Letter 22 if you made any errors. Print a copy for your portfolio. Then compose a short paragraph describing the differences between block-style and modified-block style business letters. Decide which style you would prefer to use, and explain why you chose that style.

Teacher Notes

TEACH

Letter 22. Explain to students that they should use the most simple, straightforward language possible when writing letters. For each word they choose, they should ask themselves if it best describes what they want to say.

ASSESS

- Monitor students as they complete Technique Timings and provide individualized assistance as needed.
- As students begin typing the letters, walk around the room and point out correct and incorrect formatting to individual students.
- After students finish typing the letters, have them view their work on the screen to see if they made any errors. If errors were made, have students edit their work and make corrections.

CLOSE

If students do not finish Letter 22 during the class period, make sure they save their work so that they can complete it the next time this class meets.

Remind students to clean up their workstation when they leave.

FOCUS

- Use Preview Practice to build speed and accuracy.
- Use 3-minute timings to build speed.
- Learn how to format and type a resume.

BELLRINGER

As soon as students arrive at their workstations and log in, have them type the Warmup. Go over the purpose of each line as shown to the left of the copy.

TEACH

Activity B. Point out that words in the Preview Practice are used in the timing that follows.

Activity C. Remind students that the goal for these timings is to type 33 words a minute for 3 minutes with no more than 5 errors.

LESSON 58

RESUMES

OBJECTIVES:

- Refine keyboarding skill.
- Learn about resumes.
- Type 33/3'/5e.

A. WARMUP

Type each line 2 times.

```
Speed            1 Building typing skill seems easier if you type short words.
Accuracy         2 Maxine will become eloquent over a zany gift like jodhpurs.
Language Link    3 Evi went to math, history, and art; but she missed English.
Numbers/Symbols  4 She decided that 1/3 of $36 = $12 and that 20% of $30 = $6.
                   | 1 | 2 | 3 | 4 | 5 | 6 | 7 | 8 | 9 | 10 | 11 | 12
```

SKILLBUILDING

B. PREVIEW PRACTICE

Type each line 2 times as a preview to the 3-minute timings that follow.

```
Accuracy  5 co-op solved picture resume training opportunity experience
Speed     6 learn other will give when some work stay you job not do or
```

C. 3-MINUTE TIMINGS

Take two 3-minute timings on lines 7–15. Note your speed and errors.

Goal: 33/3'/5e

```
 7      Picture this. You go to look for work. You do not get     11
 8 the job since you have no work experience. You cannot get     23
 9 work experience. No one will give you the opportunity. It     34
10 may seem like a big problem to you, but students who enroll   46
11 in a co-op work class have solved it. While still in high     58
12 school, they earn as they learn. Some stay on the job full    70
13 time. Some go on to college or other training. In any case,   81
14 they will have work experience to list on their resumes       92
15 when they complete high school.                               99
   | 1 | 2 | 3 | 4 | 5 | 6 | 7 | 8 | 9 | 10 | 11 | 12 SI 1.27
```


RESOURCES

 Lesson Plan 58

 Courseware Lesson 58

Student Data Disk

Student Manual

Supplementary Production Activities

Grading and Evaluation

D. Resumes

Once you decide to apply for a job, you will need to prepare a resume. A resume is a summary of your training, background, and qualifications for the job. There are a variety of acceptable formats for resumes, but there is basic information that should be included no matter which format you choose.

1. **Heading.** Your name, address, telephone number (with area code), and e-mail address if you have one.
2. **Objective.** A statement about the type of job you are seeking.
3. **Education.** A list of your educational background beginning with the highest level of and most recent education first. Include the school name and address, any diplomas or degrees, the year you earned them, the year you graduated, and your major area of study.
4. **Experience.** A list of your work experience beginning with the most recent. Include the name, address, and telephone number of the company; dates of employment; your job titles(s); and the name and title of your supervisor. You may also want to include a brief description of your duties.
5. **Honors, Awards, and Activities.** Any special activities or achievements that relate to the position for which you are applying. (These may give you an "edge" over other applicants.)
6. **References.** A list of at least three people who can tell a prospective employer about what kind of worker you are. Include their names, job titles, addresses, and telephone numbers. You may want to use teachers, former supervisors, and former employers as references. Before you use a person's name as a reference, you *must* get permission from that person. Another option for References is to include the statement, "References will be furnished upon request."

FACT FILE

'he Internet is being ısed more and more y companies and ndividuals to match vailable jobs to the eople who have the equired skills. You an now post your esume on the nternet at a variety f sites. When you repare a resume or electronic posting, you should keep ; simple. Use a ninimum number of onts, do not use old or italic, and ıse a minimum umber of other pecial features.

TEACH

Activity D. Explain to students that a resume is the only way a prospective employer knows who you are. A resume should be brief (1 or 2 pages long) and give an accurate picture of the individual's education, work history, and abilities.

Stress the importance of proofreading a resume so that it is free of errors.

SCHOOL TO CAREER

Explain to students that they may want to have several resumes, each one geared to a different type of business. Have students choose three ads in different fields from the newspaper and create a resume to match the type of business.

TECHNOLOGY TIP

Many large companies scan the paper resumes they receive into a resume database. Job candidates asked to prepare a scannable resume should not use fancy type fonts, lines, bullets, or visuals. They should include as many keywords and industry buzzwords as possible.

Illustration

Tell students there are many possible formats they can use for resumes. There are hundreds of books available that contain resume samples. These books may be available at your school's guidance office. In addition they can find samples of resume templates in their word processing software.

This is one example of a formatted resume. There are many acceptable styles.

Martina Valdez
4101 Fuller Apartments
Clio, MI 48240
313-555-2714
E-mail: martina@valdez.net

OBJECTIVE

To obtain an office position with word processing responsibilities.

EDUCATION

Clio High School, Clio, MI 48420

Graduated: June 1998
Major: Office Technology
Grade Point Average: 3.66

Business Subjects: Accounting, keyboarding (75 wam), word processing (Word and WordPerfect)

Honors and Activities: Student Council president during senior year; concert choir for four years; Business Student of the Year in 1998

EXPERIENCE

Rathjen Moving Co., 471 Vienna Road, Flushing, MI 48433
Telephone: 313-555-5420

June 1998 to present
Position: General Office Assistant
Supervisor: Joyce Wiesnewski, Administrative Assistant

Duties: Composing and typing routine correspondence; preparing invoices

REFERENCES

References will be furnished upon request.

206 *Word Processing*

JOURNAL ENTRY

Have students write about the following: What do you think of your resume? What would you like it to look like? How do what it looks like and how you would like it to look differ? What can you do to reach your goal?

REPORT 15
Resume

Type the resume that is illustrated on page 206 using the same format. Follow these steps:

1. Use default side and bottom margins.
2. Vertically center the page.
3. Center and type the name in bold.
4. Center and type each line in the heading; then press ENTER 2 times.
5. Type the side heading *OBJECTIVE* in all caps and bold; then press ENTER 2 times.
6. Align the remaining text at the left margin. Leave a blank line between sections.
7. Leave a blank line before and after the bold side headings.

REPORT 16
Resume

Prepare a resume for yourself using the guidelines in this lesson. Include all sections that are applicable to your background. Do not include a section if you have no entries to place in that section.

PORTFOLIO *Activity*

Once you create your resume, continue to "fine-tune" it as you continue taking courses or gaining additional work experience. Prepare a list of people you want to use as references, and ask those people for permission to list their names. Create a sheet with their names, titles, addresses, and telephone numbers. Update the list periodically so that when you are looking for a job you have the most complete, up-to-date information.

TEACH

Report 15. Refer students to the Reference Manual in the textbook to review the formats for typing a resume.

Report 16. Remind students that their resumes must be accurate and truthful.

ASSESS

- Check to see if students are increasing their word a minute speeds as they complete each 3-minute timing.
- After students finish typing the resumes, have them view their work on the screen to see if they made any errors. If errors were made, have students edit their work and make corrections.

CLOSE

If students do not finish Report 16 during the class period, make sure they save their work so that they can complete it the next time this class meets.

PORTFOLIO *Activity*

Students' resumes should be included in their portfolio for two reasons: resumes provide basic information about the students and are an example of their work in this course.

Teacher Notes

LESSON 59

FOCUS

- Use 12-second timings to build speed.
- Use Pretest/Practice/ Posttest routine to build speed and accuracy
- Learn how to format and type an application letter.
- Practice typing personal business letters.

BELLRINGER

As soon as students arrive at their workstations and log in, have them type the Warmup. Go over the purpose of each line as shown to the left of the copy.

TEACH

Activity B. Remind students that their goal for 12-second sprints is improved speed.

APPLICATION LETTERS

OBJECTIVES:

- Improve keyboarding skill.
- Learn to format application letters.

A. WARMUP

Type each line 2 times.

Speed	1	Janet works after school four hours a day at the town bank.
Accuracy	2	Buzz quickly designed five new projects for the wax museum.
Language Link	3	I waited for my best friend, and she was late getting here.
Numbers/Symbols	4	Interest charged on the $7,000 loan is 15% (down from 17%).

| 1 | 2 | 3 | 4 | 5 | 6 | 7 | 8 | 9 | 10 | 11 | 12

FACT FILE

Thanksgiving is celebrated around the world throughout the year. Thanksgiving in the United States is the fourth Thursday of November. Thanksgiving in Canada is the second Monday in October. In the Virgin Islands, Thanksgiving is celebrated on October 25, which marks the end of the hurricane season.

SKILLBUILDING

B. 12-SECOND SPRINTS

Take three 12-second timings on each line. Try to increase your speed on each timing.

5 The time had come for Bev to study for college final exams.
6 Be sure to relax, rest, and have a good meal before a test.
7 Sean scored better on this test than on the test last week.
8 This drill was written to be easy to read and fast to type.

| | | | 5 | | | | 10 | | | | 15 | | | | 20 | | | | 25 | | | | 30 | | | | 35 | | | | 40 | | | | 45 | | | | 50 | | | | 55 | | | | 60

RESOURCES

 Lesson Plan 59

 Courseware Lesson 59

Student Data Disk

Student Manual

Supplementary Production Activities

COURSEWARE OVERVIEW

When the personal information dialog box appears, remind students to type their first and last names exactly as they did in the login box.

C. PRETEST

Take a 1-minute timing on the paragraph. Note your speed and errors.

```
 9      Most people work hard to improve their writing skills.   11
10 They make the nucleus of what they wish to say more clear     23
11 by poring over their rough drafts. They bring home their      34
12 point by rewriting, if necessary, and replacing some words.   46
   | 1 | 2 | 3 | 4 | 5 | 6 | 7 | 8 | 9 | 10 | 11 | 12
```

D. PRACTICE

SPEED: ***If you made 2 or fewer errors on the Pretest, type lines 13–20 two times each.***

ACCURACY: ***If you made more than 2 errors on the Pretest, type lines 13–16 as a group two times. Then type lines 17–20 as a group two times.***

Adjacent Reaches

```
13 tr trip trade trait strain trolls truck strive tromp trials
14 po polka potter pomp point pot pork power poster poker pore
15 re renter remember resting rewrite reptiles referees recite
16 sa sample sank salmon sap sack saws sags sable savor sabers
```

Jump Reaches

```
17 mo money motor motley most mock mower mop mobile monkey moo
18 br break brake brain bracket brick brook broke brat bramble
19 nu nut number nurture nude null nurse nuclear knuckle nutty
20 ce recede center cellular celery cement certain censor celt
```

E. POSTTEST

Repeat the Pretest. Compare your Posttest results with your Pretest results.

COMMUNICATION FOCUS

The purpose of an application letter is to get an interview. When you go for an interview, dress neatly and appropriately. Be prepared to answer questions such as: Why do you think we should hire you for this job? How would you best describe yourself? What experience do you have? In addition, listen carefully to the interviewer, look at the interviewer when you speak, avoid nervous gestures, speak clearly, and answer questions honestly.

TEACH

Activities C–E. Remind students they should improve both their speed and accuracy from the Pretest to the Posttest.

PRETEST/PRACTICE/POSTTEST

The ***Pretest/Practice/Posttest*** routines are designed to improve speed or accuracy.

- The ***Pretest*** identifies students' speed or accuracy needs.
- The ***Practice*** provides a variety of improvement drills.
- The ***Posttest*** (a repeat of the Pretest) measures improvement.

Language Arts Connections

Have students make a list of concerns they have about their future careers. Ask them to put this list into the form of an article, including at least one quotation from someone they have talked to about this career. Have students revise the article three times.

Multiple Learning Styles

Explain that different people learn through different methods. Students who learn best through hearing do well when they read the text aloud or hear it read aloud. They also benefit from soft music being played. Have students try reading aloud and playing soft music when they study.

TEACH

Activity F. Remind students that the application letter is the first impression a potential employer has of them. The letter must be free of errors and include their potential worth to an employer.

Letter 23. Refer students to the Reference Manual in the software to review the formats for typing a block-style personal business letter.

FORMATTING

F. Application Letters

An application letter is written to apply for a position. Your resume should be enclosed with the letter. Since this may be the first impression an employer has of you, be sure that your letter and resume are each a single page, neat, accurate, and contain all essential information.

An application letter should contain the following paragraphs:

Paragraph 1: The purpose of the letter, the job for which you are applying, and how you learned of the opening.
Paragraph 2: The qualifications that make you especially suited for the position. Mention skills you have that can help the employer and the company. Refer to the resume you are enclosing.
Paragraph 3: Special skills that will set you apart from other applicants. For example, do you work well with other people? Are you very well organized? Are you proficient at using various machines?
Paragraph 4: A request for an interview. Restate your interest in the job and indicate when you will be available. Include a telephone number where an employer can easily reach you.

WORD PROCESSING APPLICATIONS

LETTER 23
Block Style

Format the following application letter in block style. Review the format of a personal-business letter in Lesson 48.

June 12, {year}

Mrs. Carlotta Drain
Richardson Insurance Agency
One Washington Boulevard
Fort Worth, TX 76126

Dear Mrs. Drain:

One of the participants in a career fair at my high school, Mr. Curtiss Hall, mentioned that you have an opening for an office assistant in your downtown office. I would like to be considered as an applicant for that position.

JOURNAL ENTRY

Have students finish this sentence: "My potential worth to an employer is ________________." Have students also write why they chose these attributes and how they can achieve them.

My extensive training and experience in the use of various software programs will enable me to serve Richardson Insurance Agency as a competent employee. As you will see on my enclosed resume, my computer skills helped me win two awards in competitions at the regional and state levels. Also, I have excellent grades in all of my high school business courses.

I have taken an active leadership role in school. I was president of our local chapter of Future Business Leaders of America, and I served as secretary of my class during my junior and senior years. These activities have provided me with valuable leadership and teamwork skills. They also gave me an opportunity to put my office skills to practical use.

I am very interested in working for Richardson Insurance Agency. I will telephone your office by the end of this week to arrange for an interview with you at your convenience. If you would like to speak with me before that time, please telephone me at my home number, 901-555-3245, after 4 p.m.

Sincerely,

Patrice McCrea
2316 S. Cravens
Fort Worth, TX 76132

Enclosure

TEACH

Letter 24. Remind students that in block style they do not indent paragraphs.

LETTER 24
Block Style

Format the following handwritten application letter in block style. Remember to include the current date and an enclosure notation. Use your name and address in the closing lines.

Mr. Darnell Makulski
Human Resources Department
The Rogers Group
21771 Telegraph, Suite 3000
Columbus, OH 43231

Dear Mr. Makulski:

SCHOOL TO CAREER

Have students review the classified advertising section of a Sunday newspaper and select a job for which they would like to apply. Instruct students to cut out the advertisement and bring it to class. Have students compose a letter to apply for the job.

interNET ACTIVITY

Have students search the World Wide Web for sites related to careers. Ask students to compose and type a one-page report about one Website. The report should include the name of the site, the URL and a description of its content and unique features.

ASSESS

- Check to see if students are increasing their word a minute speeds as they complete each 12-second timing.
- Check to see if students show signs of improvement from the Pretest to the Posttest.
- As students begin typing the letters, walk around the room and point out correct and incorrect formatting to individual students.
- After students finish typing the letters, have them view their work on the screen to see if they made any errors. If errors were made, have students edit their work and make corrections.

CLOSE

If students do not finish Letter 24 during the class period, make sure they save their work so that they can complete it the next time this class meets.

PORTFOLIO *Activity*

If students' portfolio goals include demonstrating progress, they may want to include one or both of the letters from this lesson. Encourage students to evaluate their work and include comments in their portfolio.

I would like to apply for the position of Administrative Assistant for your company. My high school English teacher, Ms. Lorie Gold, informed me of this position.

The experience I gained working summers as a volunteer office clerk for the American Heart Society qualifies me for the position with your company. My enclosed resume shows that most of my duties involved daily use of keyboarding, filing, and communications skills. This experience would be especially beneficial to your company.

My computer skills and my English skills are well above average, and I feel that I could perform any of the jobs I would be called upon to do with a high degree of competence.

It would be a pleasure to work for your company as an administrative assistant. Please allow me the opportunity to discuss my special qualifications with you in greater detail during an interview. You can reach me at my home number, 301-555-4774, any time after 3 p.m.

Sincerely,

PORTFOLIO *Activity*

Search your local newspaper for a job you think you would be interested in applying for. Then, compose a letter of application for the position. In the letter mention that you are enclosing a resume. Format the letter correctly, and be sure to proofread carefully and correct all errors. Ask your teacher to review your letter for content. Once you are sure you have a well-written letter, print a copy and add it to your portfolio.

212 **Word Processing**

Teacher Notes

LESSON 60 REVIEW

OBJECTIVES:

- Review personal-business and business letters.
- Review application letters.
- Learn rules for semicolons.
- Type 33/3'/5e.

A. WARMUP

Type each line 2 times.

```
Speed          1 The old man paid for the yard work before he left for town.
Accuracy       2 Ezra jokingly vowed to question tax payments for his cabin.
Language Link  3 The woman, however, was unable to provide proper childcare.
Numbers        4 Send them to 6738 East 29 Street, Chicago, 60610 by May 19.
                 | 1 | 2 | 3 | 4 | 5 | 6 | 7 | 8 | 9 | 10 | 11 | 12
```

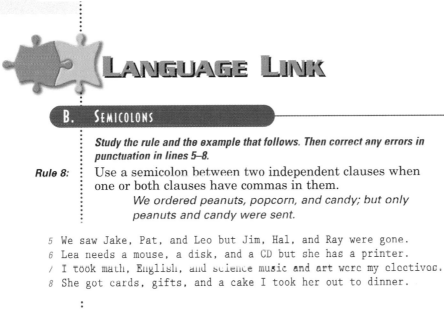

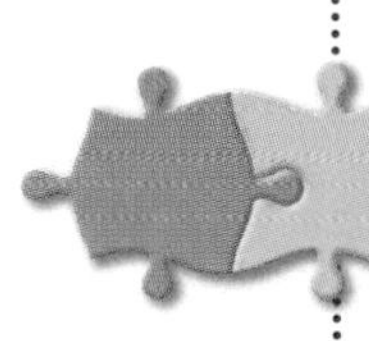

LANGUAGE LINK

B. SEMICOLONS

Study the rule and the example that follows. Then correct any errors in punctuation in lines 5–8.

Rule 8: Use a semicolon between two independent clauses when one or both clauses have commas in them.

We ordered peanuts, popcorn, and candy; but only peanuts and candy were sent.

```
5 We saw Jake, Pat, and Leo but Jim, Hal, and Ray were gone.
6 Lea needs a mouse, a disk, and a CD but she has a printer.
7 I took math, English, and science music and art were my electives.
8 She got cards, gifts, and a cake I took her out to dinner.
```


RESOURCES

-  Lesson Plan 60
-  Courseware Lesson 60
- Student Data Disk
- Student Manual
- Reteaching and Reinforcement
- Language Link Worksheets
- Unit 3 Tests
- Grading and Evaluation

LESSON 60

FOCUS

- Apply Language Link rules for semicolon usage.
- Use Preview Practice to build accuracy and speed.
- Use 3-minute timings to build speed.
- Compose and type an application letter
- Practice typing a modified-block style business letter.

BELLRINGER

As soon as students arrive at their workstations and log in, have them type the Warmup. Go over the purpose of each line as shown to the left of the copy.

TEACH

Activity B. After students complete the activities, have them rewrite the sentences so they do not use a semicolon. They may need to make two sentences out of each sentence. Have them type these sentences, and then type the original sentences using semicolons.

Solutions: We saw Jake, Pat, and Leo; but Jim, Hal, and Ray were gone.

Lea needs a mouse, a disk, and a CD; but she has a printer.

I took math, English, and science; music and art were my electives.

She got cards, gifts, and a cake; I took her out to dinner.

TEACH

Activity C. Point out that words in the Preview Practice are used in the timing that follows.

Activity D. Remind students to be aware of their posture, to sit up, keep their elbows in, and their feet flat on the floor.

Letter 25. Have students exchange their work with a partner to check each other's letter for accuracy.

SKILLBUILDING

C. Preview Practice

Type each line 2 times as a preview to the timings that follow.

```
Accuracy   9 type being learn classes example students keyboard accuracy
   Speed  10 future choose skills that more plan good will able work big
```

D. 3-Minute Timings

Take two 3-minute timings on lines 11–19. Note your speed and errors.

Goal: 33/3'/5e

```
11      Once you leave school, you should know that you must      11
12 acquire additional skills. On the job you will need good       22
13 work habits, teamwork skills, and technical skills. Plan to    34
14 take some courses that will help you advance in your career.   45
15      You should also realize that the skill you learn in       56
16 this class is just one example of the kind of skill you        67
17 will need on the job. Just about every job now requires        79
18 using a keyboard. Learn this skill as well as you can so       90
19 that you can succeed in your career choice.                    99
   | 1 | 2 | 3 | 4 | 5 | 6 | 7 | 8 | 9 | 10 | 11 | 12   SI 1.25
```

CULTURAL CONNECTIONS

The length of the workday and days of the week people work are different in various countries. Many companies, especially those in warmer climates, close their business for two to four hours during the middle of the day. In some countries, Thursday and Friday are days off with one day reserved for worship. The Korean workweek is Monday through Saturday and sometimes Sunday.

WORD PROCESSING APPLICATIONS

LETTER 25
Block Style

Compose and type a letter of application for the position in the classified ad shown on the next page. Review Lesson 59 before you begin composing. Review the format for personal-business letters and block-style letters in Lesson 48.

SCHOOL TO CAREER

Ask students to scan classified ads in your local newspaper. Have them cut out three jobs that sound interesting. Then have them find out the education or training needed. Have students type the information, tape the classified ad to this page, and display it in the classroom.

Out-of-Class Activity

Ask students to interview an adult they know who is employed. Students should find out what types of skills the person uses in the job they now have. They should ask whether the person had these skills at the beginning of his or her career. If not, how were the skills acquired?

ADMINISTRATIVE ASSISTANT
Fast-paced, downtown office seeks full-time administrative assistant. Applicants must type 40 wam, be proficient in word processing, have some desk-top publishing knowledge, and be detailed oriented. We offer competitive salary and bene-fits. Send resume to:
Human Resources Office
Suite 200
4700 Village Road
Columbus, Ohio 43235

LETTER 26
Modified-Block Style

Type the following letter in modified-block style. Use the current date and remember to add an enclosure notation and your reference initials.

Ms. Marcia Chisholm / 15 Lynch Street / Mobile, AL 36604 / Dear Ms. Chisholm: /
¶Our conference on November 3 and 4 was a great success. Your expertise helped to generate solid plans for the program, and I thank you for two positive days.
¶Enclosed are the summary of notes from our meeting, a new outline of your book, and a list of concerns about the outline. Please review these materials and let me know if you have any changes. As you recall, we did not have time to discuss everything on our agenda at the meeting.
¶As you review the outline, please check for the correct sequence and whether or not it is complete. Please provide your suggestions and concerns to me by December 4. I look forward to hearing from you.
Sincerely yours, / Diane Daniels / Editorial Advisor

LESSON 60

TEACH

Letter 26. Remind students to add an enclosure notation and their initials at the end of the letter.

ASSESS

- Check to see if students are increasing their speed as they complete each 3-minute timings.
- Watch students as they complete the Language Link activity to see if they can apply the rules cor-rectly.
- As students begin typing the letters, walk around the room and point out corrrect and incorrect formatting to individual students.
- After students finish typing the letters, have them view their work on the screen and make any necessary corrections.

CLOSE

If students do not finish Letter 26 during the class period, make sure they save their work so that they can complete it the next time this class meets.

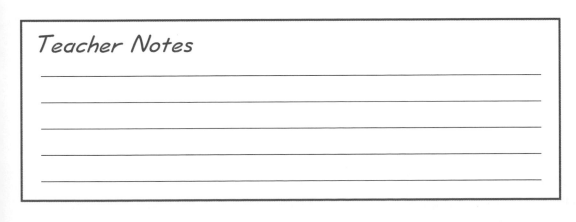

Teacher Notes

UNIT 4 ORGANIZER

KEYBOARDING

Lesson	Focus	Special Features	Skillbuilding	Pretest/ Practice/ Posttest	Documents	GO TO Activities
61	Letters: Copy and Delivery Notations	Portfolio Activity, p. 221	p. 218		Letter 27, p. 220 Letter 28, p. 220 Letter 29, p. 221	
62	Letters: Postscripts	Language Link, p. 222 Fact File, p. 222 Journey Activity, p. 223	p. 223		Letter 30, p. 224 Letter 31, p. 225 Letter 32, p. 225	
63	Letters: Reinforcement	Language Link, p. 226	p. 227		Letter 33, p. 227 Letter 34, p. 228 Letter 35, p. 229	
64	Letters: Review		p. 230	pp. 230–231	Letter 36, p. 231 Letter 37, p. 232 Letter 38, p. 233	
65	Tables: Create	Language Link, p. 234 Fact File, p. 236	p. 235		Table 1, p. 236 Table 2, p. 236	p. 236
66	Tables: Column Size and Position	Internet Activity, p. 237 Language Arts Connection, p. 239	pp. 237–238		Table 3, p. 239 Table 4, p. 239 Table 5, p. 239	p. 238
67	Tables: Column Heading	Language Link, p. 240 Fact File, pp. 240, 242, 243	p. 241	p. 241	Table 6, p. 242 Table 7, p. 242 Table 8, p. 243	
68	Tables: Number Columns	Internet Activity, p. 244	pp. 244–245		Table 9, p. 246 Table 10, p. 246 Table 11, p. 246	p. 245
69	Tables: Reinforcement	Language Link, p. 247 Fact File, p. 248	p. 248		Table 12, p. 249 Table 13, p. 249 Table 14, p. 249	
70	Tables: Titles, Subtitles, and Braced Column Headings		pp. 250–251		Table 15, p. 252 Table 16, p. 252	p. 252

UNIT 4 RESOURCE MANAGER

MULTIMEDIA
- **Courseware:** Lessons 61–80
- **Student Data Disk**
- **Student Manual:** Lessons 61–80

TEACHING TOOLS
- **Lesson Plans:** Lessons 61–80
- **Block Scheduling Guide, Unit 4**
- **Language Link Worksheets:** Lessons 61–80
- **Multicultural Applications:** Lessons 61–80
- **Academic Report Guide**
- **Solution Keys**
- **Cross-Curricular Activities:** Lessons 61–80

RETEACHING/REINFORCEMENT
- **Reteaching and Reinforcement Activities:** Lessons 61–80
- **Supplemental Production Activities:** Lessons 61–80

ASSESSMENT and EVALUATION

- **Pretest/Practice/Posttest:** pp. 230–231, 241, 254–255, 288–289
- **Portfolio Activity:** pp. 221, 287
- **Unit 4 Test**
- **Timings:** pp. 223, 238, 245, 258, 269, 285
- **Production Jobs:** Letters 27–39; Reports 17–31; Tables 1–21
- **Grading and Evaluation**

Electronic Teacher Classroom Resources

For your convenience, the teacher's materials are available on a CD-ROM. Having these resources available electronically enables you to print exactly what you need and revise materials as necessary.

Lesson	Focus	Special Features	Skillbuilding	Pretest/ Practice/ Posttest	Documents	GO TO Activities
71	Tables: Review	Language Link, p. 253 Fact File, p. 256	p. 254	pp. 254–255	Table 17, p. 255 Table 18, p. 255 Table 19, p. 256	
72	Reports: Parenthetical References and Quotes	Internet Activity, p. 259	pp. 257–258		Report 17, p. 260	p. 259
73	Reports: Works Cited Page	Language Link, p. 261 Math Connection, p. 264	p. 262		Report 18, pp. 263–264	p. 263
74	Reports: Review	Journal Activity, p. 267	p. 265		Report 19, p. 265 Report 20, pp. 266–267	
75	Reports: Footnotes and Endnotes	Language Link, p. 268 Communication Focus, p. 272	p. 269		Report 21, pp. 271–272	p. 270
76	Reports: Multipage, Bound	Communication Focus, p. 273	p. 273		Report 22, pp. 274–275	
77	Reports: Multipage, Bound	Language Link, pp. 276–277 Internet Activity, p. 280 Social Studies Connection, p. 280	p. 277		Report 23, pp. 278–279	
78	Reports: Title Page, Contents, Bibliography		p. 281		Report 24, p. 283 Report 25, p. 283 Report 26, p. 283	p. 283
79	Reports: Review	Language Link, p. 284 Fact File, pp. 284, 285 Portfolio Activity, p. 287	p. 285		Report 27, p. 286 Report 28, p. 287 Report 29, p. 287 Report 30, p. 287	
80	Simulation	Internet Activity, p. 288	pp. 288–289	pp. 288–289	Letter 39, p. 290 Report 31, pp. 290–291 Tables 20–21, p. 291	

SCANS Competencies in Glencoe Keyboarding with Computer Applications

Resources	Interpersonal Skills	Information	Systems	Technology
Throughout the course, students deal specifically with resources: allocating time for completing drills and documents, maintaining workstations, caring for computers and software.	Communication Focus, pp. 272, 273 Language Arts Connection, p. 239	Career Bit, p. 217 Fact File, pp. 222, 236, 240, 242, 243, 248, 256, 284, 285 Internet Connection, pp. 237, 244, 249, 280, 288 Social Studies Connection, p. 280	Internet Connection, pp. 237, 244, 249, 280, 288	Lessons 61–80 Internet Connection, pp. 237, 244, 249, 280, 288 Communication Focus, p. 272 Social Studies Connection, p. 280

INTRODUCING THE UNIT

Have different students read each of the objectives for Unit 4. Address each objective as it's read. Explain that the goal in this unit is to reach a typing speed of 35 words a minutes for 3 minutes with 5 or fewer errors. Encourage students to believe this is an achievable goal.

Students also will be using word processing features, proofreaders' marks, and formatting skills on tables, reports, and other documents. In this unit, students reach the point where they can compose short sentences and short paragraphs at the keyboard.

FUN Facts

The first emperor of China, Qin shi huangdi, had 7,000 life-size statues sculptured of uniformed soldiers. No two faces of these terra-cotta warriors were the same. Each was painted a brilliant color and armed with an actual weapon. Clay charioteers and horses were attached to real chariots. The clay army was buried in battle formation around Qin shi huangdi's tomb to protect his spirit.

UNIT 4 WORD PROCESSING

LESSONS 61–80

OBJECTIVES

- Demonstrate keyboarding speed and accuracy on straight copy with a goal of 35 words a minute for 3 minutes with 5 or fewer errors.
- Demonstrate correct use of word processing features.
- Demonstrate an understanding of proofreaders' symbols by editing copy marked for revision.
- Demonstrate basic formatting skills on a variety of tables, reports with special features, and multipage reports from a variety of copy—arranged, unarranged, rough draft, and handwritten.
- Compose sentences and short paragraphs at the keyboard.

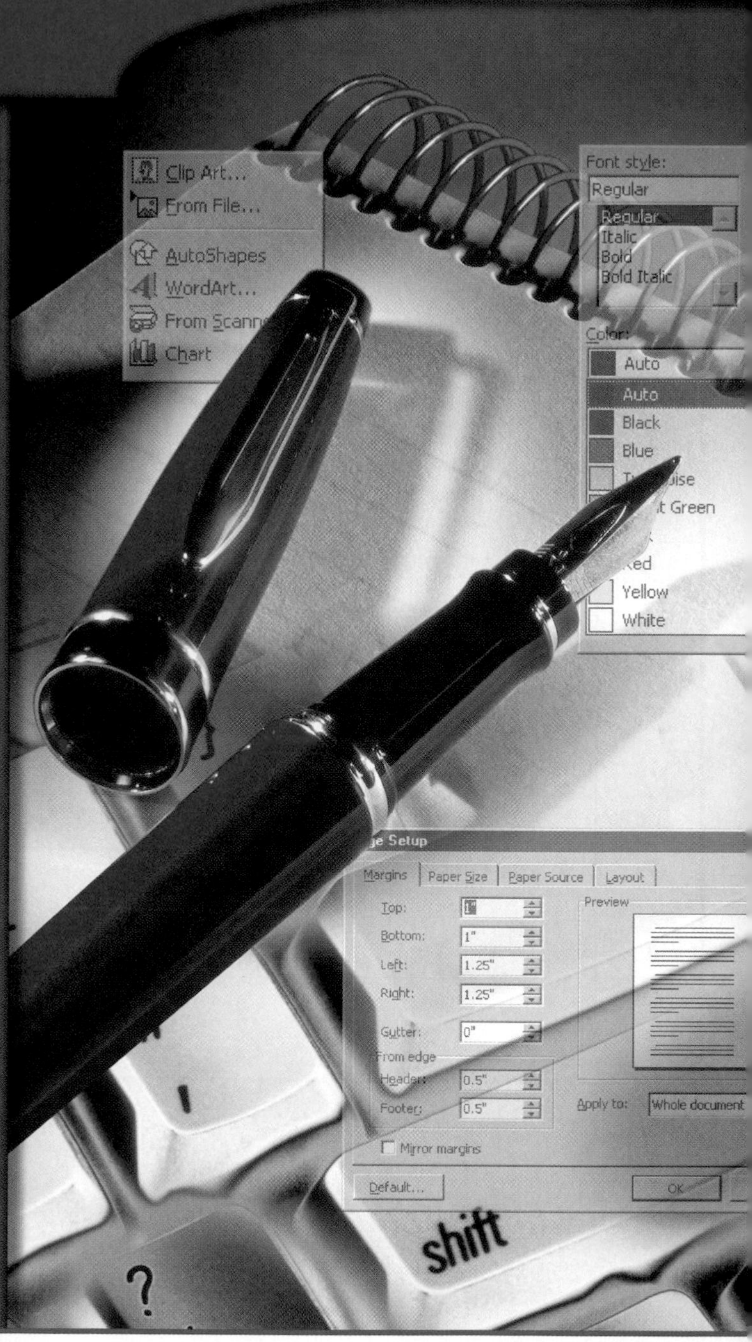

COURSEWARE OVERVIEW

The courseware provides several reports to help students keep track of their progress and to review their completed exercises. These reports can be viewed and printed. Students can link to the word processor outside of the program through the File menu. However, they will have to name and save these documents.

WORDS TO LEARN

adjusting column widths
dot leaders
endnotes
footnotes
hanging indent
header/footer
join/merge cells
left indent
margins
number columns
table create
table position

CAREER BIT

AIR TRAFFIC CONTROLLER Air traffic controllers ensure the safe operation of commercial and private aircraft. Their main responsibility is to organize the flow of aircraft in and out of the airport. Relying on radar and visual observation, they closely monitor each plane. In addition, controllers keep pilots informed about changes in weather conditions. The Federal Aviation Administration (FAA) is currently developing and implementing a new automated air traffic control system. As a result, more powerful computers will help controllers deal with the demands of increased air traffic. Some traditional air traffic controller tasks— like determining how far apart planes should be kept—will be done by computer. Improved communication between computers on airplanes and those on the ground is making the controller's job a little easier.

217

WORDS TO LEARN

The terms in Words to Learn are defined in the Glossary at the back of the book. Ask students if they are familiar with any of the terms. Have them define the terms they know. Compare their definitions with those in the Glossary.

CAREER BIT

Air traffic controllers may belong to a labor union. Membership in a labor union gives employees more power in bargaining with their employers. One tool that unions use when negotiation fails is to go on strike. When air traffic controllers threaten to strike the lives of many people are endangered. The president of the United States has the power to decide how to handle the situation. Thirteen thousand members of the air traffic controllers union went on strike in August of 1981. President Reagan fired all of the controllers and their positions were filled with substitute workers. Divide students into small groups to debate the issue:userid Do you think the air traffic controllers union should have the same right as other labor unions to strike? Why or why not?

COURSEWARE OVERVIEW

The Teacher Management program tracks student scores and progress. You may change the grading parameters through the Teacher Management program and override the grade for any exercise for any student. You may also change the weights of the components used to compute course grades. See the courseware manual for complete instructions.

LESSON 61

FOCUS

- Use 30-second timings to build speed.
- Use Diagnostic Practice to identify areas that need improvement.
- Learn how to format letters with copy and delivery notations.
- Type letters with copy and delivery notations.

BELLRINGER

As soon as students arrive at their workstations and log in, have them type the Warmup. Go over the purpose of each line as shown to the left of the copy.

TEACH

Activity B. Remind students that their goal for 30-second timings is improved speed with each of the timings.

Activity C. Make sure that students understand that this Diagnostic Practice activity is designed to help identify areas that need improvement and provide needed practice.

LESSON 61

LETTERS WITH COPY AND DELIVERY NOTATIONS

OBJECTIVES:

- Improve keyboarding skills.
- Format letters with copy and delivery notations.

A. WARMUP

Type each line 2 times.

Speed 1 I feel sure he will be here in time to drive the boys home.
Accuracy 2 Six jumped from the quarry blaze, right into Lake Cragview.
Language Link 3 Club dues must be paid now; however, you can pay next week.
Numbers/Symbols 4 Ryan saw Jack's dog's leash on Tim's brother's front porch.
| 1 | 2 | 3 | 4 | 5 | 6 | 7 | 8 | 9 | 10 | 11 | 12

SKILLBUILDING

B. 30-SECOND TIMINGS

Take two 30-second timings on lines 5–6. Then take two 30-second timings on lines 7–8. Try to increase your speed on each timing.

5 Rush to finish the drill lines before time runs out. 11
6 Keep wrists and arms quiet as your fingers strike the keys. 23

7 When the batter heard that sound of breaking glass, he 11
8 knew without looking that the home run had truly gone home. 23
| 1 | 2 | 3 | 4 | 5 | 6 | 7 | 8 | 9 | 10 | 11 | 12

C. DIAGNOSTIC PRACTICE: ALPHABET

Turn to the Diagnostic Practice: Alphabet routine on page SB-1. Type one of the Pretest/Posttest paragraphs and note your errors. Then type the corresponding drill lines 2 times for each letter on which you made 2 or more errors and 1 time for each letter on which you made only 1 error. Finally, repeat the same Pretest and compare your performance.

RESOURCES

 Lesson Plan 61

 Courseware Lesson 61

Student Data Disk

Student Manual

Supplementary Production Activities

Grading and Evaluation

D. Copy Notations

When you send a copy of a letter to someone in addition to the addressee, type a **copy notation** on the letter.

1. Type the copy notation on the line below the reference initials or below the enclosure or attachment notation.
2. At the left margin, type a lowercase *c* followed by a colon *(c:)*.
3. Press the tab and type the name of the person receiving the copy. If more than one person is to receive a copy, type each name on a separate line, aligned at the tab.
4. Use a title before the name only if the first name or initial is unknown.

When you do not want the addressee to know that someone else is to receive a copy, use the notation *bc:* (blind copy). To add a blind copy notation:

1. Print one copy of the letter.
2. Type the *bc* notation 2 lines below the last item in the letter, and print another copy.

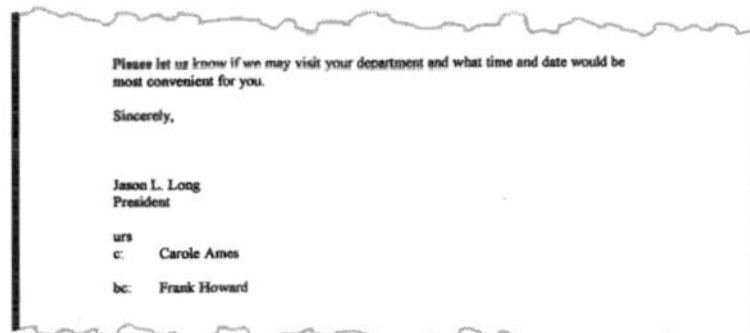

Please let us know if we may visit your department and what time and date would be most convenient for you.

Sincerely,

Jason L. Long
President

urs
c: Carole Ames

bc: Frank Howard

E. Delivery Notations

When a letter is being sent by a special method (fax, registered, certified, etc.), type the appropriate notation on the line below the reference initials. For example, a letter that is being faxed would have the notation *By fax* below the reference initials.

jrt
By Fax

jrt
By Registered Mail
c: Chris Brunet

jrt
Enclosure
By Federal Express

TEACH

Activity D. Inform students that before copiers, fax machines, and computers, sending a copy of a document required making a carbon copy. The copy notation was *cc* rather than *copy*. Tell students they may still run across the old copy notation in some correspondence.

Activity E. Discuss with students the different special methods for sending letters—fax, registered mail, certified mail, FedEx, Priority mail, and so on.

Illustration

Have students refer to these illustrations for correct formatting of notations.

FACT FILE

In Classical Greece (800 B.C.) the god Hermes was thought to be the messenger of the gods. Artwork depicts him wearing winged golden sandals and holding a magical herald's staff. Messages are delivered more easily today. Have students research other ways messages have been delivered through history.

TEACH

Letter 27. Remind students that in modified-block style they may or may not indent paragraphs. Also remind them to leave a blank line between paragraphs.

Letter 28. Suggest to students that whenever they write a letter, they should always read it aloud. This will help them both hear and see what they wrote, which will help them edit the letter so it says what they want it to say. It also will help them catch any errors they have made.

WORD PROCESSING APPLICATIONS

LETTER 27
Modified-Block Style

Format this letter in modified-block style. Address a No. 10 envelope to the addressee, and append/add it to the document.

(Current Date) / Mr. Theodis Chamberlin / 17934 Roscommon Lane / Detroit, MI 48227 / Dear Mr. Chamberlin:
¶Enclosed is the TSA loan form that you requested when we talked today. Please complete the form by filling out the highlighted areas, and return the form to me in the enclosed envelope.
¶If you elect to pay via checking account, please attach a voided check. If you elect to pay by savings account, fill out the information requested about your savings account.
¶I am pleased to tell you that I have been assigned as your financial advisor as of today. Call me if you have any questions about completing the form.
Yours truly, / Tamika Murphy / urs / Enclosure / c: Karl Mendoza

LETTER 28
Block Style

Format this letter in block style. Address a No. 10 envelope and append/add it to the document.

(Current Date) / Ms. Annette Birdsong / General Manager / Fabric Palace / 3799 Tower Place / Waterbury, CT 06704-0543 / Dear Ms. Birdsong:
¶I am happy to report that we do have washed silk in a variety of colors. It can be shipped to you the same day that your order is received.
¶Simply choose the colors you want from the attached sample card; then call 1-800-555-9877 to place your order. If you prefer, you can mail the order using the form on the back of the sample card. Hopefully, you will be able to take advantage of our "quantity discounts" that will allow you to pass along the savings to your customers.
¶We look forward to receiving your order soon. / Sincerely, / Stephen Leiberman / Sales Manager / Attachment / urs / c: James Hollingshead / Mary Lee / bc: Richard Holiday

Career Exploration

Break students into three groups to investigate careers in banking, textiles, and financial planning. Have students write a list of questions to ask people who work in these industries. Invite someone from each industry to speak to your class.

Have students use an Internet search engine and the keywords banking, textiles, and financial planning to locate professional organizations within these industries. Search to see if any of the professional organizations have student groups in your region.

LETTER 29
Modified-Block Style

Format this letter in modified-block style.

(Current Date) / Mr. Julio Sanchez / 233 Orchard Drive / Topeka, KS 66605 / Dear Mr. Sanchez:
¶Your financial planner, Craig Fulton, has shared with me your request to surrender your annuity policy with National Investors. Please consider the financial strength of our company before you make your final decision about this matter.
¶Before we process your request, we want to be sure you understand that a portion of the funds you withdraw may represent taxable income. You should contact your tax advisor to learn of the possible tax consequences of this withdrawal.
¶Please sign and return the enclosed Request for Surrender Information form indicating whether you wish to proceed with your request for surrender. If you have any questions, call our toll free number at 1-800-555-4885. / Yours truly, / Ali Faruk / Chief Executive Officer / urs / c: C. Fuller / Enclosure / By fax

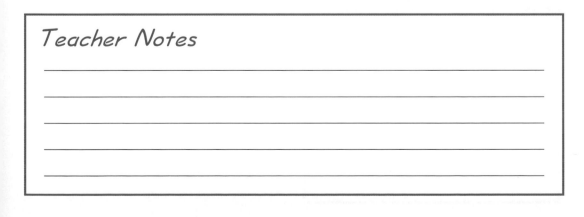

PORTFOLIO *Activity*

Open one of the letters you completed in this lesson and correct any errors you may have made. Then, print a copy of the letter and add it to your portfolio. Next, explain why it is important to add delivery notations to letters. List some other methods of deliveries that might be used.

Teacher Notes

LESSON 61

TEACH

Letter 29. Ask students what the difference is between block style and modified-block style. Ask them if they are to indent the paragraphs in this letter. (Directions do not specify, so students may or may not indent the paragraph.)

ASSESS

- Check to see if students are increasing their word a minute speeds as they complete each of the 30-second timings.
- Monitor students as they complete the Diagnostic Practice and provide individualized assistance as needed.
- As students begin typing the letters, walk around the room and point out correct and incorrect formatting to individual students.
- After students finish typing the letters, have them view their work on the screen to see if they made any errors. If errors were made, have students edit their work and make corrections.

CLOSE

If students do not finish the letters during the class period, make sure they save their work so that they can complete it the next time this class meets.

LESSON 62

FOCUS

- Compose answers for the Language Link activity using complete sentences.
- Use 3-minute timings to build speed.
- Learn how to format and type letters with post-scripts.

BELLRINGER

As soon as students arrive at their worksta-tions and log in, have them type the Warmup. Go over the purpose of each line as shown to the left of the copy.

TEACH

Activity B. After students have answered the following questions with a complete sentence, have several of them read their sentences to the class. Then have students compose a one-page essay around one of the sentences. Read several of the essays in class as well.

Solutions: Answers will vary

LESSON 62

LETTERS WITH POSTSCRIPTS

OBJECTIVES:

- Compose at the keyboard.
- Format letters with postscripts.
- Type 35/3'/5e.

A. WARMUP

Type each line 2 times.

Speed	1	It is easier to build good habits than to break bad habits.
Accuracy	2	Fritz quietly welcomed the five tax guides back from Japan.
Language Link	3	Each student has two chances; therefore, the odds are good.
Numbers	4	The 28 boys chose 29 books, 30 bags, 31 pens, and 32 disks.

| 1 | 2 | 3 | 4 | 5 | 6 | 7 | 8 | 9 | 10 | 11 | 12

B. COMPOSING AT THE KEYBOARD

Answer the following questions with complete sentences.

5 How have computers changed our lives?
6 Why is appearance important when going for a job interview?
7 If you could write a book, what topic would you choose? Why?

FACT FILE

A computer virus is a program that "infects" computers. Some viruses are mild and may only cause messages to appear on screen. Other viruses are extremely destructive and can erase everything stored on a computer. Computer viruses are usually spread from machine to machine by infected disks or through Internet connections to unsafe sites.

RESOURCES

 Lesson Plan 62

 Courseware Lesson 62

Student Data Disk

Student Manual

Supplementary Production Activities

Grading and Evaluation

C. Preview Practice

Type each line 2 times as a preview to the timings that follow.

```
stack enough quickly produce reference examining Organizing
finished leaving within pencil permit spend small time such
```

D. 3-Minute Timings

Take two 3-minute timings on the paragraph. Note your speed and errors.

Goal: 35/3'/5e

```
     Organizing the work space where you spend most of your   11
time will permit you to work more quickly and also produce    23
more. Check to see that all work still to be done is in one   35
stack and all work just finished is in another. Do you have   47
enough pens and sharp pencils? Are small things, such as      58
paper clips, staples, and tape, kept in a handy place? Are    70
reference books easy to reach from the work station? Time     82
spent examining your work space now can save time later.      93
Getting organized can lead to better use of time and space.  105
| 1 | 2 | 3 | 4 | 5 | 6 | 7 | 8 | 9 | 10 | 11 | 12  SI 1.25
```

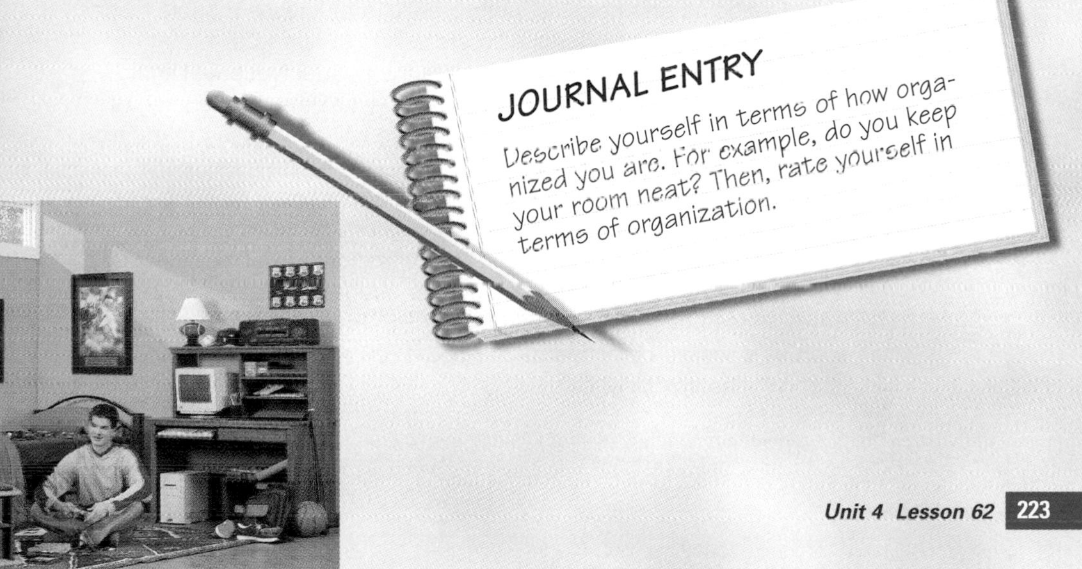

JOURNAL ENTRY
Describe yourself in terms of how organized you are. For example, do you keep your room neat? Then, rate yourself in terms of organization.

TEACH

Activity C. Remind students to take a deep breath and tell themselves to relax before beginning a timing. This will help them do better in the timings.

Activity D. The goal for these timings is 35 words a minute for 3 minutes with no more than 5 errors.

Remind students to be aware of their posture, to sit up, keep their elbows in, and their feet flat on the floor.

JOURNAL ENTRY

Have students use the following prompt: "I believe my organization skills are __________, and I demonstrate them through the way I __________." Give students a few additional minutes to proofread.

TEACH

Activity E. Point out to students that the notation PS does not contain periods.

Letter 30. Point out that the postcript in this letter should be indented like the paragraphs.

FORMATTING

E. Letters With Postscripts

A **postscript** (PS:) is an additional message in paragraph form at the end of a letter. To format a postscript:

1. Press ENTER 2 times after the last item in the letter.
2. If letter paragraphs are blocked, type the postscript at the left margin. If paragraphs are indented, indent the postscript.
3. Type *PS:* followed by 1 space; then type the message.

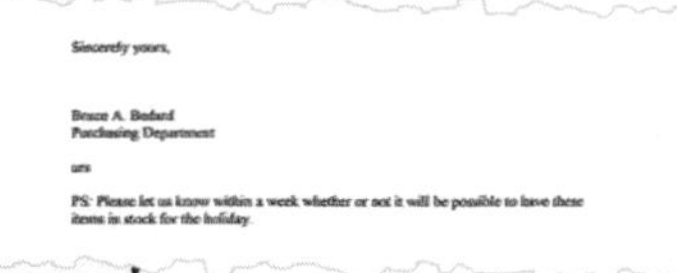
Sincerely yours,

Bruce A. Bedard
Purchasing Department

urs

PS: Please let us know within a week whether or not it will be possible to have these items in stock for the holiday.

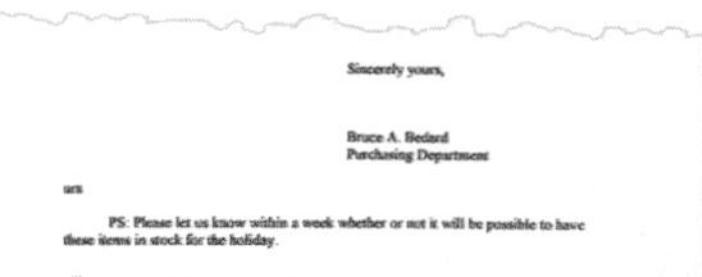
Sincerely yours,

Bruce A. Bedard
Purchasing Department

urs

PS: Please let us know within a week whether or not it will be possible to have these items in stock for the holiday.

WORD PROCESSING APPLICATIONS

LETTER 30

Modified-Block Style With Indented Paragraphs

Format the following letter in modified-block style with indented paragraphs. Remember to indent the first line of the postscript.

(Current Date) / Ms. Rachael Goldstein / 65 Sparks Avenue / Portland ME 04102 / Dear Ms. Goldstein:

¶As you know, the National High School Student Council is having its annual meeting in Denver, Colorado, next summer. As president of your school student council, you were recommended to our National Board as being an energetic, enthusiastic, and knowledgeable leader.

¶We are looking for students who are willing to spend two to three weeks during June or July to help plan the annual National High School Student Council event. You would fly to Denver and stay with one of our host families. Each weekday we will be working at my high school, Lincoln High, for four to six hours. We will be making minor revisions to a general outline from last year's national meeting.

¶I look forward to hearing from you with your acceptance to be a part of this national high school event. Your participation will certainly be well received by any college you plan to attend. / Sincerely, / Nicholas Bono, President / urs / c: Jamie Bluto / PS: Please contact me as soon as possible by phone at 303-555-1800 or by e-mail at nbono@alhs.dpsd.k12.co.us.

Teacher Notes

LETTER 31
Block Style

Format the following letter in block style.

(Current Date) / Mr. Jon Nagata / Takata Motor Company / 5800 Alder Drive S. / Tempe, AZ 85283 / Dear Mr. Nagata:
¶Surprisingly, many of us do not want to say no--to customers, salespeople, or employees--especially if they smother us with kindness and cheer. As we deal with these types of people more often, we begin to think of them as family. And, we all know how difficult it is to say no to family members.
¶That is the ploy of many salespeople worldwide. In America, we know the push of the salesperson who takes us to lunch, finds us tickets to the ball game, finds us tickets to the theater, or tells us how much he or she thinks of our spouse or children. This is all done with the purpose of making us feel guilty when we are ready to negotiate on price or terms.
¶Do not be afraid to set limits. The more precise your limits, the greater respect you will receive. Most of us want to be liked, but we should not let human feelings get in the way of business judgment. Saying no and saying it firmly will make you feel better--and will help your organization.
¶I hope this "hint" about our culture will help you when you visit other companies in the United States next month, Mr. Nagata. / Sincerely yours, / Nick DelVichicco / Consultant / urs / By fax / bc: Carole Schmidt / PS: Our representative, Christine Chung, will meet you on the 20th and accompany you on your visits.

LETTER 32
Modified-Block Style

Format the following letter in modified-block style. Use the current date.

Ms. Heidi Flaharty / 2039 Northrup Street, Apt. 224 / Denver, CO 80205 / Dear Miss Flaharty:
¶Thank you for agreeing to speak to the students in my Word Processing 2 class on the topic of the office of the future. I heard your interesting presentation on this topic at the Vocational Training Association Convention. I know your ideas are going to be interesting to my students. ¶The class meets on Mondays at 10:30 a.m. in the Buhl Building of our campus in Westchester. I am hopeful that your schedule will permit you to grant this request. ¶Please contact at me at 303-555-3298 to let me know what date would be convenient for you to speak. After I speak with you, I will be able to finalize my syllabus. / Yours sincerely, / Sybil Belletarre / Instructor / urs / By Next Day Express

FACT FILE

When doing business with Japanese companies, we must remember that their culture is different from ours. Many Japanese people define themselves by who they work for, not the job they do. An employer's influence may even command an employee's social time. Discuss the importance of understanding other cultures.

LESSON 62

TEACH

Letter 31. Tell students that a good question to ask themselves when writing letters is: Would I want to receive this letter?

Letter 32. Explain to students that when they write letters, they must organize their thoughts in a logical sequence.

ASSESS

- Check to see if students are increasing their word a minute speeds as they complete each 3-minute timing.
- Review the accuracy of students' responses to questions in the Language Link composing activity.
- Check to see if students improve from the Pretest to the Posttest.
- As students begin typing the letters, walk around the room and point out correct and incorrect formatting to individual students.
- After students finish typing the letters, have them view their work on the screen to see if they made any errors. If errors were made, have students edit their work and make corrections.

CLOSE

If students do not finish the letters during the class period, make sure they save their work so they can complete it the next time this class meets.

LESSON 63

FOCUS

- Apply the Language Link rule for using semicolons with independent clauses.
- Use 30-second OK timings to improve accuracy.
- Use Diagnostic Practice to identify areas that need improvement.
- Practice formatting and typing letters.

BELLRINGER

As soon as students arrive at their workstations and log in, have them type the Warmup. Go over the purpose of each line as shown to the left of the copy.

TEACH

Activity B. After students have completed correcting errors in lines 5–8, have them choose a partner to check each other's work. Then have students write a paragraph about what they are saving money for. Ask them to use at least one semicolon in their paragraph.

Solutions: Last year I invested in stocks; after that I had less cash.

They gave an excellent presentation; mine was not terrific.

Rene was saving his money; he looked forward to his cruise.

LESSON 63

REINFORCEMENT: LETTERS

OBJECTIVES:

- Learn about semicolons with independent clauses.
- Refine keyboarding skill.
- Format letters in a variety of styles.

A. WARMUP

Type each line 2 times.

Speed 1 All of the fans were glad to hear news that their team won.
Accuracy 2 Jan very quickly froze both mixtures in the deep brown jar.
Language Link 3 The legal offices will move; however, her office will stay.
Numbers/Symbols 4 Our Orders #207 and #208 and #209 were paid by Check #1317.
| 1 | 2 | 3 | 4 | 5 | 6 | 7 | 8 | 9 | 10 | 11 | 12

B. SEMICOLONS WITH INDEPENDENT CLAUSES

Study the rule and the examples that follow. Then correct any errors in punctuation in lines 5–8.

Rule 9: Use a semicolon to join two closely related independent clauses that are not connected by a conjunction (such as *and, but, or,* or *nor*).

Melissa wanted to climb to the top of the mountain; Harry did not.

Harry was studying long hours; he was working days.

5 Last year I invested in stocks after that I had less cash.
6 They gave an excellent presentation mine was not terrific.
7 Rene was saving his money he looked forward to his cruise.
8 Buy bananas while you are out I will get the other fruits.

RESOURCES

 Lesson Plan 63
 Courseware Lesson 63
Student Data Disk
Student Manual
Language Link Worksheet
Reteaching and Reinforcement
Grading and Evaluation

SKILLBUILDING

C. 30-Second OK Timings

Take two 30-second OK (error-free) timings on lines 9–10. Then take two 30-second OK timings on lines 11–12. Goal: no errors.

```
 9      People make decisions each day; most are just routine,   11
10  but some require exact thinking and the ability to analyze. 23

11      Maxine had five jobs requiring zest and nearly perfect   11
12  work habits; I explained that a few jobs involve hazards.    23
    | 1 | 2 | 3 | 4 | 5 | 6 | 7 | 8 | 9 | 10 | 11 | 12
```

D. Diagnostic Practice: Numbers

Turn to the Diagnostic Practice: Numbers routine on page SB-4. Type one of the Pretest/Posttest paragraphs and identify any errors made. Then type the corresponding drill lines 2 times for each number on which you had 2 or more errors and 1 time for each number on which you made only 1 error. Finally, repeat the Pretest and compare your performance.

WORD PROCESSING APPLICATIONS

LETTER 33

Block Style

Format this letter in block style.

January 20, {year}/ Mrs. Blair Piapot / 706 Middleton Avenue / Tunica, MS 39175 / Dear Mrs. Piapot:

¶We at Dream Vacations are certainly able to assist you with your travel plans. We have years of experience helping our customers get the most for their travel dollar. One of our agents, Theresa Sullivan, will be happy to help you with ideas to make your trip to Alaska a memorable one.

¶I have enclosed several brochures giving descriptions both of cruises and airfare/hotel packages. Take some time now to look them over. Theresa will call you to work out the best time to meet as soon as you are ready.

¶If you have any questions or need additional information, please do not hesitate to call. It is a pleasure to be of service to you.

Cordially yours, / Carole Defazio / urs / Enclosures /c: Theresa Sullivan / bc: Carmella Rosito

LESSON 63

TEACH

Buy bananas while you are out; I will get the other fruits.

Activity C. Remind students that the goal for 30-second OK timings is no errors.

Activity D. Remind students that Diagnostic Practice activities help them identify areas they need to improve.

Letter 33. Remind students that to write a letter correctly means to produce an error-free letter. If they make errors, they must correct them before the letter is sent.

Social Studies Connections

Have students research these questions: In 1959 Alaska became the fiftieth state right behind ______. (Hawaii) Alaska is in what part of the U.S.? (extreme northwestern) What is the midnight sun? (daylight at night)

Multiple Learning Styles

Explain to students that different people learn through different methods. Some students, called kinetic learners, do best when they can experience the lessons through movement. Ask students to experiment with associating what they are learning with particular hand and finger movements.

TEACH

Letter 34. Have students look at the first paragraph of this letter. Ask them why they think the person receiving this letter will be receptive to helping the writer.

LETTER 34

Personal-Business in Modified-Block Style

Format this personal-business letter in modified block style.

June 4, {year}/ Mr. Lyle Martin / Director, Customer Relations / Speedy Striders, Inc. / 8406 Hull Street / Henderson, NV 89015 / Dear Mr. Martin:

¶I purchased a pair of Speedy Striders, Model X7, from The Sports Store in the Dequindre Mall on April 15. Although I have always had good service from your shoes, this pair turned out to be defective.

¶I ran practice laps in the shoes during April and May with no problem. When I wore them in the Memorial Day Fun Run on May 30, I had a problem with my right shoe. The sole of the shoe ripped apart from the sides of the shoe; I was forced to drop out of the race. This was a serious problem for me because participation in the marathon was a requirement in my Health 155 class at Hillsdale College.

¶When I took the shoes back to the store, the manager refused to exchange the shoes or refund my money. This situation has been very frustrating for me. I would appreciate your help in getting a refund and clearing up this matter with the instructor of my physical education class. A copy of my sales slip is enclosed along with a photograph of the shoes.

Yours truly, / Kia Strobe / 45 East Windside Street / Thousand Oaks, CA 91360 / Enclosures / By registered mail

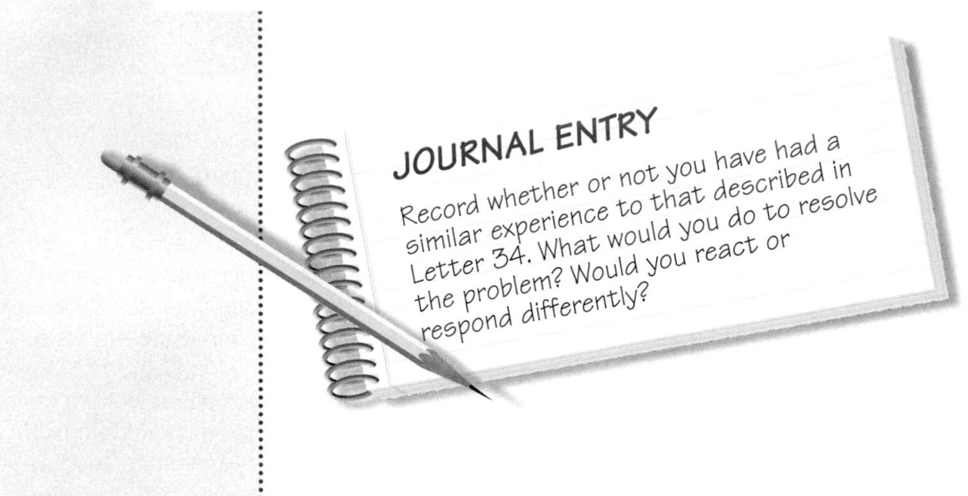

JOURNAL ENTRY
Record whether or not you have had a similar experience to that described in Letter 34. What would you do to resolve the problem? Would you react or respond differently?

JOURNAL ENTRY

Use the following prompts: (1) "I am afraid to get a job in the business world because ________." (2) "I am excited about getting a job in the business world because ________."

LETTER 35

Modified-Block With Indented Paragraphs

Format the following letter in modified-block style with indented paragraphs.

June 15, (year)

Ms. Juvetta Dishman
7337 Westfalia Street
Charlotte, TN 37036
Dear Ms. Dishman:

Thank you for volunteering to participate in the PLSO study. Enclosed are two consent forms, a baseline questionnaire, a baseline locator form, and a postage-paid envelope in which to return these forms.

Please read the entire consent form carefully before signing it. Keep one copy of the consent form for your records. If you have any questions about the form, please call Lynn or Vanda at 555-8706. Answer each question to the best of your ability. If there are some questions you are not able to answer, indicate that on the form, and an interviewer will telephone you for more information.

Place the completed forms (unfolded) in the envelope provided and mail them back to us. We would appreciate it if you would take time right now to fill out the forms and return them. Thank you for your assistance in this important health study of older adults.

Sincerely,

Nolan Goydos, M.D.
Principal Investigator
Enclosures
c: M. Bryant, M.D.
R. Welsh, M.D.

Teacher Notes

LESSON 63

TEACH

Letter 35. Remind students that in modified-block style, they can indent paragraphs.

ASSESS

- Check to see if students are completing 30-second OK timings without any errors.
- Monitor students as they complete the Diagnostic Practice and provide individualized assistance as needed.
- Watch students as they complete the Language Link activity to see if they are able to apply the semicolon rule correctly.
- As students begin typing the letters walk around the room and point out correct and incorrect formatting to individual students.
- After students finish typing the letters, have them view their work on the screen to see if they made any errors. If errors were made, have students edit their work and make corrections.

CLOSE

If students do not finish the letters during the class period, make sure they save their work so that they can complete it the next time this class meets.

Remind students to clean up their workstation when they leave.

FOCUS

- Use 12-second timings to build speed.
- Use Pretest/Practice/Posttest routine to build speed and accuracy.
- Practice formatting and typing letters.

BELLRINGER

As soon as students arrive at their workstations and log in, have them type the Warmup. Go over the purpose of each line as shown to the left of the copy.

TEACH

Activity B. Remind students to type at a fast pace during the 12-second timing. At the end of the first and second timings, encourage students to type just one or two strokes faster on the next timing.

LESSON 64

LETTER REVIEW

OBJECTIVES:

- Improve keyboarding speed and accuracy.
- Review various letter formats.

A. WARMUP

Type each line 2 times.

```
Speed          1 They do not feel it is their duty to fix the flat for free.
Accuracy       2 Did she realize big yellow quilts from Jack were expensive?
Language Link  3 Seven-digit codes were assigned; you should have yours now.
Numbers        4 2301 3402 4503 5604 6705 7806 8907 2301 3402 4503 5604 6705
                 | 1 | 2 | 3 | 4 | 5 | 6 | 7 | 8 | 9 | 10 | 11 | 12
```

SKILLBUILDING

B. 12-SECOND SPRINTS

Take three 12-second timings on each line. Try to increase your speed on each timing.

```
5 When you go to get your pen, will you also please get mine.
6 He did the job well and was paid by the maid who was there.
7 Now that we have the time to sit back and read, it is cold.
8 The red leaves fell from the maple tree when the wind blew.
  | 1 | 2 | 3 | 4 | 5 | 6 | 7 | 8 | 9 | 10 | 11 | 12
```

C. PRETEST

Take a 1-minute timing on the paragraph. Note your speed and errors.

```
9       The name high tech is given to a basic and useful type   12
10  of design that is changing our concept of modern living and  24
11  things we use daily. It has long enjoyed a quiet appeal in   36
12  places like restaurants and stores.                          43
    | 1 | 2 | 3 | 4 | 5 | 6 | 7 | 8 | 9 | 10 | 11 | 12
```


RESOURCES

 Lesson Plan 64

 Courseware Lesson 64

Student Data Disk

Student Manual

Reteaching and Reinforcement

Grading and Evaluation

D. PRACTICE

In the chart below, find the number of errors you made on the Pretest. Then, type each of the designated drill lines 2 times.

Pretest Errors	0–1	2	3	4+
Drill Lines	16–20	15–19	14–18	13–17

Accuracy

```
13 own basic quiet stores design concept expensive restaurants
14 built style pipes range bright rubber window appeal designs
15 use and are wild tech living modern useful quietly changing
16 now but used come water things colors coming places enjoyed
```

Speed

```
17 glass daily wide sign such tire come like home with has not
18 homes given high tech name type long used they last now are
19 appeal living useful given basic things daily long type use
20 colors bright stores water pipes style glass range wind are
```

E. POSTTEST

Repeat the Pretest. Compare your Posttest results with your Pretest results.

WORD PROCESSING APPLICATIONS

LETTER 36

Modified-Block Style

Format this letter in modified-block style.

June 18, {year}

Ms. Kia Strobe
45 E. Windside Street
Thousand Oaks, CA 93160

Dear Ms. Strobe:

You were justified in being angry. We are sorry for the problems you had with your Speedy striders, model X7, which forced you to drop out of the Memorial Day Fun Run. I have telephoned your physical education instructor and sent her a letter explaining your reason for not completing the class assignment. We are grateful to you for bringing this matter to our attention. The photo you sent was especially helpful.

TEACH

Activities C–E. Remind students they should improve both their speed and accuracy from the Pretest to the Posttest.

PRETEST/PRACTICE/POSTEST

The ***Pretest/Practice/Posttest*** routines are designed to improve speed or accuracy.

- The ***Pretest*** identifies students' speed or accuracy needs.
- The ***Practice*** provides a variety of improvement drills.
- The ***Posttest*** (a repeat of the Pretest) measures improvement.

Letter 36. Inform students that their ability to communicate effectively in writing will be one of their most important assets in business.

CULTURAL CONNECTIONS

In ancient Egypt, scribes wrote in hieroglyphics. These were pictures that symbolize words. Hieroglyphics were drawn on papyrus paper made of reeds. Have students research to learn a fact about writing in another ancient culture.

TEACH

Letter 37. Remind students to work for clarity in the letters they write. Clarity ensures their messages will more likely be understood.

After we recieved your letter, we conducted an investigation of our equipment. We discovered that the equipment use in sewing the Model 7X shoe is faulty. All of our dealers now have been informed of this situation, and the Model X7 Shoes have been removed from store shelves. Please take the damaged shoes to the Dequinder Mall store. The Store Manager, Mr. Kelly, has been contacted and instructed to refund your money in full.

Sincerely yours,

Lyle Martin
Director, Customer Relations

Enclosure
c: Paul Kelly

PS: We have enclose a coupon entitling you to a free pair of shoes of your choice. We hope that this will restore your faith in speedy striders and that you enjoy many more miles of successful marathon runs.

By Overnight Express

LETTER 37
Block-Style

Format this letter in block style. Make the corrections indicated by the proofreaders' marks.

(Current Date)

Mrs. Christine Piantidosi
824 England avenue
Kansas City, KS 66801

Dear Mrs. Piantidosi:

After our telephone conversation thismorning concerning late delivery of three model 60 camcorders to your store, I found that

Out-of-Class Activity

Have students write a letter of praise or complaint regarding a product or service. Make sure they add the company's address to the letter and any enclosures. Have students bring their letters to class and pair with another student to check each other's letters for accuracy.

interNET ACTIVITY

Have students use a search engine and search the Internet for information about running events in their community or big events such as the New York or Boston marathons. Ask them to write a paragraph about the event.

the cam corders were shiped in error to Kansas City, MO. Our headquaters upgraded the system computer which required many hours of re-entering invoices. Obviously, the error in your order happened at that time. Our records are now correct. Because of the inconvenence this errors has caused you the shipping and handling charges have been removed from the your bill. Your orders is being sent today by express delivery, and you should receive it in 24 hours. We value your patronage and we look forward to serving you for many years to come.

Sincerely,

Marlon Chevron
Manger
c:Darryl Adams
By fax

LETTER 38

Modified-Block Style With Indented Paragraphs

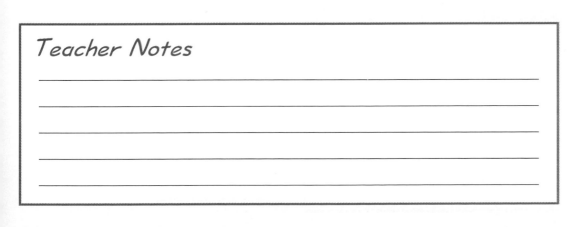

Current Date
Mr. Taylor Coates
President, News Guild
28 West Adams Street, Suite 1308
Alamonte Springs, FL 32714
Dear Mr. Coates:

Because of the extraordinarily high number of claims, we have found it necessary to increase our rates. This increase is required under Part 5, page 3-PR, of Policy Amendment 15. Accordingly, we are increasing the life insurance rate to .80/$1,000 for active members and .94/$1,000 for retirees.

In addition, the amount of dependent life insurance will be reduced from $10,000 to $5,000 along with extending the current policy for one year. If you think it would help, I am willing to come to your next membership meeting to answer questions.

Sincerely,
Patrick Tecumseh
Account Representative
PS: A summary of all changes we are recommending is enclosed for your review.

Teacher Notes

TEACH

Letter 38. Remind students that with modified-block style they can either indent paragraphs or leave a line blank between paragraphs. In this letter, they are to indent.

ASSESS

- Check to see if students are increasing their word a minute speeds as they complete each of the 12-second timings.
- Check to see if students show signs of improvement from the Pretest to the Posttest.
- As students begin typing the letters, walk around the room and point out correct and incorrect formatting to individual students.
- After students finish typing the letters, have them view their work on the screen to see if they made any errors. If errors were made, have students edit their work and make corrections.

CLOSE

If students do not finish the letters during the class period, make sure they save their work so that they can complete it the next time this class meets.

Remind students to clean up their workstation when they leave.

LESSON 65

FOCUS

- Apply the Language Link rule for subject/verb agreement.
- Use technique timings to improve technique.
- Take 2-minute Paced Practice timings.
- Learn how to create a table.

BELLRINGER

As soon as students arrive at their workstations and log in, have them type the Warmup. Go over the purpose of each line as shown to the left of the copy.

TEACH

Activity B. After students have edited lines 5–8 for subject/verb agreement, have them underline the subject in each sentence, then have students check each other's work for accuracy.

Solutions: The books in the bookcase were rearranged by May last week.

The students working on the project are doing a very nice job.

One of the programmers has written and tested the program.

The contract, including all attachments, is due to be submitted today.

LESSON 65

TABLES: CREATING

OBJECTIVES:

- Learn about subject/verb agreement.
- Improve keyboarding techniques.
- Learn to create tables.

A. WARMUP

Type each line 2 times.

Speed	*1*	`Heavy rain fell fast and hard on the game later in the day.`
Accuracy	*2*	`Jeff quickly took away five dozen more boxes of light pens.`
Language Link	*3*	`The express elevator broke; I had to walk up eight flights.`
Numbers/Symbols	*4*	`($95.15) ($59.26) ($60.37) ($71.48) ($82.59) ($90.60) ($$$)`
		| 1 | 2 | 3 | 4 | 5 | 6 | 7 | 8 | 9 | 10 | 11 | 12

LANGUAGE LINK

B. SUBJECT/VERB AGREEMENT

Study the rule and examples that follow. Then edit lines 5–8 for subject/verb agreement.

Rule 10: Disregard any intervening words that come between the subject and verb when establishing agreement.

The lost box of books has been found.

The buses covered with green paint were moving very fast.

5 The books in the bookcase (was/were) rearranged by May last week.
6 The students working on the project (is/are) doing a very nice job.
7 One of the programmers (has/have) written and tested the program.
8 The contract, including all attachments, (is/are) due to be submitted today.

RESOURCES

 Lesson Plan 65

 Courseware Lesson 65

Student Data Disk

Student Manual

Language Link Worksheets

Supplementary Production Activities

C. Technique Timings

Take two 30-second timings on each line. Focus on the technique at the left.

Press the space bar with a quick down-and-in motion.

```
 9 go to it go do so go be on us we do to on it at bet tip top
10 We want to go on and see that band at the park play for us.
11 Now it is my turn to tell them that we do not want it done.
12 How do you get it all done and stay in top form for us now?
   | 1 | 2 | 3 | 4 | 5 | 6 | 7 | 8 | 9 | 10 | 11 | 12
```

D. Paced Practice

Turn to the Paced Practice routine beginning on page SB-7 Take three 2-minute timings, starting at the point where you left off the last time.

FORMATTING

E. Parts of a Table

1. Tables consist of vertical columns and horizontal rows. Where a column and row meet is called a **cell**. Information is typed in the cells.
2. Tables may be formatted with lines (a boxed table) or without lines (an open table). A boxed table is shown in the illustration.
3. When a table appears on a page by itself, it should be vertically and horizontally centered.
4. Align text columns at the left; align number columns at the right.

Accounting and Finance	Richards College of Business
Management and Business Systems	Richards College of Business
Mass Communications	College of Arts and Sciences
Physical Education and Recreation	College of Education

TEACH

Activity C. Remind students that proper technique is a building block for speed and accuracy.

Activity D. Review the procedure for the Paced Practice routine.

Activity E. Ask students what the difference is between a boxed table and an open table. Make sure students understand the difference between horizontal and vertical.

Illustration

Point out that this is a boxed table. Explain that they will learn more about tables in later lessons.

Out-of-Class Activity

Have students locate tables in magazines, newspapers, or textbooks for other courses. Bring these examples to class. Make overhead projections of three different types of tables. Put these on the overhead projector and ask students to format them.

TECHNOLOGY TIP

Many word processing software packages include a feature that allows the user to apply built-in formats to tables. This feature changes the appearance of the tables by automatically formatting headings, lines, borders, fonts, and colors.

TEACH

Activity F. Explain the Tables, Create software feature presented in this activity.

STUDENT MANUAL
Be sure students turn to the correct lesson in their Student Manual.

Table 1. Remind students to use the tab key to move from column to column.

Table 2. Ask students how they see themselves using tables in their lives.

ASSESS

- Watch students as they complete the Language Link activity.
- Make sure students are able to create tables.
- Monitor students as they complete Technique Timings and provide individualized assistance as needed.

CLOSE

If students do not finish the tables during the class period, make sure they save their work so that they can complete it the next time this class meets.

F. SOFTWARE FEATURES

STUDENT MANUAL
Tables, Create

Study Lesson 65 in your student manual. Complete all the practice activities while at your computer. Then complete the following jobs.

WORD PROCESSING APPLICATIONS

TABLE 1

Create a table with 2 columns and 4 rows. Use the tab key to move from column to column as you fill in information.

Accounting and Finance	Richards College of Business
Management and Business Systems	Richards College of Business
Mass Communications	College of Arts and Sciences
Physical Education and Recreation	College of Education

TABLE 2

Create a table with 3 columns and 4 rows. Use the tab key to move from column to column as you fill in information.

The Great Barrier Reef	Australia	1,200 miles long
The Grand Canyon	United States	217 miles long
Nile River	Egypt and Sudan	4,160 miles long
Mt. Everest	Nepal and Tibet	29,000 feet high (est.)

FACT FILE

The koala is native only to Australia. Koalas are marsupials—mammals whose young grow and mature inside a pouch on the mother's belly. Koalas live in southeastern Australia in eucalyptus trees. These animals spend approximately 20 hours a day sleeping. The only food koalas eat is eucalyptus leaves, and they eat about 2.5 pounds of these leaves every day.

Teacher Notes

Tables: Column Size and Position

OBJECTIVES:

- Adjust column widths.
- Center tables on a page.
- Type 35/3'/5e.

A. Warmup

Type each line 2 times.

Speed	1	He may find time to go today if Dan will help with the car.
Accuracy	2	James Boxell, the banquet speaker, analyzed a few carvings.
Language Link	3	Twenty boys will be five; they cannot register before then.
Symbols	4	Attention: Dear Mr. Westin: Subject: Gentlemen: Ladies: Re:

| 1 | 2 | 3 | 4 | 5 | 6 | 7 | 8 | 9 | 10 | 11 | 12

Using the Internet, search for information about carpel tunnel syndrome. Try searching by name or locate a medical information site. Learn what causes this problem and what can be done to help relieve the pain. Compose a short paragraph describing what you learned.

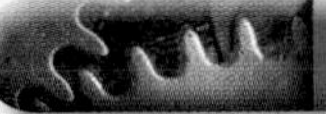

SKILLBUILDING

B. Preview Practice

Type each line 2 times as a preview to the timings that follow.

Accuracy	5	hesitate Extended computer different stretching revitalized
Speed	6	cause work give seat step desk walk neck mind your time not

LESSON 66

FOCUS

- Use Preview Practice to build speed and accuracy
- Use 3-minute timings to build speed.
- Learn word processing features: Adjusting Column Width and Table Position.
- Learn how to adjust column widths and center tables on a page.

BELLRINGER

As soon as students arrive at their workstations and log in, have them type the Warmup. Go over the purpose of each line as shown to the left of the copy.

TEACH

Activity B. Point out that words in the Preview Practice are used in the 3-minute timing that follows.

RESOURCES

 Lesson Plan 66

 Courseware Lesson 66

Student Data Disk

Student Manual

Supplementary Production Activities

Grading and Evaluation

Multicultural Activities

TEACH

Activity C. Remind students that the goal for this timing is to type 35 words a minute for 3 minutes with no more than 5 errors.

Activity D. Provide students with this tip to help them remember the difference between horizontal and vertical: horizontal is the same direction as the horizon—across.

Activity E. Explain why it may be necessary to adjust column widths.

- Demonstrate table position.
- Demonstrate how to adjust column width.

STUDENT MANUAL

Be sure students turn to the correct lesson in their Student Manual.

C. 3-Minute Timings

Take two 3-minute timings on the paragraph. Note your speed and errors.

Goal: 35/3'/5e

Workers may hesitate to take work breaks because they 11
feel they should not take the time. Extended sitting at a 22
computer can cause muscle pain. Experts say we should take 34
short breaks to refresh body and mind. Get out of your seat 46
and step around your desk. Walk to a different section of 58
the office. Do exercises that will relax your shoulders and 70
your neck. Just stretching at your desk will help to ease 81
stress. A quick change of pace can give your mind a chance 93
to shift gears. Then, you can return to work revitalized. 105

| 1 | 2 | 3 | 4 | 5 | 6 | 7 | 8 | 9 | 10 | 11 | 12 SI 1.30

FORMATTING

D. Column Widths and Table Position

When you create a table, the table is horizontally centered between the margins and extends from the left margin to the right margin. All columns are the same width. If a column contains long entries or short entries, you may want to change the width of the columns to make the table more readable or more attractive.

Once you change the column widths, the table will no longer be horizontally centered. Therefore, you must reposition the table so that it is centered horizontally.

E. Software Features

STUDENT MANUAL

Table Position Adjusting Column Width

Study Lesson 66 in your student manual. Complete all the practice activities while at your computer. Then complete the jobs that follow.

FACT FILE

Of the 191 countries in the world, the United States ranks 20th in life expectancy and 26th in infant mortality rate. Sweden ranks 3rd in life expectancy and 4th in infant mortality. Have students create a table to illustrate ten other countries' life expectancy and infant mortality ranks.

TABLE 3

Create a table with 3 columns and 4 rows. Enter the information in the cells. Use the tab key to move from cell to cell. Automatically adjust the column widths. Center the table vertically and horizontally.

Your table should look like the following table when you have completed it.

Chevrolet	October	Julia Renfro
Ford	May	Mark Karen
Chrysler	June	James Hill
Toyota	August	Meridy Street

TABLE 4

Language Arts Connections

Create a table with 3 columns and 5 rows. Automatically adjust the column widths. Center the table vertically and horizontally.

adapt	adopt	adept
lose	loose	loss
rein	rain	reign
site	sight	cite
too	to	two

TABLE 5

Create a table with 3 columns and 5 rows. Automatically adjust the column widths. Center the table vertically and horizontally.

Coca Cola	KO	NYSE
Intel Corporation	INTC	NASDAQ
Microsoft	MSFT	NASDAQ
Nike	NKE	NYSE
Walt Disney Co.	DIS	NYSE

LANGUAGE ARTS CONNECTIONS

Table 4 contains a list of confusing words. Look up the definition for each of the words in the table; then, for each word, compose a sentence in which the word is correctly used.

LESSON 66

TEACH

Table 3. Remind students to use the tab key to move from column to column.

Table 4. Make sure students are clear about what is a column and what are rows.

Table 5. Make sure students have centered tables both vertically and horizontally.

ASSESS

- Check to see if students are increasing their word a minute speeds as they complete each 3-minute timing.
- Make sure students are able to adjust column widths and position tables correctly.

CLOSE

If students do not finish the tables during the class period, make sure they save their work so that they can complete it the next time this class meets.

Remind students to clean up their workstation when they leave.

PORTFOLIO *Activity*

If students' portfolio goals include demonstrating progress, they may want to include one or more tables from this lesson. Encourage students to evaluate their work and include comments in their portfolio.

Teacher Notes

FOCUS

- Compose answers using complete sentences for the Language Link activity.
- Use 12-second timings to build speed.
- Use the Pretest/Practice/ Posttest routine to build speed and accuracy.
- Learn how to format and type tables with column headings.
- Type tables with column headings.

BELLRINGER

As soon as students arrive at their workstations and log in, have them type the Warmup. Go over the purpose of each line as shown to the left of the copy.

TEACH

Activity B. After students have answered the questions with complete sentences, have them exchange their work with another student to check each other's work for accuracy.

Solutions: Answers will vary.

LESSON 67

TABLES: COLUMN HEADINGS

OBJECTIVES:

- Improve keyboarding speed and accuracy.
- Compose at the keyboard.
- Format tables with column headings.

A. WARMUP

Type each line 2 times.

Speed	1	Take good care of this car, and it should last a long time.
Accuracy	2	Jeff's size had helped him to win quickly over Gene Baxter.
Language Link	3	Lucia had a pretty silver bracelet; she wore it constantly.
Numbers/Symbols	4	Using the 8% increase, we bought 25# of #112 and #64 nails.
		| 1 | 2 | 3 | 4 | 5 | 6 | 7 | 8 | 9 | 10 | 11 | 12

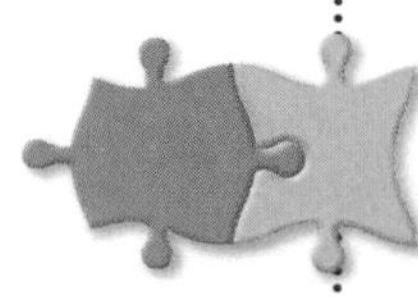

LANGUAGE LINK

B. COMPOSING AT THE KEYBOARD

Answer the following questions with complete sentences.

5 Why do we need automobile insurance?
6 What are some of your bad habits, and how can you change them?
7 What are two things that annoy you, and why do they annoy you?

FACT FILE

The Model T Ford automobile, which was built between 1908 and 1927, was nicknamed the "Tin Lizzie."

RESOURCES

 Lesson Plan 67

 Courseware Lesson 67

Student Data Disk

Student Manual

Supplementary Production Activities

Cross-Curricular Activities

SKILLBUILDING

C. 12-Second Sprints

Take three 12-second timings on each line. Try to increase your speed on each timing.

```
 8 It is always a good idea to take time to do your best work.
 9 Take enough time to think about it and plan each step well.
10 If you rush into a job, you may just make many more errors.
11 Now is the time you should use these tips to do a good job.
   ||||5||||10||||15||||20||||25||||30||||35||||40||||45||||50||||55||||60
```

D. PRETEST

Take a 1-minute timing on the paragraph. Note your speed and errors.

```
12      Cecil must know more about my past than he does about   11
13 his own. As we walked in the hazy sunshine with friends, he  23
14 spoke above the noise around us. I was pleased that he was   35
15 able to remember things we did when we were young.           45
   | 1 | 2 | 3 | 4 | 5 | 6 | 7 | 8 | 9 | 10 | 11 | 12
```

E. PRACTICE

SPEED: ***If you made 2 or fewer errors on the Pretest, type lines 16–23 two times each.***

ACCURACY: ***If you made more than 2 errors on the Pretest, type lines 16–19 as a group two times. Then type lines 20–23 as a group two times.***

Up Reaches

```
16 ce cell once mice rice slice cease cedar fleece niece juice
17 me lime mime meal mere melon plume metal become slime smell
18 hi high hits hive nigh thigh chime whine chirps whips hires
19 lo lost love flow loam plods solos clots slower plops loans
```

Down Reaches

```
20 ca case cast pica carp carve cards cable capers laces cabin
21 im whim slim aims time limps crimp blimp chimes limes prime
22 rm harm worm arms army perms alarm charm squirm farms warms
23 ba bask bark barb paba bards bawls balms turban samba baits
```

F. POSTTEST

Repeat the Pretest. Compare your Posttest results with your Pretest results.

TEACH

Activity C. Remind students that the goal for 12-second timings is improved speed with each timing.

Activities D–F. Remind students they should improve both their speed and accuracy from the Pretest to the Posttest.

PRETEST/PRACTICE/POSTTEST

The ***Pretest/Practice/Posttest*** routines are designed to improve speed or accuracy.

- The ***Pretest*** identifies students' speed or accuracy needs.
- The ***Practice*** provides a variety of improvement drills.
- The ***Posttest*** (a repeat of the Pretest) measures improvement.

JOURNAL ENTRY

Ask students to write using the following prompt: "I don't always do the best I can do because ______." Remind them the idea is to get their thoughts down on paper.

TEACH

Activity G. Go over the instructions with students to make sure they understand how to format column headings.

Table 6. Remind students to center their tables both vertically and horizontally.

Table 7. Ask students what month they were born. If their birth month is not included in this table, have them add it to the list along with their month's birthstone.

FACT FILE

If students don't know the birthstone for their birth month, provide them with the following information:

July	Ruby
August	Peridot
September	Sapphire
October	Opal
November	Topaz
December	Turquoise

FORMATTING

G. Tables: Column Headings

Column headings describe the data in each column of a table. To format column headings:

Salesperson	Territory	No. of Units
Dawson, Angelique	Midwest	1,245
Goodfellow, Robin	Southeast	1,137
Karampalas, Stephen	Northeast	1,089
Saad, Gamal	Western	1,764

1. Type the column headings in initial caps and bold.
2. Align column headings at the left over text columns, at the right over number columns, or centered over all columns.
3. If a column heading is much wider than the data in the column (See Table 6, column 2), you may want to let it wrap to the next line or break the heading into two lines by pressing ENTER at an appropriate point.

WORD PROCESSING APPLICATIONS

TABLE 6

Language Arts Connections

Create a 3-column, 6-row table. Type the column headings in bold. Adjust the column widths; then center the table vertically and horizontally.

Past Tense	**Present Tense**	**Past Participle**
go	went	have/had gone
run	ran	have/had run
do	did	have/had done
see	saw	have/had seen
ring	rang	have/had rung

TABLE 7

Create a 2-column, 7-row table. Adjust the column widths; then center the table vertically and horizontally.

Month	**Birthstone**
January	Garnet
February	Amethyst
March	Aquamarine
April	Diamond
May	Emerald
June	Pearl

FACT FILE

Emerald refers to a bright green beryl (mineral). The word emerald is derived from the word smaragdos, a name given to a number of stones having little in common except the color green.

Language Arts Connections

Refer students to Table 6. Have students compose and type sentences using each verb correctly. They should have 15 sentences when complete. For each verb, students can use the same sentence and change it to agree with the verb.

Multiple Learning Styles

Explain to students that some people learn best through seeing things and are called visual learners. Many visual learners do well with seeing videos, pictures, or other visual forms. Have students create a drawing of what they are trying to learn.

TABLE 8

Create a 3-column, 7-row table. Press* E*NTER* *to break the column headings as shown. Then adjust the column widths, and center the table vertically and horizontally.

City of Origin	**City of Destination**	**Date of Travel**
Anchorage	Vancouver	January 1
Chicago	Quebec	March 15
New York City	Montreal	May 27
Niagara Falls	Halifax	September 10
San Francisco	Toronto	October 7
Atlanta	Calgary	December 13

FACT FILE

Did you know that a praying mantis is not a religious insect? In fact, it is a cannibal. When a mantis appears to be praying, it is actually preying. The reverential-looking position of its forelegs is really an attack position. An insect that gets within reach of a mantis is quickly captured, then eaten. This happens so quickly, that it's almost impossible to see. A praying mantis eats only live insects, and will often eat another mantis.

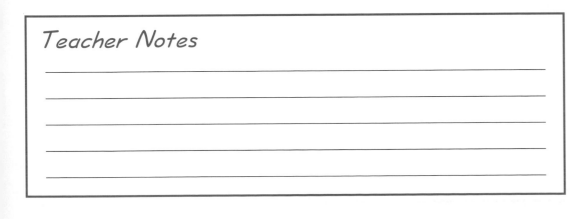

Teacher Notes

LESSON 67

TEACH

Table 8. Remind students to press ENTER to break the column headings.

ASSESS

- Check to see if students are increasing their word a minute speeds as they complete each 12-second timing.
- Review the accuracy of students' responses to questions in the Language Link composing activity.
- Check to see if students show signs of improvement from the Pretest to the Posttest.
- As students begin typing the tables, walk around the room and point out correct and incorrect formatting to individual students.
- After students finish typing the tables, have them view their work on the screen to see if they made any errors. If errors were made, have students edit their work and make corrections.

CLOSE

If students do not finish the tables during the class period, make sure they save their work so that they can complete it the next time this class meets.

Remind students to clean up their workstation when they leave.

LESSON 68

FOCUS

- Use 3-minute timings to build speed.
- Learn a word processing feature: Number Columns.
- Learn how to create and type tables with number columns.

BELLRINGER

As soon as students arrive at their workstations and log in, have them type the Warmup. Go over the purpose of each line as shown to the left of the copy.

TEACH

Activity B. Point out that words in the Preview Practice are used in the timing that follows.

LESSON 68

TABLES: NUMBER COLUMNS

OBJECTIVES:

- Format tables with number columns.
- Type 35/3′/5e.
- Learn software features.

A. WARMUP

Type each line 2 times.

Speed	1	We took a long trip and saw many fine sights while on tour.
Accuracy	2	Joe Pott quickly won over six men because of his good size.
Language Link	3	The teacher gave careful directions; the pupils understood.
Numbers	4	5201 6202 7203 8204 9205 1206 2207 3208 4209 5210 6211 7212
		| 1 | 2 | 3 | 4 | 5 | 6 | 7 | 8 | 9 | 10 | 11 | 12

interNET CONNECTION

Use the Internet to research the effects of stress on your health. You may want to try some of these sites:

www.lifetimetv.com/wosport/gogetfit
www.nhlbi.nih.gov/chd
www.vitality.com

SKILLBUILDING

B. PREVIEW PRACTICE

Type each line 2 times as a preview to the timings that follow.

Accuracy	5	health thoughts feelings physical positive Practice friends
Speed	6	person habit think music comes when urge say hug day the we

RESOURCES

 Lesson Plan 68

 Courseware Lesson 68

Student Data Disk

Student Manual

Supplementary Production Activities

Grading and Evaluation

C. 3-Minute Timings

Take two 3-minute timings on the paragraphs. Note your speed and errors.

Goal: 35/3'/5e

When it comes to health, our minds matter more than 11
we know. Some studies say that a person may have feelings 22
and beliefs that can improve physical well-being. People 34
might act quite differently when they realize that how 45
they think could affect how they feel. 52
Relax more. Be positive. Enjoy each day. Get back to 63
nature. Listen to the music you like. Practice the habit 75
of a hug a day from friends or family. Take breaks and 86
quiet time for yourself. Smile more often. Doctors urge 97
us to think good thoughts so we can live better lives. 108
| 1 | 2 | 3 | 4 | 5 | 6 | 7 | 8 | 9 | 10 | 11 | 12 SI 1.34

FORMATTING

D. Tables: Number Columns

To format numbers in table columns:

1. Align the numbers at the right.
2. Align column headings over number columns at the right, except when all column headings are centered.
3. If necessary, adjust the width of narrow number columns to balance them with the remaining columns in the table.

E. Software Features

STUDENT MANUAL

Number Columns

Study Lesson 68 in your student manual. Complete all the practice activities while at your computer. Then complete the jobs that follow.

TEACH

Activity C. Remind students that the goal for these timings is to type 35 words a minute for 3 minutes with no more than 5 errors.

Activity D. Demonstrate for students how to align right and how to center headings.

Activity E. Explain why numbers are aligned at the right.

STUDENT MANUAL

Be sure students turn to the correct lesson in their Student Manual.

CULTURAL CONNECTIONS

The ancient Chinese practices of meditation and Tai Chi are widely practiced in the Western world. Meditation is a way of stilling the mind and body. Tai Chi employs slow, graceful movements. Invite a meditation or Tai Chi teacher to speak to your class.

TECHNOLOGY TIP

Computer-aided design (CAD) uses computers and special graphics software to design products. CAD allows a designer to modify a design and even send a design over the Internet. Have students research careers that use CAD, including what higher education is needed and jobs available.

TEACH

Table 9. Remind students to center the table vertically and horizontally.

Table 10. Remind students to use the tab key to move from one column to the next.

Table 11. Check to make sure students are aligning the columns either left or right.

ASSESS

- Check to see if students are increasing their word a minute speeds as they complete each 3-minute timing.
- Make sure students are aligning columns corrrectly.
- As students begin typing the tables, walk around the room and point out correct and incorrect formatting to individual students.
- After students finish typing the tables, have them view their work on the screen to see if they made any errors. If errors were made, have students edit their work and make corrections.

CLOSE

If students do not finish the tables during the class period, make sure they save their work so that they can complete it the next time this class meets.

Remind students to clean up their workstation when they leave.

WORD PROCESSING APPLICATIONS

TABLE 9

Create a 3-column, 6-row table. Align the column headings and the text columns at the left; align the column heading and the number column at the right. Automatically adjust the column widths. Center the table vertically and horizontally.

Teacher	Course	Room
B. Blackhawk	Word Processing	109
S. Maxey	Applied Economics	2570
M. Gorman	Financial Planning	110
P. Wicker	Music Appreciation	2957
B. Sykes	Beginning Japanese	315

TABLE 10

Create a 3-column, 8-row table. Center all column headings (break them as shown). Align the number columns at the right. Automatically adjust the column widths. Center the table vertically and horizontally.

Snack Items	Total Caloric Count	Percent of Calories From Fat
Cheddar Wafers	200	12
Mini Bits of Chips	290	10
Sell Well Chips	340	21
Frizzell's Snack Crackers	190	8
Bagel Bits	120	0
Snacker Crackers	150	8
Munchos	215	11

TABLE 11

3-Column Boxed

Create a 3-column, 6-row table. Align the first column heading at the left. Align the second and third column headings at the right. Align the number columns at the right. Automatically adjust the column widths. Center the table vertically and horizontally.

Name	Gross Pay ($)	Tax ($)
Boldt, David	1,246	248
Johnson, Jay	942	188
Miller, Joan	846	168
Sipowitz, Andrew	1,050	210
Vandenburg, Harlan	976	194

Teacher Notes

LESSON 69 TABLES: REINFORCEMENT

OBJECTIVES:

- Learn about subject/verb agreement.
- Improve keyboarding skill.
- Reinforce table formats.

A. WARMUP

Type each line 2 times.

Speed	1	Rita will go to town and order two pairs of shoes for them.
Accuracy	2	Brown jars prevented the mixture from freezing too quickly.
Language Link	3	David went to the fair; he won first prize with his squash.
Numbers/Symbols	4	You will get (1) more for the money and (2) better quality.

| 1 | 2 | 3 | 4 | 5 | 6 | 7 | 8 | 9 | 10 | 11 | 12

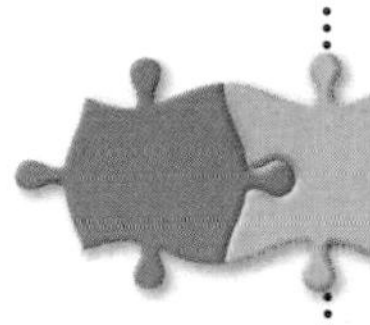

LANGUAGE LINK

B. SUBJECT/VERB AGREEMENT

Study the rule and the examples below. Then correct any errors in subject/verb agreement in lines 5–8.

Rule 11: Subjects joined by *and* take a plural verb unless the compound subject is preceded by *each, every,* or *many a (an).*

Many a computer and printer was purchased during the first quarter.

The physician and the anesthesiologist were in a patient conference.

Every student and instructor is hoping to obtain the test results soon.

5 Each girl and boy (have/has) a ticket to the senior play.
6 Many a skier and skater (has/have) taken a really bad fall.
7 Both Jean and Ricki (is/are) taking a trip to Europe this fall.
8 Every dog and cat (has/have) to get rabies shots to be safe.

JOURNAL ENTRY

Have students use the following prompt: "When I feel bad about myself and my skills, I ________ and when I feel good about myself and my skills, I ________."

LESSON 69

FOCUS

- Apply the Language Link rule for subject/verb agreement.
- Use Diagnostic Practice to identify areas that need improvement.
- Practice formatting and typing tables.

BELLRINGER

As soon as students arrive at their workstations and log in, have them type the Warmup. Go over the purpose of each line as shown to the left of the copy.

TEACH

Activity B. Explain the subject-verb agreement rule to students before they edit lines 5–8 on page 248. After they have edited these lines, have them pair with another student to check their work.

Solutions: Each girl and boy has a ticket to the senior play.

Many a skier and skater has taken a really bad fall.

Both Jean and Ricki are taking a trip to Europe this fall.

Every dog and cat has to get rabies shots to be safe.

TEACH

Activity C. Make sure that students understand that this Diagnostic Practice activity is designed to help identify areas that need improvement and provide needed practice.

Activity D. Tell students that all letters of the alphabet are used in this review. Have students who make errors use this as a homework assignment and bring to class an error-free copy.

PORTFOLIO *Activity*

If students' portfolio goals include demonstrating progress, they may want to include one or more tables from this lesson. Encourage students to evaluate their work and include comments in their portfolio.

SKILLBUILDING

C. Diagnostic Practice: Alphabet

Turn to the Diagnostic Practice: Alphabet routine on page SB-1 Type one of the Pretest/Posttest paragraphs and identify any errors made. Then type the corresponding drill lines 2 times for each letter on which you made 2 or more errors and 1 time for each letter on which you made only 1 error. Finally, repeat the Pretest and compare your performance.

D. Alphabet Review

Type each line 2 times. Repeat if time permits.

```
 9 axle aide ache away bite brag brim bowl caps come crew chip
10 duet drag down dive east etch ends exit feud fame from flat
11 gale give glow grip hope have hill help ills into iced idea

12 joke jump jail jest knit kiln keep know line late lump lost
13 maze more mist melt norm nice nail numb odor over oath open
14 paid pour prod pest quad quip quiz quay ride reap rake room

15 sing stay sort shop team task thin tray ugly upon used unit
16 vote vast vine vest wage when wire worm axis oxen exit flax
17 yell yard year yolk yawl type zinc zeal zone zero zany buzz
```

FACT FILE

An emperor penguin can hold its breath for 15 to 20 minutes and lives an average of 15-20 years. Emperor penguins cannot fly, but small flippers help it to swim very fast. The flippers are strong enough to break a person's wrist. In the Ross Sea in Antarctica, an emperor penguin once dove to a depth of 1,584 feet. This dive, which was recorded in 1990, is the deepest dive on record for any bird.

RESOURCES

 Lesson Plan 69

 Courseware Lesson 69

Student Data Disk

Student Manual

Language Link Worksheets

Reteaching and Reinforcement

Grading and Evaluation

TABLE 12

Create a 3-column, 7-row table. Center the column headings. Center the table vertically and horizontally.

Name of Show	Day/Date	Time
Learning Rainbow	Monday-Friday	2:30 p.m.-3:00 p.m.
The Science Guru	Monday-Friday	4:00 p.m.-4:30 p.m.
Hooping It Up	Wed., November 15	10:30 a.m.-11:00 a.m.
All Against Violence	Wed., October 16	3:30 p.m.-5:00 p.m.
Rock and Roll Times	Sunday-Thursday	8:00 p.m.-10:00 p.m.
Magic Schoolroom	Sundays	10:30 a.m.-11:00 a.m.

TABLE 13

Create a 3-column, 8-row table, and align the column headings as follows: Align the first column heading at the left (press ENTER 1 time before you type it so that it aligns with the multiline column headings at the bottom). Align the second and third column headings at the right. Break the column headings into 2 lines as shown. Automatically adjust the column widths. Center the table vertically and horizontally.

Sandwich Items	Total Calorie Count	% of Calories From Fat
Lucy's Grilled Chicken	290	6
Barbey's Chicken Lite	276	7
Barbey's Lite Beef	294	10
Lucy's Junior Burger	270	9
O'Brien's Lean Burger	320	10
BQ Broiler Chicken	280	10
Andy's Turkey Lite	260	6

TABLE 14

Open Table 8 and make the following changes:

1. Center all of the column headings.
2. Remember to delete the hard return in each column heading.
3. Recenter the table horizontally.

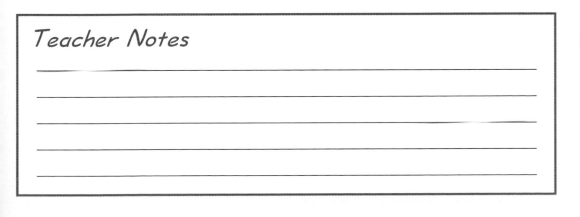

Teacher Notes

LESSON 69

TEACH

Table 12. Remind students to center the table vertically and horizontally. Remind students that vertically is up and down and horizontally is across.

Table 13. Ask students what the difference is between a row and a column. Remind them to use the tab key to move from one column to the next.

Table 14. Have students check each other's work for accuracy.

ASSESS

- Watch students as they complete Language Link activity to see if they are able to apply the rule correctly.
- Monitor students as they complete the Diagnostic Practice and provide individualized assistance as needed.
- As students begin typing the tables, walk around the room and point out correct and incorrect formatting to individual students.
- After students finish typing the tables, have them view their work on the screen to see if they made any errors.

CLOSE

If students do not finish the tables during the class period, make sure they save their work so that they can complete it the next time this class meets.

LESSON 70

FOCUS

- Use 30-second timings to build speed.
- Learn a word processing feature: Join Cells.
- Learn how to type tables with titles, subtitles, and braced column headings.

BELLRINGER

As soon as students arrive at their workstations and log in, have them type the Warmup. Go over the purpose of each line as shown to the left of the copy.

TEACH

Activity B. Remind students that the goal for 30-second timings is improved speed with each timing.

TABLES: TITLES, SUBTITLES, AND BRACED COLUMN HEADINGS

OBJECTIVES:

- Improve keyboarding skill.
- Format tables with subtitles and braced column headings.
- Learn software features.

A. WARMUP

Type each line 2 times.

Speed	To reach your goal, you must learn to keep your mind on it.
Accuracy	Jars prevented the brown mixture from freezing too quickly.
Language Link	Each pattern and bow requires at least two yards of ribbon.
Numbers	Today's homework is to study Chapter 15, pages 136 and 137.
	| 1 | 2 | 3 | 4 | 5 | 6 | 7 | 8 | 9 | 10 | 11 | 12

SKILLBUILDING

B. 30-SECOND TIMINGS

Take two 30-second timings on the first paragraph. Then take two 30-second timings on the second paragraph. Try to type with no more than 2 errors on each timing.

Very seldom will you be asked to type from exact copy 11
that has no errors. You will often have to make changes. 22

Most typing is done from rough-draft copy. On the job 11
you must be able to make a decision about correct format. 22

| 1 | 2 | 3 | 4 | 5 | 6 | 7 | 8 | 9 | 10 | 11 | 12

RESOURCES

 Lesson Plan 70

 Courseware Lesson 70

Student Data Disk

Student Manual

Supplementary Production Activities

C. Number and Symbol Review

Type each line 2 times.

```
 9 They found 10 @ 56, 56 @ 47, 47 @ 38, 38 @ 29, and 29 @ 10.
10 Our new scale shows #10 at 29#, #38 at 47#, and #29 at 56#.
11 Gray,* Moletti,* Young,* Hernandez,* and Jones* won prizes.

12 Our show tickets should cost us $10, $29, $38, $47, or $56.
13 Your sales increased 10%, 29%, 38%, 47%, and 56% last year.
14 Lea & Madera, Yung & Poe, and Day & Cole are all attorneys.

15 Label the square cartons as 47-10, 56-38, 38-47, and 10-29.
16 We know that 38 + 47 = 85, 29 + 10 = 39, and 56 + 70 = 126.
17 Lund (Utah), Leon (Iowa), and Troy (Ohio) were represented.
```

FORMATTING

D. Tables With Titles and Subtitles

VISITATION REPORT June 30, {year}			
First Quarter		Second Quarter	
Month	City	Month	City
January	New York City	April	New Orleans
February	San Francisco	May	Kansas City
March	Philadelphia	June	Jacksonville

Most tables have titles to identify what is in the table and column headings to identify what is in the columns. Tables may also have subtitles that further describe the information in the table. Titles and subtitles are typed in the first row of the table. To format a table with a title and a subtitle:

1. Join the cells in the first row of the table.
2. Center and type the title in all caps and bold.
3. Press ENTER 1 time.
4. Center and type the subtitle in initial caps (no bold).
5. Press ENTER 1 time to leave a blank line.

E. Braced Column Headings

Braced column headings are headings that apply to more than one column of a table. In Table 16, *First Quarter* and *Second Quarter* are braced headings. To create a braced heading:

1. Determine which cells need to be joined.
2. Select the cells and join them.
3. Because braced headings apply to more than one column, they should always be centered.

TEACH

Activity C. If students seem to slow down on this review, assign it as homework to have them practice typing numbers and symbols.

Activity D. Go over the information in items 1–5 with students. Walk around the room and check on students' progress as they practice formatting tables with titles and subtitles.

Activity E. Go over the method for creating braced column headings.

Social Studies Connections

Create seven groups. Assign each group one of the natural wonders in Table 15. Have groups use the Internet to research, then write a report on the assigned natural wonder. If possible, have students download pictures and post these along with the typed reports around the room.

interNET ACTIVITY

Check an Internet weather site, such as The Weather Channel (www.weather.com) or WeatherNet (www.weathernet.com), or have students search to determine the average high and low temperatures for one of the cities in Table 16.

TEACH

Activity F. Demonstrate how to join cells.

STUDENT MANUAL

Be sure students turn to the correct lesson in their Student Manual.

Table 15. Make sure students join the cells in the first row and center and type the title and subtitle. Also check to make sure they leave a blank line after the subtitle.

Table 16. Remind students to center the column headings.

ASSESS

- Check to see if students are increasing their word a minute speeds as they complete each 30-second timing.
- As students begin typing the tables walk around the room and point out correct and incorrect formatting to individual students.
- After students finish typing the tables, have them view their work on the screen to see if they made any errors. If errors were made, have students edit their work and make corrections.

CLOSE

If students do not finish the tables during the class period, make sure they save their work so that they can complete it the next time this class meets.

F. SOFTWARE FEATURES

STUDENT MANUAL

Join Cells

Study Lesson 70 in your student manual. Complete the practice activities while at your computer. Then complete the jobs that follow.

WORD PROCESSING APPLICATIONS

TABLE 15

Create a 2-column, 9-row table. Join the cells in the first row and center and type the title and subtitle. Remember to leave a blank line after the subtitle. Center the column headings. Center the table vertically and horizontally.

NATURAL WONDERS OF THE WORLD (Listed by World Travelers and Explorers)	
Name	**Location**
Carlsbad Caverns	United States (New Mexico)
Caves and Prehistoric Paintings	France and Spain
Giant Sequoia Trees	United States (California)
Grand Canyon	United States (Colorado River)
Great Barrier Reef	Australia
Paricutin (young volcano)	Mexico
Victoria Falls	Zimbabwe

TABLE 16

Create a 4-column, 6-row table. Join the cells in the first row and center and type the title and subtitle. Join the cells in columns 1 and 2 in the second row; then join the cells in columns 3 and 4 in the second row. Center all of the column headings. Center the table vertically and horizontally.

SEMI-ANNUAL VISITATION REPORT June 30, {year}			
First Quarter		**Second Quarter**	
Month	**City**	**Month**	**City**
January	New York City	April	New Orleans
February	San Francisco	May	Kansas City
March	Philadelphia	June	Jacksonville

Teacher Notes

LESSON 71 TABLES: REVIEW

OBJECTIVES:

- Learn about subject/verb agreement.
- Improve keyboarding speed and accuracy.
- Review table formats.

A. WARMUP

Type each line 2 times.

Speed	1 The goal of the girl is to work to be the best she can be.
Accuracy	2 Dave froze the mixtures in the deep brown jug too quickly.
Language Link	3 On January 9 my insurance premium will increase by $93.95.
Numbers/Symbols	4 I purchased 13 dozen pens @ $11.05. (The sale ends today!)

| 1 | 2 | 3 | 4 | 5 | 6 | 7 | 8 | 9 | 10 | 11 | 12

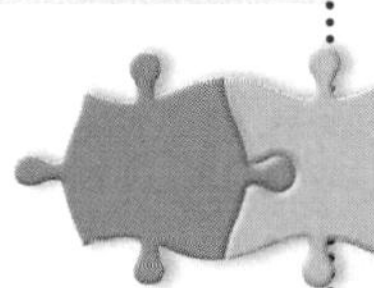

LANGUAGE LINK

B. SUBJECT/VERB AGREEMENT

Study the rule and the examples that follow. Then correct any errors in subject/verb agreement in lines 5–8.

Rule 12: If two subjects are joined by *or, either / or, neither / nor,* or *not only / but also,* the verb should agree with the subject nearer to the verb.

Either the lifeguard or the swimmers have reported a shark in the water.

Not only the page proofs but also the color template is ready to be returned.

5 Either my supervisor or the vice president (has/have) to sign my expense report.
6 Neither I nor my children (was/were) watching that particular program.
7 Not only the assistants but also the managers (wants/want) to attend.
8 Either you or your classmates (is/are) able to take up a collection for that.

RESOURCES

 Lesson Plan 71

 Courseware Lesson 71

Student Data Disk

Student Manual

Language Link Worksheets

Reteaching and Reinforcement

Grading and Evaluation

LESSON 71

FOCUS

- Apply the Language Link rule for subject/verb agreement.
- Use 30-second OK timings to improve accuracy.
- Use Pretest/Practice/Posttest routine to build speed and accuracy.
- Practice formatting and typing tables.

BELLRINGER

As soon as students arrive at their workstations and log in, have them type the Warmup. Go over the purpose of each line as shown to the left of the copy.

TEACH

Activity B. Explain the subject/verb agreement rule to students. Go over the examples with students, then have them type lines 5–8 using the correct word. Have students check each other's work.

Solutions: Either my supervisor or the vice president has to sign my expense report.

Neither I nor my children were watching that particular program.

Not only the assistants but also the managers want to attend.

Either you or your classmates are able to take up a collection for that.

SKILLBUILDING

TEACH

Activity C. Point out that 30-second OK timings are designed to encourage accuracy.

Activities D–F. Remind students they should improve both their speed and accuracy from the Pretest to the Posttest.

PRETEST/PRACTICE/POSTEST

The ***Pretest/Practice/Posttest*** routines are designed to improve speed or accuracy.

- The ***Pretest*** identifies students' speed or accuracy needs.
- The ***Practice*** provides a variety of improvement drills.
- The ***Posttest*** (a repeat of the Pretest) measures improvement.

C. 30-Second OK Timings

Take two 30-second OK (error-free) timings on lines 9–10. Then take two 30-second OK timings on lines 11–12. Goal: no errors.

```
9       I quickly explained that only a few big jobs involve      11
10  hazards, but the managers say we need more safety measures.  23

11      Peter reviewed the subject before giving Kay and Max a    11
12  quiz. Both of them like using the computer to take tests.     23
    | 1 | 2 | 3 | 4 | 5 | 6 | 7 | 8 | 9 | 10 | 11 | 12
```

D. PRETEST

Take a 1-minute timing on the paragraph. Note your speed and errors.

```
13      Can you name the five steps in the cycle of processing    11
14  information? First is input. The next step is processing.     23
15  Output is the third step. The fourth step is distribution.    35
16  The last step is storage.                                     40
    | 1 | 2 | 3 | 4 | 5 | 6 | 7 | 8 | 9 | 10 | 11 | 12
```

E. PRACTICE

In the chart below find the number of errors you made on the Pretest. Then type each of the designated drill lines 2 times.

Pretest Errors	0–1	2	3	4+
Drill Lines	20–24	19–23	18–22	17–21

Accuracy

```
17  quire words future format mailed certain involves publicize
18  saves input phase public fourth output retrieval processing
19  modes backs third others lasted storage changed information
20  next steps named saving inform getting require distribution
```

Speed

```
21  files other words done this back last all the can use on be
22  store disks forms some them five mode and has job put up to
23  first cycle right name form have been rib you out for is in
24  names which third mail that four sets may mat his her of or
```

F. POSTTEST

Repeat the Pretest. Compare your Posttest results with your Pretest results.

TABLE 17

Create a 3-column, 9-row table. Center the column headings. Align the number column on the right. Automatically adjust the column widths. Center the table vertically and horizontally.

MAJOR U.S. RIVERS (From *U.S. Geographic Textbook*)		
River	**Length**	**Origin**
Arkansas	1,460	Colorado
Colorado	1,450	Colorado
Columbia	1,240	British Columbia
Mississippi	2,350	Minnesota
Missouri	2,320	Montana
Tennessee	900	North Carolina

TABLE 18

Create a 4-column, 10-row table. Center the column headings. Align the number columns on the right. Automatically adjust the column widths. Center the table vertically and horizontally.

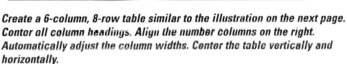

PARKS HIGH SCHOOL HONOR GRADUATES (GPA From 3.50 to 4.00)			
3.75 GPA to 4.00 GPA		**3.50 GPA to 3.74 GPA**	
Student	**GPA**	**Student**	**GPA**
Bryce Bynum	4.00	Aaron Christopher	3.73
Jennifer Click	4.00	Shelley Lyons	3.70
Samuel Dornbusch	3.98	Kelley Lavender	3.65
Rose Barstow	3.97	James Crawford	3.62
Isaac Heyman	3.90	Brandon Lee	3.57
Charlotte Mendosa	3.85	Karen Brackett	3.52
Neil Pacioni	3.80	Charlotte Diaz	3.50

TABLE 19

Create a 6-column, 8-row table similar to the illustration on the next page. Center all column headings. Align the number columns on the right. Automatically adjust the column widths. Center the table vertically and horizontally.

TEACH

Table 17. If you have not done so lately, remind students to be aware of their posture, to sit up, keep their elbows in, and their feet flat on the floor.

Table 18. Ask students what the advantages are of being on the honor roll. Why would they want to try to achieve this honor, or why isn't this a goal for them? How might it help or hurt their lives?

Out-of-Class Activity

Discuss careers related to rivers, such as waiters on steamboat cruise vessels, barge captains, dock workers, and so forth. Have students search the classified ads and the backs of magazines for careers related to rivers. Bring these ads to class and create a bulletin board.

Math Connections

Have students add another column titled "Length in Kilometers" between "Length" and "Origin." Convert the miles to kilometers and add these figures to this column. (Multiply miles by 1.6 to get kilometers.)

Table 19. Remind students to center all headings and to align the number columns on the right.

ASSESS

- Check to see if students are completing 30-second OK timings without any errors.
- Watch students as they complete the Language Link activity to see if they are able to apply the subject/verb agreement rule.
- Check to see if students show signs of improvement from the Pretest to the Posttest.
- After students finish typing the tables, have them view their work on the screen to see if they made any errors.

CLOSE

If students do not finish the tables during the class period, make sure they save their work so that they can complete it the next time this class meets.

PORTFOLIO Activity

If students' portfolio goals include showcasing their best work, they may want to include one of the tables from this lesson. Encourage students to evaluate their work and include comments in their portfolio.

ANTARCTICA EXPLORATIONS
(Expeditions to the South Pole)

1772–1928			1929–1989		
Year	**Explorer**	**Mode of Travel**	**Year**	**Explorer**	**Mode of Travel**
1773	Cook	Ship	1929	Byrd	Airplane
1908	Shackleton	Pony sled	1935	Ellsworth	Airplane
1911	Amundsen	Dog sled	1946	Ronne	Airplane
1912	Scott	Dog sled	1958	Thiel	Tractor
1928	Wilkins	Airplane	1989	Murden & Metz	Skis

FACT FILE

The blue whale is the largest animal in the world—probably the largest that ever lived. Antarctic blue whales can be over 100 feet long and weigh more than 150 tons. A blue whale's heart alone may weigh as much as 2,000 pounds (as much as a small car).

In spite of their huge size, most blue whales are gentle, placid browsers that strain vast amounts of ocean for the krill (small shrimp) on which they feed. Blue whales are known to migrate from the South Pole to the Equator in small packs.

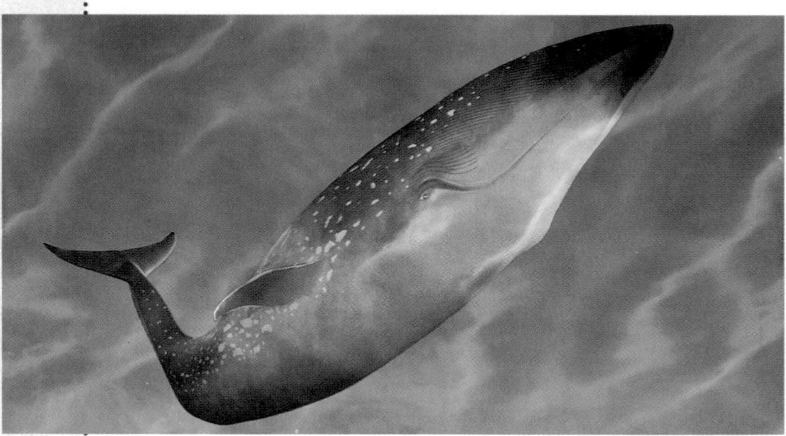

Teacher Notes

LESSON 72

Reports With Parenthetical References and Quotes

OBJECTIVES:

- Review the format for an academic report.
- Learn the format for long quotes and works cited.
- Learn software features.
- Type 35/3'/5e.

A. Warmup

Type each line 2 times.

Speed	1 The team has worked hard to solve the problem for the firm.
Accuracy	2 Six big jet planes quickly zoomed over the five old towers.
Language Link	3 I visited Western High School located in western Milwaukee.
Numbers	4 Our 15 girls and 25 boys ate 8 pies, 8 cakes, and 9 pizzas.
	| 1 | 2 | 3 | 4 | 5 | 6 | 7 | 8 | 9 | 10 | 11 | 12

SKILLBUILDING

B. Preview Practice

Type each line 2 times as a preview to the 3-minute timings that follow.

Accuracy	5 several everyone stressful management inadequate everything
Speed	6 people time gift less seem have they plan want tips item up

LESSON 72

FOCUS

- Use 3-minute timings to build speed.
- Learn word processing features: Left Indent, Right Indent, and Hanging Indent.
- Learn how to format and type reports with parenthetical references and quotes.
- Type reports with parenthetical references and quotations.

BELLRINGER

As soon as students arrive at their workstations and log in, have them type the Warmup. Go over the purpose of each line as shown to the left of the copy.

TEACH

Activity B. Point out that words in the Preview Practice are used in the timing that follows.

RESOURCES

 Lesson Plan 72

 Courseware Lesson 72

Student Data Disk

Student Manual

Academic Report Format Guide

Supplementary Production Activities

Grading and Evaluation

TEACH

Activity C. The goal for these timings is to type 35 words a minute for 3 minutes with no more than 5 errors.

Remind students to be aware of their posture, to sit up, keep their elbows in, and their feet flat on the floor.

Activity D. Provide the class with an MLA style book for reference. Go over the guidelines for parentheses. Go over the five examples of parenthetical references in class.

C. 3-Minute Timings

Take two 3-minute timings on the paragraph. Note your speed and errors.

Goal: 35/3'/5e

```
    Time is a gift we all have. A day is the same length      11
for all of us. Some people always seem to have time for       22
everything and everyone. Other people just never seem to      33
have enough time to do all the things they want to do. This   45
difference may be due to people not having an adequate plan   57
to manage the time they do have. Experts in time management   69
have decided on several tips for better use of time. Make     81
lists of things to do and check each item as it is done.      92
Your day will be less stressful if you manage your time      104
wisely.                                                      105
 | 1 | 2 | 3 | 4 | 5 | 6 | 7 | 8 | 9 | 10 | 11 | 12  SI 1.26
```

FORMATTING

D. Reports With Parenthetical References

When you use facts, ideas, and information of others in a report, you must give credit to those people. One acceptable format to use is the MLA (Modern Language Association) style for **parenthetical references.** In this style, a quotation is followed by the author's or source's name in parentheses. Follow these guidelines to format parenthetical references:

1. Include the author's name and the page number(s) of the source in parentheses; for example, (Adams 157–158).
2. If the author's or source's name is used before the quote, include only the page number(s) in parentheses; for example, (157–158).
3. If there are two or three authors of the source, include all authors' names in parentheses; for example, (Jones, Cass, and Noel 199).

FACT FILE

Psychologists say it takes 21 days to form a habit. Have students make a chart to record the way they spend their time for three weeks. Then have them change their schedule to help better manage their time. Ask them to stick to their new schedule for 21 days. At the end of this time, check with students.

4. If there are four or more authors, include the first author's name followed by *et al.;* for example, (Martin et al. 215–217).
5. If there is no author, include a shortened version of the title and the page number(s) in parentheses; for example, (Critical Essays 59).

E. Quotations In Reports

Short Quotations (less than 4 lines):

1. Enclose direct quotations in quotation marks. Do not use quotation marks with indirect quotes or paraphrased remarks.
2. Type the parenthetical reference 1 space after the closing quotation mark or the last word of an indirect quote. Type the ending punctuation mark after the reference.
   Example: ". . . until we receive confirmation" (Barton 96).

Long Quotations (4 or more lines):

1. Leave a blank line before and after the quote.
2. Do not use quotation marks.
3. Indent the quote 1 inch from the left margin.
4. Type the parenthetical reference 1 space after the ending punctuation mark.
   Example: . . . by tomorrow at the latest. (Johnson 41)

F. Software Features

STUDENT MANUAL

Left Indent | Right Indent | Hanging Indent

Study Lesson 72 in your student manual. Complete all the practice activities while at your computer. Then complete the jobs that follow.

*inter*NET CONNECTION

Use the Internet to search for Websites that provide information on time management. Try the site, http://www.day-timer.com. Take the time management quiz. Then, prepare a brief paragraph describing the results of the test of your time management skills.

LESSON 72

TEACH

Activity E. Go over both the short and long quotations with students. Make sure they understand the proper use of quotation marks.

Activity F. Explain the software features presented in this activity.

- Demonstrate a left indent.
- Demonstrate a right indent.
- Demonstrate a hanging indent.

STUDENT MANUAL

Be sure students turn to the correct lesson in their Student Manual.

JOURNAL ENTRY

Have students write about how technology affects their lives and how they feel about technology. Does it help or hinder their lives? How?

TEACH

Report 17. Remind students to double-space. Have them proofread their work and make any necessary corrections. Have students check each other's work.

ASSESS

- Check to see if students are increasing their word a minute speeds as they complete the 3-minute timings.
- Make sure students are able to use the Left Indent, Right Indent, and Hanging Indent software features.
- As students begin typing the reports, walk around the room and point out correct and incorrect formatting to individual students.
- After students finish typing the reports, have them view their work on the screen to see if they made any errors. If errors were made, have students edit their work and make corrections.

CLOSE

If students do not finish the report during the class period, make sure they save their work so that they can complete it the next time this class meets.

Remind students to clean up their workstation when they leave.

WORD PROCESSING APPLICATIONS

REPORT 17

Type the following report in academic style. Double-space the report.

If necessary, refer to formatting instructions on page 139 for academic reports.

(Your Name)
(Your Teacher's Name)
(Class Name)
(Current Date)

Employee Absenteeism

"Absence makes the heart grow fonder" (Bayly 1). This quote may apply to the absence of a loved one; however, it is not true in the case of employee absence.

Some feel that a paycheck is enough incentive to come to work. Others feel that what happens once employees arrive can increase absenteeism. Hawkens writes in his book, Management by Communication:

> It will help to work with employees rather than manage them and to keep open lines of communication. There is no greater obstacle to successful communications than the refusal of a manager to willingly communicate with those who are under his or her direct line of control and an unwillingness to practice this activity on a day-to-day basis. (22–23)

Employers have studied reports explaining why employees are absent. They have found that lack of good quality child care is one big factor. In response to this need, some employers have set up child care facilities at the work site (Stone and Burlingham 47).

The solution to the problem of employee absenteeism will take effort on the part of both workers and employers. Workers must understand how their job performance affects business success—and whether or not they will even have a job. Employers need to continue to try to help employees overcome factors that cause them to be absent.

Teacher Notes

LESSON 73 REPORTS WITH WORKS CITED PAGE

OBJECTIVES:

- Improve keyboarding technique.
- Compose at the keyboard.
- Learn software features.
- Learn to format a Works Cited page.

A. WARMUP

Type each line 2 times.

Speed	1	You will need to learn new ways to work and save more time.
Accuracy	2	The judge quickly gave back six of the prizes to the women.
Language Link	3	Not only they but also I am playing golf and swimming soon.
Numbers/Symbols	4	Report #R102 (prepared by Rothe & Roy) shows a 2% increase.
		| 1 | 2 | 3 | 4 | 5 | 6 | 7 | 8 | 9 | 10 | 11 | 12

LANGUAGE LINK

B. COMPOSING AT THE KEYBOARD

Answer the following questions with complete sentences.

5 Who are three people you would most like to meet, and why would you like to meet them?

6 If you could travel with a famous person, who would that be, and why did you choose that person?

7 If you could design your dream vacation spot, what would it look like?

RESOURCES

 Lesson Plan 73

 Courseware Lesson 73

Student Data Disk

Student Manual

Supplementary Production Activities

Grading and Evaluation

Cross-Curricular Activities

LESSON 73

FOCUS

- Compose answers for the Language Link activity using complete sentences.
- Use Technique Timings to improve technique.
- Learn how to format and type reports with a Works Cited Page.
- Learn a word processing feature: Header/Footer.
- Type a report in academic style.

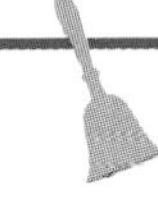

BELLRINGER

As soon as students arrive at their workstations and log in, have them type the Warmup. Go over the purpose of each line as shown to the left of the copy.

TEACH

Activity B. After students have completed the sentences, have them check each other's work for accuracy. For the students who make errors, have them retype their answers error-free as a homework assignment.

Solutions: Answers will vary.

TEACH

Activity C. Remind students that proper technique is a building block for speed and accuracy. The focus for this timing: space without pausing.

Activity D. Review with students the steps for citing works in reports as explained in the MLA style book.

Illustration

Explain that this illustration does not show all possible entries.

SKILLBUILDING

C. Technique Timings

Take two 30-second timings on each line. Focus on the technique at the left.

Space without pausing.

```
 8 Now that I have my own car, I can drive to all of my games.
 9 If I have to see him just now, he must come to this window.
10 My dad took a long trip and fished in the river for a week.
11 Our mom went to a spa to rest and relax while our dad read.
   | 1 | 2 | 3 | 4 | 5 | 6 | 7 | 8 | 9 | 10 | 11 | 12
```

FORMATTING

D. Works Cited Page

Molvide 4

Works Cited

Blue, Leslie. Free College Cash. Detroit: Fact File Press, 1997.

Drake, M. L. "Your Guide to Finding College Cash." Business Week 14 September 1998: 112-113.

Kent, Dennis M. Financial Aid Opportunities for Undergrads: Step-by-Step. New York: Visible Ink Press, 1996.

Redburn, Philana H. Secrets to Finding Maximum College Financial Aid. 9th ed. Chicago: Student College Aid Publishing Division, 1998.

Spinner, June Ann and David R. Webster. Scholarships and Financial Aid for the Disabled Student. Redwood City: Redwood Publishers.

In MLA-style reports, the **Works Cited page** is an alphabetical list of all the sources you have cited. To format a list of works cited:

1. Begin the Works Cited section on a new page, continuing the page numbers from the report.
2. Use the same side margins as in the report, and use double spacing.
3. Create a header with the report author's name and page number aligned at the right margin; for example, Sanders 4. Press ENTER 1 time after typing the page number.
4. Center and type the title *Works Cited* in initial caps approximately 1 inch from the top of the page.
5. Arrange the list alphabetically by authors' last names.
6. Begin each entry at the left margin, and indent carryover lines 0.5 inch (use a hanging indent).

interNET ACTIVITY

Have students access MLA online (www.mla.org/) by going directly to the site or by using a search engine and typing in the words Modern Language Association. Have students first read the FAQs and then access other areas from the home page.

Multiple Learning Styles

Experiment with playing different music in class while students work. Have students create a chart on the computer of the different pieces of music. Post this in the classroom. Have students vote on which music helps improve their performance (both accuracy and speed).

E. Software Features

STUDENT MANUAL

Header/Footer

Study Lesson 73 in your student manual. Complete all the practice activities while at your computer. Then complete the jobs that follow.

WORD PROCESSING APPLICATIONS

REPORT 18

Type the following report in academic style. Type the Works Cited page as the last page of the report. Use your name, your teacher's name, your course title, and the current date in the heading. Use only your last name with the page number.

Paying College Costs

¶It is assumed that students will continue their education beyond high school. Some graduates will attend community colleges or four-year colleges and universities immediately after high school graduation. Some graduates will work part-time and take classes over an extended period of years. Redburn states that:

> Some will obtain vocational skills by attending career-specific schools and training programs. No matter what path is taken, all who seek post-high-school training face the problem of paying the ever-increasing costs of higher education. Next to your home, this may be the most expensive investment you make. (2)

¶Financial aid can be the answer. It is best to begin by examining the several types of financial aid available. There are scholarships, loans, and grants that do not have to be repaid. There are work-study programs and internships, which allow students to work and earn tuition. Some scholarships are granted by extracurricular organizations and may require a formal membership or a period of active participation. It is important to start your research early so that you have enough time to locate and meet application deadlines for a variety of awards (Kent 97).

¶The U. S. Department of Education offers six main student financial aid programs: Pell Grants, Supplemental Education Opportunity Grants, College Work Study, Perkins Loans, Stafford Loans, and Plus Loans (Blue 202). Published guidelines showing the requirements needed to qualify for each of these programs are available. Everyone, no matter what his or her income level, can benefit by completing the paperwork for governmental financial aid.

TEACH

Activity E. Go over the information on headers and footers in the Student Manual with students. Walk around the room while they work through the steps to make sure each student understands each step.

STUDENT MANUAL

Be sure students turn to the correct lesson in their Student Manual.

Report 18. Remind students this report is an academic report and should be typed in MLA style.

JOURNAL ENTRY

Have students write about the questions they want to ask their guidance counselor concerning financial aid for trade or business schools or college.

ASSESS

- Review students' responses to questions in the Language Link composing activity.
- Make sure students are able to add a header to a report.
- Monitor students as they complete Technique Timings and provide individualized assistance as needed.
- As students begin typing the reports, walk around the room and point out correct and incorrect formatting to individual students.
- After students finish typing the reports, have them view their work on the screen to see if they made any errors. If errors were made, have students edit their work and make corrections.

CLOSE

If students do not finish the report during the class period, make sure they save their work so that they can complete it the next time this class meets.

Remind students to clean up their workstation when they leave.

¶There are even financial aid programs earmarked for students with disabilities (Spinner and Webster 16). Each year millions of dollars are available as assistance for disabled students and their families. These programs are open to disabled applicants from high school through postdoctoral studies. Students with physical disabilities as well as learning disabilities (such as dyslexia) are eligible.
¶Probably the best place to begin the search for information on sources for college financial aid is in the counseling office of your school. Also, contact the financial aid office at the schools you are interested in attending as suggested by Drake (112). The task of locating ways to fund college costs may seem overwhelming. It is made easier if you start early and are well-organized in your search.

Works Cited

Blue, Leslie. Free College Cash. Detroit: Fact File Press, 1997.

Drake, M. L. "Your Guide to Finding College Cash." Business Week 14 September 1998: 112–113.

Kent, Dennis M. Financial Aid Opportunities for Undergrads: Step-by-Step. New York: Visible Ink Press, 1996.

Redburn, Philana H. Secrets to Finding Maximum College Financial Aid, 9th ed. Chicago: Student College Aid Publishing Division, 1998.

Spinner, June Ann and David R. Webster. Scholarships and Financial Aid for the Disabled Student. Redwood City: Redwood Publishers, 1998.

MATH CONNECTIONS

Use whatever sources are available such as the Internet, the library, or local colleges to determine what tuition rates for various schools are. Then, calculate how much you would need to earn or save every week in order to pay the tuition. Based on money you currently earn either through working or an allowance, calculate how long it would take you to save the entire amount of tuition.

Teacher Notes

LESSON 74 REPORTS REVIEW

OBJECTIVES:

- Improve keyboarding speed and accuracy.
- Review report formats.

A. WARMUP

Type each line 2 times.

```
Speed          1 When you go to look for a job, dress well and arrive early.
Accuracy       2 Jackie quietly gave most of his prize boxers to dog owners.
Language Link  3 His surgery was May 4; he returned to work six weeks later.
Numbers        4 You can telephone Myron at 318-555-2647 or at 318-555-2648.
                 | 1 | 2 | 3 | 4 | 5 | 6 | 7 | 8 | 9 | 10 | 11 | 12
```

SKILLBUILDING

B. PACED PRACTICE

Turn to the Paced Practice routine beginning on page SB-7 Take three 2-minute timings, starting at the point where you left off the last time.

WORD PROCESSING APPLICATIONS

REPORT 19

Agenda

Type the following agenda in the correct format.

ASIF TECHNOLOGY CONFERENCE / Meeting Agenda / August 12-15, {year}

1. Registration/Lobby
2. Demonstration: Virtual Reality/Mott Suite
3. Break/Curtise Suite
4. Computerized Accounting Software/Carriage B
5. Awards Luncheon/Chrysler A/B
6. Managing Files on a Computer/Carriage B
7. Break/Curtise Suite
8. Introduction: Interactive Communications/Mott Suite
9. Discussion and Evaluation/Chrysler B

RESOURCES

- Lesson Plan 74
- Courseware Lesson 74
- Student Data Disk
- Student Manual
- Reteaching and Reinforcement
- Grading and Evaluation

LESSON 74

FOCUS

- Use the Paced Practice 2-minute timings.
- Practice formatting and typing reports.

BELLRINGER

As soon as students arrive at their workstations and log in, have them type the Warmup. Go over the purpose of each line as shown to the left of the copy.

TEACH

Activity B. Review the procedure for the Paced Practice routine with students.

Report 19. Remind students to use the numbering command for the list.

TEACH

Report 20. Keep a classroom copy of the MLA style book handy for student reference. Encourage them to use it and to become familiar with it. You might also keep copies of other style books in the classroom, such as *APA* and *The Chicago Manual of Style*.

REPORT 20

Type the following report in academic style, including the Works Cited page as the last page of the report.Use your name, your teacher's name, your course title, and the current date in the heading.

Managing Your Money 101

¶It is not easy to manage money, but this is a very important part of becoming an independent adult. When you start your first job (which will probably be a part-time job), you will be expected to take on some of the financial responsibilities for your own care that were previously met by your parents or guardians. Perhaps you will have to buy your own clothes. You will certainly have to pay for your own lunches and for your transportation to and from work. "You will have to learn to live within your means, which means spending no more than you earn, or not buying things for which you cannot pay" (Krammer and Petrie 154).

¶If you are to be successful in living within your means, you must have a plan for spending. People who do not plan often end up in trouble with credit accounts. College students are particularly at risk of overdoing it with credit if they use the many unsolicited credit cards that come to them in the mail almost as soon as they check into the dormitory. Jones tells parents to be sure that their college-age students leave for college with a sensible spending plan and lessons on how to use credit (29).

¶In order to have a realistic spending plan, you need to think about your plans—both long-range and short-range. If you want to purchase a house, for example, you will need to begin saving money for a down payment.

> One of the most important things you can do is to think of saving as you think of paying your bills—something you do every month without fail. In fact, you should think of savings as a bill you pay yourself. You may be one of the many people who are always planning to save but are constantly confronted with other ways of spending money earmarked for savings. Certainly, saving requires discipline. (Porter 163)

¶Single adults and families with young children should consider saving money for the future or providing for emergencies by investing in insurance (Topolnicki 45). Income-protection insurance will provide income for the single person or young family in case the breadwinner is unable to work. There is homeowner's insurance to cover unexpected losses of property. Car insurance is also a must. For many people, the purchase of insurance is a good way to save money for future expenses. There are many different kinds of insurance to be considered when putting together a spending plan.

Career Exploration

Invite a financial planner, a banker, an accountant, and a stock broker to be part of a panel to speak to your class about careers in money management. Have students type a list of questions before the panel arrives. Review the questions in class, editing and changing as necessary.

*inter*NET ACTIVITY

Have students choose one of the money management topics discussed in Report 20 and search to find more information on the topic. Have them compose a paragraph at the keyboard using the information they find.

¶There is help available for people who find themselves in need of help with money matters. General information can be obtained free of charge from government publications. Also, banks employ people who can provide you with information on savings and investments (Garnet et al. 194–201). It would be worth your while to invest your time and money in a class to learn how to manage your money. Remember, no matter how much you earn, how you manage your money will determine the type of lifestyle you will be able to achieve.

Works Cited

Garner, Christopher et al. Personal Finance Guide for Working Couples. New York: John Wiley & Sons, Inc. 1995.

Jones, Gregory. "Teaching Young Children About Spending Money." Essence April 1996, 29–30.

Krammer, Gloria and Sylvia B. Petrie. Succeeding in the World of Finance. Bloomington: Wright Publishing 1998.

Porter, Harold. Managing Family Finances. San Francisco: Prentice Hall Press 1993.

Topolnicki, Dillard. "Getting in Touch With Your Finances." Money December 1997, 142–146.

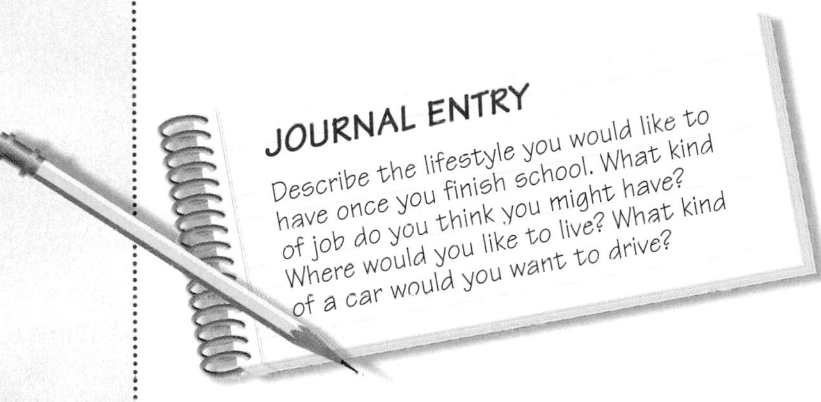

JOURNAL ENTRY
Describe the lifestyle you would like to have once you finish school. What kind of job do you think you might have? Where would you like to live? What kind of a car would you want to drive?

Teacher Notes

ASSESS

- Review students' performance on the Paced Practice 2-minute timings.
- As students begin typing the reports, walk around the room and point out correct and incorrect formatting to individual students.
- After students finish typing the reports, have them view their work on the screen to see if they made any errors. If errors were made, have students edit their work and make corrections.

CLOSE

If students do not finish the reports during the class period, make sure they save their work so that they can complete it the next time this class meets.

Remind students to clean up their workstation when they leave.

PORTFOLIO *Activity*

If students' portfolio goals include showcasing their best work, they may want to include one of the reports from this lesson. Encourage students to evaluate their work and include comments in their portfolio.

LESSON 75

FOCUS

- Apply the Language Link rule for commas.
- Use 3-minute timings to build speed.
- Learn word processing features: Footnotes and Endnotes.
- Learn how to format and type footnotes and endnotes in reports.

BELLRINGER

As soon as students arrive at their workstations and log in, have them type the Warmup. Go over the purpose of each line as shown to the left of the copy.

TEACH

Activity B. After students have completed the sentences, have them check each other's work. Next have students compose five new sentences that use introductory expressions.

Solutions: As we discussed yesterday, you must type this entire document for Larry.

After you see the package, you may decide that it isn't what you really want.

In 1998 several explorers had to be rescued from the top of the mountain.

During this same period, global warming was blamed for the avalanches.

LESSON 75

FOOTNOTES AND ENDNOTES IN REPORTS

OBJECTIVES:

- Learn about commas with introductory expressions.
- Type 35/3'/5e.
- Format reports with footnotes and endnotes.
- Learn software features.

A. WARMUP

Type each line 2 times.

Speed	1	We know that a good thing to do is to rest and read a book.
Accuracy	2	The lazy judge was very quick to pay tax money for the box.
Language Link	3	Kia understands that the classroom rules apply to everyone.
Numbers/Symbols	4	Lee & Lou and Nate & Nat paid for 534# of #80 tape @ $1.28.

| 1 | 2 | 3 | 4 | 5 | 6 | 7 | 8 | 9 | 10 | 11 | 12

B. COMMAS

Study the rule and the examples below. Then correct any errors in comma usage in lines 5–8.

Rule 13: Use a comma after an introductory expression (unless it is a short prepositional phrase).

In my opinion, the cars should be repaired immediately.

No, you may not take the ferry to the island.

After the flood, we sold our house and moved to a condominium.

RESOURCES

 Lesson Plan 75

 Courseware Lesson 75

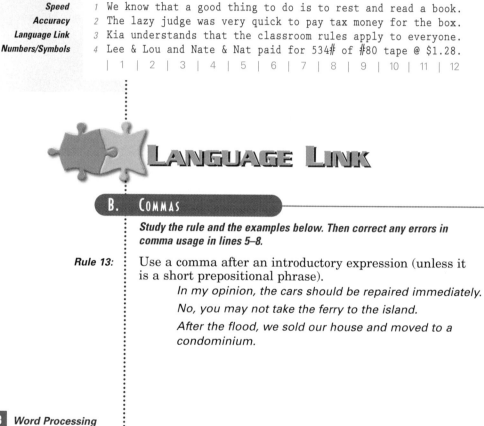

Student Data Disk

Student Manual

Language Link Worksheets

Supplementary Production Activities

Grading and Evaluation

5 As we discussed yesterday you must type this entire document for Larry.
6 After you see the package you may decide that it isn't what you really want.
7 In 1998 several explorers had to be rescued from the top of the mountain.
8 During this same period global warming was blamed for the avalanches.

SKILLBUILDING

C. Preview Practice

Type each line 2 times as a preview to the 3-minute timings below.

Accuracy 9 start resume realize involved business Employers activities
Speed 10 apply work deal good soon have help make will ask use so in

D. 3-Minute Timings

Take two 3-minute timings on the paragraph. Note your speed and errors.

Goal: 35/3'/5e

11 You will soon be asked to write a resume to use when 11
12 you inquire about your first job. Employers realize that 22
13 you may not have a great deal of work experience, so they 34
14 tend to look more at school activities and interests. It 45
15 would be a good idea to get involved in the activities of 57
16 any clubs for business students. Your school is sure to 68
17 have at least one. If not, ask your teacher to help you 79
18 start one. You will apply what you have learned in your 90
19 classes, gain leadership skills, and make friends who have 102
20 like interests. 105

| 1 | 2 | 3 | 4 | 5 | 6 | 7 | 8 | 9 | 10 | 11 | 12 SI 1.36

LESSON 75

TEACH

Activity C. Point out that words in the Preview Practice are used in the timing that follows.

Activity D. Remind students that they should try to improve speed with each of the 3-minute timings. The goal for this 3-minute timing is to type 35 words a minute with no more than 5 errors.

JOURNAL ENTRY

Have students write about the information they would like to put into their resume. Remind them to include school activities, interests, and any work experience they have. Include reasons they want to work.

TEACH

Activity E. Ask students to explain the difference between footnotes and endnotes. Make sure they understand the difference.

Activity F. Have students complete the practice activities while at the computer. While they work on the jobs, walk around the room to make sure they are doing the work accurately.

STUDENT MANUAL

Be sure students turn to the correct lesson in their Student Manual.

FORMATTING

E. Footnotes and Endnotes

In Lesson 72 you gave credit to sources of information in reports using parenthetical references. Two other acceptable methods for giving credit are **footnotes** and **endnotes.** Footnotes and endnotes should include the name of the author, the title of the book or article, the publisher, the place and year of publication, and the page numbers being referenced.

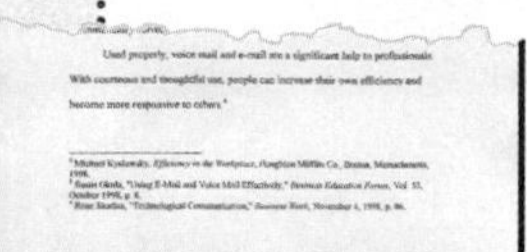

Footnotes

1. Footnotes are indicated in the body of a report by superior figures.
2. Footnotes are consecutively numbered.
3. Footnotes appear at the bottom of the page on which the reference appears.

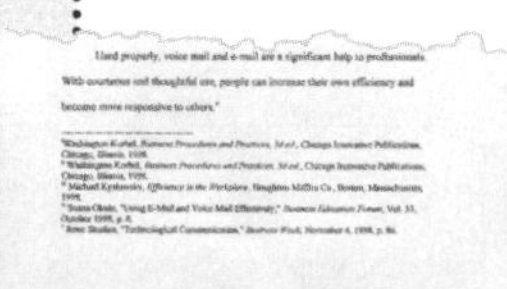

Endnotes

1. Endnotes are indicated in the body of a report by superior figures.
2. Endnotes are numbered consecutively.
3. Endnotes appear at the end of a report, either on the last page or on a separate page.

F. Software Features

STUDENT MANUAL

Footnotes Endnotes

Study Lesson 75 in your student manual. Complete all the practice activities while at your computer. Then complete the jobs that follow.

Out-of-Class Activity

Have students search magazines and books for footnotes and endnotes, and bring in one example written on a 3″ x 5″ card and note whether this is an endnote or footnote. Mix up the cards, have each student draw one, and then write a short report, using the footnote or endnote.

Language Arts Connections

Ask students what plagiarism is. (to steal another's writing and use it as your own) Explain that plagiarism is both ethically and legally wrong. Footnotes and endnotes allow you to give credit to the original authors for work you are using. Hold a class discussion on plagiarism.

REPORT 21

Type the following business report with double spacing. Format all references as footnotes. The text for the footnotes is at the end of the report.

COMMUNICATING IN THE NEW MILLENNIUM

¶Just a few short years ago, the way we most often communicated with others was by telephone or letter. Often, using the telephone meant playing what business workers referred to as "telephone tag."[1] This name resulted from a caller's having to leave a message for someone to call back, then not being available when the call was returned. If you communicated via letters, you could never be sure exactly when the letter would be delivered.

¶With advances in technology, we now have many more options available. Among these options are voice mail and e-mail. Voice mail enables you to leave a message for someone even if you know the person is not available. It enables the person being called to answer the telephone or wait until a more convenient time to get any messages. E-mail enables you to send "written" messages to anyone at any time and have those messages delivered instantly. This is particularly useful if you must communicate with someone in a different time zone. You can send your message at a convenient time for you, and the receiver can respond at a convenient time for him or her.

¶Each of these options also has negative aspects. Many people do not like voice mail because they do not like to be greeted by a recording; others refuse to leave messages. Companies that rely on voice mail to answer and route all incoming calls risk losing the business of people who want to speak with a "real" person.[2] Have you ever been frustrated by having to listen to a long recording or a list of options before your call could be completed?

¶E-mail has provided us with a way to send instantaneous messages. However, this ease of sending messages has dramatically increased the number of unimportant messages being sent. (In other instances, using e-mail has proved to be very costly. The informality of e-mail often causes people to respond without thinking and send messages that should never be sent.) In addition, e-mail is not totally secure. Information that you don't want others to know should not be sent via e-mail.

TEACH

Report 21. As students type the report, walk around the room and make sure they remember to add the footnotes.

FACT FILE

Many employers believe any files created on company computers belong to the company, including private e-mail messages and even personal resumes. Divide the class into two groups. Have one group debate the right of privacy in the workplace; have the other group debate the employer's viewpoint. Make sure the arguments are logical.

ASSESS

- Check to see if students are increasing their word a minute speeds as they complete each 3-minute timing.
- Watch students as they complete the Language Link activity to see if they are able to apply the comma rule correctly.
- Make sure students are able to use the Footnote and Endnote software feature.
- As students begin typing the report, walk around the room and point out correct and incorrect formatting to individual students.
- After students finish typing the report, have them view their work on the screen to see if they made any errors. If errors were made, have students edit their work and make corrections.

CLOSE

If students do not finish the report during the class period, make sure they save their work so that they can complete it the next time this class meets.

Remind students to clean up their workstation when they leave.

¶Here are four general guidelines for using voice mail and e-mail. Whichever one you use, keep your message professional, clear, and courteous. If you are dealing with extremely sensitive information, you may want to deliver the message face-to-face or over the telephone so that there are no misunderstandings. Remember that neither voice mail nor e-mail is totally secure. If you are saying or writing something that you do not want anyone other than the recipient to know about, speak directly to him or her. Finally, be sure your messages are clear, concise, and grammatically correct.[3]

¶Used properly, voice mail and e-mail are a significant help to professionals. With courteous and thoughtful use, people can increase their own efficiency and become more responsive to others.[4]

1. Washington Korbel, *Business Procedures and Practices,* 3d ed., Chicago Innovative Publications, Chicago, Illinois, 1998.
2. Michael Kyslowsky, *Efficiency in the Workplace,* Houghton Mifflin Co., Boston, Massachusetts, 1998.
3. Susan Okula, "Using E-Mail and Voice Mail Effectively," *Business Education Forum,* Vol. 53, October 1998, p. 8.
4. Rene Shadira, "Technological Communication," *Business Week,* November 4, 1998, p. 86.

COMMUNICATION FOCUS

When you are leaving a message on voice mail, be sure to speak clearly, state the essential facts quickly, and give your name and telephone number slowly. It is also a good idea to repeat your telephone number again at the end of the message. If your message contains any unusual names, you may want to spell those names. Analyze your messages and think of ways in which you can improve them.

If you use e-mail, always remember that the person receiving your message cannot see your expression or hear the tone of your voice. Because of this, be careful what you write. Be sure that nothing you say can be taken in a way that you didn't intend. And always spell check and proofread your messages before you send them.

Teacher Notes

LESSON 76

REPORTS: MULTIPAGE, LEFT BOUND

OBJECTIVES:

- Improve keyboarding speed.
- Format multipage, bound reports.

A. WARMUP

Type each line 2 times.

Speed	1	When the cat rests, it wants to lie down in the same place.
Accuracy	2	Jack was too lazy for the farm job; he proved quite vexing.
Language Link	3	On Tuesday, it rained more than it did on Friday or Sunday.
Numbers/Symbols	4	We will earn 12% more on #31 & #46 if they are sold @ $200.
		| 1 | 2 | 3 | 4 | 5 | 6 | 7 | 8 | 9 | 10 | 11 | 12

SKILLBUILDING

B. 12-SECOND SPRINTS

Take three 12-second timings on each line. Try to increase your speed on each timing.

```
5 He may not play ball if he did not yet take that math test.
6 We might have a very nice profit if the order is a big one.
7 That job might very well take much longer than you thought.
8 Justin had time to do the job because it was planned early.
  ||||5||||10||||15||||20||||25||||30||||35||||40||||45||||50||||55||||60
```

COMMUNICATION FOCUS

Follow these steps to improve your listening: Choose to listen. Listen actively. Listen for ideas and feelings. Know when to keep silent. Be flexible when taking notes. Resist distractions. Keep an open mind.

LESSON 76

FOCUS

- Use 12-second timings to build speed.
- Learn how to format and type multipage, left-bound reports.

BELLRINGER

As soon as students arrive at their workstations and log in, have them type the Warmup. Go over the purpose of each line as shown to the left of the copy.

TEACH

Activity B. Remind students that the goal for 12-second sprints is improved speed with each timing.

RESOURCES

 Lesson Plan 76

Courseware Lesson 76

Student Data Disk

Student Manual

Supplementary Production Activities

TEACH

Activity C. Remind students they are changing only the left margin, not the right margin.

Report 22. Ask students what the left margin of this report should be. (1.5 inches)

FORMATTING

C. Left-Bound Reports

In a left-bound report, the left margin must be wider to allow room for the binding. To format a left-bound report, change the left margin to 1.5 inches. Do not change the default right margin.

WORD PROCESSING APPLICATIONS

REPORT 22

Type the following business report as a left-bound report. Format all the references as endnotes. Remember to add the page number to the second page of the report.

LISTENING

Everyone appreciates a good listener. Good listeners make good friends. People who are good listeners not only gain insight into other people, but they also learn about the world around them. If you want to be a good listener, you must make a conscious decision to listen. The following suggestions should help you become a better listener.

BE QUIET

Pause for several seconds before you start to talk after the one speaking to you stops. This pause allows the speaker to catch a breath and gather his or her thoughts. The speaker may want to continue. This pause also gives you time to form your response. Preparing your response while you are trying to listen often leads to missing the main point.

MAINTAIN EYE CONTACT

Look at the person who is speaking. It shows you are listening and keeps your mind from wandering. Looking directly at the speaker enables you to watch body language and behavior. Don't stare, but look into the speaker's eyes often.

Out-of-Class Activity

Give students the following listening tips and ask them to practice in other classes for a day: take notes; focus; bring their thoughts back to what is being said when their minds drift; after class, tell someone what was said; associate what is said with something more familiar.

Multiple Learning Styles

Have students close their eyes while you read a paragraph from the text. Ask students to imagine their primary learning style is through listening. Ask them what they might do to make learning easier for them. Have them free write about this, then share these ideas in class.

DISPLAY OPENNESS

Your facial expressions and body positions convey openness. Sit or stand up straight; correct posture conveys interest. Never cross your arms or legs; such posture conveys boredom or disagreement. Do not have any physical barriers, such as a desk or a pile of books, between you and the other person.

LISTEN WITHOUT RESPONSE

Don't interrupt the speaker even if you feel that you cannot wait to express your opinions, suggestions, and comments. Marie C. Ford suggests, "Don't always have a bigger or better one of whatever the speaker is telling you about."[1] Watch your nonverbal expressions, such as shrugs and frowns. They may keep the other person from finishing the message.

SEND ACKNOWLEDGMENTS

Send acknowledgments. It is important to let the speaker know you are still listening throughout the conversation. A frequent "OK," "Yes," or nod of the head lets the speaker know that you are interested in what is being said. These signals do not imply that you agree with the speaker; they indicate only that you are hearing what is being said.[2]

Being a good listener is hard work. Sometimes it takes more effort to be a good listener than it does to be a good speaker. If you put these suggestions into practice, they will pay you big dividends.

1. Marie C. Ford and W. Ernest Ford, "The Power of Listening," *Communications Journal,* January 1998, p. 21.
2. Earl L. Belcher, *Communications for Daily Living,* Beeline Press, College Station, Texas, 1997, p. 65.

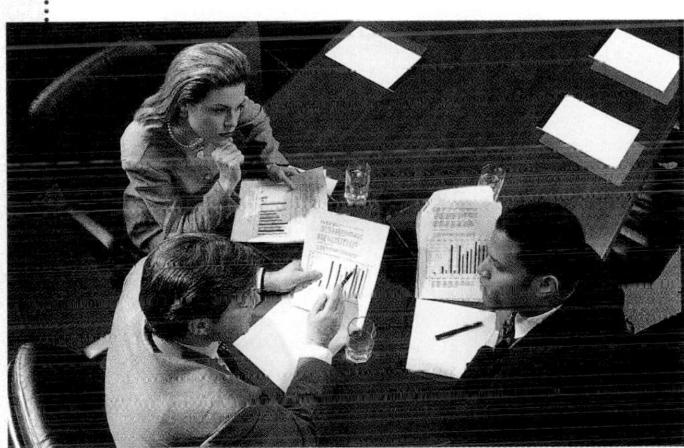

ASSESS

- Make sure students are able to change margins.
- As students begin typing the report, walk around the room and point out correct and incorrect formatting to individual students.
- After students finish typing the report, have them view their work on the screen to see if they made any errors. If errors were made, have students edit their work and make corrections.

CLOSE

If students do not finish the report during the class period, make sure they save their work so that they can complete it the next time this class meets.

Remind students to clean up their workstation when they leave.

PORTFOLIO *Activity*

If students' portfolio goals include demonstrating progress, they may want to include the report from this lesson. Encourage students to evaluate their work and include comments in their portfolio.

Teacher Notes

LESSON 77

FOCUS

- Apply the Language Link rules for capitalization.
- Use 30-second timings to build speed.
- Practice formatting and typing a multipage, left-bound report.

BELLRINGER

As soon as students arrive at their workstations and log in, have them type the Warmup. Go over the purpose of each line as shown to the left of the copy.

TEACH

Activity B. Review the rules for capitalization. Once students understand the rules, have them correct any errors in lines 5–8 on page 277. Have students check each other's work.

Solutions: The editorial staff of the Office Technology Unit worked very well together.

He took one class in word processing and another in database management.

The Computer Support Unit works with us to keep our computers running smoothly.

I studied economics and took the course Business Communications 301.

REPORTS: MULTIPAGE, LEFT BOUND

OBJECTIVES:

- Learn the rules for capitalization.
- Improve keyboarding speed.
- Format multipage, bound reports.

A. WARMUP

Type each line 2 times.

Speed	*1*	`You should always be honest with yourself about your goals.`
Accuracy	*2*	`David quickly put the frozen jars away in small gray boxes.`
Language Link	*3*	`Although Bill said it wasn't, Jason thought it was further.`
Numbers/Symbols	*4*	`Two items (#20 & #21) were sold for $33 each--a great loss!`
		| 1 | 2 | 3 | 4 | 5 | 6 | 7 | 8 | 9 | 10 | 11 | 12

B. CAPITALIZATION

Study the following rules and examples. Then correct any errors in capitalization in lines 5–8.

Rule 14: Capitalize common organizational terms (such as *advertising department* and *finance committee*) when they are the actual names of the units in your own organization and when they are preceded by the word *the.*

The monthly update will be presented by our Marketing Department today.

I applied for a position as an assistant in a marketing department.

RESOURCES

 Lesson Plan 77

 Courseware Lesson 77

Student Data Disk

Student Manual

Language Link Worksheets

Supplementary Production Activities

Rule 15: Capitalize names of specific course titles but not the names of subjects or areas of study.

She enrolled in Advanced Physics 201 and will also take a psychology course.

5 The editorial staff of the office technology unit worked very well together.

6 He took one class in word processing and another in database management.

7 The computer support unit works with us to keep our computers running smoothly.

8 I studied economics and took the course business communications 301.

SKILLBUILDING

C. 30-Second Timings

Take two 30-second timings on lines 9–10. Then take two 30-second timings on lines 11–12. Try to increase your speed on each timing.

```
 9      Driving in the country in the fall is a real treat if   11
10 you can stop and visit some local vendors along the way.      22

11      A visit to some small villages is like a trip back in   11
12 time because they work to keep things the way they were.      22
   | 1 | 2 | 3 | 4 | 5 | 6 | 7 | 8 | 9 | 10 | 11 | 12
```

TEACH

Activity C. Remind students that the goal for 30-second timings is improved speed with each timing.

TEACH

Report 23. Remind students to change the left margin for a left-bound report. Also remind students to remember the footnotes for this report.

FACT FILE

During World War I, women worked in munitions factories and war-related industries, filled service jobs, and were essential to the running of industry. Have students research what happened to women's role in industry at the end of World War I.

REPORT 23

Type the following report as a left-bound business report. Format all references as footnotes. The text for each footnote follows the superscript number and is enclosed in brackets.

VOICE RECOGNITION: INTO THE FUTURE

¶Many newspapers, magazines, and technology demonstrations are featuring voice recognition as the wave of the future. But, is voice recognition really new?

HISTORICAL PERSPECTIVES ON VOICE RECOGNITION

¶People have been able to recognize each other's voices since language first began. You need only to watch the face of a cat or dog when its owner speaks to know that the animal has heard and recognized the voice. Call centers and other kinds of businesses have been using a type of voice (speech) recognition for years.

¶Think for a moment, though, how exciting it would be to speak to your computer and have it understand what you said. Then, it would format what you said into what you need—a letter, a report, a table, a memo, or whatever, all with your voice telling your computer what to do. Is this really possible?

SPEECH RECOGNITION IN ITS INFANCY

¶While Bell Laboratories of Lucent Technologies created the first speech recognizer in 1952, the first speech recognition capability for PCs was finally developed in the 80s. The world's first discrete speech dictation system was developed by Dragon Systems in 1990. Following that innovation was the world's first commercially available software-only dictation system.[1] [1. "Dragon Systems Leading the Industry," *Dragon Naturally Speaking Mobile Edition Product Specifications*, November 12, 1998, pp.2-4.]

¶In 1997, Jim and Janet Baker excited the speech recognition arena with the first dictation software to handle continuous speech. The spotlight focused on *Naturally Speaking,* another Dragon Systems' product.[2] [2. "Let's Talk! Special Report," *Business Week*, February 23, 1998, p. 67.]

VOICE RECOGNITION MARCHES ON

¶The technology movement had begun in earnest. Several companies jumped into the race to capture the market and produce software capable of higher and higher feats of accuracy. Software and portable device manufacturers came out with new programs and devices. Companies such as Sony, Norcom, Olympus, Dragon Systems, Lernout & Hauspie, and IBM, to name a few, began to find this field exciting.[3] [3. Marie E. Flatley, "Voice Recognition Software," *Business Education Forum*, December 1998, p. 44.] Philips, Grover Industries, and others followed the thrill of voice recognition development with hardware and software utilities. For example, Grover Industries'

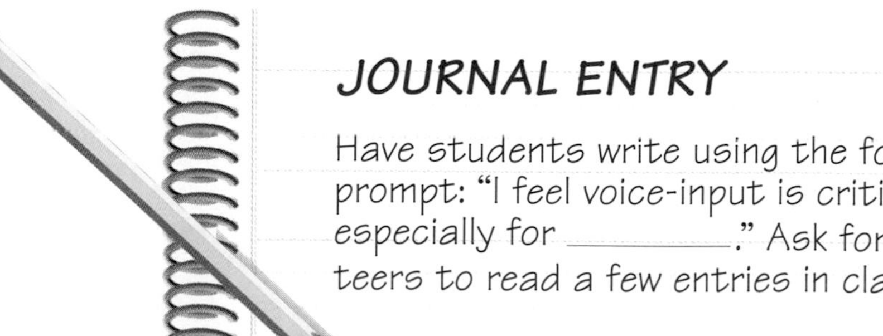

JOURNAL ENTRY

Have students write using the following prompt: "I feel voice-input is critical, especially for ________." Ask for volunteers to read a few entries in class.

Web-TalkIt is an easy-to-use voice command and control utility for your default Web browser. Just say the Website you wish to visit and Web-TalkIt will go to the URL address.

USERS OF VOICE RECOGNITION

¶Large mail order and customer service companies as well as utilities, banks, airlines, stockbrokers, manufacturers, and couriers are some of the major users of voice recognition. Customers or clients can use these voice recognition systems to obtain information, service, or to order products without human contact in most instances. Adding natural language processing to speech recognition gives us an entirely new user interface, notes Michael J. Miller of *PC Magazine*.[4] [4. Michael J. Miller, "Built for Speed," *PC Magazine,* September 22, 1998, p. 4.]

¶Voice recognition programs are enabling many physically challenged persons to use their computers more efficiently and effectively. Adrian Clifton, the inspiration for Adrian's Closet, which produces a line of clothing for young people with various disabilities, is beginning to use a voice-activated computer. He cannot use his hands, but he is able to enter invoices into files with his voice-activated computer.[5] [5. Tamar Asedo Sherman, "Threads of Love," *USA Weekend*, December 4-8, 1998, pp. 18-19.]

¶Financial traders, lawyers, and physicians are using voice recognition software. Pat Higgerty, a lawyer who cannot type, firmly believes in voice recognition technology. Higgerty creates most of his own documents and enjoys preparing a document while the client is in the office, printing it, and having the client sign the document before he or she leaves the office. Higgerty emphasizes that proper training on how to use the technology is a necessity for the 98 percent accuracy that he wants to attain.[6] [6. Paul McLaughlin, "Hands-free Computing: A Voice Recognition Technology Story," *NETWORK2D Newsletter*, Spring 1997, ABA Law Practice Management Section, 1997-98, American Bar Association, pp. 8-9.]

¶Physicians are finding voice recognition ideal for dictating chart notes after patient sessions. They say they often get more accurate notes because they can say more than if they were writing charts by hand.

¶More and more applications will be developed and more people will avail themselves of voice recognition technology as it is perfected and as accuracy levels improve above the 95-98 percent level.

TAKING IT ONE STEP FURTHER INTO THE FUTURE

¶What does the future hold for voice recognition technology? Forecasters say the sky is the limit. Computers will probably arrive loaded with voice recognition software; you will be able to access the Internet quickly, and you will be able to go from link to link just by saying what topic you want to request. Innovative software and equipment will make the lives of the blind, the deaf, and others with different physical difficulties more efficient by enabling them to access their computers without using their hands.

¶Some new processors can zoom through the math used in speech recognition, making it possible to "train" the new computer to understand the user

TEACH

Report 23. While students are typing this report, walk around the room to make sure they have changed the left margin and that they are remembering the footnotes.

CULTURAL CONNECTIONS

People of ancient cultures worshipped both goddesses and gods, which represented both the female and male. This is not true of some religions in modern culture (Christianity, Judaism, Islam), which typically worship a patriarchal god. Have a class discussion about how this change has affected the roles women play in business in our culture today.

Teacher Notes

LESSON 77

ASSESS

- Watch students as they complete the Language Link activity to see if they are able to apply the capitalization rules correctly.
- Check to see if students are increasing their speeds with each 30-second timing.
- As students begin typing the report, walk around the room and point out correct and incorrect formatting to individual students.
- After students finish typing the report, have them view their work on the screen to see if they made any errors. If errors were made, have students edit their work and make corrections.

CLOSE

If students do not finish the report during the class period, make sure they save their work so that they can complete it the next time this class meets.

Remind students to clean up their workstation when they leave.

PORTFOLIO *Activity*

If students' portfolio goals include showcasing their best work, they may want to include one of the reports from this lesson. Encourage students to evaluate their work and include comments in their portfolio.

in less than five minutes. Software developers that harness the power of these new processors predict that speech recognition will be a standard PC feature by the end of the year.[7] [7.Andy Reinhardt, "Computers with Sharp Ears," *Business Week*, March 8, 1999, p. 6.]
¶Is voice recognition in your future? Keep your ears sharp, watch for new developments, and you'll probably be a voice recognition technology user soon!

*inter*NET CONNECTION

Using the Internet, search for additional information on voice-recognition technology. You may want to search for products such as *Via Voice* or *Dragon Naturally Speaking.* Make a list of advantages and disadvantages of using this technology. Discuss with your classmates whether or not voice-recognition technology is appropriate for everyone.

SOCIAL STUDIES CONNECTIONS

Electronic engineers John Pierce and Harold Rosen designed the first successful communication satellites in the 1960s. Because of their developments, we are now able to enjoy cellular phones and watching far away television stations. Information is beamed up to satellites and sent back down to different places on Earth.

Social Studies Connections

Have students work in groups to discuss the use and the abuse of cellular phones and satellite television, and then to type a list of each. Have the whole class come together to compare their lists.

LESSON 78

Reports: Title Page, Contents, Bibliography

OBJECTIVES:

- Improve keyboarding accuracy.
- Format title, contents, and bibliography pages.

A. Warmup

Type each line 2 times.

Speed	1	Edward saved his files on the hard drive and on a diskette.
Accuracy	2	Vic quickly mixed grape juice with the frozen strawberries.
Language Link	3	It is too soon for Will to know whether he passed spelling.
Numbers/Symbols	4	Hamilton & Jones expected a 12% increase in sales--$35,890.

| 1 | 2 | 3 | 4 | 5 | 6 | 7 | 8 | 9 | 10 | 11 | 12

SKILLBUILDING

B. 30-Second OK Timings

Take two 30-second OK (error-free) timings on lines 5–6. Then take two 30-second OK timings on lines 7–8. Goal: no errors.

5 Peg was amazed by the fact that time management skills 11
6 are magic tools for learning very quickly how to mix tasks. 23

7 Sixty men went to a quaint village in the back country 11
8 of western New Zealand and fished for pike, jack, and gar. 23

| 1 | 2 | 3 | 4 | 5 | 6 | 7 | 8 | 9 | 10 | 11 | 12

RESOURCES

 Lesson Plan 78

 Courseware Lesson 78

Student Data Disk

Student Manual

Supplementary Production Activities

Multicultural Activities

FOCUS

- Use 30-second OK timings to improve accuracy.
- Learn a word processing feature: Dot Leaders.
- Learn how to format and type a title page, table of contents, and bibliography for a report.

BELLRINGER

As soon as students arrive at their workstations and log in, have them type the Warmup. Go over the purpose of each line as shown to the left of the copy.

TEACH

Activity B. Remind students that 30-second OK timings are designed to encourage accuracy.

TEACH

Activity C. Call on different students to read the five instructions on creating a title page. Make sure each student understands the steps.

Activity D. Have students open their books to the table of contents. Inform them that books, reports, magazines, and other printed materials have a table of contents that gives the reader an outline of headings. Go over the five steps to format a table of contents with students.

Activity E. Call on different students to read the six instructions on creating a bibliography on page 283. Check to make sure each student understands the steps.

FORMATTING

C. Title Page

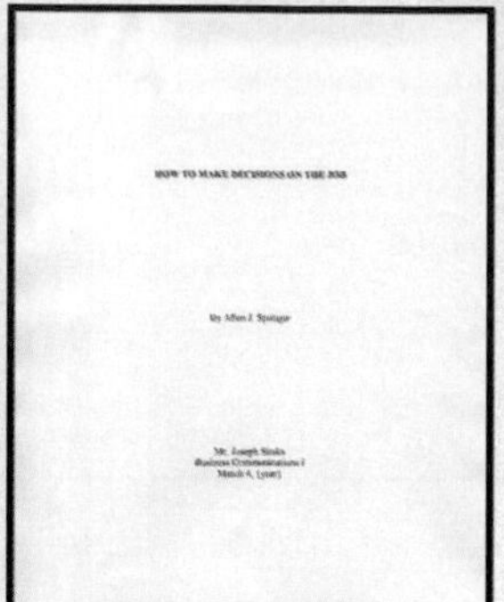

HOW TO MAKE DECISIONS ON THE JOB

By Allen J. Sprague

Mr. Joseph Sinks
Business Communications I
March 4, [year]

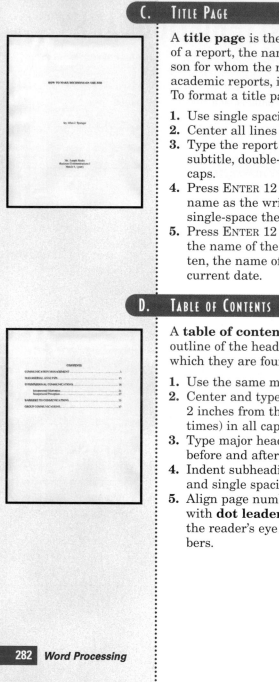

A **title page** is the first page of a report. It gives the title of a report, the name of the writer, the name of the person for whom the report was prepared, and the date. For academic reports, it also contains the name of the course. To format a title page:

1. Use single spacing, and center the page vertically.
2. Center all lines of text horizontally.
3. Type the report title in all caps and bold. If there is a subtitle, double-space and type the subtitle in initial caps.
4. Press ENTER 12 times and type *By* followed by your name as the writer. If there is more than one writer, single-space the names of the writers.
5. Press ENTER 12 times. Then, using single spacing, type the name of the person for whom the report was written, the name of the course (if appropriate), and the current date.

D. Table of Contents

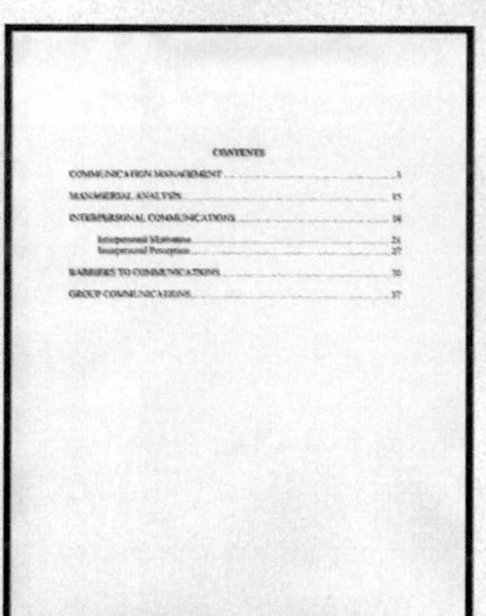

CONTENTS

COMMUNICATION MANAGEMENT
MANAGERIAL ANALYSIS
INTERPERSONAL COMMUNICATIONS
Interpersonal Motivation
Interpersonal Perception
BARRIERS TO COMMUNICATIONS
GROUP COMMUNICATIONS

A **table of contents** may follow the title page. It is an outline of the headings in a report and the pages on which they are found. To format a table of contents:

1. Use the same margins as those used in the report.
2. Center and type the word *CONTENTS* approximately 2 inches from the top of the page (press ENTER 6 times) in all caps and bold, followed by a double space.
3. Type major headings in all caps; leave a blank line before and after them.
4. Indent subheadings and type them with initial caps and single spacing.
5. Align page numbers at the right and precede them with **dot leaders**—a series of periods that help guide the reader's eye from the headings to the page numbers.

Out-of-Class Activity

Have students bring examples of tables of contents from books, magazines, annual reports, or other printed material. Each student should bring in one example. Have students meet in groups and look just at the table of contents and "guess" what the book is about.

SCHOOL TO CAREER

Have students analyze the parts of a book and make up a table of contents for a book about careers in the book publishing industry. Each heading in the table of contents should be a career. Under each heading, list a few attributes of the job. Have students bring their tables of contents to class.

E. Bibliography

A **bibliography** is an alphabetical listing of sources used in a report. It is very similar to a Works Cited page. It follows the text of the report. To format a bibliography:

1. Use the same side margins as those used in the report and use single spacing.
2. Center and type the title, ***BIBLIOGRAPHY,*** in all caps and bold, approximately 2 inches from the top of the page (press ENTER 6 times). Press ENTER 2 times after the title.
3. Use a hanging indent for each entry and leave a blank line between entries (press ENTER 2 times).
4. List entries in alphabetical order by authors' last names. If there is no author, alphabetize by the title of the article or book.
5. Arrange book entries as follows: author's name, title (in italics), publisher, place of publication, and year.
6. Arrange journal articles as follows: author's name, article title (in quotation marks), journal title (in italics), followed by information on the journal issue (series, volume, issue numbers; date and page numbers).

F. Software Features

STUDENT MANUAL

Dot Leaders

Study Lesson 78 in your student manual. Complete all the practice activities while at your computer. Then complete the jobs that follow.

WORD PROCESSING APPLICATIONS

REPORT 24 ***Prepare a cover page for Report 23. Use your name, the name of your keyboarding teacher, and the current date.***

REPORT 25 ***Prepare a table of contents for Report 23. Use the side headings for the major entries.***

REPORT 26 ***Prepare a bibliography for Report 23. Use the footnotes as the entries for the bibliography. Number the bibliography as the final page of the report.***

LESSON 78

TEACH

Activity F. Explain the use and different styles of dot leaders.

STUDENT MANUAL

Be sure students turn to the correct lesson in their Student Manual.

Report 24. Review the steps in preparing a cover page with students.

Report 25. Review the steps in preparing a table of contents with students.

Report 26. Review the steps in preparing a bibliography with students.

ASSESS

- Check to see if students type with no errors on the 30-second OK timings.
- Make sure students are able to add dot leaders.
- After students finish typing the reports, have them view their work on the screen to see if they made any errors. If errors were made, have students edit their work and make corrections.

CLOSE

If students do not finish the reports during the class period, make sure they save their work so that they can complete it the next time this class meets.

Teacher Notes

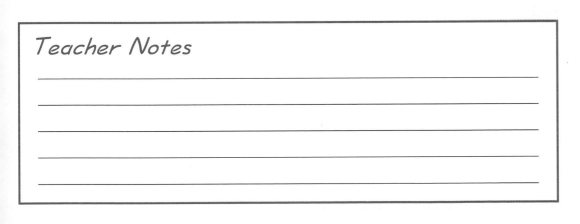

LESSON 79

FOCUS

- Compose answers for the Language Link activity using complete sentences.
- Use 3-minute timings to build speed.
- Practice formatting and typing a report including a title page, table of contents, and bibliography.

BELLRINGER

As soon as students arrive at their workstations and log in, have them type the Warmup. Go over the purpose of each line as shown to the left of the copy.

TEACH

Activity B. After students have completed their sentences, have them exchange their work with another student to check for typing accuracy.

Solutions: Answers will vary.

LESSON 79 REVIEW

OBJECTIVES:

- Reinforce report formats.
- Compose at the keyboard.
- Type 35/3′/5e.

A. WARMUP

Type each line 2 times.

Speed	1	The grass has grown tall, and it must be mowed by Thursday.
Accuracy	2	Paz visited the Zagros Mountains near the Strait of Hormuz.
Language Link	3	In the past, we have had our Billing Department sell candy.
Numbers/Symbols	4	If 33% (1/3 of total) attends #26 or #45, we will earn $90.

| 1 | 2 | 3 | 4 | 5 | 6 | 7 | 8 | 9 | 10 | 11 | 12

B. COMPOSING AT THE KEYBOARD

Answer each of the following questions with complete sentences.

5 If money were no object, what kind of a car would you like to have and why?
6 If you could live anywhere in the United States, where would you live and why?
7 If you could travel overseas, where would you like to go and why?

FACT FILE

Do not remove a disk from your computer's disk drive until the drive light is off. Removing the disk while the light is on could corrupt your disk.

RESOURCES

 Lesson Plan 79
 Courseware Lesson 79
Student Data Disk
Student Manual
Grading and Evaluation

SKILLBUILDING

C. Preview Practice

Type each line 2 times as a preview to the timings that follow.

Accuracy enjoy quite pursuit difficult aptitudes analyzing happiness
Speed choices future their small along must life ten way not do a

D. 3-Minute Timings

Take two 3-minute timings on the paragraphs. Note your speed and errors.

Goal: 35/3'/5e

Students seldom think about their future careers in 11
the first six or seven years of school. They do not know 22
what they want to do or what skills they need to acquire 33
over the next few years. 38
It is important for students to think about and plan 49
for their careers. They must analyze their personal goals 61
and aptitudes when they choose a career. They also must set 73
goals throughout their lives. Any failures must not become 85
roadblocks in their pursuit of their goals. They should 96
enjoy their careers if they want to be happy. 105
| 1 | 2 | 3 | 4 | 5 | 6 | 7 | 8 | 9 | 10 | 11 | 12 SI 1.32

FACT FILE

Football appears to have its origins in rugby. In the 1800s, Princeton University students were also playing a game called ballown. Organized football games were held on the Boston Common starting in about 1860. In 1865, after the Civil War ended, colleges began to organize football games. The Princeton rules were established and the first football was patented in 1867. It is also believed that the first intercollegiate football game was between Rutgers and Princeton in 1867.

LESSON 79

TEACH

Activity C. Point out that words in the Preview Practice are used in the timing that follows.

Activity D. Remind students that they should try to improve speed with each of the 3-minute timings. The goal for this timing is to type 35 words a minute for 3 minutes with no more than 5 errors.

FACT FILE

Have students name their favorite sport. Write five or six of these sports on the board. Have students form groups and research their sport and prepare a short oral report. Reports should include the origins of the sport.

TEACH

Report 27. Ask students what the margin should be for a left-bound report. Remind them to use this margin.

FACT FILE

Basketball was first played in December, 1891, in Springfield, Massachusetts. In the late 1970s, a law called Title IX prohibited discrimination on the basis of gender in educational institutions' sports programs. Discuss students' beliefs about discrimination in sports.

WORD PROCESSING APPLICATIONS

REPORT 27

Type the following business report as a left-bound report. Add a byline below the title (press ENTER 1 time) that contains the word By followed by your name. Format the references as footnotes. The text for each footnote follows the superscript number and is enclosed in brackets.

BASKETBALL SPECIFICS

INTRODUCTION

The game of basketball is one of the most widely played and watched sports in the world. The game is played by two teams consisting of five players each. Nearly all elementary schools, high schools, and colleges in the United States have organized basketball teams.[1] [Bill Sullivan, "Basketball," *Encyclopedia Americana,* 1989 ed., p. 106–107.]

Basketball is truly America's game since it was invented in the United States in 1891. The popularity of the game has steadily increased over the years because it is exciting to play and to watch. Three very important features of the official game include the specific dimensions of the basketball, the court, and the basket and backboard.

The Basketball. The ball measures about 30 inches in circumference and weighs from 20 to 22 ounces. It can be made of leather, plastic, rubber, or similar material, and it is inflated with air.

The Court. The basketball court is a hard, level surface. Most indoor courts are made of wood. Outdoor courts are made of asphalt, concrete, or any other solid material. Most high school courts measure 84 feet long by 50 feet wide. College and professional courts measure 94 feet long by 50 feet wide. The court has two sidelines, a division line, which divides the court in halves, two free-throw lanes, and two free-throw lines. Two circles, the center circle and the restraining circle, mark the middle of the court.[2] [Wiley Thomaston and Leslie Richards, *Basketball Standards and Regulations,* Daily Publishing Company, Columbia, South Carolina, 1986, p. 234–235.]

The Basket and Backboard. A white-cord net basket attached to a backboard hangs above the middle of each end line. The net hangs down 15 to 18 inches from the ring and slows the ball as it passes through the basket. The backboard is made of glass, metal, wood, or any other hard material. It must be white or transparent and rectangular or fan-shaped. Rectangular backboards measure 72 inches wide by 48 inches high. Fan-shaped backboards are 54 inches wide by 35 inches high. The backboard must be mounted 4 feet inside the end line.[3] [James McLendon, "Basketball—America's Sport," *Sports Today,* December 1994, p. 23.]

Career Exploration

Brainstorm with students about careers in sports other than professional athletes. Examples might be careers in sports management, broadcasting, officiating, sports medicine, high school coaching, etc. Write the list on the board and have small groups research one career.

interNET ACTIVITY

Check out these sites, then have students access those you feel are appropriate: basketball—NBA (www.nba.com); WNBA (www.wnba.com); running—Running Online (www.runningonline.com). Have students find three facts and bring them to class.

Official games played in elementary school, high school, and college and by professionals use regulation basketballs, courts, baskets, and backboards. Following these standards makes the game fairer for both teams.

CLOSING

Basketball has grown in the past decade to become one of the most popular spectator sports. It is played in almost every country in the world, is popular with both young and old, and attracts both men and women players. It has been an Olympic sport for many years and will likely grow in popularity in years to come.

REPORT 28

Prepare a title page for Report 27. Use your keyboarding teacher's name, the keyboarding course in which you are enrolled, and the current date.

REPORT 29

Prepare a table of contents from the information in Report 27. Use the side headings and paragraph headings as your entries.

REPORT 30

Prepare a bibliography from the sources in Report 27. Number the bibliography as the final page in the report.

PORTFOLIO *Activity*

Review the work you have done in the past ten lessons. Choose the best of each type of document. If you had any errors in any of these documents, correct the errors. Then print copies of these documents and place them in a folder as a representation of your best work. Also, print a copy of your best timing for your portfolio as an example of your speed and accuracy.

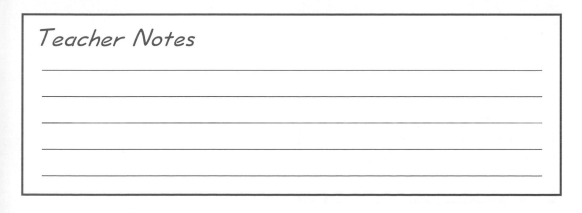

Teacher Notes

LESSON 79

TEACH

Report 28. On the board, write your name, the name of this course, and the current date for students.

Report 29. Students' table of contents may vary. Go over a few in class. Ask students why they chose these headings.

Report 30. Make sure students have the correct information in their bibliographies. Everyone should have the same information.

ASSESS

- Check to see if students are increasing their word a minute speeds as they complete each 3-minute timing.
- Review the accuracy of students' responses to questions in the Language Link composing activity.
- As students begin typing the reports, walk around the room and point out correct and incorrect formatting to individual students.
- After students finish typing the reports, have them view their work on the screen to see if they made any errors. If errors were made, have students edit their work and make corrections.

CLOSE

If students do not finish the reports during the class period, make sure they save their work so that they can complete it the next time this class meets.

LESSON 80

FOCUS

- Use the Pretest/Practice/ Posttest routine to build speed and accuracy
- Practice formatting and typing a letter, report, and tables.

BELLRINGER

As soon as students arrive at their workstations and log in, have them type the Warmup. Go over the purpose of each line as shown to the left of the copy.

TEACH

Activity B. Use the P/P/P routine to build skill. Have students note their speed and errors when typing the Pretest lines.

PRETEST/PRACTICE/POSTEST

The ***Pretest/Practice/Posttest*** routines are designed to improve speed or accuracy.

- The ***Pretest*** identifies students' speed or accuracy needs.
- The ***Practice*** provides a variety of improvement drills.
- The ***Posttest*** (a repeat of the Pretest) measures improvement.

LESSON 80

SIMULATION

OBJECTIVES:

- Improve keyboarding speed and accuracy.
- Format and type a variety of office documents.

A. WARMUP

Type each line 2 times.

Speed	1	Dale saw a small cabin at the end of the winding dirt road.
Accuracy	2	Four lawyers quickly rejected a luxury prize given to them.
Language Link	3	Marge sent the project to the advertising department today.
Numbers/Symbols	4	Their tax was $35,489 (26% sales + 10% excise)--incredible!

interNET CONNECTION

Use the Internet to search for information about wind chill factors (the topic of the Pretest). One site you may want to try is: http://www.nws.noaa.gov/er/iln/tables.htm. Learn about calculating wind chill. Search for information about the coldest temperatures and highest winds. Discuss your findings with the class.

SKILLBUILDING

B. PRETEST

Take a 1-minute timing on the paragraph. Note your speed and errors.

Science Connections

5 The presence of wind makes it seem colder out than is 11
6 indicated by a thermometer. This can be pleasing when the 23
7 temperature is high. When temperatures are low, wind chill 34
8 becomes a threat to human beings and may cause death. 45

| 1 | 2 | 3 | 4 | 5 | 6 | 7 | 8 | 9 | 10 | 11 | 12 |

RESOURCES

 Lesson Plan 80

 Courseware Lesson 80

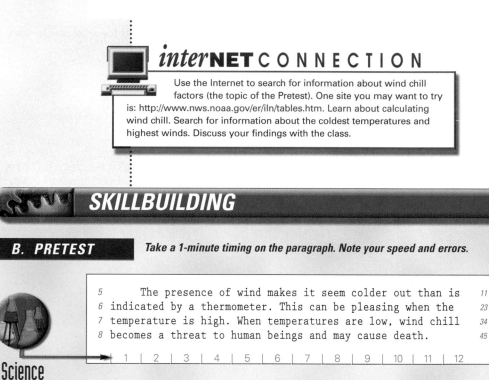

Student Data Disk

Student Manual

Reteaching and Reinforcement

Unit 4 Test

Grading and Evaluation

C. PRACTICE

In the chart below, find the number of errors you made on the Pretest. Then, type each of the designated drill lines 2 times.

Pretest Errors	0–1	2	3	4+
Drill Lines	12–16	11–15	10–14	9–13

Accuracy

```
9  thermometer indicate presence pleasing threats humans cause
10 winter becomes highest chilling pleasure pleasant temperate
11 beings please making thermal windiest chilliest threatening
12 by colder become pleasing indicated thermometer temperature
```

Speed

```
13 a to of it is by be the out are can low than when high wind
14 a this cold make come chill cause death please threat human
15 be to on dear come when wind cloth treat threat death there
16 mom hen his ten man see low his hill that meter press three
```

D. POSTTEST

Repeat the Pretest. Compare your Posttest results with your Pretest results.

WORD PROCESSING APPLICATIONS

E. ORIENTATION

LETTER 39

Please send this letter today. Correct any errors.

You will be working in the offices of the Community Way, City Center, Suite 100, 14 South Main, Akron, OH 44308. Community Way is a nonprofit, community-service organization. Today is June 6. Mrs. Alice Emerson is the director. Her assistant is Hugh Michaelson. You will help him get documents ready for Mrs. Emerson's approval. She depends on her assistant (and on you) to format the documents correctly and to catch any errors she may have missed. Mrs. Emerson prefers letters done in modified-block style with blocked paragraphs. She uses Sincerely yours, followed by her name and title on separate lines.

Mr. Lester Romero / Romero Industries, Inc. / 272 Burdette Street / Akron, OH 44319 / Dear Mr. Romero:
We are indebted to you for allowing Community Way to use your facility as the site for this year's fund-raising dinner. Last Friday, 300 guests enjoyed fine dining, listening to music, and dancing. Your lovely ballroom provided the perfect setting for this exciting event.

TEACH

Activity C. Point out to students that they are to type lines 12–16 twice if they made 0–1 errors on the Pretest; type lines 11–15 twice if they made 2 errors; type lines 10–14 twice if they made 3 errors; and type lines 9–13 twice if they made more than 4 errors.

Activity D. Remind students they should improve both their speed and accuracy from the Pretest to the Posttest.

Activity E. Have a student read the information in this activity aloud. Have them pay close attention to the information they'll need to complete the letters and reports on the following pages.

*inter*NET ACTIVITY

Have students use the key word "job" or provide them with the address for JobBank USA (www.jobbankusa.com). Have them search for a job that sounds interesting, and then write a resume and cover letter for that job.

Science Connections

Invite a meteorologist to speak to the class. Have students type a list of questions and edit the list as a class. Have students ask about weather patterns, wind chill factors, and national, international, and local weather.

TEACH

Letter 39. Remind students to use modified-block style with blocked paragraphs. Have students check each other's work for accuracy.

Report 31. When students have completed the report, go over the errors in spelling, punctuation, and grammar that should have been caught and corrected.

As you probably know, this event is one of our major fund-raising activities. This year, our major project is Project Upgrade, which will provide training for displaced workers in our community. Thanks to the support of caring individuals such as you, Community Way will be able to provide valuable services to some of our less fortunate neighbors.
Again, thank you for your kind support.

REPORT 31

Prepare this left-bound report Correct errors in spelling, punctuation, and grammar.

FITNESS FOR WORK

The company expects all employees to be physically able to perform their jobs and other wise meet the demands of there jobs and condition of employ except as required by applicable law. the company provides medical and dental benefits, which are fully described in the benefit information material, and counseling services, which are part of our employee assistance program.

This section explains the responsibility of the manager and the employee when a employee cannot report to work because of a medical condition.

~~Employee absences due to illness or injury~~

ILLNESSES AND INJURIES

The Employees Responsibilities. An employee who is incapable of performing his/her job adequately because of a medical condition or whose presence at work might effect other employees, should remain at home. In the case of a contagious disease, an employee should inform the manager of the extent to which he or she may have exposed co-workers.

The Manager's Responsibility. When an employee is absent due to a medical condition for 6 or more consecutive working days, or due to a job related injury for 1 or more days, the employee's manager must notify the human resources office by completing an absence notification form. When the employee returns to work, the manager must complete a return to work form and send it to the human resources office.

JOURNAL ENTRY

Have students write about how they feel about being absent from school. What do they consider a good excuse? Have they ever been absent for a reason other than illness? Why?

ABSENTEE AND TARDINESS

The company counts on it's employees to be at work time and a regular basis, to carry out the responsibilities of their jobs. The company expects employees to be conscientious about their attendance and punctuality. Although some absence or tardiness can be accepted, poor or excessive absence or tardiness will not be tolerated and will be cause for discipline, up to and including termination of employment.

Employees are not "given" a number of sick days per year. The company plan protects employees when they need it, but the plan is not a "time-off" plan. If an employee's absence becomes poor or excessive, he/she may be subject to disciplin action.

If employees must be delayed or absent, they must notify their managers, of the fact and the reason for the delay or absence as far in advance of their starting time as possible.

Employees who are absent for 3 or more consecutive working days without notifying their managers may have their employment terminated.

TABLES 20–21

Prepare these tables as 2 separate documents. Center them vertically and horizontally, and automatically adjust the column widths.

ABSENCE GUIDELINES		
	Days Absent in a 6-Month Period	**Days Absent in a 12-Month Period**
Poor	4–5 days	7–8 days
Excessive	6 or more days	9 or more days

TARDINESS GUIDELINES		
	Times Late in a 6-Month Period	**Times Late in a 12-Month Period**
Poor	7–8 times	11–12 times
Excessive	9 or more times	13 or more times

Teacher Notes

TEACH

Tables 20–21. Remind students to prepare the documents as two separate tables.

ASSESS

- Check to see if students show signs of improvement from the Pretest to the Posttest.
- As students begin typing, walk around the room and point out correct and incorrect formatting to individual students.
- After students finish typing the documents, have them view their work on the screen to see if they made any errors. If errors were made, have students make corrections.

CLOSE

If students do not finish the documents during the class period, make sure they save their work so that they can complete it the next time this class meets.

PORTFOLIO *Activity*

If students' portfolio goals include showcasing their best work, they may want to include the documents from this lesson. Encourage students to evaluate their work and include comments in their portfolio.

UNIT 5 ORGANIZER

WORD PROCESSING

Lesson	Focus	Special Features	Skillbuilding	Pretest/ Practice/ Posttest	Documents	GO TO Activities
81	Skillbuilding	Language Link, pp. 294–295 Fact File, p. 296	pp. 295–296	pp. 295–296		
82	Skillbuilding	Science Connection, p. 298	pp. 297–298	pp. 297–298		
83	Letters: Two-Page		pp. 299–300		Letter 40, pp. 301–302	
84	Letters: Attention and Subject Lines	Internet Activity, p. 303 Fact File, p. 307	pp. 303–304		Letter 41, p. 305 Letter 42, pp. 305–306 Letter 43, pp. 306–307	
85	Letters: Form Letter Merge	Language Link, p. 308 Language Arts Connection, p. 308	p. 309		Letters 44–45, p. 310	p. 310
86	Letters: Form Letter Merge		pp. 311–312	p. 312	Letters 46–49, p. 313	
87	Letters: Review	Fact File, p. 314 Science Connection, p. 314 Math Connection, p. 315	pp. 314–315		Letter 50, p. 316 Letters 51–53, p. 317	
88	Letters: Numbered Lists	Language Link, p. 318 Technology Tip, p. 321	p. 319	p. 319	Letter 54, p. 320 Letter 55, p. 321	
89	Memos: Templates	Language Link, p. 322 Social Studies Connection, p. 323	p. 323		Memo 1, p. 324 Memo 2, p. 324	p. 324
90	Review	Fact File, p. 326 Fact File, p. 328	p. 325		Letter 56, p. 326 Letter 57, p. 327 Memo 3, p. 327 Memo 4, p. 328	p. 252
91	Tables: Reversing Lines	Language Arts Connection, p. 330 Internet Activity, p. 332	pp. 329–330		Table 22, p. 331 Table 23, p. 332 Table 24, p. 332	p. 331

UNIT 5 RESOURCE MANAGER

MULTIMEDIA
- Courseware: Lessons 81–100
- Student Data Disk
- Student Manual: Lessons 81–100

TEACHING TOOLS
- Lesson Plans: Lessons 81–100
- Block Scheduling Guide, Unit 5
- Language Link Worksheets: Lessons 81–100
- Multicultural Applications
- Academic Report Guide
- Solution Keys
- Cross-Curricular Activities: Lessons 81–100

RETEACHING/REINFORCEMENT
- Reteaching/Reinforcement Activities: Lessons 81–100
- Supplemental Production Activities: Lessons 81–100

ASSESSMENT and EVALUATION

Pretest/Practice/Posttest: pp. 295–296, 297–298, 312, 319, 345, 347–348
Portfolio Activity: pp. 343, 357, 360
Unit 5 Test
Timings: pp. 300, 311, 315, 330, 333, 337, 341, 354
Production Jobs: Letters 40–62; Memos 1–8; Tables 22– 42
Grading and Evaluation

Electronic Teacher Classroom Resources

For your convenience, the teacher's materials are available on a CD-ROM. Having these resources available electronically enables you to print exactly what you need and revise materials as necessary.

Lesson	Focus	Special Features	Skillbuilding	Pretest/ Practice/ Posttest	Documents	GO TO Activities
92	Tables: Borders/Fill	Social Studies Connection, p. 334 Science Connection, p. 335 Fact File, p. 335	p. 333		Table 25, p. 334 Table 26, p. 335 Table 27, p. 335	p. 334
93	Tables: Reinforcement	Language Link, p. 336 Internet Activity, p. 336 Fact File, p. 339	p. 337		Table 28, p. 338 Table 29, p. 338 Table 30, p. 339	
94	Tables: Page Orientation	Language Link, pp. 340–341 Portfolio Activity, p. 343	p. 341		Table 31, p. 342 Table 32, p. 343	p. 341
95	Tables: Add/Delete Columns and Rows	Language Link, p. 344 Fact File, p. 346	p. 345	p. 345	Table 33, p. 346 Table 34, p. 346 Table 35, p. 346	p. 345
96	Tables: Totals	Fact File, p. 347 Internet Activity, p. 349	pp. 347–348	pp. 347–348	Table 36, p. 349 Table 37, p. 349 Table 38, p. 349	p. 348
97	Review	Fact File, p. 350 Cultural Connection, p. 352	pp. 350–351		Table 39, p. 351 Table 40, p. 352 Table 41, p. 352	
98	Letters: International Addresses	Language Link, p. 353 Cultural Connection, p. 356 Portfolio Activity, p. 357	p. 354		Letter 58, p. 355 Letter 59, p. 356 Letter 60, p. 357	
99	Memos: Copy Notations and Attachments	Portfolio Activity, p. 360	p. 358		Memo 5, p. 359 Memo 6, p. 360 Memo 7, pp. 360–361	
100	Formatting Review	Language Link, pp. 362–363	p. 363		Letter 61, p. 376 Letter 62, p. 364 Memo 8, p. 364 Table 42, p. 365	

SCANS Competencies in Glencoe Keyboarding with Computer Applications

Resources	Interpersonal Skills	Information	Systems	Technology
Throughout the course, students deal specifically with resources: allocating time for completing drills and documents, maintaining workstations, caring for computers and software.	Cultural Connection, pp. 352, 356	Career Bit, p. 293 Fact File, pp. 296, 307, 314, 326, 328, 335, 339, 346, 347, 350 Internet Connection, pp. 303, 332, 336, 349 Math Connection, p. 315 Science Connection, pp. 298, 314, 335 Social Studies Connection, pp. 323, 334	Internet Connection, pp. 303, 332, 336, 349	Lessons 61–80 Internet Connection, pp. 303, 332, 336, 349 Technology Tip, p. 321 Language Arts Connection, p. 330

UNIT 5 WORD PROCESSING

Lessons 81–100

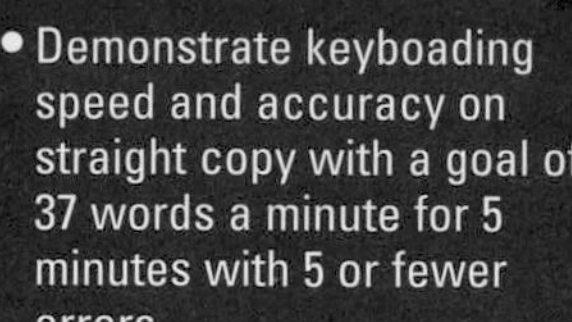

OBJECTIVES

- Demonstrate keyboarding speed and accuracy on straight copy with a goal of 37 words a minute for 5 minutes with 5 or fewer errors.
- Demonstrate correct use of word processing features.
- Demonstrate an understanding of proofreaders' symbols by editing copy marked for revision.
- Demonstrate advanced formatting skills on a variety of reports, letters, memos, and tables from a variety of copy—arranged, unarranged, rough draft, and handwritten.
- Compose paragraphs at the keyboard.

INTRODUCING THE UNIT

Have different students read Unit 5. Address each objective as it's read. Explain that the goal in this unit is to reach a typing speed of 37 words a minute for 5 minutes with 5 or fewer errors. Encourage students to believe this is an achievable goal.

Students will continue to use word processing features and edit copy using proofreaders' symbols. Students will learn advanced formatting skills, including how to arrange and unarrange text on rough drafts and handwritten copy. Lastly, students will learn how to compose paragraphs at the keyboard.

FUN Facts

Levi's, the blue denim jeans many students wear, were patented in 1873 by Levi Strauss and Jacob Davis, a tailor. The copper-riveted waist overalls were popular with miners, cowboys, lumberjacks, and people who needed comfortable, durable pants. Levi's were sold to retail stores for $1.50 a pair. In 1998 Levi Strauss & Co. had sales of $6 billion. The company employs approximately 30,000 people worldwide.

COURSEWARE OVERVIEW

The directions for a mail merge differ slightly between the courseware and the student manual so that the documents can be scored by the courseware. In the courseware, students are told to access KCA Help, *How to Merge Files in KCA*. Students should print and save these instructions.

WORDS TO LEARN

add/delete columns, rows
borders/fill (shading)
data file
form file
formulas
landscape
mail merge
page orientation
reverse lines
templates

CAREER BIT

COURT REPORTER Court reporters take verbatim reports of speeches, conversations, legal proceedings, meetings, or other events when written accounts of spoken words are necessary for correspondence, records, or legal proof. Court reporters use stenotype machines, which enable them to record combinations of letters representing sounds, words, or phrases. The symbols are recorded on computer disks, which are then loaded into a computer that translates and displays the symbols in English. Stenotype machines that link directly to the computer are used for real-time captioning. That is, as the reporter types the symbols, the computer instantly transcribes them. This is used for closed captioning for the deaf or hearing-impaired on television, in courts, classrooms, or meetings.

COURSEWARE OVERVIEW

All memos are done using the first memo template in the word processor. You may want to have students experiment with different memo templates and have them open other kinds of templates. Remind students to use default formats that have already been established on the templates.

WORDS TO LEARN

The terms in Words to Learn are defined in the Glossary at the back of the book. Ask students if they are familiar with any of the terms. Have them define the terms they know. Compare their definitions with those in the Glossary.

CAREER BIT

After students have read the information on court reporting, have them brainstorm to create a list of other law-related occupations in which computers may be used. Write these occupations on the board. Ask students to interview someone who works in one of these fields to learn how computers are used on the job. Have students meet in small groups to discuss what they learned. Have the small groups prepare a short report, then have one representative from each group give the report to the whole class. Have students discuss as a class how they think computers will be used in law and in courtrooms in the future.

LESSON 81

FOCUS

- Apply the Language Link rule for expressing numbers.
- Use the Pretest/Practice/Posttest routine to build speed and accuracy.
- Focus on technique with Technique Checkpoint.
- Use the Paced Practice 2-minute timings.

BELLRINGER

As soon as students arrive at their workstations and log in, have them type the Warmup. Go over the purpose of each line as shown to the left of the copy.

TEACH

Activity B. Go over the Language Link rules with students to make sure they understand number expressions.

Solutions: Jan got two dozen pastries and a pot of coffee.

The agenda listed 25 items to be covered today.

Seven hundred seventy-nine students were there.

The musician recorded 7 six-track demo tapes.

After taxes, he was worth four million dollars.

Only one-third of the students had summer jobs.

SKILLBUILDING

OBJECTIVES:

- Learn the rules for number expression.
- Reinforce good keyboarding techniques.
- Improve keyboarding skill.

A. WARMUP

Type each line 2 times.

Speed	1	The little black puppy ran to the door to greet his master.
Accuracy	2	Jeff amazed the audience by quickly giving six new reports.
Language Link	3	Terry is taking English Literature 215 on Tuesday mornings.
Numbers/Symbols	4	Can't they find Check #953 for $840, which is dated May 16?

| 1 | 2 | 3 | 4 | 5 | 6 | 7 | 8 | 9 | 10 | 11 | 12

B. NUMBER EXPRESSION

Study the rules and examples below. Then edit lines 5–10 to correct any errors in number usage.

Rule 16: In general, spell out numbers 1 through 10. Use figures for numbers above 10.

Only three walls have been painted.

We purchased 15 pairs of socks, 11 jackets, and 23 scarves.

Rule 17: Spell out numbers used as the first word in a sentence. Also spell out the smaller of two adjacent numbers.

Nineteen applications were processed today.

Each participant will receive three 45-minute tapes to listen to.

RESOURCES

 Lesson Plan 81

 Courseware Lesson 81

Student Data Disk

Student Manual

Language Link Worksheets

Multicultural Activities

Rule 19: Spell out the words *million* and *billion* in even amounts. Do not use decimals with even amounts. Spell out fractions.

The multimillionaire gave almost 2 million dollars to charity.

About one-half of the graduating class participated in the graduation ceremony.

Each of them paid $50 for a ticket and $12.50 for parking.

```
Jan got 2 dozen pastries and a pot of coffee.
The agenda listed twenty-five items to be covered today.
779 students were there.
The musician recorded 7 6-track demo tapes.
After taxes, he was worth $4,000,000.00.
Only 1/3 of the students had summer jobs.
```

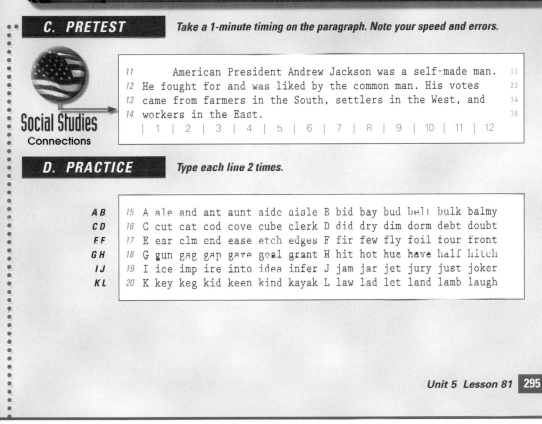

SKILLBUILDING

C. PRETEST

Take a 1-minute timing on the paragraph. Note your speed and errors.

Social Studies Connections

```
     American President Andrew Jackson was a self-made man.   11
He fought for and was liked by the common man. His votes      23
came from farmers in the South, settlers in the West, and     34
workers in the East.                                          38
| 1 | 2 | 3 | 4 | 5 | 6 | 7 | 8 | 9 | 10 | 11 | 12
```

D. PRACTICE

Type each line 2 times.

```
AB  A ale and ant aunt aide aisle B bid bay bud belt bulk balmy
CD  C cut cat cod cove cube clerk D did dry dim dorm debt doubt
EF  E ear elm end ease etch edges F fir few fly foil four front
GH  G gun gag gap gaze goal grant H hit hot hue have half hitch
IJ  I ice imp ire into idea infer J jam jar jet jury just joker
KL  K key keg kid keen kind kayak L law lad let land lamb laugh
```


Teacher Notes

LESSON 81

TEACH

Activities C–E. Remind students they should improve both their speed and accuracy from the Pretest to the Posttest.

PRETEST/PRACTICE/POSTEST

The ***Pretest/Practice/Posttest*** routines are designed to improve speed or accuracy.

- The ***Pretest*** identifies students' speed or accuracy needs.
- The ***Practice*** provides a variety of improvement drills.
- The ***Posttest*** (a repeat of the Pretest) measures improvement.

TEACH

Activity F. Remind students that proper technique is a building block for speed and accuracy. The focus for this timing: Space between words without pausing.

Activity G. Go over the routine for the 2-minute Paced Practice timings. (See Lesson 34, page 119.)

ASSESS

- Watch students as they complete the Language Link activity to see if they are able to apply the rules for number expression correctly.
- Check to see if students show signs of improvement from the Pretest to the Posttest.
- Monitor students as they complete Technique Checkpoint and provide individualized assistance as needed.

CLOSE

Remind students to clean up their workstation when they leave.

M N	21 M may mix mad make mind month N new nor now note next noise
O P	22 O own old oil oath ouch ought P peg par pay prod plea purge
Q R	23 Q qua qui quo quip quit quest R rod rig rug raft ream right
S T	24 S ski six sod salt sent scale T tag tin toy tend toil toast
U V	25 U uke urn use undo unit using V vow van vie volt vile virus
W X	26 W why won wet wipe wrap waver X vex fox mix lynx text waxen
Y Z	27 Y yam yes yaw yoke year yards Z zag zip zoo zinc zing zesty

E. POSTTEST

Repeat the Pretest. Compare your Posttest results with your Pretest results.

F. TECHNIQUE CHECKPOINT

Type each line 2 times. Repeat if time permits. Focus on the technique at the left.

Space between words without pausing.

```
28 He is the one who will pay if we go to the ball game today.
29 When all of us have gone out, you need to stay in the room.
30 You need to save as much of your pay as you can to be safe.
31 There is no one but you who knows how to lead the band now.
```

G. PACED PRACTICE

Turn to the Paced Practice routine beginning on page SB7. Take three 2-minute timings, starting at the point where you left off the last time.

FACT FILE

Jeffrey Hudson who was just 18 inches tall, served as a captain of the cavalry in the British Army. Hudson, who lived from 1619-1682, made his first public appearance inside a pie served at the table of the Duke of Buckingham. When Hudson was about thirty years old, he "shot up" in size, reaching a height of 3 feet, 9 inches.

FACT FILE

Have students measure 18 inches, then use their imaginations to write a one-page story about the heroics of Jeffrey Hudson. Have them use one of the facts in the Fact File.

LESSON 82 SKILLBUILDING

OBJECTIVES:

- Improve keyboarding skill.
- Reinforce good keyboarding techniques.

A. WARMUP

Type each line 2 times.

Speed 1 Four students from our school will run in the state finals.
Accuracy 2 The quadrant has been a survey device since medieval times.
Language Link 3 The accountant had 100 five-column pads in his desk drawer.
Numbers/Symbols 4 Invoice 836-259 for $1,274.50 is subject to a 12% discount.

| 1 | 2 | 3 | 4 | 5 | 6 | 7 | 8 | 9 | 10 | 11 | 12

SKILLBUILDING

B. PRETEST

Take a 1-minute timing on the paragraph. Note your speed and errors.

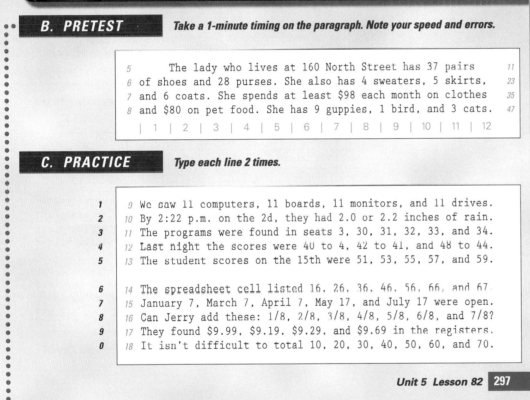

5 The lady who lives at 160 North Street has 37 pairs 11
6 of shoes and 28 purses. She also has 4 sweaters, 5 skirts, 23
7 and 6 coats. She spends at least $98 each month on clothes 35
8 and $80 on pet food. She has 9 guppies, 1 bird, and 3 cats. 47

| 1 | 2 | 3 | 4 | 5 | 6 | 7 | 8 | 9 | 10 | 11 | 12

C. PRACTICE

Type each line 2 times.

1 9 We saw 11 computers, 11 boards, 11 monitors, and 11 drives.
2 10 By 2:22 p.m. on the 2d, they had 2.0 or 2.2 inches of rain.
3 11 The programs were found in seats 3, 30, 31, 32, 33, and 34.
4 12 Last night the scores were 40 to 4, 42 to 41, and 48 to 44.
5 13 The student scores on the 15th were 51, 53, 55, 57, and 59.

6 14 The spreadsheet cell listed 16, 26, 36, 46, 56, 66, and 67.
7 15 January 7, March 7, April 7, May 17, and July 17 were open.
8 16 Can Jerry add these: 1/8, 2/8, 3/8, 4/8, 5/8, 6/8, and 7/8?
9 17 They found $9.99, $9.19, $9.29, and $9.69 in the registers.
0 18 It isn't difficult to total 10, 20, 30, 40, 50, 60, and 70.

RESOURCES

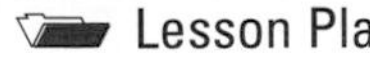

- Lesson Plan 82
- Courseware Lesson 82
- Student Data Disk
- Student Manual
- Multicultural Activities

LESSON 82

FOCUS

- Use the Pretest/Practice/Posttest routines to build speed and accuracy.
- Use the Paced Practice 2-minute timings.
- Use Technique Checkpoint to improve technique.

BELLRINGER

As soon as students arrive at their workstations and log in, have them type the Warmup. Go over the purpose of each line as shown to the left of the copy.

TEACH

Activity B. Remind students to be aware of their posture, to sit up, keep their elbows in, and their feet flat on the floor.

Activities C–D. Remind students they should improve both their speed and accuracy from the Pretest to the Posttest.

TEACH

Activity E. Go over the routine for Paced Practice 2-minute timings with students.

Activity F. Remind students that proper technique is a building block for speed and accuracy. The focus for this timing: Press and release shift keys without hesitating.

Activities G–I. Remind students they should improve both their speed and accuracy from the Pretest to the Posttest.

ASSESS

- Check to see if students show signs of improvement from the Pretest to the Posttest.
- Monitor students as they complete the Technique Checkpoint and provide individualized assistance as needed.

CLOSE

Remind students to clean up their workstation when they leave.

D. POSTTEST

Repeat the Pretest. Compare your Posttest results with your Pretest results.

E. Paced Practice

Turn to the Paced Practice routine beginning on page SB7. Take three 2-minute timings, starting at the point where you left off the last time.

F. Technique Checkpoint

Type each line 2 times. Repeat if time permits. Focus on the technique at the left.

Press and release the shift keys without hesitating.

```
19 Hal traveled to the Isle of Hope to visit Kelly and Jackie.
20 Nancy traveled to London, Paris, Madrid, and Oslo in March.
21 Frances passed West Dublin on the way to East Dublin today.
22 As in the past, the Wild West Rodeo will be in Thomasville.
```

G. PRETEST

Take a 1-minute timing on the paragraph. Note your speed and errors.

Science Connections

```
23      Recycling is the process of using goods more than one   11
24 time. Since many kinds of wastes can be reused, we must      22
25 learn just how important it is to start recycling. Glass,    34
26 cans, plastic, newspapers, and old tires can be used again.  46
   | 1 | 2 | 3 | 4 | 5 | 6 | 7 | 8 | 9 | 10 | 11 | 12
```

H. PRACTICE

In the chart below, find the number of errors you made on the Pretest. Then type each of the designated drill lines 2 times.

Pretest Errors	0–1	2	3	4+
Drill Lines	30–34	29–33	28–32	27–31

Accuracy

```
27 melted process ground turned products purposes requirements
28 paper bottles realize materials gasoline recycled newsprint
29 pulp reuse exact useful bottle highway substances important
30 such used make glass using tires clean should wastes melted
```

Speed

```
31 kinds more than time many cans into then made tires one how
32 paper ones just meet that very from must can be for new car
33 items tires then from are and for the how be if to as is it
34 goods clean down into down made time make news than old off
```

I. POSTTEST

Repeat the Pretest. Compare your Posttest results with your Pretest results.

298 ***Word Processing***

Teacher Notes

LESSON 83 TWO-PAGE LETTERS

OBJECTIVES:

- Format two-page business letters.
- Learn word processing features.
- Type 37/5'/5e.

A. WARMUP

Type each line 2 times.

Speed	1	We must drive cautiously during the rush hours in the city.
Accuracy	2	Gazelles are Bovidae herbivores living from India to Egypt.
Language Link	3	We need to buy 16 bars of soap. We have seven bars on hand.
Numbers/Symbols	4	Martin & Wills sent a check for $2,195; the bill is $3,468.
		| 1 | 2 | 3 | 4 | 5 | 6 | 7 | 8 | 9 | 10 | 11 | 12

SKILLBUILDING

B. PREVIEW PRACTICE

Type each line 2 times as a preview to the timings that follow.

Accuracy	5	pollution pesticides fertilizers surroundings unjustifiably
Speed	6	litter marine water fouls ruins food used our be can all of

RESOURCES

- Lesson Plan 83
- Courseware Lesson 83
- Student Data Disk
- Student Manual
- Supplementary Production Activities
- Grading and Evaluation

LESSON 83

FOCUS

- Use 5-minute timings to build speed.
- Learn how to format and type two-page letters.

BELLRINGER

As soon as students arrive at their workstations and log in, have them type the Warmup. Go over the purpose of each line as shown to the left of the copy.

TEACH

Activity B. Point out that words in the Preview Practice are used in the timing that follows.

TEACH

Activity C. Remind students that they should try to improve speed with each of the 5-minute timings. The goal for the timings is to type 37 words a minute for 5 minutes with no more than 5 errors.

Activity D. Point out to students that the top margin on the second page of a two-page business letter should be 1-inch rather than 2-inches like the first page.

Illustration
Use the illustration to show students how to correctly format a second page heading.

C. 5-Minute Timings

Take two 5-minute timings on the paragraphs. Note your speed and errors.

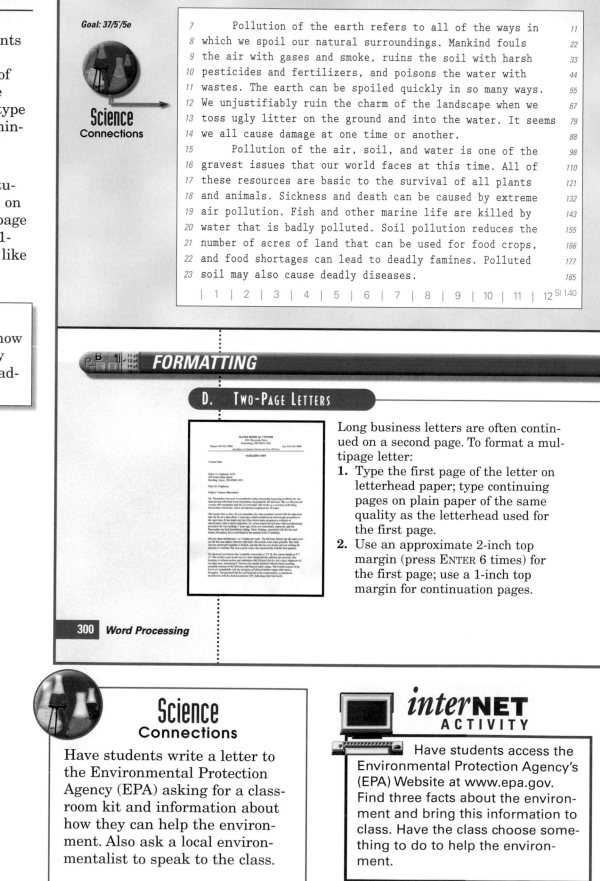

Goal: 37/5'/5e

Science Connections

Pollution of the earth refers to all of the ways in 11
which we spoil our natural surroundings. Mankind fouls 22
the air with gases and smoke, ruins the soil with harsh 33
pesticides and fertilizers, and poisons the water with 44
wastes. The earth can be spoiled quickly in so many ways. 55
We unjustifiably ruin the charm of the landscape when we 67
toss ugly litter on the ground and into the water. It seems 79
we all cause damage at one time or another. 88

Pollution of the air, soil, and water is one of the 98
gravest issues that our world faces at this time. All of 110
these resources are basic to the survival of all plants 121
and animals. Sickness and death can be caused by extreme 132
air pollution. Fish and other marine life are killed by 143
water that is badly polluted. Soil pollution reduces the 155
number of acres of land that can be used for food crops, 166
and food shortages can lead to deadly famines. Polluted 177
soil may also cause deadly diseases. 185

| 1 | 2 | 3 | 4 | 5 | 6 | 7 | 8 | 9 | 10 | 11 | 12 SI 1.40

FORMATTING

D. Two-Page Letters

Long business letters are often continued on a second page. To format a multipage letter:

1. Type the first page of the letter on letterhead paper; type continuing pages on plain paper of the same quality as the letterhead used for the first page.
2. Use an approximate 2-inch top margin (press Enter 6 times) for the first page; use a 1-inch top margin for continuation pages.

Science Connections

Have students write a letter to the Environmental Protection Agency (EPA) asking for a classroom kit and information about how they can help the environment. Also ask a local environmentalist to speak to the class.

interNET ACTIVITY

Have students access the Environmental Protection Agency's (EPA) Website at www.epa.gov. Find three facts about the environment and bring this information to class. Have the class choose something to do to help the environment.

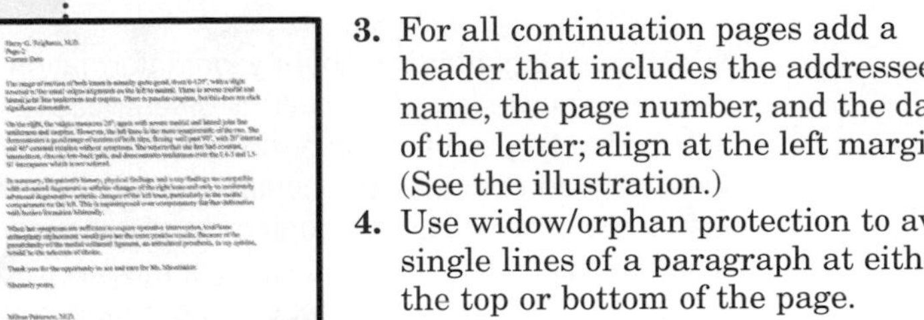

3. For all continuation pages add a header that includes the addressee's name, the page number, and the date of the letter; align at the left margin. (See the illustration.)
4. Use widow/orphan protection to avoid single lines of a paragraph at either the top or bottom of the page.

WORD PROCESSING APPLICATIONS

LETTER 40
Modified-Block Style

Type this letter in modified-block style. Create a header for the second page.

(Current Date) / Ms. Josephine Morello / 348 Douglas Boulevard / Atlanta, GA 30303 / Dear Ms. Morello:
¶Thank you for your request for travel information.
¶You have several options for travel arrangements. You can use a travel agency, your company's travel department, or your computer (for online reservation service), or you can make all the contacts yourself. Travelers are more and more frequently using the Internet to make their airline reservations.
¶If you choose a travel agency, you will receive assistance in making airline, rental car, or hotel/motel reservations. Travel agencies use computerized databases and can find the lowest fares and most convenient flight schedules. So that you can get the exact flight and fare you want, you will need to provide the travel agent with your preferred arrival and departure dates, and cities from which you will depart. Also provide your arrival time, times of travel, and travelers' names. You may also need to provide photographs or birth certificates if you are traveling to overseas destinations.
¶Travel agencies will make hotel and rental car reservations. You can tell your travel agent exactly what you want in the way of a rental car, specify a certain hotel or motel, and ask for reservations on a specific airline. Usually, your agent will be able to fulfill the majority of your requests.

LESSON 83

TEACH

Letter 40. Remind students to type the letter in modified-block style and to create a header for the second page of this letter.

Career Exploration

Brainstorm with students about careers in the travel industry. Help them look beyond the obvious. Include careers such as administrative assistants for travel departments in companies. Have students collect travel brochures and cut pictures from magazines to create a classroom collage.

Social Studies Connections

Put the names of several foreign countries on index cards and have each student choose one. Ask students to write a letter to the foreign embassy asking for brochures and information about the customs and culture of that country.

ASSESS

- Check to see if students are increasing their word a minute speeds as they complete each of the 5-minute timings.
- As students begin typing the letter, walk around the room and point out correct and incorrect formatting to individual students.
- After students finish typing the letter, have them view their work on the screen to see if they made any errors. If errors were made, have students edit their work and make corrections.

CLOSE

If students do not finish the letter during the class period, make sure they save their work so that they can complete it the next time this class meets.

Remind students to clean up their workstation when they leave.

PORTFOLIO *Activity*

If students' portfolio goals include demonstrating progress, they may want to include the letter from this lesson. Encourage students to evaluate their work and include comments in their portfolio.

¶Before visiting a foreign country, get information about customs and cultures. Knowledge about cultural differences is vital. It will help you avoid offending someone in a foreign country. Don't be surprised if foreigners do not make eye contact. Some may make long eye contact, while others view eye contact as disrespectful. If you're confused about cultural differences, question someone who knows the culture. Most countries have days that commemorate special events. Information about social customs is very important.
¶Get to know a country's currency, and bring a translation dictionary with you so that you can refer to it for some of your basic communication needs.
¶GLOBAL TRAVEL can easily make airplane and hotel reservations for you. By making reservations in advance, you can save money and be certain you're getting the schedules you want.
¶Next week, we will be sending you a helpful booklet, *Traveling Abroad,* containing numerous helpful tips for traveling. Also included in the booklet are several detailed maps of the most popular travel destinations. These maps identify travel mileage between many cities and also highlight major scenic attractions that you may wish to visit during your trip.
¶We hope you will consider using GLOBAL TRAVEL for your travel needs. We look forward to helping you make your reservations for what we believe will be your most enjoyable travel adventure. / Sincerely, / Conrad McMurphy / Travel Agent / urs

Teacher Notes

LESSON 84

Letters With Attention and Subject Lines

OBJECTIVES:

- Improve keyboarding skill.
- Format letters with attention and subject lines.

A. Warmup

Type each line 2 times.

Speed	1	A strong dollar makes it easier for interest to be lowered.
Accuracy	2	An aqueous liquid was used externally to prevent abscesses.
Language Link	3	We bought seven pies and seven dozen cookies for the party.
Numbers/Symbols	4	The S & P's 500 index (dividends + gains) was just over 9%.
		| 1 | 2 | 3 | 4 | 5 | 6 | 7 | 8 | 9 | 10 | 11 | 12

interNET CONNECTION

Use the Internet to search for information about the environment. Search specifically for things such as water pollution and air pollution. Discuss your findings with your classmates.

SKILLBUILDING

B. 12-Second Sprints

Take three 12-second timings on each line. Try to increase your speed on each timing.

```
5 Many good stocks showed slow gains even in the bull market.
6 Your credit card rate will go up if you pay late too often.
7 The people in this country save much less than they should.
8 A bank savings account is a safe way to save your earnings.
  | | | | 5 | | | | 10 | | | | 15 | | | | 20 | | | | 25 | | | | 30 | | | | 35 | | | | 40 | | | | 45 | | | | 50 | | | | 55 | | | | 60
```


LESSON 84

FOCUS

- Use 12-second timings to build speed.
- Use a Concentration Drill to improve concentration.
- Learn how to format and type letters with attention and subject lines.
- Type modified-block and block style letters from rough draft and handwritten copy.

BELLRINGER

As soon as students arrive at their workstations and log in, have them type the Warmup. Go over the purpose of each line as shown to the left of the copy.

TEACH

Activity B. Remind students that their goal for 12-second sprints is improved speed with each timing.

RESOURCES

- Lesson Plan 84
- Courseware Lesson 84
- Student Data Disk
- Student Manual
- Supplementary Production Activities
- Grading and Evaluation

TEACH

Activity C. Tell students that concentration is a matter of continuing to bring their awareness back to the task at hand. As they practice concentration, they will improve it.

Activity D. Have different students read aloud the steps for creating an attention line.

Activity E. Explain to students that different organizations may format subject lines differently from the illustration.

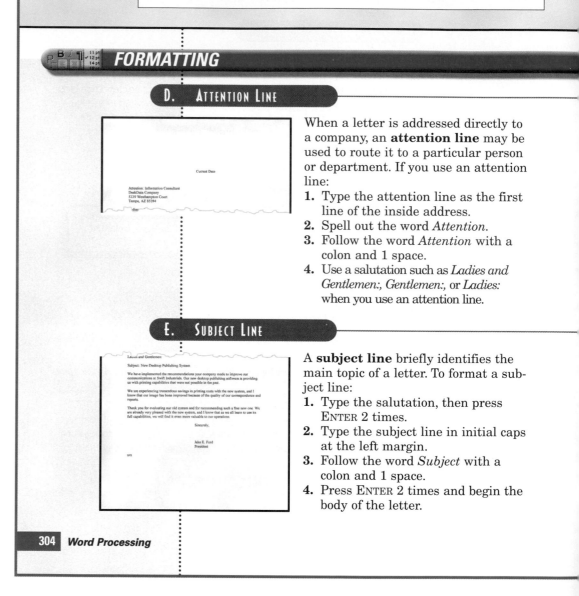

C. Concentration

***Type the following lines. As you type, change every masculine pronoun to a feminine pronoun* (his *to* her)*, and change every feminine pronoun to a masculine pronoun* (she *to* he).**

```
She will complete the sales report as soon as she receives it.
He must give her the sales figures so that she can compile it.
Her final copy is past-due; her boss has already asked for it.
Her boss will then give it to his boss, the director of sales.
```

FORMATTING

D. Attention Line

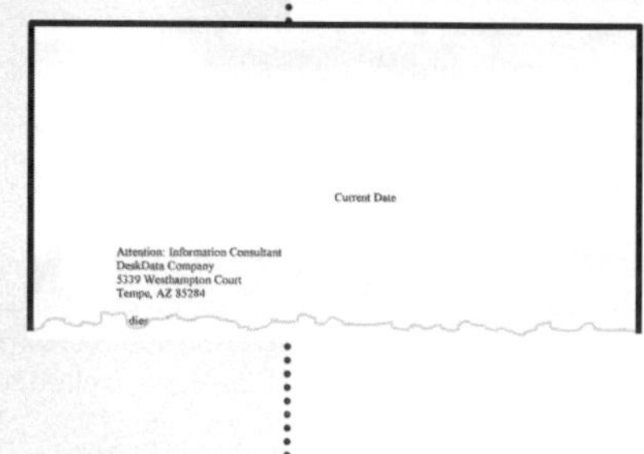
Current Date

Attention: Information Consultant
DeskData Company
5339 Westhampton Court
Tempe, AZ 85284

When a letter is addressed directly to a company, an **attention line** may be used to route it to a particular person or department. If you use an attention line:

1. Type the attention line as the first line of the inside address.
2. Spell out the word *Attention.*
3. Follow the word *Attention* with a colon and 1 space.
4. Use a salutation such as *Ladies and Gentlemen:, Gentlemen:,* or *Ladies:* when you use an attention line.

E. Subject Line

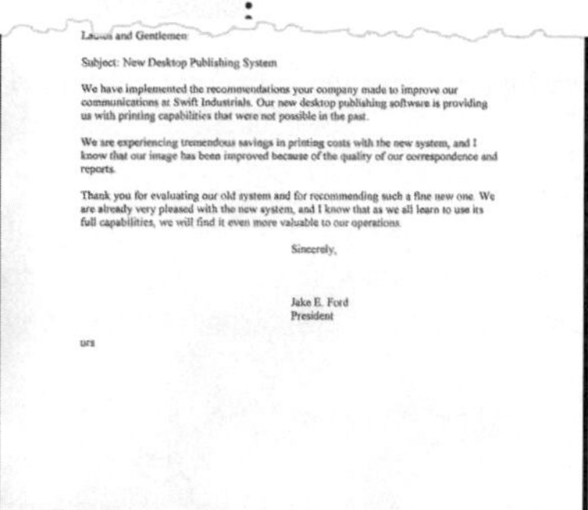
Ladies and Gentlemen:

Subject: New Desktop Publishing System

We have implemented the recommendations your company made to improve our communications at Swift Industrials. Our new desktop publishing software is providing us with printing capabilities that were not possible in the past.

We are experiencing tremendous savings in printing costs with the new system, and I know that our image has been improved because of the quality of our correspondence and reports.

Thank you for evaluating our old system and for recommending such a fine new one. We are already very pleased with the new system, and I know that as we all learn to use its full capabilities, we will find it even more valuable to our operations.

Sincerely,

Jake E. Ford
President

urs

A **subject line** briefly identifies the main topic of a letter. To format a subject line:

1. Type the salutation, then press ENTER 2 times.
2. Type the subject line in initial caps at the left margin.
3. Follow the word *Subject* with a colon and 1 space.
4. Press ENTER 2 times and begin the body of the letter.

FACT FILE

About 800 B.C. an alphabet was adopted in Classical Greece. For the first time in Europe, a popular literary culture developed. Theater became a popular form of entertainment and the works of great thinkers were written down. Have students research Greek thinkers and type a report on one of them.

LETTER 41
Modified-Block Style

Type the following letter in modified-block style.

(Current Date) / Attention: Customer Relations Department / Allied Automotive Corporation / 3259 Bellevue Boulevard / Novato, CA 94949 / Ladies and Gentlemen:

¶A few weeks ago I purchased a new SouthStar from AAA Motors in Carrollton, Georgia. Since I have worked as a sales representative for an automobile dealership in the past, I know it is not too often that you receive letters that say, "Thank you." That is the reason I want to take a few minutes to tell you how pleased I am with my new SouthStar and how much I appreciate the way I was treated by your two AAA sales representatives.

¶Everything about this vehicle has measured up to my expectations. The salespeople were most courteous and helpful—there was no high-pressure sales pitch. They gave me some valuable information about the use and upkeep of the vehicle, too.

¶Congratulations! You have a fine vehicle and a super dealership in Carrollton, Georgia! / Sincerely, / David Jackson / urs

LETTER 42
Block Style

Type the following letter in block style. Make any needed changes as you type.

Current Date

Attention Purchasing Agent
Ladies and gentlemen

Solar supply co.
917 west madison street
Johnson City, tn 37601

We appreciate your check in payment of order no. 16543, however, I'm returning the check to you by registered mail since the correct amount of $195.18 and your signature were omitted. Please fill in these items and return the check to us.

(Handwritten corrections: ":" inserted after "Attention" and after "gentlemen"; salutation moved below the inside address; capitalization marks under g, s, c, w, m, s, tn, n, t; "the check should be" inserted before "$195.18"; "s" inserted after "$195.18"; "since" replaced by ";"; "were" changed to "as"; period after "mail".)

TEACH

Letter 41. Ask students if they have ever sent a thank-you note to someone. Why did they write the note? How did writing the note make them feel? Have they ever received a thank-you note? How did this make them feel? Help students to understand that even in a busy world, every-one appreciates receiving a short note of thanks. Sending a thank-you note is an act of kindness.

Letter 42. Remind students this is a rough draft. They are to correct any errors they find.

JOURNAL ENTRY

Have students write about acts of kind-ness they have done or can do to make the world a gentler and kinder place. Have volunteers read their entries.

TEACH

Letter 43. Remind students that they need to stretch their fingers and relax their shoulders while they are typing.

PORTFOLIO *Activity*

If students' portfolio goals include showcasing their best work, they may want to include one of the letters from this lesson. Encourage students to evaluate their work and include comments in their portfolio.

¶ Your order for the compact disc player model no. 34109 has been forwarded to our regional office in Dallas Texas. We should receive it in this office by the 28th of this month. When it arrives, I will inspect it personally and send it to you immediately. Please let us know if there is any other way we can be of service to you.

sincerely,

charles l. walker
sales manager

LETTER 43

Modified-Block Style
handwritten

Type the following letter in modified-block style. Use the current date and be sure to add your initials as reference initials.

DeskData Company
5339 Westhampton Court
Tempe, AZ 85284
Attention: Information Consultant

Ladies and Gentlemen:
Subject: New Desktop Publishing System

We have implemented the recommendations your company made to improve our communications at Swift Industrials. Our new desktop publishing software is providing us with printing capabilities that were not possible in the past.

We are experiencing tremendous savings in printing costs with the new system, and I know that our image has been improved because of the quality of our correspondence and reports.

FACT FILE

Before computers, typesetting was done through typecasting. This process began with a mold of a letter. The mold was placed in a holder, then molten metal was poured in to form a piece of type. Type was arranged upside down and right to left into words on a tray.

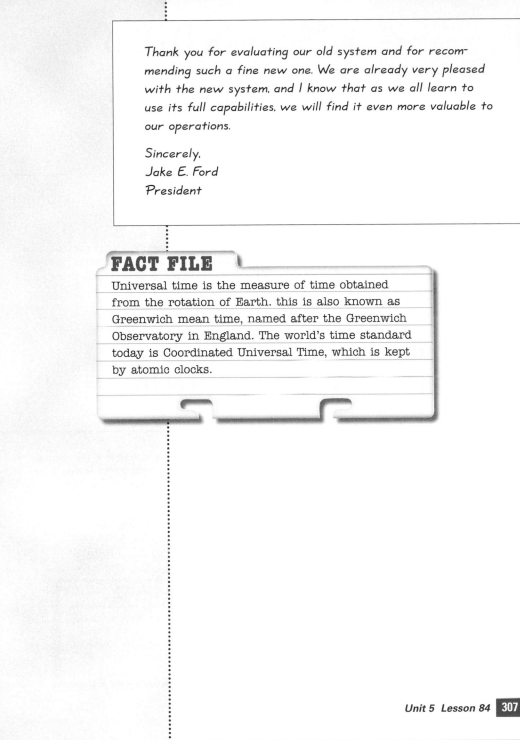

Thank you for evaluating our old system and for recommending such a fine new one. We are already very pleased with the new system, and I know that as we all learn to use its full capabilities, we will find it even more valuable to our operations.

Sincerely,
Jake E. Ford
President

FACT FILE

Universal time is the measure of time obtained from the rotation of Earth. this is also known as Greenwich mean time, named after the Greenwich Observatory in England. The world's time standard today is Coordinated Universal Time, which is kept by atomic clocks.

ASSESS

- Check to see if students are increasing their word a minute speeds as they complete each of the 12-second timings.
- As students begin typing the letters, walk around the room and point out correct and incorrect formatting to individual students.
- After students finish typing the letters, have them view their work on the screen to see if they made any errors. If errors were made, have students edit their work and make corrections.

CLOSE

If students do not finish the letters during the class period, make sure they save their work so that they can complete it the next time this class meets.

Remind students to clean up their workstation when they leave.

Teacher Notes

LESSON 85

FOCUS

- Compose a paragraph for the Language Link activity.
- Use the Pretest/Practice/Posttest routine to build speed and accuracy.
- Learn a word processing feature: Mail Merge.
- Create and type a data file of names and addresses and a form letter.

BELLRINGER

As soon as students arrive at their workstations and log in, have them type the Warmup. Go over the purpose of each line as shown to the left of the copy.

TEACH

Activity B. Ask for volunteers to read their paragraphs to the class. Have students check each other's work. For those who made errors, have them retype their paragraphs as a homework assignment.

Solutions: Answers will vary.

LESSON 85 MERGE: FORM LETTERS

OBJECTIVES:

- Reinforce good keyboarding technique.
- Compose at the keyboard.
- Learn to do a mail merge.

A. WARMUP

Type each line 2 times.

Speed	1	You can learn to type at a fast speed if you will practice.
Accuracy	2	Olmec, Zapotec, Mixtec, and Aztec were early civilizations.
Language Link	3	The homework for math class was problems 45-49 on page 549.
Numbers/Symbols	4	Our company will buy 1/3 of their stock @ 22 7/8 per share.
		| 1 | 2 | 3 | 4 | 5 | 6 | 7 | 8 | 9 | 10 | 11 | 12

B. COMPOSING AT THE KEYBOARD

Choose one of the sentence fragments below, complete it, and continue composing until you have created a short paragraph with at least three sentences.

5 I was never a believer in UFOs until . . .
6 The road was dark and deserted. All of a sudden . . .
7 My phone never stopped ringing after I . . .
8 While sailing on a very windy day, we suddenly . . .

LANGUAGE ARTS CONNECTIONS

A *constellation* is an easily recognized group of stars that appear close together in the sky. These stars form a picture if you can imagine lines connecting them (connect the dots). Constellations are usually named after an animal, a character from mythology, or a common object. One well-known constellation is the Big Dipper.

RESOURCES

 Lesson Plan 85
 Courseware Lesson 85
Student Data Disk
Student Manual
Supplementary Production Activities
Grading and Evaluation
Multicultural Activities

COURSEWARE OVERVIEW

For KCA to score mail merges, documents must be saved with specific file names. Special instructions are provided in Help for completing merges. Students are instructed on screen to print and and save these instructions.

SKILLBUILDING

C. PRETEST

Take a 1-minute timing on the paragraph. Note your speed and errors.

```
 9      To merge many addresses with one letter is truly quite   11
10  a job for certain people. However, this vexing task can be   23
11  completed very simply and in an amazingly little amount of   35
12  time with concentrated effort to learn the right technique.   47
    | 1 | 2 | 3 | 4 | 5 | 6 | 7 | 8 | 9 | 10 | 11 | 12
```

D. PRACTICE

SPEED: If you made 2 or fewer errors on the Pretest, type lines 13–20 two times each.

ACCURACY: If you made more than 2 errors on the Pretest, type lines 13–16 as a group two times. Then type lines 17–20 as a group two times.

Left Reaches

```
13  rer red were crow break dread cheer chore dream toast clerk
14  asa ask base lane flash saint hasty sauce spasm salty treat
15  rtr art dirt trim ports chart tract short trade sport train
16  tet jet team kite meter beets meets sweet liter miter white
```

Right Reaches

```
17  iui suit quit unit ruin build equip quiet quick guilt fruit
18  oio toil coil riot boil joins lions joist avoid doing onion
19  pop pods chop pose stop spoil sport adopt depot topic power
20  lol poll lots jolt told molds older holds soles folds holes
```

E. POSTTEST

Repeat the Pretest. Compare your Posttest results with your Pretest results.

FORMATTING

F. MERGE: DATA SOURCE/FORM FILE

Often it is necessary to send the same letter to many different people. A **form letter** is a letter that is typed only once but can be sent to many different people. To prepare a form letter:

1. Create a data file that contains the variable information within the letter (for example, the names and addresses of all the people to whom you want to send the letter).
2. Create a form letter with fields for the missing data.
3. Merge the form letter with the data.

TEACH

Activities C–E. Remind students they should improve both their speed and accuracy from the Pretest to the Posttest.

PRETEST/PRACTICE/POSTTEST

The ***Pretest/Practice/Posttest*** routines are designed to improve speed or accuracy.

- The ***Pretest*** identifies students' speed or accuracy needs.
- The ***Practice*** provides a variety of improvement drills.
- The ***Posttest*** (a repeat of the Pretest) measures improvement.

Activity F. Ask a student to read aloud to the class the steps for creating a form letter. As students practice, walk around the room and make sure they understand the directions.

FACT FILE

Form letters often are used in direct mail advertising and marketing. Many businesses develop a customer database that includes the name and address of each customer as well as the types and amounts of products each has purchased. This allows the businesses to send sales letters that are precisely targeted to specific customers.

TEACH

Activity G. Explain and demonstrate a Mail Merge.

STUDENT MANUAL
Be sure students turn to the correct lesson in their Student Manual.

Letters 44–45. This data will be merged with the letter.

ASSESS

- Review the typing accuracy of students' paragraphs in the Language Link composing activity.
- Check to see if students show signs of improvement from the Pretest to the Posttest.
- Make sure students are able to complete the Mail Merge.
- As students begin typing, walk around the room and point out correct and incorrect formatting to individual students.

CLOSE

If students do not finish the merge during the class period, make sure they save their work so that they can complete it the next time this class meets.

G. Software Features

STUDENT MANUAL

Mail Merge: Data File   Form File

Study Lesson 85 in your student manual. Complete all the practice activities while at your computer. Then complete the jobs that follow.

WORD PROCESSING APPLICATIONS

LETTERS 44–45

Create a data file with the field names shown below; then create the two records. After the data records are complete, type the form letter in block style. Merge the data file and form letter to create Letters 44-45.

Field Names	Record 1	Record 2
Title	Ms.	Mr.
FirstName	Teresa	Tom
LastName	Belle	Carlisle
Address	7168 Olympia Avenue	16687 E. Latimer Place
City	Dalton	Westlake
State	GA	OH
ZIP	30720	44145

January 19, {Year}

<<Title>> <<FirstName>> <<LastName>>
<<Address>>
<<City>>, <<State>> <<ZIP>>

Dear <<FirstName>>:

¶Congratulations! You are a winner in the Bold Journey Contest sponsored by *Outdoor Magazine*. You have won an entire week at Outdoor Adventure Camp in Big Branch, Utah—all expenses paid. We hope, <<FirstName>>, that you are looking forward to joining the other 49 high school students across the country who are also winners.
¶Next week we will send you all the details concerning your travel arrangements, needed equipment, and the type of clothing you should bring.
¶We look forward to seeing you at Big Branch.
Sincerely, / Brandon T. Dillard / Editor in Chief / urs

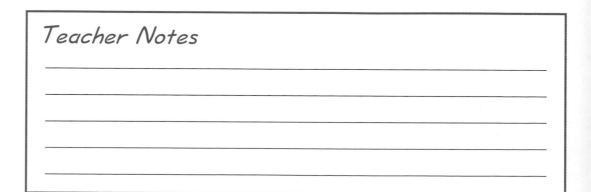

Teacher Notes

LESSON 86

MERGE: FORM LETTERS

OBJECTIVES:

- Improve keyboarding skill on symbol keys.
- Create a form letter and a data file.
- Merge the form letter with the data file.

A. WARMUP

Type each line 2 times.

Speed	1	The report cover is the first part of a report that we see.
Accuracy	2	Joey requested help to research weekly executive magazines.
Language Link	3	Atlanta, Georgia, is the home office for many corporations.
Numbers/Symbols	4	You may reach Don any weekday at (404) 555-7139, Ext. 3286.
		| 1 | 2 | 3 | 4 | 5 | 6 | 7 | 8 | 9 | 10 | 11 | 12

SKILLBUILDING

B. 30-SECOND TIMINGS

Take two 30-second timings on lines 5–6. Then take two 30-second timings on lines 7–8. Try to increase your speed on each timing.

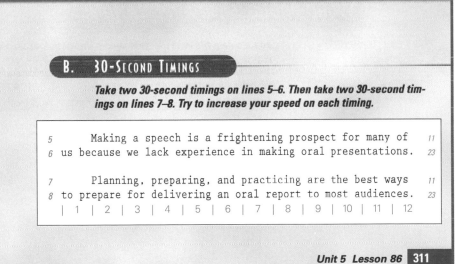

5 Making a speech is a frightening prospect for many of 11
6 us because we lack experience in making oral presentations. 23

7 Planning, preparing, and practicing are the best ways 11
8 to prepare for delivering an oral report to most audiences. 23
| 1 | 2 | 3 | 4 | 5 | 6 | 7 | 8 | 9 | 10 | 11 | 12

RESOURCES

 Lesson Plan 86

 Courseware Lesson 86

Student Data Disk

Student Manual

Supplementary Production Activities

Multicultural Activities

LESSON 86

FOCUS

- Use 30-second timings to build speed.
- Use the Pretest/Practice/Posttest routine to build speed and accuracy.
- Create a form letter and merge data.

BELLRINGER

As soon as students arrive at their workstations and log in, have them type the Warmup. Go over the purpose of each line as shown to the left of the copy.

TEACH

Activity B. Remind students that their goal for 30-second timings is improved speed with each of the timings.

TEACH

Activity C. The P/P/P routine in this lesson reviews symbols students have learned.

Activity D. Be sure students repeat the lines that contain symbols they had trouble with in the Pretest.

Activity E. Remind students they should improve both their speed and accuracy from the Pretest to the Posttest.

PRETEST/PRACTICE/POSTEST

The ***Pretest/Practice/Posttest*** routines are designed to improve speed or accuracy.

- The ***Pretest*** identifies students' speed or accuracy needs.
- The ***Practice*** provides a variety of improvement drills.
- The ***Posttest*** (a repeat of the Pretest) measures improvement.

Activity F. Ask students what a form file is. Have them create a form file with the data file they created in Lesson 85 for practice.

TEACH

Letters 46–49. Have students check each other's work. Make sure students have inserted the appropriate fields.

C. PRETEST

Take a 1-minute timing on the paragraph. Note your speed and errors.

Symbol Diagnostic

```
 9      J&J Nursery numbered their plants. They sold 5 of #76,   11
10 69 of #42, and 25 of #38. I bought 20 bulbs* @ $2.49; now I   23
11 have to plant them. This is 20 + 40 = 60 that I have bought.  35
12 Red flowers @ $2.49 each show a profit of 8%. I'm thrilled!   47
   | 1 | 2 | 3 | 4 | 5 | 6 | 7 | 8 | 9 | 10 | 11 | 12
```

D. PRACTICE

Type lines 13–21 once. Then repeat any of the lines that stress the symbol errors you noted in the Pretest.

```
@    13 Frank sold 15 @ 11, 20 @ 22, 25 @ 33, 30 @ 44, and 35 @ 55.
*    14 Earl selected *Rome, *Venice, *Paris, *Berlin, and *Madrid.
#    15 We see that #9 weighs 56#, #7 weighs 34#, and #8 weighs 2#.

$    16 The seven girls saved $9, $10, $38, $47, $56, $72, and $89.
%    17 On those days the market rose 3%, 5%, 7%, 8%, 12%, and 18%.
&    18 The leaders are Kim & Dave, Robert & Mary, and Kay & Peter.

()   19 Li chose Marco (Florida), Daisy (Georgia), and Alta (Utah).
-    20 The cartons were labeled as 29-92, 38-56, 47-10, and 59-28.
+ =  21 Eb said that 28 + 65 = 93, 47 + 15 = 62, and 10 + 99 = 109.
```

E. POSTTEST

Repeat the Pretest. Compare your Posttest results with your Pretest results.

WORD PROCESSING APPLICATIONS

LETTERS 46–49

Create a data file with the field names shown below, then create the four records. After the data records are complete, type the form letter in block style. Insert the fields where necessary. Merge the data file and form letter to create Letters 46-49.

Field Names: Title, FirstName, LastName, Address, City, State, ZIP

Record 1	**Record 2**
Mrs.	Dr.
Jasmine	Lewis
Graham	Garcia
7457 S. Hudson Avenue	3284 S. Utica Street
Tulsa	Tulsa
OK	OK
74136	74105

312 *Word Processing*

TECHNOLOGY TIP

Explain to students that when they create form letters using the mail merge feature, it is a good idea to test the merge with a few letters before running the whole job. Ask students why this is so. Have them practice this method.

SCHOOL TO CAREER

Have students form small groups and discuss ways that form letters might be used in different careers. Have each group type a list of careers, with a sentence or two about the career and how form letters are used. Have students collect form letters they or their families receive and bring these to class to discuss.

Record 3	**Record 4**
Mr.	Mrs.
Cameron	Nichole
Wingert	McCullum
8130 S. College Avenue	948 S. Winston Avenue
Tulsa	Tulsa
OK	OK
74136	74112

October 1, {year}

<<Title>> <<FirstName>> <<LastName>>
<<Address>>
<<CityStateZIP>>

Dear <<Title>> <<LastName>>:

We appreciate your recent purchase of an appliance from our Shalimar Mall store. A coupon book is enclosed that should be used to make your monthly payments.

Please be sure that our mailing address shows in the window part of the envelopes that are also enclosed. For your convenience, payments may also be made at the store. We look forward, <<Title>> <<LastName>>, to serving your appliance needs in the coming years.

Sincerely,

Wilbert Crawford
Accounts Manager

Enclosures

Teacher Notes

ASSESS

- Check to see if students are increasing their word a minute speeds as they complete the 30-second timings.
- Check to see if students show signs of improvement from the Pretest to the Posttest.
- As students begin typing the form letter, walk around the room and point out correct and incorrect formatting to individual students.
- After students finish merging data, have them view their work on the screen to see if they made any errors. If errors were made, have students edit their work and make corrections.

CLOSE

If students do not finish the letters during the class period, make sure they save their work so that they can complete it the next time this class meets.

PORTFOLIO Activity

If students' portfolio goals include demonstrating specific skills, they may want to include the form letters from this lesson. Encourage students to evaluate their own work and include comments in their portfolio.

LESSON 87

FOCUS

- Use 5-minute timings to build speed.
- Practice typing letters and using mail merge features.

BELLRINGER

As soon as students arrive at their workstations and log in, have them type the Warmup. Go over the purpose of each line as shown to the left of the copy.

TEACH

Activity B. Point out that words in the Preview Practice are used in the timing that follows.

LESSON 87 REVIEW

OBJECTIVES:

- Review business letter formats.
- Type 37/5'/5e.

A. WARMUP

Type each line 2 times.

Speed	1	You can stay in shape with a brisk walk three times a week.
Accuracy	2	Dr. Baxter was quick to analyze the four major food groups.
Language Link	3	We now have two kittens I adopted after they were deserted.
Numbers/Symbols	4	Donald and Darlene paid $5.08 for 4 pamphlets @ $1.27 each.

| 1 | 2 | 3 | 4 | 5 | 6 | 7 | 8 | 9 | 10 | 11 | 12

SKILLBUILDING

B. PREVIEW PRACTICE

Type each line 2 times as a preview to the timings that follow.

Accuracy	5	jump steady difficult realize purchases extremely establish
Speed	6	credit afford result stable good time cash will job not has

FACT FILE

High temperatures and humidity can quickly lead to heat exhaustion. To ward of serious consequences, know these early signs and symptoms: headache, nausea, fatigue, dizziness or lightheadedness, actively sweating. Generally heat exhaustion is caused by loss of body fluids and important salts. If untreated, heat exhaustion can lead to heat stroke. To treat heat exhaustion, get into the shade or a cool place, increase fluids, and use cold, wet towels to cool down.

RESOURCES

 Lesson Plan 87

 Courseware Lesson 87

Student Data Disk

Student Manual

Reteaching and Reinforcement

Grading and Evaluation

C. 5-Minute Timings

Take two 5-minute timings on the paragraphs. Note your speed and errors.

Goal: 37/5′/5e

```
     The term credit means buying now and paying later. It      11
is similar to borrowing cash. One reason people use credit      23
is because they do not have the cash to pay for something       34
at the time they want to buy it.                                41
     Many people now use credit cards to purchase things.       52
Credit cards are easy to obtain and use, and people are         63
quick to use them as borrowed money for extra things they       75
cannot afford. They build up debts they just cannot pay.        86
     People of all ages and all income levels can easily        97
get into debt with credit cards. They do not realize that      108
using credit comes with a high price. Often, cardholders       120
pay finance charges or interest on unpaid bills for their      131
purchases.                                                     133
     In spite of this, most people will need to establish      144
a good credit record. They will need a steady job with         155
stable income, and they must prove that they will repay        166
any money they borrow. Once people have their good credit      178
ratings, they must maintain them.                              185
| 1 | 2 | 3 | 4 | 5 | 6 | 7 | 8 | 9 | 10 | 11 | 12 SI 1.38
```

MATH CONNECTIONS

Check your local newspapers or use the Internet to determine the various interest rates on most credit cards. Based on your findings, determine how long it would take and how much interest you would pay if you bought something that cost $700 and paid a minimum amount of $10 every month toward your bill. Have your teacher check your math.

TEACH

Activity C. Remind students that they should try to improve speed with each of the 5-minute timings. The goal for these timings is to type 37 words a minute for 5 minutes with no more than 5 errors.

Math Connections

Discuss the advantages and disadvantages of credit cards. To help students understand what careers are open to them in this industry, have them brainstorm about careers related to the credit card industry. Write these on the board.

TEACH

Letter 50. Remind students to indent the paragraphs in this modified-block style letter.

WORD PROCESSING APPLICATIONS

LETTER 50
Modified-Block Style

Type the following letter in modified-block style with indented paragraphs.

(Current Date) / Ms. Kateri Tahoma / Administrative Assistant / Diabo Construction Company / 330 Cooper Avenue / Lincoln, NE 68506 / Dear Ms. Tahoma:

¶You are invited to attend a seminar entitled "Listening Skills—Do You Hear When You Listen?" It will be held at the Cornhusker Hotel in Lincoln on June 17 from 9 a.m. until 3 p.m.

¶The registration fee of $50 includes the seminar and a luncheon from noon until 1:30. During lunch you will be able to view fashions from DeLilli Designs. Your employer, Diabo Construction, will pay your registration fee.

¶This professional seminar will be well worth the time away from the office if you take the right approach. Here are a few suggestions that will help you turn this seminar into a valuable experience. Prepare yourself by reading the information provided by your company. List at least five specific questions you want answered. Use break time to network and talk to your peers. Bring business cards to exchange. When you receive one, make a note on the back about the person giving it to you. Collect handouts from all the speakers. Read your notes. Review and prepare a summary of what you experienced and learned. You also might listen for suggestions on how to be a better listener. The presenters will give the audience time to role-play and use specific techniques of listening.

¶If you follow these little hints, the seminar will be informative as well as enjoyable for you. We are looking forward to seeing you at the Cornhusker. / Sincerely, / Dana Olsen, Coordinator / Climbing the Ladder, Inc.

SCHOOL TO CAREER

Have students break into small groups and develop a list of ten careers centered around listening skills. Help students get started by suggesting careers such as producers of videos on listening skills or training coordinators in companies who plan listening seminars. Then discuss how listening skills are used in all careers.

Multiple Learning Styles

To help students with hand coordination, have them practice the following exercise: Put both hands on the table top. Begin with the dominant hand. Tap the index finger several times. Tap the index finger and little finger at the same time. Switch to the non-dominant hand and repeat.

LETTERS 51–53
Block Style

Create a data file with these field names:* Title, FirstName, LastName, Address, CityStateZIP, Physician, State. *After you have created the data file with these field names, create the following three records.

Record 1	**Record 2**	**Record 3**
Ms. Faye Hayes	Mr. Alvin Morgan	Mr. Lloyd Blairstone
450 Marshall Avenue	742 Huck Road	7500 Lada Lane
Hickory, NC 28611	Lexington, SC 29072	Thomaston, GA 30286
Dr. Millhouse	Dr. Stewart	Dr. Abernathy
North Carolina	South Carolina	Georgia

After you create the data records, type the following form letter in block style. Note that two of the data fields appear within the body of the letter. Then, merge the data records with the form letter to create Letters 51–53.

June 6, {year}

<<Title>> <<FirstName>> <<LastName>>
<<Address>>
<<CityStateZIP>>

Dear <<Title>> <<LastName>>:

¶Your physician, <<Physician>>, recommended you as a person who might benefit from participating in a research study on the problems of aging. This study is being conducted through the medical school at Wayne State University. The examinations included in the study will be at no cost to you.

¶Please read the brochure describing the study, complete the enclosed questionnaire, and return it to me by June 30. A postage-paid return envelope is also enclosed for your convenience.

¶Your participation in this study will help us reach our goal for the number of respondents we hope to include from <<State>>. If you have any questions, call me at 810-555-4575. I look forward to including you in this study.

Sincerely,

Donald L. Gaddis, M.D.
Project Director

urs
Enclosures

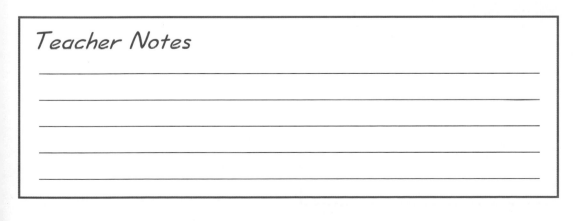

Teacher Notes

LESSON 87

TEACH

Letters 51–53. Have students check the titles of their data file to make sure they are correct. After they have completed the letter and merged the data, have students check each other's work.

ASSESS

- Check to see if students are increasing their word a minute speeds as they complete each 5-minute timing.
- As students begin typing the letters, walk around the room and point out correct and incorrect formatting to individual students.
- After students finish typing the letters, have them view their work on the screen to see if they made any errors. If errors were made, have students edit their work and make corrections.

CLOSE

If students do not finish the letters during the class period, make sure they save their work so that they can complete it the next time this class meets.

Remind students to clean up their workstation when they leave.

FOCUS

- Apply the Language Link rule for capitalization.
- Use the Pretest/Practice/Posttest routine to build speed and accuracy.
- Learn how to format and type letters with numbered lists.

BELLRINGER

As soon as students arrive at their workstations and log in, have them type the Warmup. Go over the purpose of each line as shown to the left of the copy.

TEACH

Activity B. Explain the capitalization rule to students. After they have completed typing, go over the sentences in class and have students check their own work. Assign as homework any sentences in which they had errors.

Solutions: If you are traveling to the North today, be careful of fog.

Paula lived in the North until she moved south to Florida.

Karen sold the most homes in the southern part of the city.

The flooding was severe in the Southeast and Midwest.

LESSON 88

LETTERS WITH NUMBERED LISTS

OBJECTIVES:

- Learn capitalization rules for compass points.
- Improve keyboarding skills.
- Format letters with numbered lists.

A. WARMUP

Type each line 2 times.

Speed	1	Richard can ask what size tent he should take for the trip.
Accuracy	2	Jena quickly seized the wax buffer and removed a big patch.
Language Link	3	Publisher's Clearing House gave away three million dollars.
Numbers/Symbols	4	The booklets are AB-GN, catalog item XH479/162CLW @ $13.50.

| 1 | 2 | 3 | 4 | 5 | 6 | 7 | 8 | 9 | 10 | 11 | 12

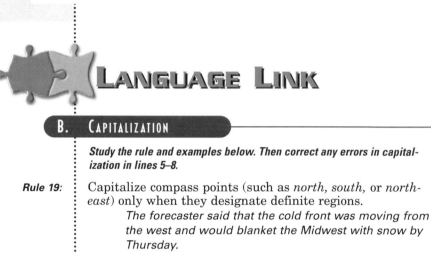

B. CAPITALIZATION

Study the rule and examples below. Then correct any errors in capitalization in lines 5–8.

Rule 19: Capitalize compass points (such as *north, south,* or *northeast*) only when they designate definite regions.

The forecaster said that the cold front was moving from the west and would blanket the Midwest with snow by Thursday.

5 If you are traveling to the north today, be careful of fog.
6 Paula lived in the north until she moved south to Florida.
7 Karen sold the most homes in the southern part of the city.
8 The flooding was severe in the southeast and midwest.

RESOURCES

 Lesson Plan 88

 Courseware Lesson 88

Student Data Disk

Student Manual

Language Link Worksheets

Supplementary Production Activities

SKILLBUILDING

C. PRETEST

Take a 1-minute timing on the paragraph. Note your speed and errors.

```
 9       In the past decade, computers have affected almost      12
10   every job in the business office. Today, it is very common  22
11   to see computers being used that are smaller and six to ten 34
12   times quicker than they were only a few short years ago.    45
     | 1 | 2 | 3 | 4 | 5 | 6 | 7 | 8 | 9 | 10 | 11 | 12
```

D. PRACTICE

In the chart below, find the number of errors you made on the Pretest. Then type each of the designated drill lines 2 times.

Pretest Errors	0–1	2	3	4+
Drill Lines	16–20	15–19	14–18	13–17

Accuracy

```
13 just during decade faster smaller invaded business addition
14 past about coming become common powerful possible computers
15 now have would popular horizon machines business technology
16 six more find would quite become smaller possible computers
```

Speed

```
17 office being today every this task all now are the it in so
18 years their time more were used find this that not of is to
19 become makes will hard that they then much new and on be or
20 times today find such does much just work few ago use on of
```

E. POSTTEST

Repeat the Pretest. Compare your Posttest results with your Pretest results.

LANGUAGE ARTS CONNECTIONS

In 1962, Martin K. Specter invented the word *interrobang.* When some one shouts with alarm and asks a question at the same time, the sentence could end with an interrobang. The first part of the word, *interro,* is short for interrogation point, which is another name for a question mark. An interrogation is a questioning, which comes from the Latin *inter.* The ending, *bang,* was originally a printer's slang word for an exclamation point. Interrobang has now migrated into the world of computer terminogy.

TEACH

Activities C–E. Remind students they should improve both their speed and accuracy from the Pretest to the Posttest. For the Practice activity, go over the drill lines they should type twice for the number of Pretest errors they make.

PRETEST/PRACTICE/POSTTEST

The ***Pretest/Practice/Posttest*** routines are designed to improve speed or accuracy.

- The ***Pretest*** identifies students' speed or accuracy needs.
- The ***Practice*** provides a variety of improvement drills.
- The ***Posttest*** (a repeat of the Pretest) measures improvement.

EXTENDING THE CONTENT

Business people use computers to communicate with other employees using e-mail. They also use computers to make business decisions. Managers use a management information system (MIS) to process and report information. An MIS typically includes financial information, production and inventory information, marketing information and human resources information.

TEACH

Activity F. Remind students to leave a blank line before the first and after the last numbered item and to single-space a numbered list within the body of a letter.

Letter 54. Tell students that numbered lists are helpful when they are providing a list for the reader, such as the list in Letter 54. Ask students for other types of lists that may be in a letter.

FORMATTING

F. Letters With Numbered Lists

A numbered list is often included in the body of a letter. Use the automatic numbering feature to create the list. Leave a blank line before the first and after the last numbered item. Single-space the list.

WORD PROCESSING APPLICATIONS

LETTER 54
Modified-Block Style

Type the following letter in modified-block style.

(Current Date) / Dr. Jaune Sakyesva / 2042 East Bellview Parkway / Suite 109 / Denver, CO 80202-1956 / Dear Dr. Sakyesva:
¶We are happy to respond to your letter requesting information about our next seminar on current ISSUES IN SOCIETY. This series of seminars has been successful because we have addressed some of the major issues our society faces today, and we have offered helpful suggestions on how to deal with them.

1. The seminar will be held August 21 from 9 a.m. until 3 p.m. at the Inn of the Rockies, 404 West Mountain Drive. A map is enclosed with this letter.
2. Lunch will be provided by Epicurean Delight. Call 699-555-1245 to specify your luncheon choice from those items listed in our brochure.
3. There will be three speakers and a chance for questions after each talk.
4. Tapes from other seminars will be available for purchase in the lobby during the luncheon break and at the conclusion of the seminar.

¶As soon as we have confirmations from the speakers, I'll send you literature regarding each speaker and his/her qualifications. Thank you for your interest in the seminar.
Sincerely, / Maya Harris / Public Relations Director / urs / Enclosures

FACT FILE

The human ear is a complex instrument. Sound waves entering the external ear canal travel through the middle ear and into the inner ear and are converted to nerve impulses, which allow us to hear.

LETTER 55
Block Style

Type this letter in block style.

(Current Date) / Mr. Sullivan D'Amico / D'Amico & McGrawth Legal Firm / 404 West Broadway / Suite 220 / Denver, CO 80501 / Dear Mr. D'Amico:

¶Thank you for your letter asking about my new book, *Listening Is an Art.* In the book, I stress that listening is not a spectator sport. It requires active participation.

¶As a listener, you need to encourage your speaker by visibly paying close attention. Body language on your part is often a great encouragement to the speaker. Listed below are several of the topics I cover in the book:

1. Paraphrase the content. In your own words, repeat what you are hearing. Encourage the speaker by letting him/her know that you are listening.
2. Be involved in the conversation. Go beyond paraphrasing to enforce understanding by adding comments to the person's discussion.
3. Feed back feelings. Reflect the feelings you hear by expressing your opinion about the topic being discussed. If you can, ask direct questions of the speaker.

¶I hope, Mr. D'Amico, that this gives you an idea of what I'm writing about. I've mailed you an autographed copy of my book for your enjoyment.

Yours truly, / Bonnie Ryan, Author / urs

FACT FILE

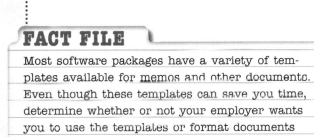

Most software packages have a variety of templates available for memos and other documents. Even though these templates can save you time, determine whether or not your employer wants you to use the templates or format documents differently.

Teacher Notes

LESSON 88

TEACH

Letter 55. Use the tips in this letter as ways students can practice good listening skills.

ASSESS

- Watch students as they complete the Language Link activity to see if they are able to apply the capitalization rule correctly.
- Check to see if students show signs of improvement from the Pretest to the Posttest.
- After students finish typing the letters, have them view their work on the screen to see if they made any errors. If errors were made, have students edit their work and make corrections.

CLOSE

If students do not finish the letters during the class period, make sure they save their work so that they can complete it the next time this class meets.

PORTFOLIO *Activity*

If students' portfolio goals include showcasing their best work, they may want to include one of the letters from this lesson. Encourage students to evaluate their work and include comments in their portfolio.

LESSON 89

FOCUS

- Apply the Language Link rule concerning confusing words.
- Use 30-second OK timings to improve accuracy.
- Use Technique Checkpoint to improve technique.
- Learn a word processing feature: Templates.
- Learn how to format and type memos using templates.

BELLRINGER

As soon as students arrive at their workstations and log in, have them type the Warmup. Go over the purpose of each line as shown to the left of the copy.

TEACH

Activity B. Ask students which words they have the most trouble with. Go over the rules with them before they type the assignment.

Solutions: Rather than stay home, we saw a movie and then had pizza.

After studying the map further, we realized we were 50 miles farther than we should have been.

First we visited Niagara Falls, then we drove farther into Canada to visit Toronto.

The board members agreed to discuss the matter further.

LESSON 89 MEMO TEMPLATES

OBJECTIVES:

- Learn about confusing words.
- Learn word processing features.
- Format memos using templates.

A. WARMUP

Type each line 2 times.

Speed	1	We are planning to have a cookout when we meet at the lake.
Accuracy	2	All four mixtures in the deep brown jug froze very quickly.
Language Link	3	We usually vacation at a place that is south of the border.
Numbers/Symbols	4	Invoice #70-2 read: 653# "Extra" @ $4.89 per lb., less 10%.

| 1 | 2 | 3 | 4 | 5 | 6 | 7 | 8 | 9 | 10 | 11 | 12

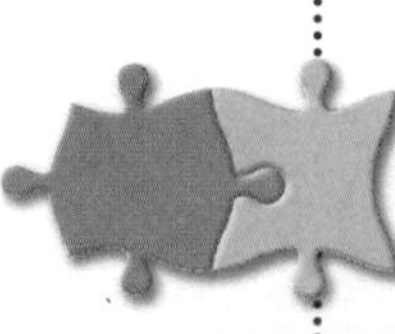

LANGUAGE LINK

B. CONFUSING WORDS

Study the confusing words and their meanings shown below. Then edit lines 5–8 by selecting the correct word.

than (conj. or prep.)	in comparison with
then (adv.)	at that time
farther (adv.)	to a greater distance
further (adv.)	in addition to

5 Rather (then/than) stay at home, we saw a movie and (then/than) had pizza

6 After studying the map (further/farther), we realized we were 50 miles (further/farther) (then/than) we should have been.

7 First we visited Niagara Falls, (then/than) we drove (further/farther) into Canada to visit Toronto.

8 The board members agreed to discuss the matter (further/farther).

RESOURCES

 Lesson Plan 89

 Courseware Lesson 89

Student Data Disk

Student Manual

Supplementary Production Activities

Multicultural Activities

SKILLBUILDING

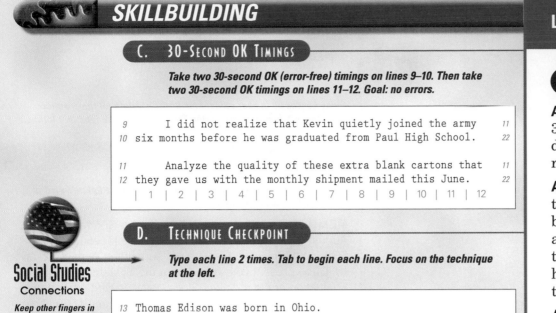

C. 30-Second OK Timings

Take two 30-second OK (error-free) timings on lines 9–10. Then take two 30-second OK timings on lines 11–12. Goal: no errors.

```
9       I did not realize that Kevin quietly joined the army      11
10  six months before he was graduated from Paul High School.    22

11      Analyze the quality of these extra blank cartons that     11
12  they gave us with the monthly shipment mailed this June.      22
```

Social Studies
Connections

Keep other fingers in home position while reaching to the tab.

D. Technique Checkpoint

Type each line 2 times. Tab to begin each line. Focus on the technique at the left.

```
13  Thomas Edison was born in Ohio.
14  His childhood home is now a museum.
15  He is best known for inventing the lightbulb.
16  He also invented a talking doll.
17  He was a close friend of Henry Ford.
```

FORMATTING

E. Memo Templates

Memos are written messages sent from one person to another in the same organization or business. Memos are less formal than letters and do not have salutations or closing lines.

Most word processing programs now include memo templates. **Templates** are forms that have been designed so that you can move quickly from one data entry area to the next to fill in necessary information. Memo templates usually include the guide words *TO:, FROM:, DATE:,* and *SUBJECT:*.

TEACH

Activity C. Point out that 30-second OK timings are designed to encourage accuracy.

Activity D. Remind students that proper technique is a building block for speed and accuracy. The focus for this timing: Keep other fingers in home position while reaching to the tab.

Activity E. Make sure students understand the purpose for each of the guide words used in the memo template: ***TO***:, ***FROM***:, ***DATE***:, and ***SUBJECT***:.

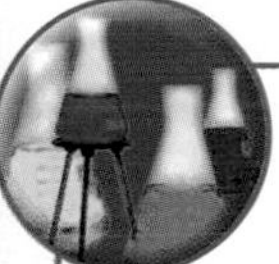

Science
Connections

Have students choose one of the sentences in Activity D (lines 13–17). Research the topic and write a one-page report. Remind students to follow the correct format for their reports. They are to have at least one footnote or endnote in their reports.

Social Studies
Connections

Have students research your state's history and write a short report on five significant persons. Reports should include names, where they were born and lived, and their contribution. Students are to cite at least one footnote or endnote.

TEACH

Activity F. Show students the different memo templates.

STUDENT MANUAL
Be sure students turn to the correct lesson in their Student Manual.

Memos 1–2. Point out the first memo template in the word processing software to students. Make sure each student finds the template.

ASSESS

- Check to see if students are completing 30-second OK timings without any errors.
- Make sure students are able to use the Templates software feature.
- As students type the memos, walk around the room and point out correct and incorrect formatting.
- Have students view their work on the screen to see if they made any errors. If errors were made, have students make corrections.

CLOSE

If students do not finish the memos during the class period, make sure they save their work so that they can complete it the next time this class meets.

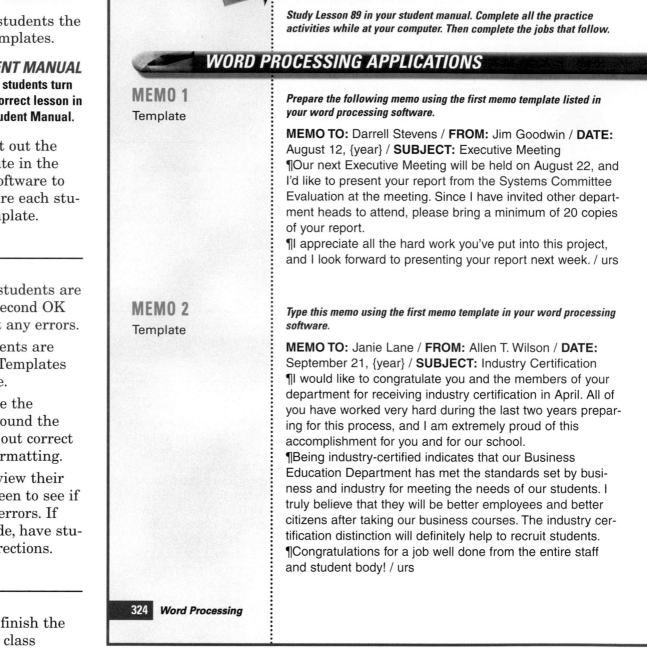

F. Software Features

STUDENT MANUAL
Templates

Study Lesson 89 in your student manual. Complete all the practice activities while at your computer. Then complete the jobs that follow.

WORD PROCESSING APPLICATIONS

MEMO 1
Template

Prepare the following memo using the first memo template listed in your word processing software.

MEMO TO: Darrell Stevens / **FROM:** Jim Goodwin / **DATE:** August 12, {year} / **SUBJECT:** Executive Meeting
¶Our next Executive Meeting will be held on August 22, and I'd like to present your report from the Systems Committee Evaluation at the meeting. Since I have invited other department heads to attend, please bring a minimum of 20 copies of your report.
¶I appreciate all the hard work you've put into this project, and I look forward to presenting your report next week. / urs

MEMO 2
Template

Type this memo using the first memo template in your word processing software.

MEMO TO: Janie Lane / **FROM:** Allen T. Wilson / **DATE:** September 21, {year} / **SUBJECT:** Industry Certification
¶I would like to congratulate you and the members of your department for receiving industry certification in April. All of you have worked very hard during the last two years preparing for this process, and I am extremely proud of this accomplishment for you and for our school.
¶Being industry-certified indicates that our Business Education Department has met the standards set by business and industry for meeting the needs of our students. I truly believe that they will be better employees and better citizens after taking our business courses. The industry certification distinction will definitely help to recruit students.
¶Congratulations for a job well done from the entire staff and student body! / urs

324 ***Word Processing***

Teacher Notes

LESSON 90 REVIEW

OBJECTIVES:

- Reinforce keyboarding techniques.
- Improve keyboarding skill.
- Reinforce letter and memo formats.

A. WARMUP

Type each line 2 times.

Speed	1	Elaine invited several of her friends over for the evening.
Accuracy	2	Why would quick brown foxes want to jump over any lazy dog?
Language Link	3	Rather than go any farther, they stopped to get directions.
Numbers/Symbols	4	Only 4% of our current PCs are equipped with CD-ROM drives.
		| 1 | 2 | 3 | 4 | 5 | 6 | 7 | 8 | 9 | 10 | 11 | 12

SKILLBUILDING

B. TECHNIQUE TIMINGS

Take two 30-second timings on lines 5–6. Then take two 30-second timings on lines 7–8. Focus on the technique at the left.

Keep your eyes on the copy.

5	Try to type each letter of the alphabet as quickly as	11
6	you can without having to stop to look where the keys are.	23
7	As you type, think about where each letter is located.	11
8	Then type with your eyes closed to see if you learned well.	23
	| 1 | 2 | 3 | 4 | 5 | 6 | 7 | 8 | 9 | 10 | 11 | 12	

C. PACED PRACTICE

Turn to the Paced Practice routine beginning on page SB7 Take three 2-minute timings, starting at the point where you left off the last time.

LESSON 90

FOCUS

- Use Technique Timings to improve technique.
- Use Paced Practice 2-minute timings.
- Type a letter in modified-block style.
- Type memos using a memo template.

BELLRINGER

As soon as students arrive at their workstations and log in, have them type the Warmup. Go over the purpose of each line as shown to the left of the copy.

TEACH

Activity B. Remind students that proper technique is a building block for speed and accuracy. The focus for this timing: Keep your eyes on the copy.

Activity C. Go over the routine for the Paced Practice 2-minute timings. (See Lesson 34, page 119.)

RESOURCES

 Lesson Plan 90

 Courseware Lesson 90

Student Data Disk

Student Manual

Reteaching and Reinforcement

Grading and Evaluation

TEACH

Letter 56. Remind students to use automatic numbering, and to leave a blank line before and after the numbered list.

WORD PROCESSING APPLICATIONS

LETTER 56

Block Style

Type the following letter in block style.

(Current Date) / Ms. Ruthe Barichello, Department Chair / English Department / Central High School / 3474 Maple Avenue / Carrollton, GA 30118 / Dear Ms. Barichello:
Subject: Effective Leadership
¶As we discussed at our meeting last week, there are certainly several traits that we should be aware of when selecting the next members of the department. Are leaders born or made? No one is really sure, but there are four specific actions that successful leaders should carry out regardless of the organization they lead. Effective leaders should:

1. Make others feel important and emphasize others' strengths and contributions, not their own. If leaders' goals are self-centered, followers will lose their enthusiasm quickly.
2. Promote a vision. Followers need a clear idea of where they are being lead. A leader needs to provide that vision. Followers need to understand that vision or goal and buy into it.
3. Follow the golden rule. A leader should treat followers the way he/she likes to be treated. That means admitting mistakes.
4. Criticize others only in private. Public praise encourages others to excel.

¶Our first interview is scheduled for next Monday in the board conference room at 9 a.m. I look forward to seeing you then. / Sincerely, / Casey Javonovich / Board Chairman / urs

FACT FILE

Herbert Hoover was a mining engineer. He managed gold mines in Australia and later worked in mines in China and started a mining company. Herbert Hoover was also the thirty-first president of the United States.

FACT FILE

Tell students there is a Herbert Hoover National Historic Site. Have each of five groups answer one of these questions: Where is the site? What does it commemorate? Who administers the site? What surrounds the site? What do visitors to the site see? Have each group type a report and present it to the class.

LETTER 57

Modified-Block Style

Type this letter in modified-block style.

(Current Date) / Attention: Human Resources / Alkens Industries / 750 South Filmore Street / Denver, CO 80209-5072 / Ladies and Gentlemen:
¶Mr. Warren Thomas was recently treated by me at Wilson Hospital. During his hospitalization, I placed him on a disability leave. I felt his condition was such that he could not return to work until his symptoms had resolved.
¶Mr. Thomas has continued in my care. He has shown good progress in recovery. On reevaluation, it is apparent that he would be able to return to work on the 15th of next month. This is sooner than I anticipated, but it reflects his positive progress.
¶If there are any other questions, please contact my office. Sincerely, / John Blackburn, M.D. / urs / c: Mr. Warren Thomas

MEMO 3

Template

Type the following memo. Use the first memo template in your word processing software.

TO: Shelby Taylor / FROM: Kenneth Anderson / DATE: July 12, {year} / SUBJECT: Company Newsletter
¶Your first issue of the *Brownfield Quarterly* was fantastic, and I want to extend my heartfelt congratulations for a job well done. Even though this was your first edition of the newsletter using our new desktop publishing software, I think the finished product was great!
¶The Projects Update on page 2 was especially informative because you let us know the major projects our employees have been working on this quarter. We certainly need to know what is going on throughout the plant. I have heard many other employees make very favorable comments about the newsletter, especially this section.
¶Keep up the good work, Shelby. / urs

LESSON 90

TEACH

Letter 57. Tell students that a letter provides them with a record of what they have said and can even be used as a legal document in court.

Memo 3. Ask students if they have ever sent someone a congratulations letter for something well done. Have they ever received one? Suggest they write a letter to someone they know just to congratulate them for something—maybe just for smiling so brightly!

JOURNAL ENTRY

Have students write about how they feel when they do something nice for another person. Their entries should tell what they did. Remind students to free write, then go back and proofread. Read the entries in class.

TEACH

Memo 4. Tell students that before they write a business letter, they need to plan what they want to say. This will help them keep their letters to the point and well organized.

ASSESS

- Monitor students as they complete Technique Timings and provide individualized assistance as needed.
- As students begin typing the letters and memos, walk around the room and point out correct and incorrect formatting to individual students.
- After students finish typing the letters and memos, have them view their work on the screen to see if they made any errors. If errors were made, have students edit their work and make corrections.

CLOSE

If students do not finish the letters and memos during the class period, make sure they save their work so that they can complete it the next time this class meets.

Remind students to clean up their workstation when they leave.

MEMO 4

Template

Type the following memo. Use the first memo template in your word processing software.

TO: David J. Bacon / FROM: Wayne S. Goodin / DATE: Current / SUBJECT: Marketing Questionnaire
¶One of the questionnaires that was sent to your office at the beginning of the month should be completed by the 31st of this month. As a reminder, Section III must be completed for questions 8, 12, 18, 24, and 27. The results of the questionnaires are going to be used to compare our product sales with those of the other district offices in the eastern region. Thank you very much for your immediate response. / urs

FACT FILE

The expression "two bits" is used to indicate that you have a quarter. The origin of the word "bit" for a coin goes back to the seventeenth century when any coin in Great Britain could be called a bit. The slang migrated to the southwestern part of the United States where Mexican coins were commonly used as currency. The Mexican real (ray-AHL), which was worth about 12 and a half cents, was called a bit. When the U.S. quarter came out, it was worth about two reals, or two bits.

Teacher Notes

LESSON 91 TABLES: REVERSING LINES

OBJECTIVES:

- Reinforce keyboarding skill.
- Type 37/5'/5e.
- Learn software features.
- Reverse table lines.

A. WARMUP

Type each line 2 times.

Speed	1	The temperature last night dropped below the freezing mark.
Accuracy	2	Jack typed four dozen requisitions for hollow moving boxes.
Language Link	3	Then Coach said the prize went to whoever ran the farthest.
Numbers/Symbols	4	The citation for the case is 795 F.2D 1423 (9th Cir. 1996).

| 1 | 2 | 3 | 4 | 5 | 6 | 7 | 8 | 9 | 10 | 11 | 12

SKILLBUILDING

B. TECHNIQUE CHECKPOINT

Type each line 2 times. Focus on the techniques at the left.

Lines 5–6: Space without pausing.

5 You can do much more work than you do each day of the week.
6 They will use the pay for the one day of work that she did.

Lines 7–8: Press and release the Caps Lock key without pausing.

7 Our SEVENTH ANNUAL MEETING will be held in MOBILE, ALABAMA.
8 The DAY COMPANY will sponsor our ADVISORY COUNCIL luncheon.

RESOURCES

 Lesson Plan 91

 Courseware Lesson 91

Student Data Disk

Student Manual

Supplementary Production Activities

Grading and Evaluation

LESSON 91

FOCUS

- Use the Technique Checkpoint to improve technique.
- Use 5-minute timings to build speed.
- Learn a word processing feature: Table Lines.
- Learn how to reverse lines in tables.
- Create tables.

BELLRINGER

As soon as students arrive at their workstations and log in, have them type the Warmup. Go over the purpose of each line as shown to the left of the copy.

TEACH

Activity B. Remind students that proper technique is a building block for speed and accuracy. The focus for lines 5–6: Space without pausing. The focus for lines 7–8: Press and release the caps lock key without pausing.

TEACH

Activity C. Point out that words in the Preview Practice are used in the timing that follows.

Activity D. Remind students that they should try to improve speed with each of the 5-minute timings. The goal is to type 37 words a minute for 5 minutes with no more than 5 errors.

COMMUNICATION ACTIVITY

Divide students into groups of three. Explain to students that they are going to speak for themselves by standing and speaking for 30 seconds about something that concerns them. This is not a gripe session but a time for each student in turn to practice speaking up. Two of the students are to practice listening skills while the third one speaks. Each student is to take a turn speaking.

C. Preview Practice

Type each line 2 times as a preview to the timings that follow.

Accuracy
Speed

```
express respect negative yourself effectively communication
situations essential feelings realize beyond ideas high own
```

D. 5-Minute Timings

Take two 5-minute timings on the paragraphs. Note your speed and errors.

Goal: 37/5'/5e

Language Arts Connections

```
     In high school and beyond, the communication of ideas,    11
needs, wants, and feelings in the right way is a skill that    23
must be acquired. Parents and teachers may not be around       35
when you need them later. It is up to you to realize the       46
need for learning how to get your ideas and feelings across    58
to others clearly and to do so in a way that shows respect     70
both for yourself and for others.                              77
     Think of times when you wished you had the skill to       87
make your point. Perhaps you needed to know how to respond     99
in a job interview or how to bargain for work hours. These    111
situations call for good communication skills. Some people    123
find it easy to speak up for themselves, but many others      134
frequently receive negative reactions for their attempts.     146
     It is up to you to examine your own needs and learn      156
how to express your ideas or feelings in an effective way.    168
This skill is essential in all dealings with other people.    180
Practice this skill often.                                    185
 | 1 | 2 | 3 | 4 | 5 | 6 | 7 | 8 | 9 | 10 | 11 | 12 SI 1.37
```


Language Arts Connections

Ask students to free write for ten minutes about a time when communication was difficult for them. Who were they trying to communicate with? Why was the communication difficult? Did they feel heard by the other person? Were they listening to the other person? What parts do speakers and listeners play in communication?

SCHOOL TO CAREER

Help students understand that all careers require communication skills by challenging them to name a career where they wouldn't need communication skills. Explain that since the beginning of time, humankind has endeavored to communicate with one another. Have students make a list of ways humans have communicated.

FORMATTING

E. Reversing Lines in Tables

As you learned in Lesson 65, tables are created either without lines (open tables) or with lines (boxed tables). In this lesson, you will reverse this feature in the tables you create.

F. Software Features

STUDENT MANUAL

Table Lines

Study Lesson 91 in your student manual. Complete all the practice activities while at your computer. Then complete the jobs that follow.

WORD PROCESSING APPLICATIONS

TABLE 22

Create a 2-column, 8-row boxed table. Automatically adjust the column widths. Center the table vertically and horizontally.

HOMONYMS	
there	their
allowed	aloud
principal	principle
it's	its
stationery	stationary
forward	foreword
patience	patients

Teacher Notes

TEACH

Activity E. Go over the instructions with students to make sure they understand what they are to do.

Activity F. Explain and demonstrate the Table Lines software feature presented in this lesson.

STUDENT MANUAL

Be sure students turn to the correct lesson in their Student Manual.

Table 22. Ask students how they might use tables in their personal lives. Challenge them to come up with ten applications. Write these on the board. Have students develop a list of other homonyms.

LESSON 91

Table 23. Remind students to center the column headings and to center the table vertically and horizontally.

Table 24. Remind students to center the table vertically and horizontally and to automatically adjust the column widths.

ASSESS

- Monitor students as they complete the Technique Checkpoint and provide individualized assistance as needed.
- Check to see if students are increasing their word a minute speeds as they complete each of the 5-minute timings.
- Make sure students are able to use the Table Lines software feature.
- As students begin typing the tables, walk around the room and point out correct and incorrect formatting to individual students.
- After students finish typing the tables, have them view their work on the screen to see if they made any errors. If errors were made, have students edit their work and make corrections.

CLOSE

If students do not finish the tables during the class period, make sure they save their work so that they can complete it the next time this class meets.

TABLE 23

Create a 4-column, 7-row open table. Center the braced column headings. Center the table vertically and horizontally. Automatically adjust the column widths.

BASEBALL SCHEDULE
July 14, {year}

American League Games		**National League Games**	
Toronto Blue Jays	Cleveland Indians	Atlanta Braves	New York Mets
Minnesota Twins	Detroit Tigers	Florida Marlins	Montreal Expos
Seattle Mariners	Boston Red Sox	Chicago Cubs	Pittsburgh Pirates
Baltimore Orioles	Texas Rangers	Houston Astros	Cincinnati Reds
Oakland Athletics	Anaheim Angels	San Diego Padres	Colorado Rockies

TABLE 24

Create a 2-column, 8-row boxed table. Center the table vertically and horizontally. Automatically adjust the column widths.

HONOR SOCIETY OFFICERS Central High School	
Kathy Chou	President
LaTasha Bennett	Vice President
Marcus Wilson	Secretary
Angel Florez	Treasurer
Holly Koskoski	Reporter
Kahlid Jordan	Historian
Benjamin Hertz	Parliamentarian

*inter*NET CONNECTION

Use the Internet to update Table 23. Determine which cities and/or teams have changed. See if you can find information about why teams have changed cities or changed names over the years.

FACT FILE

Native American tribes spoke different languages and dialects, so to communicate they developed a sign language that is still used today. To say buffalo, for example, the hands are placed on either side of the head with the index fingers slightly hooked. Ask students what sign language they use today to communicate with each other.

LESSON 92 TABLES: BORDERS/FILL

OBJECTIVES:

- Improve keyboarding skill.
- Learn word processing features.
- Format table lines and fill.

A. WARMUP

Type each line 2 times.

Speed	1 We can all speak well if we think about what we are saying.
Accuracy	2 Because he was very lazy, Jake paid for six games and quit.
Language Link	3 The chapter was much longer than she had expected it to be.
Numbers/Symbols	4 Hasn't our July Check #830 for $149.56 been mailed to them?
	| 1 | 2 | 3 | 4 | 5 | 6 | 7 | 8 | 9 | 10 | 11 | 12

SKILLBUILDING

B. 12-SECOND SPRINTS

Take three 12-second timings on each line. Try to increase your speed on each timing.

5 The goal is to do the work we have to do as well as we can.
6 Type at the speed that is well within your zone of control.
7 She can save a lot of time and effort by planning the work.
8 She cannot count on luck as a means of getting ahead today.
| | | | 5 | | | | 10 | | | | 15 | | | | 20 | | | | 25 | | | | 30 | | | | 35 | | | | 40 | | | | 45 | | | | 50 | | | | 55 | | | | 60

FORMATTING

C. BORDERS AND FILL/SHADING

U.S. PRESIDENTS, PARTY, AND YEARS IN OFFICE 1945-1993		
President	**Party**	**Term**
Harry S Truman	Democrat	1945-1953
Dwight D. Eisenhower	Republican	1953-1961
John F. Kennedy	Democrat	1961-1963
Lyndon B. Johnson	Democrat	1963-1969
Richard M. Nixon	Republican	1969-1974
Gerald R. Ford	Republican	1974-1977
James E. Carter, Jr.	Democrat	1977-1981
Ronald W. Reagan	Republican	1981-1989
George H. W. Bush	Republican	1989-1993

To highlight table cells, rows, or columns, you can change borders and add fill or shading to rows or individual cells. You can also delete all of the borders to create an open

LESSON 92

FOCUS

- Use 12-second timings to build speed.
- Learn word processing features: Borders and Shading/Fill.
- Learn how to change borders and add fill or shading to columns, rows, or individual cells in tables.
- Create and type 3-column tables.

BELLRINGER

As soon as students arrive at their workstations and log in, have them type the Warmup. Go over the purpose of each line as shown to the left of the copy.

TEACH

Activity B. Remind students to type at a fast pace during the 12-second timings. At the end of the first and second timings, encourage students to type one or two strokes faster on the next timing.

RESOURCES

 Lesson Plan 92

 Courseware Lesson 92

Student Data Disk

Student Manual

Supplementary Production Activities

Multicultural Activities

TEACH

Activity C. Ask students why they should use 20 percent or less when selecting a fill pattern. (so the cell will be easy to read) Have them experiment with using more than 20 percent.

Activity D. Walk around the room while students are completing Lesson 92 in their Student Manuals. Make sure they understand what they are to do and that they are doing the assignment correctly.

STUDENT MANUAL

Be sure students turn to the correct lesson in their Student Manual.

TEACH

Table 25. Remind students to change the lines above and below the column headings to double lines.

Social Studies Connections

Have students work with Table 25 and choose one of the presidents to research. Have them create a table that includes the president's name, party affiliation, term, a few keywords about his platform, and one other fact of the student's choice. Post these tables around the room.

U.S. PRESIDENTS, PARTY, AND YEARS IN OFFICE 1945-1993		
President	Party	Term
Harry S Truman	Democrat	1945-1953
Dwight D. Eisenhower	Republican	1953-1961
John F. Kennedy	Democrat	1961-1963
Lyndon B. Johnson	Democrat	1963-1969
Richard M. Nixon	Republican	1969-1974
Gerald R. Ford	Republican	1974-1977
James E. Carter, Jr.	Democrat	1977-1981
Ronald W. Reagan	Republican	1981-1989
George H. W. Bush	Republican	1989-1993

table. In Illustration 1 on page 333, a different line style was used to separate the table title from the columns. In Illustration 2, column-heading cells were highlighted with 20 percent shading.

When you select a fill pattern or shading, use 20 percent or less so that any text in the cell will be easy to read.

D. Software Features

STUDENT MANUAL

Borders and Shading/Fill

Study Lesson 92 in your student manual. Complete all the practice activities while at your computer. Then complete the jobs that follow.

WORD PROCESSING APPLICATIONS

TABLE 25

Create a 3-column, 11-row boxed table. Adjust the column widths so they look similar to the illustration. Center the table vertically and horizontally. Change the lines above and below the column headings to double lines. Center the column headngs.

Social Studies Connections

U.S. PRESIDENTS, PARTY, AND YEARS IN OFFICE 1945–1993		
President	**Party**	**Term**
Harry S Truman	Democrat	1945–1953
Dwight D. Eisenhower	Republican	1953–1961
John F. Kennedy	Democrat	1961–1963
Lyndon B. Johnson	Democrat	1963–1969
Richard M. Nixon	Republican	1969–1974
Gerald R. Ford	Republican	1974–1977
James E. Carter, Jr.	Democrat	1977–1981
Ronald W. Reagan	Republican	1981–1989
George H. W. Bush	Republican	1989–1993

SOCIAL STUDIES CONNECTIONS

Gerald Ford, who succeeded Richard Nixon as president, was the first U.S. president who was never elected to the office of president or vice president.

Science Connections

Have students research average monthly temperatures for your community. Research can be done through the Internet, library, or by contacting a local radio or television station. Create a table of average monthly temperatures for your community.

interNET ACTIVITY

Have students access the Website for a sports team. The team can be a local or professional team. Ask students to create a table similar to Table 27 that lists the date of games, the name of the team, and where the team will play each game.

TABLE 26

Create a 3-column, 14-row boxed table. Add 20 percent shading to the column heading row. Center the table vertically and horizontally. Adjust the column widths so that all columns are equal.

FACT FILE

The highest recorded temperature was 136.4 degrees in El Azizia, Libya, on September 13, 1932.

AVERAGE MONTHLY TEMPERATURES Anchorage, Alaska		
Month	**High**	**Low**
January	20	6
February	27	10
March	34	16
April	44	27
May	55	36
June	63	45
July	65	49
August	64	47
September	56	40
October	43	29
November	29	16
December	20	7

TABLE 27

Create a 3-column, 8-row boxed table. Add 20-percent shading to the column-heading row. Center the table vertically and horizontally. Automatically adjust the column widths. Add a double line above and below the column headings and to the left and right of the center column.

GIRLS' TRACK SCHEDULE Spring Hills High School		
Date	**School**	**Location**
March 3	Walton City High School	Home
March 10	Peachtree Heights Academy	Away
March 16	Bentwood Day Academy	Away
March 22	Trenton Valley High School	Home
March 27	J. C. Carlton High School	Away
March 30	Addison County High School	Home

LESSON 92

TEACH

Table 27. Remind students to add 20-percent shading to the column heading row.

ASSESS

- Check to see if students are increasing their word a minute speeds as they complete each of the 12-second timings.
- Make sure students are able to use the Borders and Shading/Fill software features.
- As students begin typing the tables, walk around the room and point out correct and incorrect formatting to individual students.
- After students finish typing the tables, have them view their work on the screen to see if they made any errors. If errors were made, have students edit their work and make corrections.

CLOSE

If students do not finish the tables during the class period, make sure they save their work so that they can complete it the next time this class meets.

Remind students to clean up their workstation when they leave.

Teacher Notes

LESSON 93

FOCUS

- Compose short paragraph answers for the Language Link activity.
- Use 5-minute timings to build speed.
- Practice creating and typing 3-column tables.

BELLRINGER

As soon as students arrive at their workstations and log in, have them type the Warmup. Go over the purpose of each line as shown to the left of the copy.

TEACH

Activity B. After students have completed one of the sentence fragments, have several read their selections aloud in class. Inform students that reading their writing aloud will help them catch errors.

Solutions: Answers will vary

LESSON 93

REINFORCEMENT: TABLES

OBJECTIVES:

- Compose at the keyboard.
- Type 37/5'/5e.
- Review table formats.

A. WARMUP

Type each line 2 times.

Speed	1	Some people seem to have more hours in the day than others.
Accuracy	2	Jeff quietly moved a dozen boxes last night by power truck.
Language Link	3	First we washed our hands, then it was time to enjoy lunch.
Numbers/Symbols	4	The invoice #740 for $189.32 is subject to a 6.5% discount.

| 1 | 2 | 3 | 4 | 5 | 6 | 7 | 8 | 9 | 10 | 11 | 12

B. COMPOSING AT THE KEYBOARD

Choose one of the scenarios below and complete it. Then continue composing until you have created a short paragraph of several sentences.

5 My friend and I were walking home after class when all of a sudden we saw . . .

6 I was driving home when I hit a patch of ice on the road. Next thing I knew . . .

7 Several of us were hiking up the steep mountain path when all of a sudden . . .

8 The building started to shake. As soon as I realized it was an earthquake, I . . .

interNET CONNECTION

Use the Internet site http://wwwneic.cr.usgs.gov/ to gather information from the National Earthquake Information Center, which is located 10 miles west of Denver, Colorado. Find out when and where the last earthquake in the world occurred. Find out when the largest earthquake in the United States occurred.

RESOURCES

 Lesson Plan 93

 Courseware Lesson 93

Student Data Disk

Student Manual

Reteaching and Reinforcement

Grading and Evaluation

C. Preview Practice

Type each line 2 times as a preview to the timings that follow.

Accuracy who next rapid strong require training relations innovative
Speed technology graduates creative economy growth swift grow for

D. 5-Minute Timings

Take two 5-minute timings on the paragraphs. Note your speed and errors.

Goal: 37/5'/5e

Many factors are changing the workplace as we move 10
into the next century. A strong force in the economy at 22
this time is the rapid growth in the information industry. 33
The picture for employment is quickly being changed by 44
advances in technology. Just a few years ago, high school 56
graduates who were trained in most business skills could 67
be hired in entry jobs and grow in these same fields with 79
little or no more training. 85

This is no longer true. Most office jobs now require 95
workers with creative and innovative talents as well as 107
good human relations and computer skills. Many technical 118
school and college students are soon realizing that most 129
of the skills they have learned may be outdated in five 141
or six years because of these swift changes. The world of 152
work is being changed so fast that workers must be willing 164
and able to adapt. The workers who will be able to compete 176
are going to be those who are learners for life. 185

| 1 | 2 | 3 | 4 | 5 | 6 | 7 | 8 | 9 | 10 | 11 | 12 SI 1.40

TEACH

Activity C. Point out that words in the Preview Practice are used in the timing that follows.

Activity D. Remind students that they should try to improve speed with each 5-minute timing. The goal for these timings is to type 37 words a minute for 5 minutes with no more than 5 errors.

JOURNAL ENTRY

Have students write about how they feel about learning. What do they enjoy about learning? What do they not enjoy about learning. How might learning add to their lives 10 years from now? 20 years? 50 years?

TEACH

Table 28. Remind students to adjust their table so it looks similar to the one in the text.

Table 29. Remind students to add a double line between each of the columns and shade the column-heading row with a 10-percent fill.

WORD PROCESSING APPLICATIONS

TABLE 28

Create a 3-column, 8-row boxed table. Shade the column-heading row and the single performance cells with 20-percent shading. Change the lines above and below the column-heading row to double lines. Center the table vertically and horizontally. Adjust the column widths so that your table looks similar to the illustration.

ALEXANDER THEATER Fall Performance Dates		
Name of Show	**Day/Date**	**Time**
Learning Rainbow	Monday–Friday	2:30 p.m.–3:00 p.m.
The Science Guru	Monday–Friday	4:00 p.m.–4:30 p.m.
Hooping It Up	November 15	10:30 a.m.–11:00 a.m.
All Against Violence	October 16	3:30 p.m.–5:00 p.m.
Rock and Roll Times	Sunday–Thursday	8:00 p.m.–10:00 p.m.
Magic Schoolroom	Sundays	10:30 a.m.–11:00 a.m.

TABLE 29

Create a 3-column, 9-row boxed table. Center the column headings. Add a double line between each of the columns. Shade the column-heading row with a 10 percent fill. Automatically adjust the column widths.

LBO'S HAMBURGER STAND Calorie Count for Selected Menu Items		
Sandwich Item	**Calories**	**Calories From Fat**
Lucy's Grilled Chicken	290	6
Barbey's Chicken Lite	276	7
Barbey's Lite Beef	294	10
Lucy's Junior Burger	270	9
O'Brien's Lean Burger	320	10
BQ Broiler Chicken	280	10
Andy's Turkey Lite	260	6

Out-of-Class Activity

Provide students with a copy of this week's menu from your school cafeteria. Have them make a table with the menu information. Add two additional columns for the day and date. Then have students make up a table of the foods they would like to eat for lunch for one week.

Science Connections

Have students collect menus from their favorite fast-food restaurants. Then have them make a table with the menu information that includes the following column headings: name of food, calories, calories from fat, other nutritional information.

TABLE 30

Create a 3-column, 10-row boxed table. Center the table vertically and horizontally. Center the column headings and add 10 percent shading. Add a double line below the column headings.Automatically adjust the column widths.

DOUGLAS COUNTY STAR STUDENTS
(Highest Grade Point Averages)

Student	School	Teacher
Richard Milton	Lakewood High School	Katherine Godwin
Leslie Littlefield	Green Meadow Academy	Daniel L. Smithers
Marilyn Edenfield	Trapp High School	Clemmons Watson
Larry Adamson	J. W. Briggs High School	Francis Jackson
Brock Simpson	Coosa Mountain Academy	Bernadette Franklin
Marie Teakwitha	Lithia Springs High School	Alton Williamson
Wesley Kaufman	Chappel Hill High School	Anna Ford
Edward Wue	Edison High School	Rebecca Thompson

FACT FILE

Did you know that fjords are deep, narrow valleys that stretch inland from the coasts of northern Europe, Scandinavia, and South America? Fjords were carved by huge glaciers that descended from mountains. As the glaciers flowed seaward, their enormous weight carved deep valleys—some more than 300 feet deep.

Teacher Notes

LESSON 93

TEACH

Table 30. Remind students to add a double line below the column headings and a 10-percent shading over the centered column headings.

ASSESS

- Review the accuracy of students' responses to the questions in the Lanugage Link composing activity.
- Check to see if students are increasing their word a minute speeds as they complete each of the 5-minute timings.
- As students begin typing the tables, walk around the room and point out correct and incorrect formatting to individual students.
- After students finish typing the tables, have them view their work on the screen to see if they made any errors. If errors were made, have students edit their work and make corrections.

CLOSE

If students do not finish the tables during the class period, make sure they save their work so that they can complete it the next time this class meets.

Remind students to clean up their workstation when they leave.

LESSON 94

FOCUS

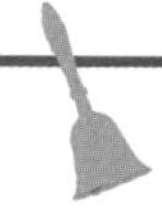

- Use 30-second OK timings to improve accuracy.
- Use the Pretest/Practice/Posttest routine to build speed and accuracy.
- Learn a word processing feature: Page Orientation.
- Format and type tables in landscape orientation.

BELLRINGER

As soon as students arrive at their workstations and log in, have them type the Warmup. Go over the purpose of each line as shown to the left of the copy.

TEACH

Activity B. Ask students which of these words is most difficult for them. Give them the following tip for "to" and "too": Too, which means also, has an extra o in it.

Solutions: Sean passed the cycle driver too quickly to see who he was.

From past experience, I have learned how to handle the job.

The two sisters were much too shy to go to the party alone.

Don said that he will go to the committee meeting tomorrow.

TABLES: PAGE ORIENTATION

OBJECTIVES:

- Improve keyboarding skill.
- Recognize confusing words.
- Format tables in landscape orientation.

A. WARMUP

Type each line 2 times.

```
Speed              1 We have to learn to make introductions with poise and ease.
Accuracy           2 Mo brought back five or six dozen pieces of quaint jewelry.
Language Link      3 The trip to Grandma's house was farther than they expected.
Numbers/Symbols    4 She will visit our top offices (#1 & #2): DALLAS & EL PASO.
                     | 1 | 2 | 3 | 4 | 5 | 6 | 7 | 8 | 9 | 10 | 11 | 12
```

B. CONFUSING WORDS

Study the confusing words and their meanings below. Then edit lines 5–8 by selecting the correct word.

passed (v.) past tense of *pass;* move beyond; transfer of ownership; to be approved; surpass; to happen

past (adj.) elapsed; former
(adv.) beyond
(n.) time before the present

to (prep.) toward
too (adv.) besides, also
two (adj.) one more than one

As we passed the house, we had fond memories of the past.
He too left to shop at the two stores.

RESOURCES

 Lesson Plan 94

 Courseware Lesson 94

Student Data Disk

Student Manual

Supplementary Production Activities

5 Sean (passed, past) the cycle driver (to, too, two) quickly to see who he was.
6 From (passed, past) experience, I have learned how (to, too, two) handle the job.
7 The (to, too, two) sisters were much (to, too, two) shy to go (to, too, two) the party alone.
8 Don said that he will go (to, too, two) the committee meeting tomorrow.

SKILLBUILDING

C. 30-Second OK Timings

Take two 30-second OK (error-free) timings on lines 9–10. Then take two 30-second OK timings on lines 11–12. Goal: no errors.

```
 9      We are expecting two quite sizable contracts in June      11
10  from Houston Federal Credit Union and Yonkers Savings Bank.   23

11      They were amazed that they were able to cut expenses      11
12  so quickly by reducing their television advertising budget.  23
    | 1 | 2 | 3 | 4 | 5 | 6 | 7 | 8 | 9 | 10 | 11 | 12
```

FORMATTING

D. Tables: Page Orientation

The default page orientation for 8.5- × 11-inch paper is vertical, or **portrait.** A page may also be formatted in horizontal orientation, or **landscape.**

E. Software Features

STUDENT MANUAL

Page Orientation

Study Lesson 94 in your student manual. Complete all the practice activities while at your computer. Then complete the jobs that follow.

LESSON 94

TEACH

Activity C. Remind students that their goal for 30-second OK timings is improved speed with each of the timings.

Activity D. Ask students which direction portrait orientation is. (vertical) Which direction is landscape? (horizontal)

Activity E. Have students turn to Lesson 94 in their Student Manual and read the explanation for Page Orientation. Then have them complete the practice activities that follow.

STUDENT MANUAL

Be sure students turn to the correct lesson in their Student Manual.

Multiple Learning Styles

Visual learners see pictures in their minds. Have students close their eyes. Read the following and ask if they can see the picture: "In the dark of night, I walk into the open meadow. A canopy of stars lights the sky. On a full moon night the light washes over Earth and I see past the horizon."

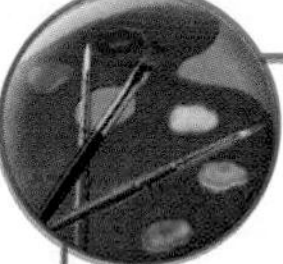

Art Connections

Native American art was also useful. A headdress of buffalo horns, eagle feathers, and horse hair was worn during the Buffalo Dance, a ceremony to lure the herds within hunting range. Have students create art objects that reflect their lives.

TEACH

Table 31. Remind students to use landscape orientation, to insert a double line below the column headings, and to use 20-percent shading for the column-heading row.

TABLE 31

Change the paper orientation to landscape. Then create a boxed table with 5 columns and 12 rows. Center the table vertically and horizontally. Insert a double line below the column headings and use 20-percent fill/shading for the column-heading row. Center the column headings and align text columns at the left and number columns at the right. Automatically adjust the column widths.

TOP TEN GEORGIA OCCUPATIONS
(Ranked by Growth Rate)

Rank	Occupation	Annual Growth Rate (%)	1990 Employment	Average Job Openings
1	Home Health Aides	10.0	3,310	388
2	Computer Engineers	7.6	1,410	137
3	Physical Therapists	6.4	2,000	172
4	Systems Analysts	6.2	11,160	789
5	Technical Writers	5.3	1,190	88
6	Physical Therapy Assistants	5.3	1,450	90
7	Medical Assistants	4.9	4,880	285
8	Medical Secretaries	4.8	4,970	351
9	Surgical Technicians	4.8	1,170	66
10	Respiratory Therapists	4.6	1,680	114

interNET ACTIVITY

Have students search or check the Website for My Future (www.myfuture.com) to explore the growth rate of five careers that interest them. Have students then make a table that includes pertinent information about the careers.

Career Exploration

Have students write a short paragraph about each career they researched in the interNet Activity on this page. Paragraphs should tell about the career, what education is needed, its growth potential, and what interests the student.

TABLE 32

Change the paper orientation to landscape. Then create a 4-column, 7-row boxed table. Center the table vertically and horizontally. Shade the column-heading row with 20 percent fill. Center all column headings. Align the first column on the left; align the remaining columns at the center. Note that the column heading in the first column is only a single line and the other column headings are 2 and 3 lines. Press ENTER 2 times before typing the first column heading and 1 time before typing the last one. Adjust the column widths so that the entries in column 1 are on a single line.

FIVE FASTEST-GROWING CAREERS FOR THE 21ST CENTURY (Requiring a College Degree)			
Career	**% Increase in Positions by 2005**	**Average Starting Pay ($) for 1994 Grads**	**Recommended College Degree**
Computer Scientist/ Systems Analyst	79	33,957	Computer Science
Physical Therapist	76	31,432	Health Sciences
Psychologist	64	20,270	Psychology
Marketing Manager	47	24,721	Marketing
Preschool Teacher	41	17,393	Education

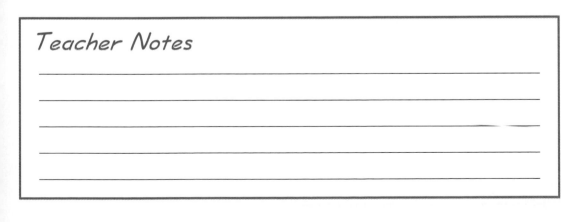

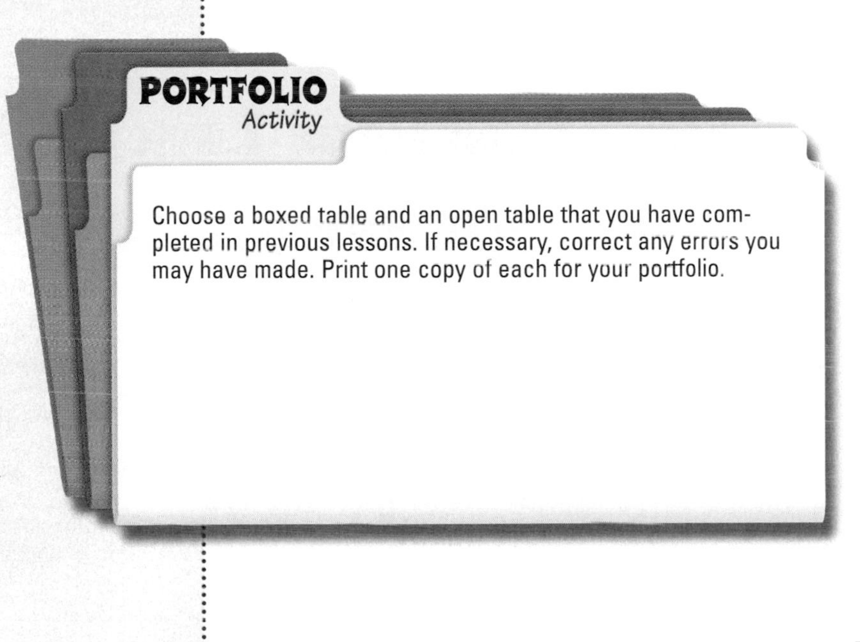

Choose a boxed table and an open table that you have completed in previous lessons. If necessary, correct any errors you may have made. Print one copy of each for your portfolio.

Teacher Notes

LESSON 94

TEACH

Table 32. Ask students which direction landscape orientation is. Remind them to align the first column on the left.

ASSESS

- Check to see if students are completing 30-second OK timings without any errors.
- Watch students as they complete the Language Link activity to see if they choose the correct words.
- Make sure students are able to change the page orientation.
- As students begin typing the tables, walk around the room and point out correct and incorrect formatting to individual students.
- After students finish typing the tables, have them view their work on the screen to see if they made any errors. If errors were made, have students edit their work and make corrections.

CLOSE

If students do not finish the tables during the class period, make sure they save their work so that they can complete it the next time this class meets.

Remind students to clean up their workstation when they leave.

LESSON 95

FOCUS

- Apply the Language Link rule for using quotation marks with direct quotes.
- Use a Pretest/Practice/Posttest routine to build speed and accuracy.
- Learn how to add and delete columns and rows in tables.

BELLRINGER

As soon as students arrive at their workstations and log in, have them type the Warmup. Go over the purpose of each line as shown to the left of the copy.

TEACH

Activity B. Explain the rule about using quotation marks with direct quotes, then have students complete the activity.

Solutions: Mrs. Woo said, "Rea is being considered for the promotion."

"Yes, Jill, you're still in the running," replied Ms. Paul.

Ben cried, "Someone stole the library book I need tomorrow."

Diane asked me, "When did they come to take your computer?"

TABLES: ADD/DELETE COLUMNS AND ROWS

OBJECTIVES:

- Learn about quotation marks.
- Improve keyboarding speed and accuracy.
- Format tables in landscape format.
- Add and delete columns and rows.

A. WARMUP

Type each line 2 times.

Speed	1 Business law governs transactions in the world of business.
Accuracy	2 Had Jeff's size helped him to win quickly over Gene Baxter?
Language Link	3 It takes two hands to flatten out the dough for pizza, too.
Symbols	4 The word court can be a location. (I'll see them in court!)
	| 1 | 2 | 3 | 4 | 5 | 6 | 7 | 8 | 9 | 10 | 11 | 12

B. QUOTATION MARKS WITH DIRECT QUOTATIONS

Study the rule and examples below. Then edit lines 5–8 to correct any errors in the use of quotation marks.

Rule 20: Use quotation marks to enclose a **direct quotation,** that is, the exact words of a speaker or a writer.

Robert said, "That is the highest grade on this project."

5 Mrs. Woo said, Rea is being considered for the promotion.
6 Yes, Jill, you're still in the running, replied Ms. Paul.
7 Ben cried, Someone stole the library book I need tomorrow.
8 Diane asked me, When did they come to take your computer?

RESOURCES

 Lesson Plan 95

 Courseware Lesson 95

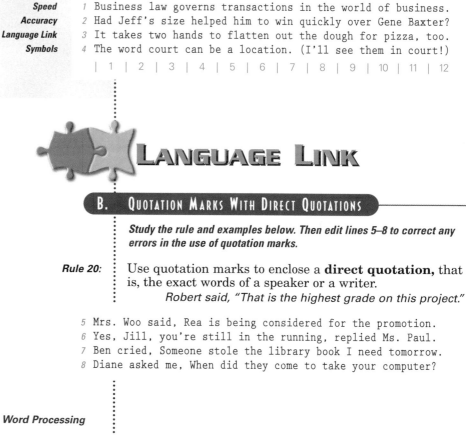

Student Data Disk

Student Manual

Language Link Worksheets

Supplementary Production Activities

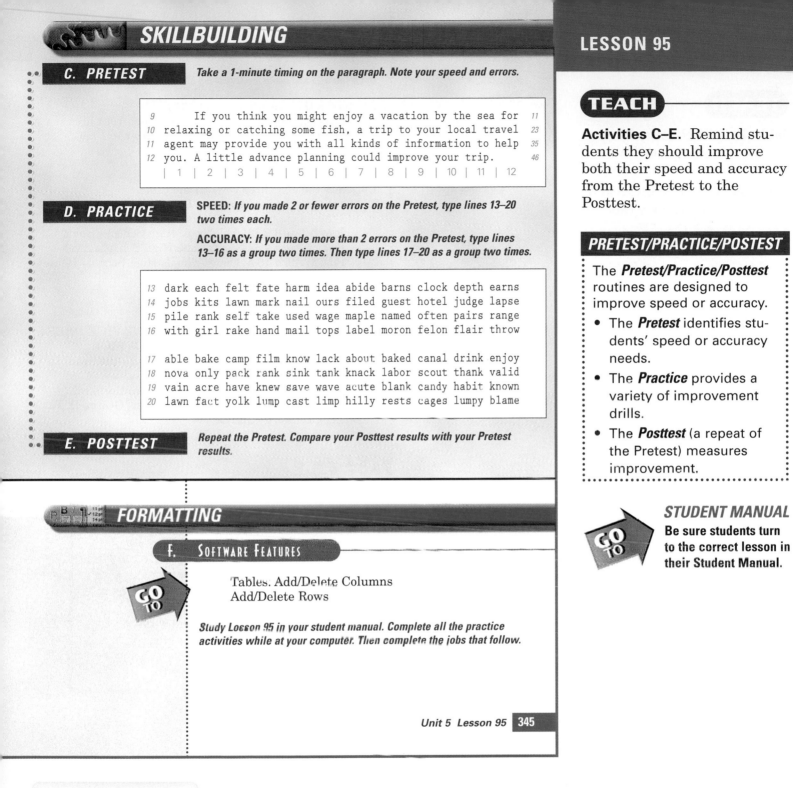

SKILLBUILDING

C. PRETEST *Take a 1-minute timing on the paragraph. Note your speed and errors.*

```
9       If you think you might enjoy a vacation by the sea for   11
10  relaxing or catching some fish, a trip to your local travel  23
11  agent may provide you with all kinds of information to help  35
12  you. A little advance planning could improve your trip.      46
    | 1 | 2 | 3 | 4 | 5 | 6 | 7 | 8 | 9 | 10 | 11 | 12
```

D. PRACTICE SPEED: *If you made 2 or fewer errors on the Pretest, type lines 13–20 two times each.*

ACCURACY: *If you made more than 2 errors on the Pretest, type lines 13–16 as a group two times. Then type lines 17–20 as a group two times.*

```
13  dark each felt fate harm idea abide barns clock depth earns
14  jobs kits lawn mark nail ours filed guest hotel judge lapse
15  pile rank self take used wage maple named often pairs range
16  with girl rake hand mail tops label moron felon flair throw

17  able bake camp film know lack about baked canal drink enjoy
18  nova only pack rank sink tank knack labor scout thank valid
19  vain acre have knew save wave acute blank candy habit known
20  lawn fact yolk lump cast limp hilly rests cages lumpy blame
```

E. POSTTEST *Repeat the Pretest. Compare your Posttest results with your Pretest results.*

FORMATTING

F. SOFTWARE FEATURES

Tables: Add/Delete Columns
Add/Delete Rows

Study Lesson 95 in your student manual. Complete all the practice activities while at your computer. Then complete the jobs that follow.

TEACH

Activities C–E. Remind students they should improve both their speed and accuracy from the Pretest to the Posttest.

PRETEST/PRACTICE/POSTTEST

The ***Pretest/Practice/Posttest*** routines are designed to improve speed or accuracy.

- The ***Pretest*** identifies students' speed or accuracy needs.
- The ***Practice*** provides a variety of improvement drills.
- The ***Posttest*** (a repeat of the Pretest) measures improvement.

STUDENT MANUAL

Be sure students turn to the correct lesson in their Student Manual.

FACT FILE

Eskimos have many names for snow. "Apun" means snow on the ground; "mauja" means soft snow; "pukak" means snow that causes avalanches; "oaliq" means snow that collects on trees; and "oannik" means snowflake.

TEACH

Table 33. Check to make sure students have opened Table 25.

Table 34. Check to make sure students have opened Table 27.

Table 35. Check to make sure students have opened Table 33.

ASSESS

- Watch students as they complete the Language Link activity to see if they are able to apply the rule correctly.
- Check to see if students show signs of improvement from the Pretest to the Posttest.
- As students begin typing the tables, walk around the room and point out correct and incorrect formatting to individual students.
- After students finish typing the tables, have them view their work on the screen to see if they made any errors. If errors were made, have students edit their work and make corrections.

CLOSE

If students do not finish the tables during the class period, make sure they save their work so that they can complete it the next time this class meets.

WORD PROCESSING APPLICATIONS

TABLE 33

Open Table 25 and make the following changes:

1. Change the subtitle to 1969-1993.
2. Fill the column-heading cells with 20-percent fill.
3. Delete the rows representing years prior to 1969.

TABLE 34

Open Table 27 and make the following changes:

1. Delete the last three rows in the table.
2. Insert three new rows at the bottom of the table and add the following information:
   Row 6: April 7 / Pebblebrook High School / Home
   Row 7: April 12 / North Cobb High School / Away
   Row 8: April 15 / Dorsett Shoals High School / Home

TABLE 35

Open Table 33 and make the following changes:

1. Change the orientation to landscape.
2. Change the title to **U.S. PRESIDENTS, VICE PRESIDENTS, PARTY, AND YEARS IN OFFICE.**
3. Insert a new column after column A with the heading **Vice President**.
4. Add the following entries to the column: Gerald R. Ford, Spiro T. Agnew, Walter F. Mondale, George H. W. Bush, J. Danforth Quayle.

FACT FILE

The White House in which U.S. presidents live has 3 elevators, 5 major floors, 2 basements, 7 staircases, 12 chimneys, 32 bathrooms, 132 rooms, 160 windows, and 412 doors. Here are some other interesting facts about the White House. The first baby born in the White House was Thomas Jefferson's grandson in 1806. The first wedding at the White House was for Dolly Madison's sister in 1812. Cows grazed on the front lawn of the White House until 1913. The only president married in the White House was Grover Cleveland in 1886.

Teacher Notes

TOTALS IN TABLES

OBJECTIVES:
- Increase keyboarding skills.
- Use the SUM formula feature in tables.
- Reinforce the use of lines in tables.

A. WARMUP

Type each line 2 times.

Speed	1	Our world is very different now from the way it used to be.
Accuracy	2	Six big men quickly won over Jeff despite his greater size.
Language Link	3	Mom said, "Who wants cake?" to which Becky replied, "I do."
Numbers/Symbols	4	Invoice #23654, dated March 19, for 73 A-18 was 2/10, n/30.

| 1 | 2 | 3 | 4 | 5 | 6 | 7 | 8 | 9 | 10 | 11 | 12

FACT FILE

We live in a galaxy called the Milky Way. The Milky Way is made up of about 400 billion stars of which our Sun is one. There are many other galaxies in the universe, but one of the closest ones is the Andromeda Galaxy which is 2 million light years away.

SKILLBUILDING

B. PRETEST

Take a 1-minute timing on the paragraph. Note your speed and errors.

```
     Effective writing always involves the choice of words     11
and expressions. Sentences may express similar ideas, but      23
style is what makes the words affect readers in different      35
ways. Your style should be appropriate to your subject.        46
| 1 | 2 | 3 | 4 | 5 | 6 | 7 | 8 | 9 | 10 | 11 | 12
```


RESOURCES

- Lesson Plan 96
- Courseware Lesson 96
- Student Data Disk
- Student Manual
- Supplementary Production Activities

LESSON 96

FOCUS

- Use a Pretest/Practice/Posttest routine to build speed and accuracy.
- Use Diagnostic Practice to identify areas that need improvement.
- Learn a word processing feature: Formulas.
- Learn how to use the SUM function in tables.

BELLRINGER

As soon as students arrive at their workstations and log in, have them type the Warmup. Go over the purpose of each line as shown to the left of the copy.

TEACH

Activities B–D. Remind students they should improve both their speed and accuracy from the Pretest to the Posttest.

PRETEST/PRACTICE/POSTEST

The ***Pretest/Practice/Posttest*** routines are designed to improve speed or accuracy.

- The ***Pretest*** identifies students' speed or accuracy needs.
- The ***Practice*** provides a variety of improvement drills.
- The ***Posttest*** (a repeat of the Pretest) measures improvement.

TEACH

Activity E. Make sure that students understand that this Diagnostic Practice activity is designed to help identify areas that need improvement and provide needed practice.

Activity F. Explain that the SUM function is a formula that may be inserted into a table cell to add a row or column of numbers.

Activity G. Walk around the room while students are completing Lesson 96 in their Student Manuals. Make sure they understand what they are to do and that they are doing the assignment correctly.

STUDENT MANUAL

Be sure students turn to the correct lesson in their Student Manual.

C. PRACTICE

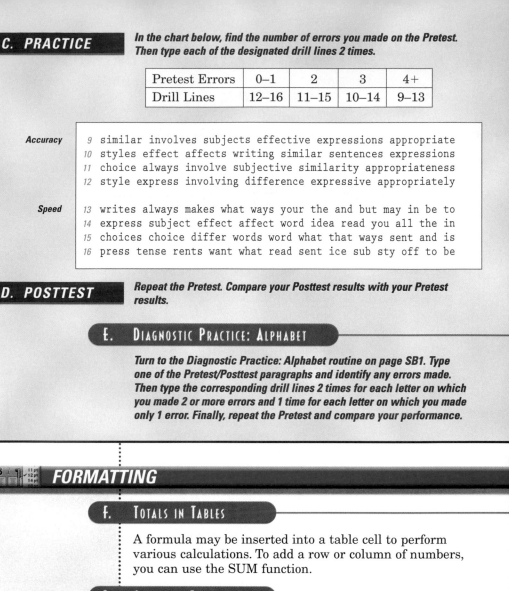

In the chart below, find the number of errors you made on the Pretest. Then type each of the designated drill lines 2 times.

Pretest Errors	0–1	2	3	4+
Drill Lines	12–16	11–15	10–14	9–13

Accuracy

```
 9 similar involves subjects effective expressions appropriate
10 styles effect affects writing similar sentences expressions
11 choice always involve subjective similarity appropriateness
12 style express involving difference expressive appropriately
```

Speed

```
13 writes always makes what ways your the and but may in be to
14 express subject effect affect word idea read you all the in
15 choices choice differ words word what that ways sent and is
16 press tense rents want what read sent ice sub sty off to be
```

D. POSTTEST

Repeat the Pretest. Compare your Posttest results with your Pretest results.

E. DIAGNOSTIC PRACTICE: ALPHABET

Turn to the Diagnostic Practice: Alphabet routine on page SB1. Type one of the Pretest/Posttest paragraphs and identify any errors made. Then type the corresponding drill lines 2 times for each letter on which you made 2 or more errors and 1 time for each letter on which you made only 1 error. Finally, repeat the Pretest and compare your performance.

FORMATTING

F. TOTALS IN TABLES

A formula may be inserted into a table cell to perform various calculations. To add a row or column of numbers, you can use the SUM function.

G. SOFTWARE FEATURES

STUDENT MANUAL

Formulas

Study Lesson 96 in your student manual. Complete all the practice activities while at your computer. Then complete the jobs that follow.

Math Connections

Point out Table 36 on page 349 to students. Have them add the numbers in the second and third columns without using SUM. Then have students add the same numbers using SUM. Discuss how much easier it is to use SUM.

Multiple Learning Styles

Have students type flash cards for table formatting and word processing skills. On one side type a word or process; on the other side type the directions. Ask students to choose a partner. One partner holds up the side of the card with the word or process. The other partner explains the directions.

TABLE 36

Create a 3-column, 8-row boxed table. Center the column headings. Center the table vertically and horizontally, and automatically adjust the columns. Total columns 2 and 3.

QUARTERLY SALES REPORT First Quarter		
Salesperson	**Quarterly Total ($)**	**Quarterly Average ($)**
Cochran, Richard	34,757	11,586
Duffy, Theodora	39,154	15,829
Frances, Parker	49,721	16,778
Hebert, Theresa	43,198	13,862
Minichiello, Pat	40,500	13,754
TOTAL		

TABLE 37

***Open Table 31. Insert a TOTAL row after the last entry. Join cells A13, B13, and C13. Change the alignment in the joined cell to left. Delete the left and right borders in cell D13. In cell A13, type* TOTAL EMPLOYMENT. *Format cell D13 with commas and no decimal places. Then calculate a total for* 1990 Employment.**

TABLE 38

***Open Table 29. Insert a TOTAL row after the last entry. Place a double line above the last row in the table. In cell A10, type* TOTAL CALORIES. *Format cells B10 and C10 with commas and no decimal places. Then calculate totals for* Calories *and* Calories From Fat.**

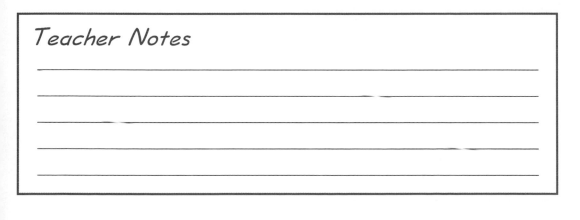

interNET CONNECTION

Use the Internet to search for information on calories and fats in your favorite foods. You may want to try the Website http://www.vitality.com/ to learn more about health and fitness. Write a brief summary of your findings, and share your findings with the class.

TEACH

Table 36. Remind students to use the SUM function to total columns 2 and 3.

Table 37. Suggest to students they read the directions once for overall comprehension.

Table 38. While students work, walk around the room to make sure each student understands the directions and is completing the activity correctly.

ASSESS

- Check to see if students show signs of improvement from the Pretest to the Posttest.
- Monitor students as they complete Diagnostic Practice and provide individualized assistance as needed.
- As students begin typing the tables, walk around the room and point out correct and incorrect formatting to individual students.
- After students finish typing the tables, have them view their work on the screen to see if they made any errors.

CLOSE

If students do not finish the tables during the class period, make sure they save their work so that they can complete it the next time this class meets.

Teacher Notes

LESSON 97

FOCUS

- Use a Pretest/Practice/Posttest routine to build speed and accuracy.
- Practice creating and typing tables.

BELLRINGER

As soon as students arrive at their workstations and log in, have them type the Warmup. Go over the purpose of each line as shown to the left of the copy.

TEACH

Activity B. Remind students they should improve both their speed and accuracy from the Pretest to the Posttest.

LESSON 97 REVIEW

OBJECTIVES:

- Improve keyboarding skill.
- Review tables with sums.

A. WARMUP

Type each line 2 times.

Speed	1	You must work very hard at this job to improve your skills.
Accuracy	2	Brown jars would prevent the mixture from freezing quickly.
Language Link	3	The president said, "Let's give support to our leadership."
Numbers/Symbols	4	The L & C 10 3/4% bonds (due 2013) are at 175; bid 169 3/8.

| 1 | 2 | 3 | 4 | 5 | 6 | 7 | 8 | 9 | 10 | 11 | 12

FACT FILE

According to the Guinness Book of World Records, Shakuntala Devi completed the fastest mathematical computation in June 1980. She multiplied (in her head!) two randomly selected 13-digit numbers in just 28 seconds. A computer can accomplish this same feat in less than one second.

SKILLBUILDING

B. PRETEST

Take a 1-minute timing on the paragraph. Note your speed and errors.

5 A spreadsheet is a useful software tool if you know 11
6 how to use one. You can save hours of effort if you are 22
7 required to work with rows and columns of numbers by using 34
8 formulas to add, subtract, multiply, and divide numbers. 45

| 1 | 2 | 3 | 4 | 5 | 6 | 7 | 8 | 9 | 10 | 11 | 12

RESOURCES

 Lesson Plan 97
Courseware Lesson 97
Student Data Disk
Student Manual
Reteaching and Reinforcement
Grading and Evaluation

C. PRACTICE

In the chart below, find the number of errors you made on the Pretest. Then type each of the designated drill lines 2 times.

Pretest Errors	0–1	2	3	4+
Drill Lines	12–16	11–15	10–14	9–13

Accuracy

```
 9 useful column divide multiply formulas required spreadsheet
10 work using useful effort subtract numbers software required
11 numbs numeric division formulate subtraction multiplication
12 actions addition columnar requisite effortless requisitions
```

Speed

```
13 column meets with will used know kind for one use and of by
14 tool soft save hour form ware sheet one can use add row how
15 working rowing tools knows your full cane can you use if to
16 subs work add use the add are you how add it an if is on or
```

D. POSTTEST

Repeat the Pretest. Compare your Posttest results with your Pretest results.

WORD PROCESSING APPLICATIONS

TABLE 39

Create a 5-column, 7-row boxed table in landscape orientation. Shade the column headings with 20 percent fill. Insert a double line below the column headings. Align the entries in columns 1, 2, and 5 on the left; align the entries in columns 3 and 4 on the right. Adjust the column widths so that all entries fit on a single line.

DATA WORKS, INC.
Monthly Hardware Purchases
April {year}

Customer Name	Account No.	Price	Telephone No.	Item Description
Ferstad, Rhonda	F901-76-3488	535.75	505-555-8900	17″ .42 mm flat screen monitor
Keller, Tenille	K854-00-3550	375.99	505-555-3409	24-bit color scanner
LaBerge, Paul	L258-04-3891	325.75	505-555-7833	Color laser printer
Persson, Andrew	P789-00-3548	98.99	505-555-6673	10X CD-ROM drive
Toring, Jan	T901-75-3487	315.95	505-555-7834	15″ .28 mm flat screen monitor

TEACH

Activities C–D. Remind students they should improve both their speed and accuracy from the Pretest to the Posttest.

PRETEST/PRACTICE/POSTTEST

The ***Pretest/Practice/Posttest*** routines are designed to improve speed or accuracy.

- The ***Pretest*** identifies students' speed or accuracy needs.
- The ***Practice*** provides a variety of improvement drills.
- The ***Posttest*** (a repeat of the Pretest) measures improvement.

JOURNAL ENTRY

Have students write about important moments in their lives. Ask them to add another entry about what connection to careers these moments might have. Tell students to write whatever comes into their mind.

LESSON 97

TEACH

Table 40. Ask students what direction portrait orientation is. Make sure they all understand portrait orientation is vertical.

Table 41. Be sure students use the correct formula to get the total.

ASSESS

- Check to see if students show signs of improvement from the Pretest to the Posttest.
- As students begin typing the tables, walk around the room and point out correct and incorrect formatting to individual students.
- After students finish typing the tables, have them view their work on the screen to see if they made any errors. If errors were made, have students edit their work and make corrections.

If students do not finish the tables during the class period, make sure they save their work so that they can complete it the next time this class meets.

CLOSE

Remind students to clean up their workstation when they leave.

TABLE 40

Create a boxed table with 3 columns and 9 rows in portrait orientation. Merge the first two cells in row 9. Shade the column headings with 20-percent fill. Insert a double line below the column headings and above the TOTAL line. Align the entries in columns 1 and 2 at the left; align the entries in column 3 at the right. Use the SUM feature to calculate the total salaries. Apply a numeric format of currency with no decimal places to the total.

BRANCH MANAGER SALARIES
January 1, {year}

Office	Manager	Salary
Atlanta	Harrison Wilson	69,750
Boston	Audrey Pritchett	63,900
Chicago	Martin Sellers	62,800
Dallas	Leigh Martinez	68,500
Salt Lake City	William Beauchamp	64,350
Tulsa	Isabella Montgomery	68,890
TOTAL SALARIES		

TABLE 41

Open Table 39. Insert a TOTAL row after the last entry. In cell A8, type TOTAL PRICE. Delete all inside vertical lines in row 8. Format all the cells in column C (but not the column heading) with dollar signs and two decimal places. Then calculate a total for Price.

CULTURAL CONNECTIONS

Ukraine, which was once a part of the Soviet Union, became an independent republic in 1991. The rich fertile soil and plentiful rainfall in Ukraine are ideal for farming. Farmers grow a variety of grains as well as potatoes and sugar beets. Because of the abundant grain harvests, Ukraine is often called the breadbasket of Europe.

Teacher Notes

LESSON 98 LETTERS WITH INTERNATIONAL ADDRESSES

OBJECTIVES:

- Compose at the keyboard.
- Type 37/5'/5e.
- Learn to type letters with international addresses.

A. WARMUP

Type each line 2 times.

Speed	1	You can opt to leave things as they are and make no change.
Accuracy	2	Jacqueline was vexed by the folks who got the money prizes.
Language Link	3	The vice president said, "Let's use dates we can maintain."
Numbers/Symbols	4	Take a 3-, 4-, and 5-minute timing on 186-C, pages 279-280.

| 1 | 2 | 3 | 4 | 5 | 6 | 7 | 8 | 9 | 10 | 11 | 12

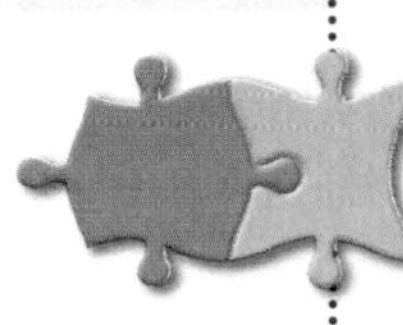

LANGUAGE LINK

B. COMPOSING AT THE KEYBOARD

Redundancy is using several words that mean the same thing. For example, instead of using the phrase, "the same identical items," use just the word *identical.*

Type the following paragraph eliminating the redundant wording.

5 When driving to school, I take the same identical
6 route each day. I have a car that is small in size.
7 Two friends ride along with me. Each and every day we
8 get to class at about the same time. One day we tried
9 another different route and got lost. We rode around in
10 circles before we found our way. We repeatedly asked
11 many times for directions. The only other alternative
12 we had was to not repeat again the exact same route. We
13 decided we would continue using our original old route.

RESOURCES

 Lesson Plan 98

 Courseware Lesson 98

Student Data Disk

Student Manual

Supplementary Production Activities

Grading and Evaluation

LESSON 98

FOCUS

- Eliminate redundant wording in the Language Link composing activity.
- Use 5-minute timings to build speed.
- Learn to format and type letters with international addresses.
- Type letters in block style and modified-block style.

BELLRINGER

As soon as students arrive at their workstations and log in, have them type the Warmup. Go over the purpose of each line as shown to the left of the copy.

TEACH

Activity B. Have students see how many redundancies they can find before they begin the activity. Go over lines 5–10 while students check their work.

Solution: Students' answers will vary.

When driving to school, I take the same route each day. I have a car that is small. Two friends ride with me. Each day we get to class about the same time. One day we tried another route and got lost. We rode in circles before we found our way. We asked many times for directions. The only alternative we had was not to repeat the same route. We decided we would continue using our old route.

TEACH

Activity C. Point out that words in the Preview Practice are used in the timing that follows.

Activity D. Remind students that they should try to improve speed with each 5-minute timing. The goal is to type 37 words a minute for 5 minutes with no more than 5 errors.

SKILLBUILDING

C. Preview Practice

Type each line 2 times as a preview to the timings that follow.

Accuracy who true quite traits choices realized examining individual
Speed describe lifestyle identity achieve personal start will you

D. 5-Minute Timings

Take two 5-minute timings on the paragraphs. Note your speed and errors.

Goal: 37/5'/5e

Most decisions about your present lifestyle have been 11
made for you by your parents. Your current way of life is 23
quite often defined by your role as a member of a family 34
and as a student. Your personal identity is closely related 46
to how you live. In fact, your lifestyle and who you are as 58
an individual are often linked. 64

As an adult, you will make almost all of the choices 75
that will determine your lifestyle. These decisions might 87
help you define your personal identity. It is never too 98
early to begin examining lifestyle features that you want 110
to have when you are older. When you can describe those 121
traits, you can start setting goals and selecting options 132
that will help you achieve the way of life you want to have 144
as an adult. 147

To live your life in a way that gives you peace and 158
joy, your needs must be satisfied, most of your wants must 169
be realized, and your style of living should be true to the 181
values you hold. 185

| 1 | 2 | 3 | 4 | 5 | 6 | 7 | 8 | 9 | 10 | 11 | 12 SI 1.35

CULTURAL CONNECTIONS

Have students think about the lifestyle of a student from a different part of the country or a different cultural background than theirs. Have them type a list of differences and similarities between their lives and that of the person from the different region or heritage.

FORMATTING

E. International Addresses

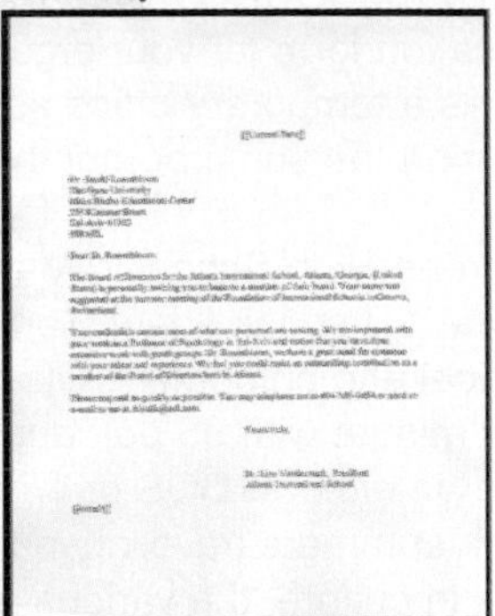

International mailing addresses are similar to domestic mailing addresses. International addresses may also include:

1. Numbers to identify the routing of the correspondence.
2. The name of the country typed in all capital letters as the final line of the address.

WORD PROCESSING APPLICATIONS

LETTER 58
Block Style

Type the following business letter in block style.

(Current Date) / Mr. George Grinderemann / Arnoldstrabe 56 / 22256 Hamburg / GERMANY / Dear Mr. Grinderemann: /
¶The VanHughes School of Fine Arts is pleased to notify you of your acceptance into our program. George, you realize that only a select few new students are accepted each year.
¶We considered your outstanding scholastic record at your school in Hamburg, Germany, and looked favorably upon your many extracurricular activities. Our Board of Directors unanimously voted you to be our foreign exchange student of the year.
¶Next month we will be sending you more information regarding the VanHughes School of Fine Arts, its housing choices, courses of study, and the many extracurricular activities we have available. You'll find that our faculty and staff are skilled, knowledgeable, and interested only in helping you succeed in a career in fine arts.
¶We look forward to hearing from you soon.
Sincerely yours, / Dr. Paula Toddsworthy / President / urs

TEACH

Activity E. Ask students what international means. Ask what domestic means. Make sure all students understand the meaning of both words.

Letter 58. Remind students that paragraphs are not indented in block-style letters.

FACT FILE

At one time, more than 25 different languages were spoken by dozens of Native American tribes in the Pacific Northwest. Many built totem poles that portrayed in a visual language the stories of their clans (families). Have students research one clan's totem and write a short report.

LESSON 98

TEACH

Letter 59. Tell students they may want to keep a copy of the letter and modify it to use as a model when writing for an employment application.

LETTER 59

Modified-Block Style

Type this personal-business letter in modified-block style.

(Current Date) / Michael Renard / EuroBureau Interim / Rue de Hesperange 5 / L-1731 / LUXEMBOURG / Dear Mr. Renard:
¶Please send me an application form for your organization. I am interested in applying for a job as a temporary office assistant/computer operator in Luxembourg during the summer months of June, July, and August.
¶I will graduate from Evergreen High School in May and will be available for employment on June 1. I speak fluent German as well as French and Italian. My clerical and computer skills are excellent. My typing speed is 90 words a minute with 95 percent accuracy; I can efficiently use any computer in either a DOS or Windows environment.
¶I have spent the past three summers traveling in Europe, so I am familiar with the differences in culture, the various governments, and the transportation systems.
Sincerely, / Michele LaGare / 4810 South Longs Peak Road / Longmont, CO 80501

CULTURAL CONNECTIONS

Color should be taken into consideration if you are dressing for business abroad. In some cultures, only royalty wears certain colors, and other colors may convey grief. For example, in Malaysia, you should not wear yellow, blue, or white; in Thailand, you should not wear black or purple; in Japan, you should not wear mauve; in Greece, you should not wear black.

*inter*NET ACTIVITY

Have students use the name of your school or community as the keyword in an Internet search. Have them access information they find of interest. Students should track and type a record of their paths and bring it to class.

CULTURAL CONNECTIONS

Have students research the resources in your community to find a businessperson who can speak about cultural differences between Europeans and Americans in the ways of doing business. Students should write a letter inviting this person to speak to the class.

LETTER 60

Modified-Block Style With Indented Paragraphs

Type this business letter in modified-block style with indented paragraphs.

(Current Date) / Oksana Khizir / Elbrussky Prospekt 78-3 / Tyrnyanz, KBR 361600 / RUSSIA / Dear Ms. Khizir:

¶Careers in international marketing are everywhere, not only with firms involved directly with international business, but also with those that might be entering the global marketplace in the foreseeable future. Our firm, U.S. Industries, Inc., is one of those just entering the global market.

¶The CEO of our company met you last month when she was in Russia. She was impressed with your knowledge of politics, geography, and world history. Also, your sensitivity to the differences between cultures impressed her. You have mastered the English language, both written and spoken. These are all qualities necessary to have a successful career in international marketing.

¶We are hopeful that you will accept our offer of a position in our International Marketing Department.

Yours truly, / Joseph R. Murray / International Marketing Director / urs

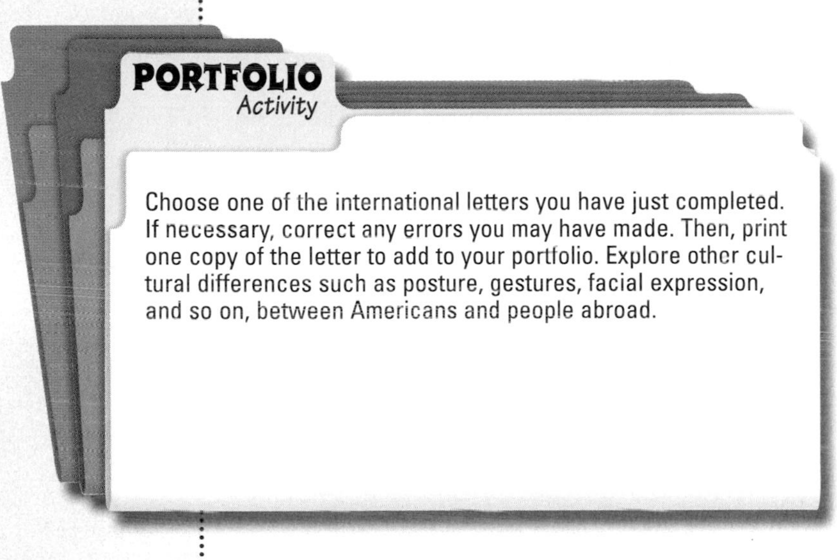

Choose one of the international letters you have just completed. If necessary, correct any errors you may have made. Then, print one copy of the letter to add to your portfolio. Explore other cultural differences such as posture, gestures, facial expression, and so on, between Americans and people abroad.

LESSON 98

TEACH

Letter 60. Remind students that kindness in their communications will get them more of what they want out of life.

ASSESS

- Review students' responses to the Language Link redundancy activity.
- Check to see if students are increasing their speeds.
- As students begin typing the letters, walk around the room and point out correct and incorrect formatting to individual students.
- After students finish typing the letters, have them view their work on the screen to see if they made any errors.

CLOSE

If students do not finish the letters during the class period, make sure they save their work so that they can complete it the next time this class meets.

PORTFOLIO *Activity*

If students' portfolio goals include showcasing their best work, they may want to include one of the letters from this lesson. Encourage students to evaluate their work and include comments in their portfolio.

Teacher Notes

LESSON 99

FOCUS

- Use Technique Timings to improve technique.
- Use Diagnostic Practice to identify areas that need improvement.
- Learn to format and type memos with copy notations and attachments.

BELLRINGER

As soon as students arrive at their workstations and log in, have them type the Warmup. Go over the purpose of each line as shown to the left of the copy.

TEACH

Activity B. Remind students that proper technique is a building block for speed and accuracy. The focus for this timing: Keep your eyes on the copy.

Activity C. Make sure that students understand that this Diagnostic Practice activity is designed to help identify areas that need improvement and provide needed practice.

LESSON 99

MEMOS WITH COPY NOTATIONS AND ATTACHMENTS

OBJECTIVES:

- Improve keyboarding skill.
- Format memos with copy notations and attachments.
- Reinforce typing from script and rough draft copy.

A. WARMUP

Type each line 2 times.

```
Speed             1 All of the errors have been corrected in the final project.
Accuracy          2 Pat quickly froze the gold mixtures in five old brown jars.
Language Link     3 The old woman in the shoe said, "No more children, please."
Numbers/Symbols   4 Kenny & April ordered 50# of potatoes (red) @ $.45 a pound.
                    | 1 | 2 | 3 | 4 | 5 | 6 | 7 | 8 | 9 | 10 | 11 | 12
```

SKILLBUILDING

B. TECHNIQUE TIMINGS

Take two 30-second timings on lines 5–6. Then take two 30-second timings on lines 7–8. Focus on the technique at the left.

Keep your eyes on the copy.

```
5      We sit and toss rocks in the lake as the sun sets, but    11
6 we cannot see if they are going to skip over the big waves.    23

7      The lane that goes to the lake turns and goes to town,    11
8 but we do not know if you can use it all the way right now.    23
  | 1 | 2 | 3 | 4 | 5 | 6 | 7 | 8 | 9 | 10 | 11 | 12
```

C. DIAGNOSTIC PRACTICE: ALPHABET

Turn to the Diagnostic Practice: Alphabet routine on page SB1 Type one of the Pretest/Posttest paragraphs and identify any errors made. Then type the corresponding drill lines 2 times for each letter on which you made 2 or more errors and 1 time for each letter on which you made only 1 error. Finally, repeat the Pretest and compare your performance.

RESOURCES

 Lesson Plan 99

 Courseware Lesson 99

Student Data Disk

Student Manual

Supplementary Production Activities

Multicultural Activities

FORMATTING

D. Copy Notations

When you send a copy of a memo to someone in addition to the addressee, type a copy notation on the memo. Many memo templates already have a field where you can simply insert the names of the people to whom you want to send copies of the memo. If there is no field, then type the copy notation as follows:

1. Type the copy notation on the line below the reference initials or below the enclosure or attachment notation.
2. At the left margin, type a lowercase *c* followed by a colon (*c:*)
3. Press the tab and type the name of the person receiving the copy.

E. Attachments

When material is physically attached to a memo (either clipped or stapled), type an attachment notation below the reference initials. To type the attachment notation:

1. Press enter once after typing your reference initials.
2. Type the word *Attachment* at the left margin.

WORD PROCESSING APPLICATIONS

MEMO 5

Template

Complete this memo using the first memo template listed in your word processing software. Use today's date.

TO:/ Katrina Stevens / **CC:** / Marshall McElreath **FROM:**/ Justine O'Neal / **SUBJECT:** / Evaluation Criteria
¶Please refer to the attachment as you develop your suggestions for the evaluation criteria for the new department personnel brochure. Please give thought to developing at least five suggestions.
¶Submit your suggestions to me via e-mail by October 1. My personal e-mail address is joneal@jobs.personnel.gov.co.us. I assure you that all of your suggestions will be kept confidential in my personal mailbox. We will meet on October 5 in the Spruce Conference Oval Room to review all of your suggestions, develop a list of 25 criteria for personnel evaluation, and plan the brochure. / urs / Attachment

TEACH

Activity D. Explain that including these notations on a memo is very similar to a letter.

Memo 5. Make sure all students have accessed the correct template.

FACT FILE

William Shakespeare (1564–1616) is the greatest English playwright. Often he acted at the Globe Theater in London. Since Shakespeare's time, our language has lost thousands of words. Have students research one of Shakespeare's works and type a list of ten words in the work with which they are not familiar.

TEACH

Memo 6. Be sure students use the correct template.

Memo 7. Remind students to be aware of their posture, to sit up, keep their elbows in, and their feet flat on the floor.

PORTFOLIO *Activity*

If students' portfolio goals include demonstrating specific skills, they may want to include the one or more of the tables from this lesson. Encourage students to evaluate their own work and include comments in their portfolio.

MEMO 6
Template

Complete this memo using the first memo template listed in your word processing software. Use today's date.

TO: Daniel Whitebuffalo / **FROM:** Ellen Herrera / **SUBJECT:** Technology in Education Conference
¶The TIE conference will be held again this year in Snowmass.
¶There will be rooms available at the Aspen Lodge for all of our personnel. I've asked that the management make our stay more personal by reserving the entire west wing of the lodge for our group.
¶I've attached directions to the lodge; however, the company will provide us with a minivan. If you wish to ride in the minivan, please contact me via e-mail. The address is: eherrera@ccsd.k12.ca.us. The minivan will pick us up in front of the school. We will leave promptly at 8 a.m. on Thursday, September 16. I hope you choose to join me in the ride to Snowmass. The fall tree colors will be beautiful at that time. I look forward to seeing you then. / urs / Attachment

MEMO 7
Template

Complete the following memo using the first memo template listed in your word processing software. Use today's date.

TO: Nina Lewis, Supervisor / **CC:** Marc Pak / **FROM:** Sam Roshdy / **SUBJECT:** Employees' Gym
¶The new gym and the Olympic swimming pool are now open for employee use. Thanks to your support of this effort, the company has equipped this gym for their personnel with most of the exercise equipment needed for a good 30-minute workout.

SCHOOL TO CAREER

Have students choose an interesting career. Have them design a brochure about the career. The brochure should include titles and information about what the career is, what education is needed, and what a person in this career does. Display the brochures in the classroom.

¶You know that there is now an hour and a half for the lunch break. This will give employees time to work out, eat their lunches, and attend to personal matters before the afternoon shift begins.

¶Please encourage all those employees that you supervise to use this modern, new workout facility. It's free to employees during the week and open on Saturdays for employees and their families. / urs

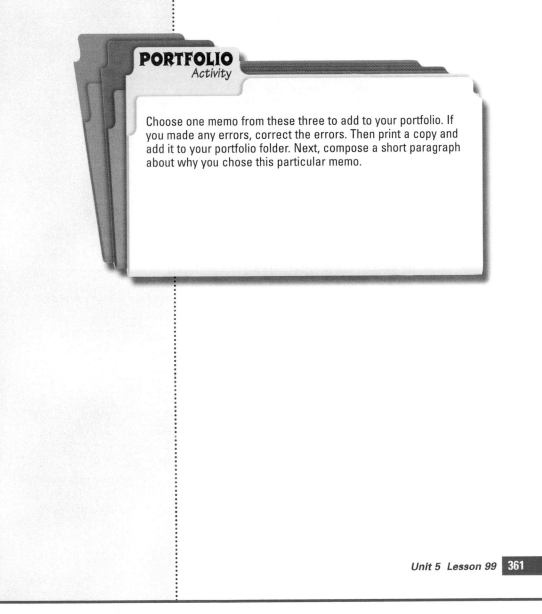

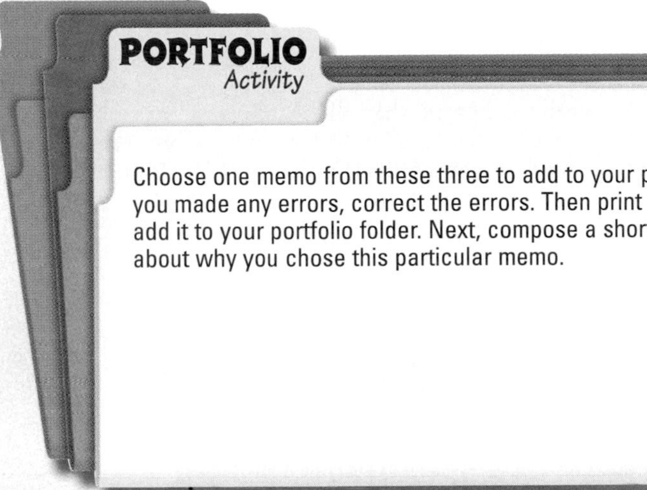

Choose one memo from these three to add to your portfolio. If you made any errors, correct the errors. Then print a copy and add it to your portfolio folder. Next, compose a short paragraph about why you chose this particular memo.

LESSON 99

ASSESS

- Monitor students as they complete Technique Timings and assess individual student's technique.
- Monitor students as they complete Diagnostic Practice and provide individualized assistance as needed.
- As students begin typing the memos, walk around the room and point out correct and incorrect formatting to individual students.
- After students finish typing the memos, have them view their work on the screen to see if they made any errors. If errors were made, have students edit their work and make corrections.

CLOSE

If students do not finish the memos during the class period, make sure they save their work so that they can complete it the next time this class meets.

Remind students to clean up their workstation when they leave.

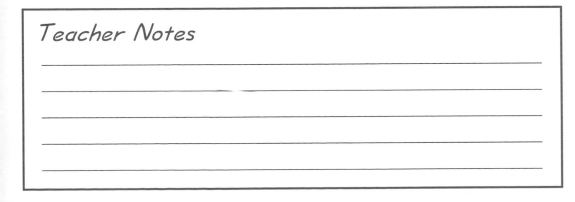

Teacher Notes

LESSON 100

FOCUS

- Apply the Language Link rule concerning comma use with direct quotations.
- Use Concentration Drills to improve concentration.
- Practice formatting and typing letters, memos, and tables.

BELLRINGER

As soon as students arrive at their workstations and log in, have them type the Warmup. Go over the purpose of each line as shown to the left of the copy.

TEACH

Activity B. Explain the Language Link rules for using commas with direct quotations. Then have students complete the activity. Have students check each other's work.

Solutions: "Remember," said Sara, "turn off the lights when you leave."
Sharon asked, "Would you like to have half of my sandwich?"
"If you have not eaten lunch yet," said Bev, "let's eat."
"I can hardly believe it is afternoon," said the professor.

LESSON 100 FORMATTING REVIEW

OBJECTIVES:

- Learn to use commas with direct quotations.
- Review formats for letters, memos, and tables.

A. WARMUP

Type each line 2 times.

Speed	1	Shaun typed by touch in order to type at his fastest speed.
Accuracy	2	Viv poured a liquid that froze quickly into the beige jars.
Language Link	3	Alana asked, "Did you record that book on a separate disk?"
Numbers/Symbols	4	By October 10 you need to order 253# of Item #46 @ $798.15.

| 1 | 2 | 3 | 4 | 5 | 6 | 7 | 8 | 9 | 10 | 11 | 12

B. COMMAS WITH DIRECT QUOTATIONS

Study the rules and examples below. Then edit lines 5–8 to correct any errors in punctuation.

Rule 21: Use a comma before a direct quotation.

The magician said, "Hokus pokus."

The officer replied, "The fingerprints are in the lab for analysis."

Rule 22: Use a comma after a direct quotation.

"Over here," shouted the traffic officer.

"All books are to be returned within one week," the statement read.

Rule 23: Use a comma before and after a direct quotation.

"When you go outside," said Mom, "be sure to wear a coat."

"When you drive my car," said Dad, "be very careful!"

RESOURCES

 Lesson Plan 100

 Courseware Lesson 100

Student Data Disk

Student Manual

Language Link Worksheets

Reteaching and Reinforcement

Unit 5 Test

Grading and Evaluation

"Remember" said Sara "turn off the lights when you leave."
Sharon asked "Would you like to have half of my sandwich?"
"If you have not eaten lunch yet" said Bev "let's eat."
"I can hardly believe it is afternoon" said the professor.

SKILLBUILDING

C. Concentration

***Type the following paragraph 1 time. Every time a number appears, replace it with a number that is two greater. For example, replace* two *with* four *and* five *with* seven.**

Three students wanted five notebooks, three calendars, six mechanical pencils, four black markers, seven sheets of poster paper, and eight ink pens for the school store. They planned to market these items to students to make a profit.

WORD PROCESSING APPLICATIONS

LETTER 61

Block Style

Type the following business letter in block style. Use today's date.

Ms. Wynona Foster / Owner / Frills & Fluff Fine Fashion / 560 James Naismith Drive / Gloucester, Ontario / CANADA /K1B5N / Dear Ms. Foster:
¶Thank you for your clothing merchandise order. The New York Fashion Show was the best we have presented. We were delighted that you could attend.
¶Your purchase entitles you to a 25-percent discount on your next order. We know that our business relationship with Frills & Fluff Fine Fashion will be long-lasting. / Sincerely yours, / Yolanda McDonald / Merchandise Marketing / urs

LESSON 100

TEACH

Activity C. Go over the instructions with students to make sure they understand this activity. Give them a few more examples: "Replace three with ______." (five) "Replace six with ______." (eight).

Letter 61. Be sure students type the international address correctly.

JOURNAL ENTRY

Have students write about how they feel about continuing their education. Do they plan to go on to trade or business school or college? What will their lives be like if they do/do not go on to school?

LESSON 100

TEACH

Letter 62. Be sure students use date insert for the date.

Memo 8. Remind students to replace urs with their initials.

Table 42. Remind students to add 10-percent fill to column headings, adjust the column widths, and center the table vertically and horizontally.

LETTER 62
Modified-Block Style

Type the following business letter in modified-block style. Use today's date.

Dr. David Rosenbloom / The Open University / Maks Rhoho Educational Center / 255 Klausner Street / Tel-Aviv 61392 / ISRAEL / Dear Dr. Rosenbloom:
¶The Board of Directors for the Atlanta International School, Atlanta, Georgia, (United States) is personally inviting you to become a member of their board. Your name was suggested at the summer meeting of the Foundation of International Schools in Geneva, Switzerland.
¶Your credentials contain most of what our personnel are seeking. We are impressed with your work as a Professor of Psychology in Tel-Aviv and notice that you have done extensive work with youth groups. Dr. Rosenbloom, we have a great need for someone with your talent and experience. We feel you could make an outstanding contribution as a member of the Board of Directors here in Atlanta.
¶Please respond as quickly as possible. You may telephone me at 404-555-1454 or send an e-mail to me at Aistalk@aol.com.
Yours truly, / Dr. Lien Vandermark, President / Atlanta International School / urs

MEMO 8
Template

Complete the following memo using the first memo template listed in your word processing software.

TO: Allison Wong / **CC:** Zachary Barkley / **FROM:** Rocio Cunningham / **DATE:** February 15, (year) / **SUBJECT:** Council Meeting
¶The office council meeting originally scheduled for Tuesday, February 23, has been changed to Thursday, February 25, upon the advice of Mr. Brown, our company's legal counsel. A revised agenda is attached.
¶There will be time for each person to voice his/her feelings on all major issues concerning changing personnel. Everyone's personal opinion will be taken into consideration before final decisions are made.
¶If you cannot attend the meeting, please send a representative who can speak for your department.
urs / Attachment /

SCHOOL TO CAREER

Ask students about careers in sales and marketing. Write these careers on the board, and have students form groups. Have each group choose a career, research the career, and write a report. Reports should include the education needed for the career and what forces are affecting modern marketing.

TABLE 42
Boxed Table

Create a 5-column, 10-row boxed table. Add 10-percent fill to the braced column headings. Sum columns B–E. Automatically adjust the column widths. Center the table vertically and horizontally.

SALES ANALYSIS Borden Manufacturing Company June 30, {year}				
	1st Quarter		**2nd Quarter**	
Salesperson	**Units**	**Gross Sales ($)**	**Units**	**Gross Sales ($)**
Robert Brazinski	10	427.70	29	1,240.33
Carol Dawkins	18	769.86	17	727.09
Janice Greene	20	855.40	28	1,197.56
Carlos Bieseda	17	727.09	24	1,026.48
Diane Kessler	15	641.55	25	1,069.25
Charles Young	19	812.63	32	1,368.64
TOTAL				

Teacher Notes

LESSON 100

ASSESS

- Watch students as they complete Language Link activity to see if they are able to apply the rules correctly.
- As students begin typing, walk around the room and point out correct and incorrect formatting to individual students.
- After students finish typing the documents, have them view their work on the screen to see if they made any errors. If errors were made, have students make corrections.

CLOSE

If students do not finish the jobs during the class period, make sure they save their work so that they can complete it the next time this class meets.

Remind students to clean up their workstation when they leave.

PORTFOLIO *Activity*

If students' portfolio goals include showcasing their best work, they may want to include one of the letters or memos from this lesson. Encourage students to evaluate their work and include comments in their portfolio.

UNIT 6 ORGANIZER

DESKTOP PUBLISHING

Lesson	Focus	Special Features	Skillbuilding	Pretest/ Practice/ Posttest	Documents	GO TO Activities
101	Desktop Publishing: Special Characters	Fact File, p. 368	p. 368		Report 32, p. 369 Report 33, p. 370 Report 34, p. 371	p. 369
102	Desktop Publishing: Font Colors and Features	Internet Connection, p. 372 Portfolio Activity, p. 375	pp. 372–373		Report 35, pp. 374–375	p. 374
103	Desktop Publishing: Borders and Fill	Language Link, p. 376 Fact File, p. 377	p. 377	p. 377	Report 36, pp. 378–379 Report 37, p. 379 Report 38, p. 379 Report 39, p. 379	p. 378
104	Desktop Publishing: Graphic Lines/Rules	Internet Connection, p. 380 Journal Entry, p. 382	p. 380		Report 40, p. 381 Report 41, p. 381 Report 42, p. 382	p. 381
105	Desktop Publishing: Drawing	Language Link, pp. 383–384	p. 384	p. 384	Report 43, p. 385 Report 44, p. 385	p. 385
106	Desktop Publishing: Text and Graphic Boxes	Fact File, p. 387	p. 386		Report 45, p. 387 Report 46, p. 387	p. 387
107	Desktop Publishing: Boxes: Fill, Borders	Language Link, p. 388 Internet Connection, p. 389 Science Connection, p. 390 Fact File, p. 391	p. 389		Report 47, p. 390 Report 48, p. 391 Report 49, p. 391	p. 390
108	Desktop Publishing: Boxes: Wrapping Text	Communication Focus, p. 392 Portfolio Activity, p. 394	p. 392		Report 50, p. 393 Report 51, p. 394	p. 393
109	Desktop Publishing: Personal Notepads	Language Link, p. 395 Fact File, p. 395 Cultural Connection, p. 397 Art Connection, p. 398	p. 396	p. 396	Report 52, p. 397 Report 53, p. 398	p. 397

UNIT 6 RESOURCE MANAGER

MULTIMEDIA
- Courseware: Lessons 101–120
- Student Data Disk
- Student Manual: Lessons 101–120

TEACHING TOOLS
- Lesson Plans: Lessons 101–120
- Block Scheduling Guide, Unit 6
- Language Link Worksheets: Lessons 101–120
- Multicultural Applications
- Academic Report Guide
- Solution Keys
- Cross-Curricular Activities: Lessons 101–120

RETEACHING/REINFORCEMENT
- Reteaching/Reinforcement Activities: Lessons 101–120
- Supplemental Production Activities: Lessons 101–120

ASSESSMENT and EVALUATION

Pretest/Practice/Posttest: pp. 377, 384, 396, 411–412, 428
Portfolio Activity: pp. 375, 394
Unit 6 Test
Timings: pp. 373, 389, 400, 415, 424
Production Jobs: Reports 32–71
Grading and Evaluation

Electronic Teacher Classroom Resources

For your convenience, the teacher's materials are available on a CD-ROM. Having these resources available electronically enables you to print exactly what you need and revise materials as necessary.

Lesson	Focus	Special Features	Skillbuilding	Pretest/ Practice/ Posttest	Documents	GO TO Activities
110	Desktop Publishing: Personal Stationery	Fact File, p. 399 Internet Connection, p. 401	pp. 399–400		Report 54, p. 401 Report 55, p. 401	
111	Desktop Publishing: Text/Word Art	Language Link, pp. 402–403 Fact File, p. 405	p. 403		Report 56, p. 404 Report 57, p. 405	p. 404
112	Desktop Publishing: Review		p. 406		Report 58, p. 407	
113	Desktop Publishing: Flyer Design	Language Link, pp. 408–409 Communication Focus, p. 410 Internet Connection, p. 410	p. 409		Report 59, pp. 409–410 Report 60, p. 410	
114	Desktop Publishing: Certificate Design	Fact File, p. 411 Cultural Connection, p. 413	pp. 411–412	pp. 411–412	Report 61, p. 413	
115	Desktop Publishing: Invitation Design	Language Link, p. 414 Science Connection, p. 415 Fact File, p. 416	p. 415		Report 62, pp. 415–416 Report 63, p. 416	
116	Desktop Publishing: Columns	Journal Entry, p. 419	p. 417		Report 64, p. 418 Report 65, p. 419	p. 418
117	Desktop Publishing: Newsletters	Language Link, pp. 420–421	p. 421		Report 66, p. 422 Report 67, p. 422	
118	Desktop Publishing: Newsletters	Internet Connection, p. 423 Fact File, p. 426	pp. 423–424		Report 68, pp. 424–426	
119	Desktop Publishing: Newsletters	Language Link, p. 427	p. 428	p. 428	Report 69, pp. 429–430	
120	Desktop Publishing: Review	Science Connection, p. 432 Journal Entry, p. 433	p. 431		Report 70, pp. 432–433 Report 71, p. 422	

SCANS Competencies in Glencoe Keyboarding with Computer Applications

Resources	Interpersonal Skills	Information	Systems	Technology
Throughout the course, students deal specifically with resources: allocating time for completing drills and documents, maintaining workstations, caring for computers and software.	Cultural Connection, p. 413 Communication Focus, pp. 392, 410 Fact File, p. 416	Career Bit, p. 367 Fact File, pp. 368, 377, 387, 391, 395, 399, 405, 411, 416, 426 Internet Connection, pp. 372, 380, 389, 401, 423 Science Connection, pp. 390, 415, 432	Internet Connection, pp. 372, 380, 389, 401, 423	Lessons 101–120 Internet Connection, pp. 372, 380, 389, 401, 423 Art Connection, p. 398

INTRODUCING THE UNIT

Have different students read each of the objectives for Unit 6. Address each objective as it's read. Explain that the goal in this unit is to reach a typing speed of 38 words a minute for 5 minutes with 5 or fewer errors. Encourage students to believe this is an achievable goal.

Students also will learn the correct use of word processing features and the basic design and formatting skills to create variety of reports. In addition, students will compose short reports on the keyboard.

FUN Facts

Bicycle riding is even more popular in Europe than it is here in the United States. In Europe bicycling also is a popular competitive sport. The first bicycle race was held in France in 1869. The Tour de France, which is still held today, is the most prestigious bicycle race in the world. Many Americans participate in this race that runs for 25 to 30 days and covers about 2,000 miles (3200 km).

UNIT 6 DESKTOP PUBLISHING

Lessons 101–120

OBJECTIVES

- Demonstrate keyboarding speed and accuracy on straight copy with a goal of 38 words a minute for 5 minutes with 5 or fewer errors.
- Demonstrate correct use of word processing features.
- Demonstrate basic design and formatting skills on a variety of reports including flyers, invitations, stationery, certificates, and newsletters.
- Compose short reports at the keyboard.

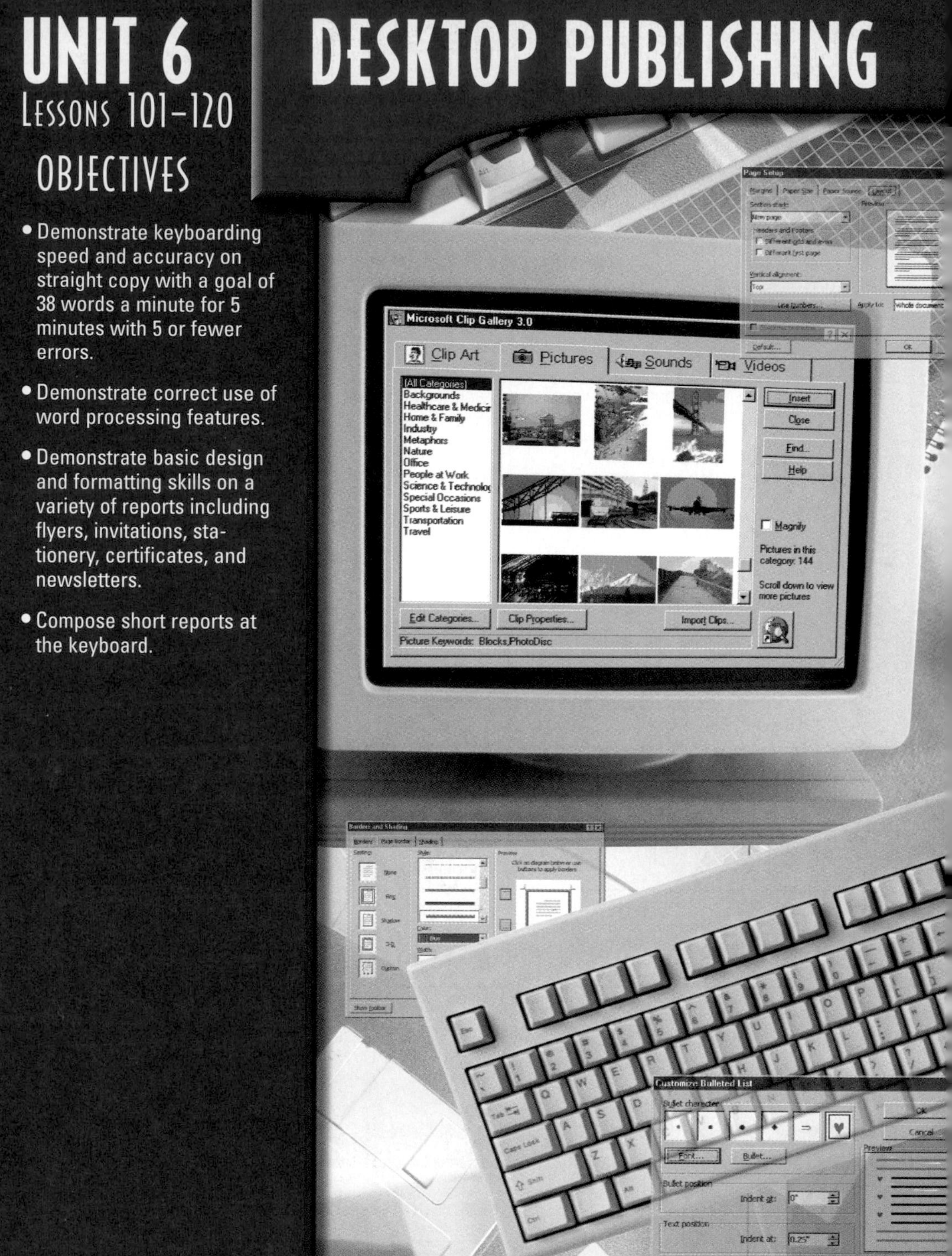

COURSEWARE OVERVIEW

As students begin desktop publishing, check your word processing software to see what graphics are available. If necessary, show students how to access these graphics on your system. As they complete documents, view them on screen to check color and format, or view the documents through the Teacher Management program.

WORDS TO LEARN

automatic hyphenation
clip art
drawing tools
drop caps
graphics
newspaper columns
special characters
text color
text/word art
vertical lines
vertical text

CAREER BIT

GRAPHIC ARTIST Graphic artists may create promotional copy for new products, visual designs for annual reports and other corporate literature, or distinctive logos for products or businesses. Graphic artists use a variety of print, electronic, and film media to create art. Most graphic artists now use computer software to design new images; some of this work appears on the Internet and CD-ROM. Artists may be assigned to create the overall layout and design of magazines, newspapers, journals, and other publications. They may also be asked to create graphics for television and computer-generated media, for example, home pages on the Internet.

367

WORDS TO LEARN

The terms in Words to Learn are defined in the Glossary at the back of the book. Ask students if they are familiar with any of the terms. Have them define the terms they know. Compare their definitions with those in the Glossary.

CAREER BIT

Ask a student to read the Career Bit aloud to the class. In the center of the board write the word Graphic Artist. Ask students to brainstorm about people in other careers who work with graphic artists, including advertising managers, copywriters, project managers, administrative assistants, editors, computer programmers, and so on. Write these occupations on the board around the word Graphic Artist. Have students contact a local newspaper, advertising agency, corporation, or graphic arts firm to invite a speaker to your class. Request that the speaker bring samples of graphic designs and explain the scope of the graphic artists' job.

COURSEWARE OVERVIEW

Have students experiment with various lines, shapes, drawings, and so forth. To view the character map and corresponding keystrokes for Wingdings or other special fonts, expand the Character Map icon in the Windows Accessories group.

LESSON 101

FOCUS

- Use 12-second timings to build speed.
- Learn desktop publishing feature: Special Characters.
- Type and format paragraphs using special characters.
- Type and format a flyer using special characters.

BELLRINGER

As soon as students arrive at their workstations and log in, have them type the Warmup. Go over the purpose of each line as shown to the left of the copy.

TEACH

Activity B. Remind students to type at a fast pace during the 12-second timings. At the end of the first and second timings, encourage students to type just one or two strokes faster on the next timing.

DESKTOP PUBLISHING: SPECIAL CHARACTERS

OBJECTIVES:

- Improve keyboarding speed.
- Learn about desktop publishing.
- Learn about special characters.

A. WARMUP

Type each line 2 times.

```
Speed          1 The goal of the rich girls is to fix a bike for an old man.
Accuracy       2 Dave froze the mixtures in the deep brown jugs too quickly.
Language Link  3 One runner from our high school races in the June 12 event.
Numbers        4 Fabra will mark the board at 10, 29, 38, 47, and 56 inches.
                 | 1 | 2 | 3 | 4 | 5 | 6 | 7 | 8 | 9 | 10 | 11 | 12
```

SKILLBUILDING

B. 12-SECOND SPRINTS

Take three 12-second timings on each line. Try to increase your speed on each timing.

```
5 She said the four girls can swim across the lake with ease.
6 Please take one of these big boxes down to the post office.
7 May we go to the game with you, or do you have other plans?
8 The short words are often typed faster than the long words.
  ||||5||||10||||15||||20||||25||||30||||35||||40||||45||||50||||55||||60
```

FACT FILE

Opals are made up of many spheres of silica molecules. They are not, however, crystals.

RESOURCES

 Lesson Plan 101

 Courseware Lesson 101

Student Data Disk

Student Manual

Supplementary Production Activities

COURSEWARE OVERVIEW

You may want to have students experiment with the various Wingdings and special characters. To view the character map and the corresponding keystrokes, expand the Character Map icon in the Windows Accessories group. Also remember that documents are scored only for keystrokes, not for formats.

FORMATTING

C. Orientation to Desktop Publishing

Desktop publishing (DTP) is the process of using special word processing features to make your documents fun and visually appealing. Through the use of different font styles, colors, boxes, and graphics, you can create a variety of special documents such as letterheads, flyers, and newsletters.

For documents to be effective, however, they should be fairly simple, have a limited number of different font styles, and contain a lot of white space.

D. Software Features

STUDENT MANUAL

Special Characters

Study Lesson 101 in your student manual. Complete all the practice activities while at your computer. Then complete the jobs that follow.

DESKTOP PUBLISHING APPLICATIONS

REPORT 32

Follow these steps to type the paragraph:

1. Change the font size to 20 points.
2. Type the paragraph in Times New Roman, but replace the words in brackets with Wingdings. To do this, change the font to Wingdings; then use the following keystrokes to create the symbols. (Before you continue typing, be sure to change the font back to Times New Roman.)

letter	+ (plus)
mailbox	- (hyphen)
air	Q (capital *Q*)
telephoned	((left parenthesis)
happy	J (capital *J*)

I wrote a [letter] and rushed to get it into the [mailbox]. I was sending it by [air] to get it delivered quickly. Once the [letter] was sent, I [telephoned] my friend, who was [happy] to learn it was coming.

LESSON 101

TEACH

Activity C. Tell students they are about to learn about desktop publishing. Ask students how they might use this knowledge in their lives.

Activity D. Have students turn to Lesson 101 in their Student Manual and complete all the practice activities and jobs that follow.

STUDENT MANUAL

Be sure students turn to the correct lesson in their Student Manual.

Report 32. Have students read the steps in Report 32 carefully.

Illustration

The illustration shows the words in brackets in Report 32 replaced with Wingdings.

Out-of-Class Activity

Have students compose a couple paragraphs about how they might use desktop publishing in their lives today and in the future. They should use some of the special characters introduced in this lesson as well as additional ones from the special characters list in their software.

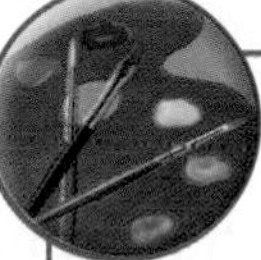

Art Connections

Have students write a letter to a graphics arts company inviting someone to speak to the class about how visual elements enhance messages. Request the speaker to bring samples of such work.

TEACH

Illustration

The illustration contains copy that students will use to type Report 33.

Report 33. Read each step aloud, stopping between steps to make sure students understand the instructions. Have students execute each step before reading the next.

Report 34. Remind students to follow directions carefully to complete Report 34. Have students check each other's work once it is completed.

PORTFOLIO *Activity*

If students' portfolio goals include demonstrating progress, they may want to include one or more of the reports from this lesson. Encourage students to evaluate their own work and include comments in their portfolio.

REPORT 33
Flyer

Create the flyer in the illustration following these steps:

1. Center the text vertically and horizontally.
2. Type the heading using Arial 36-point.
3. Add the symbols on either side of the heading using Wingdings 36-point (8).
4. Double-space after the heading.
5. Change to Arial 20-point and type the remaining text. Quadruple-space before and after the list; double-space before typing the last line.
6. Add the diamond shapes to the listed items using Wingdings (t). Leave a space after the symbol at the beginning of a line and before the symbol at the end of a line.

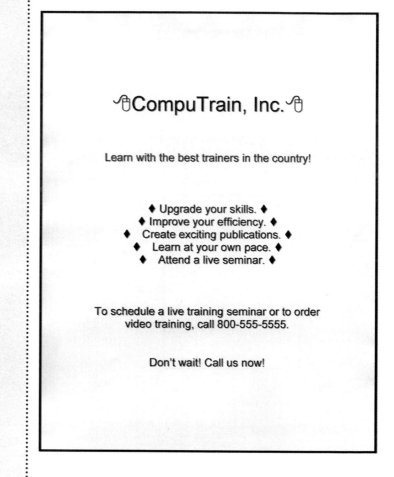

CompuTrain, Inc.

Learn with the best trainers in the country!

♦ Upgrade your skills. ♦
♦ Improve your efficiency. ♦
♦ Create exciting publications. ♦
♦ Learn at your own pace. ♦
♦ Attend a live seminar. ♦

To schedule a live training seminar or to order video training, call 800-555-5555.

Don't wait! Call us now!

JOURNAL ENTRY

Have students write a letter that begins Dear (*their name*). The letter should include ways studens pick up their spirits when they are down and praise for things they like about themselves.

REPORT 34

Follow these steps to type the paragraph:

When my ⏲ rang, I was ☹. I turned on some ♫ to make me ☺; then I read the paper. There were several articles I ✂ out to send to my friends. Of course, that meant I had ✍ to them first. As someone ☞ out, ✉ may be the ☼ in someone's day.

1. Change the font size to 24 points.
2. Change the font to WPIconicSymbolsA; replace the words in brackets; then use the following keystrokes to create the symbols. (Before you continue typing, be sure to change the font back to Times New Roman.)

clock	@	cut	C
unhappy	;	write	N
		pointed	L
music	+	letters	J
happy	(	sunshine	z

When my [alarm clock] rang, I was [unhappy]. I turned on some [music] to make me [happy]; then I read the paper. There were several articles I [cut] out to send to my friends. Of course, that meant I had to [write] to them first. As someone [pointed] out, [letters] may be the [sunshine] in someone's day.

LESSON 101

ASSESS

- Check to see if students are increasing their word a minute speeds as they complete each of the 12-second timings.
- Make sure students are able to use the Special Characters software feature.
- After students finish typing the reports, have them view their work on the screen to see if they made any errors. If errors were made, have students edit their work and make corrections.

CLOSE

If students do not finish the reports during the class period, make sure they save their work so that they can complete it the next time this class meets.

Remind students to clean up their workstation when they leave.

Teacher Notes

LESSON 102

FOCUS

- Use 5-minute timings to build speed.
- Learn word processing features: Font Color and Drop Caps.
- Type and format a report using font color and drop caps.

BELLRINGER

As soon as students arrive at their workstations and log in, have them type the Warmup. Go over the purpose of each line as shown to the left of the copy.

interNET CONNECTION

Be sure to preview the Internet site before assigning this activity to students to make sure the site is appropriate.

Activity B. Point out that words in the Preview Practice are used in the timing that follows.

LESSON 102

FONT COLORS AND FEATURES

OBJECTIVES:

- Learn to change font color.
- Learn to use drop caps.
- Type 38/5'/5e.

A. WARMUP

Type each line 2 times.

Speed	*1*	`They may go to town for the pens if they are not both busy.`
Accuracy	*2*	`We amazed six judges by quietly giving back the four pages.`
Language Link	*3*	`He told Aunt Joan to buy Major Michael an anniversary gift.`
Numbers/Symbols	*4*	`Jo & Don bought 20 cookies @ $.25 from the You & Me Bakery.`

| 1 | 2 | 3 | 4 | 5 | 6 | 7 | 8 | 9 | 10 | 11 | 12

interNET CONNECTION

Keeping track of dates and required information should be simple and easy. Search the World Wide Web for types of tickler files. You may want to start with this URL: http://www.tamu.edu/cis/property/software/doc/files.html

SKILLBUILDING

B. PREVIEW PRACTICE

Type each line 2 times as a preview to the timings that follow.

Accuracy	*5*	`extract planner realize penciled calendar reminder benefits`
Speed	*6*	`on if of as may day for use the can jot your each with help`

RESOURCES

 Lesson Plan 102

 Courseware Lesson 102

Student Data Disk

Student Manual

Supplementary Production Activities

Grading and Evaluation

C. 5-Minute Timings

Take two 5-minute timings on the paragraphs. Note your speed and errors.

Goal: 38/5'/5e

You can realize many benefits from using a computer 11
calendar program. At times, however, even with computers, 22
there still may be a need for a desk calendar. A desk 32
calendar can be quite useful if entries are neatly written 45
in pencil so that you can change them quickly as you need 56
to. If your calendar is visible on the desk and your notes 68
are clear, your coworkers and your boss can extract needed 80
details of your schedule when you are out of the office. Do 92
not jot your private notes on the calendar. 101
A daily planner can also help you manage your time. 111
This record might have ruled or blank paper with places to 123
mark each hour of your day. Some people prefer to use a 134
weekly planner, which shows the schedule for a whole week. 146
The pages are split into parts and may have a blank space 158
for routine entries. 162
Another daily reminder tool is a tickler file. The 172
tickler file uses dated index cards. You can then place 184
reminders behind the correct date. 190

| 1 | 2 | 3 | 4 | 5 | 6 | 7 | 8 | 9 | 10 | 11 | 12 *SI 1.39*

FORMATTING

D. Font Colors and Drop Caps

In addition to changing font sizes and styles, you can also create special effects by using color throughout a document and by using special treatments such as drop caps at the beginning of paragraphs. Keep in mind that you should limit the number of font styles and colors to keep your document readable.

Unit 6 Lesson 102 **373**

TEACH

Activity C. Remind students that they should try to improve speed with each 5-minute timing. The goal for these timings is to type 38 words a minute for 5 minutes with no more than 5 errors.

Activity D. Have students experiment with different colors to see what is and is not readable.

Art Connections

Many calendars today are about works of art and even may be works of art themselves. Have students create a calendar on the computer. Students can use letters, symbols, different fonts and font sizes, and different colors. Display students' work.

Social Studies Connections

Explain to students there are three principal calendars in use today—Gregorian, Hebrew, and Moslem. Ask students which calendar our calendar is based on (Gregorian). What are the other two calendars used for? (Hebrew and Islamic religions)

TEACH

Activity E. Explain and demonstrate the Font Color and Drop Caps features presented in Lesson 102. Walk around the room while students are completing the Lesson. Make sure they are doing the assignment correctly.

STUDENT MANUAL

Be sure students turn to the correct lesson in their Student Manual.

Report 35. Go over each of the eight steps with students before asking them to type Report 35. Make sure each student understands how to proceed.

E. Software Features

STUDENT MANUAL

Font Color Drop Caps

Study Lesson 102 in your student manual. Complete all the practice activities while at your computer. Then complete the jobs that follow.

DESKTOP PUBLISHING APPLICATIONS

REPORT 35

Follow these directions to format the report that follows:

1. Turn on widow/orphan control.
2. Center and type the title in a 20-point sans serif font, such as Arial, approximately 2 inches from the top of the page.
3. Add a diamond symbol to either side of the title with Wingdings (t).
4. Change the title color to red.
5. Center and type your name in a 16-point sans serif font. Leave a blank line between the title and your name.
6. Type the body of the report in Times New Roman 16-point, single-spaced with full justification. Leave a blank line between paragraphs, but do not indent the paragraphs.
7. Use a blue drop cap for the first letter of each paragraph.
8. Number the pages at the bottom center.

AN EFFECTIVE RESUME / By Your Name

¶The main goal of a resume is to create enough interest to secure an interview for a job. A resume should be brief—no more than one page. It should reflect your education, skills, accomplishments, and experience in a positive way.
¶Before you begin writing your resume, do a self-evaluation. Determine your abilities and your goals and ensure that they are compatible. Know what you want to do, why you want to do it, and why someone should hire you to do this.

Multiple Learning Styles

To help kinetic learners, have students write instructions on flash cards. Then have them walk in rhythm while they repeat the instructions as a chant to the rhythm they are walking. Students should emphasize keywords by lightly stomping, or stopping and tapping their toe.

SCHOOL TO CAREER

Have students write a self-evaluation, determining their abilities and goals. Remind students that these should be compatible. Then have students write a resume, including any new information since they wrote their last resume.

¶The next step is to prepare a draft of your resume. Start with your name, address, and telephone number. You may want to include an objective such as "Obtain a position that utilizes my skills and provides an opportunity for growth." Next, include your educational background. Include school names, dates, special courses, and your grade point average.

¶Next, list your work experience, if any. This list should be arranged in chronological order, with the most recent experience first. Include the name and address of your employer, your supervisor's name, and a brief description of your duties. If you have no work experience, you may want to describe activities in which you participated that have provided you with valuable skills.

¶Finally, develop a list of references. Before doing so, ask people for permission to use their names. References should consist of teachers, employers, supervisors, or other people who can vouch for your work ethics and other important traits.

¶Once you determine what should be on your resume, type the final copy. Be sure to proofread carefully. Your resume will often make the first impression an employer will have of you, and you want it to be perfect. Then, print your resume on high-quality paper that matches the paper you will use for your cover letter and the envelope.

¶While sending a perfect resume will maximize your chances of securing a job, it does not guarantee that everyone to whom you send your resume will interview you.

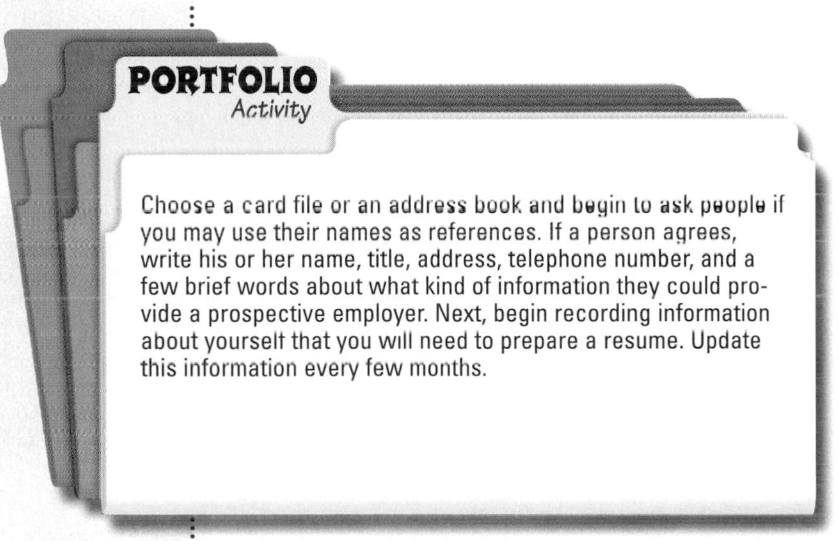

PORTFOLIO *Activity*

Choose a card file or an address book and begin to ask people if you may use their names as references. If a person agrees, write his or her name, title, address, telephone number, and a few brief words about what kind of information they could provide a prospective employer. Next, begin recording information about yourself that you will need to prepare a resume. Update this information every few months.

LESSON 102

ASSESS

- Check to see if students are increasing their word a minute speeds as they complete each 5-minute timing.
- Make sure students are able to use the Font Colors and Drop Cap software features.
- As students begin typing the report, walk around the room and point out correct and incorrect formatting to individual students.
- After students finish typing the report, have them view their work on the screen to see if they made any errors. If errors were made, have students edit their work and make corrections.

CLOSE

If students do not finish the report during the class period, make sure they save their work so that they can complete it the next time this class meets.

PORTFOLIO *Activity*

If students' portfolio goals include demonstrating progress, they may want to include the report from this lesson. Encourage students to evaluate their work and include comments in their portfolio.

Teacher Notes

LESSON 103

FOCUS

- Use the Language Link activity to eliminate redundant wording in sentences.
- Use a Pretest/Practice/Posttest routine to build speed and accuracy.
- Learn word processing features: Borders, Drop Shadows, and Fill.
- Type and format reports using borders, drop shadows, and fill.

BELLRINGER

As soon as students arrive at their workstations and log in, have them type the Warmup. Go over the purpose of each line as shown to the left of the copy.

TEACH

Activity B. After students have completed typing the activity, go over lines 5–10 with them. Help students to find any redundancies they missed.

Solutions: Answers will vary.

LESSON 103 BORDERS AND FILL

OBJECTIVES:

- Improve keyboarding skill.
- Compose at the keyboard.
- Learn about borders and fill.
- Learn about drop shadows.

A. WARMUP

Type each line 2 times.

```
Speed          1 The six forms she got from the firm may do for the problem.
Accuracy       2 The judge quickly gave six of the prizes to the able woman.
Language Link  3 There at the bank their personnel gave personal statements.
Technique      4 I need TWO or THREE or FOUR, but ONE or FIVE are good also.
                 | 1 | 2 | 3 | 4 | 5 | 6 | 7 | 8 | 9 | 10 | 11 | 12
```

B. COMPOSING AT THE KEYBOARD

To make your writing easier to read and understand, use concise wording. Replace lengthy phrases such as *due to the fact that* with *because*.

Revise the following paragraph to eliminate the redundant wording.

```
     Last week I completed my term paper in a satis-
factory manner. The paper was six pages in length and
was written for the purpose of describing what happened
during the Civil War. For the simple reason that I had
done my research for the purpose of completing this
report, I know that my grade will meet with my approval.
It would appear that my instructor plans to extend to
me an invitation to read the report to the class. Due
to the fact that I am not a good speaker, I am experi-
encing nervousness about doing this.
```


RESOURCES

 Lesson Plan 103

 Courseware Lesson 103

Student Data Disk

Student Manual

Supplementary Production Activities

Cross-Curricular Activities

SKILLBUILDING

C. PRETEST

Take a 1-minute timing on the paragraph. Note your speed and errors

```
15      You should join those who have learned how to use       10
16 their typing skill on the job. This skill can be used in     22
17 many walks of life, and it is just what you will need to     33
18 help you succeed. Most jobs now require computer typing.     44
   | 1 | 2 | 3 | 4 | 5 | 6 | 7 | 8 | 9 | 10 | 11 | 12
```

D. PRACTICE

SPEED: ***If you made 2 or fewer errors on the Pretest, type lines 19–26 two times each.***

ACCURACY: ***If you made more than 2 errors on the Pretest, type lines 19–22 as a group two times. Then type lines 23–26 as a group two times.***

Left-Hand Reaches

```
19 ded den dear deaf dread greed horde stead adept defer dried
20 wew wet week weed weave swear where worse weigh wheat wheel
21 cdc cod clad cord cedar crowd cloud cadet child crude cider
22 rtr art wart cart track train start trail tramp parts troop
```

Right-Hand Reaches

```
23 uyu your duly yule duty lucky young youth dusty yucca murky
24 jhj just huge join harm joist hunch jumpy house judge heart
25 klk milk folk walk silk silky balky milky links polka stalk
26 opo pop poor stop snoop whoop spoon ponds pound polka scope
```

E. POSTTEST

Repeat the Pretest. Compare your Posttest results with your Pretest results.

FACT FILE

Silly putty was originally known as "gupp." This popular material was invented in 1945 by engineers at GE.

LESSON 103

TEACH

Activities C–E. Remind students they should improve both their speed and accuracy from the Pretest to the Posttest.

PRETEST/PRACTICE/POSTEST

The ***Pretest/Practice/Posttest*** routines are designed to improve speed or accuracy.

- The ***Pretest*** identifies students' speed or accuracy needs.
- The ***Practice*** provides a variety of improvement drills.
- The ***Posttest*** (a repeat of the Pretest) measures improvement.

SCHOOL TO CAREER

Have students choose a partner. One student is the interviewer; the other, the interviewee. Before mock interviews begin, have students list questions the interviewer should ask. Provide time for each student to be the interviewer and the interviewee. Have students critique each other.

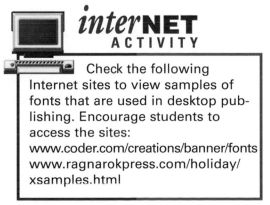

interNET ACTIVITY

Check the following Internet sites to view samples of fonts that are used in desktop publishing. Encourage students to access the sites:
www.coder.com/creations/banner/fonts
www.ragnarokpress.com/holiday/xsamples.html

TEACH

Activity F. Provide classroom time for students to experiment with borders, drop shadows, and fill.

Activity G. Have students turn to Lesson 103 in their Student Manual and complete the practice activities and jobs that follow.

STUDENT MANUAL

Be sure students turn to the correct lesson in their Student Manual.

Report 36. Remind students to use the default top margins and to leave a blank line between paragraphs.

FORMATTING

F. Borders, Drop Shadow, Fill

In addition to different fonts and colors, there are other special formatting techniques that will make documents more eye-catching. For example, you can use **borders** (frames), around text or pages; **drop shadows** (shading), to make text look three-dimensional; or **fill** (shading), options to call attention to text.

G. Software Features

STUDENT MANUAL

Borders Drop Shadows Fill

Study Lesson 103 in your student manual. Complete all the practice activities while at your computer. Then complete the jobs that follow.

DESKTOP PUBLISHING APPLICATIONS

REPORT 36

Type the following report single-spaced. Use the default top margin. Leave a blank line between paragraphs.

¶It is important to display good manners at all times. Manners are especially important during a job interview. Good manners show that you are sociable and civilized and may be a potentially good member of the company's team.
¶Arriving for an interview on time is one way to demonstrate your good manners. This indicates that you are reliable and will be on time for work. Being late for an interview could harm your chances of being hired.
¶Go to your interview alone. Even if someone must drive you to the interview, do not have him or her accompany you to the interview site. If possible, leave your hat and coat in the outer office. Carrying or wearing them into the interviewer's office may be awkward, and it may give the interviewer the impression that you are anxious to leave!

FACT FILE

Have students work in groups to come up with a list of ten business etiquette tips. When the groups have completed typing their lists, have one member read the group's list to the class. Combine the groups' lists into one class list and post it in the classroom.

¶When you arrive for an interview, be sure to introduce yourself to the receptionist or assistant. Be pleasant and courteous. You can be assured that the manager will receive feedback on your manners and appearance from this person.
¶Once you are in the interviewer's office, wait until you are invited to sit. This shows that you have respect for the interviewer's position. If someone comes into the office during the interview, stand up and be prepared to shake hands with this person—it might be the interviewer's boss.

REPORT 37

Open Report 36 and make the following changes:

1. Center and type in all caps and bold the title *GOOD MANNERS FOR JOB INTERVIEWS* approximately 2 inches from the top of the page.
2. Add a thin border around the title.
3. Add a drop shadow to the title border.
4. Add a 10-percent fill inside the border.
5. Add a thick border to the entire page.
6. Change the paragraphs to a bulleted list.

REPORT 38

Open Report 37 and revise it following these steps:

1. Change the border around the title to a double line.
2. Change the page border to a heavy double line.
3. Delete the fill inside the title border.
4. Change the justification of the paragraphs to full justification.
5. Vertically center the page.

REPORT 39

Open Report 33 and make these changes:

1. Add a heavy border around the heading.
2. Add a heavy, double-line border around the page.
3. Add a broken-line border to the last line.
4. Add a 5-percent fill/shading to the last line.

Teacher Notes

LESSON 103

TEACH

Report 37. Have a student read each step aloud.

Report 38. As students work, walk around the room to make sure each student is completing the assignment according to the directions.

Report 39. Have students check each other's work for accuracy.

ASSESS

- Watch students as they complete the Language Link activity to see if they are able to revise the paragraph to eliminate redundant wording.
- Check to see if students show signs of improvement from the Pretest to the Posttest.
- Make sure students are able to use the Borders, Drop Shadows, and Fill software features.
- After students finish typing the reports, have them view their work on the screen to see if they made any errors. If errors were made, have students edit their work and make corrections.

CLOSE

If students do not finish the reports during the class period, make sure they save their work so that they can complete it the next time this class meets.

LESSON 104

ASSESS

- Use 30-second timings to build speed.
- Learn desktop publishing features: Lines, Line Position, Line Size, and Line Style.
- Type and format flyers using graphic lines and rules.

BELLRINGER

As soon as students arrive at their workstations and log in, have them type the Warmup. Go over the purpose of each line as shown to the left of the copy.

TEACH

Activity B. Remind students that the goal for 30-second timings is improved speed with each timing.

LESSON 104 GRAPHIC LINES/RULES

OBJECTIVES:

- Refine keyboarding skill.
- Learn to select, size, and position lines.
- Learn about line styles.

A. WARMUP

Type each line 2 times.

```
Speed             1 Clair may wish to blame me for both of these big work jams.
Accuracy          2 By quietly giving back six tops, we amazed the four judges.
Language Link     3 The French student will visit the Grand Canyon in February.
Numbers/Symbols   4 Rick sold 64 tickets on 10/23/99, and then he sold 75 more.
                    | 1 | 2 | 3 | 4 | 5 | 6 | 7 | 8 | 9 | 10 | 11 | 12
```

SKILLBUILDING

B. 30-SECOND TIMINGS

Take two 30-second timings on lines 5–6. Then take two 30-second timings on lines 7–8. Try to increase your speed on each timing.

```
5      I think that we might cut down our staff loss if you      11
6  will make a pay scale that shows all are being paid fairly.   23

7      We have not been able to cut costs. We do not know how    11
8  a boss set up the pay scale to show we are all paid fairly.   23
   | 1 | 2 | 3 | 4 | 5 | 6 | 7 | 8 | 9 | 10 | 11 | 12
```

interNET CONNECTION

Connect to the Internet. Enter the following URL: http://www.almaz.com/nobel/literature.html. Prepare a short report from the information you have read.

RESOURCES

Lesson Plan 104

Courseware Lesson 104

Student Data Disk

Student Manual

Supplementary Production Activities

FORMATTING

C. Graphic Lines/Rules

Vertical and/or horizontal lines, or rules, can be used to enhance the appearance of a printed page or to separate text to make it more readable. There are a variety of line styles from which to choose. Lines may be light, heavy, solid, broken, double, and so on. In addition, lines can be positioned in different ways to make your document visually appealing.

D. Software Features

STUDENT MANUAL

Lines	Line Position
Line Size	Line Style

Study Lesson 104 in your student manual. Complete all the practice activities while at your computer. Then complete the jobs that follow.

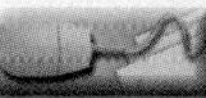

DESKTOP PUBLISHING APPLICATIONS

REPORT 40
Flyer

Open and revise Report 33 as follows:

1. Add a heavy line the length of the heading above and below the heading.
2. Add a heavy line the length of the longest text line approximately 0.5 inch below the last line of text.
3. Delete the Wingdings diamonds and extra spaces from both sides of each item in the list.
4. Draw a geometric shape around the items in the list.

REPORT 41
Flyer

Open Report 38. Give it a new look by following these steps:

1. Delete the border around the title.
2. Delete the page border.
3. Change the page layout so that the title starts approximately 2 inches from the top of the page.
4. Change the title to Times New Roman 20-point blue.
5. Add a thick horizontal blue line beneath the title.
6. Change the bullets to 20-point red.
7. Add a 5-inch horizontal double blue line 0.5 inch below the last line of text.

Teacher Notes

TEACH

Activity C. Ask students to collect copies of brochures and other documents that illustrate vertical and/or horizontal lines. Post these around the room as models.

Activity D. Walk around the room while students are completing Lesson 104 in their Student Manual. Make sure they understand what they are to do and that they are doing the assignment correctly.

STUDENT MANUAL
Be sure students turn to the correct lesson in their Student Manual.

Report 40. If you haven't done so for awhile, remind students to be aware of their posture, to sit up, keep their elbows in, and their feet flat on the floor.

Report 41. Have students help each other with the steps in this report. Also have students check each other's work.

Be sure to preview the Internet site before assigning this activity to students to make sure the site is appropriate.

TEACH

Report 42. Have different students read aloud the steps for completing Report 42. Stop after each step to make sure all students understand the directions.

ASSESS

- Check to see if students are increasing their word a minute speeds as they complete each 30-second timing.
- Make sure students are able to use the software features concerning lines.
- As students begin typing the reports, walk around the room and point out correct and incorrect formatting to individual students.
- After students finish typing the flyers, have them view their work on the screen to see if they made any errors. If errors were made, have students edit their work and make corrections.

CLOSE

If students do not finish the flyers during the class period, make sure they save their work so that they can complete it the next time this class meets.

Remind students to clean up their workstation when they leave.

REPORT 42
Flyer

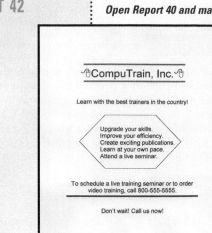

CompuTrain, Inc.

Learn with the best trainers in the country!

Upgrade your skills.
Improve your efficiency.
Create exciting publications.
Learn at your own pace.
Attend a live seminar.

To schedule a live training seminar or to order video training, call 800-555-5555.

Don't wait! Call us now!

Open Report 40 and make the following changes.

1. Change the listed items so that they left-align approximately 1.5 inches from the margin.
2. Adjust the geometric shape so that it still wraps around the list.
3. Delete the line at the bottom of the page.
4. Add a thick horizontal line from margin to margin below the section containing the telephone number.
5. Change the color of the rules above and below the title to red.
6. Change the border of the geometric shape to red.

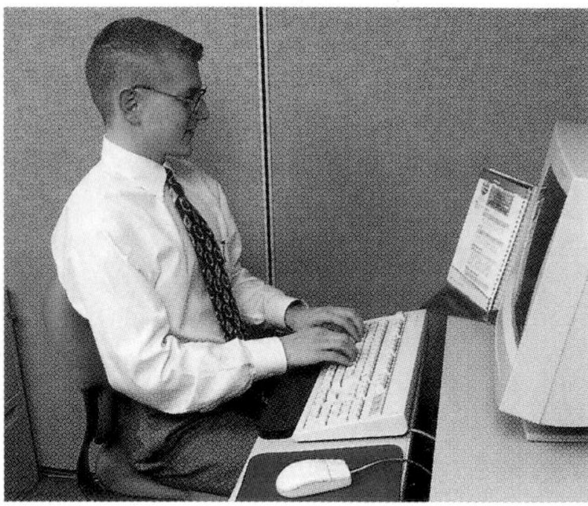

JOURNAL ENTRY

Study the photograph; then write about the importance of correct position while working at a keyboard. Answer: why is it important; what is the correct position; what are some results of incorrect position.

Math Connections

Have students create a 3-column table of 5 items they want to buy. The first column is the name of the item; the second is the price at a trendy store; the third is the price at a discount store. Have them calculate price differences.

Out-of-Class Activity

Have students type a list of the documents they come across in two days that use desktop publishing. Have students try to duplicate one of the documents. They should bring their list, their document, and the original document to class.

LESSON 105 DRAWING

OBJECTIVES:

- Improve keyboarding skills.
- Learn about quotation marks and italics.
- Learn to insert various shapes into documents.

A. WARMUP

Type each line 2 times.

Speed	1	Norma may go for a walk on this nice day to visit that boy.
Accuracy	2	A dozen big witches quickly jumped over six long red sofas.
Language Link	3	Their friends saw the footballs over there in Dave's field.
Numbers/Symbols	4	They bought #2 lead pencils @ $.24 each at Penzey's Papers.

| 1 | 2 | 3 | 4 | 5 | 6 | 7 | 8 | 9 | 10 | 11 | 12

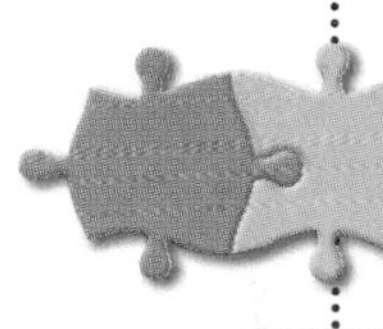

LANGUAGE LINK

B. QUOTATION MARKS AND ITALICS

Study the following rules and examples. Then edit lines 5–8 to correct any errors in the use of quotation marks and italics.

Rule 24: Use quotation marks around the titles of newspaper articles, magazine articles, chapters in a book, conferences, and similar items.

The next assignment is to read the chapter entitled "The Kennedy Years."

Kurt read and reread the article, "An Interview With Joe Montana."

Rule 25: Italicize (or underline) the titles of books, magazines, newspapers, and other complete published works.

The Fifties *by David Halberstam gives an excellent portrait of the decade.*

The article in <u>Sports Illustrated</u> covered the new basketball rules changes.

RESOURCES

 Lesson Plan 105

 Courseware Lesson 105

Student Data Disk

Student Manual

Language Link Worksheets

Supplementary Production Activities

LESSON 105

FOCUS

- Use a Pretest/Practice/Posttest routine to build speed and accuracy.
- Learn desktop publishing features: Inserting/Drawing Shapes, Sizing, and Moving.
- Learn how to format a variety of shapes.
- Type and format reports.

BELLRINGER

As soon as students arrive at their workstations and log in, have them type the Warmup. Go over the purpose of each line as shown to the left of the copy.

TEACH

Activity B. Explain the Language Link rules for using quotation marks and italics. Discuss the difference between titles of magazines and titles of the articles in the magazines; titles of books and chapter titles.

Solutions: The interest rates were discussed in the November 24 *Tribune*.

"Types of Life Insurance" is an excellent chapter in your text.

Her proposed title for the report was "Vacations Versus Trips."

The December 2 issue of *Newsweek* had most excellent coverage.

Activities C–E. Remind students they should improve both their speed and accuracy from the Pretest to the Posttest.

PRETEST/PRACTICE/POSTEST

The ***Pretest/Practice/Posttest*** routines are designed to improve speed or accuracy.

- The ***Pretest*** identifies students' speed or accuracy needs.
- The ***Practice*** provides a variety of improvement drills.
- The ***Posttest*** (a repeat of the Pretest) measures improvement.

Activity F. Have different students draw the different shapes on the board. Label the shapes.

Activity G. Walk around the room while students are completing Lesson 105 in their Student Manuals. Make sure they understand what they are to do and that they are doing the assignment correctly.

STUDENT MANUAL
Be sure students turn to the correct lesson in their Student Manual.

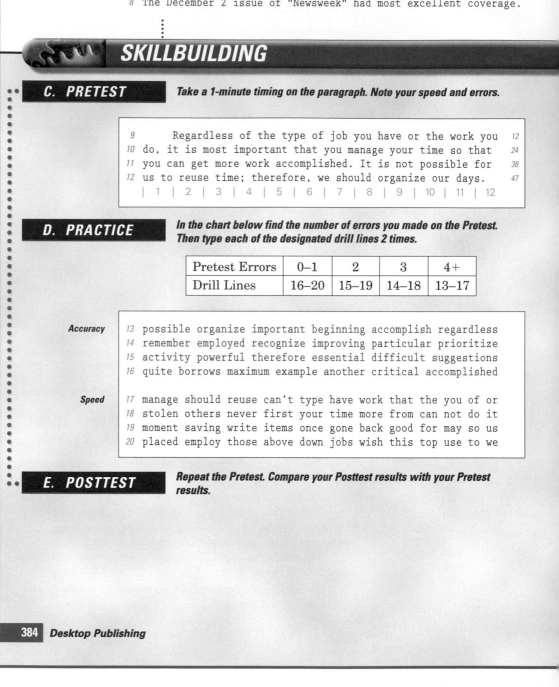

```
5 The interest rates were discussed in the November 24 Tribune.
6 Types of Life Insurance is an excellent chapter in your text.
7 Her proposed title for the report was Vacations Versus Trips.
8 The December 2 issue of "Newsweek" had most excellent coverage.
```

SKILLBUILDING

C. PRETEST

Take a 1-minute timing on the paragraph. Note your speed and errors.

```
 9      Regardless of the type of job you have or the work you   12
10 do, it is most important that you manage your time so that    24
11 you can get more work accomplished. It is not possible for    36
12 us to reuse time; therefore, we should organize our days.     47
   | 1 | 2 | 3 | 4 | 5 | 6 | 7 | 8 | 9 | 10 | 11 | 12
```

D. PRACTICE

In the chart below find the number of errors you made on the Pretest. Then type each of the designated drill lines 2 times.

Pretest Errors	0–1	2	3	4+
Drill Lines	16–20	15–19	14–18	13–17

Accuracy

```
13 possible organize important beginning accomplish regardless
14 remember employed recognize improving particular prioritize
15 activity powerful therefore essential difficult suggestions
16 quite borrows maximum example another critical accomplished
```

Speed

```
17 manage should reuse can't type have work that the you of or
18 stolen others never first your time more from can not do it
19 moment saving write items once gone back good for may so us
20 placed employ those above down jobs wish this top use to we
```

E. POSTTEST

Repeat the Pretest. Compare your Posttest results with your Pretest results.

FACT FILE

Tell students that it is important to protect computers with anti-virus software to keep out the "bugs." The first computer "bug" was in a Navy computer. It was an actual bug—a moth caught in a relay switch that caused errors. Have students investigate anti-virus software.

FORMATTING

F. Circles, Ellipses (Ovals), and Other Shapes

By using a variety of shapes such as circles, rectangles, and ellipses (ovals), you can make page layouts more interesting. Once these shapes are inserted into a document, they can be repositioned and resized.

G. Software Feature

STUDENT MANUAL

Inserting/Drawing Shapes
Sizing Moving

Study Lesson 105 in your student manual. Complete all the practice activities while at your computer. Then complete the jobs that follow.

DESKTOP PUBLISHING APPLICATIONS

REPORT 43

Follow these directions to create a snowperson similar to the illustration at the left.

1. Draw an oval approximately 3 inches wide and 2.5 inches high.
2. Drag the oval to the lower half of the page.
3. Create a circle and size it so that it is approximately 2 inches in diameter.
4. Place this circle on the top of the oval and center it.
5. Create another circle and size it so that it is approximately 1 inch in diameter.
6. Place this circle on top of the other circle in the approximate horizontal center.
7. Add the face, arms, and other features using drawing tools.

REPORT 44

Open Report 35 and make the following changes:

1. Insert a right arrow beside the title. Size the arrow so that it is approximately the height of the title and does not overlay the text.
2. Add a 100-percent red fill to the arrow.
3. Insert a rounded rectangle approximately 4 inches wide and 0.25 inch high at the end of the document.
4. Change the border to red.

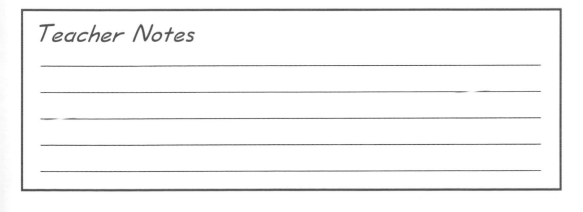

Teacher Notes

TEACH

Illustration
The illustration shows a snowperson created by following the directions.

Report 43. Have students read and follow the instructions carefully.

Report 44. Read the instructions aloud to students, stopping after each step to make sure students understand what they are to do.

ASSESS

- Watch students as they complete the Language Link activity to see if they are able to apply the rules for using quotation marks and italics.
- Check to see if students show signs of improvement from the Pretest to the Posttest.
- Make sure students are able to use the drawing software features.
- After students finish typing the reports, have them view their work on the screen to see if they made any errors.

CLOSE

If students do not finish the reports during the class period, make sure they save their work so that they can complete it the next time this class meets.

LESSON 106

FOCUS

- Use 30-second timings to build speed.
- Learn word processing features: Text Boxes and Graphics or Figure Boxes.
- Type and format flyers.

BELLRINGER

As soon as students arrive at their workstations and log in, have them type the Warmup. Go over the purpose of each line as shown to the left of the copy.

TEACH

Activity B. Remind students that the goal for 30-second OK timings is improved accuracy.

Activity C. Have students collect samples of desktop publishing documents that use boxes and bring these to class.

Activity D. Have students turn to Lesson 106 in their Student Manual and complete all practice activities and jobs that follow.

STUDENT MANUAL

Be sure students turn to the correct lesson in their Student Manual.

Report 45. Have students read and follow the instructions carefully.

LESSON 106

BOXES: TEXT AND GRAPHIC BOXES

OBJECTIVES:

- Improve keyboarding speed.
- Learn about text and graphic boxes.
- Learn to add text and graphics to boxes.

A. WARMUP

Type each line 2 times.

Speed	1	All my friends met Tom at the mall and went on to the play.
Accuracy	2	Judy gave a quick jump as the zebra and lynx fought wildly.
Language Link	3	She counseled and gave advice, but the advice did not work.
Technique	4	Anne saw RCA, BBS, US, and MTV written on the PTO brochure.
		| 1 | 2 | 3 | 4 | 5 | 6 | 7 | 8 | 9 | 10 | 11 | 12

SKILLBUILDING

B. 30-SECOND OK TIMINGS

Take two 30-second OK (error-free) timings on lines 5–6. Then take two 30-second OK timings on lines 7–8. Goal: no errors.

5	Roxie picked yellow jonquils as Delbert watched; then	12
6	he zipped off to the cavern to tell of the amazing event.	24
7	Holly received a prize for jumping over six feet, and	12
8	Mac quickly explained that some big jumps involved risks.	24
	| 1 | 2 | 3 | 4 | 5 | 6 | 7 | 8 | 9 | 10 | 11 | 12	

FORMATTING

C. INSERTING BOXES

Boxes can be used to highlight text and graphics. Text inside a box can be formatted using different font styles and sizes. Whether a box contains text or graphics, its borders and fill can be changed, and it can be repositioned and resized.

RESOURCES

 Lesson Plan 106

 Courseware Lesson 106

Student Data Disk

Student Manual

Supplementary Production Activities

D. SOFTWARE FEATURES

GO TO

STUDENT MANUAL

Text Boxes   Graphic or Figure Boxes

Study Lesson 106 in your student manual. Complete all the practice activities while at your computer. Then complete the jobs that follow.

DESKTOP PUBLISHING APPLICATIONS

REPORT 45

Flyer

Create a flyer following these steps:

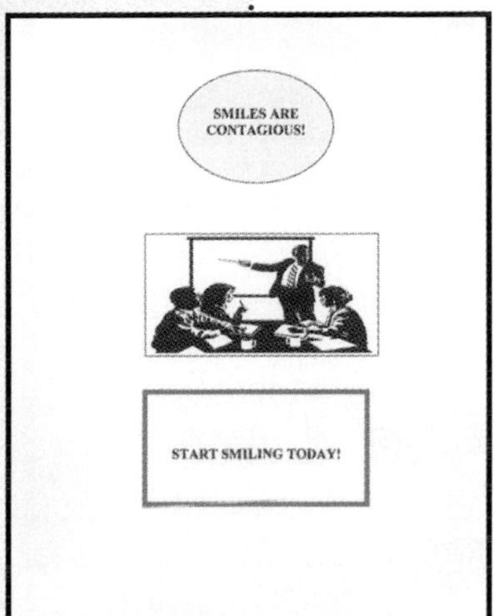

1. Create a circle at the top of the page and horizontally center it.
2. In the circle, center and type in Times New Roman 18-point bold, *SMILES ARE CONTAGIOUS,* and size the circle to fit the text on 2 lines.
3. Approximately 1 inch below the circle, insert a text box that is 4 inches wide and 2 inches high.
4. In the text box, vertically and horizontally center and type in Times New Roman 18-point bold, *HELP START AN EPIDEMIC!*
5. Approximately 1 inch below the text box, insert another text box and center and type in Times New Roman 18-point bold, *START SMILING TODAY!*

REPORT 46

Flyer

Open Report 45 and revise it following these steps:

1. Change the background of the circle to light yellow.
2. Replace the text in the first text box with a graphic of a group of people.
3. Adjust the size of the graphic and/or the text box so that the graphic looks proportionally correct and fills the text box without increasing the size of the text box.
4. Change the border of the bottom text box to a thick green border.

FACT FILE

The act of smiling apparently has some positive effect on the mood chemicals released from the brain, thereby making smiling a method to relieve stress.

Teacher Notes

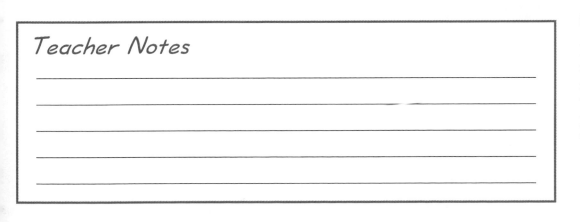

TEACH

Illustration

The illustration shows the flyer created by following the directions.

Report 46. Have different students read aloud the steps for creating this flyer. Stop after each step to make sure all students understand the directions.

ASSESS

- Check to see if students are improving their accuracy as they complete 30-second timings.
- Make sure students are able to use the Text Boxes and Graphics or Figure Boxes software features.
- As students begin typing the flyers, walk around the room and point out correct and incorrect formatting to individual students.
- After students finish typing the flyers, have them view their work on the screen to see if they made any errors. If errors were made, have students edit their work and make corrections.

CLOSE

If students do not finish the flyers during the class period, make sure they save their work so that they can complete it the next time this class meets.

LESSON 107

FOCUS

- Apply the Language Link rules concerning comma usage.
- Use 5-minute timings to build speed.
- Learn word processing features: Fill and Borders.
- Type reports.

BELLRINGER

As soon as students arrive at their workstations and log in, have them type the Warmup. Go over the purpose of each line as shown to the left of the copy.

TEACH

Activity B. Go over the comma rules with students. Give them time to study these rules in class; then ask what their questions are concerning them. When students have completed the assignment, have them check each other's work.

Solutions: The warehouse building will be ready in September 2000.

The lawyer told the clerk to use May 3, 1999, as the date.

The reports were sent to Nagoya, Japan, on March 14, 1999.

The move to Toledo, Ohio, was scheduled for August 2001.

LESSON 107

BOXES: FILL, BORDERS

OBJECTIVES:

- Type 38/5'/5e.
- Learn rules for commas.
- Learn to change box borders and fill.

A. WARMUP

Type each line 2 times.

Speed	1 I came to work for this firm and have been here since then.
Accuracy	2 Jacques picked five boxes of oranges while Diz stayed home.
Language Link	3 The council gave advice; a counselor advised Flora to stay.
Numbers	4 Please clean Rooms 4, 6, and 7 but not Rooms 9, 29, and 38.

| 1 | 2 | 3 | 4 | 5 | 6 | 7 | 8 | 9 | 10 | 11 | 12

B. COMMAS

Study the following rules and examples for comma usage. Then edit lines 5–8 to correct any errors.

Rule 26: Use a comma before and after the year in a complete date.

On December 7, 1996, the Tribune *reviewed the Pearl Harbor events.*

BUT: *The* News Monthly *printed December 1996 reviewed the same events.*

Rule 27: Use a comma before and after a state or country that follows a city, but not before a ZIP Code.

Sioux City, Iowa, is a lovely place in which to live.

BUT: *Sioux City, IA 51102, is where she plans to live.*

5 The warehouse buildings will be ready in September, 2000.
6 The lawyer told the clerk to use May 3, 1999 as the date.
7 The reports were sent to Nagoya, Japan on March 14, 1999.
8 The move to Toledo, Ohio, was scheduled for August, 2001.

RESOURCES

 Lesson Plan 107

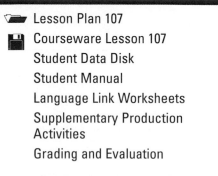

 Courseware Lesson 107

Student Data Disk

Student Manual

Language Link Worksheets

Supplementary Production Activities

Grading and Evaluation

C. Preview Practice

Type each line 2 times as a preview to the timings that follow.

Accuracy merit fortunate promotion beforehand experience individuals
Speed a do be in the you not set are now own how why than what

D. 5-Minute Timings

Take two 5-minute timings on the paragraphs. Note your speed and errors.

Goal: 38/5'/5e

If you feel fortunate to have a job today, this might 11
not be in your best interest. In fact, this feeling will 22
prevent some individuals from taking the risks needed to 34
keep up with salary trends in their field. 42

You should realize that getting a raise is harder now 53
than it was ten years ago. When you believe you merit one, 65
do not be afraid to seek it out. Usually, a promotion comes 77
with a raise. In this case, your good work already is being 89
recognized and rewarded. However, there are times when an 101
employee must take the initiative to seek what is due. 112

Take inventory of yourself. Be sure you know what your 123
strengths are and how your experience makes you a valuable 135
employee. Know why you deserve the raise so you can justify 147
it to your employer. 151

Requesting a raise on your own may mean you need to 162
meet a different set of job standards. Your employer might 173
expect something more from you. You might want to think 185
about a response beforehand. 190

| 1 | 2 | 3 | 4 | 5 | 6 | 7 | 8 | 9 | 10 | 11 | 12 SI 1.36

interNET CONNECTION

Connect to the Internet and enter the following URL:
http://www.dac.neu.edu/coop.careerservices/interview.html
Select one of the topics of interest about interviews. You may be especially interested in the topic "Salary Negotiation."

TEACH

Activity C. Point out that words in the Preview Practice are used in the timing that follows.

Activity D. Remind students that they should try to improve speed with each 5-minute timing. The goal for these timings is to type 38 words a minute for 5 minutes with no more than 5 errors.

Be sure to preview the Internet site before assigning this activity to students to make sure the site is appropriate.

FACT FILE

Introduce students to career resources that include salary information from Bureau of Labor Statistics publications such as Occupational Outlook Handbook, Occupational Quarterly, and Dictionary of Occupational Titles. Have students find these publications in the library and bring three facts from them to class.

TEACH

Activity E. Walk around the room while students are completing Lesson 107 in their Student Manual. Make sure they understand what they are to do and that they are doing the assignment correctly.

STUDENT MANUAL

Be sure students turn to the correct lesson in their Student Manual.

Report 47. Remind students to single-space this report.

Report 48. Have students read and follow the instructions carefully.

FORMATTING

E. SOFTWARE FEATURES

STUDENT MANUAL

Fill Borders

Study Lesson 107 in your student manual. Complete all the practice activities while at your computer. Then complete the jobs that follow.

DESKTOP PUBLISHING APPLICATIONS

REPORT 47

Type the following report single-spaced. Press ENTER 6 times to leave an approx. 2-inch margin. Do not include a title. Do not leave a blank line between paragraphs.

Different animals behave in a variety of ways. An animal's behavior is dependent on a number of factors. One factor that affects its behavior is the environment. The environment consists not only of living things but also of physical characteristics such as temperature, types of soil, amount of rainfall, and amount of light.
¶Animal behavior is greatly affected by the temperature of the environment where the animal lives. Animals' body temperatures can vary greatly. Some animals are described as cold-blooded—such as snakes and frogs. *Cold-blooded* means that their body temperature changes as the temperature of their environment changes. Although the body temperature of cold-blooded animals is not always the same as the environment, it is usually close to it.
¶Warm-blooded animals—including tigers and humans—maintain the same body temperature nearly all the time. Warm-blooded animals usually maintain the temperature at which they function best. People, for example, maintain an average body temperature of 37 degrees Celsius.
¶Some warm-blooded animals hibernate during the winter. Groundhogs and woodchucks are examples of mammals that hibernate. Their body activities come to almost a complete halt. Bears are often thought, erroneously, to hibernate. However, they have been known to occasionally wake up and walk around.

Science Connections

Science Connections

February 2 is Ground-hog Day. According to legend, the ground hog emerges from hibernation on this day and returns to its burrow if it sees its shadow, predicting long winter weather. Have students write about a warm-blooded animal.

interNET ACTIVITY

Have students search with the keyword weather or access The Weather Channel (www.weather.com) to learn about weather patterns in your area. Then have them write a short report on one type of weather in your region.

REPORT 48

Open Report 47 and modify it as follows:

1. Beginning with the first paragraph, change the line spacing to 1.5.
2. Add the page number at the bottom center.
3. Create a text box at the beginning of the first paragraph.
4. Choose an animal graphic and insert it into the box.
5. Resize the graphic and the text box so that the graphic remains proportional.
6. Position the text box so that it does not cover any text.
7. Delete the text box border.

REPORT 49

Open Report 48 and make the following changes:

1. Create a text box at the top of the report.
2. Horizontally center the text box.
3. Inside the text box, center and type in Times New Roman 20-point bold, *ANIMAL BEHAVIOR*.
4. Shade the text box with a 15-percent fill in a color that complements the graphic.
5. Change the body of the report to full justification.
6. Add the same animal graphic that appears at the beginning of the page after the last line of text.
7. Position the graphic so that it does not cause text to shift, and delete the border.

FACT FILE

The cheetah is the fastest mammal on record. Cheetahs can travel at speeds of 60 to 70 miles an hour. Cheetahs are usually found in east Africa, Iran, Afghanistan, and Turkmenistan.

Teacher Notes

LESSON 107

TEACH

Report 49. Have different students read aloud the steps for this report. Stop after each step to make sure all students understand the directions.

Illustration

The illustration shows Report 49 created by following the directions.

ASSESS

- Check to see if students are increasing their word a minute speeds as they complete each 5-minute timing.
- Watch students as they complete the Language Link activity to see if they are able to apply the rules.
- Make sure students are able to use the Fill and Borders software features.
- As students type the reports, walk around the room and point out correct and incorrect formatting.

CLOSE

If students do not finish the reports during the class period, make sure they save their work so that they can complete it the next time this class meets.

LESSON 108

FOCUS

- Use 12-second timings to build speed.
- Use Paced Practice 2-minute timing routines.
- Learn a word processing feature: Wrapping Text.
- Learn how to wrap text around boxes.
- Type and format reports.

BELLRINGER

As soon as students arrive at their workstations and log in, have them type the Warmup. Go over the purpose of each line as shown to the left of the copy.

TEACH

Activity B. Remind students that the goal for 12-second timings is improved speed with each timing.

Activity C. Go over the procedure for Paced Practice 2-minute timing routines with students. (See Lesson 34, page 119.)

LESSON 108

BOXES: WRAPPING TEXT

OBJECTIVES:

- Improve keyboarding techniques.
- Learn to wrap text around boxes.

A. WARMUP

Type each line 2 times.

Speed	*1*	Show her what a nice day it is so that she may take a walk.
Accuracy	*2*	Expert jockeys quickly led a horse away from a blazing van.
Language Link	*3*	Because we stopped to eat, we got home well after midnight.
Numbers/Symbols	*4*	Jon & Bev paid for 674# of #95 glue @ $1.92 at Quill & Ink.

| 1 | 2 | 3 | 4 | 5 | 6 | 7 | 8 | 9 | 10 | 11 | 12

SKILLBUILDING

B. 12-SECOND SPRINTS

Take three 12-second timings on each line. Try to increase your speed on each timing.

Keep your eyes on the copy.

5 Irene was to make the cake for the office party this month.
6 He bought a new computer from the dealer at the mall today.
7 My courses were given in the rooms of the old school house.
8 When you go to the dance, be sure to take her some flowers.

5 | 10 | 15 | 20 | 25 | 30 | 35 | 40 | 45 | 50 | 55 | 60

C. PACED PRACTICE

Turn to the Paced Practice routine beginning on page SB7. Take three 2-minute timings, starting at the point where you left off the last time.

COMMUNICATION FOCUS

A *smiley* or *emoticon* is sometimes used to mean a grin or some other emotion. Ask your friends and a few business associates how they feel about receiving these symbols in messages.

RESOURCES

 Lesson Plan 108

 Courseware Lesson 108

Student Data Disk

Student Manual

Supplementary Production Activities

FORMATTING

D. Wrapping Text

Once a text or graphic box is inserted into a document, it can be positioned anywhere on the page. In order to keep the original text on the page readable, you may want to wrap the text around the box or have the text appear above, below, or beside the box.

E. Software Features

STUDENT MANUAL

Wrapping Text

Study Lesson 108 in your student manual. Complete all the practice activities while at your computer. Then complete the jobs that follow.

DESKTOP PUBLISHING APPLICATIONS

REPORT 50

Open Report 46 and revise it as follows:

1. Type the paragraph following the numbered steps at the top of the page.
2. Wrap the text around the sides of the circle containing the words *SMILES ARE CONTAGIOUS.* Make any adjustments that may be necessary to attractively arrange the text and circle.
3. Add a 48-point smiley face symbol centered below the type in the circle.
4. Delete the graphic from the text box.
5. Insert four 78-point smiley face symbols in the text box, horizontally center them, and adjust the size of the text box as necessary.
6. Add a 48-point smiley face symbol centered below the text in the last text box.
7. Add a heavy black border to the page.

Much has been said about the effect of smiles on human beings. Perhaps you have heard some of the following well-known sayings. "A smile is an expression your face wears when your heart is happy." "A smile is your umbrella during stormy times." "A smile is a frown turned upside down." "Smile, it gives your face something to do."

TEACH

Activity D. Bring to class examples of text wrapped around photos. Pass these examples around for students to see.

Activity E. Have students turn to Lesson 108 in their Student Manual and complete the practice activities and jobs that follow.

STUDENT MANUAL

Be sure students turn to the correct lesson in their Student Manual.

Report 50. Read the instructions aloud to students, stopping after each step to make sure students understand what they are to do.

Illustration

The illustration shows Report 50 completed by following the directions.

TECHNOLOGY TIP

Electrical surges are swells of electricity that move like a wave through electrical lines. Electrical surges can harm, or even destroy, documents. An electrical surge protector protects the computer from electrical surges. This device allows you to plug several electrical plugs in to it.

Multiple Learning Styles

Have students work in groups to create a rap/hip-hop song about smiling. While groups are brainstorming about the lyrics of their songs, walk around the room and assist where necessary. Students should type their lyrics, make copies, and pass them around.

TEACH

Report 51. Read the instructions aloud to students, stopping after each step to make sure students understand what they are to do.

Illustration

The illustration shows Report 51 completed by following the directions.

ASSESS

- Check to see if students are increasing their word a minute speeds as they complete each 12-second timing.
- Make sure students can use the Wrapping Text software feature.
- As students begin typing the reports, walk around the room and point out correct and incorrect formatting to individual students.
- After students finish typing the reports, have them view their work on the screen to see if they made any errors. If errors were made, have students edit their work and make corrections.

CLOSE

If students do not finish the reports during the class period, make sure they save their work so that they can complete it the next time this class meets.

Remind students to clean up their workstation when they leave.

"Frowns cause wrinkles; smile now—avoid wrinkles later." "Smile—everyone will wonder what you are up to." "Smile and the world smiles with you—cry and you cry alone." "Smiles beget smiles." "It takes fewer face muscles to smile than to frown." Why not give smiling a try?

REPORT 51

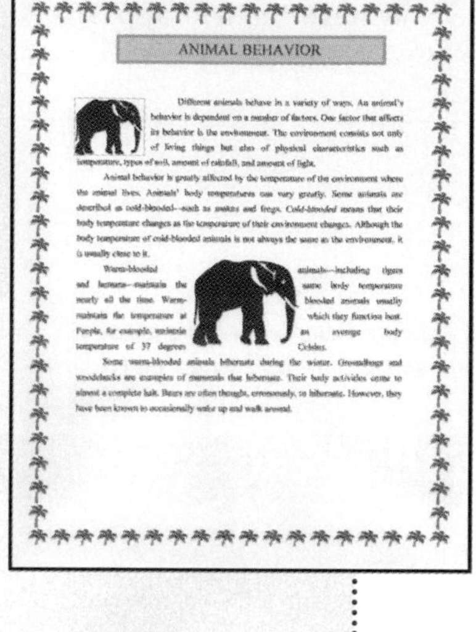

ANIMAL BEHAVIOR

Different animals behave in a variety of ways. An animal's behavior is dependent on a number of factors. One factor that affects its behavior is the environment. The environment consists not only of living things but also of physical characteristics such as temperature, types of soil, amount of rainfall, and amount of light.

Animal behavior is greatly affected by the temperature of the environment where the animal lives. Animals' body temperatures can vary greatly. Some animals are described as cold-blooded—such as snakes and frogs. *Cold-blooded* means that their body temperature changes as the temperature of their environment changes. Although the body temperature of cold-blooded animals is not always the same as the environment, it is usually close to it.

Warm-blooded animals—including tigers and humans—maintain the same body temperature nearly all the time. Warm-blooded animals usually maintain the temperature at which they function best. People, for example, maintain an average body temperature of 37 degrees Celsius.

Some warm-blooded animals hibernate during the winter. Groundhogs and woodchucks are examples of mammals that hibernate. Their body activities come to almost a complete halt. Bears are often thought, erroneously, to hibernate. However, they have been known to occasionally wake up and walk around.

Open Report 49 and make the following changes:

1. Change the border of the title to a heavy line.
2. Resize the graphic at the top of the page to approximately 1.5 by 1.5 inches, and add a thin border the same color as the title border.
3. Move the graphic to the beginning of the first paragraph, and wrap the text to the right of the graphic.
4. Move the graphic at the end of the report to the end of the second paragraph, and size it to approximately 2 inches wide.
5. Wrap the text around both sides of the graphic.
6. To the entire page, add a fancy border that relates to the content of the report.

PORTFOLIO *Activity*

Using what you have learned so far about desktop publishing, create a document that incorporates this knowledge. Think of a theme relating to health, manners, careers, or other topics of interest. If necessary, search the Internet for information about your topic to include in your document. Print the final product and save it as an example of your work.

Teacher Notes

LESSON 109 PERSONAL NOTEPADS

OBJECTIVES:

- Compose at the keyboard.
- Improve keyboarding skill.
- Learn about reverse text.
- Create personal notepads.

A. WARMUP

Type each line 2 times.

Speed	1 Nan said she may go back to her job by the end of the week.
Accuracy	2 Jane quickly seized the wax buffer and removed a big patch.
Language Link	3 Bert lost his shoes Tuesday on Flight 567; they are size 9.
Technique	4 q z p / w x o . e c I , r v u m t b y n a ; s l d k f j g h
	| 1 | 2 | 3 | 4 | 5 | 6 | 7 | 8 | 9 | 10 | 11 | 12

LANGUAGE LINK

B. COMPOSING AT THE KEYBOARD

Choose one of the following topics and compose a short three-paragraph report.

5 My Greatest Fear
6 My Proudest Moment
7 My Future Plans

FACT FILE

In 1987, Astronomer Ian Shelton discovered a supernova (exploding star). This event was the first such discovery visible with the naked eye since 1604.

LESSON 109

FOCUS

- Compose a multiparagraph report.
- Use a Pretest/Practice/Posttest routine to build speed and accuracy.
- Learn a word processing feature: Reverse Text
- Type and format reports using the reverse text feature.

BELLRINGER

As soon as students arrive at their workstations and log in, have them type the Warmup. Go over the purpose of each line as shown to the left of the copy.

TEACH

Activity B. After students have completed their paragraphs, ask for volunteers to read their work in class.

Solutions: Answers will vary.

RESOURCES

Lesson Plan 109

Courseware Lesson 109
Student Data Disk
Student Manual
Supplementary Production Activities

TEACH

Activities C–E. Remind students they should improve both their speed and accuracy from the Pretest to the Posttest.

PRETEST/PRACTICE/POSTEST

The ***Pretest/Practice/Posttest*** routines are designed to improve speed or accuracy.

- The ***Pretest*** identifies students' speed or accuracy needs.
- The ***Practice*** provides a variety of improvement drills.
- The ***Posttest*** (a repeat of the Pretest) measures improvement.

SKILLBUILDING

C. PRETEST

Take a 1-minute timing on the paragraph. Note your speed and errors.

8 Reading a book during a weekend is a wise choice. You 10
9 can increase your word power even by reading popular books. 22
10 Enjoy yourself; join a number of those who choose to read a 33
11 good book. Invest your weekend time wisely by reading. 44
| 1 | 2 | 3 | 4 | 5 | 6 | 7 | 8 | 9 | 10 | 11 | 12

D. PRACTICE

SPEED: ***If you made 2 or fewer errors on the Pretest, type lines 12–19 two times each.***

ACCURACY: ***If you made more than 2 errors on the Pretest, type lines 12–15 as a group two times. Then type lines 16–19 as a group two times.***

Adjacent Reaches

12 we weak wean wept weave wedge sweat weigh weary dowel sweet
13 oi soil toil boil hoist point joist poise spoil avoid noise
14 po pond port pour pound pouch poach point polka power polar
15 rt tort sort dart short court party warts sorts forth mirth

Jump Reaches

16 ce cede cell cent cease hence sauce grace niece cedar cello
17 um numb jump lump chump mumps crumb gummy stump thumb bumpy
18 in bind find grin brain cabin cling brink drain faint grain
19 om come pomp some bloom romps domes homes tombs zooms rooms

E. POSTTEST

Repeat the Pretest. Compare your Posttest results with your Pretest results.

FORMATTING

F. SOFTWARE FEATURES

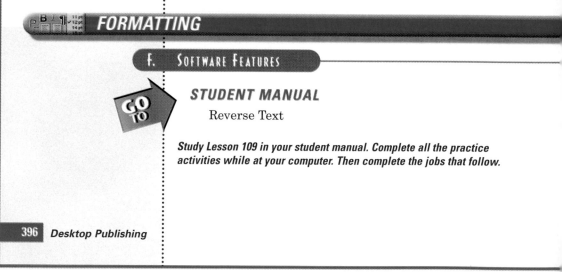

GO TO

STUDENT MANUAL

Reverse Text

Study Lesson 109 in your student manual. Complete all the practice activities while at your computer. Then complete the jobs that follow.

JOURNAL ENTRY

Have students write about how they feel about reading. Do they like to read? Why? If they don't, have them write about why this is so. Remind students to free write for five to ten minutes.

REPORT 52

From the desk of Your Name . . .

- Urgent
- Do Today
- Do As Soon As Possible
- Follow Up

Create the notepad illustrated here by following these steps:

1. Create a boxed table with 1 column and 1 row.
2. Change the font to Times New Roman Bold Italic 24-point.
3. Type *From the desk of* and your name followed by a space and then by three periods. Leave a space between the periods.
4. Apply a 100-percent fill in the color of your choice to the box and reverse the type to white.
5. Create a footer.
6. Change the font to Wingdings 16-point, type the letter *q* to create a check box, and space once.
7. Change the font to Times New Roman Bold Italic 16-point, type *Urgent,* and press ENTER once.
8. Repeat steps 5–7 for the remaining lines, using the words indicated in the illustration.
9. Change the color of the text in the footer to match the color you chose for the top section.

CULTURAL CONNECTIONS

Writing styles and stationery used may vary from country to country. Interview someone from another country to find out how that country writes business letters. Ask what type of stationery is used and what style of letters they use.

TEACH

Activity F. Walk around the room while students are completing Lesson 109 in their Student Manual. Make sure they understand reverse text and that they are doing the assignment correctly.

STUDENT MANUAL

Be sure students turn to the correct lesson in their Student Manual.

Report 52. Have students read and follow the instructions carefully.

Illustration

The illustration shows Report 52 completed by following the directions.

SCHOOL TO CAREER

Stress the importance of writing thank-you notes to the interviewer after an interview. In addition to being good manners, a thank-you note puts your name in front of the prospective employer again, which gives you an advantage over other candidates. Have students create a model.

Out-of-Class Activity

Have students create a table with four columns. Title the columns as follows: *Times Roman key*, *Wingdings key*, *Times Roman shift1*key, *and Wingdings shift1*key. Have students then fill in the chart beginning with the alphabet, then numbers, then symbol keys.

TEACH

Report 53. Go over each step with students for creating this report. Make sure all students understand every step before proceeding.

Illustration

The illustration shows Report 53 completed by following the directions.

ASSESS

- Review the typing accuracy in students' Language Link composing activity paragraphs.
- Check to see if students show signs of improvement from the Pretest to the Posttest.
- Make sure students are able to use the Reverse Text software feature.
- As students begin typing the reports, walk around the room and point out correct and incorrect formatting to individual students.
- After students finish typing the reports, have them view their work on the screen to see if they made any errors. If errors were made, have students edit their work and make corrections.

CLOSE

If students do not finish the reports during the class period, make sure they save their work so that they can complete it the next time this class meets.

REPORT 53

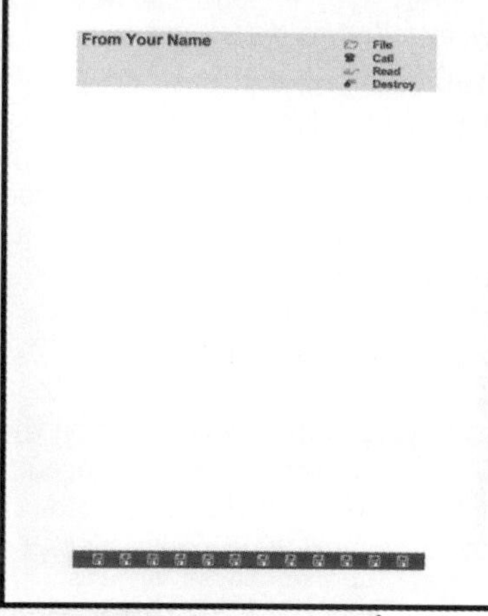

Create a different notepad following these steps:

1. Create a boxed table with 1 column and 1 row, and apply a 20-percent color fill to the row.
2. Set tabs at 4.5 inches and 5 inches from the left margin.
3. Change the font to Arial Bold 20-point, and type *From* and your name. Then press CTRL + TAB to move to the first tab stop.
4. Change the font to Wingdings 14-point, and type the number *1* to create the file folder.
5. Press CTRL + TAB, change the font to Arial Bold 14-point, and type *File.* Then, press ENTER once.
6. Repeat steps 4–6 for the remaining words and symbols (= telephone; $ = glasses; M = bomb).
7. Create a footer, insert a 1-column, 1-row table, and apply a 100-percent color fill.
8. Change the font to Wingdings 18-point, space once, and type < to create a disk. Space once before creating the next disk. Type as many disks as needed to fill the row. Reverse the type to white.

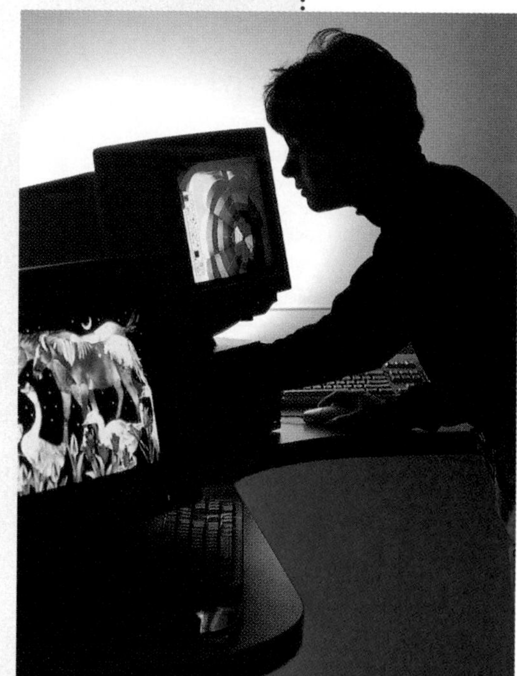

ART CONNECTIONS

Graphic artists and designers use computers and a variety of software programs in their work. They design everything from business logos to multimedia productions.

Teacher Notes

LESSON 110 PERSONAL STATIONERY

OBJECTIVES:

- Improve keyboarding skill.
- Type 38/5'/5e.
- Create personal stationery.

A. WARMUP

Type each line 2 times.

Speed	1 The home row keys are easy to find as you type, type, type.
Accuracy	2 Why did Professor Black give you a quiz on the major texts?
Language Link	3 Blue and red are very popular colors found on today's cars.
Numbers	4 I saw on page 38 that 47 times 29 was much less than 1,560.
	| 1 | 2 | 3 | 4 | 5 | 6 | 7 | 8 | 9 | 10 | 11 | 12

FACT FILE

Stationery comes in many colors, sizes, and qualities. Research the types of stationery for sale in a local supply store. Prepare a short report as your teacher directs.

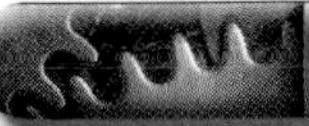

SKILLBUILDING

B. PREVIEW PRACTICE

Type each line 2 times as a preview to the timings that follow.

Accuracy	5 team firms foreign creative Employers confidence management
Speed	6 able ways some the are how who and not key if do as to in a

LESSON 110

FOCUS

- Use 5-minute timings to build speed.
- Design personal letterhead.

BELLRINGER

As soon as students arrive at their workstations and log in, have them type the Warmup. Go over the purpose of each line as shown to the left of the copy.

TEACH

Activity B. Point out that words in the Preview Practice are used in the timings that follow.

RESOURCES

Lesson Plan 110

Courseware Lesson 110

Student Data Disk

Student Manual

Supplementary Production Activities

Reteaching and Reinforcement

Grading and Evaluation

TEACH

Activity C. Remind students that they should try to improve speed with each 5-minute timing. The goal for these timings is to type 38 words a minute for 5 minutes with no more than 5 errors.

CULTURAL CONNECTIONS

Have students interview in person or by letter the human resources manager of a medium or large corporation. Ask the manager what he or she looks for in prospective employees in addition to education and experience. Choose one of the managers to speak to the class. Have students type questions ahead of time.

Activity D. Explain to students that many word processing programs provide templates for designing letterheads. These letterheads range from informal styles used for personal letters to formal styles used for business letters.

C. 5-Minute Timings

Take two 5-minute timings on the paragraphs. Note your speed and errors.

Goal: 38/5'/5e

```
     American companies used to be content with people who     11
showed up for work on time, performed their jobs, and did      23
as they were told. Now, managers want to find better ways      34
to run the business.                                           38
     As they have in the past, workers still need to have      49
such skills as being able to read, to write, and to do         60
math. But those skills alone are not enough. Employers         71
want to hire workers who have creative ideas, good manners,    83
and confidence. Workers should also be strong in technical     85
areas. Other pluses are being willing to learn, a team        106
player, a good listener, and a quick thinker.                 115
     Although employers might provide training, they still    126
seek workers who have at least some of the above traits.      138
Employers also say that if they could hire enough bright,     149
able workers, middle management wouldn't be needed. They      161
realize this could lead to more profits. American companies   173
looked at the success of foreign rivals and found ways to     184
improve how they do business.                                 190
| 1 | 2 | 3 | 4 | 5 | 6 | 7 | 8 | 9 | 10 | 11 | 12  SI 1.40
```

FORMATTING

D. Designing Letterhead

When you are designing stationery, you should take into consideration how it will be used. For example, if you are designing a letterhead for writing letters to friends, you can use a less formal font and style. If the letterhead is going to be used to write a personal-business letter, such as a letter of application for employment, you should use a more traditional, formal style.

Career Exploration

Ask students to bring to class samples of business letterheads. They may ask an adult relative or request a letterhead from a local company. Have students meet in groups of three or four to discuss the common elements in all business letterheads. Have groups create a letterhead for their group.

Out-of-Class Activity

After students have created their personal letterhead, have them write a cover letter for their resume using the letterhead. The letter should answer a classified ad from the newspaper for a job that sounds interesting to the student.

REPORT 54

Create informal personal stationery for yourself. Be sure to include your full name, your address including ZIP Code, and your telephone number.

1. Insert a shape of your choice from the shapes available in your word processor.
2. Center the shape at the top of the page.
3. Choose a font to use for your initials, which will be typed inside the shape.
4. Center your main initial (the first letter of your last name) between your first initial and your middle initial. Make the main initial twice as large as the others.
5. Center your name, address, telephone number, and e-mail address below the shape (either on one line with spaces between sections or on several lines).
6. Create a table in a footer and insert a series of shapes or symbols of your choice for the bottom of the page.

REPORT 55

Create a more formal letterhead for yourself.

1. Use Times New Roman 16-point.
2. Center and type your name in all capital letters.
3. Press ENTER once.
4. Change the font to Times New Roman 12-point, and center your address on 2 lines. Use initial caps.
5. Press ENTER once.
6. Center and type your telephone number, beginning with your area code.
7. Press ENTER once.
8. Center and type your e-mail address.
9. Add a heavy line above and below your name and address.

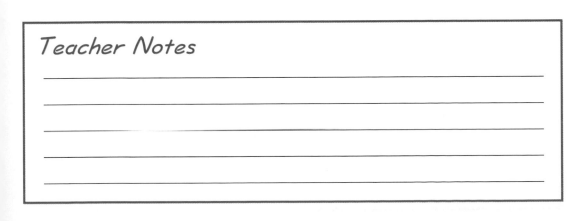

***interNET* CONNECTION**

Companies often design a special logo to use on their letterhead stationery. Search the World Wide Web for information on logos and trademarks.

LESSON 110

TEACH

Report 54. Have students read and follow the instructions carefully.

Report 55. Read the instructions aloud to students, stopping after each step to make sure students understand what they are to do.

ASSESS

- Check to see if students are increasing their word a minute speeds as they complete each 5-minute timing.
- As students begin creating their letterhead, walk around the room and praise or give suggestions to individual students.
- After students finish creating their letterhead, have them view their work on the screen and evaluate the content and appearance. Have students edit their work as necessary.

CLOSE

If students do not finish the letterhead during the class period, make sure they save their work so that they can complete it the next time this class meets.

Remind students to clean up their workstation when they leave.

Teacher Notes

LESSON 111

FOCUS

- Apply a Language Link rule for comma usage.
- Use 12-second timings to build speed.
- Use Diagnostic Practice to identify areas that need improvement.
- Learn desktop publishing features: Drawing Tools, Vertical Text, and Text/Word Art.
- Format page designs using text art and drawing tools.

BELLRINGER

As soon as students arrive at their workstations and log in, have them type the Warmup. Go over the purpose of each line as shown to the left of the copy.

TEACH

Activity B. Explain the Lanuage Link rule to students. Once they have completed the assignment, have them check each other's work for accuracy. Go over as a class where commas belong.

Solutions: Karen has what I would call a dynamic, forceful presentation.

The sleek, colorful tractor won first prize at the contest.

Last week they went to a long, boring movie at the theater.

The space shuttle is transported on a long, sturdy vehicle.

LESSON 111 TEXT/WORD ART

OBJECTIVES:

- Increase keyboarding speed.
- Learn comma usage rules.
- Learn about the drawing toolbar.
- Learn to use text/word art.

A. WARMUP

Type each line 2 times.

Speed	1 The six girls held a social to pay for a visit to the lake.
Accuracy	2 Why would quick brown foxes want to jump over any lazy dog?
Language Link	3 My cousin's winter ski jacket is much warmer than my parka.
Numbers/Symbols	4 Ed & Zoe sold 59# of sugar @ $1.67, for a total of $103.84.
	| 1 | 2 | 3 | 4 | 5 | 6 | 7 | 8 | 9 | 10 | 11 | 12

B. COMMA USAGE

Study the rule and examples that follow. Then edit lines 5–8 to correct any errors in comma usage.

Rule 28: Use a comma between two adjacent adjectives that modify the same noun. To determine whether the adjectives do describe the same noun, use the following test.

Read the sentence, "Chris gave a *short, emotional* speech." Now change the order to say, "A speech was short *and* emotional." If it makes sense, it proves that both adjectives describe *speech,* and a comma is necessary.

Read the sentence, "She mailed a *new spring* schedule. Now change the order to say, "A schedule is new *and* spring." It doesn't make sense, so no comma is needed.

RESOURCES

 Lesson Plan 111

 Courseware Lesson 111

Student Data Disk

Student Manual

Language Link Worksheets

Supplementary Production Activities

The soft Angora kitten slept peacefully near the fireplace.
Roger purchased a noise shield for the loud, rapid printer.

```
5 Karen has what I would call a dynamic forceful presentation.
6 The sleek colorful tractor won first prize at the contest.
7 Last week they went to a long, boring movie at the theater.
8 The space shuttle is transported on a long sturdy vehicle.
```

SKILLBUILDING

C. 12-Second Sprints

Take three 12-second timings on each line. Try to increase your speed on each timing.

```
9  Mark can quickly type the words for, the, but, can, and go.
10 The four of them had to get to the bus by the time it left.
11 Sue says that she can fix the vase that fell from the desk.
12 Jane and the girl kept their title to the farm on the hill.
   ||||5||||10||||15||||20||||25||||30||||35||||40||||45||||50||||55||||60
```

D. Diagnostic Practice: Numbers

Turn to the Diagnostic Practice: Numbers routine on page SB4. Type one of the Pretest/Posttest paragraphs and identify any errors made. Then type the corresponding drill lines 2 times for each number on which you made 2 or more errors and 1 time for each number on which you made only 1 error. Finally, repeat the same Pretest paragraph and compare your performance.

FORMATTING

E. Page Design

The design of a page can be made more exciting by creating special effects with text. **Text art** enables you to curve, distort, and twist text into a variety of shapes and sizes. In addition, you can shade the text and make it three-dimensional. Treating text as art is useful in creating unique company or personal logos on letterhead and business cards.

LESSON 111

TEACH

Activity C. Remind students that the goal for 12-second sprints is improved speed with each timing.

Activity D. Make sure that students understand that this Diagnostic Practice activity is designed to help identify areas that need improvement and provide needed practice.

Activity E. Provide time for students to experiment with drawing several shapes using the drawing tool feature in their word processing software.

JOURNAL ENTRY

Write the following prompt on the board for a journal entry: "I am feeling __________ about my future career because...." Have students write for about five or ten minutes, then have them read what they have written.

TEACH

Activity F. Walk around the room while students are completing Lesson 111 in their Student Manual. Make sure they understand what they are to do and that they are doing the assignment correctly.

STUDENT MANUAL

Be sure students turn to the correct lesson in their Student Manual.

Report 56. Have different students read aloud the steps for this report. Stop after each step to make sure all students understand the directions.

Illustration

The illustration shows Report 56 completed by following the directions.

Report 57. Have students read the instructions once, then have them read the instructions again.

Illustration

The illustration shows Report 57 completed by following the directions.

F. Software Features

STUDENT MANUAL

Drawing Tools Text/Word Art
Vertical Text

Study Lesson 111 in your student manual. Complete all the practice activities while at your computer. Then complete the jobs that follow.

DESKTOP PUBLISHING APPLICATIONS

REPORT 56

GOOD MANNERS FOR JOB INTERVIEWS

GET THE JOB YOU WANT!

Open Report 37 and make the following changes:

1. Change the title to a wavy shape.
2. Adjust the width of the title to fit within the margins of the page.
3. Remove the bullets and begin each paragraph with a drop cap in a color that complements the title.
4. Add the following text to print vertically on the right side of the page: *GET THE JOB YOU WANT!* If necessary, change the color to complement the title and drop caps.
5. Add an appropriate graphic at the bottom center of the page and size it appropriately.

Out-of-Class Activity

Have students collect examples of desktop publishing features in magazines, newspapers, brochures, and other print documents. Then have students create a collage of their examples. Each example should be labeled. Encourage students to make their collages colorful and expressive.

Career Exploration

Have students brainstorm about different art careers. Write the careers on the board. Organize them into different categories such as graphic arts, art history, art museums, fine arts, and so on. Invite someone in an art career to speak to the class.

REPORT 57

Open Report 51 and make the following changes:

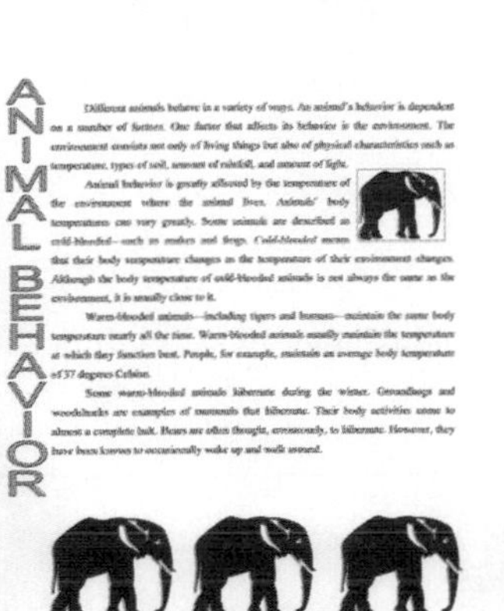

1. Change the title to a vertical style at the left of the page.
2. Position the vertical type so that it extends from the top of the text to the bottom of the text.
3. Change the color of the type to green.
4. Move the graphic at the beginning of the first paragraph to the end of that same paragraph.
5. Change the wrap so that the text wraps to the left.
6. Move the graphic at the end of the last paragraph to just below the vertical text.
7. Adjust the size of the graphic and copy and paste it so that three of them extend from the left margin to the right margin.

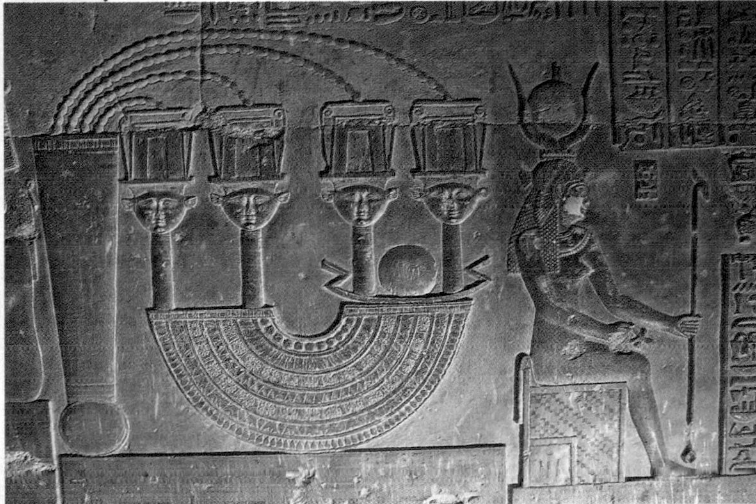

FACT FILE

Hieroglyphics were used by the ancient Egyptians as a type of communication in pictorial characters. How do they compare with logos.

Teacher Notes

LESSON 111

ASSESS

- Watch students to see if they complete the Language Link activity correctly.
- Check to see if students are increasing their word a minute speeds as they complete each timing.
- Monitor students as they complete Diagnostic Practice and provide individualized assistance.
- Make sure students are able to use the Drawing Tools, Vertical Text, and Text/Word Art features.
- After students finish their reports, have them view their work on the screen to see if they made any errors.

CLOSE

If students do not finish the reports during the class period, make sure they save their work so that they can complete it the next time this class meets.

PORTFOLIO *Activity*

If students' portfolio goals include showcasing their best work, they may want to include a report from this lesson. Encourage students to evaluate their work and include comments in their portfolio.

LESSON 112

FOCUS

- Use 30-second timings to build speed.
- Create and type a customer survey form.

BELLRINGER

As soon as students arrive at their workstations and log in, have them type the Warmup. Go over the purpose of each line as shown to the left of the copy.

TEACH

Activity B. Remind students that the goal for 30-second timings is improved speed with each timing.

Report 58. To help students create the survey form in this activity review the following elements: formatting a drop cap, creating a graphic box, applying special symbols, and shading a graphic box. Also recommend a source for students to find an appropriate graphic image.

Illustration

The illustration shows Report 58 completed by following the directions.

LESSON 112 DESKTOP PUBLISHING REVIEW

OBJECTIVES:

- Improve keyboarding skill.
- Practice using desktop publishing features.

A. WARMUP

Type each line 2 times.

Speed	1	The six forms she got from the firm may do for the problem.
Accuracy	2	Jack typed four dozen requisitions for hollow moving boxes.
Language Link	3	He was always trying to be a helpful, courteous individual.
Numbers/Symbols	4	Type the problems: 100 - 74 = 26; 86 + 17 = 103; 4 - 3 = 1.
		| 1 | 2 | 3 | 4 | 5 | 6 | 7 | 8 | 9 | 10 | 11 | 12

SKILLBUILDING

B. 30-SECOND TIMINGS

Take two 30-second timings on lines 5–6. Then take two 30-second timings on lines 7–8. Try to increase your speed on each timing.

5	Things seem to happen right for some people; they know	11
6	when a good chance comes along and can quickly seize it.	22
7	They are quick to get an exact vision of how this luck	11
8	can work for them; it may make their lives very different.	22
	| 1 | 2 | 3 | 4 | 5 | 6 | 7 | 8 | 9 | 10 | 11 | 12	

RESOURCES

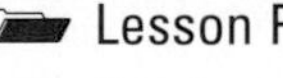
Lesson Plan 112

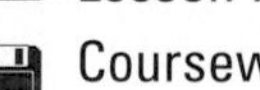
Courseware Lesson 112
Student Data Disk
Student Manual
Reteaching and Reinforcement
Grading and Evaluation

REPORT 58

Survey Form

Create a customer survey form similar to the one shown below.

1. Use Times New Roman 36-point italic with a shadow for the title.
2. Choose an appropriate graphic for the upper right corner of the page.
3. Use Times New Roman 16-point for the remaining text except for the bottom box.
4. Add a drop cap to the first line.
5. Draw red check boxes that are large enough to write a number from 1 to 5 inside.
6. Leave an appropriate amount of space between the parts of the form.
7. Add a light shading to the bottom box and type the text in red Times New Roman 36-point italic bold.

What do you think?

Please rate our business today.

Excellent = 5   Poor = 1

You may use any number from 1 through 5. The higher the number, the more positive the rating. Use the boxes at the left to fill in your rating.

☐ How would you rate our overall service today?

☐ How friendly were our employees?

☐ Please rate the appearance of the store.

What can we do to make your next visit better?

____

____

Please write the names of any employees you feel were especially helpful to you.

____

____

Thank you for your help.

ASSESS

- Check to see if students are increasing their word a minute speeds as they complete each timing.
- As students begin typing the customer survey, walk around the room and point out correct and incorrect formatting to individuals.
- After students finish typing the survey, have them view their work on the screen to see if they made any errors. If errors were made, have students make corrections.

CLOSE

If students do not finish the customer survey during the class period, make sure they save their work so that they can complete it the next time this class meets.

Remind students to clean up their workstation when they leave.

PORTFOLIO *Activity*

If students' portfolio goals include showcasing their best work, they may want to include the customer survey from this lesson. Encourage students to evaluate their work and include comments in their portfolio.

Teacher Notes

LESSON 113

FOCUS

- Apply a Language Link rule for comma usage.
- Use 30-second OK timings to improve accuracy.
- Type and format a flyer.

BELLRINGER

As soon as students arrive at their workstations and log in, have them type the Warmup. Go over the purpose of each line as shown to the left of the copy.

TEACH

Activity B. Go over the Language Link rule for comma usage with students, including reviewing the sample sentences. Make sure students are comfortable with this comma rule before they begin the activity.

Solutions: He will, therefore, take all precautions before proceeding.

Can she, however, be certain that all the reports are there?

I would, under most circumstances, approve the merger today.

Hillary is, as you can see, the perfect candidate for them.

LESSON 113

DESKTOP PUBLISHING DESIGNS: FLYERS

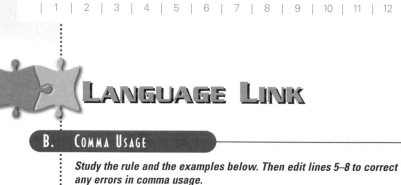

OBJECTIVES:

- Improve keyboarding skill.
- Learn comma usage.
- Prepare documents using DTP features.

A. WARMUP

Type each line 2 times.

Speed	1	The man got a snap of an authentic whale by the big island.
Accuracy	2	I quickly explained that few big jobs involve many hazards.
Language Link	3	The twins' book had big print and the book's cover was red.
Numbers/Symbols	4	Ed had 789 birds there in 1982; but by 1992 there were 823.

| 1 | 2 | 3 | 4 | 5 | 6 | 7 | 8 | 9 | 10 | 11 | 12

B. COMMA USAGE

Study the rule and the examples below. Then edit lines 5–8 to correct any errors in comma usage.

Rule 29: Use a comma *before* and *after* a nonessential expression. Nonessential expressions include words, phrases, or clauses that are not necessary for the meaning of a sentence. Names in direct address are also considered nonessential. Use one comma if a nonessential element appears at the end or at the beginning of a sentence.

We are willing, as you know, to renegotiate the offer.

Therefore, the lease will be terminated next Thursday.

Lisa requested, however, that she retain her position.

You will be notified, Mr. Samuel, of our new location.

RESOURCES

 Lesson Plan 113

 Courseware Lesson 113

Student Data Disk

Student Manual

Language Link Worksheets

Cross-Curricular Activities

```
5 He will therefore, take all precautions before proceeding.
6 Can she however be certain that all the reports are there?
7 I would under most circumstances approve the merger today.
8 Hillary is as you can see the perfect candidate for them.
```

SKILLBUILDING

C. 30-Second OK Timings

Take two 30-second OK (error-free) timings on lines 9–10. Then take two 30-second OK timings on lines 11–12. Goal: no errors.

```
9       Paula reviewed the subject before giving Raylynn and     11
10 Monte a quiz and quietly reviewed the next game with Buzz.    22

11      Even with all kinds of gripes, Maxine had a zest for     11
12 quiet living; Zeke examined all work and rejected most all.   22
   | 1 | 2 | 3 | 4 | 5 | 6 | 7 | 8 | 9 | 10 | 11 | 12
```

DESKTOP PUBLISHING APPLICATIONS

REPORT 59

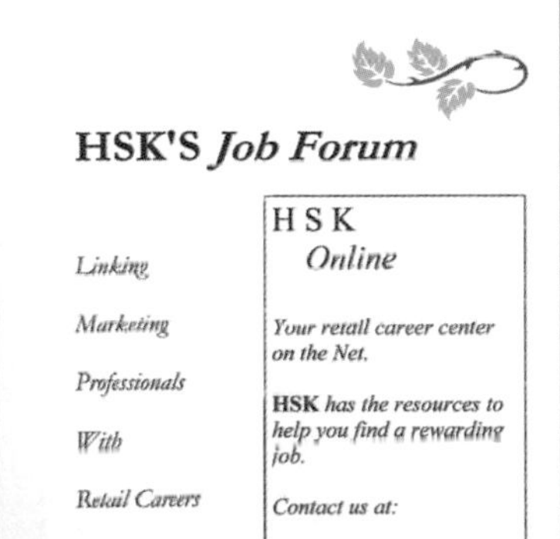
HSK'S Job Forum
Linking
Marketing
Professionals
With
Retail Careers
HSK
Online
Your retail career center on the Net.
HSK has the resources to help you find a rewarding job.
Contact us at:
www.hsk.org

Create the flyer in the illustration following these steps:

1. At the top right of a page, insert a graphic element similar to the one shown in the illustration.
2. Change the font to 48-point bold, and select a font style such as Garamond.
3. Approximately 2 inches from the top of the page, type the beginning of the title in regular type; type the remainder of the line in italic.
4. Press ENTER 3 times, change the font to 28-point italic, and type the copy at the left of the page with initial caps.
5. Create a text box similar in size to the one shown, position it at the right side of the page, and set the wrap to the left of the box.

TEACH

Activity C. Point out that OK timings are designed to encourage accuracy.

Report 59. Before beginning Report 59, let students experiment with creating various text/word art characters using the text/word art feature in their word processing software.

Illustration

The illustration shows Report 59 completed by following the directions.

FACT FILE

Modern medical technology allows us to read the brain so that we can see how it functions with different activities. A procedure known as a PET scan records different areas of the brain used in aspects of language activity. Have students research how language is processed in the brain and type a short report.

TEACH

Report 60. Have different students read aloud the steps for this report. Stop after each step to make sure all students understand the directions.

Illustration
The illustration shows Report 60 completed by following the directions.

ASSESS

- Check to see if students are completing 30-second OK timings without any errors.
- Watch students as they complete the Language Link activity to see if they are able to apply the comma usage rule correctly.
- After students finish typing and formatting the flyer, have them view their work and make corrections.
- Check the positioning of the text and the graphic boxes to see if they are similar to the illustration.
- Check the point sizes of text throughout the flyer to see if they match the guidelines stated in the textbook.

CLOSE

If students do not finish the flyers during the class period, make sure they save their work so that they can complete it the next time this class meets.

6. Type the information into the text box as follows: Use Times New Roman 36-point for the first line, and insert a space between the letters; change to italic for the second line.
7. Press ENTER 2 times, change the font size to 24-point, and type the next sentence.
8. Press ENTER 2 times, type *HSK* in bold (no italic), then complete the rest of the sentence in italic (no bold).
9. Press ENTER 2 times and type the next line.
10. Press ENTER 2 times and center and type the Internet address in regular type.
11. Add a blank line between each line of text at the left of the text box, and position the text box so that the copy appears to be vertically centered beside the box.
12. Create another text box at the lower left of the page, and insert the text in Times New Roman 10-point. Position the box so that the bottom of both boxes align.

REPORT 60

HSK'S Job Forum
Linking
Marketing
Professionals
With
Retail Careers
H S K
Online
Your retail career center on the Net.
HSK has the resources to help you find a rewarding job.
Contact us at:
www.hsk.org

Open Report 59 and make the following changes:

1. Change the color of the title to red, and add a shadow.
2. Change the text at the left of the text box to bold.
3. Add blue shading to the text box at the right.
4. Add a shadow to the first two lines of text in the text box at the right.

interNET CONNECTION

The Internet is an excellent source of information and can be used to locate people and businesses. Enter the following URL to locate information about a business in a particular city: http://netscape.yahoo.com/guide/yellow pages.html

Teacher Notes

LESSON 114

DESIGNING A CERTIFICATE

OBJECTIVES:

- Improve keyboarding skill.
- Design a certificate.

A. WARMUP

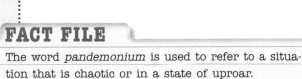

Type each line 2 times.

```
Speed             1 When did he go to the city and pay them for the world maps?
Accuracy          2 Five brown ibexes quickly zipped up among the jagged rocks.
Language Link     3 My best friend, Carlene, liked the new soft leather saddle.
Numbers/Symbols   4 Ronda knew that 3/4 of $84 = $63 and that 30% of $90 = $27.
                    | 1 | 2 | 3 | 4 | 5 | 6 | 7 | 8 | 9 | 10 | 11 | 12
```

FACT FILE

The word *pandemonium* is used to refer to a situation that is chaotic or in a state of uproar.

SKILLBUILDING

B. PRETEST

Take a 1-minute timing on the paragraph. Note your speed and errors.

```
5      Information that is presented in a graph or a chart is   11
6 frequently referred to as graphics. Many writers like this    23
7 manner of presentation because they recognize that a reader   35
8 will best understand a message when it includes graphics.     46
  | 1 | 2 | 3 | 4 | 5 | 6 | 7 | 8 | 9 | 10 | 11 | 12
```

C. PRACTICE

In the chart below find the number of errors you made on the Pretest. Then type each of the designated drill lines 2 times.

Pretest Errors	0–1	2	3	4+
Drill Lines	12–16	11–15	10–14	9–13

RESOURCES

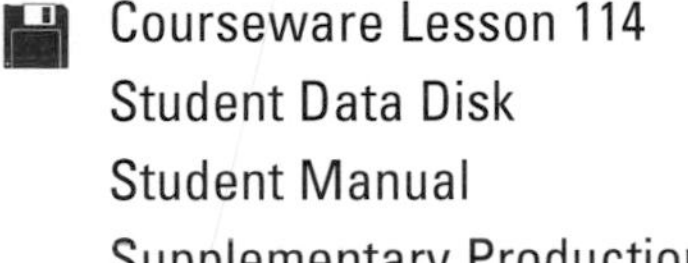

- Lesson Plan 114
- Courseware Lesson 114
- Student Data Disk
- Student Manual
- Supplementary Production Activities

LESSON 114

FOCUS

- Use a Pretest/Practice/Posttest routine to build speed and accuracy.
- Format and type a certificate.

BELLRINGER

As soon as students arrive at their workstations and log in, have them type the Warmup. Go over the purpose of each line as shown to the left of the copy.

TEACH

Activities B–C. Remind students that they should improve both their speed and accuracy from the Pretest to the Posttest.

TEACH

Activity D. Remind students to compare their Posttest results with their Pretest.

PRETEST/PRACTICE/POSTEST

The ***Pretest/Practice/Posttest*** routines are designed to improve speed or accuracy.

- The ***Pretest*** identifies students' speed or accuracy needs.
- The ***Practice*** provides a variety of improvement drills.
- The ***Posttest*** (a repeat of the Pretest) measures improvement.

Report 61. Review the formatting of a document in landscape orientation with students. Also review the use of word/text art. Remind students to leave adequate space above the signature line.

Illustration

The illustration shows Report 61 completed by following the directions.

Accuracy

```
is exist message selection computer comparison presentation
are common variety software referred supported relationship
it's because writers although choosing recognize frequently
pie format written graphic excellent information understand
```

Speed

```
reader sliced number chart their order items they most line
manner pieces change kinds graph looks right will used work
better reveal period today three often makes that when want
support report choice print forms parts like this show over
```

D. POSTTEST ***Repeat the Pretest. Compare your Posttest results with your Pretest results.***

DESKTOP PUBLISHING APPLICATIONS

REPORT 61
Certificate

Create a certificate similar to the illustration on the next page.

1. Change your page orientation to landscape (11 × 8½ inches).
2. Vertically center the page.
3. Using text/word art, select a slightly curved style of type and an interesting font. Change the type size to 40-point, and center and type the certificate title.
4. Center and type the text of the certificate using a script font set at 24 points. Type the name of the student in a heavier but complementary 24-point font.
5. Below the certificate title, insert a graphic that relates to academic achievement, such as the seal in the illustration.
6. Change to 12-point type, and create a table for the signature and date line at least 1 inch below the last line of the text.
7. Type the signer's title, *RCTC Training Specialist,* beneath the signature line, and type the word *Date* beneath the date line.

CULTURAL CONNECTIONS

Have students work in groups to choose a country, and then compose a letter to the embassy of that country requesting information on what is required by an American citizen to work in the country.

CERTIFICATE OF PROFICIENCY

This certifies that
Jonathan Riley
has successfully completed the requirements of the
Level 1 Desktop Publishing Training
offered by
Rodgers Career Technical Center

RCTC Training Specialist *Date*

CULTURAL CONNECTIONS

Interview customs may vary from country to country. Select someone from another country to interview about the types of questions a prospective employee is asked by an interviewer.

Teacher Notes

LESSON 114

ASSESS

- Check to see if students show signs of improvement from the Pretest to the Posttest.
- As students begin typing and formatting the certificate, walk around the room and point out correct and incorrect formatting.
- Check to see if the selected graphics are appropriate for certificates and that there is adequate spacing between the various parts of the certificate.
- After students finish typing and formatting the certificate, have them view their work on the screen to see if they made any errors.

CLOSE

If students do not finish the certificate during the class period, make sure they save their work so that they can complete it the next time this class meets.

PORTFOLIO Activity

If students' portfolio goals include demonstrating specific skills, they may want to include the certificate from this lesson. Encourage students to evaluate their work and include comments in their portfolio.

LESSON 115

FOCUS

- Compose a short, multi-paragraph report.
- Use 5-minute timings to build speed.
- Type and format invitations.

BELLRINGER

As soon as students arrive at their workstations and log in, have them type the Warmup. Go over the purpose of each line as shown to the left of the copy.

TEACH

Activity B. After students have completed their reports, ask for volunteers to read a few of them in class.

Solutions: Answers will vary

LESSON 115 DESIGNING AN INVITATION

OBJECTIVES:

- Compose at the keyboard.
- Type 38/5'/5e.
- Create a party invitation.

A. WARMUP

Type each line 2 times.

Speed	1	The profit she got for the corn and hay may make them rich.
Accuracy	2	Jim saw five dozen extra quilts by peeking under the truck.
Language Link	3	The cost is one's own even if somebody's hat was left here.
Symbols	4	Mr. Edward C. Jones joined Smith & Smythe, Inc., last June.

B. COMPOSING AT THE KEYBOARD

Choose one of the following topics and compose a short, three-paragraph report. Use the topic as the report title.

5 My Most Embarrassing Moment
6 My Favorite Relative
7 My Favorite Memory

SKILLBUILDING

C. PREVIEW PRACTICE

Type each line 2 times as a preview to the 5-minute timings that follow.

```
8 waxy zapped needles quality September antifreeze broadleafs
9 enough leaves change types green where that name all the to
```


RESOURCES

 Lesson Plan 115

 Courseware Lesson 115

Student Data Disk

Student Manual

Supplementary Production Activities

Grading and Evaluation

D. 5-Minute Timings

Take two 5-minute timings. Note your speed and errors.

Goal: 38/5'/5e

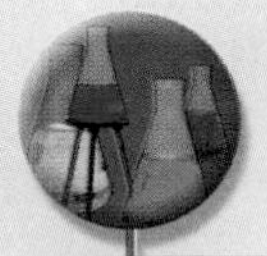

Science Connections

Many leaves change colors in the fall. The two main 11
types of trees are evergreens and broadleafs. Evergreen 22
trees have green needles all year round. The needles form a 34
quality heavy waxy cover that protects them. They also have 46
natural antifreeze inside that will usually protect them. 57
Broadleaf trees are just as the name implies. These 68
trees have leaves that are flat and wide. They do not have 80
a wax covering or natural antifreeze that will protect them 92
from being zapped by winter's cold. When the weather gets 103
cold enough and the leaves die, they usually fall off. 114
Some broadleaf trees are considered to be evergreens, 125
such as holly. They are green all year. In warmer areas, 136
some broadleaf trees do not turn colors. Those trees that 148
turn beautiful fall colors are where the weather gets below 160
freezing. Usually, they turn fall colors just before the 171
leaves fall off the trees. The usual season to see fall 182
foliage is September through October. 190

| 1 | 2 | 3 | 4 | 5 | 6 | 7 | 8 | 9 | 10 | 11 | 12 SI 1.40

DESKTOP PUBLISHING APPLICATIONS

REPORT 62
Invitation

Follow these steps to create an invitation similar to the one in the Illustration on the next page:

1. Select a piece of clip art that has something to do with either graduation or a celebration.
2. Adjust the size of the clip art to form a 2.5-inch square, and horizontally center it on the page.
3. Using word/text art and an attractive font set for 30 or 32 points, arrange the words *GRADUATION TIME!* vertically down the left side of the page. Insert *CELEBRATION TIME!* vertically down the right side of the page.

TEACH

Activity C. Point out that words in the Preview Practice are used in the timing that follows.

Activity D. Remind students that they should try to improve speed with each timing. The goal for these timings is to type 38 words a minute for 5 minutes with no more than 5 errors.

Report 62. Review the formatting of vertical text with students. Demonstrate how students should stretch the text/word art so that it extends from the top margin to the bottom margin of the page.

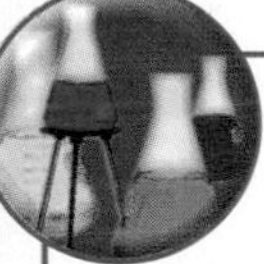

Science Connections

Research the resources in your community to learn about nature reserves, parks, and other natural areas that are protected. Invite someone to speak about the importance of protecting the ecological systems of the world.

Out-of-Class Activity

Have students work in groups to create a flyer about an upcoming school event or an invitation to a class gathering. Suggest they plan what they want to draw and say beforehand. Have them design and create the flyers and invitations. Post them around the classroom.

TEACH

Report 63. Have students check each other's work.

Illustration
The illustration shows Report 62 completed by following the directions

ASSESS

- Check to see if students are increasing their word a minute speeds as they complete each 5-minute timing.
- Review the typing accuracy of students' responses in the Language Link composing activity.
- As students begin typing and formatting the invitations, walk around the room and point out correct and incorrect formatting.
- Check to see if the graphics that students select are appropriate.
- Check spacing to see if it is adequate between the various invitation parts.
- After students finish typing and formatting invitations, have them view their work on the screen to see if they made any errors.

CLOSE

If students do not finish the invitations during the class period, make sure they save their work so that they can complete it the next time this class meets.

GRADUATION TIME!
CELEBRATION TIME!
You are cordially invited
to join family and friends
in a celebration to honor
our graduate:
FAYE MARIE THEMUS
Date: Sunday, June 2, (year)
Time: 5 p.m. to 8 p.m.
Place: 21337 Kenwyck Circle
West Columbia, SC 29170
Please respond before May 22.
Call 803-555-3219

4. Adjust the size of the word/text art so that it extends from the top margin to the bottom margin of the page.
5. Insert a text box below the clip art and horizontally center it.
6. Select an attractive, easy-to-read font style and size; then type the copy as illustrated in the text box horizontally centered, breaking the lines as shown. Type the graduate's name in bold in a slightly larger type size. Double-space before and after the graduate's name and between the separate sections (see the illustration).
7. If you have additional clip art available, you may want to add it to the bottom of the invitation.
8. Size the box so that the bottom aligns evenly with the text on the right and left. If necessary, adjust the font style and/or size to fit all of the text in the box.

> You are cordially invited
> to join family and friends
> in a celebration to honor
> our graduate
> Faye Marie Themus
>
> Date: Sunday, June 2, (year)
> Time: 5 p.m. to 8 p.m.
> Place: 21337 Kenwyck Circle
> West Columbia, SC 29170
>
> Please respond before May 22.
> Call 803-555-3219.

REPORT 63

Design an invitation to your own birthday party, which will be held at your house.

FACT FILE

Ethical employees always apply the rules of proper business etiquette and always treat their colleagues and customers with respect.

Teacher Notes

LESSON 116 COLUMNS

OBJECTIVES:

- Improve keyboarding skill.
- Learn to format text in columns.

A. WARMUP

Type each line 2 times.

Speed	1	Sue is to pay the man to fix the bicycle for the six girls.
Accuracy	2	Pete quickly froze the egg mixtures in five old brown jars.
Language Link	3	One of the students rides the bus all the way from Fordham.
Numbers	4	The 10 men lived 29 days at 3847 Bluff Way and 5 days here.
		| 1 | 2 | 3 | 4 | 5 | 6 | 7 | 8 | 9 | 10 | 11 | 12

SKILLBUILDING

B. 30-SECOND TIMINGS

Take two 30-second timings on lines 5–6. Then take two 30-second timings on lines 7–8. Try to increase your speed on each timing.

5	Ida will go to the movie with Jay and take her small	11
6	dog to a vet today. Tom will also be there with his dog.	22
7	We had the box of new books in our office and got the	11
8	new pens before he did. My boss gave us a ride to the city.	23
	| 1 | 2 | 3 | 4 | 5 | 6 | 7 | 8 | 9 | 10 | 11 | 12	

C. DIAGNOSTIC PRACTICE: ALPHABET

Turn to the Diagnostic Practice: Alphabet routine on page SB1. Type one of the Pretest/Posttest paragraphs and identify any errors made. Then type the corresponding drill lines 2 times for each letter on which you made 2 or more errors and 1 time for each number on which you made only 1 error. Finally, repeat the same Pretest paragraph and compare your performance.

RESOURCES

Lesson Plan 116

Courseware Lesson 116

Student Data Disk

Student Manual

Supplementary Production Activities

LESSON 116

FOCUS

- Use 30-second timings to build speed.
- Use a Paced Practice 2-minute timing routine.
- Learn a desktop publishing feature: Columns.
- Type and format a report using columns.

BELLRINGER

As soon as students arrive at their workstations and log in, have them type the Warmup. Go over the purpose of each line as shown to the left of the copy.

TEACH

Activity B. Remind students that their goal for 30-second timings is improved speed with each timing.

Activity C. Go over the procedure for the Diagnostic Practice: Alphabet routine with students. Make sure students understand that this activity is designed to help identify areas that need improvement and provide needed practice.

FORMATTING

D. Columns

In desktop publishing, columns are often used to create documents such as brochures and newsletters. Arranging text in columns often makes the text easier to read and provides more visual interest. In addition, the length and width of columns can be varied and lines and boxes can be added to columns.

E. Software Features

STUDENT MANUAL

Columns

Study Lesson 116 in your student manual. Complete all the practice activities while at your computer. Then complete the jobs that follow.

DESKTOP PUBLISHING APPLICATIONS

REPORT 64

Single-space the following copy. Begin at the top margin, and indent paragraphs 0.5 inch. Do not leave a blank line between paragraphs.

¶For any organization to run smoothly, the organization must have a highly skilled, well-trained support staff. In today's fast-paced business world, executive secretaries and administrative assistants are an essential element. As businesses streamline their operations, executive secretaries and administrative assistants become increasingly important as they take on key managerial roles. In fact, according to a survey conducted several years ago, managers have now turned over more than 70 percent of their responsibilities to their support staff.
¶Support staff must have a combination of finely tuned management, interpersonal, and technical skills; a positive work attitude; and a willingness to promote change in order to advance the organization. Assistants now negotiate, manage projects, coordinate the office, and handle many other managerial responsibilities that used to be handled by their bosses.

TEACH

Activity D. Emphasize that a title that spans both columns must be entered before the column command is used. Also emphasize that a columnar format, once initiated, will continue in a document until it is discontinued.

Activity E. Have students turn to Lesson 116 in their Student Manual and complete all the practice activities and jobs that follow.

STUDENT MANUAL

Be sure students turn to the correct lesson in their Student Manual.

Report 64. Point out Report 64 to students. Ask a student to read the report aloud to the class. Ask students how the information in this report is important to them.

Career Exploration

Have students collect classified ads for administrative assistants, executives, and other support staff positions from newspapers and magazines. Have students write a cover letter and resume geared to one of these ads. Students should stress their positive work attitude as well as their technical skills.

Out-of-Class Activity

Over the next week, have students make a list of different desktop publishing elements used in documents they see. Ask them to bring some examples to class (newspapers, magazines, brochures). Encourage students to look everywhere, including billboards and other unusual places.

¶Assistants must develop vital management skills. They must be able to manage priorities and projects, communicate effectively, creatively solve problems, and much more. Assistants must be team players who can manage increasing responsibility and get things done.

REPORT 65

Open Report 64 and revise it as follows:

1. Add the title *THE EXCEPTIONAL ASSISTANT* in a font that resembles a newspaper heading (for example, Times New Roman Bold Italic or Arial Black. Place it at the top of the page and increase the font size so that the title spans both columns.
2. Arrange the report into two balanced newspaper columns.
3. Add a line between the columns.

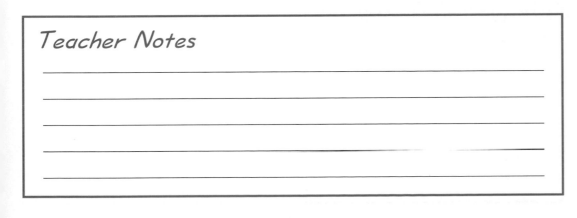

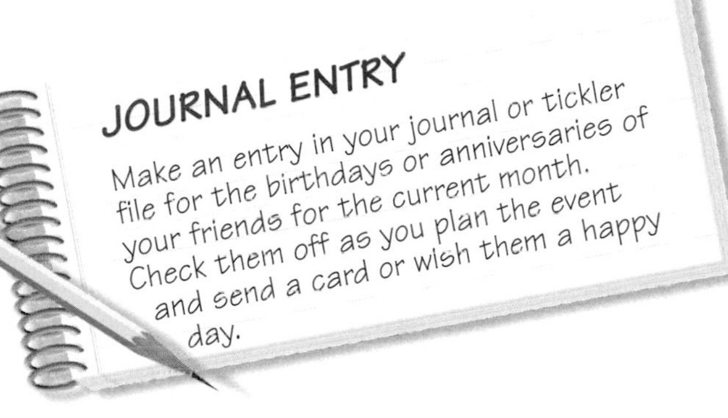

JOURNAL ENTRY
Make an entry in your journal or tickler file for the birthdays or anniversaries of your friends for the current month. Check them off as you plan the event and send a card or wish them a happy day.

Teacher Notes

TEACH

Report 65. Have different students read aloud the steps for this report. Stop after each step to make sure all students understand the directions.

Tell students that the content of Report 65 will be used in the newsletter they will create in Report 66.

Illustration

The illustration shows Report 65 completed by following the directions.

ASSESS

- Check to see if students are increasing their word a minute speeds as they complete each timing.
- Make sure students are able to use the Columns software feature.
- As students begin typing and formatting the reports, walk around the room and point out correct and incorrect formatting to individual students.
- After students finish typing and formatting the reports, have them view their work on the screen to see if they made any errors.

CLOSE

If students do not finish the report during the class period, make sure they save their work so that they can complete it the next time this class meets.

LESSON 117

FOCUS

- Apply the Language Link rules concerning number expression.
- Use a Paced Practice 2-minute timing routine.
- Type and format newsletters.

BELLRINGER

As soon as students arrive at their workstations and log in, have them type the Warmup. Go over the purpose of each line as shown to the left of the copy.

TEACH

Activity B. Explain the Language Link rules concerning number expression to students. Make sure all students understand these rules before beginning the activity.

Solutions: We bought 15 pairs of socks, 7 jackets, and 23 scarves.

On the 3rd of July, he made plans for the July 4 parade.

At 9 a.m. we delivered the $500 rent check to the owner.

On the 6th of December, we got ten tickets for January 2.

LESSON 117

DESKTOP PUBLISHING: NEWSLETTERS

OBJECTIVES:

- Improve keyboarding speed.
- Learn rules for typing numbers.
- Create a newsletter.

A. WARMUP

Type each line 2 times.

```
Speed            1 If they pay me for the emblem, I may make it to the social.
Accuracy         2 Six big men quickly won over Jeff despite his greater size.
Language Link    3 The students working on the project will resolve the issue.
Numbers/Symbols  4 With the 8% increase, Ed bought 29# of #134 and #56 for $7.
                   | 1 | 2 | 3 | 4 | 5 | 6 | 7 | 8 | 9 | 10 | 11 | 12
```

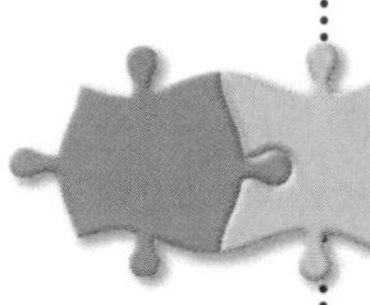

LANGUAGE LINK

B. NUMBER EXPRESSION

Study the rules and examples that follow. Then edit lines 5–8 to correct any errors in number usage.

Rule 30: Use figures for dates (use *st, d,* or *th* with a date only if it precedes the month) and all numbers if two or more related numbers both above and below ten are used in the same sentence.

Rule 31: Use figures for measurements (time, money, distance, weight, and percentage) and mixed numbers.

She ordered 2 printers, 3 keyboards, and 12 printer cartridges on May 1 at 10 a.m.

On the 4th of July, we spent $65 to buy 20 pounds of meat for the picnic, which was being held 3⅝ miles away.

RESOURCES

 Lesson Plan 117

 Courseware Lesson 117

Student Data Disk

Student Manual

Language Link Worksheets

Supplementary Production Activities

5 We bought 15 pairs of socks, seven jackets, and 23 scarves.
6 On the third of July, he made plans for the July 4th parade.
7 At nine a.m. we delivered the $500 rent check to the owner.
8 On the sixth of December, we got ten tickets for January 2.

SKILLBUILDING

C. Paced Practice

Turn to the Paced Practice routine beginning on page SB7. Take three 2-minute timings, starting at the point where you left off the last time.

FORMATTING

D. Newsletters

Professional Journal

THE EXCEPTIONAL ASSISTANT

ACCOUNTABILITY

Newsletters are one of the best ways to communicate a variety of information to a wide range of people. A well-planned newsletter will be attractive and easy-to-read; it will use graphics to draw readers' attention and other DTP features to add interest and emphasize text. Most newsletters have these standard elements:

1. **Nameplate/masthead:** section located on the first page giving the name of the newsletter, the name of the organization, and possibly a logo. The nameplate sometimes includes a tagline that explains the newsletter's purpose.
2. **Date line:** line under the nameplate that includes the volume number, issue number, and the date of publication.
3. **Headline:** large-type title stating the subject of an article. (Some articles may also have a byline giving the name of the writer.)
4. **Body text**: the information in an article.
5. **Credits:** a list of the names and locations of the newsletter's staff.

LESSON 117

TEACH

Activity C. Go over the Paced Practice 2-minute timing routine with students. (See Lesson 34, page 119.)

Activity D. Ask students what type of newsletters they are familiar with. How might a business use a newsletter?

Illustration

The illustration shows Report 66 completed by following the directions for Reports 66 and 67.

PORTFOLIO *Activity*

If students' portfolio goals include demonstration of progress, they may want to include one or more of the newsletters from this lesson. Encourage students to evaluate their own work and include comments in their portfolio.

FACT FILE

Carpal Tunnel Syndrome is caused by inflammation and swelling of the tendons in the wrists caused by repetitive motions, such as typing. To avoid, exercise by squeezing a ball and keep your wrists properly supported when typing.

TEACH

Report 66. Show students that drawing shapes and text/word art are similar to graphic boxes in that document text will wrap around them.

Report 67. Have different students read aloud the steps for this report. Stop after each step to make sure all students understand the directions. Refer students to the illustration of Report 67 shown on page 421.

ASSESS

- Watch students as they complete the Language Link activity to see if they are able to apply the rules correctly.
- After students finish typing and formatting the newsletter, have them view their work on the screen to see if they made any errors.

CLOSE

If students do not finish the newsletters during the class period, make sure they save their work so that they can complete it the next time this class meets.

Remind students to clean up their workstation when they leave.

DESKTOP PUBLISHING APPLICATIONS

REPORT 66

Open Report 65 and add the following text in two balanced columns as a separate section beginning below the first section.

¶Accountability involves asking for help when necessary to produce the desired results. It means knowing how to delegate and making sure each person knows exactly what needs to be done. Accountability is not saying, "It was all my fault." It is looking calmly at what caused a problem and determining how to prevent it from happening again. Accountability is promising only what can be delivered. It means constantly sorting out priorities and taking responsibility for ongoing communication about the status of projects. It involves asking questions in order to understand the big picture and what is expected. It is also acknowledging work that is well done. If your boss doesn't practice accountability, you must still be accountable.

REPORT 67

Open Report 66 and revise it as follows:

1. Create a masthead using text/word art and Arial 36-point type. The name of the newsletter is *PROFESSIONAL JOURNAL*.
2. Add a heavy line beneath the masthead.
3. Before you press ENTER, change the font to Times New Roman 12-point; then press ENTER once.
4. Type the volume and number at the left and the current date at the right. This newsletter is *Vol. 6, No. 3*.
5. Add a lighter line beneath the date line and leave some space between this line and the headline type.
6. Add to the second article the title *ACCOUNTABILITY* in Times New Roman 22-point.
7. Add a byline in Times New Roman 10-point. Use your name in the byline.
8. At the end of the first article, insert a graphic of people working in an office. Size the graphic appropriately, and keep the columns balanced.

Out-of-Class Activity

Have students contact local businesses and organizations to request copies of newsletters. Have students choose one newsletter and duplicate it as a homework assignment. Post the newsletters around the room.

Career Exploration

Brainstorm with students about careers related to newsletters. Have several 3″ x 3″ squares of different colors available to students and a couple of markers and tape. On the board, write: Careers and Newsletters. Under this title, have each student write a career on one of the colored squares and tape it to the board under the title.

LESSON 118 NEWSLETTERS

OBJECTIVES:

- Improve keyboarding skill.
- Type 38/5'/5e.
- Complete the first page of a two-page newsletter.

A. WARMUP

Type each line 2 times.

Speed	1	Both of the men may go soon if he pays them for their work.
Accuracy	2	Brown jars would prevent the mixture from freezing quickly.
Language Link	3	At 2 p.m. this afternoon, my 21-year-old son located a job.
Numbers	4	There are 539 students and 68 faculty members at this camp.

| 1 | 2 | 3 | 4 | 5 | 6 | 7 | 8 | 9 | 10 | 11 | 12

interNET CONNECTION

Connect to the Internet. Search the Web for the latest information on voice recognition technology. Go to your nearest office supply or computer store to learn which types of voice recognition software are in stock. Report to the class on the technology involved in this software.

SKILLBUILDING

B. PREVIEW PRACTICE

Type each line 2 times as a preview to the timings that follow.

Accuracy	5	new realize quality foreign exporter Technology competition
Speed	6	know with help stay use the job all our of is in to do we a

RESOURCES

- Lesson Plan 118
- Courseware Lesson 118
- Student Data Disk
- Student Manual
- Reteaching and Reinforcement
- Grading and Evaluation

LESSON 118

FOCUS

- Use 5-minute timings to build speed.
- Type and format a newsletter.

BELLRINGER

As soon as students arrive at their workstations and log in, have them type the Warmup. Go over the purpose of each line as shown to the left of the copy.

TEACH

Activity B. Remind students to be aware of their posture, to sit up, keep their elbows in, and their feet flat on the floor.

TEACH

Activity C. Remind students that they should try to improve speed with each timing. The goal for these timing is to type 38 words a minute for 5 minutes with no more than 5 errors.

Report 68. Read the instructions aloud to students, stopping after each step to make sure students understand what they are to do.

Illustration
The illustration shows Report 68 completed by following the directions.

C. 5-Minute Timings

Take two 5-minute timings on the paragraphs. Note your speed and errors.

Goal: 38/5'/5e

Almost everything we use today is made with the help 11
of machines. Technology has caused a great change in how we 23
produce our goods. People first invent and then run the 34
machines. They also come up with new ideas for all of the 46
quality items that these machines can produce. 55

Human hands never examine some goods. In some cases, 66
all workers have to do is push a button. But, employees do 78
need to know which button to push so that they can get the 89
job done. 91

The producers in our country realize they must sell 102
their goods abroad to stay competitive. It is said that we 114
are the world's biggest exporter. Our country offers a big 126
market for producers in other countries as well. For that 137
reason, foreigners want to sell their goods here. There is 149
strong competition from foreign products. We are reported 161
also to have the most productive workers in the world. Our 173
product worth has improved because our employees are well- 184
trained, diverse, and skilled. 190

| 1 | 2 | 3 | 4 | 5 | 6 | 7 | 8 | 9 | 10 | 11 | 12 SI 1.42

DESKTOP PUBLISHING APPLICATIONS

REPORT 68

Create the first page of a newsletter following these directions:

1. Set the top and bottom margins at 0.75 inch and the left and right margins at 1.2 inches.
2. Press ENTER until you reach approximately 2.5 inches, then move the cursor to the top of the page.
3. Create the nameplate, *THE REPORTER,* using colorful word/text art. Use Arial Black 36-point for the font.
4. Add a thick horizontal line from margin to margin under the nameplate.

interNET ACTIVITY

Have students use the Internet to access Learning Kingdom (www.ce.vt.edu/evd/). Have students bring three new facts to class. Type these fun facts and display them around the room.

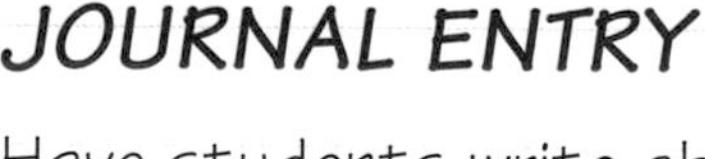

JOURNAL ENTRY

Have students write about how they see their lives changing as technology changes. Start with what they have experienced and then write about the future. Ask a few students to read their entries.

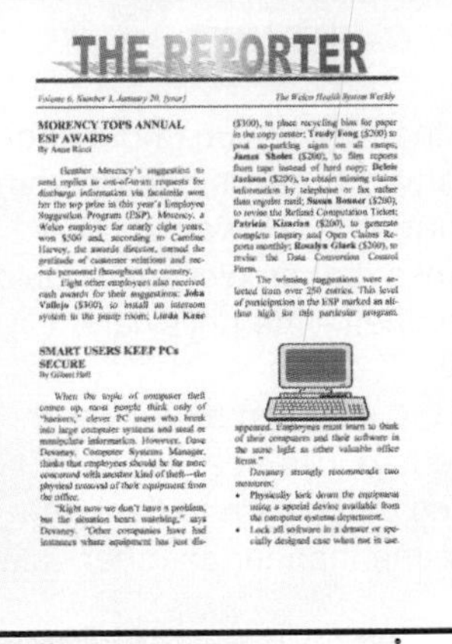
THE REPORTER

MORENCY TOPS ANNUAL ESP AWARDS

SMART USERS KEEP PCs SECURE

5. Add the date line below the nameplate. Align the volume number and date at the left; align the tag line at the right. Use Times New Roman 11-point italic. The line should read: *Volume 6, Number 3, January 20, {year} / The Welco Health System Weekly.*
6. Add a thin horizontal line from margin to margin below the date line.
7. Type the headline for article 1 in all capital letters and bold at the left margin using Times New Roman 14-point.Type the byline in Times New Roman 10-point.
8. Type the body of the article in Times New Roman 12-point. Indent paragraphs approximately 0.25 inch, justify the text, and use automatic hyphenation.
9. Type the names of the eight other winners in bold.
10. Balance the columns.
11. Follow steps 7–8 for the second article.
12. Add an appropriate graphic at the top of the second column of the second article. Balance the columns.
13. Adjust the spacing as necessary to fit everything on one page.

Article 1 headline: *MORENCY TOPS ANNUAL ESP AWARDS*
Byline: By Anne Ricci
Article 1 text: ¶Heather Morency's suggestion to send out-of-town requests for discharge information via facsimile won her the top prize in this year's Employee Suggestion Program (ESP). Morency, a Welco employee for nearly eight years, won $500 and, according to Caroline Harvey, the awards director, earned the gratitude of customer relations and records personnel throughout the country.
¶Eight other employees also received cash awards for their suggestions: John Vallejo ($300), to install an intercom system in the pump room; Linda Kane ($300), to place recycling bins for paper in the copy center; Trudy Fong ($200), to post no-parking signs on all ramps; James Sholes ($200), to film reports from tape instead of hard copy; Delois Jackson ($200), to obtain missing claims information by telephone or fax rather than regular mail; Susan Bonner ($200), to revise the Refund Computation Ticket; Patricia Kizarian ($200), to generate complete Inquiry and Open Claims Reports monthly; Rosalyn Gluck ($200), to revise the Data Conversion Control Form.
¶The winning suggestions were selected from more than 250 entries. This level of participation in the ESP marked an all-time high for the suggestion program.

TEACH

Report 68. As students continue to work on Report 68, walk around the room to make sure they understand the directions and are able to execute them. If you notice several students having trouble with the same step, go over this step again with the whole class. Refer them to page 424 for an illustration of Report 68.

FACT FILE

Do you wonder why naturally curly hair becomes frizzy and straight hair becomes limp as the humidity rises? Human hair grows longer as the humidity rises and shorter as it falls. The hair absorbs more water when there's more vapor in the air, which pushes the hair molecules apart.

ASSESS

- Check to see if students are increasing their word a minute speeds as they complete each 5-minute timing.
- As students begin typing and formatting the newsletter, walk around the room and point out correct and incorrect formatting to individual students.
- After students finish the first page of the newsletter, have them view their work on the screen to see if they made any errors. If errors were made, have students edit their work and make corrections.

CLOSE

If students do not finish the first page of the newsletter during the class period, make sure they save their work so that they can complete it the next time this class meets.

Remind students to clean up their workstation when they leave.

Article 2 headline: *SMART USERS KEEP PCs SECURE*
Byline: By Gilbert Hall
Article 2 text: When the topic of computer theft comes up, most people think only of "hackers," clever PC users who break into large computer systems and steal or manipulate information. However, Dave Devaney, Computer Systems Manager, thinks that employees should be far more concerned with another kind of theft—the physical removal of their equipment from the office.
¶"Right now we don't have a problem, but the situation bears watching," says Devaney. "Other companies have had instances where equipment has just disappeared. Employees must learn to think of their computers and their software in the same manner as other valuable office items."
¶Devaney strongly recommends two measures:
- Physically lock down the equipment using a special device available from the computer systems department.
- Lock all software in a drawer or specially designed case when not in use.

FACT FILE

Usually companies bring lawsuits against those who have stolen equipment or information from them. A court reporter may be used to record the testimony presented during the trial.

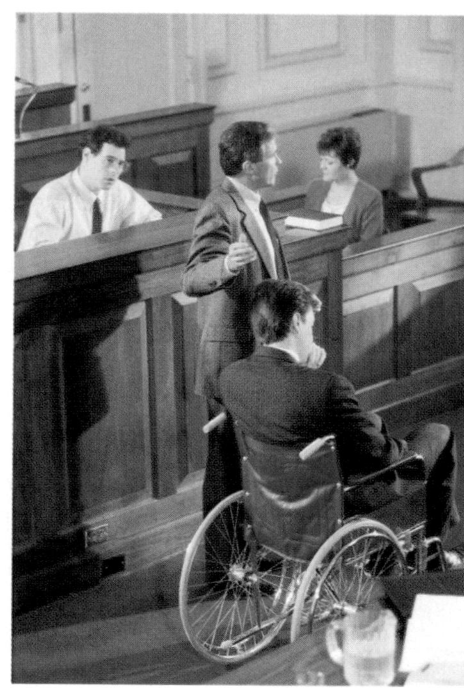

Teacher Notes

LESSON 119 NEWSLETTERS

OBJECTIVES:

- Improve keyboarding skill.
- Learn about confusing words.
- Complete the second page of a newsletter.

A. WARMUP

Type each line 2 times.

Speed	1	Andy may pay me for the bicycle if he is paid for the work.
Accuracy	2	Jacqueline was vexed by the folks who got the money prizes.
Language Link	3	My savings account pays low interest of only 4 5/8 percent.
Numbers	4	She sold 1,234 in June, 3,456 in July, and 7,890 in August.

| 1 | 2 | 3 | 4 | 5 | 6 | 7 | 8 | 9 | 10 | 11 | 12

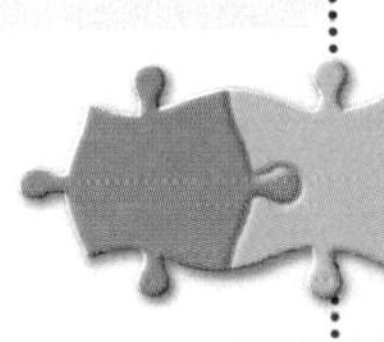

LANGUAGE LINK

B. CONFUSING WORDS

Study the confusing words and their meanings shown below. Then edit lines 5–8 by selecting the correct word to complete each sentence.

personal (adj.) private; of, relating to, or affecting a person;
personnel (n.) employees; a staff making up a work-force;human resources workers
their (pron.) possessive form of *they*
there (adv.) at or in that place
(pron.) used to introduce a clause

5 The letters are (personal/personnel) and should not be read at (there/ their) party.
6 All of the teachers expressed (their/there) (personal/personnel) concerns about the problems.
7 Over (their/there) are our neighbors; (their/there) family is very pleasant.
8 The (personal/personnel) staff are (their/there) to help you.

RESOURCES

 Lesson Plan 119
 Courseware Lesson 119
Student Data Disk
Student Manual
Supplementary Production Activities

LESSON 119

FOCUS

- Apply the Language Link rule concerning confusing words.
- Use a Pretest/Practice/ Posttest routine to build speed and accuracy.
- Type and format a newsletter.

BELLRINGER

As soon as students arrive at their workstations and log in, have them type the Warmup. Go over the purpose of each line as shown to the left of the copy.

TEACH

LANGUAGE LINK

Activity B. Ask students which of these words they have difficulty with. Give them this tip to help them remember personnel: both personnel and employee have an e.

Solutions: The letters are personal and should not be read at their party.

All of the teachers expressed their personal concerns about the problems.

Over there are our neighbors; their family is very pleasant.

The personnel staff are there to help you.

TEACH

Activities C–E. Remind students they should improve both their speed and accuracy from the Pretest to the Posttest.

PRETEST/PRACTICE/POSTTEST

The ***Pretest/Practice/Posttest*** routines are designed to improve speed or accuracy.

- The ***Pretest*** identifies students' speed or accuracy needs.
- The ***Practice*** provides a variety of improvement drills.
- The ***Posttest*** (a repeat of the Pretest) measures improvement.

SKILLBUILDING

C. PRETEST

Take a 1-minute timing on the paragraph. Note your speed and errors.

```
 9      It is our civic duty to vote for the mayor of this      10
10 city. We may also need to audit the books so that we have    22
11 proof that the manner in which we do business is correct.    34
12 We will have to go through channels for this to work out.    45
    | 1 | 2 | 3 | 4 | 5 | 6 | 7 | 8 | 9 | 10 | 11 | 12
```

D. PRACTICE

SPEED: ***If you made 2 or fewer errors on the Pretest, type lines 13–20 two times each.***

ACCURACY: ***If you made more than 2 errors on the Pretest, type lines 13–16 as a group two times. Then type lines 17–20 as a group two times.***

```
13 nn funny cannon cannot dinner manner runner winner channels
14 oo good wood room soon proof spoon foods tooth groom booths
15 tt kitty bottle button attach cattle fitted attacks attends
16 mm rummy tummy drummer summer simmer summit yummy hammer mm

17 duck duty bush busy city clay audit blend civic cycle field
18 dock down both bowl buck burn flaps girls goals panel risks
19 dial corn cork body also auto rocks spend their tight vivid
20 dark pens kept coal gyms pent fight right tight burnt socks
```

E. POSTTEST

Repeat the Pretest. Compare your Posttest results with your Pretest results.

DESKTOP PUBLISHING APPLICATIONS

REPORT 69

Complete the second page of the newsletter you created in Lesson 118. Follow these steps:

1. Set the top and bottom margins at 0.75 inch and the left and right margins at 1.2 inches.
2. Format the text in two columns, justify the text, and use automatic hyphenation.
3. Type the headline for the first article in all caps and bold at the left margin using Times New Roman 14-point. Add a flag to the left of the title (Wingdings, O), and make it red, 36 points. Insert a space after the flag.
4. Type the byline on the next line in Times New Roman 10-point.

JOURNAL ENTRY

Have students write about a newsletter they could write. What would they put into their newsletter? To whom would they send it? Students' newsletters can be about them or a cause that interests them.

BRIGHTON HOSTS 70TH EAGLE CELEBRATION
By Collette Searle

Hugh Brighton, Welco Civic Affairs Director, hosted the 70th birthday festivities for the Golden Order of Eagles earlier this week in Baltimore. Brighton, who was recently elected president of the local chapter of the organization, hosted the order's national president, Milton Land. The highlight of the three-day celebration was the dedication of the New Eagle Wing of Children's Hospital. The 200-bed facility will provide free care to children who have been referred there from 12 eastern states.

COMPANY ANNOUNCEMENTS

You and Your W-2
Most employees should have received their W-2 forms by now. Employees who were on the accident and sickness program administered by Blue Banner will receive their forms this week. If you have any questions about your W-2 forms, contact Gary Ashford in the Accounting Department at Ext. 589.

Short-Term Parking Passes
Because of road repairs near Wesley Tower and Building H, additional parking has been arranged for employees. If you work at either building, you can obtain a special parking permit from Roger Loucks, Mail Code 1209.

The permits are valid for spaces in Lot A on the northwest corner of Logan and [illegible] Streets.

Conference Tickets
If there is sufficient interest by Welco employees in seeing *West Side Story,* which is coming to the Palm Theater, the company will purchase a block of discount tickets for the Friday, March 16 performance. The show begins at 8 p.m. If you are interested in purchasing tickets, please call Diane Cohen, Civic Affairs Dept., Ext. 479, before March 2.

◇ **Las Vegas Night** ♡

The Five-Year Club is sponsoring a Las Vegas Night fundraiser on April 26 at 8 p.m. at the Town Line House. All proceeds from this event will be donated to those charities supported by the club. Please call Helen Oldhoff at Ext. 291 for details.

Community Service
Welco continues to support the local school system by providing employees with release time to speak at schools or career fairs with students who are making career decisions. If you are interested, please contact Diane Cohen, Ext. 479.

THE REPORTER is published weekly by Welco. Letters should be addressed to the editor at New Center Building, 609 Griswold, Room 703, Detroit, Michigan 48030. Editor: *Phillip S. DeRoy;* Reporters: *Gilbert Hall, Diane Novak, Ann Ricci, Collette Searle;* Designer/Desktop Specialist: *Betty [illegible]*

2

5. Type the body of the article in Times New Roman 12-point.
6. Insert a text box with a black border and yellow fill, and type *COMPANY ANNOUNCEMENTS* in bold Times New Roman 14-point. Center and type each announcement head in initial caps, bold, Times New Roman 14-point. Type the announcement text in 12-point Times New Roman, full-justified.
7. Add a diamond on one side of *Las Vegas Night,* and add a heart on the other side. Make both symbols red, 36 points. Insert a space between each symbol and the text. (Use WPIconic Symbols A, diamond = ", heart = !)
8. Insert an appropriate graphic above the community service article.
9. Insert a text box for the credits at the end of the second column. Add a double-line border, shade the box light yellow, and type the credits in Times New Roman 11-point.
10. Adjust the columns and text boxes so that your page looks similar to the illustration.
11. Number the page (2) at the bottom center of the page.

Headline: *BRIGHTON HOSTS 70TH EAGLE CELEBRATION*
Byline: By Collette Searle
¶Hugh Brighton, Welco Civic Affairs Director, hosted the 70th birthday festivities for the Golden Order of Eagles earlier this week in Baltimore. Brighton, who was recently elected president of the local chapter of the organization, hosted the order's national president, Milton Land. The highlight of the three-day celebration was the dedication of the New Eagle Wing of Children's Hospital. The 200-bed facility will provide free care to children who have been referred there from 12 eastern states.
Company Announcements:
You and Your W-2: Most employees should have received their W-2 forms by now. Employees who were on the accident and sickness program administered by Blue Banner will receive their forms this week. If you have questions about your W-2 forms, contact Gary Ashford in the Accounting Department at Ext. 589.

TEACH

Report 69. Have students read the instructions for Report 69 aloud in class. Make sure all students understand them.

As students work on this report, walk around the room to make sure they are able to execute the steps. If you notice several students having trouble with the same step, go over it again with the class.

Illustration

The illustration shows Report 69 completed by following the directions.

interNET ACTIVITY

Have students use the keyword newsletter and explore different Websites dedicated to newsletters. Have students find three sites they think their classmates might like. Take a vote and give a prize for the most popular site.

Career Exploration

Have students choose a career of interest to them, research the career, then design and write a one-page newsletter about the career. Newsletters should include what training or education is needed for the career. Use as many different desktop publishing elements as possible, including color.

ASSESS

- Check to see if students are increasing their word a minute speeds as they complete each 5-minute timing.
- Watch students as they complete the Language Link activity to see if they apply the rules correctly.
- Check to see if students show signs of improvement from the Pretest to the Posttest.
- As students begin typing and formatting the newsletter, walk around the room and point out correct and incorrect formatting.
- After students finish typing and formatting the newsletter, have them view their work on the screen.

CLOSE

If students do not finish the newsletter during the class period, make sure they save their work so that they can complete it the next time this class meets.

PORTFOLIO *Activity*

If students' portfolio goals include showcasing their best work, they may want to include the newsletter from this lesson. Encourage students to evaluate their own work and include comments in their portfolio.

Short-Term Parking Passes: Because of road repairs near Wesley Tower and Building H, additional parking has been arranged for employees. If you work in either building, you can obtain a special parking permit from Roger Loucks, Mail Code 1209.
¶The permits are valid for spaces in Lot A on the northwest corner of Logan and Beaubien Streets.
Theater Tickets: If there is sufficient interest by Welco employees in seeing *West Side Story,* which is coming to the Palm City Theater, the company will purchase a block of discount tickets for the Friday, March 16, performance. The show begins at 8 p.m. If you are interested in purchasing tickets, please call Diane Cohen, Civic Affairs Dept., Ext. 479, before March 2.
Las Vegas Night: The Five-Year Club is sponsoring a Las Vegas Night fundraiser on April 26 at 8 p.m. at the Town Line House. All proceeds from this event will be donated to those charities supported by the club. Please call Helen Oldhoff at Ext. 291 for details.
Community Service: Welco continues to support the local school system by providing employees with release time to speak at schools or career fairs with students who are making career decisions. If you are interested, please contact Diane Cohen, Ext. 479.
Credits: *THE REPORTER* is published weekly by Welco. Letters should be addressed to the editor at New Center Building, 609 Griswold, Room 703, Detroit, Michigan 48030. Editor: *Phillip S. DeRoy*; Reporters: *Gilbert Hall, Diane Novick, Anne Ricci, Collette Searle*; Designer/Desktop Specialist: *Betty Lynclyff.*

430 **Desktop Publishing**

Teacher Notes

LESSON 120

Desktop Publishing Review

OBJECTIVES:

- Improve keyboarding skill.
- Review desktop publishing features.

A. Warmup

Type each line 2 times.

Speed	1 It is now time for all of us to take the time to save more.
Accuracy	2 Pat quickly froze the gold mixtures in five old brown jars.
Language Link	3 The personnel department sent out their recognition awards.
Numbers/Symbols	4 The total bill was \$5.78 + \$9.64 + \$2.13, less 5% = \$16.67.
	| 1 | 2 | 3 | 4 | 5 | 6 | 7 | 8 | 9 | 10 | 11 | 12

SKILLBUILDING

B. 12-Second Sprints

Take three 12-second timings on each line. Try to increase your speed on each timing.

5 They will be able to amend the votes that were taken today.
6 She sent a note about an issue to four kind men who helped.
7 When you take a tour, you may see four new members at work.
8 The first court passed one new law today that we must read.
| | | | 5 | | | | 10 | | | | 15 | | | | 20 | | | | 25 | | | | 30 | | | | 35 | | | | 40 | | | | 45 | | | | 50 | | | | 55 | | | | 60

C. Diagnostic Practice: Alphabet

Turn to the Diagnostic Practice: Alphabet routine beginning on page SB1. Type one of the Pretest/Posttest paragraphs and identify any errors made. Then type the corresponding drill lines 2 times for each letter on which you made 2 or more errors and 1 time for each letter on which you made only 1 error. Finally, repeat the same Pretest paragraph and compare your performance.

RESOURCES

- Lesson Plan 120
- Courseware Lesson 120
- Student Data Disk
- Student Manual
- Reteaching and Reinforcement
- Unit 6 Test
- Grading and Evaluation

LESSON 120

FOCUS

- Use 12-second timings to build speed.
- Use Diagnostic Practice to identify areas that need improvement.
- Type and format a newsletter.
- Type and format an invitation.

Bellringer

As soon as students arrive at their workstations and log in, have them type the Warmup. Go over the purpose of each line as shown to the left of the copy.

TEACH

Activity B. Remind students to type at a fast pace during the 12-second timing. At the end of the first and second timings, encourage students to type just one or two strokes faster on the next timing.

Activity C. Make sure that students understand that this Diagnostic Practice activity is designed to help identify areas that need improvement and provide needed practice.

TEACH

Report 70. Read the instructions aloud to students, stopping after each step to make sure all students understand what they are to do.

Illustration

The illustration shows Report 70 completed by following the directions.

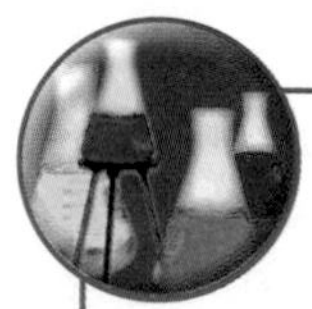

Science Connections

Have students contact a local environmental organization that is dedicated to protecting endangered natural resources or endangered wildlife and ask for someone to speak to the class. As a class, choose one environmental issue the class can work on. Write letters, volunteer time, or perform other activities to help the environment.

DESKTOP PUBLISHING APPLICATIONS

REPORT 70
Newsletter

Create a newsletter by following these steps:

1. Use text/word art and Times New Roman 36-point to create the title *OUR WORLD*.
2. Type the body of the newsletter in two columns using Times New Roman 13-point and full justification. Insert a vertical line between the columns.
3. Indent paragraphs 0.25 inch.
4. Insert a graphic of a globe between the third and fourth paragraphs.
5. Type the heading *Promoting Conservation* so that the type reverses to white in a green box.
6. Add an appropriate page border to the newsletter.

¶When the first pictures from space appeared in *Life* magazine several decades ago, we gained a new perspective on the planet Earth. Science was not just the study of land, sea, air, and living things. It was also the study of an entire planet—the only one in our solar system—that so far has been found suitable for life.

¶Earth is the only planet where water is stable at the surface. Seas are important because water has been the catalyst for the development of life on our planet.

¶As the population of humanity continues to grow and use more and more of the world's resources, it is more important than ever that everyone realize the impact this is having and will continue to have on the environment.

¶Concern for the environment and ecology has led to the formation of about 3,000 environmental interest groups. Their goals range from protecting endangered natural resources to protecting endangered wildlife.

Promoting Conservation

¶The Forest Service has restored millions of acres of forests used for outdoor recreation, for timber, and for wildlife habitats.

¶The federal government created the Environmental Protection Agency to help clean up our air, water, land, and other natural resources.

Science Connections

interNET ACTIVITY

Have half of your students access the NASA Website (www.nasa.gov) and half access the EPA Website (www.epa.gov). Ask students to explore these sites for information that helps them understand the importance of protecting the environment.

Career Exploration

Have students work in groups of three or four to learn about careers related to protecting endangered natural resources or endangered wildlife. Students can contact the EPA, wildlife services, forest services, and other organizations. Each group should write a short report.

¶Recycling has now become more important than ever. Business and industry are finding new ways to recycle waste products such as paper, plastics, glass, oil, animal by-products, tires, and other trash. In many places, trash is being burned to create electricity.
¶There is a wealth of information available on global environmental changes. There are CDs, videodiscs, and other materials available to help explore the various aspects of Earth's systems. Everyone needs to be aware of what he or she can do to help protect life on Earth.

REPORT 71
Invitation

Create an invitation to a formal dinner dance using the desktop publishing features that you have learned.

1. The dance is called the Washington Ball.
2. It will be held on September 23.
3. Dinner will begin at 7:30 p.m. and dancing will begin at 9 p.m.
4. The dance will be held at the Mt. Washington Hotel in Bretton, New Hampshire.
5. The cost is $60 per couple, and reservations must be made.
6. The telephone number is 603-555-0203, and all reservations must be received by September 1.

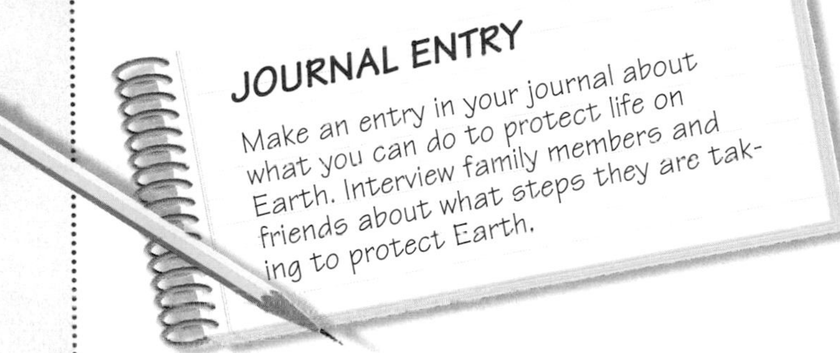

JOURNAL ENTRY
Make an entry in your journal about what you can do to protect life on Earth. Interview family members and friends about what steps they are taking to protect Earth.

LESSON 120

TEACH

Report 71. As students work on Report 71, walk around the room to make sure students understand the directions and are able to execute them. If you notice several students having trouble with the same step, go over this step again with the class.

ASSESS

- Check to see if students are increasing their word a minute speeds as they complete each 12-second timing.
- Monitor students as they complete Diagnostic Practice and provide individualized assistance as needed.
- As students begin typing and formatting the documents, walk around the room and point out correct and incorrect formatting to individual students.
- After students finish typing and formatting the documents, have them view their work on the screen to see if they made any errors. If errors were made, have students edit their work and make corrections.

CLOSE

If students do not finish the documents during the class period, make sure they save their work so that they can complete it the next time this class meets.

Teacher Notes

UNIT 7 ORGANIZER

SPREADSHEETS

Lesson	Focus	Special Features	Skillbuilding	Pretest/ Practice/ Posttest	Documents	GO TO Activities
121	Spreadsheets: Orientation	Language Link, p. 436	pp. 436–437			p. 438
122	Spreadsheets: Navigating	Fact File, p. 439 Internet Connection, p. 441	pp. 439–440	pp. 439–440	Spreadsheet 1, pp. 440–441	p. 440
123	Spreadsheets: Entering Data	Language Link, pp. 442–443 Fact File, p. 444	p. 443		Spreadsheet 1, p. 444	
124	Spreadsheets: Create, Align Columns	Fact File, p. 447	p. 445		Spreadsheet 2, pp. 446–447 Spreadsheet 3, p. 446 Spreadsheet 4, p. 447	p. 445
125	Spreadsheets: Copying Data, Changing Column Widths	Language Link, pp. 448–449 Journal Entry, p. 450 Cultural Connection, p. 452	p. 449		Spreadsheet 5, p. 451 Spreadsheet 6, p. 452	p. 450
126	Spreadsheets: Moving Data, Changing Row Height	Communication Focus, p. 456	pp. 453–454	p. 454	Spreadsheet 7, p. 455 Spreadsheet 8, p. 456 Spreadsheet 9, p. 456	p. 455
127	Spreadsheets: Formatting Values	Language Link, p. 457 Communication Focus, p. 457 Social Studies Connection, p. 458 Fact File, p. 459	p. 458		Spreadsheet 10, pp. 459–460 Spreadsheet 11, p. 460 Spreadsheet 12, p. 460	p. 459
128	Spreadsheets: Printing		p. 461		Spreadsheet 5, p. 463 Spreadsheet 3, p. 463 Spreadsheet 6, p. 463 Spreadsheet 7, p. 463	p. 462
129	Spreadsheets: Entering Formulas	Language Link, p. 464 Math Connection, p. 465 Internet Connection, p. 466	p. 465		Spreadsheet 13, p. 467 Spreadsheet 14, p. 468 Spreadsheet 15, p. 468 Spreadsheet 16, p. 468	p. 466
130	Spreadsheets: Entering Formulas	Social Studies Connection, p. 469 Fact File, p. 471	pp. 469–470	pp. 469–470	Spreadsheet 17, pp. 470–471 Spreadsheet 18, p. 471	

UNIT 7 RESOURCE MANAGER

MULTIMEDIA
- **Courseware:** Lessons 121–140
- **Student Data Disk**
- **Student Manual:** Lessons 121–140

TEACHING TOOLS
- **Lesson Plans:** Lessons 121–140
- **Block Scheduling Guide, Unit 7**
- **Language Link Worksheets:** Lessons 121–140
- **Multicultural Applications**
- **Academic Report Guide**
- **Solution Keys**
- **Cross-Curricular Activities:** Lessons 121–140

RETEACHING/REINFORCEMENT
- **Reteaching/Reinforcement Activities:** Lessons 121–140
- **Supplemental Production Activities:** Lessons 121–140

ASSESSMENT and EVALUATION

Pretest/Practice/Posttest: pp. 439–440, 454, 467–470, 477, 510–511
Portfolio Activity: pp. 487, 505, 513
Unit 7 Test
Timings: pp. 437, 449, 458, 473, 489, 498
Production Jobs: Spreadsheets 1–48
Grading and Evaluation

Electronic Teacher Classroom Resources

For your convenience, the teacher's materials are available on a CD-ROM. Having these resources available electronically enables you to print exactly what you need and revise materials as necessary.

Lesson	Focus	Special Features	Skillbuilding	Pretest/ Practice/ Posttest	Documents	GO TO Activities
131	Spreadsheets: Sum Function, Center Data	Language Link, pp. 472–473	p. 473		Spreadsheet 20, p. 475 Spreadsheet 21, p. 475	
132	Spreadsheets: Average Function	Internet Connection, pp. 476, 479 Science Connection, p. 477 Communication Focus, p. 478	pp. 476–477	p. 477	Spreadsheet 22, p. 478 Spreadsheet 23, p. 478 Spreadsheet 24, p. 479	p. 478
133	Spreadsheets: InsertingRows/ Sorting Data	Language Link, p. 480 Fact File, pp. 480, 482 Internet Connection, p. 483	p. 481		Spreadsheet 25, p. 482 Spreadsheet 26, p. 482 Spreadsheet 27, p. 482 Spreadsheet 28, p. 483	p. 481
134	Spreadsheets: Inserting Columns, Borders, and Shading	Fact File, pp. 484, 487 Portfolio Activity, p. 487	p. 484		Spreadsheet 29, p. 486 Spreadsheet 30, p. 486 Spreadsheet 31, p. 487	p. 485
135	Spreadsheets: Clear Cells, Delete Rows and Columns	Language Link, p. 488 Social Studies Connection, p. 489 Science Connection, p. 489 Cultural Connection, p. 490	p. 489		Spreadsheet 32, p. 491 Spreadsheet 33, p. 491	p. 490
136	Spreadsheets: Fill Right/Fill Down Commands	Fact File, p. 493 Communication Focus, p. 495 Math Connection, p. 495	p. 492		Spreadsheet 34, pp. 493–494 Spreadsheet 35, p. 494 Spreadsheet 36, p. 495	p. 493
137	Spreadsheets: Creating Bar Charts	Language Link, pp. 496–497 Social Studies Connection, pp. 497, 498 Internet Connection, p. 500	pp. 497–498		Spreadsheet 37, pp. 499–500 Spreadsheet 38, p. 501	p. 499
138	Spreadsheets: Creating Pie Charts	Fact File, p. 502 Math Connection, p. 504 Portfolio Activity, p. 505	p. 502		Spreadsheet 39, p. 503 Spreadsheet 40, p. 504 Spreadsheet 41, p. 505 Spreadsheet 42, p. 505	p. 502
139	Spreadsheets: Review	Language Link, p. 506 Fact File, p. 507	p. 507		Spreadsheet 43, pp. 507–508 Spreadsheet 44, pp. 508–509	
140	Spreadsheets: Review	Fact File, p. 510 Internet Connection, p. 513 Portfolio Activity, p. 513	pp. 510–511	pp. 510–511	Spreadsheet 45, p. 511 Spreadsheet 46, p. 512 Spreadsheet 47, p. 512 Spreadsheet 48, p. 513	

SCANS Competencies in Glencoe Keyboarding with Computer Applications

Resources	Interpersonal Skills	Information	Systems	Technology
Throughout the course, students deal specifically with resources: allocating time for completing drills and documents, maintaining workstations, caring for computers and software.	Cultural Connection, pp. 452, 590 Communication Focus, pp. 456, 457, 478, 495	Career Bit, p. 435 Fact File, pp. 439, 444, 447, 459, 471, 480, 482, 484, 487, 493, 502, 507, 510 Internet Connection, pp. 441, 466, 476, 479, 483, 500, 513 Social Studies Connection, pp. 458, 469, 489, 497, 498 Science Connection, pp. 477, 487 Math Connection, pp. 467, 504, 495	Internet Connection, pp. 441, 466, 476, 479, 483, 500, 513	Lessons 121–140 Internet Connection, pp. 441, 466, 476, 479, 483, 500, 513 Communication Focus, p. 456 Fact File, p. 502

INTRODUCING THE UNIT

Have different students read each of the objectives for Unit 7. Address each objective as it's read. Explain that the goal in this unit is to reach a typing speed of 39 words a minute for 5 minutes with 5 or fewer errors. Encourage students to believe this is an achievable goal.

Students also will learn the basic parts of a spreadsheet, how to create a spreadsheet, and how to manipulate data within a spreadsheet. Plus, they will learn to compose letters and short stories at the keyboard.

FUN Facts

Rap music originated in the South Bronx area of New York City in the African-American community. Rap comes out of rhythm and blues and the cross-culture of its early practitioners—Kool Herc, D.J. Hollywood, and Afrika Bambaataa—who were either first- or second-generation Americans of Caribbean ancestry. The first rap recording was made in 1979.

UNIT 7 SPREADSHEETS

LESSONS 121–140

OBJECTIVES

- Demonstrate keyboarding speed and accuracy on straight copy with a goal of 39 words a minute for 5 minutes with 5 or fewer errors.
- Demonstrate knowledge of the basic parts of a spreadsheet.
- Demonstrate the ability to create a spreadsheet and manipulate the data.
- Demonstrate the ability to use spreadsheets to ask "what if" questions.
- Compose letters and short stories at the keyboard.

COURSEWARE OVERVIEW

The courseware will automatically launch the available spreadsheet program but will not put a KCA menu item on the menu bar. Therefore, show students how to use Alt + Tab to return to KCA or to click the KCA button on the status bar.

WORDS TO LEARN

AVERAGE
bar chart
cell ranges
fill down
fill right
fill series
formula
functions
gridlines
operators
pie chart
row height
sort
SUM
values
what if
worksheet
X axis
Y axis

CAREER BIT

METEOROLOGIST Meteorology is the study of the atmosphere. Meteorologists study the atmosphere's physical characteristics, motions, and processes, and the way it affects the rest of our environment. The best known application of this knowledge is in weather forecasting. Meteorologists study information on air pressure, temperature, humidity, and wind velocity, and apply physical and mathematical relationships to make short-and long-range weather forecasts. Their data come from weather satellites, weather radar, and remote sensors and observers in many parts of the world. Weather information and meteorological research are also applied in air-pollution control, agriculture, air and sea transportation, defense, and the study of trends in Earth's climate such as global warming or ozone depletion.

WORDS TO LEARN

The terms in Words to Learn are defined in the Glossary at the back of the book. Ask students if they are familiar with any of the terms. Have them define the terms they know. Compare their definitions with those in the Glossary.

CAREER BIT

After students have read the information on meteorologists, have them brainstorm to create a list of ways meteorologists use computers. Have students meet in small groups to discuss how they think computers will be used in predicting the weather in the future. Have the small groups prepare a short report, then have one representative from each group give the report to the whole class. If possible invite a meteorologist to your class to discuss how he or she uses computers.

COURSEWARE OVERVIEW

Spreadsheet activities are not scored. Since spreadsheets take longer to print than text documents, you may want to check students' spreadsheets on screen to ensure that they are correctly formatting cells and inputting numbers and formulas.

LESSON 121

FOCUS

- Compose the body of a short letter in the Language Link activity.
- Use 5-minute timings to build speed.
- Learn parts of spreadsheets: Row, Column, Cell, Cell Name or Address, Entry Bar, and Active Cell.

BELLRINGER

As soon as students arrive at their workstations and log in, have them type the Warmup. Go over the purpose of each line as shown to the left of the copy.

TEACH

Activity B. Remind students to include the address of the museum and the date. Have students check each other's work for errors.

Solutions: Answers will vary.

Activity C. Point out that words in the Preview Practice are used in the timing that follows.

LESSON 121

SPREADSHEETS: ORIENTATION

OBJECTIVES:

- Identify the basic parts of a spreadsheet.
- Compose at the keyboard.
- Type 39/5'/5e.

A. WARMUP

Type each line 2 times.

Speed	1 Just see how well his fingers are flying over the keys now.
Accuracy	2 Kaz quickly mixed the two squeezed juices in the brown jug.
Language Link	3 The personal note he got said they were on their way there.
Technique	4 Do NOT type any CAPITAL in lowercase; always use UPPERCASE.

B. COMPOSING AT THE KEYBOARD

Compose the body of a short letter requesting information from a nearby museum. Ask for a program of scheduled events, the hours of operation, and the cost of admission.

SKILLBUILDING

C. PREVIEW PRACTICE

Type each line 2 times as a preview to the timings that follow.

Accuracy	5 United dispute quality criticize organization international
Speed	6 fixing other over were most keep with came and not is to up

RESOURCES

 Lesson Plan 121

 Courseware Lesson 121

Student Data Disk

Student Manual

Grading and Evaluation

COURSEWARE OVERVIEW

Students must close their spreadsheet program by using File, Exit to return to KCA. Note that the software does not score the spreadsheets. Once students learn how to print spreadsheets, you may want to have students print copies of their spreadsheets for you to check.

SKILLBUILDING

D. 5-MINUTE TIMINGS

Take two 5-minute timings on the paragraphs. Note your speed and errors.

Goal: 39/5'/5e

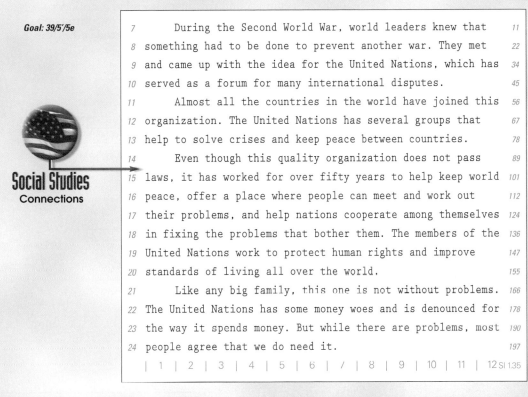

Social Studies Connections

```
     During the Second World War, world leaders knew that       11
something had to be done to prevent another war. They met       22
and came up with the idea for the United Nations, which has     34
served as a forum for many international disputes.              45
     Almost all the countries in the world have joined this     56
organization. The United Nations has several groups that        67
help to solve crises and keep peace between countries.          78
     Even though this quality organization does not pass        89
laws, it has worked for over fifty years to help keep world    101
peace, offer a place where people can meet and work out        112
their problems, and help nations cooperate among themselves    124
in fixing the problems that bother them. The members of the    136
United Nations work to protect human rights and improve        147
standards of living all over the world.                        155
     Like any big family, this one is not without problems.    166
The United Nations has some money woes and is denounced for    178
the way it spends money. But while there are problems, most    190
people agree that we do need it.                               197
| 1 | 2 | 3 | 4 | 5 | 6 | 7 | 8 | 9 | 10 | 11 | 12 SI 1.35
```

FORMATTING

E. SPREADSHEET ORIENTATION

A **spreadsheet** is an electronic worksheet or grid that is used to organize and analyze information and calculate projections (for instance, to answer "what ifs").

For example, suppose you have your English grades entered and averaged in a spreadsheet. On Friday, you

TEACH

Activity D. Remind students that they should try to improve speed with each 5-minute timing. The goal for these timings is to type 39 words a minute for 5 minutes with no more than 5 errors.

Activity E. Provide students with several examples of spreadsheets before beginning this activity. Use the illustration to discuss with students the parts of a spreadsheet.

Out-of-Class Activity

Have students write to the United Nations and request a packet of information appropriate for schools. Also have students read newspapers and news magazines and cut out any articles that talk about United Nations' activities, including the peace-keeping forces. Discuss these.

interNET ACTIVITY

Have students access the United Nations Website (www.un.org). After students have had a chance to study the site, continue the class discussion on the UN to show its relevance in the modern world and to students' lives.

LESSON 121

TEACH

Illustration
The illustration shows the parts of a spreadsheet.

Activity F. Have students turn to Lesson 121 in their Student Manual and read the explanation for the software they are using. Then have them complete the practice activities.

STUDENT MANUAL
Be sure students turn to the correct lesson in their Student Manual.

ASSESS

- Check to see if students are increasing their word a minute speeds as they complete each 5-minute timing.
- Review the letter students have typed for the Language Link composing activity.
- Make sure students are able to use the spreadsheet features.
- As students begin Lesson 121 in the Student Manual, walk around the room and provide assistance to individual students as needed.

CLOSE

Remind students to clean up their workstation when they leave.

will be taking a major test and want to know what your final grade would be if you received a test grade of 85. You could enter the 85 and have the spreadsheet recalculate your grade average.

Spreadsheets consist of rows and columns. Vertical columns are identified with letters of the alphabet. Horizontal rows are identified with numbers. The rectangle where a column and row meet is called a **cell**. A cell name or address is the column letter and row number. For example, the cell name of the highlighted cell in the example is D10.

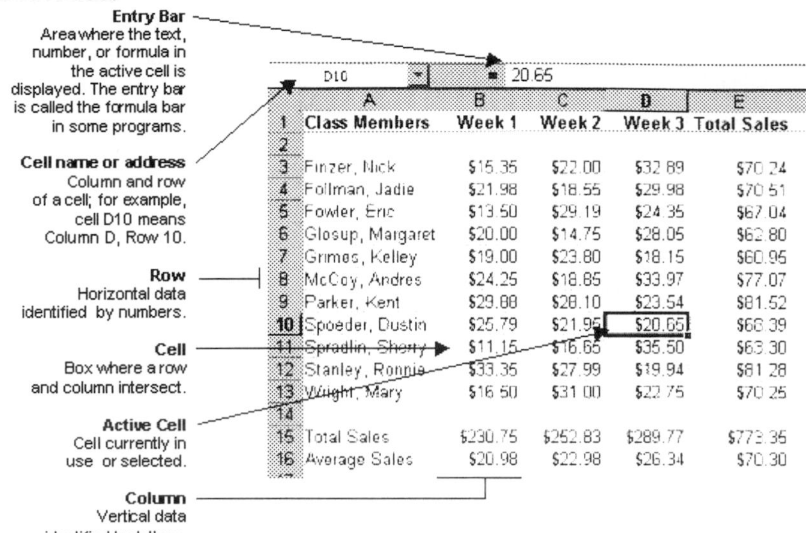

	A	B	C	D	E
1	Class Members	Week 1	Week 2	Week 3	Total Sales
2					
3	Finzer, Nick	$15.35	$22.00	$32.89	$70.24
4	Follman, Jadie	$21.98	$18.55	$29.98	$70.51
5	Fowler, Eric	$13.50	$29.19	$24.35	$67.04
6	Glosup, Margaret	$20.00	$14.75	$28.05	$62.80
7	Grimes, Kelley	$19.00	$23.80	$18.15	$60.95
8	McCoy, Andres	$24.25	$18.85	$33.97	$77.07
9	Parker, Kent	$29.88	$28.10	$23.54	$81.52
10	Spoeder, Dustin	$25.79	$21.95	$20.65	$68.39
11	Spradlin, Sherry	$11.15	$16.65	$35.50	$63.30
12	Stanley, Ronnie	$33.35	$27.99	$19.94	$81.28
13	Wright, Mary	$16.50	$31.00	$22.75	$70.25
14					
15	Total Sales	$230.75	$252.83	$289.77	$773.35
16	Average Sales	$20.98	$22.98	$26.34	$70.30

F. SOFTWARE FEATURES

GO TO ***STUDENT MANUAL***
Spreadsheets

Study Lesson 121 in your student manual. Complete all the practice activities while at your computer.

Teacher Notes

LESSON 122

SPREADSHEETS: NAVIGATING

OBJECTIVES:

- Improve keyboarding speed and accuracy.
- Move around within a spreadsheet.

A. WARMUP

Type each line 2 times.

```
Speed          The firm sent the forms over an hour after she called them.
Accuracy       These women quietly gave back the prizes of the six judges.
Language Link  They're planning to eat there for their brother's birthday.
Numbers        Those five passengers are 10, 29, 38, 47, and 56 years old.
               | 1 | 2 | 3 | 4 | 5 | 6 | 7 | 8 | 9 | 10 | 11 | 12
```

FACT FILE

A high school diploma or General Equivalency Diploma (GED) is required for entry into almost every job you can name today. Along with the high school diploma and each level of education that you complete thereafter, you usually have an increase in salary.

SKILLBUILDING

B. PRETEST

Take a 1-minute timing on the paragraph. Note your speed and errors.

```
     Finishing high school can open up many doors for those     11
who wish to go on to complete a two- or four-year degree in    23
college. It may also open up opportunities for those who       35
wish to find jobs after high school.                           42
| 1 | 2 | 3 | 4 | 5 | 6 | 7 | 8 | 9 | 10 | 11 | 12
```


LESSON 122

FOCUS

- Use a Pretest/Practice/Posttest routine to build speed and accuracy.
- Learn spreadsheet features: Select Cells and Deselect Cells.
- Learn how to move around within a spreadsheet.

BELLRINGER

As soon as students arrive at their workstations and log in, have them type the Warmup. Go over the purpose of each line as shown to the left of the copy.

TEACH

Activity B. Remind students they should improve both their speed and accuracy from the Pretest to the Posttest.

RESOURCES

 Lesson Plan 122

 Courseware Lesson 122

Student Data Disk

Student Manual

Cross-Curricular Activities

COURSEWARE OVERVIEW

Students are instructed to minimize their spreadsheet program and maximize KCA as they work through the textbook problems. You may want to provide them with detailed instructions on how to do this.

TEACH

Activities C–D. Remind students they should improve both their speed and accuracy from the Pretest to the Posttest.

PRETEST/PRACTICE/POSTEST

The ***Pretest/Practice/Posttest*** routines are designed to improve speed or accuracy.

- The ***Pretest*** identifies students' speed or accuracy needs.
- The ***Practice*** provides a variety of improvement drills.
- The ***Posttest*** (a repeat of the Pretest) measures improvement.

Activity E. Walk around the room while students are completing Lesson 122 in their Student Manual. Make sure they understand the instructions and that they are carrying them out correctly.

STUDENT MANUAL

Be sure students turn to the correct lesson in their Student Manual.

Activity 1. Have students read the instructions once, then have them read the instructions again to be sure they understand what to do.

C. PRACTICE

In the chart below, find the number of errors you made on the Pretest. Then type each of the following designated drill lines 2 times.

Pretest Errors	0–1	2	3	4+
Drill Lines	12–16	11–15	10–14	9–13

Accuracy

```
9  those seize whether require advanced training opportunities
10 two- high capable colleges graduates finishing communicates
11 want watched getting complete employers carefully coworkers
12 up judged failing criterion four-year essential exceptional
```

Speed

```
13 degree demand others after often while open many for can go
14 finish judged worker there doors these wish also who but on
15 people person school right thing prime find jobs may the is
16 listed reason skills along going being will than one get of
```

D. POSTTEST

Repeat the Pretest. Compare your Posttest results with your Pretest results.

FORMATTING

E. SOFTWARE FEATURES

STUDENT MANUAL

Select Cells   Deselect Cells

Study Lesson 122 in your student manual. Complete all the practice activities while at your computer. Then complete the jobs that follow.

SPREADSHEET APPLICATIONS

ACTIVITY 1

Spreadsheet 1

Open the file SS1 and practice selecting and deselecting cells.

1. Click on cell A3, *Finzer, Nick.*
2. Use the arrow keys to move to cell A7, *Grimes, Kelly.* Check the entry bar at the top of the spreadsheet to be sure you are in the correct cell.
3. Use the arrow keys to move to cell C1, *Week 2.*

FACT FILE

Seventeen thousand years ago on a wall of the Lascaux cave in the French Dordogne, Cro-Magnon people painted pictures of themselves and the events of their lives. The paintings were their communication. Have students think about and then write an essay on what their communications will tell people thousands of years from now.

4. Select a group of cells by clicking cell D3 and dragging down through cell D13. Note that the entry bar shows only cell D3 and its contents.
5. Deselect cells D3 through D13 by clicking outside the shaded area.

ACTIVITY 2
Spreadsheet 1

If necessary, open the file SS1, and follow these steps:

1. Select cells A3 through E3.
2. Deselect cells A3 through E3.
3. Select cells A3 through E9.
4. Deselect cells A3 through E9.
5. Move the cell pointer to cell E5. Note the formula in the entry bar and the results in cell E5.

ACTIVITY 3
Spreadsheet 1

If necessary, open the file SS1, and do the following:

1. Move the cell pointer to cell C16 and note the formula in the entry bar.
2. Move the cell pointer to cell C15 and note the formula in the entry bar.
3. Select all of column D by clicking once on the letter D.
4. Deselect column D.
5. Select all of row 11 by clicking once on the number 11.
6. Deselect row 11.
7. Select the entire spreadsheet by clicking once on the Select All button in the upper-left corner where the row and column headings meet. Note what is displayed in the entry bar.
8. Deselect the spreadsheet.
9. Close the file.

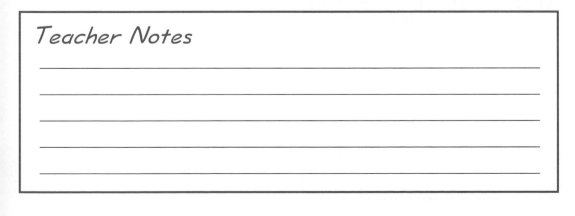

*inter*NET CONNECTION

Connect to the Internet. In the location text box of your browser, enter the name(s) of two-year colleges or universities in which you are interested. You may want to look at the information found in http://cset.sp.utoledo.edu/twoyrcol.html. From this site, you can select a particular state to search.

TEACH

Activity 2. As students work through this activity walk around the room to make sure they understand the directions and are able to execute them. If you notice several students having trouble with the same step, go over it again with the class.

Activity 3. Read the instructions aloud to students, stopping after each step to make sure students understand what they are to do.

ASSESS

- Check to see if students show signs of improvement from the Pretest to the Posttest.
- Make sure students are able to use the Select Cells and Deselect Cells spreadsheet features.

CLOSE

Remind students to clean up their workstation when they leave.

Teacher Notes

LESSON 123

FOCUS

- Apply the Language Link rules for confusing words.
- Use 30-second OK timings to improve accuracy.
- Learn how to enter spreadsheet data.

BELLRINGER

As soon as students arrive at their workstations and log in, have them type the Warmup. Go over the purpose of each line as shown to the left of the copy.

TEACH

Activity B. Ask students which of these words they have trouble with. Use each word in a sentence to help students understand the differences.

Solutions: The student sought advice from the school's student council president.

I advise you to not answer until you have retained reputable counsel.

The AMA Council on Aging advises people to stop smoking.

Her advice is based on years of experience giving advice to others.

The archeologist advised the town council to take action quickly.

The Tribal Council gave the group good advice.

LESSON 123

SPREADSHEETS: ENTERING DATA

OBJECTIVES:

- Learn about confusing words.
- Improve keyboarding accuracy.
- Enter and change spreadsheet data.

A. WARMUP

Type each line 2 times.

Speed	1 Their firm is paid to paint half the signs for those towns.
Accuracy	2 Jacqueline of Hainaut lost Zeeland and Holland to a cousin.
Language Link	3 You need these personal traits: tact, quick wit, and humor.
Numbers/Symbols	4 Certain sales are 15% or 20% off and one is $10 or $15 off.
	| 1 | 2 | 3 | 4 | 5 | 6 | 7 | 8 | 9 | 10 | 11 | 12

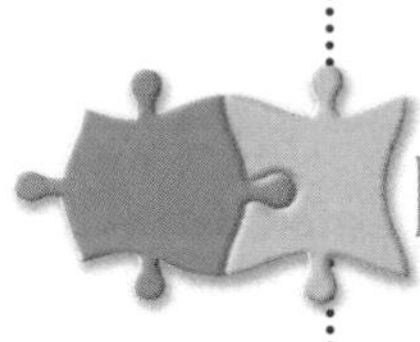

LANGUAGE LINK

B. CONFUSING WORDS

Study the confusing words and their meanings shown below. Then edit lines 5–10 by choosing the correct word.

advice (n.) An opinion, recommendation, information, or notice given

advise (v.) To give information or advice to; to counsel

council (n.) An organization or group

counsel (v.) To give advice as a result of a consultation
(n.) A policy or plan of action or behavior; a lawyer

RESOURCES

 Lesson Plan 123

 Courseware Lesson 123

Student Data Disk

Student Manual

Supplementary Production Activities

5 The student sought (advise/advice) from the school's (counsel/council) president.
6 I (advise/advice) you not to answer until you have retained reputable (counsel/council).
7 The AMA (Counsel/Council) on Aging (advises/advices) people to stop smoking.
8 Her (advise/advice) is based on years of experience giving (advise/advice) to others.
9 The archeologist (advised/adviced) the town (counsel/council) to take action quickly.
10 The Tribal (Counsel/Council) gave the group good (advise/advice).

SKILLBUILDING

C. 30-Second OK Timings

Take two 30-second OK (error-free) timings on lines 11–12. Then take two 30-second OK timings on lines 13–14. Goal: no errors.

```
11      It is not just the size of fingers but their quickness   11
12 that builds every extra word per minute in a timed writing.   23

13      Exercise maintains good health and gives you zest when   11
14 you adjust for the pace required to keep your body healthy.   23
   | 1 | 2 | 3 | 4 | 5 | 6 | 7 | 8 | 9 | 10 | 11 | 12
```

FORMATTING

D. Entering Spreadsheet Data

Words entered into a spreadsheet are called **labels**. Numbers, dates, or times entered into a spreadsheet are called **values**. Mathematical calculations that are entered into a spreadsheet cell are called **formulas**. You can use formulas to add, subtract, multiply, or average the contents of cells.

Changing how information is displayed in a spreadsheet cell is called **formatting**. Data can be displayed in bold or italics and with different font styles and sizes. Numbers, times, and dates can also be displayed in a variety of formats.

TEACH

Activity C. Point out that 30-second OK timings are designed to encourage accuracy.

Activity D. On the board write *labels*, *values*, and *formulas*. Ask students to define each word as it pertains to spreadsheets.

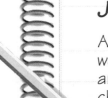

JOURNAL ENTRY

Ask students to write about today's weather and how they think they are or are not affected by weather and weather changes. Remind students to free write.

Provide time for proofreading.

Illustration
Be sure students study the illustration to understand formats and alignment.

TEACH

Activity 4. Have students read the instructions once, then have them read the instructions again to be sure they understand what they are to do.

ASSESS

- Check to see if students are completing 30-second OK timings without any errors.
- Watch students as they complete the Language Link activity to see if they are able to apply the rules concerning confusing words.
- Make sure students are able to enter data into spreadsheets.

CLOSE

Remind students to clean up their workstation when they leave.

The positioning of data at the left, center, or right of a cell is called **alignment**. The default alignment for labels is left, and the default alignment for values is right. Alignment can be easily changed.

Study the spreadsheet illustration below. Note that the contents of cells A1 through E1 are displayed in bold. Labels (words) are aligned at the left. Values (numbers) are aligned at the right. A formula was entered into cells B15–E15 to calculate the total sales.

	A	B	C	D	E
1	**Class Members**	**Week 1**	**Week 2**	**Week 3**	**Total Sales**
2					
3	Finzer, Nick	$15.35	$22.00	$32.89	$70.24
4	Follman, Jadie	$21.98	$18.55	$29.98	$70.51
5	Fowler, Eric	$13.50	$29.19	$24.35	$67.04
6	Glosup, Margaret	$20.00	$14.75	$28.05	$62.80
7	Grimes, Kelley	$19.00	$23.80	$18.15	$60.95
8	McCoy, Andres	$24.25	$18.85	$33.97	$77.07
9	Parker, Kent	$29.88	$28.10	$23.54	$81.52
10	Spoeder, Dustin	$25.79	$21.95	$20.65	$68.39
11	Spradlin, Sherry	$11.15	$16.65	$35.50	$63.30
12	Stanley, Ronnie	$33.35	$27.99	$19.94	$81.28
13	Wright, Mary	$16.50	$31.00	$22.75	$70.25
14					
15	Total Sales	$230.75	$252.83	$289.77	$773.35
16	Average Sales	$20.98	$22.98	$26.34	$70.30

SPREADSHEET APPLICATIONS

ACTIVITY 4
Spreadsheet 1

FACT FILE
The first standardized measurement unit was created around 2700 B.C. in Mesopotamia. The cubit and the shekel were measurements created then.

Open the file SS1 and save it as SS1-B. Then do the following:

1. In cell A1, change the label to *Students*.
2. In cell A7, change the name *Grimes, Kelly* to *Grimes, Kerry*.
3. In cell A10, type the name *Soeder, Dean*.
4. In cell A12, type *Stanley, Robert*.
5. In cell A13, type *Wright, Wendy*.
6. Type the following numbers in cells C3 through C13: C3, 15.05; C4, 22.37; C5, 13.75; C6, 20.02; C7, 17.54; C8, 24 (notice what happens after you press ENTER); C9, 31.53; C10, 23.88; C11, 18.51; C12, 22.52; C13, 26.60.You do not need to type the dollar sign. Notice how the numbers in cells C15, C16, E15, and E16 change as you type the new numbers. Formulas have been entered into these cells to recalculate the sums and averages. If you enter the numbers correctly, cell E16 will show 68.75.

Teacher Notes

SPREADSHEETS: CREATE, ALIGN COLUMNS

OBJECTIVES:

- Improve keyboarding speed.
- Create a spreadsheet and align columns.
- Enter data into a spreadsheet.

A. WARMUP

Type each line 2 times.

Speed	1	Jane and the man got five fish and kept them on the island.
Accuracy	2	Maizie quickly paid Jane for the five new taxis she bought.
Language Link	3	If you follow your counsel's advice, you will plea-bargain.
Technique	4	Saul Kent Dora Mary Alva Paul Ruth Kate Zora Lena Rick Juan

| 1 | 2 | 3 | 4 | 5 | 6 | 7 | 8 | 9 | 10 | 11 | 12

SKILLBUILDING

B. PACED PRACTICE

Turn to the Paced Practice routine beginning on page SB-7. Take three 2-minute timings, starting at the point where you left off the last time.

FORMATTING

C. SOFTWARE FEATURES

STUDENT MANUAL

Create a Spreadsheet   Align Columns

Study Lesson 124 in your student manual. Complete all the practice activities while at your computer. Then complete the jobs that follow.

RESOURCES

 Lesson Plan 124
 Courseware Lesson 124
Student Data Disk
Student Manual
Supplementary Production Activities

LESSON 124

FOCUS

- Use a Paced Practice 2-minute timing routine.
- Learn spreadsheet features: Create a Spreadsheet and Align Columns.
- Learn how to create a spreadsheet.

BELLRINGER

As soon as students arrive at their workstations and log in, have them type the Warmup. Go over the purpose of each line as shown to the left of the copy.

TEACH

Activity B. Go over the Paced Practice 2-minute timing routine with students. (See Lesson 34, page 119.)

Activity C. Have students turn to Lesson 124 in their Student Manual and read the explanation for the software they are using. Then have them complete the practice activities that follow.

STUDENT MANUAL

Be sure students turn to the correct lesson in their Student Manual.

Activity 5. Tell students that the spreadsheets they create may not always be exactly like the ones in the text because the printers they use may allow more or fewer words per line and/or column.

Illustration

Remind students to refer to the illustration shown to complete Activity 5.

Activity 6. Have students read the instructions once, then have them read the instructions again to be sure they understand what they are to do.

ACTIVITY 5
Spreadsheet 2

Create a new spreadsheet and save it as SS2.

1. In cell A1, type the label *Paint Inventory*. Notice that the portion of the label that doesn't fit in cell A1 displays in cell B1 because that cell is empty.
2. In cell A2, type *Prepared by* followed by your full name.
3. Type the labels and values as shown in the illustration.
4. Select cells A1 through C4 and bold the contents.
5. Select cells A4 through C4 and center the contents.

	A	B	C
4	Colors	Gallons	Cost
5	Black	8	5.79
6	Blue	13	3.99
7	Green	9	6.88
8	Pink	11	9.75
9	Red	7	4.89
10	White	5	5.95
11	Yellow	6	4.97

ACTIVITY 6
Spreadsheet 3

Open the file SS3. Then complete the following steps:

1. In cell A2, enter your name.
2. Enter the information shown in the illustration on page 447 that is missing from the spreadsheet into the correct cells. The amounts in column D will change because formulas have been entered into these cells. Remember, you do not need to type the dollar signs or decimals. The column has been formatted to insert them automatically.
3. When you finish typing the data, proofread carefully and correct any errors. If you have entered the correct numbers, cell D18 will show $35.00.
4. Save the file with your changes.

SCHOOL TO CAREER

Have students work in groups of three or four to determine how spreadsheets can be used in different careers. Have each group type their list. On the board write the top ten careers suggested by the groups. Have students research the career that they find the most interesting and write a paragraph about it.

Math Connections

Have students brainstorm as a class about careers that use math. Help students see that math is used in nearly every career. Also have students add the numbers in Column C in Activity 5 using SUM and again without using SUM.

	A	B	C	D
1	Budget for the Month of July			
2	Your Name			
3				
4	Income			
5		Allowance	$30.00	
6		Baby-sitting	$80.00	
7		Lawn Care	$20.00	
8				$130.00
9				
10	Expenses			
11		Clothes	$50.00	
12		Movies	$20.00	
13		Loan from Dad	$10.00	
14		Savings	$15.00	
15				
16	Total Expenses			$95.00
17				
18	Money for Misc. Expenses			$35.00

ACTIVITY 7

Spreadsheet 4

If necessary, open SS3 and save it as SS4. Enter the data from the following "what if" questions and see what changes result in the spreadsheet.

1. What if your allowance was increased to $55? (Your total income increases to $155, and miscellaneous money increases to $60.)
2. Type the original amount of $30 in cell C5 before continuing.
3. What if you do extra baby-sitting and earn $95?
4. What if rain reduces your lawn care income to $10?
5. What if you spend $75 on clothes?
6. What if you put $30 in savings?
7. Save the file.
8. Now try some of your own "what if" situations.
9. Close the file without saving your changes.

FACT FILE

Having a standardized measurement unit made the trade of larger quantities of goods possible.

Teacher Notes

TEACH

Illustration

The illustration shown on this page should be used to complete Activity 6.

Activity 7. Have different students read aloud the steps for this report. Stop after each step to make sure all students understand the directions.

ASSESS

- Make sure students are able to create a spreadsheet and align columns.
- As students begin creating the spreadsheets, walk around the room and provide assistance to individual students as needed.
- After students create each spreadsheet, have them view their work on the screen to see if they made any errors. If errors were made, have students edit their work and make corrections.

CLOSE

If students do not finish the spreadsheets during the class period, make sure they save their work so that they can complete it the next time this class meets.

Remind students to clean up their workstation when they leave.

LESSON 125

FOCUS

- Apply the Language Link rules for apostrophes and possessives.
- Use 5-minute timings to build speed.
- Learn spreadsheet features: Copying Data and Changing Column Widths.
- Copy spreadsheet data and change column widths in a spreadsheet document.

BELLRINGER

As soon as students arrive at their workstations and log in, have them type the Warmup. Go over the purpose of each line as shown to the left of the copy.

TEACH

Activity B. Explain the Language Link rules on apostrophes and possessives to students. Then have students complete lines 5–8. When students are finished, have them check each other's work.

Solutions: At the customer's request, she sent a copy of the company's report.

The men's watches and the women's shoes are on sale today.

The child's boots were a gift from her friend's parents.

The secretaries' computers were purchased with funds from the government's retraining program.

LESSON 125

SPREADSHEETS: COPYING DATA, CHANGING COLUMN WIDTHS

OBJECTIVES:

- Learn the rules for apostrophes and possessives.
- Copy data within a spreadsheet and change column width.
- Type 39/5'/5e.

A. WARMUP

Type each line 2 times.

Speed	1	They may end the big fight by the lake by the usual signal.
Accuracy	2	Jody typed white requisitions for moving large-sized boxes.
Language Link	3	Follow the advice of your legal counsel to sign the papers.
Numbers	4	Read Chapters 129 and 374 and summarize Chapters 48 and 56.

| 1 | 2 | 3 | 4 | 5 | 6 | 7 | 8 | 9 | 10 | 11 | 12

B. APOSTROPHES AND POSSESSIVES

Study the rules and examples below. Then edit lines 5–8 by deciding whether an apostrophe or an apostrophe and* s *are needed.

Rule 32: Use 's to form the possessive of singular nouns.

The hurricane caused major damage to Georgia's crops.

Rule 33: Use only an apostrophe to form the possessive of plural nouns that end in *s*.

The investors' goals were outlined in the annual report.

Rule 34: Use 's to form the possessive of plural nouns that do not end in *s*.

The women's offices were next door to the gym.

RESOURCES

 Lesson Plan 125

 Courseware Lesson 125

Student Data Disk

Student Manual

Language Link Worksheets

Supplementary Production Activities

Grading and Evaluation

5 At the customers request, she sent a copy of the companys report.
6 The mens watches and the womens shoes are on sale today.
7 The childs boots were a gift from her friends parents.
8 The secretaries computers were purchased with funds from the governments retraining program.

SKILLBUILDING

C. Preview Practice

Type each line 2 times as a preview to the timings that follow.

Accuracy	9 handles quality favorable vacations experience achievements
Speed	10 their might after when late cite pact job few for can up by

D. 5-Minute Timings

Take two 5-minute timings on the paragraphs. Note your speed and errors.

Goal: 39/5'/5e

11 Job seekers can get a head start by starting their 10
12 search in late summer. This can be a good time to start a 22
13 job hunt because by late August, most managers have taken 34
14 their vacations and are back at work, sizing up the quality 46
15 of their staff. It also might be easier to get an interview 58
16 in the late summer when business is somewhat slower. Most 69
17 job openings are found by referrals or through personal 80
18 contacts. Meeting someone in person will sometimes give you 92
19 the best chance to make the most favorable impression. 103
20 When you search for a job, you will need a resume. It 114
21 should include a list of what you have done in your career. 126
22 Realize that you are trying to make a positive impact. You 138
23 can cite a few of your achievements. Also, you should send 150
24 a cover letter with a resume to the person who does the 161
25 hiring for the firm where you wish to work. Your letter and 173
26 resume should list each of your unique abilities and skills 185
27 and include all of your experience and training. 195

| 1 | 2 | 3 | 4 | 5 | 6 | 7 | 8 | 9 | 10 | 11 | 12 SI 1.44

JOURNAL ENTRY

Explain that a network is a group of people who help each other out. Students have a network of other students, parents, teachers, and others. Have students write about how they can best use their network.

LESSON 125

TEACH

Activity C. Point out that words in the Preview Practice are used in the timing that follows.

Activity D. Remind students that they should try to improve speed with each 5-minute timing. The goal for these timings is to type 39 words a minute for 5 minutes with no more than 5 errors.

TEACH

Activity E. After you demonstrate for students, have them copy several cells to practice.

Activity F. Remind students that they may have to adjust column widths in order to see all the data in a column.

Activity G. Have students turn to Lesson 125 in their Student Manual and read the explanation for the software they are using. Then have them complete the practice activities that follow.

STUDENT MANUAL

Be sure students turn to the correct lesson in their Student Manual.

Activity 8. Have different students read aloud the steps for this spreadsheet. Stop after each step to make sure all students understand the directions.

FORMATTING

E. Copying Spreadsheet Data

Sometimes it is necessary to enter the same information in several cells. Copying a cell's contents is faster and more accurate than typing the same information repeatedly. However, you must be sure that the information you are going to copy is correct before you copy it.

F. Changing Column Widths

When you enter data into a spreadsheet, some data may be hidden because the column is too narrow to display the data. When this occurs, you will have to adjust the width of the column to fit the data.

G. Software Features

STUDENT MANUAL

Copying Data   Changing Column Widths

Study Lesson 125 in your student manual. Complete all the practice activities while at your computer. Then complete the jobs that follow.

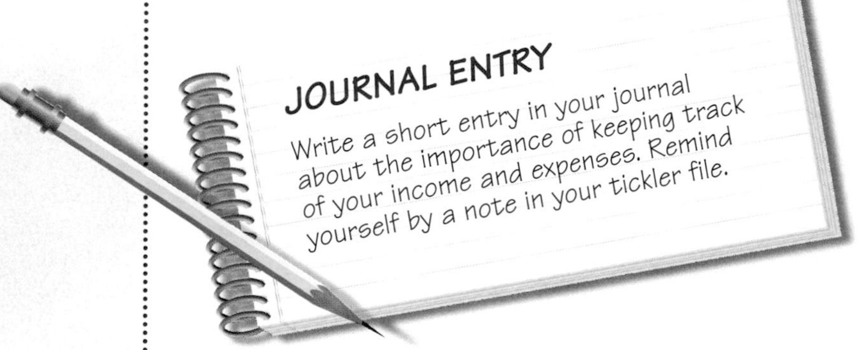

JOURNAL ENTRY
Write a short entry in your journal about the importance of keeping track of your income and expenses. Remind yourself by a note in your tickler file.

FACT FILE

In the second largest country in the world, with a population of 28.2 million, two languages are spoken—English and French. Ask students which country they believe this is. Write the name Canada on the board. Ask students to look on a map and locate the French-speaking area of Canada. (Quebec)

ACTIVITY 8

Spreadsheet 5

Open the file SS5, save it as SS-5B, and follow these steps:

1. Type your name after the words *Prepared by* in cell A2.
2. Center and bold the column headings (*Teachers*, *Period 1*, *Period 2*, and so on).
3. Add the names as shown from the illustration that follows. Copy the name in cell B6 to the other columns as shown.
4. Copy other names that are repeated in other columns.
5. Proofread your work carefully.

	A	B	C	D	E	F	G
1	**Teacher Assistant Schedule**						
2	**Prepared by**						
3							
4	**Teachers**	**Period 1**	**Period 2**	**Period 3**	**Period 4**	**Period 5**	**Period 6**
5							
6	Akins, Jason	Bunnell, N.					
7	Bailey, Karen			Graham, T.			
8	Brawner, Seth					Graham, T.	
9	Carter, Crystal					Walker, O.	
10	Clawson, Anna		Graham, T.				
11	Cowley, Rhonda			Bunnell, N.			
12	Green, Brad				Graham, T.		
13	Holloway, Nicholas	Graham, T.					
14	Ivie, Karla				Bunnell, N.		
15	Lane, Kathleen						Bunnell, N.
16	Morrison, Molly		Walker, O.				
17	Parish, James				Walker, O.		
18	Quillian, Harris		Bunnell, N.				
19	South, Suzette						Graham, T.
20	Sprock, Daniel			Walker, O.			
21	Turner, Wilson						Walker, O.
22	Williams, Virginia					Bunnell, N.	
23	Zobel, Adrian	Walker, O.					Walker, O.

TEACH

Illustration

The illustration shown is to be used to complete Activity 8.

Activity 8. As students continue to work on the spreadsheet in Activity 8, walk around the room to make sure students understand the directions and are able to execute them. If you notice several students having trouble with the same step, go over this step again with the whole class.

Teacher Notes

LESSON 125

TEACH

Activity 9. Read the instructions aloud to students, stopping after each step to make sure students understand what they are to do.

ASSESS

- Check to see if students are increasing their word a minute speeds as they complete each 5-minute timing.
- Watch students as they complete the Language Link activity to see if they are able to apply the rules for apostrophes and possessives.
- Make sure students are able to use the Copying Data and Changing Column Widths spreadsheet features.
- As students begin creating the spreadsheets, walk around the room and provide assistance to individual students as needed.
- After students create each spreadsheet, have them view their work on the screen to see if they made any errors. If errors were made, have students edit their work and make corrections.

CLOSE

If students do not finish the spreadsheets during the class period, make sure they save their work so that they can complete it the next time this class meets.

ACTIVITY 9
Spreadsheet 6

Create a new spreadsheet file and save it as SS6. Then follow these steps:

1. In cell A1, type the label *Favorite Amusement Parks.*
2. In cell A2, type *Prepared by* and your name.
3. Enter the remaining data as shown in the illustration, copying cell contents whenever possible.
4. Select cell range A1 through D4 and bold the cell contents.
5. Select cell range A4 through D4 and center the cell contents.
6. Select cell range A6 through D14 and change the width of columns so that all information is displayed.

	A	B	C	D
1	**Favorite Amusement Parks**			
2	**Prepared by Your Name**			
3				
4	**State**	**City**	**Park**	**Attraction**
5				
6	California	Anaheim	Disneyland	Indiana Jones Adventure
7	California	Hollywood	Universal Studios	Back to the Future—The Ride
8	Florida	Orlando	Universal Studios	Back to the Future—The Ride
9	Florida	Orlando	Universal Studios	Terminator 2 3-D
10	New York	Lake George	The Great Escape	Comet
11	Ohio	Sandusky	Cedar Point	Raptor
12	Pennsylvania	Elysburg	Knoebels Amusement Resort	Haunted House
13	Pennsylvania	Hershey	Hersheypark	Wildcat
14	Texas	Arlington	Six Flags Over Texas	Texas Giant

CULTURAL CONNECTIONS

Learning to add, subtract, multiply, and divide are important skills that students learn early in life. Ask a student from another country how old he or she was when these skills were taught to him or her.

Career Exploration

Have students work in small groups to investigate careers related to amusement parks. Students can list people who run the rides, but they should also think of people behind the scenes, like engineers, landscapers, clerical staff, etc. Give a prize to the group that has the longest list.

interNET ACTIVITY

Have students use a search engine to access information on amusement parks throughout the world. Have students then create a spreadsheet that includes the name of the park and two other pieces of information about the park.

LESSON 126

SPREADSHEETS: MOVING DATA, CHANGING ROW HEIGHT

OBJECTIVES:

- Reinforce skill on left and right reaches.
- Move data in a spreadsheet.
- Change row heights in a spreadsheet.

A. WARMUP

Type each line 2 times.

Speed	1	The road to the left is the right one to take on our drive.
Accuracy	2	Wolf gave Jake an extra dozen quarts, but he can't pay him.
Language Link	3	Ruth's sister went to the Women's Center to look for a job.
Numbers/Symbols	4	I can guess the prices for #32 and #48 within 5% error now!
		| 1 | 2 | 3 | 4 | 5 | 6 | 7 | 8 | 9 | 10 | 11 | 12

SKILLBUILDING

B. 12-SECOND SPRINTS

Take three 12-second timings on each line. Try to increase your speed on each timing.

5 We will stop to rest as soon as we finish the last section.
6 The roof on our old shed is in need of repair at this time.
7 The cafe down the road has both good food and good service.
8 Chuck says rain is likely during the early part of the day.
||||5||||10||||15||||20||||25||||30||||35||||40||||45||||50||||55||||60

RESOURCES

- Lesson Plan 126
- Courseware Lesson 126
- Student Data Disk
- Student Manual
- Supplementary Production Activities

LESSON 126

FOCUS

- Use 12-second timings to build speed.
- Use a Pretest/Practice/Posttest routine to build speed and accuracy.
- Learn spreadsheet features: Moving Spreadsheet Data and Changing Row Height.
- Move data and change row heights in a spreadsheet document.

BELLRINGER

As soon as students arrive at their workstations and log in, have them type the Warmup. Go over the purpose of each line as shown to the left of the copy.

TEACH

Activity B. Remind students that the goal for 12-second timings is improved speed with each timing.

TEACH

Activities C–E. Remind students they should improve both their speed and accuracy from the Pretest to the Posttest.

PRETEST/PRACTICE/POSTEST

The ***Pretest/Practice/Posttest*** routines are designed to improve speed or accuracy.

- The ***Pretest*** identifies students' speed or accuracy needs.
- The ***Practice*** provides a variety of improvement drills.
- The ***Posttest*** (a repeat of the Pretest) measures improvement.

Activity F. Remind students to always pay attention to the new location they are moving the cell to so that they do not overwrite data they still need.

Activity G. Point out to students that adjusting rows with values or labels in them will not affect font size.

C. PRETEST

Take a 1-minute timing on the paragraph. Note your speed and errors.

```
9      You may get a better grade in your courses if you will   11
10 allow enough time to find and fix any errors in a paper as   23
11 you prepare the final draft. A neat paper will impress most  35
12 people who read it.                                          39
   | 1 | 2 | 3 | 4 | 5 | 6 | 7 | 8 | 9 | 10 | 11 | 12
```

D. PRACTICE

SPEED: ***If you made 2 or fewer errors on the Pretest, type lines 13–20 two times each.***

ACCURACY: ***If you made more than 2 errors on the Pretest, type lines 13–16 as a group two times. Then type lines 17–20 as a group two times.***

Left Reaches

```
13 fad bar bag era few best data acted beads brass cards caves
14 get raw sat sea tea cage case debts defer edges erase faces
15 bed beg eve fat war debt rest fewer grade refer seats state
16 cat fed tar tab rat vest star gages water fever waste taxes
```

Right Reaches

```
17 him hop ill boil clip coil cool fill full allow ample ankle
18 ink inn joy gulp hill hold hole hook hope built child chips
19 mop oil pin hung hunt jump like lime lips clips color drill
20 pin pop hop kiln pump poll joke loan lump plump jolly plums
```

E. POSTTEST

Repeat the Pretest. Compare your Posttest results with your Pretest results.

FORMATTING

F. MOVING SPREADSHEET DATA

At times, you may need to move the contents of a cell to a different location within a spreadsheet. Unlike copying, which duplicates the cell contents, moving removes the contents from the original cell and inserts the contents into the new cell. Moving replaces the contents of the new cell. Be careful not to overwrite data that you still need.

G. CHANGING ROW HEIGHT

The height of a spreadsheet row automatically adjusts to fit the size of the font being used. For example, if you change to 18-point, the row height will automatically be adjusted to fit the new font. However, you may want to adjust the height of a row. Adjusting rows with values or labels in them will not affect font size.

FACT FILE

Tell students that there are about 5,000 languages in the world. Have each student choose a different language and research how that language came into being and something about the people who speak the language. Have students write a short report and bring it to class. Read a few of the reports in class.

H. Software Features

STUDENT MANUAL

Moving Spreadsheet Data
Changing Row Heights

Study Lesson 126 in your student manual. Complete all the practice activities while at your computer. Then complete the jobs that follow.

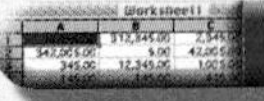

SPREADSHEET APPLICATIONS

ACTIVITY 10

Spreadsheet 7

Create a new spreadsheet and save it as SS7. Add the necessary data by following these steps.

1. In cell A1, type the label *Flight Departure Schedule for Tours of Summer*.
2. In cell A2, type the label *Prepared by* and your name.
3. Enter the data into the correct cells as shown in the illustration.
4. Select cell range A1 through F3, and bold the cell contents.
5. Save your changes and close the file.

	A	B	C	D	E	F
1	Flight Departure Schedule for Tours of Summer					
2	Prepared by Your Name					
3	Carrier		Boston	Phoenix	Omaha	Seattle
4						
5						
6						
7						
8						
9	American		4:50 p.m.	3:25 p.m.	3:10 p.m.	6:20 p.m.
10	Continental		7:10 p.m.	4:30 p.m.	2:45 p.m.	3:35 p.m.
11	Delta		6:25 p.m.	2:50 p.m.	4:17 p.m.	5:50 p.m.
12	Northwest		NA	3:50 p.m.	5:30 p.m.	NA
13	Southwest		NA	4:15 p.m.	2:15 p.m.	4:15 p.m.
14	United		5:45 p.m.	6:45 p.m.	2:15 p.m.	5:55 p.m.
15	US Airways		4:40 p.m.	7:25 p.m.	3:55 p.m.	5:55 p.m.
16	America West		NA	6:30 p.m.	NA	5:35 p.m.

TEACH

Activity H. Have students turn to Lesson 126 in their Student Manual and read the explanation for the software they are using. Then have them complete the practice activities that follow.

STUDENT MANUAL

Be sure students turn to the correct lesson in their Student Manual.

Activity 10. Have students read the instructions once, then have them read the instructions again to be sure they understand what to do.

JOURNAL ENTRY

Have students write about how they would celebrate their birthday if they could do anything they wanted to do. Tell them to have fun with this entry and to be creative. Read a few entries in class.

TEACH

Activity 11. Read the instructions aloud to students, stopping after each step to make sure students understand what they are to do.

Activity 12. Have different students read aloud the steps for this report. Stop after each step to make sure all students understand the directions.

ASSESS

- Check to see if students are increasing their word a minute speeds as they complete each timing.
- Check to see if students show signs of improvement from the Pretest to the Posttest.
- Make sure students are able to use the Moving Spreadsheet Data and Changing Row Height software features.
- As students begin working on the spreadsheets, walk around the room and provide individual assistance.
- After students finish working on each spreadsheet, have them view their work on the screen to see if they made any errors.

CLOSE

If students do not finish the activities in this lesson during the class period, make sure they save their work so that they can complete it the next time this class meets.

ACTIVITY 11
Spreadsheet 8

Open the file SS7 and save it as SS8. Then follow these steps:

1. Select cell range A3 through F3, and center the cell contents.
2. While cell range A3 through F3 is still selected, move the contents to cells A4 through F4.
3. Select cell range A16 through F16, and move the contents to A8 through F8.
4. Select cell range A8 through F16, and move the contents to A6 through F13.
5. Select cell range C4 through C13, and move the contents to B4 through B13.
6. Select row 4, and change the point size to 16.
7. Change row 3 to approximately 2 times the default height.
8. Change row 5 to approximately 1.5 times the default height.
9. Select row 4, and automatically widen the columns.
10. Save your changes and close the file.

ACTIVITY 12
Spreadsheet 9

Open the file SS8 and save it as SS9. Then follow these steps to move cell contents and change row heights:

1. Select cell range E4 through E13, and move the contents to C4 through C13.
2. Select cell range F4 through F13, and move the contents to E4 through E13.
3. Select cell range B6 through E13, and align the cell contents on the right.
4. Select cell range A4 through E13, and automatically widen the columns.
5. In cell A1, delete the words *for Tours of Summer.*
6. Select row 1, and change the point size to 20.
7. Select row 2, and change the point size to 18.
8. Select cell range A1 through A2, and move the contents to C1 and C2. Then center the column data.
9. Save your changes and close the file.

COMMUNICATION FOCUS

Spreadsheets and other graphics are important aids to communication. Ask an office worker if he or she uses spreadsheets or other graphics in reports or other documents.

Out-of-Class Activity

Have students write a short story about something that has happened in their lives. Then have students exchange their story with another student to proofread each other's stories. After students make corrections, have them bring their stories to class. Create a bound book of their stories.

SCHOOL TO CAREER

Have students write about the ideal job for them, including the lifestyle they want to create with this job, such as time spent at work, environment, and so forth. Then have students research the career to find out about job openings, education, and training needed.

LESSON 127

SPREADSHEETS: FORMATTING VALUES

OBJECTIVES:

- Compose at the keyboard.
- Format values in a spreadsheet.
- Type 39/5'/5e.

A. WARMUP

Type each line 2 times.

```
Speed          1 If you find the small blue ball, please toss it to our dog.
Accuracy       2 Gwyn exceeds the speed limit by zigzagging through traffic.
Language Link  3 The teacher's day was full of her children's fun and games.
Numbers        4 Dale should use cars 47, 38, 29, or 10 if 56 laps are left.
                 | 1 | 2 | 3 | 4 | 5 | 6 | 7 | 8 | 9 | 10 | 11 | 12
```

LANGUAGE LINK

B. COMPOSING AT THE KEYBOARD

Compose the body of a letter to a large computer or software company and ask them for information on their latest developments. Explain that you are studying the future of computing and that you need to write a report on the topic of how computing is going to change the future.

COMMUNICATION FOCUS

A letter is an important type of business communication. A letter requesting information should be easy to follow so that the receiver can include all the requested information quickly. One way to make it easy is to put each requested item in a separate paragraph or bullet each item to be checked off by the receiver.

LESSON 127

FOCUS

- Compose the body of a letter for the Language Link activity.
- Use 5-minute timings to build speed.
- Learn a spreadsheet feature: Formatting Values.
- Format values in a spreadsheet document.

BELLRINGER

As soon as students arrive at their workstations and log in, have them type the Warmup. Go over the purpose of each line as shown to the left of the copy.

TEACH

LANGUAGE LINK

Activity B. Write today's date on the board for students. Remind them to add the date to their letters. Have students check each other's work for errors.

Solutions: Answers will vary

RESOURCES

Lesson Plan 127

Courseware Lesson 127

Student Data Disk

Student Manual

Supplementary Production Activities

Grading and Evaluation

TEACH

Activity C. Point out that words in the Preview Practice are used in the timing that follows.

Activity D. Remind students that they should try to improve speed with each 5-minute timing. The goal for these timings is to type 39 words a minute for 5 minutes with no more than 5 errors.

SKILLBUILDING

C. Preview Practice

Type each line 2 times as a preview to the timings that follow.

Accuracy hazard produced expansion equipment inventions refrigerated
Speed shipped comfort tracks vital fuel wood rail raw one air car

D. 5-Minute Timings

Take two 5-minute timings on the paragraphs. Note your speed and errors.

Goal: 39/5′/5e

After the Civil War, the railroad played a vital role 11
in the growth of America. Expansion of the railroads helped 23
the iron and coal mining and lumber industries grow through 35
the need for iron tracks, engines, fuel, and wood railway 47
ties. New jobs were opened for people who built stations, 58
laid tracks, and produced equipment. 66

At the start, each train line built tracks of varied 76
widths. This made long-distance travel slow and difficult. 88
Later, rail widths were set to a standard size. This meant 100
that goods could be shipped more quickly using just one 111
train to cross the country. Trains shipped produce, raw 122
materials, and finished goods from place to place. 133

Four inventions improved rail transport a great deal. 144
Air brakes decreased the hazard of stopping a train. The 155
Janney car coupler made it simpler to link one car to the 167
next. Pullman sleeping cars increased the comfort of long 178
trips, and refrigerated cars allowed food to be shipped 189
without the risk of spoiling. 195

| 1 | 2 | 3 | 4 | 5 | 6 | 7 | 8 | 9 | 10 | 11 | 12 SI 1.45

FACT FILE

Westward expansion of the railroads began with the building of a line between Albany and Buffalo, New York, in 1842. The locomotive was the DeWitt Clinton. The first American transcontinental railroad was completed May 10, 1869, at Promontory, Utah. Have students research to find additional facts about the railroad expansion.

FORMATTING

E. Formatting Spreadsheet Values

A **value** is a spreadsheet entry that begins with a number or a mathematical sign. Because spreadsheets are designed to work with values, you can format numbers, dates, and times in many different ways. For example, the number *15.75* can be formatted as 15¾, *$15.75, 15.8,* or *16*. The date *November 13, 2002* can be formatted *11/13/02*. Remember that if a value is too wide to fit in a column, you will see only number signs (#####). When you widen the column, the value will be displayed.

F. Software Features

STUDENT MANUAL

Formatting Values

Study Lesson 127 in your student manual. Complete all the practice activities while at your computer. Then complete the jobs that follow.

FACT FILE

Abraham Lincoln met with Confederate vice president Alexander H. Stephens on February 3, 1865, in an attempt to end the Civil War. Because Lincoln would not yield on the subjects of emancipation and reunion, the conference was a failure, and the war continued for three more months.

SPREADSHEET APPLICATIONS

ACTIVITY 13
Spreadsheet 10

Create a new spreadsheet and save it as SS10. Then follow these steps to format the values:

1. In cell A1, type the label *Small Caribbean Islands*.
2. In cell A3, type the date as *10/25*.
3. In cell A4, type the time as *2:35:49 p.m.*
4. In cell A5, type *Prepared by* and your name.
5. Enter the data as shown in the illustration on the next page into the correct cells.
6. Save your changes and close the file.

TEACH

Activity E. On the board, write the symbol #####. Ask students what this means if they see it in a spreadsheet column. (value is too wide to fit in the column) Ask how they can fix the situation. (widen the column)

Activity F. Have students turn to Lesson 127 in their Student Manual and read the explanation for the software they are using. Then have them complete the practice activities that follow.

STUDENT MANUAL

Be sure students turn to the correct lesson in their Student Manual.

Activity 13. Have different students read aloud the steps for this report. Stop after each step to make sure all students understand the directions.

Social Studies Connections

Railroads were built by daring men who worked on mountains and in deserts. Have students research railroad tycoons, such as Leland Stanford, T.C. Durant, or J.P. Morgan, and write an essay about why they do or do not admire them.

Multiple Learning Styles

To help students strengthen their audio perception, listening skills, and typing skills, read slowly to students, and have them type what you are reading. Have students use blindfolds or ask them to keep their eyes closed. Read for about 60 seconds. Repeat the exercise without blindfolds.

TEACH

Illustration

The illustration shown here should be used to complete Activity 13.

Activity 14. Have students read the instructions once, then have them read the instructions again to be sure they understand what to do.

Activity 15. Read the instructions aloud to students, stopping after each step to make sure students understand what they are to do.

ASSESS

- Check to see if students are increasing their word a minute speeds.
- Review students' letters in the Language Link activity.
- Make sure students are able to format spreadsheet values correctly.
- As students begin working, walk around the room and provide assistance as needed.
- After students finish working on each spreadsheet, have them view their work on the screen to see if they made any errors.

CLOSE

If students do not finish the spreadsheets in this lesson during the class period, make sure they save their work so that they can complete it the next time this class meets.

	A	B	C	D	E
8	Name	Square Miles	Population	Lodging	Cost
9					
10					
11					
12	Anegada	15	250	Coral Reef Estate	180
13	Beguia	7	5000	Parrot's Roost	78
14	Little Cayman	10	100	The Farm House	120
15	Mayreau	1.5	250	Pirate's Hideaway	90
16	Saba	5	1200	The Gang Plank	240

ACTIVITY 14

Spreadsheet 11

Open the file SS10, save it as SS11, and make the following changes:

1. Select row 1, and change the point size to 16.
2. Move cell A5 to A2.
3. Select cell A3, and format the date as *MM/DD/YY.*
4. Select cell A4, and format the time as *H:MM:PM*.
5. Change rows 3 and 4 to 12-point size.
6. Move cell range A8 through E8 to A6 through E6.
7. Save your changes and close the file.

ACTIVITY 15

Spreadsheet 12

Open the file SS11, save it as SS12, and make the following changes:

1. Bold row 6.
2. Move cell range A12 through E16 to A8 through E12.
3. Format cell range B8 through B12 to have 1 decimal place.
4. Format cell range C8 through C12 to have commas and no decimals.
5. Format cell range E8 through E12 to have dollar signs and no decimals.
6. Select cell range A6 through E12, and automatically widen the columns.
7. Horizontally center the text in rows 1 through 4 between columns A through E.
8. Change row 5 to double the default height.
9. Change row 7 to 1.5 times the default height.
10. Save your changes and close the file.

Teacher Notes

LESSON 128 SPREADSHEETS: PRINTING

OBJECTIVES:

- Improve keyboarding speed and accuracy.
- Print a worksheet and cell ranges.
- Print with and without gridlines.
- Print with and without row and column headings.

A. WARMUP

Type each line 2 times.

Speed 1 The girls had fun playing games in the park near our house.
Accuracy 2 A sequence of jobs, or queue, is held in auxiliary storage.
Language Link 3 The building's exterior was so worn, he questioned its age.
Symbols 4 less than = <; greater than = >; backslash = \; a tilde = ~
| 1 | 2 | 3 | 4 | 5 | 6 | 7 | 8 | 9 | 10 | 11 | 12

SKILLBUILDING

B. 30-SECOND TIMINGS

Take two 30-second timings on lines 5–6. Then take two 30-second timings on lines 7–8. Try to increase your speed on each timing.

5 A resume must be entirely free of errors; an employer 11
6 will view it as a reflection of how you will do on the job. 23

7 Before you go to an interview, learn all you can about 11
8 that company by spending some time in your public library. 23
| 1 | 2 | 3 | 4 | 5 | 6 | 7 | 8 | 9 | 10 | 11 | 12

C. DIAGNOSTIC PRACTICE: ALPAHBET

Turn to the Diagnostic Practice: Alphabet routine on page SB1. Type one of the Pretest/Posttest paragraphs and identify any errors made. Then type the corresponding drill lines 2 times for each letter on which you made 2 or more errors and 1 time for each letter on which you made only 1 error. Finally, repeat the same Pretest and compare your performance.

RESOURCES

 Lesson Plan 128

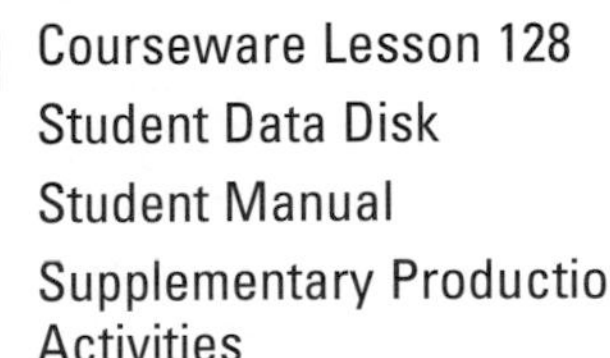

Courseware Lesson 128
Student Data Disk
Student Manual
Supplementary Production Activities

LESSON 128

FOCUS

- Use 30-second timings to build speed.
- Use the Diagnostic Practice to identify areas that need improvement.
- Learn spreadsheet features: Print Spreadsheets, Print Cell Ranges, Print Gridlines, Print Row and Column Headings.
- Create spreadsheets and learn to print spreadsheets.

BELLRINGER

As soon as students arrive at their workstations and log in, have them type the Warmup. Go over the purpose of each line as shown to the left of the copy.

TEACH

Activity B. Remind students that the goal for 30-second timings is improved speed with each timing.

Activity C. Make sure that students understand that this Diagnostic Practice activity is designed to help identify areas that need improvement and provide needed practice.

FORMATTING

TEACH

Activity D. Ask students what page orientation is. (direction of the page) Have students change the page orientation several times for practice.

Illustration
The illustrations show examples of documents printed in portrait and in landscape.

Activity E. Have students turn to Lesson 128 in their Student Manual and read the explanation for the software they are using. Then have them complete the practice activities that follow.

STUDENT MANUAL
Be sure students turn to the correct lesson in their Student Manual.

D. Printing Spreadsheets

Many spreadsheets are too wide to print on a standard 8.5-inch-wide page. However, spreadsheets can be printed on an 11-inch-wide page. **Page orientation** is the direction of the page on which the spreadsheet is printed. The default page orientation (standard 8.5 × 11 inches) is called **portrait**. When the orientation is changed to print across the 11-inch width of a page it is called **landscape**.

Study the following illustrations.

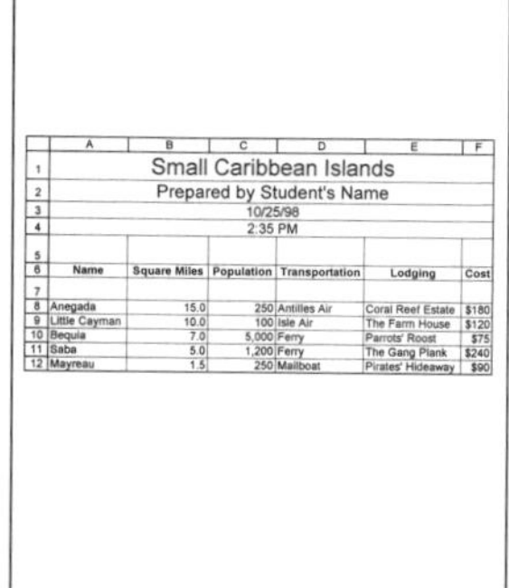

	A	B	C	D	E	F
1	Small Caribbean Islands					
2	Prepared by Student's Name					
3	10/25/98					
4	2:35 PM					
5						
6	Name	Square Miles	Population	Transportation	Lodging	Cost
7						
8	Anegada	15.0	250	Antilles Air	Coral Reef Estate	$180
9	Little Cayman	10.0	100	Isle Air	The Farm House	$120
10	Bequia	7.0	5,000	Ferry	Parrots' Roost	$75
11	Saba	5.0	1,200	Ferry	The Gang Plank	$240
12	Mayreau	1.5	250	Mailboat	Pirates' Hideaway	$90

	A	B	C	D	E	F
1	Small Caribbean Islands					
2	Prepared by Student's Name					
3	10/25/98					
4	2:35 PM					
5						
6	Name	Square Miles	Population	Transportation	Lodging	Cost
7						
8	Anegada	15.0	250	Antilles Air	Coral Reef Estate	$180
9	Little Cayman	10.0	100	Isle Air	The Farm House	$120
10	Bequia	7.0	5,000	Ferry	Parrots' Roost	$75
11	Saba	5.0	1,200	Ferry	The Gang Plank	$240
12	Mayreau	1.5	250	Mailboat	Pirates' Hideaway	$90

Spreadsheets often consist of multiple pages. However, you can print only a portion of a spreadsheet. In addition, you can print spreadsheets with or without the gridlines and with or without the row and column headings. Before you print a spreadsheet, use Print Preview to ensure you are printing what you want.

E. Software Features

STUDENT MANUAL

Print Spreadsheets	Print Cell Ranges
Print Gridlines	Print Row and Column Headings

Study Lesson 128 in your student manual. Complete all the practice activities while at your computer. Then complete the jobs that follow.

JOURNAL ENTRY

Have students write about how they can use spreadsheets to organize all their events and activities. Or they can write about using a spreadsheet to organize for writing an autobiography.

462

ACTIVITY 16
Spreadsheet 5

Open the file SS5; then follow these steps:

1. Preview the file using Print Preview. Notice that the page orientation is portrait and there are no gridlines in the spreadsheet.
2. Change the page orientation to landscape.
3. Set the gridlines to print.
4. Preview the file, and note the changes that you made.
5. If your teacher has given you instructions for printing, print the spreadsheet. Otherwise, close the file without saving your changes.

ACTIVITY 17
Spreadsheet 3

Open the file SS3; then follow these steps:

1. Preview the file.
2. Change the orientation to landscape.
3. Select cell range A13 through G13, and print-preview that range.
4. Set the gridlines and row and column headings to print, and preview the spreadsheet again.
5. If your teacher has given you instructions for printing, print the selected cell range. Otherwise, close the file without saving your changes.

ACTIVITY 18
Spreadsheet 6

Open the file SS6; then follow these steps:

1. Preview the file.
2. Select cell range A1 through E8, and preview that range.
3. Deselect the cell range.
4. Close the file without saving your changes.

ACTIVITY 19
Spreadsheet 7

Open the file SS7; then follow these steps:

1. Change the page orientation to landscape.
2. Set the gridlines and row and column headings to print.
3. Preview the spreadsheet.
4. If your teacher has given you instructions for printing, print the spreadsheet. Otherwise, close the file without saving your changes.

TEACH

Activities 16–19. Have different students read aloud the steps for these activities. Stop after each step to make sure all students understand the directions.

ASSESS

- Check to see if students are increasing their word a minute speeds as they complete each 30-second timing.
- Monitor students as they complete Diagnostic Practice and provide individualized assistance as needed.
- Make sure students understand how to use the printing features for spreadsheet software.
- As students begin working on the spreadsheets, walk around the room and provide assistance to individual students as needed.
- After students finish working on each spreadsheet, have them view their work on the screen to see if they made any errors. If errors were made, have students edit their work and make corrections.

CLOSE

Remind students to clean up their workstation when they leave.

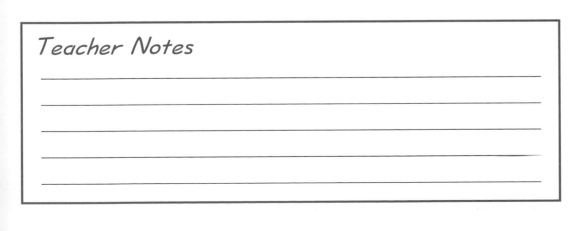

Teacher Notes

LESSON 129

FOCUS

- Apply the Language Link rules for apostrophe usage.
- Use 30-second OK timings to improve accuracy.
- Learn a spreadsheet feature: Formulas.
- Enter formulas in spreadsheet documents.

BELLRINGER

As soon as students arrive at their workstations and log in, have them type the Warmup. Go over the purpose of each line as shown to the left of the copy.

TEACH

Activity B. Go over the Language Link rules for apostrophe usage with students, then have students complete lines 5–8. When students finish, have them check each other's work for accuracy.

Solutions: The new house was hers, but now it is yours.

Somebody's lottery ticket is going to be worth millions.

Our company recycles its paper, and everyone's support is needed.

No one's desktop is running, so the laptops are ours for today.

SPREADSHEETS: ENTERING FORMULAS

OBJECTIVES:

- Learn the rules for apostrophes and possessives.
- Improve keyboarding skills.
- Learn to enter formulas into a spreadsheet.

A. WARMUP

Type each line 2 times.

Speed	1	Bill has worked as a short order cook in a small town cafe.
Accuracy	2	Ziggy James quickly paid us for the five new Rambler taxis.
Language Link	3	Sara's car required four hundred dollars' worth of repairs.
Numbers	4	Old Models 75, 83, and 96 are now Models 121, 344, and 500.

| 1 | 2 | 3 | 4 | 5 | 6 | 7 | 8 | 9 | 10 | 11 | 12

B. APOSTROPHE

Study the rules and examples below. Then edit lines 5–8 by inserting apostrophes where appropriate.

Rule 35: Use apostrophe *s* (*'s*) to form the possessive of indefinite pronouns.

She was instructed to select anybody's paper for a sample.

Rule 36: Do not use an apostrophe with possessive personal pronouns.

Each computer comes carefully packed in its own container.

5 The new house was hers, but now it is yours.
6 Somebodys lottery ticket is going to be worth millions.
7 Our company recycles its paper, and everyones support is needed.
8 No ones desktop is running, so the laptops are ours for today.

RESOURCES

 Lesson Plan 129

 Courseware Lesson 129

Student Data Disk

Student Manual

Language Link Worksheets

Supplementary Production Activities

SKILLBUILDING

C. 30-Second OK Timings

Take two 30-second OK (error-free) timings on lines 9–10. Then take two 30-second OK timings on lines 11–12. Goal: no errors.

```
 9      A quick leap from a taxi caused Gavez to hurt his arm.   11
10 He fell down and hurt his shoulder, which was already sore.   23

11      Jay's six long vans zipped quickly down the wet roads,   11
12 but they were not able to finish the entire route in time.    23
   | 1 | 2 | 3 | 4 | 5 | 6 | 7 | 8 | 9 | 10 | 11 | 12
```

FORMATTING

D. Spreadsheet Formulas

A **spreadsheet formula** simply instructs the spreadsheet to perform various calculations. For example, if you create a spreadsheet for your budget, you can enter formulas to add your income, add your expenses, and subtract your expenses from your income.

Math Connections

To enter a formula in a spreadsheet, you must use the cell names and the following **mathematical operators:**

+ (plus sign) for addition
- (hyphen) for subtraction
* (asterisk) for multiplication
/ (slash) for division
^ (caret) for exponentiation

When you enter a formula into a cell and press ENTER, only the answer will appear in the cell. The formula will be displayed in the entry bar. (See the example on the next page.)

To enter a formula, select the cell where you want the formula. Begin formulas with an equal sign (=) to indicate you are going to type a value, not a label. Formulas are typed without spaces.

Study the formula displayed in the entry bar on the next page. It adds the contents of cells B4 through B7 and displays the answer in the active cell, B9.

TEACH

Activity C. Point out that 30-second OK timings are designed to encourage accuracy.

Activity D. Have students read the information once, then have them read it again to be sure they understand how to enter formulas.

Math Connections

Have students create flash cards with mathematical symbols on one side and the operations the symbols represent on the other. Have students stand in lines facing each other. One student holds up a symbol. The other student must explain the symbol.

Career Exploration

Have students explore math careers. Ask the guidance counselor to speak to your class about careers related to math. Have students type a list of questions to ask the speaker. Have students interested in any of the careers write to educational institutions for course requirements.

TEACH

Illustration

The illustration shows parts of spreadsheet.

Activity E. Have students turn to Lesson 129 in their Student Manual and read the explanation for the software they are using. Then have them complete the practice activities that follow.

STUDENT MANUAL

Be sure students turn to the correct lesson in their Student Manual.

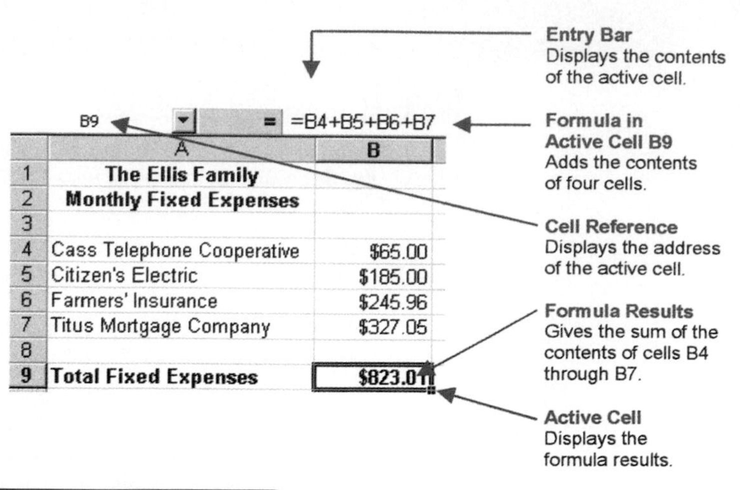

	A	B
1	**The Ellis Family**	
2	**Monthly Fixed Expenses**	
3		
4	Cass Telephone Cooperative	$65.00
5	Citizen's Electric	$185.00
6	Farmers' Insurance	$245.96
7	Titus Mortgage Company	$327.05
8		
9	**Total Fixed Expenses**	**$823.01**

E. SOFTWARE FEATURES

STUDENT MANUAL

Formulas

Study Lesson 129 in your student manual. Complete all the practice activities while at your computer. Then complete the jobs that follow.

*inter*NET CONNECTION

Connect to the Internet. Search the World Wide Web for information on income and expenses. You may want to include search words such as income, expenses, forms, capital, and gains/losses.

JOURNAL ENTRY

Explain that the key to a successful life is working in a career that matches our likes, but we may have to examine ourselves closely to find out what we like and dislike. Have students write about their likes and dislikes.

ACTIVITY 20
Spreadsheet 13

Create a new spreadsheet, and save it as SS13.

1. In cell A1, type the label *Expense Report for November.*
2. In cell A2, type *Prepared by* and your name.
3. Type the data as shown in the illustration. Use the copy feature when it is appropriate.
4. Change the font in cells A1 and A2 to 12-point bold.
5. Center the text in rows 1 and 2.
6. Bold and center the data in rows 4, 9, and 14.
7. Select cell range A4 through E17, and automatically widen the columns.
8. Align cells A7, A12, and A17 at the right.
9. Change the font in cell A19 to 12-point bold.
10. Select cell E5 and enter a formula to multiply cells C5 and D5 (C5*D5).
11. Select cell E6 and enter a formula to multiply cells C6 and D6.
12. Save the changes and close the file.

	A	B	C	D	E
4	Travel	Dates	Miles	Per Mile	Mileage
5		November 7-9	500	0.31	
6		November 18-19	175	0.31	
7	Total Travel				
8					
9	Lodging	Dates	Nights	Per Night	Total
10		November 7-9	3	75	
11		November 18-19	2	80	
12	Total Lodging				
13					
14	Meals	Dates	Days	Per Day	Total
15		November 7-9	3	40	
16		November 18-19	2	40	
17	Total Meals				
18					
19	Total Expenses for November				

TEACH

Activity 20. Have students read the instructions once, then have them read the instructions again to be sure they know what to do.

Illustration
The illustration should be used to complete Activity 20.

FACT FILE

In the middle latitudes where storms travel from west to east, rainbows are usually seen when a storm is over. In the tropics where storms travel from east to west, rainbows are often seen before a storm arrives. Have students write a poem about a rainbow or that uses the word rainbow. Post the poems around the room.

TEACH

Activities 21–23. Have different students read aloud the steps for these activities. Stop after each step to make sure all students understand the directions.

ASSESS

- Watch students as they complete the Language Link activity to see if they apply the rules correctly.
- Check to see if students are increasing their word a minute speeds as they complete each timing.
- Make sure students are able to use the Formula feature for spreadsheet software.
- As students begin working on the spreadsheets, walk around the room and provide assistance to individual students as necessary.
- After students finish working on each spreadsheet, have them view their work on the screen to see if they made any errors. If errors were made, have students edit their work and make corrections.

CLOSE

If students do not finish the activities in this lesson during the class period, make sure they save their work so that they can complete it the next time this class meets.

Remind students to clean up their workstation when they leave.

ACTIVITY 21
Spreadsheet 14

Open the file SS13, save it as SS14, and make the following changes:

1. Select cell E10 and enter a formula to multiply cells C10 and D10.
2. Enter the appropriate formula into cell E11.
3. Select cell E15 and enter a formula to multiply cells C15 and D15.
4. Enter the appropriate formula into cell E16.
5. Select cell F7 and enter a formula to add cells E5 and E6.
6. Select cell F12 and enter a formula to add cells E10 and E11.
7. Save your changes and close the file.

ACTIVITY 22
Spreadsheet 15

Open the file SS14, save it as SS15, and then do the following:

1. Enter the appropriate formula into cell F17.
2. Enter a formula into cell F19 to add cells F7, F12, and F17. Change the font to 12-point bold.
3. Format the numbers in columns E and F for currency with the dollar sign and 2 decimals.
4. Increase the height of row 3 until it is about 1.5 times the default height.
5. Select column E and change the width to 12.
6. Save your changes and close the file.

ACTIVITY 23
Spreadsheet 16

Open the file SS15, save it as SS16, and then do the following:

1. Preview the spreadsheet.
2. Change the page orientation to landscape.
3. Set the gridlines to print.
4. Preview the spreadsheet again.
5. If your teacher has given you instructions for printing, print the spreadsheet. Otherwise, save your changes and close the file.

Teacher Notes

LESSON 130 Spreadsheets: Entering Formulas

OBJECTIVES:

- Improve keyboarding skill.
- Enter formulas into a spreadsheet.

A. Warmup

Type each line 2 times.

Speed	Do not try to blame anyone else when you are late for work.
Accuracy	Mr. Jakman found exactly a quarter in the woven zipper bag.
Language Link	The towels in the Mallen's house said his and hers on them.
Numbers/Symbols	Olo saw apples @ $1.09, pears @ $1.29, and oranges @ $1.49.
	| 1 | 2 | 3 | 4 | 5 | 6 | 7 | 8 | 9 | 10 | 11 | 12

SOCIAL STUDIES CONNECTIONS

On March 1, 1961, then President John F. Kennedy signed an executive order establishing the Peace Corps, a volunteer organization that is still in operation today.

SKILLBUILDING

B. PRETEST

Take a 1-minute timing on the paragraph. Note your speed and errors.

Fur traders were the first Americans to settle in the	11
part of the country we now call Oregon. Because they spent	23
most all of their time in the mountains, they were called	34
mountain men. Many adopted the ways of Native Americans.	46
| 1 | 2 | 3 | 4 | 5 | 6 | 7 | 8 | 9 | 10 | 11 | 12	

Social Studies Connections

RESOURCES

- Lesson Plan 130
- Courseware Lesson 130
- Student Data Disk
- Student Manual
- Supplementary Production Activities
- Multicultural Activities

LESSON 130

FOCUS

- Use a Pretest/Practice/Posttest routine to build speed and accuracy
- Learn how to enter formulas in spreadsheets.

BELLRINGER

As soon as students arrive at their workstations and log in, have them type the Warmup. Go over the purpose of each line as shown to the left of the copy.

TEACH

Activity B. Remind students they should improve both their speed and accuracy from the Pretest to the Posttest.

Social Studies Connections

The Hupa Indians believed that they had a responsibility to the people who would inhabit Earth after them. They used a ten-day ceremony featuring the White Deerskin Dance to purify the people and bring abundance in the coming season. Have students create dances that celebrate their beliefs or an aspect of their lives. Have them type titles and short explanations.

TEACH

Activities C–D. Remind students they should improve both their speed and accuracy from the Pretest to the Posttest.

PRETEST/PRACTICE/POSTEST

The ***Pretest/Practice/Posttest*** routines are designed to improve speed or accuracy.

- The ***Pretest*** identifies students' speed or accuracy needs.
- The ***Practice*** provides a variety of improvement drills.
- The ***Posttest*** (a repeat of the Pretest) measures improvement.

Activity E. Read the information aloud to students. Make sure they understand order of operations and how it applies to entering spreadsheet formulas.

C. PRACTICE

In the chart below, find the number of errors you made on the Pretest. Then type each of the following designated drill lines two times.

Pretest Errors	0–1	2	3	4+
Drill Lines	12–16	11–15	10–14	9–13

Accuracy

```
9  men money enjoy living buffalo trapping moccasins Americans
10 fur spent called Oregon wearing adopted collected mountains
11 gun alone settle coffee trading because buckskin rendezvous
12 set would summer lodges friends country companies exchanged
```

Speed

```
13 native skins these traps call many wild quit try joy fur in
14 trader would Rocky times most time year with can for way of
15 friend first pelts their hers guns meet most end men and at
16 living where pants their buck good were they sum set met or
```

D. POSTTEST

Repeat the Pretest. Compare your Posttest results with your Pretest results.

SPREADSHEET APPLICATIONS

E. Entering Formulas

When you work with formulas, you may need to use several operators. Spreadsheet formulas are completed in a specific order called the **order of operations**. For example, multiplication and division are performed before addition and subtraction. If the operators are equal (such as + and −), they will be completed in the order in which they appear in the formula. To change the order, enclose what you want calculated first in parentheses.

ACTIVITY 24
Spreadsheet 17

Create a new spreadsheet and save it as SS17. Then, follow these steps:

1. In cell A1, type the label *Temperature Conversions*.
2. In cell A2, type *Prepared by* and your name.
3. In cell A4, type *Fahrenheit;* copy this label into cell E4.
4. In cell A5, type *Temperatures;* copy this into cells C5 and E5.
5. In cell B5, change the font to Wingdings. Hold down the Alt key and enter *0232* on the numeric keypad. This character should appear: → . Copy this to cell D5.

JOURNAL ENTRY

Ask students to write about someone they admire. What qualities do they admire in this person and why do they admire these qualities? Then have students write about whether they see these qualities in themselves.

FACT FILE

Temperature is very important to people when they are engaged in a strenuous activity such as mountain climbing. The normal temperature for a person in good health is 98.6°F.

6. In cell C4, type *Celsius.* Enter the following numbers below as shown from low to high (ascending order) into cell range A7 through A16.

   0, 10, 24, 32, 43, 57, 70, 86, 95, 100

7. In cell C7, enter the formula to convert Fahrenheit to Celsius: (A7-32)*5/9. To convert Fahrenheit to Celsius, you would subtract 32 from Fahrenheit degrees, multiply by 5, and divide by 9, or F-32*5/9.
8. Copy the formula from cell C7 into cell range C8 through C16.
9. Save your changes and close the file.

ACTIVITY 25

Spreadsheet 18

Open file SS17, save the file as SS18, and make the following changes:

1. In cell E7, enter the formula to convert Celsius to Fahrenheit: C7*9/5+32. To convert Celsius to Fahrenheit, you would multiply Celsius by 9, divide by 5, and add 32. Since the order of operations is correct, no parentheses are necessary.
2. Copy this formula to cell range E8 through E16.
3. Format the numbers in column C to have 1 decimal place.
4. Format the rest of the spreadsheet so that it is attractive and easy to read. Use Print Preview to see what adjustments are necessary.
5. Save your changes and close the file.

Math Connections

	A	B	C	D	E
1	Temperature Conversions				
2	Prepared by Your Name				
3					
4	Fahrenheit		Celsius		Fahrenheit
5	Temperatures	➔	Temperatures	➔	Temperatures
6					
7	0		-17.8		0
8	10		-12.2		10
9	24		-4.4		24
10	32		0.0		32
11	43		6.1		43
12	57		13.9		57
13	70		21.1		70
14	86		30.0		86
15	95		35.0		95
16	100		37.8		100

TEACH

Activity 24. Have different students read aloud the steps for these spreadsheets. Stop after each step to make sure all students understand the directions.

Activity 25. Walk around the room to make sure students understand the directions and are able to execute them. If you notice several students having trouble with the same step, go over this step again with the class.

ASSESS

- Check to see if students show signs of improvement from the Pretest to the Posttest.
- Make sure students are able to enter formulas in spreadsheets.
- As students begin working on the spreadsheets, walk around the room and provide assistance to individual students as necessary
- After students finish working on each spreadsheet, have them view their work on the screen to see if they made any errors. If errors were made, have students make corrections.

CLOSE

If students do not finish the spreadsheets during the class period, make sure they save their work so that they can complete it the next time this class meets.

interNET ACTIVITY

Have students access the weather sites to see if weather is reported in Fahrenheit or Celsius: The Weather Channel (www.weather.com); Accu-Weather (www.accuweather.com) or WeatherNet (www.weathernet.com)

Math Connections

Have students collect information about the weather in your community for a week, including temperature, precipitation, and so forth. On the board, post the weather, days, and dates. Have students create a spreadsheet that includes this data.

LESSON 131

FOCUS

- Apply the Language Link rules for singular and plural pronoun usage.
- Use 5-minute timings to build speed.
- Learn how to use functions for summing.

BELLRINGER

As soon as students arrive at their workstations and log in, have them type the Warmup. Go over the purpose of each line as shown to the left of the copy.

TEACH

Activity B. Go over the Language Link rules for singular and plural pronoun usage with students. After students have completed typing, have them check each other's work.

Solutions: All of the books in our catalog are categorized by subject.

Each of you is to bring two pencils to the test.

Neither one of us is likely to win the nomination.

One of the new cases storing books and tapes was damaged.

SPREADSHEETS: SUM FUNCTION, CENTER DATA

OBJECTIVES:

- Learn about verbs with pronouns.
- Use the SUM function.
- Center data across a spreadsheet selection.
- Type 39/5'/5e.

A. WARMUP

Type each line 2 times.

Speed	1	The loan form asked for two proofs of a good credit record.
Accuracy	2	If prizes were given for anxiety, Ms. Jaquan would qualify.
Language Link	3	An old adage says that a dog's bark is worse than its bite.
Numbers/Symbols	4	7/8, 4/5, 11/12, 1/2, 8/9, 10/11, 3/4, 6/7, 12/13, 5/6, 2/3
		| 1 | 2 | 3 | 4 | 5 | 6 | 7 | 8 | 9 | 10 | 11 | 12

B. SINGULAR AND PLURAL PRONOUNS

Study the rules and examples that follow. Then edit lines 5–8 by choosing the correct verb.

Rule 38: Some pronouns (*anybody, each, either, everybody, everyone, much, neither, no one, nobody,* and *one*) are always singular and take a singular verb. Other pronouns (*all, any, more, most, none,* and *some*) may be singular or plural, depending on the noun to which they refer.

Everybody was glad to hear that we could leave early.

Most of the workers are going to get a large raise.

Each employee is responsible for summarizing reports.

Some of the gas is being pumped into the tank.

RESOURCES

 Lesson Plan 131

 Courseware Lesson 131

Student Data Disk

Student Manual

Language Link Worksheets

Supplementary Production Activities

Grading and Evaluation

5 All of the books in our catalog (is/are) categorized by subject.
6 Each of you (is/are) to bring two pencils to the test.
7 Neither one of us (is/are) likely to win the nomination.
8 One of the new cases storing books and tapes (was/were) damaged.

SKILLBUILDING

C. Preview Practice

Type each line 2 times as a preview to the timings that follow.

Accuracy	9 trend amazing relaxed quickly powerful employee communicate
Speed	10 leisure office small great home with that room work made by

D. 5-Minute Timings

Take two 5-minute timings on the paragraphs. Note your speed and errors.

Goal: 39/5'/5e

```
     Businesses that are based in the home are booming as a    11
way to earn a good living. Also, more and more workers can      23
choose to stay at home and communicate with the company by      35
computer. An office in the home saves time and money spent      45
traveling to and from the office.                               53
     This trend is now possible because of the ease with        64
which workers can make use of small, powerful computers.        75
This means that the workplace does not need to be in the        89
corporate office building itself. Computers can fit into a      98
small part of a room in the home, and they have an amazing     110
power to communicate with each other. This ability has had     122
a great impact on where people do work. Projects worked on     134
by an employee on the computer at home can be sent quickly     145
over phone lines to the office through the use of modems,      157
faxes, and e-mail.                                             161
     Today's workers want to have a more relaxed life and      172
to enjoy more leisure time than they could in the past.        183
Thanks to powerful computers, millions of people can do so.    195
| 1 | 2 | 3 | 4 | 5 | 6 | 7 | 8 | 9 | 10 | 11 | 12    SI 1.36
```


LESSON 131

TEACH

Activity C. Point out that words in the Preview Practice are used in the timing that follows.

Activity D. Remind students that they should try to improve speed with each 5-minute timing. The goal for these timings is to type 39 words a minute for 5 minutes with no more than 5 errors.

JOURNAL ENTRY

Have students write about their favorite book, magazine, movie, or television show. They are to explain what they like about it, why they like it, and how it relates to their own lives.

TEACH

Activity E. Explain the purpose of each of the functions shown.

Activity 26. Help students through this speadsheet as they create formulas.

FORMATTING

E. Using Functions

A **function** is a formula built into a spreadsheet that enables you to make calculations or text changes quickly and easily. The following list shows some of the most common functions available with most spreadsheets.

SUM	Adds values in a cell range	=SUM(A5:A16)
AVERAGE	Averages values in a cell range	=AVERAGE(D1:D9)
MAX	Finds largest value in a cell range	=MAX(F3:F91)
MIN	Finds smallest value in a cell range	=MIN(C12:C55)
ROUND	Rounds to a specified number of digits	=ROUND(SUM(B1:B3),2)
MEDIAN	Finds middle value in a cell range	=MEDIAN(L17:1Q17)
SQRT	Finds square root of the value in a cell	=SORT(Y54)
PROPER	Changes text to initial caps	=PROPER("kathy reeves")
UPPER	Changes text to all caps	=UPPER("jamal h. fowler")
NOW	Displays current time and/or date	=NOW()

F. Software Features

STUDENT MANUAL

SUM | Insert Functions
Horizontally Centering Across Cell Ranges

Study Lesson 131 in your student manual. Complete all the practice activities while at your computer. Then complete the jobs that follow.

SPREADSHEET APPLICATIONS

ACTIVITY 26
Spreadsheet 19

Create a new spreadsheet, save it as SS19, then follow the steps below:

1. In cell A1, type the label *Grocery Store Price Comparisons.*
2. In cell A2, type *Prepared by* followed by your name.
3. In cell A3, type the date as *February 14 {year}*, or 14 Feb., {year} in bold. Note that your spreadsheet may automatically change the format of the date.
4. Type the data into the cells as shown below.
5. Save your changes and close the file.

474 *Spreadsheets*

FACT FILE

Technology has spurred a major business trend—home offices. Employees work out of their homes sending and receiving information from clients via computer modems and fax machines. Have students discuss the advantages and disadvantages of a home office, including the need for equipment, records, and discipline.

	A	B	C	D	E	F
5	Item	Size	Cost Cutter	Family Foods	Food Queen	Paul Bunyon
6						
7	Egg Subs	16 oz	2.17	2.34	1.99	2.25
8	Bully Paper Towels	80.6 sq ft	0.96	1.07	1.14	0.99
9	Zippy Pasta Sauce	26 oz	2.89	2.53	2.67	2.73
10	Fizzy Cola	2 L	1.24	1.29	1.19	1.36
11	Fruit Crunch Cereal	16 oz	2.98	3.18	3.06	3.24
12	Buzzy Bee Honey	12 oz	1.98	1.99	1.83	1.91
13						
14	Total					

ACTIVITY 27
Spreadsheet 20

Open the file SS19, save it as SS20, and then make the following changes:

1. Select cell C14, and use AutoSum/QuickSum to get the total.
2. Select cell D14, and use Insert, Function to get the total.
3. Select cell E14, type =*SUM*, and select the cell range to be added to get the total.
4. Select cell F14, type =*SUM*, and select the cell range to be added to get the total.
5. Format cell range C14 through F14 with dollar signs and two decimals.
6. Save your changes and close the file.

ACTIVITY 28
Spreadsheet 21

Open the file SS20, save it as SS21, and make the following changes:

1. Bold and center row 5.
2. Select cell range A5 through F14, and automatically change the column width.
3. Align cell range B7 through B12 at the right.
4. Change cell A1 to 16-point bold.
5. Change cell A2 to 12-point bold.
6. Add gridlines so they will print.
7. Select cell range A1 through F3; center horizontally across the selection.
8. Change the height of row 4 to approximately 1.5 times the default height.
9. If your teacher has given you instructions for printing, print the spreadsheet. Otherwise, save your changes and close the file.

Teacher Notes

TEACH

Activity 27. Explain the advantage of using the SUM function instead of creating a formula that adds the individual cells. Point out that it is more efficient to use the SUM function.

Activity 28. Have students read the instructions once, then have them read the instructions again to be sure they understand what to do.

ASSESS

- Check to see if students are increasing their word a minute speeds as they complete each 5-minute timing.
- Watch students as they complete the Language Link activity to see if they are able to apply the rule correctly.
- As students begin working on the spreadsheets, walk around the room and provide assistance to individual students as needed.
- After students finish working on each spreadsheet, have them view their work on the screen to see if they made any errors. If errors were made, have students edit their work and make corrections.

CLOSE

Remind students to clean up their workstation when they leave.

LESSON 132

FOCUS

- Use 12-second timings to build speed.
- Use a Pretest/Practice/ Posttest routine to build speed and accuracy.
- Learn spreadsheet features: AVERAGE function.
- Use the AVERAGE function in spreadsheets.

BELLRINGER

As soon as students arrive at their workstations and log in, have them type the Warmup. Go over the purpose of each line as shown to the left of the copy.

TEACH

Activity B. Remind students that the goal for 12-second timings is improved speed with each timing.

LESSON 132

SPREADSHEETS: AVERAGE FUNCTION

OBJECTIVES:

- Improve keyboarding speed and accuracy.
- Use the AVERAGE function in a spreadsheet.

A. WARMUP

Type each line 2 times.

```
Speed            1 Ruth sets her alarm so that she will wake up on time daily.
Accuracy         2 Zelda squeezed the six bouquets into a quaint antique vase.
Language Link    3 Most of the area schools are closed today due to bad roads.
Numbers/Symbols  4 I ordered #6, #7, and #34 at discounts of 5%, 15%, and 20%.
                   | 1 | 2 | 3 | 4 | 5 | 6 | 7 | 8 | 9 | 10 | 11 | 12
```

interNET CONNECTION

Workers often find they have too much to do and little time to do it. Students, too, often feel the same time crunch. Connect to the following adress on the Internet to take a time management quiz and find useful tips for managing your time: http://www.daytimer.com.

SKILLBUILDING

B. 12-SECOND SPRINTS

Take three 12-second timings on each line. Try to increase your speed on each timing.

```
5 The new desk and chair will be put in the back of the room.
6 Those boys were asked to cut and water the dry, brown lawn.
7 At long last I have a pen that will not leak on my fingers.
8 We need to turn off the light before they tell us to do it.
  ||||5||||10||||15||||20||||25||||30||||35||||40||||45||||50||||55||||60
```


RESOURCES

 Lesson Plan 132

 Courseware Lesson 132

Student Data Disk

Student Manual

Supplementary Production Activities

C. PRETEST

Take a 1-minute timing on the paragraph. Note your speed and errors.

```
9       It is essential that we get plenty of sleep so that we   11
10  are rested when we get up each morning. We must eat a good   23
11  breakfast to build up energy for the day. Physical exercise  35
12  is a must for stronger hearts and greater endurance.         45
    | 1 | 2 | 3 | 4 | 5 | 6 | 7 | 8 | 9 | 10 | 11 | 12
```

Science Connections

D. PRACTICE

In the chart below, find the number of errors you made on the Pretest. Then type each of the designated drill lines 2 times.

Pretest Errors	0–1	2	3	4+
Drill Lines	16–20	15–19	14–18	13–17

Accuracy

```
13 by friends families stronger breakfast minimize experienced
14 many rested problems run-down physical fatigued performance
15 build plenty energy increases endurance essential adversely
16 we quality morning exercise symptoms mentioned increasingly
```

Speed

```
17 hearts become energy there lives time each that when run we
18 levels active plenty tired these they good must felt our is
19 affect making crease limit spend with ways have down and it
20 friend affect rested sleep break days many just ever job of
```

E. POSTTEST

Repeat the Pretest. Compare your Posttest results with your Pretest results.

FORMATTING

F. USING THE AVERAGE FUNCTION

AVERAGE (or AVG.) is a formula that automatically adds the values in a range of cells and divides by the number of values to find the average. The average can then be formatted to have the desired number of decimal places.

TEACH

Activities C–E. Remind students they should improve both their speed and accuracy from the Pretest to the Posttest.

PRETEST/PRACTICE/POSTTEST

The ***Pretest/Practice/Posttest*** routines are designed to improve speed or accuracy.

- The ***Pretest*** identifies students' speed or accuracy needs.
- The ***Practice*** provides a variety of improvement drills.
- The ***Posttest*** (a repeat of the Pretest) measures improvement.

Activity F. Point out the AVERAGE (AVG.) formula to students. Ask them how they might use this function in their lives, both personal and in business.

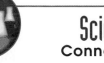

Science Connections

Have students keep a record of what they eat for breakfast and their physical activity for five days. Have them create a spreadsheet with this information, then analyze the information to see how well they are taking care of their bodies.

Multiple Learning Styles

This exercise will help audio and kinetic learners. Have students work in groups to create a rap/hip hop song about spreadsheets and how they can use them. Encourage them to be creative. Have students type their lyrics and pass them out to their classmates.

TEACH

Activity G. Have students turn to Lesson 132 in their Student Manual and read the explanation for the software they are using. Then have them complete the practice activities that follow.

STUDENT MANUAL

Be sure students turn to the correct lesson in their Student Manual.

Activity 29. Have students read the instructions once, then have them read the instructions again to be sure they understand what to do.

Activity 30. As students work on this activity, walk around the room to make sure they understand the directions and are able to execute them. If you notice several students having trouble with the same step, go over this step again with the class.

PORTFOLIO *Activity*

If students' portfolio goals include demonstrating specific skills, they may want to include a spreadsheet from this lesson. Encourage students to evaluate their work and include comments in their portfolio.

G. Software Features

STUDENT MANUAL

AVERAGE Function

Study Lesson 132 in your student manual. Complete all the practice activities while at your computer. Then complete the jobs that follow.

COMMUNICATION FOCUS

Write a short report on what you believe will be the advantages of working from home instead of from an office. Interview at least one person who has an office at home, perhaps a writer or an accountant in your city or town.

SPREADSHEET APPLICATIONS

ACTIVITY 29

Spreadsheet 22

Open the file SS1 and save it as SS22. Then follow these steps to change a spreadsheet by inserting the AVERAGE function.

1. Move cell range E1 through E16 to F1 through F16.
2. In cell E1, center and type in bold the label *Averages.*
3. In cell E3, find the average for weeks 1, 2, and 3.
4. Save your changes and close the file.

ACTIVITY 30

Spreadsheet 23

Open the file SS22, and save it as SS23. Then make the following changes:

1. In cell E4, find the average by typing the function name and selecting the cells to be averaged.
2. In cell E5, find the average by typing the function name and cell range.
3. Copy the contents of cell E5 to cell range E6 through E13.
4. Format all numbers to have two decimal places where necessary.
5. In cell E16, find the average of cell range E3 through E13.
6. Set the gridlines to print.
7. Automatically format the column width of cells E1 and F1.
8. Save your changes and close the file.

TECHNOLOGY TIP

The automatic hyphenation function helps you avoid excessive white space. At times you may still need to manually insert a hyphen to improve the appearance and readability of a page. Ask students what other adjustments can they make to improve the appearance and readability of a page.

Out-of-Class Activity

Have students choose a partner; then have student pairs develop a spreadsheet for calculating grade point averages for grades they receive in this class. Have them develop another spreadsheet for the grades they receive in all their classes so they can see their overall grade point average.

ACTIVITY 31
Spreadsheet 24

Create a new spreadsheet and save it as SS24. Then follow these steps:

1. Type the data as shown in the following table.
2. In cell G4, use the AVERAGE function to average Howard Joslin's grades.
3. Copy the contents of cell G4 to cell range G5 through G17.
4. Widen columns A, D, and F and the titles, so that you can read the names easily.
5. Save your changes and close the file.

	A	B	C	D	E	F	G
1	Students	Author	Portfolios	Persuasiv	Narrative	Descriptiv	Grade
2		Projects		Essays	Essays	Essays	Averages
3							
4	Joslin, Howard	88	92	78	83	75	
5	Calavan, Casey	97	99	91	93	89	
6	Petropoulos, Cheryl	73	81	80	65	77	
7	Figueroa, Miguel	79	90	87	82	80	
8	Vititow, Megan	75	55	81	73	69	
9	Mathis, Monica	98	94	88	95	96	
10	Quintero, Luis	84	76	66	89	92	
11	Kizer, Paula	90	87	94	88	91	
12	Yankey, Ottis	79	74	78	77	83	
13	Pfiel, Logan	95	89	96	92	87	
14	Locks, Andrea	100	97	99	98	100	
15	Flewharty, Robin	99	89	90	87	98	
16	Jimmerson, Gennifer	85	71	82	78	84	
17	Swafford, Priscilla	87	69	83	76	68	

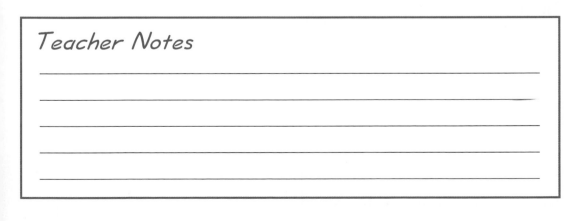

*inter*NET CONNECTION

Connect to the Internet. Enter the following address to learn about ergonomic tips for office workers: http://www.advergo.com

Teacher Notes

LESSON 132

TEACH

Activity 31. If students have trouble keeping the columns straight as they type, suggest they place a ruler across the page. Remind them to proofread their work when they finish.

ASSESS

- Check to see if students show signs of improvement from the Pretest to the Posttest.
- Make sure students are able to use the AVERAGE spreadsheet function.
- As students begin working on the spreadsheets, walk around the room and provide assistance to individual students as needed.
- After students finish working on each spreadsheet, have them view their work on the screen to see if they made any errors. If errors were made, have students edit their work and make corrections.

CLOSE

If students do not finish the spreadsheets during the class period, make sure they save their work so that they can complete it the next time this class meets.

Remind students to clean up their workstation when they leave.

FOCUS

- Compose a one-page story for the Language Link activity.
- Use 30-second timings to build speed.
- Learn spreadsheet features: Insert Rows and Sort Data.
- Insert rows and sort data in spreadsheets.

BELLRINGER

As soon as students arrive at their workstations and log in, have them type the Warmup. Go over the purpose of each line as shown to the left of the copy.

TEACH

Activity B. Have students read each other's stories to check for any errors. If time permits, read a few stories in class.

Solutions: Answers will vary.

LESSON 133 SPREADSHEETS: INSERTING ROWS/SORTING DATA

OBJECTIVES:

- Compose at the keyboard.
- Improve typing speed.
- Insert rows into a spreadsheet.
- Sort data in a spreadsheet.

A. WARMUP

Type each line 2 times.

Speed	1	Three workers left early and were paid for only half a day.
Accuracy	2	Del and Wanda Quaid are great examples of quality citizens.
Language Link	3	Everybody was warned to stay home due to the freezing rain.
Numbers/Symbols	4	18, 290, 27, 38, 851, 63, 94, 704, 91, 48, 532, 10, 76, 495

| 1 | 2 | 3 | 4 | 5 | 6 | 7 | 8 | 9 | 10 | 11 | 12

B. COMPOSING AT THE KEYBOARD

Compose the body of a one-page story which begins as follows:

> "The last thing I remember was taking the dog for a walk. When I awoke, I found myself in a hospital room, but I couldn't remember . . ."

When you finish your story, proofread it carefully and correct any errors.

FACT FILE

The planet Neptune orbits the sun once in 164 years. That is a long orbit!

RESOURCES

 Lesson Plan 133

Courseware Lesson 133

Student Data Disk

Student Manual

Supplementary Production Activities

SKILLBUILDING

C. 30-Second Timings

Take two 30-second timings on lines 5–6. Then take two 30-second timings on lines 7–8. Try to increase your speed on each paragraph.

```
5      One type of report is an agenda; it is used to inform   11
6  people of items that may be discussed at a future meeting.  23

7      Minutes of a meeting are another kind of report; they   11
8  are records of reference for what takes place in meetings.  23
   | 1 | 2 | 3 | 4 | 5 | 6 | 7 | 8 | 9 | 10 | 11 | 12
```

FORMATTING

D. Inserting Rows

Even when you carefully plan a spreadsheet, there will be times when you need to insert additional rows. When you insert a row, all of the rows after the insertion will be renumbered, and any formulas in the spreadsheet will be readjusted.

E. Sorting Data

Sorting data is arranging it in a certain order such as alphabetic or numeric. You can sort data in **ascending order** (from A to Z or low to high) or in **descending order** (from Z to A or high to low). You can also choose which column to sort first, second, and third. Before you sort data, it is a good idea to save your file. Your sort may not turn out the way you intended.

F. Software Features

STUDENT MANUAL

Insert Rows
Sort Data

Study Lesson 133 in your student manual. Complete all the practice activities while at your computer. Then complete the jobs that follow.

JOURNAL ENTRY

Have students write about what they think it would be like to be a famous fiction writer. What type of lifestyle would they live? Would they make a lot of money or small amount? What type stories would they write?

LESSON 133

TEACH

Activity C. Remind students that the goal for 30-second timings is improved speed with each timing.

Activity D. Offer some simple reasons for adding a row to a worksheet. For example, if you keep your monthly budget on a spreadsheet you might want to add a row if you have a new expense such as a monthly health club fee.

Activity E. Offer some reasons why you might want to sort data. For example, you might have a list of volunteers that you want to put in alphabetical order. You might want to take the same list and put it in order according to hours of service.

Activity F. Have students turn to Lesson 133 in their Student Manual and read the explanation for the software they are using. Then have them complete the practice activities that follow.

STUDENT MANUAL

Be sure students turn to the correct lesson in their Student Manual.

TEACH

Activities 32–34. Have students read the instructions once for each activity, then have them read the instructions again to be sure they understand what to do.

SPREADSHEET APPLICATIONS

ACTIVITY 32
Spreadsheet 25

Open the file SS1, and save it as SS25. Then follow the steps below:

1. Insert a blank row 1.
2. In cell A1, type in 14-point bold the label *Fund-Raising Report.*
3. Insert a blank row 2.
4. In cell A2, type in 12-point bold the label *Prepared by* followed by your name.
5. Insert a blank row 3.
6. Save your changes and close the file.

ACTIVITY 33
Spreadsheet 26

Open the file SS25, save it as SS26, and follow these steps:

1. In cell A3, type in 12-point bold, the label *October 12-30, {year}.*
2. Insert a blank row 4.
3. Center cell range A1 through A3 across the spreadsheet.
4. Bold the contents of rows 19 and 20.
5. Change the print orientation to landscape.
6. If the contents of any column are not visible, adjust the width.
7. Save your changes but do not close the file.

ACTIVITY 34
Spreadsheet 27

If file SS26 is not open, open it now and save it as SS27.

1. Select cell range A7 through E17.
2. Sort column E in descending order (from high to low). The names are no longer in alphabetic order but are arranged in order of highest to lowest total sales.
3. Follow your teacher's instructions for printing.
4. Save your changes and close the file.

FACT FILE

The dinosaur Mamenchisaurus had an extremely long neck. This type of dinosaur could have a neck as long as 49 feet, about 2 1/2 times as long as a giraffe's neck.

TECHNOLOGY TIP

To avoid harming floppy disks, avoid placing heavy objects on them and do not expose disks to excessive heat, sunlight, or cold. Also keep disks away from magnetic fields such as stereo speakers, telephones, headsets, monitors, or calculators.

Out-of-Class Activity

Have student pairs brainstorm an idea for a spreadsheet that would be useful in school or for an extracurricular activity or hobby. Have them plan the rows and columns and the functions they will use. Have each pair write a one-page report describing their spreadsheets.

ACTIVITY 35
Spreadsheet 28

Open the file SS24, save it as SS28, and follow these steps to change the spreadsheet by inserting rows and sorting data:

1. Insert a blank row 1.
2. In cell A1, type in 12-point bold the label *Fifth-Period Junior English Class.*
3. Insert a blank row 2.
4. In cell A2, type in bold the label *Prepared by* followed by your name.
5. Insert a blank row 3.
6. In cell A3, type in bold the label *Beginning February 10,{year}.*
7. Center cell range A1 through A3 across the spreadsheet.
8. Insert a blank row 4.
9. Bold and center cell range A5 through G6.
10. Select cell range A8 through G21, and sort the names in column A in ascending order.
11. Format all numbers to have no decimal places.
12. Insert gridlines and change the print orientation to landscape.
13. Follow your teacher's instructions for printing.
14. Save your changes and close the file.

*inter*NET CONNECTION

Connect to the Internet. Search the World Wide Web for information on the skeletal structure of the blue whale. How does it compare with that of the dinosaur?

LESSON 133

TEACH

Activity 35. Read the instructions aloud to students, stopping after each step to make sure students understand what they are to do.

ASSESS

- Review the stories students composed for the Language Link activity.
- Check to see if students are increasing their word a minute speeds as they complete each 30-second timing.
- Make sure students are able to use the Insert Rows and Sort Data spreadsheet features.
- As students begin working with the spreadsheets, walk around the room and provide assistance to individual students as needed.
- After students finish each activity, have them view their work on the screen to see if they made any errors. If errors were made, have students edit their work and make corrections.

CLOSE

Remind students to clean up their workstation when they leave.

Teacher Notes

FOCUS

- Use a Paced Practice 2-minute timing routine.
- Learn spreadsheet features: Insert Columns and Add Borders and Shading.
- Insert columns, add borders, and add shading to a spreadsheet.

BELLRINGER

As soon as students arrive at their workstations and log in, have them type the Warmup. Go over the purpose of each line as shown to the left of the copy.

TEACH

Activity B. Go over the routine for the Paced Practice 2-minute timing. (See Lesson 34, page 119.)

LESSON 134

SPREADSHEETS: INSERTING COLUMNS, BORDERS, AND SHADING

OBJECTIVES:

- Improve keyboarding skills.
- Insert columns into a spreadsheet.
- Add borders and shading.

A. WARMUP

Type each line 2 times.

Speed	1	The four women spent the day on the lake in a fishing boat.
Accuracy	2	Ximenez may jeopardize the quality of those antique quilts.
Language Link	3	None of the parents wanted their children out in the storm.
Numbers/Symbols	4	Those answers are: (a) $135, (b) $46, (c) $128, (d) $97.03.

| 1 | 2 | 3 | 4 | 5 | 6 | 7 | 8 | 9 | 10 | 11 | 12

SKILLBUILDING

B. PACED PRACTICE

Turn to the Paced Practice routine beginning on page SB7. Take three 2-minute timings, starting at the point where you left off the last time.

FACT FILE

The gray shark is a smaller version of a great white shark. Gray sharks are members of the Carcharhinidae or *man-eating* family of sharks. Gray sharks are most often found in the waters of the Mediterranean Sea and the Atlantic Ocean.

RESOURCES

 Lesson Plan 134

 Courseware Lesson 134

Student Data Disk

Student Manual

Supplementary Production Activities

Cross-Curricular Activities

C. Inserting Columns Into a Spreadsheet

Sometimes it may be necessary to insert additional columns into a spreadsheet. When you insert a column, all the columns following the insertion will be relettered, and formulas in the spreadsheet will be readjusted.

D. Adding Borders and Shading

Spreadsheets can be made more attractive and readable by using lines, or **borders,** both in and around the worksheet and darker or color backgrounds called **shading.** Choose shading that does not interfere with reading the text. Also, do not use too many special treatments in a single spreadsheet. You may need to experiment with available options to find what works best.

Borders. *Lines placed around spreadsheet cells and/or cell ranges.*

Shading. *Darkening or coloring the background of cells or cell ranges.*

CONCESSION STAND ROSTER
Tuesday, September 12

5:30-6:30	6:30-7:30	7:30-8:30	8:30-9:30	9:30-Cleanup
Gray Aubrey	Bessonett, Teri	Diener, Darren	Corbin, Curt	Daehn, Sonja
Maddox, Roy	Horvath, Jessie	Katchinska, Ken	Estes, Edith	Feddon, Lee
McNeal, Mike	Ottwell, Dionne	Roark, Randa	Geitner, Gail	Gustafson, Gunther
Owen, Beverly	Rubio, Nan	Vega, Oscar	Hosea, Jim	Nix, Nita

E. Software Features

STUDENT MANUAL

Insert Columns
Add Borders and Shading

Study Lesson 134 in your student manual. Complete all the practice activities while at your computer. Then complete the jobs that follow.

TEACH

Activity C. Offer some simple reasons why you might want to add a column to a worksheet. For example, if you keep the names, addresses, and telephone numbers for members of a committee on a spreadsheet, you might want to add a column for e-mail addresses.

Demonstrate how formulas are adjusted when you add a column. For example, if the formula in C1 is =SUM(A1:B1) and you insert a column between A and B, the data in A1 stays the same, the data that was in B1 moves to C1, and the formula that was in C1 moves to D1. The new formula is =SUM(A1:C1).

Activity D. Point out that shading and colors often look different on the screen than on a printed page. This is particularly true if you are using a black and white printer.

Activity E. Have students turn to Lesson 134 in their Student Manual and read the explanation for the software they are using. Then have them complete the practice activities that follow.

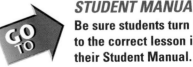

STUDENT MANUAL

Be sure students turn to the correct lesson in their Student Manual.

FACT FILE

If you fly in an airplane heading into a 100-mile-per-hour jet stream on a coast-to-coast trip, you would take about an hour and a half longer than a trip going in the same direction as the jet stream. Have students create a spreadsheet that records your local weather for one week that includes a column for direction of the jet stream.

TEACH

Activity 36. Have different students read aloud the steps for this activity. Stop after each step to make sure all students understand the directions.

Activity 37. As students work on this activity, walk around the room to make sure students understand the directions and are able to execute them. If you notice several students having trouble with the same step, go over this step again with the class.

SPREADSHEET APPLICATIONS

ACTIVITY 36
Spreadsheet 29

Open the file SS12, save it as SS29, and then follow these steps to change the spreadsheet:

1. Insert a blank column D.
2. In cell D6, center and type in bold the label *Transportation.*
3. In cell range D8 through D12, type the following entries: *Antilles Air; Ferry; Isle Air; Mailboat; Ferry.*
4. Automatically widen column D.
5. Select cell range A8 through F12, and sort column B in descending (high to low) order.
6. Follow your teacher's instructions for printing.
7. Save your changes and close the file.

ACTIVITY 37
Spreadsheet 30

Open the file SS20, save it as SS30, and follow these steps to change the spreadsheet:

1. Insert a blank column F.
2. In cell F5, type the label *Our Store.*
3. In cell range F7 through F12, enter the following values: *1.97; 1.03; 2.88; 0.99; 3.11; 1.78.*
4. Copy the formula in cell E14 to F14.
5. Automatically adjust the width of column F.
6. Insert a blank row 9.
7. In cell range A9 through G9, enter the following data: *Holstein Milk; 1 gal.; 1.56; 1.78; 1.89; 1.65; 1.49.*
8. Select cell range A7 through G13 and sort column A in ascending order.
9. If necessary, center cells A1 through A3 across the spreadsheet again.
10. Add a heavy border around cell range A1 through G15.
11. Add a border at the bottom of cell range A1 through G5.
12. Save your changes and close the file.

Teacher Notes

ACTIVITY 38
Spreadsheet 31

Open the file SS30, save it as SS31, and make the following changes:

1. Fill cell range A1 through G5 with a light shading or light horizontal lines.
2. Add a medium border at the top of cell range A15 through G15.
3. Using the same fill you used in step 1, shade the following cell ranges: A7 through G7; A9 through G9; A11 through G11; A13 through G13.
4. Save your changes and close the file.

FACT FILE
The spadefoot toad is a persistent desert dweller, digging with a projection on each hind foot. The toad experiences estivation, a type of hibernation, when drought sets in. This estivation can last eight or nine months.

PORTFOLIO *Activity*
Write a short paragraph about the importance of accuracy in temperature conversions such as those in Activity 25. What can happen if you make an error? If you made any errors in your mathematical conversions, explain why you think you made the errors and what you can do to prevent such errors in the future.

LESSON 134

TEACH
Activity 38. Read the instructions aloud to students, stopping after each step to make sure students understand what they are to do.

ASSESS
- Make sure students are able to use the Insert Columns and Add Borders and Shading spreadsheet features.
- As students begin working with the spreadsheets, walk around the room and provide assistance to individual students as needed.
- After students finish each activity, have them view their work on the screen to see if they made any errors. If errors were made, have students edit their work and make corrections.

CLOSE
If students do not finish the spreadsheets during the class period, make sure they save their work so that they can complete it the next time this class meets.

Remind students to clean up their workstation when they leave.

FACT FILE
Have students research amphibians, and then create a spreadsheet that includes the following information: type of amphibian, body temperature, fact about behavior, scientific classification, habitat, and an additional fact.

LESSON 135

FOCUS

- Apply Language Link rules for pronoun usage.
- Use 5-minute timings to build speed.
- Learn spreadsheet features: Clearing Commands and Deleting Rows and Columns.
- Clear the content of cells, delete rows, and delete columns on spreadsheets.

BELLRINGER

As soon as students arrive at their workstations and log in, have them type the Warmup. Go over the purpose of each line as shown to the left of the copy.

TEACH

Activity B. Discuss the Language Link rules for pronoun usage with students. Make sure they all understand the difference between nominative pronouns and objective pronouns.

Solutions: Rob knows art better than she, but she can't add.

She and I saw the new movie before they did.

My friends and I do not like him when he brags.

I'm sure he has more knowledge of cultures than I.

SPREADSHEETS: CLEAR CELLS, DELETE ROWS AND COLUMNS

OBJECTIVES:

- Learn nominative and objective pronoun use.
- Clear cells.
- Delete rows and columns.
- Type 39/5'/5e.

A. WARMUP

Type each line 2 times.

Speed	1 That round key that you gave me will not fit into the door.
Accuracy	2 Buzz was pleased to qualify in the men's bike extravaganza.
Language Link	3 Since school was called off, some of the students slept in.
Numbers/Symbols	4 Just 4% of the #156 ($2.36) on 3% of #78 ($1.90) were used.
	| 1 | 2 | 3 | 4 | 5 | 6 | 7 | 8 | 9 | 10 | 11 | 12

B. PRONOUN USE

Study the rules and examples that follow. Then edit lines 5–8 to correct any errors in pronoun use.

Rule 38: Use **nominative** pronouns (such as *I, he, she, we,* and *they*) as subjects of a sentence or clause.

The programmer and he are reviewing that.

It is she who likes this software.

Rule 39: Use **objective** pronouns (such as *me, him, her,* and *them*) as objects in a sentence or clause.

The folders are for Susan and him.

She went out with him and me.

5 Rob knows art better than (she/her), but (she/her) can't add.
6 (She/Her) and (I/me) saw the new movie before (they/them) did.
7 My friends and (I/me) do not like (he/him) when (he/him) brags.
8 I'm sure (he/him) has more knowledge of cultures than (I/me).

RESOURCES

 Lesson Plan 135

 Courseware Lesson 135

Student Data Disk

Student Manual

Language Link Worksheet

Supplementary Production Activities

Grading and Evaluation

C. Preview Practice

Type each line 2 times as a preview to the timings that follow.

Accuracy	how extent impaired Alexander equipment surprised telephone
Speed	hearing speech moved wires help soon just grew live but was

D. 5-Minute Timings

Take two 5-minute timings on the paragraphs. Note your speed and errors.

Goal: 39/5'/5e

Social Studies Connections

Science Connections

```
     Throughout its history, America has prospered and        10
grown with the help of countless inventions. Although he      22
could not have realized the full extent of its effects at     33
the time, Alexander Graham Bell invented a device that led    45
to a change in the way we communicate not just in our own     57
country but in the entire world.                              63
     Bell grew up in a family that had a deep interest in     74
speech and deafness. He moved from Scotland to the United     86
States where he learned how to teach the hearing impaired     97
to speak. He also began to work with equipment that would    109
send several telegraph messages over one line. From this     121
interest, he started to try to send voices over electrical   132
wires. Soon the telephone was born.                          140
     Bell might be surprised at how his work has linked our  151
world together, but we can be sure he would be most proud    162
of the strides that have been made in helping the hearing    174
impaired. Bell's inventions have enabled those who cannot    186
hear to live richer lives in a hearing world.                195
| 1 | 2 | 3 | 4 | 5 | 6 | 7 | 8 | 9 | 10 | 11 | 12  SI 1.42
```


TEACH

Activity C. Point out that words in the Preview Practice are used in the 5-minute timings that follow.

Activity D. Remind students that they should try to improve speed with each 5-minute timing. The goal for these timings is to type 39 words a minute for 5 minutes with no more than 5 errors.

Social Studies Connections

Have students research the nearest school or learning facility for deaf students. Write a letter to invite a speaker to the class to teach your students about sign language and how they can communicate with people with hearing disabilities.

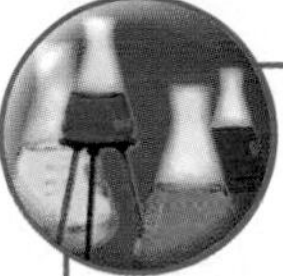

Science Connections

In the letter of invitation students write to the speaker in the Social Studies Connection, have them request that the speaker also bring instruments that aid people with hearing impairments. Have students prepare questions to ask the speaker.

FORMATTING

E. Clearing Cells

When you press delete or backspace in a cell or cell range, the contents of the cell is removed, but the formatting remains. To remove formatting properties from cells, use the clear commands. Clear usually removes basic formatting commands such as bold, italics, underline, and fonts. Some clear commands also remove shading, borders, alignments, and numeric formats. An option in the clear command is to remove both the contents and the formatting properties at the same time.

F. Deleting Rows and Columns

Spreadsheet rows and columns can be deleted by selecting the row number or column letter and using the delete command. If the spreadsheet contains formulas and a row or column is deleted, the software will adjust the addresses of the shifted cells. However, if a formula depends upon a cell that has been deleted, an error message will be displayed.

G. Software Features

STUDENT MANUAL

Clear Commands
Delete Rows and Columns

Study Lesson 135 in your student manual. Complete all the practice activities while at your computer. Then complete the jobs that follow.

CULTURAL CONNECTIONS

Dates and time are expressed in different ways from one country to another. Ask a student from another country how he or she would write today's date on a letter.

TEACH

Activity E. Demonstrate why you might want to remove the formatting from a cell or group of cells. For example, if you format a cell for a dollar amount, any number you enter will include the dollar sign unless you change the format or clear the cell.

Activity F. Demonstrate how formulas are adjusted when you delete a row or a column. For example, if the formula in C10 is =SUM(C1:C9) and you delete row 8, the data in C1 through C7 stays the same, the data that was in C9 moves to C8, and the formula that was in C10 moves to C9. The new formula is =SUM(C1:C8).

Also demonstrate how an error can result in a formula if the formula depends on a cell that is removed. For example, if the formula in E5 is =(B5+C5)/D5 and you remove column C, an error message will be displayed in E5.

Activity G. Have students turn to Lesson 135 in their Student Manual and read the explanation for the software they are using. Then have them complete the practice activities that follow.

STUDENT MANUAL

Be sure students turn to the correct lesson in their Student Manual.

JOURNAL ENTRY

Have students write about the things they like about themselves. Keep students writing nonstop for at least five minutes. Encourage students to keep writing even when they think they are out of words.

ACTIVITY 39
Spreadsheet 32

Open the file SS18, save it as SS32, and follow these steps to clear formatting properties:

1. Select cell range A1 through E16 and clear the formatting. Note what happens to your spreadsheet.
2. If the format of the numbers in column C did not change, change them to numeric, general.
3. Move the contents of cells C1 and C2 to A1 and A2.
4. Change rows 1 and 2 to 10-point bold, and center cells A1 and A2 across the spreadsheet.
5. Clear the contents of cell range A7 through A16; then enter these numbers: *7, 15, 30, 37, 45, 51, 68, 77, 93, 105.*
6. Center and bold cell range A4 through E5.
7. Change the font in cells B5 and D5 to Wingdings.
8. Format cell range C7 through C16 for no decimal places.
9. Shade cell range A1 through E5 in a shade of your choice.
10. Shade the data in rows 7, 9, 11, 13, and 15 in a shade of your choice.
11. Add a border around the entire spreadsheet.
12. Save your changes and close the file.

ACTIVITY 40
Spreadsheet 33

Open the file SS24, save it as SS33, and follow these steps:

1. Delete column C. Notice that the grade averages are either recalculated or you get an error message indicating that you must recalculate or rewrite the formula.
2. Delete the rows containing data for Robin Flewharty, Logan Pfiel, and Priscilla Swafford.
3. Shade the data in rows 4, 6, 8, 10, 12, and 14 in a shade of your choice.
4. Place a border around the entire spreadsheet.
5. Place a line at the bottom of cell range A6 through F6.
6. Save your changes and close the file.

LESSON 135

TEACH

Activity 39. Have students read the instructions once, then have them read the instructions again to be sure they understand what to do.

Activity 40. Walk around the room to make sure students understand the directions and are able to execute them. If you notice several students having trouble with the same step, go over this step again with the class.

ASSESS

- Check to see if students are increasing their word a minute speeds as they complete each 5-minute timing.
- Watch students as they complete the Language Link activity to see if they are able to apply the pronoun usage rule correctly.
- Make sure students are able to use the Clearing Commands and Deleting Rows and Columns spreadsheet features.
- As students begin working with the spreadsheets, walk around the room and provide individual assistance.
- After students finish each activity, have them view their work on the screen to see if they made any errors.

CLOSE

Remind students to clean up their workstation when they leave.

Teacher Notes

LESSON 136

FOCUS

- Use 30-second OK timings to build accuracy.
- Learn spreadsheet features: Fill Right, Fill Down, and Fill Series.
- Use the fill commands to enter data in adjacent cells in spreadsheets.

BELLRINGER

As soon as students arrive at their workstations and log in, have them type the Warmup. Go over the purpose of each line as shown to the left of the copy.

TEACH

Activity B. Point out that 30-second OK timings are designed to encourage accuracy.

LESSON 136

SPREADSHEETS: FILL RIGHT/FILL DOWN COMMANDS

OBJECTIVES:

- Improve keyboarding skill.
- Use Fill Right and Fill Down commands.
- Use Fill Series command.

A. WARMUP

Type each line 2 times.

Speed	1	The boys will not go to the zoo as was said at the meeting.
Accuracy	2	Liza quit her job, packed six new bags, and moved far away.
Language Link	3	The students hope that they can get passes to today's game.
Numbers/Symbols	4	You will set tabs for these jobs at 18, 24, 37, 42, and 54.
		| 1 | 2 | 3 | 4 | 5 | 6 | 7 | 8 | 9 | 10 | 11 | 12

SKILLBUILDING

B. 30-SECOND OK TIMINGS

Take two 30-second OK (error-free) timings on lines 5–6. Then take two 30-second OK timings on lines 7–8. Goal: no errors.

```
5      Quinn was in a daze after watching six rented movies;    11
6  she wanted to jot down the plots before she forgot them.     23

7      Marvin went to buy zippers to fix the jeans, but then    11
8  he could not squeeze his vehicle into the parking place.     23
   | 1 | 2 | 3 | 4 | 5 | 6 | 7 | 8 | 9 | 10 | 11 | 12
```


RESOURCES

 Lesson Plan 136

 Courseware Lesson 136

Student Data Disk

Student Manual

Supplementary Production Activities

FACT FILE

The term figure skating originally meant just that: skating figures (such as a figure 8) on ice.

FORMATTING

C. Fill Right, Fill Down, and Fill Series

Spreadsheet fill commands reproduce or copy the same data down a column (**Fill Down**) or across a row (**Fill Right**). Fill commands can be used with text and values, including formulas. The **Fill Series** command is used to create data with a pattern. For example, if you type *Monday* and *Tuesday* in cells A1 and B1, you can use the fill command to fill cells C1 through G1 with the rest of the days. The same is true for months and numbers that have a pattern such as *5, 10, 15* or *15, 12, 9.* The fill commands generate data quickly and accurately and are great time-savers.

D. Software Features

STUDENT MANUAL

Fill Right — Fill Down
Fill Series

Study Lesson 136 in your student manual. Complete all the practice activities while at your computer. Then complete the jobs that follow.

SPREADSHEET APPLICATIONS

ACTIVITY 41
Spreadsheet 34

Create a new spreadsheet and save it as SS34. The follow these steps:

1. Type the data as shown in the illustration, using Copy and Paste where applicable.
2. Insert 3 blank rows at row 1.
3. In cell A1, type the label *Proposed Work Schedule for Carlton, Inc.*
4. In cell A2, type *Prepared by* followed by your name.
5. Save your changes and close the file.

LESSON 136

TEACH

Activity C. Demonstrate how *fill series* is different from *fill down* and *fill right*. For example, if you type April in cell A1 and you use the *fill series* command to fill the next four cells in the column, May will appear in A2, June in A3, and July in A4. If you use *fill down*, April will appear in all four cells. Similarly, if you type 200 in cell A15 and you use the fill series command to fill the next four cells in the row, 201 will appear in B15, 202 in C15, and 203 in D15. If you use fill right, 200 will appear in all four cells.

Activity D. Have students turn to Lesson 136 in their Student Manual and read the explanation for the software they are using. Then have them complete the practice activities that follow.

STUDENT MANUAL
Be sure students turn to the correct lesson in their Student Manual.

Activity 41. Make sure students insert three rows at the top of the spreadsheet. When they finish this activity, the third row should be blank.

Multiple Learning Styles

Have students make up flash cards of different formatting skills and formulas. Suggest they put these inside their books or lockers, and in other places they frequently look. When they see the card, they are to read it aloud, then close their eyes and repeat the information.

SCHOOL TO CAREER

Invite someone from your metropolitan newspaper to speak about newspaper careers, including support staff, sales staff, and marketing personnel, as well as journalists. Or have the local community editor speak about the newspaper industry in suburban or rural settings.

TEACH

Activity 42. An illustration of the finished spreadsheet appears in the Textbook Production Solutions book.

PORTFOLIO *Activity*

If students' portfolio goals include showcasing their best work, they may want to include a spreadsheet from this lesson. Encourage students to evaluate their work and include comments in their portfolio.

	A	B	C	D	E	F	G
1		January	February				
2							
3	Monday	8 a.m.-5 p.m.	8 a.m.-5 p.m.		7 a.m.-4 p.m.	7 a.m.-4 p.m.	7 a.m.-6 p.m.
4	Tuesday	8 a.m.-5 p.m.	8 a.m.-5 p.m.		7 a.m.-4 p.m.	7 a.m.-4 p.m.	7 a.m.-6 p.m
5							
6							
7							
8		Closed					Closed

ACTIVITY 42
Spreadsheet 35

Open the file SS34, save the file as SS35, and do the following:

1. Complete the months through June in column G.
2. Complete the days through Sunday in row 12.
3. Use Fill Down or Copy and Paste to copy cells B6 through C7 to B8 through C10.
4. Use Fill Right to copy cell range C6 through C10 to D6 through D10.
5. Use Fill Down to copy cells E6 through F7 to E8 through F10.
6. Use Fill Down to copy cells G6 through G7 to G8 through G9.
7. Use Fill Right to copy cell B11 to C11 through G11 and to B10 through G10.
8. Use Fill Down to copy cell range B11 through G11 to B12 through G12.
9. Bold and center the names of the months.
10. Bold the names of the days.
11. Select cell range A6 through G12 and automatically widen the columns.
12. Change cells A1 and A2 to 12-point bold and center each line above the block A1 through G1 and A2 through G2.
13. Shade cell range A1 through G2 and add a line at the bottom of cell range A2 through G2.
14. Shade cell ranges B3 through B12; D3 through D12; and F3 through F12.
15. Place a border around cell range A1 through G12.
16. Save your changes and close the file.

JOURNAL ENTRY

Have students write about the traits they dislike about themselves. Allow about five minutes. Then have students write another entry about how these traits can be transformed into useful traits.

ACTIVITY 43
Spreadsheet 36

Create a new spreadsheet and save it as SS36.

1. Type the data as shown in the illustration.
2. Extend the numbers in cells B4 and C4 to M4. The last number should be *12*.
3. Bold the numbers.
4. Extend the numbers in cells A5 and A6 to A16. The last number should be *12*.
5. Bold the numbers.
6. Extend the numbers in cells B5 through C6 to D5 through M6.
7. Extend the numbers in cells B5 through M6 to B7 through M16. The number in M16 should be *144*.
8. Change cell A1 to 16-point bold.
9. Change cell A2 to 12-point bold.
10. Center cells A1 through A2 across the spreadsheet.
11. Shade cells B4 through M4 and A5 through A16.
12. Select cell range B5 through M16. Place a thin-line border around each cell.
13. Place a heavy-line border around the entire spreadsheet.
14. Change to landscape orientation.
15. If your teacher has given you instructions on how to print, print the spreadsheet. Otherwise, save your changes and close the file.

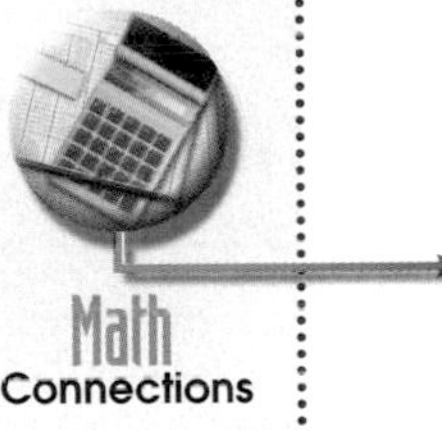

Math Connections

	A	B	C
1	Multiplication Tables		
2	Prepared by Your Name		
3			
4		1	2
5	1	1	2
6	2	2	4

COMMUNICATION FOCUS

Make a note in your journal to write a paragraph about the meaning of different expressions such as, "The grass is greener on the other side of the fence." What would this expression mean to a student from another country?

LESSON 136

TEACH

Activity 43. Have different students read aloud the steps for this activity. Stop after each step to make sure all students understand the directions.

ASSESS

- Check to see if students are increasing their word a minute speeds as they complete each 30-second timing.
- Make sure students are able to use the Fill Right, Fill Down, and Fill Series spreadsheet features.
- As students begin working with the spreadsheets, walk around the room and provide assistance to individual students as needed.
- After students finish each activity, have them view their work on the screen to see if they made any errors. If errors were made, have students edit their work and make corrections.

CLOSE

If students do not finish the spreadsheets during the class period, make sure they save their work so that they can edit it the next time this class meets.

Remind students to clean up their workstation when they leave.

Teacher Notes

LESSON 137

FOCUS

- Apply the Language Link rules for colons, dashes, and periods.
- Use 5-minute timings to build speed.
- Learn a spreadsheet feature: Bar Charts.
- Create a bar chart using spreadsheet information.

BELLRINGER

As soon as students arrive at their workstations and log in, have them type the Warmup. Go over the purpose of each line as shown to the left of the copy.

TEACH

Activity B. Point out the Language Link rules for using colons, dashes, and periods. Go over each rule separately, then have students complete lines 5–10.

Solutions: Her birthday present—a World Atlas—was finally delivered.

Since you are going to the pharmacy, will you buy vitamins.

Will you please send Guy your resume by e-mail before 11 a.m. today.

Several brands of soaps are on sale: Zest, Dial, and Ivory.

The radio station—not my favorite—was giving the weather.

Living in the country has advantages—quiet, calm, and tranquil days.

LESSON 137

SPREADSHEETS: CREATING BAR CHARTS

OBJECTIVES:

- Learn about colons, dashes, and periods with polite requests.
- Learn to create a bar chart.
- Type 40/5'/5e.

A. WARMUP

Type each line 2 times.

Speed	1 A friend would like to go to the school play with me later.
Accuracy	2 The banquet speaker, James Carvings, analyzed a few hoaxes.
Language Link	3 The flight attendant got huge, soft pillows for her and me.
Numbers/Symbols	4 Flight #1389 arrived late--7 p.m. (It was due at 6:45 p.m.)
	| 1 | 2 | 3 | 4 | 5 | 6 | 7 | 8 | 9 | 10 | 11 | 12

LANGUAGE LINK

B. COLONS, DASHES, AND PERIODS

Study the rules and examples that follow. Then edit lines 5–10 to correct any errors in the use of colons, dashes, and periods.

Rule 40: Use a colon to introduce explanatory material that follows an independent clause. (An **independent clause** is one that can stand alone as a complete sentence.)

The computer satisfies three criteria: speed, cost, and power.

There are many fine poets: Shelley, Keats, and Frost.

RESOURCES

 Lesson Plan 137

 Courseware Lesson 137

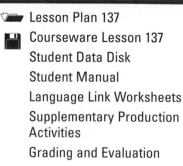

Student Data Disk

Student Manual

Language Link Worksheets

Supplementary Production Activities

Grading and Evaluation

Rule 41: Use a dash instead of a comma, semicolon, colon, or parentheses when you want to convey a more forceful separation of words within a sentence.

At the meeting, the speakers—and topics—were superb.

The icy road—slippery as a fish—was a hazard.

Rule 42: Use a period at the end of a sentence that is a polite request. (Consider a sentence a polite request if you expect the reader to act or do as you ask rather than give you a yes- or no-answer.)

Will you please fax us a copy of the insurance policy today.

Will you please close the door before you are seated.

```
5  Her birthday present a World Atlas was finally delivered.
6  Since you are going to the pharmacy, will you buy vitamins.
7  Will you please send Guy your resume by e-mail before 11 a.m.
   today?
8  Several brands of soaps are on sale Zest, Dial, and Ivory.
9  The radio station not my favorite was giving the weather.
10 Living in the country has advantages quiet, calm, and tranquil
   days.
```

SOCIAL STUDIES CONNECTIONS

President Andrew Jackson was the first U.S. president to become a victim of an assassination attempt. Luckily, the guns fired by Richard Lawrence misfired and the President was not injured.

SKILLBUILDING

C. Preview Practice

Type each line 2 times as a preview to the timings that follow.

```
11 slow Dozens textile borrowed equipment financial Depression
12 layoffs markets lumber demand crash grew main cars fail pay
```


LESSON 137

TEACH

Activity C. Point out that words in the Preview Practice are used in the timing that follows.

JOURNAL ENTRY

Have students write about a favorite gift they received. They are to tell what the gift is, the reason they received the gift (such as a birthday), who gave them the gift, and why this is a favorite gift.

TEACH

Activity D. Remind students that they should try to improve speed with each 5-minute timing. The goal for these timings is to type 40 words a minute for 5 minutes with no more than 5 errors.

Activity E. Explain to students that bar charts are often used to show relationships between fixed groups of data or to compare or contrast two sets of data.

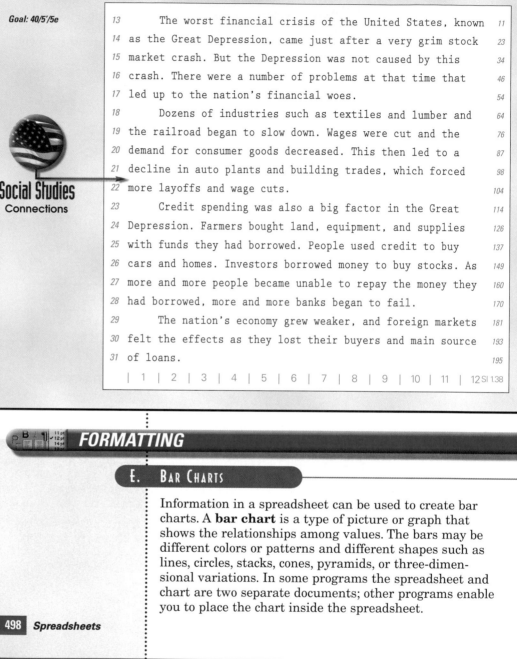

D. 5-Minute Timings

Take two 5-minute timings on the paragraphs. Note your speed and errors.

Goal: 40/5'/5e

Social Studies Connections

```
     The worst financial crisis of the United States, known   11
as the Great Depression, came just after a very grim stock    23
market crash. But the Depression was not caused by this       34
crash. There were a number of problems at that time that      46
led up to the nation's financial woes.                        54
     Dozens of industries such as textiles and lumber and     64
the railroad began to slow down. Wages were cut and the       76
demand for consumer goods decreased. This then led to a       87
decline in auto plants and building trades, which forced      98
more layoffs and wage cuts.                                  104
     Credit spending was also a big factor in the Great      114
Depression. Farmers bought land, equipment, and supplies     126
with funds they had borrowed. People used credit to buy      137
cars and homes. Investors borrowed money to buy stocks. As   149
more and more people became unable to repay the money they  160
had borrowed, more and more banks began to fail.             170
     The nation's economy grew weaker, and foreign markets   181
felt the effects as they lost their buyers and main source   193
of loans.                                                    195
 | 1 | 2 | 3 | 4 | 5 | 6 | 7 | 8 | 9 | 10 | 11 | 12 SI 1.38
```

FORMATTING

E. Bar Charts

Information in a spreadsheet can be used to create bar charts. A **bar chart** is a type of picture or graph that shows the relationships among values. The bars may be different colors or patterns and different shapes such as lines, circles, stacks, cones, pyramids, or three-dimensional variations. In some programs the spreadsheet and chart are two separate documents; other programs enable you to place the chart inside the spreadsheet.

Math Connections

Have students locate interesting charts in newspapers and magazines and bring them to class. Students should type a short report about the chart. Then have several students give a two-minute oral report that tells what their chart is about.

A bar chart uses vertical or horizontal bars to represent the values in the spreadsheet. In the illustration, the **Y axis,** or vertical scale, displays the values from the spreadsheet, which range from 0 to 6,000. The **X axis,** or horizontal scale, displays the labels or names of the schools. The legend on the right identifies the data being charted through the use of color or shading. This chart makes it very easy to see the enrollment changes in each school over a three-year period.

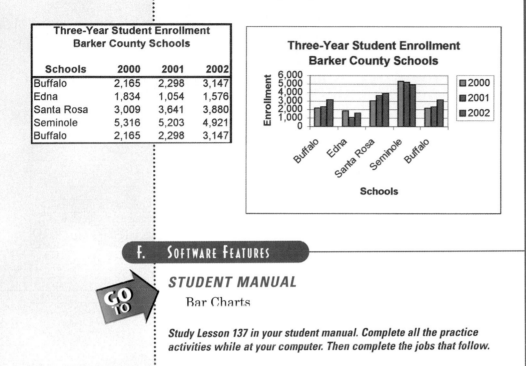

Three-Year Student Enrollment
Barker County Schools

Schools	2000	2001	2002
Buffalo	2,165	2,298	3,147
Edna	1,834	1,054	1,576
Santa Rosa	3,009	3,641	3,880
Seminole	5,316	5,203	4,921
Buffalo	2,165	2,298	3,147

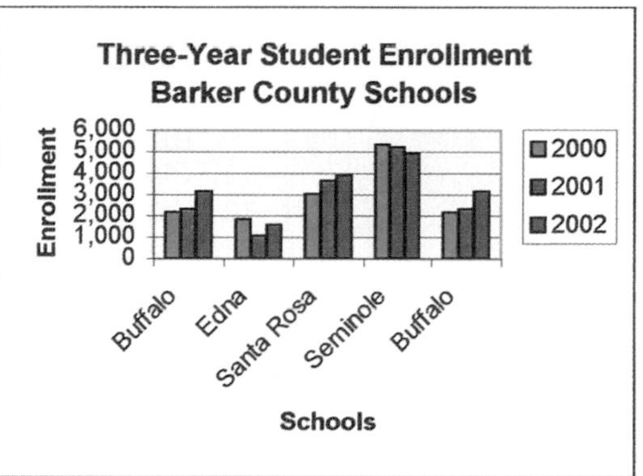

F. Software Features

STUDENT MANUAL

Bar Charts

Study Lesson 137 in your student manual. Complete all the practice activities while at your computer. Then complete the jobs that follow.

SPREADSHEET APPLICATIONS

ACTIVITY 44

Spreadsheet 37

Create a new spreadsheet, and save it as SS37.

1. Type the data as shown in the illustration on the next page. Enter the dates in cells C6 and D6 as labels. To do this, type an apostrophe before the date (*'June 5*). The apostrophe indicates that the value is to be treated like a label; it will not be visible in the cell after you press ENTER.

TEACH

Activity F. Have students turn to Lesson 137 in their Student Manual and read the explanation for the software they are using. Then have them complete the practice activities that follow.

STUDENT MANUAL

Be sure students turn to the correct lesson in their Student Manual.

Activity 44. An illustration of the finished spreadsheet appears in Textbook Production Solutions book.

Illustration

Show the original spreadsheet and the bar graph created from that spreadsheet.

FACT FILE

In July 1998, the United States Postal Service began selling a 32-cent commemorative postage stamp for 40 cents. Within two months more than 33 million stamps had been sold. Ask students why anyone would spend more for a postage stamp than they had to. (The 8¢ difference goes to breast cancer research.)

TEACH

Illustration
This illustration should be used to complete Activity 44.

PORTFOLIO *Activity*

If students' portfolio goals include demonstrating specific skills, they may want to include one or more of the bar charts from this lesson. Encourage students to evaluate their work and include comments in their portfolio.

2. Bold cell range A1 through D6.
3. Center cells A1 through A3 across the spreadsheet.
4. Center cells A5 through D6.
5. Automatically change the column width in cell range A5 through D12.
6. Place a border under A6 through D6.
7. Format all numbers to have commas and no decimal places.
8. Sort cell ranges A7 through D12 to alphabetize the park names in ascending order (A–Z).
9. Insert a blank row 12. Type the following information beginning in cell A12: *The Ball Park; 48100; 43917; 34866.*
10. Shade the odd-numbered rows beginning with row 7 through row 13.
11. Place a border around cell range A1-D13.
12. Save your changes and close the file.

	A	B	C	D
1	Baseball Game Attendance			
2	June 5-6, {year}			
3	Prepared by Your Name			
4				
5		Stadium	Attendance	Attendance
6	Park	Capacity	June 5	June 6
7	Shea Stadium	55600	15872	53210
8	Fenway Park	33870	20187	18992
9	Wrigley Field	38760	17438	38760
10	Dodger Stadium	56000	55110	30031
11	Jacobs Field	42400	42310	22764
12	Anaheim Stadium	64590	27321	58542

***inter*NET ACTIVITY**

Have students create a spreadsheet using Internet information they obtained on stadiums around the country. Have them include the stadium name, type of sports played, events being held, and whether the stadium is home to a professional sports team.

ACTIVITY 45
Spreadsheet 38

Open the file SS37, save it as SS38, and create a chart by following these steps:

1. Select cell range A6 through D13 and create a vertical bar chart.
2. Type in bold the title *Baseball Game Attendance.*
3. Type in bold the subtitle *June 5–6, [Year].*
4. Type the Y-axis label *Attendance.*
5. Type the X-axis label *Stadiums.*
6. Add the legend labels *Capacity; June 5; June 6.*
7. Place the chart to the right of the spreadsheet if your software has that capability. Otherwise, the spreadsheet and chart will be two separate documents.
8. Preview the file in landscape orientation. You may need to adjust the size of the chart or make changes in the font sizes so that all titles and labels can be read. For example, the font size of the stadium names may need to be smaller.
9. If your teacher has given you instructions to print, print the chart. Otherwise, save your changes and close the file.

*inter*NET CONNECTION

Search the Internet for other statistics about the capacity of stadiums around the country. Search for information on what kinds of events the stadiums are used for and whether any are home to professional sports teams. Share your findings with the class.

Teacher Notes

LESSON 137

TEACH

Activity 45. An illustration of the finished chart appears in the Textbook Production Solutions book.

ASSESS

- Watch students as they complete the Language Link activity to see if they are able to apply the rules for colons, dashes, and periods correctly.
- Check to see if students are increasing their word a minute speeds as they complete each 5-minute timing.
- Make sure students are able to create bar charts.
- As students begin working with the spreadsheet and bar chart, walk around the room and provide assistance to individual students as needed.
- After students finish each activity, have them view their work on the screen to see if they made any errors. If errors were made, have students edit their work and make corrections.

CLOSE

If students do not finish the activities during the class period, make sure they save their work so that they can complete it the next time this class meets.

Remind students to clean up their workstation when they leave.

LESSON 138

FOCUS

- Use 30-Second Timings to increase speed.
- Learn a spreadsheet feature: Pie Charts.
- Create a pie chart using spreadsheet information.

BELLRINGER

As soon as students arrive at their workstations and log in, have them type the Warmup. Go over the purpose of each line as shown to the left of the copy.

TEACH

Activity B. Go over with students the routine for the 30-second timings.

Spreadsheets: Creating Pie Charts

OBJECTIVES:

- Improve keyboarding skills.
- Create pie charts.

A. Warmup

Type each line 2 times.

```
Speed             1 The boy ran for the toys as fast as his short legs let him.
Accuracy          2 Squeeze that liquid gel into an opaque jar sealed with wax.
Language Link     3 The computer now works--she finally had it repaired Friday.
Numbers/Symbols   4 Horses #29, #35, #17, and #48 are racing at 2:30 Wednesday.
                    | 1 | 2 | 3 | 4 | 5 | 6 | 7 | 8 | 9 | 10 | 11 | 12
```

SKILLBUILDING

B. 30-Second Timings

Take two 30-second timings on lines 5–6. Then take two 30-second timings on lines 7–8. Try to increase your speed on each paragraph.

```
5      Some kinds of birds sleep with one half of their brain  11
6 at a time, with one eye closed and one open to spy enemies.  23

7      Dolphins sleep with only half their brains, also. They  11
8 need to remember to surface for air since they are mammals.  23
  | 1 | 2 | 3 | 4 | 5 | 6 | 7 | 8 | 9 | 10 | 11 | 12
```

FACT FILE

Workers in the laboratories of Nippon Telephone and Telegraph Corp. have invented a microchip capable of identifying fingerprints. This chip can identify a fingerprint in a half second with 99 percent accuracy.

RESOURCES

 Lesson Plan 138

 Courseware Lesson 138

Student Data Disk

Student Manual

Supplementary Production Activities

Multicultural Activities

C. Creating Pie Charts

A **pie chart** uses a circle divided into pieces or slices to visually show the relationship among values in a spreadsheet. Each piece of the pie represents one of the values in the spreadsheet; the whole circle represents the total. Pie charts are especially appropriate for displaying percentages of a whole, and the software will automatically calculate the percentages for you. In the following illustration, each slice of the pie chart represents a percentage of the total acres used for planting the top five crops in Texas. The labels and percentages make it easy to see which are the largest crops.

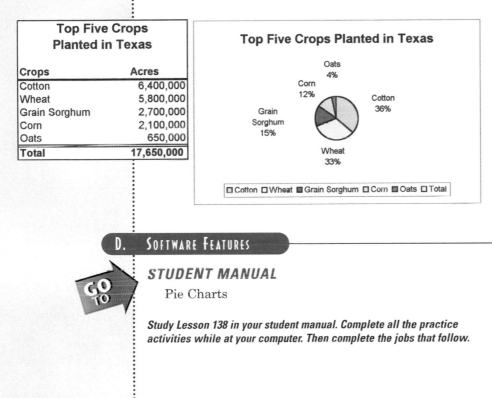

Top Five Crops Planted in Texas

Crops	Acres
Cotton	6,400,000
Wheat	5,800,000
Grain Sorghum	2,700,000
Corn	2,100,000
Oats	650,000
Total	**17,650,000**

Top Five Crops Planted in Texas

Oats 4%

Corn 12%

Cotton 36%

Grain Sorghum 15%

Wheat 33%

□ Cotton □ Wheat ■ Grain Sorghum □ Corn ■ Oats □ Total

D. Software Features

STUDENT MANUAL

Pie Charts

Study Lesson 138 in your student manual. Complete all the practice activities while at your computer. Then complete the jobs that follow.

TEACH

Activity C. Ask students how they might use a pie chart in their lives, both personal and in business. Explain that pie charts are used to show the relationships between parts and a whole.

Illustration

The illustration shows the data in the chart on the left restated as the pie chart on the right.

Activity D. Have students turn to Lesson 138 in their Student Manual and read the explanation for the software they are using. Then have them complete the practice activities that follow.

STUDENT MANUAL

Be sure students turn to the correct lesson in their Student Manual.

Activity 46. An illustration of the finished spreadsheet appears in the Textbook Production Solutions book.

Art Connections

Have students use the computer to create different pie charts using different sizes of charts and different-size sections within the charts. Also use a variety of colors. Use all the pie charts to create a colorful bulletin board collage.

Out-of-Class Activity

Provide students with colorful sheets of paper. Have students collect different pie charts that they cut out of newspapers and magazines. Then have them type the name and purpose of the chart and glue these along with the pie chart to a sheet of colorful paper. Hang these around the room.

TEACH

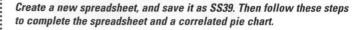

Activity 47. An illustration of the finished chart appears in the Textbook Production Solutions book.

PORTFOLIO *Activity*

If students' portfolio goals include demonstrating specific skills, they may want to include at least one chart from this lesson. Encourage students to evaluate their work and include comments in their portfolio.

SPREADSHEET APPLICATIONS

ACTIVITY 46

Spreadsheet 39

Math Connections

Create a new spreadsheet, and save it as SS39. Then follow these steps to complete the spreadsheet and a correlated pie chart.

1. Type the data as shown in the illustration.
2. Bold cells A1 through B4.
3. Align cell B4 at the right.
4. Adjust column A to be 30 points wide.
5. Center cells A1 through A2 across the spreadsheet.
6. Sort cells A5 through B10 alphabetically in ascending order (A–Z).
7. Shade rows 6, 8, and 10.
8. Place 1 line under row 4.
9. Place an outline border around cell range A1 through B10.
10. Save your changes and close the file.

MATH CONNECTION

Using the data from Spreadsheet 39, calculate the amount of snow in feet rather than inches.

	A	B	C
1	Annual Snowfall at Popular Ski Resorts		
2	Prepared by Your Name		
3			
4	Resort	Inches	
5	Squaw Valley, Calif.	450	
6	Taos, N.M.	312	
7	Aspen, Colo.	400	
8	Jackson Hole, Wyo.	400	
9	Snowbird, Utah	500	
10	Sun Valley, Idaho	220	

ACTIVITY 47

Spreadsheet 40

Open the file SS39, save it as SS40, and create a pie chart following these steps:

1. Select cell range A5 through B10, and create a pie chart similar to the illustration that appears earlier in this lesson. Note that your spreadsheet may not create a separate legend.
2. Type in bold the title *Annual Snowfall at Popular Ski Resorts.*
3. Type in bold the subtitle *Inches Per Year.*
4. Add the series labels as shown in cells A5 through A10. Have the actual values displayed on the chart instead of percentages.
5. Add a border around the chart.
6. Place the chart to the right of the spreadsheet if your software has that capability.

SCHOOL TO CAREER

On the board write the following career categories: manufacturing, service, health, and art. Students are to choose one of the categories and form a group to research five careers within the category. Then create a pie chart that shows the largest to the smallest growth potential in each career.

interNET ACTIVITY

Have students use the Internet for their research in the School to Career activity on this page. Students are to track their path and type a report that shows how they found the site of their research. They should also show the source of their research.

7. Change the page orientation to landscape and preview the document.
8. Adjust the size of the chart or make any other changes that are necessary so that all titles and labels can be read.
9. If your teacher has given you instructions for printing, print the spreadsheet. Otherwise, save your changes and close the file.

ACTIVITY 48
Spreadsheet 41

Open the file SS12, save it as SS41, and then follow these steps:

1. Delete rows 3 and 4.
2. Delete columns C, D, E, and F.
3. Change rows 1 and 2 to 10-point bold.
4. Adjust column A so that it is 20 points wide.
5. Align cell A4 at the left; align cell B4 at the right.
6. Place interior and exterior gridlines on cells A4 through B10.
7. Place a border around cell range A1 through B10.
8. Save your changes, and close the file.

ACTIVITY 49
Spreadsheet 42

Open the file SS41, save it as SS42, and create a pie chart following these steps:

1. Select cell range A6 through B10 and create a pie chart.
2. Type in bold the title *Size of Small Caribbean Islands*.
3. Type in bold the subtitle *In Square Miles*.
4. Add the series labels as shown in column A. Have the actual values displayed on the chart instead of percentages.
5. Add a border around the chart.
6. Place the chart to the right of the spreadsheet if your software has that capability.
7. Preview the file and make any necessary adjustments.
8. If your teacher has given you instructions for printing, print the spreadsheet. Otherwise, save your changes and close the file.

LESSON 138

TEACH

Activity 48. An illustration of the finished spreadsheet appears in the Textbook Production Solutions book.

Activity 49. An illustration of the finished spreadsheet and chart appears in the Textbook Production Solutions book.

ASSESS

- Make sure students are able to use the Pie Charts spreadsheet feature.
- As students begin working with the spreadsheet and pie chart, walk around the room and provide assistance to individual students as needed.
- After students finish each activity, have them view their work on the screen to see if they made any errors. If errors were made, have students edit their work and make corrections.

CLOSE

If students do not finish the activities during the class period, make sure they save their work so that they can edit it the next time this class meets.

Remind students to clean up their workstation when they leave.

Teacher Notes

LESSON 139

FOCUS

- Apply the Language Link rule for abbreviations.
- Use 30-second timings to build speed.
- Practice spreadsheet skills.

BELLRINGER

As soon as students arrive at their workstations and log in, have them type the Warmup. Go over the purpose of each line as shown to the left of the copy.

TEACH

Activity B. Provide students with a list of common nouns and proper nouns to help them understand the differences. Go over the list in class. Remind them that common nouns, such as department (dept.) and package (pkg.) are not capitalized.

Solutions: The new company fleet cars are averaging about 21 miles per gallon.

The remaining men will be transferred in January to Athens, Georgia.

On Monday, the trustee and auditor will meet with the company president.

The new product package was colorful; the book was over 33 pages.

LESSON 139

SPREADSHEETS: REVIEW

OBJECTIVES:

- Learn abbreviation rules for common nouns.
- Improve keyboarding skills.
- Strengthen spreadsheet concepts.

A. WARMUP

Type each line 2 times.

Speed	1 Our school band played in the show for four years in a row.
Accuracy	2 Our squad was amazed that Xenia would quarrel with a judge.
Language Link	3 He enjoys three types of music: popular, country, and jazz.
Numbers/Symbols	4 My check on 11/30 for $279.81 should have been for $305.06.

LANGUAGE LINK

B. ABBREVIATIONS

Study the rule and examples that follow. Then edit lines 5–8 to correct any abbreviation errors.

Rule 43: In nontechnical writing, do not use abbreviations for common nouns (such as *dept.* or *pkg.*), compass points, and units of measure, or for the names of months, days of the week, cities, or states (except in addresses).

Our sales department will meet on Tuesday, March 7, in Tempe, Arizona.

5 The new co. fleet cars are averaging about 21 miles per gal.
6 The remaining men will be transferred in Jan. to Athens, Ga.
7 On Mon., the trustee and auditor will meet with the co. pres.
8 The new product pkg. was colorful; the book was over 33 pgs.

RESOURCES

Lesson Plan 139

Courseware Lesson 139
Student Data Disk
Student Manual
Language Link Worksheets
Grading and Evaluation

SKILLBUILDING

C. 30-Second Timings

Take two 30-second timings on lines 9–10. Then take two 30-second timings on lines 11–12. Try to increase your speed on each paragraph.

```
 9      One of the best ways to learn from past mistakes is to   11
10 study what has taken place in the journal of man's history.   23

11      It is a wise person who can learn from the mistakes of   11
12 others and not have to learn those lessons from experience.   23
    | 1 | 2 | 3 | 4 | 5 | 6 | 7 | 8 | 9 | 10 | 11 | 12
```

SPREADSHEET APPLICATIONS

ACTIVITY 50

Spreadsheet 43

Create a new spreadsheet, and save it as SS43. Then complete the following steps:

1. Enter the data as shown in the illustration.
2. Insert blank rows 3, 4, and 5.
3. Center and type in bold the following column headings beginning in cell A4: *Composer, Life Span, Country, Music, Specialty.*
4. Copy the following cells to these locations: C7 to C12 and C13; C8 to C14; D7 to D8, D12, and D13; E9 to E6, E10, E11, and E13; E8 to E14.
5. Select cells A6 through E14, and sort column B in descending order.
6. Select cells A4 through E14 and automatically widen the columns.
7. Change the following fonts: cell A1 to 14-point bold; cell A2 to 12-point bold.
8. Center cells A1 and A2 across the spreadsheet.
9. Shade cells A1 through E5, and place a line under row 5.
10. Shade the odd rows beginning with row 7.
11. Place a border around the spreadsheet and interior gridlines in A6 through E14.
12. Preview the spreadsheet; then change the orientation to landscape.
13. If your instructor has given you instructions for printing, print the spreadsheet. Otherwise, save your changes and close the file.

FACT FILE

As early as 1914, a group of songwriters led by Victor Herbert met in New York. They established the American Society of Composers, Authors, and Publishers (ASCAP). This society protects the copyrighted musical compositions of its members.

Unit 7 Lesson 139 **507**

TEACH

Activity C. Remind students that the goal for 30-second timings is improved speed with each of the timings.

Activity 50. An illustration of the finished spreadsheet appears in the Textbook Production Solutions book.

Art Connections

Have students make a list of their ten favorite musicians and create a spreadsheet like the one on page 516. Categories are to be: number, name, date of birth, date of death, country of origin, type of music, and voice or name of instrument.

TEACH

Activity 51. An illustration of the finished spreadsheet appears in the Textbook Production Solutions book.

PORTFOLIO *Activity*

If students' portfolio goals include showcasing their best work, they may want to include at least one spreadsheet from this lesson. Encourage students to evaluate their work and include comments in their portfolio.

	A	B	C	D	E
1	Great Music Composers				
2	Prepared by Your Name				
3	Tchaikovsky, Piotr Ilych	1840–1893	Russia	Russian Folk Songs	
4	Haydn, Franz Joseph	1732–1809	Austria	Classical	Voice
5	Beethoven, Ludwig van	1770–1827	Germany		Organ
6	Chopin, Frederic	1810–1849	Poland	Polish Dances	Piano
7	Debussy, Claude	1862–1918	France	Impressionism	
8	Gershwin, George	1898–1937	America	Musical Comedy	
9	Mozart, Wolfgang Amadeus	1756–1791			Violin
10	Schubert, Franz	1797–1828			
11	Bach, Johann Sebastian	1685–1750		Baroque	

ACTIVITY 51
Spreadsheet 44

Create a new spreadsheet and save it as SS44. Then complete the following steps:

1. Enter the data as shown in the illustration.
2. Insert blank rows 3, 6, 12, and 14.
3. Make the following font changes: cell A1, 16-point; cell A2, 12-point italic.
4. Move cell range C4 through C5 to F4 through F5.
5. Move cell range D4 through F11 to C4 through E11.
6. Italicize cell range A4 through E5, and align cell range C4 through E5 at the right.
7. Format the date in cell A7 to *MM/DD/YYYY*.
8. Automatically set the width of columns A4 through E11.
9. Fill the following: from cell A7, fill down through cell A11. The dates should increase by 1. From cell B7, fill down through B11; from cells D7 through D8, fill down through cell D11.
10. In cell E7, enter a formula to multiply C7 by D7; then fill down through cell E11.
11. In cell C13, use SUM to add cell range C7 through C11; then copy the formula to cell E13.
12. In cell E15, enter a formula to subtract E13 from C13.
13. Format numbers as follows: in columns C and E, format numbers for 2 decimal places; in column D, format numbers as percentages with no decimal places.

JOURNAL ENTRY

Have students write about the type of music they like. Include information on why they like this music and why they like the musicians they chose in the Art Connections activity. Read a few entries in class.

14. Place a double line under cell range A3 through E3 and a single line under cell range A5 through E5.
15. Shade rows 7, 9, and 11.
16. Add a border around cell range A15 through E15, and bold the cells.
17. If your instructor has given you instructions for printing, print the spreadsheet. Otherwise, save your changes and close the file.

	A	B	C	D	E
1	Comprehensive Healthcare				
2	Statement of Benefits for Your Name				
3			Benefits	Amount	Payment
4	Dates	Procedures	Paid	Submitted	Rate
5	1/12	X-Ray/Testing		187	0.8
6				96	0.8
7				242	
8				23	
9				117	
10	Totals				
11	Patient's Responsibility				

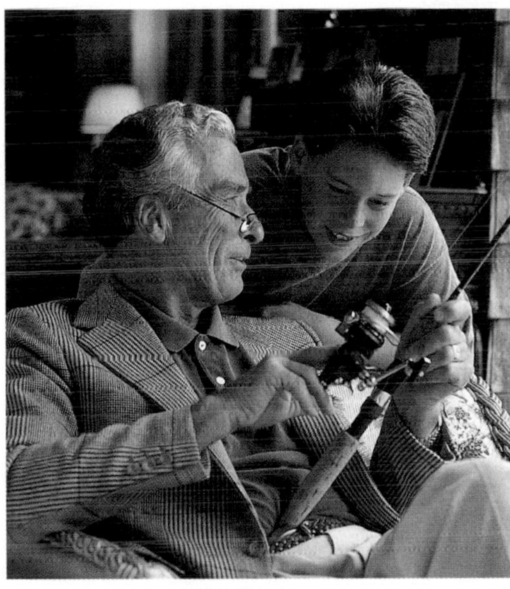

ASSESS

- Watch students as they complete the Language Link activity to see if they are able to apply the rule for abbreviations correctly.
- Check to see if students are increasing their word a minute speeds as they complete the 30-second timings.
- As students begin working with the spreadsheets, walk around the room and provide assistance to individual students as needed.
- After students finish each activity, have them view their work on the screen to see if they made any errors. If errors were made, have students edit their work and make corrections.

CLOSE

If students do not finish the activities during the class period, make sure they save their work so that they can edit it the next time this class meets.

Remind students to clean up their workstation when they leave.

Teacher Notes

LESSON 140

FOCUS

- Use a Pretest/Practice/Posttest routine to build speed and accuracy.
- Practice spreadsheet skills.

BELLRINGER

As soon as students arrive at their workstations and log in, have them type the Warmup. Go over the purpose of each line as shown to the left of the copy.

TEACH

Activity B. Remind students they should improve both their speed and accuracy from the Pretest to the Posttest.

LESSON 140

SPREADSHEETS: REVIEW

OBJECTIVES:

- Improve keyboarding skills.
- Reinforce skill on up and down reaches.
- Strengthen spreadsheet concepts.

A. WARMUP

Type each line 2 times.

Speed	1	Lee felt he could read five books by the end of this month.
Accuracy	2	Five or six dozen clubs may sign up with Karl for jonquils.
Language Link	3	Will you please make 200 copies of the agenda for tomorrow.
Numbers/Symbols	4	Within 5% error, I can guess the prices of #32 and #48 now.

| 1 | 2 | 3 | 4 | 5 | 6 | 7 | 8 | 9 | 10 | 11 | 12

FACT FILE

One proven relaxation exercise is to visualize being on vacation in the mountains or at the beach. Listening to the sound of water is very soothing.

SKILLBUILDING

B. PRETEST

Take a 1-minute timing on the paragraph. Note your speed and errors.

5 You cannot build good skills while typing if you don't 11
6 practice various reaches on the keyboard. Practice all the 23
7 reaches that are especially difficult for you while you are 35
8 taking your timings. 40

| 1 | 2 | 3 | 4 | 5 | 6 | 7 | 8 | 9 | 10 | 11 | 12

RESOURCES

 Lesson Plan 140
 Courseware Lesson 140
Student Data Disk
Student Manual
Reteaching and Reinforcement
Unit 7 Tests
Grading and Evaluation

C. PRACTICE

SPEED: ***If you made 2 or fewer errors on the Pretest, type lines 9–12 two times each.***

ACCURACY: ***If you made more than 2 errors on the Pretest, type lines 9–12 as a group two times. Then type lines 13–16 as a group two times.***

Up Reaches

```
 9 away card date earn fear fold argue baked cargo daily early
10 gift hold jury lets made nest films grade hours large meant
11 page plus rise seat tape vary plead rules stand theft voted
12 jump pink join pump limp join polka feats mumps kilts mints
```

Down Reaches

```
13 avid balk cage disc each jobs about badly cakes coach frank
14 knee lack palm rack slab taxi packs reach score snack teach
15 vary axle back calm cars sack value bales cable heavy scope
16 vice face save vase bear beat civic valor baker print copes
```

D. POSTTEST

Repeat the Pretest. Compare your Posttest results with your Pretest results.

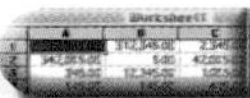

SPREADSHEET APPLICATIONS

ACTIVITY 52

Spreadsheet 45

Create a new spreadsheet, and save it as SS45.

1. Enter the data as shown in the illustration. Do not enter the commas in the numbers.
2. Format the spreadsheet in a style similar to the illustration.
3. Use SUM and Fill Right to enter totals in cells B10 through E10.
4. Select cell range A5 through E8, and sort by column B in descending order.
5. Save your changes and close the file.

Appliance Bid Sheet for Your Name
Young Quality Construction

Appliances	**TJ's Place**	**Home Store**	**Winston's**	**Kitchens**
Cooktop	429.95	339.95	549.99	469.95
Double Oven	1,095.99	1,047.89	1,337.00	1,217.79
Dishwasher	419.99	359.00	479.00	439.00
Microwave	169.99	219.00	199.00	159.00
Totals				

TEACH

Activities C–D. Remind students they should improve both their speed and accuracy from the Pretest to the Posttest.

PRETEST/PRACTICE/POSTTEST

The ***Pretest/Practice/Posttest*** routines are designed to improve speed or accuracy.

- The ***Pretest*** identifies students' speed or accuracy needs.
- The ***Practice*** provides a variety of improvement drills.
- The ***Posttest*** (a repeat of the Pretest) measures improvement.

Activity 52. An illustration of the finished spreadsheet appears in the Textbook Production Solutions book.

FACT FILE

Before computers, punched data cards were used to give instructions to machines. Have students research the history of punch cards, including information on the Jacquard loom and what it, a weaving machine, and Charles Babbage's mechanical calculating machines have to do with computers.

TEACH

Activity 53. An illustration of the finished spreadsheet appears in the Textbook Production Solutions book.

Activity 54. An illustration of the finished spreadsheet appears in the Textbook Production Solutions book.

ACTIVITY 53
Spreadsheet 46

Open the file SS45, save it as SS46, and create a chart following these steps:

1. Select cell range A4 through E8 and create a horizontal bar chart.
2. Type in bold the title *Appliance Bids.*
3. Type the labels for each appliance and each store.
4. Be sure the chart is easy to understand; a separate legend is optional.
5. Add a border and gridlines.
6. Preview the spreadsheet and check for any errors.
7. If your teacher has given you instructions for printing, print the spreadsheet. Otherwise, save your changes and close the file.

ACTIVITY 54
Spreadsheet 47

Create a new spreadsheet and save it as SS47.

1. Enter the data as shown in the illustration that follows. Remember *not* to enter commas in the numbers.
2. Format the spreadsheet in a style similar to the illustration.
3. Select cell range A5 through B11, and sort by column A in ascending order.
4. Save your changes and close the file.

A Sample of Occupational Earnings	
Occupations	*Salaries*
Lawyer	114,000
Air Traffic Controller	63,000
Secretary	25,750
Teacher	32,000
Computer Programmer	78,000
US Vice President	171,500
Registered Nurse	48,000

interNET ACTIVITY

Have each student choose a city somewhere in the world they would like to visit. Have them use the Internet to research means of traveling to and within this city. Next, have students create a spreadsheet that includes means of travel, time, and fares.

ACTIVITY 55

Spreadsheet 48

Open the file SS47, save it as SS48, and create a pie chart by doing the following:

1. Select cell range A4 through B11, and create a pie chart.
2. Type in bold the title *A Sample of Occupational Earnings.*
3. Add a border to the chart.
4. Display a percentage in each piece of the chart.
5. Select the slice of highest earnings and set it off from the rest of the chart.
6. Preview the chart and make any necessary changes.
7. If your teacher has given you instructions for printing, print the spreadsheet. Otherwise, save the changes and close the file.

*inter*NET CONNECTION

Make a list of three or four career choices in which you are interested. Search the Internet for information about the salary that you might expect from each of these career choices. Also, search for statistics on the availability of jobs in the careers you have chosen. Compare information with your classmates.

PORTFOLIO Activity

Choose one of the spreadsheets and one of the charts you have created in this unit. Print them and add them to your portfolio as a sample of your work.

LESSON 140

TEACH

Activity 55. An illustration of the finished spreadsheet appears in the Textbook Production Solutions book.

ASSESS

- Check to see if students show signs of improvement from the Pretest to the Posttest.
- As students begin working with the spreadsheets, walk around the room and provide assistance to individual students as needed.
- After students finish each activity, have them view their work on the screen to see if they made any errors. If errors were made, have students edit their work and make corrections.

CLOSE

If students do not finish the spreadsheets during the class period, make sure they save their work so that they can complete it the next time this class meets.

PORTFOLIO Activity

If students' portfolio goals include showcasing their best work, they may want to include at least one spreadsheet from this lesson. Encourage students to evaluate their work and include comments in their portfolio.

UNIT 8 ORGANIZER

DATABASES

Lesson	Focus	Special Features	Skillbuilding	Pretest/ Practice/ Posttest	Documents	GO TO Activities
141	Databases: Orientation	Language Link, pp. 516–517 Fact File, p. 517 Social Studies Connection, p. 518	p. 517			p. 518
142	Databases: Create Database Tables	Communication Focus, p. 519 Fact File, p. 520 Internet Connection, p. 521	p. 519		Database Table 1, p. 520 Database Table 2, p. 521	p. 520
143	Databases: Revise and Add Records	Language Link, p. 522 Fact File, pp. 524, 525	p. 523	p. 523	Database Table 1, p. 524 Database Table 3, pp. 524–525 Database Table 2, p. 525	p. 524
144	Databases: Rename, Add, and Position Fields	Social Studies Connection, p. 526 Journal Entry, p. 529	pp. 526–527		Database Table 2, p. 528 Database Table 3, pp. 528–529	p. 527
145	Databases: Monetary and Numeric Fields	Language Link, p. 530 Fact File, p. 530 Math Connection, p. 531 Portfolio Activity, p. 533	p. 531		Database Table 4, pp. 531–532 Database Table 5, p. 532 Database Table 5, p. 533	p. 531

UNIT 8 RESOURCE MANAGER

MULTIMEDIA
- Courseware: Lessons 141–150
- Student Data Disk
- Student Manual: Lessons 141–150

TEACHING TOOLS
- Lesson Plans: Lessons 141–150
- Block Scheduling Guide, Unit 8
- Language Link Worksheets: Lessons 141–150
- Multicultural Applications
- Academic Report Guide
- Solution Keys
- Cross-Curricular Activities: Lessons 141–150

RETEACHING/REINFORCEMENT
- Reteaching/Reinforcement Activities: Lessons 141–150
- Supplemental Production Activities: Lessons 141–150

ASSESSMENT and EVALUATION

Pretest/Practice/Posttest: pp. 523, 535
Portfolio Activity: pp. 533, 546, 559
Unit 8 Test
Timings: pp. 518, 527, 536, 545, 551
Production Jobs: Database Tables 1–6; Spreadsheet 49; Report 72
Grading and Evaluation

Electronic Teacher Classroom Resources

For your convenience, the teacher's materials are available on a CD-ROM. Having these resources available electronically enables you to print exactly what you need and revise materials as necessary.

Lesson	Focus	Special Features	Skillbuilding	Pretest/ Practice/ Posttest	Documents	GO TO Activities
146	Databases: Review	Science Connection, p. 534 Fact File, p. 537	pp. 535–536	p. 535	Database Table 3, pp. 537–538	
147	Databases: Sort and Query	Language Link, p. 539 Communication Focus, p. 540 Social Studies Connection, p. 543	p. 540		Database Table 3, pp. 541–543	p. 540
148	Databases: Reports	Social Studies Connection, p. 545 Portfolio Activity, p. 546	pp. 544–545		Database Table 4, p. 546	p. 545
149	Databases: Formulas	Language Link, p. 547	p. 548		Database Table 5, pp. 548–549	p. 548
150	Databases: Simulation	Internet Activity, pp. 550, 554 Portfolio Activity, p. 559	pp. 550–551		Spreadsheet 49, p. 552 Database Table 6, p. 552 Report 72, pp. 553–554	p. 551

SCANS Competencies in Glencoe Keyboarding with Computer Applications

Resources	Interpersonal Skills	Information	Systems	Technology
Throughout the course, students deal specifically with resources: allocating time for completing drills and documents, maintaining workstations, caring for computers and software.	Communication Focus, pp. 517, 520	Career Bit, p. 515 Fact File, pp. 517, 520, 524, 525, 530, 537 Internet Connection, pp. 521, 550, 554 Social Studies Connection, pp. 513, 526, 543, 545 Science Connection, p. 534 Math Connection, p. 531	Internet Connection, pp. 521, 550, 554	Lessons 121–140 Internet Connection, pp. 521, 550, 554

UNIT 8 DATABASES

Lessons 141–150

OBJECTIVES

- Demonstrate keyboarding speed and accuracy on straight copy with a goal of 40 words a minute for 5 minutes with 5 or fewer errors.
- Demonstrate the ability to create, navigate, and sort databases.
- Demonstrate the ability to create charts and tables and incorporate them into other applications.

INTRODUCING THE UNIT

Have different students read each of the objectives for Unit 8. Address each objective as it's read. Explain that the goal in this unit is to reach a typing speed of 40 words a minute for 5 minutes with 5 or fewer errors. Encourage students to believe this is an achievable goal.

Students will learn how to create, navigate, and sort databases. They also will learn how to create charts and tables and incorporate them into other applications.

FUN Facts

The estimated number of languages spoken in Africa ranges from 700 to 3,000. The most widely spoken languages in Africa are Arabic, Swahili, and Hausa. Each has more than 20 million speakers. Several of the languages are spoken by only a few thousand people. Only a few dozen languages have more than 1 million speakers. Very few African languages have written literature. Most have a long-standing tradition of oral storytelling.

COURSEWARE OVERVIEW

The courseware will automatically launch the available database program but will not put a KCA menu item on the menu bar. Therefore, show students how to use Alt + Tab to return to KCA or to click the KCA button on the status bar.

WORDS TO LEARN

database table
database table report
date fields
formulas
monetary fields
navigate
numeric fields
position fields
query
records
sort
windows

CAREER BIT

COMPOSER Composers create original music such as symphonies, operas, sonatas, or popular songs. They transcribe ideas into musical notations using harmony, rhythm, melody, and tonal structure. Many songwriters now compose and edit music using computers. Also, they may play the composition into the computer, which can record and play it back. Arrangers transcribe and adapt musical composition to a particular style for orchestras, bands, ballets, choral groups, or individuals. Components of music—including tempo, volume, and the mix of instruments needed—are arranged to express the composer's message. While some arrangers write directly into a musical composition, others use computer software to make changes. Compositions created with computer software can also be mailed electronically or placed on an Internet site.

515

WORDS TO LEARN

The terms in Words to Learn are defined in the Glossary at the back of the book. Ask students if they are familiar with any of the terms. Have them define the terms they know. Compare their definitions with those in the Glossary.

CAREER BIT

After students have read the information on composers in the Career Bit, have them brainstorm to create a list of people in related occupations with whom composers work. Write these occupations on the board. Ask the music teacher in your school or the music teacher of one of the students to speak to your class about careers in music and related to music. Make sure students type a list of questions ahead of time and also send a thank-you note to the speaker.

COURSEWARE OVERVIEW

Students are asked to print many of the database activities. If you choose not to have students print, you will need to check their work on screen after they complete each activity to ensure they have correctly followed the directions.

LESSON 141

FOCUS

- Apply the Language Link rules for abbreviations.
- Use Paced Practice 2-minute timing routines.
- Use 5-minute timings to build speed.
- Learn database features: Database Tables, Navigating Within a Database, Windows, and Selecting.

BELLRINGER

As soon as students arrive at their workstations and log in, have them type the Warmup. Go over the purpose of each line as shown to the left of the copy.

TEACH

Activity B. Point out the Language Link rules for abbreviations to students.

Solutions: The meeting has been changed to 1 p.m. because of room conflicts.

Auditors said sales were understated in the June e.o.m. statement.

She enlisted in the USMC after she received her Ph.D. degree.

His old research paper deals with the early history of NATO.

Denise said I should call about the paralegal position ASAP.

We have consulted with AAA about our upcoming European trip.

DATABASES: DATABASE ORIENTATION

OBJECTIVES:

- Learn rules of abbreviation.
- Improve keyboarding skill.
- Navigate within a database.
- Learn about database tables, windows, and selecting.
- Type 40/5'/5e.

A. WARMUP

Type each line 2 times.

Speed	1	She wanted low rates but did not want to lose any services.
Accuracy	2	I quickly explained that few big jobs involve many hazards.
Language Link	3	Ned knew that he would soon need to return his dad's tools.
Numbers/Symbols	4	Tell each student to get his/her parents/guardians on 9/17.

| 1 | 2 | 3 | 4 | 5 | 6 | 7 | 8 | 9 | 10 | 11 | 12

B. ABBREVIATIONS

Study the rules and examples that follow. Then edit lines 5–10 to correct any abbreviation errors.

Rule 44: In lowercase abbreviations made up of single initials, use a period after each initial but no internal spaces.

We will include several states in our tour (e.g., Maine, New Hampshire, and Vermont).

We will begin our travel at 8 a.m. so that we can see everything.

RESOURCES

 Lesson Plan 141

 Courseware Lesson 141

Student Data Disk

Student Manual

Language Link Worksheets

Multicultural Activities

Grading and Evaluation

COURSEWARE OVERVIEW

Students must close their database program by using File, Exit to return to KCA. Note that the software does not score the databases. Once students learn how to print databases, you may want to have students print copies of their databases for you to check.

Rule 45: In all-capital abbreviations made up of single initials, do not use periods or internal spaces. (Exception: Keep the periods in most academic degrees and in abbreviations of geographic names other than two-letter state abbreviations.)

You will need to call the EEO office for clarification on that issue.

He earned an M.A. in business administration.

```
 5 The meeting has been changed to 1 pm because of room conflicts.
 6 Auditors said sales were understated in the June eom statement.
 7 She enlisted in the U.S.M.C. after she received her PhD degree.
 8 His old research paper deals with the early history of N A T O.
 9 Denise said I should call about the paralegal position A.S.A.P.
10 We have consulted with A.A.A. about our upcoming European trip.
```

FACT FILE

Grizzly bears are surprisingly agile. They are also the fastest bears and can run at speeds up to 30 miles per hour. Adults may be 7 feet long and weigh 900 pounds.

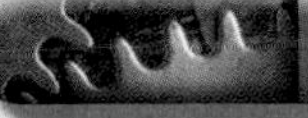

SKILLBUILDING

C. PACED PRACTICE

Turn to the Paced Practice routine beginning on page SB7. Take three 2-minute timings, starting at the point where you left off the last time.

D. PREVIEW PRACTICE

Type each line 2 times as a preview to the timings that follow.

Accuracy	11 neighbors competition, economically international Americans
Speed	12 foreign conduct require people become world study major who

TEACH

Activity C. Go over the Paced Practice 2-minute timing routine with students.

Activity D. Point out that words in the Preview Practice are used in the 5-minute timings that follow.

Language Connections

Have students do library research to find the origins and meanings of the following abbreviations: **i.e.** [L. *id est*] that is (to say); **etc.** et cetera, and so on; **et al.** [L. *et alii*] and others; **e.g.** [L. *exempli gratia*] for the sake of example, for example; **ibid.** [L. *ibidem*] in the same place: used in referring again to the book, page, etc., cited just before.

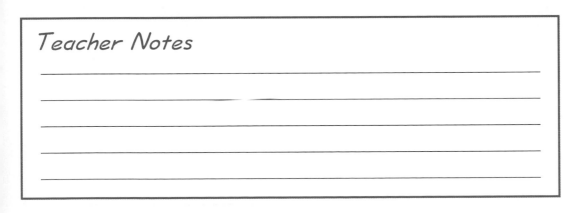

Teacher Notes

TEACH

Activity E. Remind students that they should try to improve speed with each 5-minute timing. The goal for this timing is to type 40 words a minute for 5 minutes with no more than 5 errors.

Activity F. Have students turn to Lesson 141 in their Student Manual and read the explanation for the software they are using. Then have them complete the practice activities that follow.

STUDENT MANUAL
Be sure students turn to the correct lesson in their Student Manual.

ASSESS

- Watch students as they complete the Language Link activity to see if they are able to apply the abbreviation rules correctly.
- Check to see if students are increasing their word a minute speeds as they complete each 5-minute timing.
- Make sure students are able to use the Database Tables, Navigating Within a Database, Windows, and Selecting software features.
- As students begin working with the databases, walk around the room and provide assistance to individual students as needed.

CLOSE

Remind students to clean up their workstation when they leave.

E. 5-Minute Timings

Take two 5-minute timings on the paragraphs. Note your speed and errors.

Goal: 40/5'/5e

```
     As this world shrinks daily, we become neighbors to           11
people who live in nations across the oceans. One major            22
issue now facing the United States and the world is that of        34
global competition. Some college students will find that           45
work in a global environment is a part of their lives.             56
     American students are less apt to be ready to work and        67
conduct business with those from different nations than are        79
students from other cultures. As countries continue to work        91
together, there is more and more demand to build skills for       103
this global marketplace.                                          108
     More than half of the schools in the United States now       120
include the study of a foreign language as a requirement          131
for a degree, especially for students in their school of          143
business. According to a study done by the research office        154
of the Department of Education, some American corporations        166
require that graduates they employ possess some knowledge         177
of international affairs. This knowledge is essential for         189
those who are employed in banking and communications.             200
 | 1 | 2 | 3 | 4 | 5 | 6 | 7 | 8 | 9 | 10 | 11 | 12 SI 1.54
```

Social Studies Connections

FORMATTING

F. Software Features

STUDENT MANUAL

Database Tables
Navigating Within a Database
Windows
Selecting

Study Lesson 141 in your student manual. Complete all the practice activities while at your computer.

Social Studies Connections

A trend in U.S. banking has been to open branches in foreign countries. In 1960, 8 U.S. banks had foreign offices. By 1987, about 150 banks had about 900 foreign branches. Have students write about the importance of a second language.

SCHOOL TO CAREER

Create groups of students to research the banking industry. Have the groups make a list of ten major banks, then create a spreadsheet with the following categories: name of bank, corporate headquarters, number of branches in the United States, and number of branches in foreign countries.

LESSON 142 DATABASES: CREATE DATABASE TABLES

OBJECTIVES:

- Improve keyboarding skill.
- Create database tables.

A. WARMUP

Type each line 2 times.

```
Speed              1 I went to visit my aunt who lives down the street from Sue.
Accuracy           2 Max had a zest for quiet living and placed work before joy.
Language Link      3 Leo was, of course, very surprised to hear his name called.
Numbers/Symbols    4 Do it now! Pay Bruce *(Adams) 10% and Pauline *(Drake) 15%.
                   | 1 | 2 | 3 | 4 | 5 | 6 | 7 | 8 | 9 | 10 | 11 | 12
```

SKILLBUILDING

B. 12-SECOND SPRINTS

Take three 12-second timings on each line. Try to increase your speed on each timing.

```
5 Take time to drop in on us if you are now in town sometime.
6 The girl is in the third grade and does fine work for them.
7 You have made the best use you could of all that free time.
8 If he visits with us, we shall call them at once from town.
  ||||5||||10||||15||||20||||25||||30||||35||||40||||45||||50||||55||||60
```

COMMUNICATION FOCUS

Learning another language takes practice and study. Ask a student from another country for tips he or she has used in learning another language.

RESOURCES

- Lesson Plan 142
- Courseware Lesson 142
- Student Data Disk
- Student Manual
- Supplementary Production Activities

COURSEWARE OVERVIEW

Students are instructed to minimize their database program and maximize KCA as they work through the textbook problems. You may want to provide them with detailed instructions on how to do this.

LESSON 142

FOCUS

- Use 12-second timings to build speed.
- Learn a database feature: Create Database Tables.
- Create database tables.

BELLRINGER

As soon as students arrive at their workstations and log in, have them type the Warmup. Go over the purpose of each line as shown to the left of the copy.

TEACH

Activity B. Remind students to type at a fast pace during the 12-second timings. At the end of the first and second timings, encourage students to type just one or two strokes faster on the next timing.

TEACH

Activity C. Have students turn to Lesson 142 in their Student Manual and read the explanation for the software they are using. Then have them complete the practice activities that follow.

STUDENT MANUAL
Be sure students turn to the correct lesson in their Student Manual.

Activity 1. Remind students to name this Database Activity DT1. This database will be used again in Lesson 143.

CULTURAL CONNECTIONS

The study of names and their origins is called onomastics. In medieval life, surnames (last names) often reflected a person's occupation, such as the name Chapman, which is a merchant or trader. Names also reflected where people lived; for example, John where-the-apples-grow became John Appleby. Have students research the origin of their names.

FORMATTING

C. SOFTWARE FEATURES

GO TO

STUDENT MANUAL
Create Database Tables

Study Lesson 142 in your student manual. Complete all the practice activities while at your computer. Then complete the jobs that follow.

DATABASE APPLICATIONS

ACTIVITY 1
Database Table 1

Follow these steps to create Database Table 1. Name the file DT1.

1. Create a database and name it *Activities.*
2. Define the five fields as shown.
3. Specify the size of each field as indicated by the numbers above the columns.
4. Enter the records.
5. Print the table.
6. Close the table window.

12	12	32	5	7
First Name	**Last Name**	**E-mail Address**	**Area Code**	**ZIP Code**
Jung	Kim	jkim5642@aol.com	303	80015
Steven	Stein	steven-stein@ccsdl.shhs.k12.com	719	80012
Jay J.	Baldwin	jjbald@csn.com	790	82211
Carla	Davis	cdavis547@aol.com	303	80013
Jentry P.	Mitchell	jpmitchell@nesd.sbhs.k12.com	303	80215
Karey	Fletcher	12946@netserve.net	719	82211
Felix	Gonzales	felixg@landnet.com	818	90144
Osana	Kiux	ok5466@wallnet.com	818	90128

FACT FILE

The pteranodon was called the "flying reptile" and lived in Europe where its fossils were found in Germany in 1784.

TECHNOLOGY TIP

A URL or Uniform Resource Locator is an address for an Internet Website. The three parts in a URL are *http*, or HyperText Transfer Protocol; the domain address; and the path to a specific page in an address. An address in blue and underlined is a hyperlink.

Out-of-Class Activity

Have students create a database address book of their friends. Before beginning they should make a list of ten friends. Create the following eight columns: last name, first name, e-mail address, home address, city, state, ZIP code, and phone number. Name the database *Addresses*.

ACTIVITY 2
Database Table 2

Follow these steps to create Database Table 2 and name it DT2:

1. Define the three fields as shown in the illustration; do not identify the first field as a date field.
2. Specify the size of each field as shown above the columns.
3. Enter the records.
4. Print the table.
5. Close the table window.

15	18	12
Date	**Competition**	**Start Time**
February 9	Speed Skating	10:30 a.m.
February 12	Luge	11:45 a.m.
February 13	Figure Skating	9:15 a.m.
February 14	Curling	3:30 p.m.
February 24	Downhill Skiing	2:45 p.m.

*inter*NET CONNECTION

Search the Internet for the names of champions in each of the competitions listed above. Also search for information about other Olympic sports such as ice hockey. Determine when each sport became an Olympic event.

LESSON 142

TEACH

Activity 2. Read the instructions aloud to students, stopping after each step to make sure students understand what they are to do. Point out to students that they should name the file DT2. They will use DT2 in Activity 5 in Lesson 143 and Activity 6 in Lesson 144.

ASSESS

- Check to see if students are increasing their word a minute speeds as they complete each 12-second timing.
- Make sure students are able to create database tables.
- As students begin working with the database activities, walk around the room and provide assistance to individual students.
- After students finish each activity, have them view their work on the screen to see if they made any errors. If errors were made, have students edit their work and make corrections.

CLOSE

If students do not finish the activities during the class period, make sure they save their work so that they can complete it the next time this class meets.

Remind students to clean up their workstation when they leave.

Teacher Notes

LESSON 143

FOCUS

- Apply the Language Link rule for using comparative and superlative adjectives and adverbs.
- Use a Pretest/Practice/Posttest routine to build speed and accuracy.
- Learn database features: Revise and Add Records and Date Fields.
- Revise and add records to database tables.

BELLRINGER

As soon as students arrive at their workstations and log in, have them type the Warmup. Go over the purpose of each line as shown to the left of the copy.

TEACH

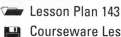

Activity B. Go over the Language Link rule with students.

Solutions: Which of these three carpets is the most practical?

Your layouts are the most appealing of any others in the display.

Both mountains have fantastic ski slopes; however, I prefer the slopes on the higher one.

Of the two computers, the one that is networked is the newer.

Of the two movies you chose, the shorter one is the more interesting.

All three classes were difficult; however, math was the least challenging.

LESSON 143

DATABASES: REVISE AND ADD RECORDS

OBJECTIVES:

- Increase keyboarding skill.
- Learn about comparative and superlative adjectives and adverbs.
- Revise and add records to database tables.

A. WARMUP

Type each line 2 times.

Speed	1	Jill has to take her time if she wants to do her best work.
Accuracy	2	Max quickly amazed Joan Bishop with five magic card tricks.
Language Link	3	Amy came by at noon to pick me up; I had left much earlier.
Numbers/Symbols	4	We ordered 130# of #8 stock @ $42.65 on April 7 and July 9.

| 1 | 2 | 3 | 4 | 5 | 6 | 7 | 8 | 9 | 10 | 11 | 12

B. COMPARATIVE AND SUPERLATIVE ADJECTIVES AND ADVERBS

Study the rule and examples below. Then edit lines 5–10 by choosing the correct word.

Rule 46: Use **comparative** adjectives and adverbs, which use *-er, more,* and *less,* when referring to two nouns; use **superlative** adjectives and adverbs, which use *-est, most,* and *least,* when referring to more than two nouns.

Of the two players, Sam is more skillful at free-throw shooting.

She is looking for the most beautiful state to visit this summer.

RESOURCES

 Lesson Plan 143

 Courseware Lesson 143

Student Data Disk

Student Manual

Language Link Worksheets

Supplementary Production Activities

5 Which of these three carpets is the (more/most) practical?
6 Your layouts are the (more/most) appealing of any others in the display.
7 Both mountains have fantastic ski slopes; however, I prefer the slopes on the (higher/highest) one.
8 Of the two computers, the one that is networked is the (newer/newest).
9 Of the two movies you chose, the (shorter/shortest) one is the (more/most) interesting.
10 All three classes were difficult; however, math was the (lesser/least) challenging.

SKILLBUILDING

C. PRETEST *Take a 1-minute timing on the paragraph. Note your speed and errors.*

```
11      You cannot build good skills while typing if you don't   12
12  practice various reaches on your keyboard. Practice all the  24
13  reaches that are especially difficult for you when you take  36
14  your timed writings. The more you type, the better you type. 48
    | 1 | 2 | 3 | 4 | 5 | 6 | 7 | 8 | 9 | 10 | 11 | 12
```

D. PRACTICE *SPEED: If you made 2 or fewer errors on the Pretest, type lines 15–22 two times each.*

ACCURACY: If you made more than 2 errors on the Pretest, type lines 15–18 as a group two times. Then type lines 19–22 as a group two times.

Up Reaches

```
15 daily card early away date earn fear fold argue baked cargo
16 page plus rise seat voted theft tape stand rules vary plead
17 meant gift large hold hours jury grade lets films made nest
18 reach hard build good don't your skill more timed take type
```

Down Reaches

```
19 very scope axle heavy cable value back calm cars sack bales
20 jobs each about disc badly cage cakes balk coach avid frank
21 taxi link packs rack reach palm score snack lack knee teach
22 wind vine blind came bland clans oxen column balm calm mine
```

E. POSTTEST *Repeat the Pretest. Compare your Posttest results with your Pretest results.*

LESSON 143

TEACH

Activities C–E. Remind students they should improve both their speed and accuracy from the Pretest to the Posttest.

PRETEST/PRACTICE/POSTEST

The ***Pretest/Practice/Posttest*** routines are designed to improve speed or accuracy.

- The ***Pretest*** identifies students' speed or accuracy needs.
- The ***Practice*** provides a variety of improvement drills.
- The ***Posttest*** (a repeat of the Pretest) measures improvement.

JOURNAL ENTRY

Have students write about a favorite trip they have taken or a trip they would like to take. Why is this a favorite place? Why did they like it or why would they like to visit it? Call for volunteers to read their entries in class.

TEACH

Activity F. Have students turn to Lesson 143 in their Student Manual and read the explanation for the software they are using. Then have them complete the practice activities that follow.

STUDENT MANUAL
Be sure students turn to the correct lesson in their Student Manual.

Activity 3. Point out to students they are to open the file DT1, which they created in Activity 1 in Lesson 142.

Activity 4. Have students read the instructions once, then have them read the instructions again to be sure they understand what to do. Make sure students name the file DT3. This file will be used in Activity 7 and then again in Activities 11 through 26.

PORTFOLIO *Activity*

If students' portfolio goals include demonstrating progress, they may want to include a database table from this lesson. Encourage students to evaluate their work and include comments in their portfolio.

FORMATTING

F. Software Features

STUDENT MANUAL

Revise and Add Records
Date Fields

Study Lesson 143 in your student manual. Complete all the practice activities while at your computer. Then complete the jobs that follow.

DATABASE APPLICATIONS

ACTIVITY 3
Database Table 1

Open the file DT1 and make the following changes:

1. Change the e-mail address for Jung Kim to *jkim6542@aol.com.*
2. Change the first name for Jay J. Baldwin to *James,* and change his e-mail address to *jbaldwin.*
3. Change the first name for Carla Davis to *Karly,* and change the e-mail address to *karlyd@aol.com.*
4. Change the e-mail address for Felix Gonzales to *felixg@buffalo.net* and the ZIP Code to *90145.*
5. Print the table.
6. Close the table window.

ACTIVITY 4
Database Table 3

Follow these steps to create Database Table 3 and name it DT3:

1. Define the three fields as shown in the illustration; identify the third field as a date field.
2. Specify the size of each field as shown above the columns.
3. Enter the records.
4. Print the table.
5. Close the table window.

FACT FILE

The Gutenberg Bible, Old Testament, was the most expensive book ever sold. It was printed in Mainz, Germany, in 1455. Tokyo booksellers purchased this book for $5.39 million.

524 ***Databases***

FACT FILE

Many databases originally contained 3 date fields: month, day, and year. The size of each field was 2 characters. Billions of dollars (and millions of hours) were spent in the last few years of the twentieth century to change the size of the year field so computers could differentiate the years 1900 and 2000.

16	16	
State Name	**Capital City**	**Date of Statehood**
Alabama	Montgomery	12/14/1819
Alaska	Juneau	1/3/1959
Arizona	Phoenix	2/14/1912
Arkansas	Little Rock	6/15/1836
California	Sacramento	9/9/1850
Colorado	Denver	8/1/1876
Connecticut	Hartford	1/9/1788
Delaware	Dover	12/7/1787

ACTIVITY 5
Database Table 2

Open the file DT2 and make the following changes:

1. Change the date for speed skating to February 12.
2. Change the start time for luge to 11:50 a.m.
3. Change the date for downhill skiing to February 14.
4. Add the following records as shown in the illustration.
5. Print the table.
6. Close the table window.

Date	Competition	Start Time
February 15	Speed Skating	9:15 a.m.
February 15	Luge	11:00 a.m.
February 16	Figure Skating	10:30 a.m.
February 17	Curling	7:00 p.m.
February 17	Downhill Skiing	1:15 p.m.

FACT FILE

Did you know that Alaska is the largest state with 591,004 square miles, and Rhode Island is the smallest state with 1,212 square miles. The last two states admitted to the Union were Alaska and Hawaii in 1959.

TEACH

Activity 5. Make sure students open the correct file. DT2 was created in Activity 2 in Lesson 142.

ASSESS

- Watch students as they complete the Language Link activity to see if they are able to apply the rule.
- Check to see if students show signs of improvement from the Pretest to the Posttest.
- Make sure students are able to revise and add records and date fields to databases.
- As students begin working with databases, walk around the room and provide assistance to individual students as needed.
- After students finish each activity, have them view their work on the screen to see if they made any errors. If errors were made, have students edit their work and make corrections.

CLOSE

If students do not finish the databases during the class period, make sure they save their work so that they can edit it the next time this class meets.

Teacher Notes

LESSON 144

FOCUS

- Use 5-minute timings to build speed.
- Learn database features: Rename, Add, and Position Fields.
- Rename, add, and position fields in databases.

BELLRINGER

As soon as students arrive at their workstations and log in, have them type the Warmup. Go over the purpose of each line as shown to the left of the copy.

TEACH

Activity B. Point out that words in the Preview Practice are used in the timing that follows.

LESSON 144

DATABASES: RENAME, ADD, AND POSITION FIELDS

OBJECTIVES:

- Improve keyboarding skill.
- Type 40/5′/5e.
- Rename, add, and position fields in a database table.

A. WARMUP

Type each line 2 times.

```
Speed          1 I hope to have the first check by the second of next month.
Accuracy       2 Jack Bowman was very excited when my quilt won first prize.
Language Link  3 His letter asked the personnel manager for a job interview.
Numbers        4 Read pages 17, 20, 35, 46, and 89 to see the right answers.
                 | 1 | 2 | 3 | 4 | 5 | 6 | 7 | 8 | 9 | 10 | 11 | 12
```

SOCIAL STUDIES CONNECTIONS

The bravery and skill under fire of the 54th Volunteer Infantry from Massachusetts set an example for all. The 54th was an African American military unit that fought during the Civil War.

COME AND JOIN US BROTHERS.

SKILLBUILDING

B. PREVIEW PRACTICE

Type each line 2 times as a preview to the 5-minute timings that follow.

```
Accuracy  5 own analyze college probably creative equipment scholarship
Speed     6 grant could print still money their music start while think
```

RESOURCES

 Lesson Plan 144

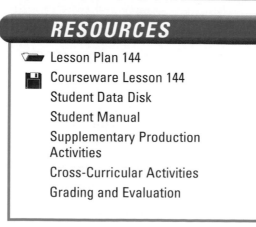

 Courseware Lesson 144

Student Data Disk

Student Manual

Supplementary Production Activities

Cross-Curricular Activities

Grading and Evaluation

C. 5-Minute Timings

Take two 5-minute timings on the paragraphs. Note your speed and errors.

Goal: 40/5'/5e

The cost of attending college is quickly rising. Have 11
you thought about how you will pay for your training after 23
high school? Will you earn a scholarship or a grant? Would 35
you be willing to take out loans that must be paid back? 46
These are some of the sources of financial aid students 57
think of first. If you give it some thought, you may find 69
additional ways to earn money for school. 77

Many students earn money for education while working 88
at part-time jobs. Others find they can start their own 99
businesses. These students often provide services that are 111
in demand by fellow students. 117

Analyze your existing level of expertise to see if 127
your keyboarding skills could earn you money. Print flyers 139
to advertise your interest in providing fast, reliable help 151
with term papers for pay. If you have the equipment and a 163
collection of music, you could sell your services as a disk 175
jockey and provide the music for campus parties. 184

A creative student can probably think of other ways to 195
earn money for college. 200

| 1 | 2 | 3 | 4 | 5 | 6 | 7 | 8 | 9 | 10 | 11 | 12 | SI 1.43

MATH CONNECTIONS

Monitor the sports section of your local newspaper for a few days. Pick two or three sports events and track their scores.

FORMATTING

D. Software Features

STUDENT MANUAL

Rename, Add, and Position Fields

Study Lesson 144 in your student manual. Complete all the practice activities while at your computer. Then complete the jobs that follow.

Unit 8 Lesson 144 527

TEACH

Activity C. Remind students that they should try to improve speed with each 5-minute timing. The goal for these timings is to type 40 words a minute for 5 minutes with no more than 5 errors.

Activity D. Have students turn to Lesson 144 in their Student Manual and read the explanation for the software they are using. Then have them complete the practice activities that follow.

STUDENT MANUAL

Be sure students turn to the correct lesson in their Student Manual.

interNET ACTIVITY

Have students access two institutions of higher learning they are interested in attending (training schools, colleges and universities, or business schools). Have them find information about available financial aid programs at these institutions.

Career Exploration

List the following categories: *technology schools*, *colleges and universities*, and *business schools*. Have students choose a category and form groups. Groups should invent ways students can make money to pay for an education at this type of institution.

TEACH

Activity 6. Make sure students open the correct file. DT2 was created in Activity 2 in Lesson 142 and was altered in Activity 5 in Lesson 143.

Activity 7. Make sure students open the correct file. DT3 was created in Activity 4 in Lesson 143.

DATABASE APPLICATIONS

ACTIVITY 6
Database Table 2

Open the file DT2 and make the following changes:

1. Change the field name *Competition* to *Event*.
2. Add a new field named *Location;* specify 16 as the field size.
3. Position the *Location* field between the *Event* and *Start Time* fields.
4. Enter the locations for events as shown in the illustration.
5. Print the table.
6. Close the table window.

Speed Skating	The Oval
Luge	Metro Park
Figure Skating	Olympic Arena
Curling	The Coliseum
Downhill Skiing	Moose Mountain

ACTIVITY 7
Database Table 3

Open the file DT3 and make the following changes:

1. Change the field name *State Name* to *State.*
2. Change the field name *Capital City* to *Capital.*
3. Add a new field named *State Bird*; specify 28 as the field size.
4. Position the field *State Bird* as the last field.
5. Enter the birds for the states indicated in the first illustration.
6. Add the records from the second illustration to the table.
7. Print the table.
8. Close the table window.

Multiple Learning Styles

Have students work with a partner. Each pair creates a list of computer terms they want to learn. Have one student close his or her eyes while the other student reads the word and the definition. What pictures come to mind? Use these mind pictures to associate the word with its meaning.

SCHOOL TO CAREER

On the board, write *Government*. Under this, list *federal*, *state*, and *local*. Have students brainstorm about careers within each category. Write students' ideas on the board. Assign students a career to research. Have students report to the class.

Alabama	Yellowhammer
Alaska	Willow ptarmigan
Arizona	Cactus wren
Arkansas	Mockingbird
California	California valley quail
Colorado	Lark bunting
Connecticut	Robin
Delaware	Blue hen chicken

State	Capital	Date of Statehood	State Bird
Florida	Tallahassee	3/3/1845	Mockingbird
Georgia	Atlanta	1/2/1788	Brown thrasher
Hawaii	Honolulu	8/21/1959	Nene
Idaho	Boise	7/3/1890	Mountain bluebird
Illinois	Springfield	12/3/1818	Cardinal
Indiana	Indianapolis	12/11/1816	Cardinal
Iowa	Des Moines	12/28/1846	Eastern goldfinch

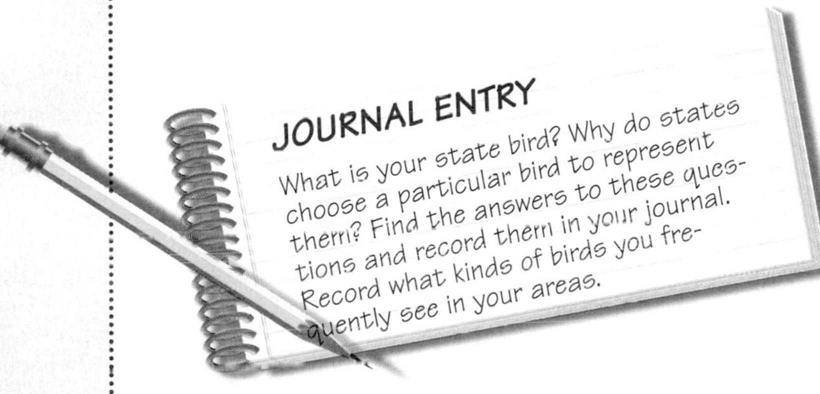

JOURNAL ENTRY
What is your state bird? Why do states choose a particular bird to represent them? Find the answers to these questions and record them in your journal. Record what kinds of birds you frequently see in your areas.

LESSON 144

ASSESS

- Check to see if students are increasing their word a minute speeds as they complete each 5-minute timing.
- Make sure students are able to rename, add, and position fields in databases.
- As students begin working with the database activities, walk around the room and provide assistance to individual students as needed.
- After students finish each activity, have them view their work on the screen to see if they made any errors. If errors were made, have students edit their work and make corrections.

CLOSE

If students do not finish the databases during the class period, make sure they save their work so that they can complete it the next time this class meets.

Remind students to clean up their workstation when they leave.

PORTFOLIO Activity

If students' portfolio goals include demonstrating progress, they may want to include a database table from this lesson. Encourage students to evaluate their work and include comments in their portfolio.

Teacher Notes

LESSON 145

FOCUS

- Compose a one-page story for the Language Link activity.
- Use the Diagnostic Practice to identify areas involving numbers that need improvement.
- Learn database features: Monetary and Numeric Fields.
- Use monetary and numeric fields in databases.

BELLRINGER

As soon as students arrive at their workstations and log in, have them type the Warmup. Go over the purpose of each line as shown to the left of the copy.

TEACH

Activity B. Have a few students read their paragraphs. Also have students check each other's work for accuracy.

Solutions: Answers will vary.

DATABASES: MONETARY AND NUMERIC FIELDS

OBJECTIVES:

- Compose at the keyboard.
- Increase keyboarding skill.
- Learn about monetary and numeric fields.

A. WARMUP

Type each line 2 times.

Speed	1	Hard rain came down very fast, so I could not see the road.
Accuracy	2	Everybody expected Jack's golf technique to win him prizes.
Language Link	3	We were told that it may be colder Friday than it is today.
Numbers/Symbols	4	Chris & David earned $7.75/hour loading 1,234# of #4 pines.

| 1 | 2 | 3 | 4 | 5 | 6 | 7 | 8 | 9 | 10 | 11 | 12

B. COMPOSING AT THE KEYBOARD

Compose a one-page story to complete the following paragraph:

I was watching the Super Bowl on television when the doorbell rang. Since I was the only one at home, I went to the door to see who would be interrupting my football game. Much to my surprise, I found the Prize Scout—complete with flowers and balloons. I could hardly believe my ears when he said, "Congratulations, you are the Publishing Giants $10 million winner!" Since that day, my life has changed, and now . . .

FACT FILE

Benjamin Franklin once proposed the turkey as the national bird of the United States instead of the eagle.

RESOURCES

 Lesson Plan 145

 Courseware Lesson 145

Student Data Disk

Student Manual

Supplementary Production Activities

SKILLBUILDING

C. Diagnostic Practice: Numbers

Turn to the Diagnostic Practice: Numbers routine on page SB4. Type one of the Pretest/Posttest paragraphs and identify any errors made. Then type the corresponding drill lines 2 times for each number on which you made 2 or more errors and 1 time for each number on which you made only 1 error. Finally, repeat the same Pretest paragraph and compare your performance.

MATH CONNECTIONS

Assume that you won $10,000,000 dollars. Determine the amount you would actually receive after taxes.

FORMATTING

D. Software Features

STUDENT MANUAL

Monetary and Numeric Fields

Study Lesson 145 in your student manual. Complete all the practice activities while at your computer. Then complete the jobs that follow.

DATABASE APPLICATIONS

ACTIVITY 8

Database Table 4

Follow these steps to create Database Table 4 and name it DT4:

1. Define the four fields as shown in the illustration.
2. Identify the third and fourth fields as monetary fields.
3. Specify the size of each text/alpha field as shown above the column.
4. Enter the records.
5. Print the table.
6. Close the table window.

TEACH

Activity C. Make sure that students understand that this Diagnostic Practice activity is designed to help identify areas that need improvement and provide needed practice.

Activity D. Have students turn to Lesson 145 in their Student Manual and read the explanation for the software they are using. Then have them complete the practice activities that follow.

STUDENT MANUAL

Be sure students turn to the correct lesson in their Student Manual.

Activity 8. Make sure students name the file correctly. They will use DT4 in activity 27 in Lesson 148.

JOURNAL ENTRY

Have students write using the following prompt: "A perfect day for me is. . . ." Remind students to get their thoughts down first and then go back and proofread what they have written. Read a few entries in class.

TEACH

Activity 9. Make sure students name the file correctly. They will use DT5 in Activity 10 later in this lesson and in Activities 29 and 30 in Lesson 149.

33	20		
Position	**Minimum Credentials**	**Low-End Salary**	**High-End Salary**
Accountant	Bachelor's Degree	$23,300.00	$29,400.00
Administrative Services Manager	Associate Degree	$39,700.00	$53,300.00
Budget Analyst	Bachelor's Degree	$24,000.00	$65,000.00
Education Administrator	Master's Degree	$34,500.00	$200,200.00
Employment Interviewer	Bachelor's Degree	$20,000.00	$54,000.00
Human Resources Specialist	Bachelor's Degree	$25,000.00	$59,000.00
Food Services Manager	Bachelor's Degree	$21,000.00	$50,000.00

ACTIVITY 9
Database Table 5

Follow these steps to create Database Table 5 and name it DT5.

1. Define the five fields as shown in the illustration; identify the fourth field as a monetary field and the fifth field as a number field.
2. Specify the size of each text/alpha field as shown above the column.
3. Enter the records.
4. Print the table.
5. Close the table window.

34	22	11		
Title	**Author**	**Binding**	**Retail Price**	**Inventory**
Out of the Dust	Karen Hesse	hardcover	$15.95	14
View From Saturday	E. L. Konigsburg	paperback	$4.50	20
The Midwife's Apprentice	Karen Cushman	hardcover	$10.95	25
Walk Two Moons	Sharon Creech	paperback	$4.95	18
Sarah, Plain and Tall	Patricia MacLachlan	hardcover	$14.95	17
The Bridge to Terabithia	Katherine Paterson	paperback	$4.95	22
Roll of Thunder, Hear My Cry	Mildred D. Taylor	hardcover	$15.99	30
Mrs. Frisby and the Rats of NIMH	Robert C. O'Brien	hardcover	$17.00	28
Summer of the Swans	Betsy Byars	paperback	$4.99	32
Sounder	William H. Armstrong	hardcover	$14.95	35
Island of the Blue Dolphins	Scott O'Dell	paperback	$5.50	15
Johnny Tremain	Esther Forbes	hardcover	$20.00	12

Career Exploration

Point out the database in Activity 8 on this page. Have students form seven groups. Assign each group one of the careers in this database to research. Groups should learn what the career consists of, the availability of jobs, and advancement potentials. Each group is to write a report about the career. Post the reports in the classroom.

Language Arts Connections

Have students form 12 groups. Assign each group one of the books in Activity 9 on this page. Have each member of the group read the assigned book, take notes, and then discuss it with their group. The group as a panel is then to give a short oral report to the class.

ACTIVITY 10
Database Table 5

Open the file DT5 and make the following changes:

1. Add a new field named *Code;* specify *5* as the field size.
2. Position the field *Code* at the beginning of the table.
3. Add a new field named *Purchase Date,* and specify it as a date field; position it between the fields *Binding* and *Retail Price*.
4. Enter the codes and dates for the titles shown in the illustration.
5. Print the table.
6. Close the table window.

Code	Title	Purchase Date
H29	Out of the Dust	4/4/--
S15	View From Saturday	4/4/--
H25	The Midwife's Apprentice	4/4/--
S33	Walk Two Moons	4/4/--
H48	Sarah, Plain and Tall	4/11/--
S36	The Bridge to Terabithia	4/11/--
H59	Roll of Thunder, Hear My Cry	4/11/--
H16	Mrs. Frisby and the Rats of NIMH	4/11/--
S45	Summer of the Swans	4/18/--
H22	Sounder	4/18/--
S61	Island of the Blue Dolphins	4/18/--
H57	Johnny Tremain	4/18/--

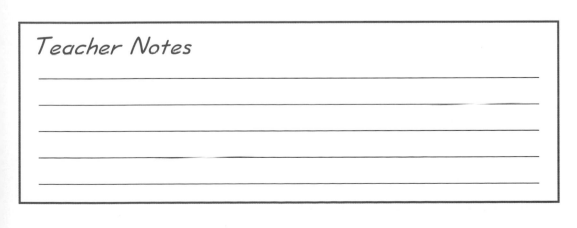

PORTFOLIO *Activity*

What would you do with the money if you won the big prize in a contest? Make a list in your portfolio of what would be the most important things you would purchase with the money. Create a database with the names and addresses of people with whom you would want to share your winnings.

LESSON 145

TEACH

Activity 10. Make sure students save the file DT5. They will use DT5 in Activities 29 and 30 in Lesson 149.

ASSESS

- Review the accuracy of students' one-page Language Link story.
- Monitor students as they complete the Diagnostic Practice and provide individualized assistance as needed.
- Make sure students are able to create monetary and numeric fields in a database.
- As students begin working with the database activities, walk around the room and provide assistance to individual students as needed.
- After students finish each activity, have them view their work on the screen to see if they made any errors. If errors were made, have students edit their work and make corrections.

CLOSE

If students do not finish the databases during the class period, make sure they save their work so that they can complete it the next time this class meets.

Remind students to clean up their workstation when they leave.

Teacher Notes

LESSON 146

FOCUS

- Use a Pretest/Practice/Posttest routine to build speed and accuracy.
- Use 5-minute timings to build speed.
- Practice creating database tables.

BELLRINGER

As soon as students arrive at their workstations and log in, have them type the Warmup. Go over the purpose of each line as shown to the left of the copy.

TEACH

Activities B–C. Remind students they should improve both their speed and accuracy from the Pretest to the Posttest.

PRETEST/PRACTICE/POSTEST

The ***Pretest/Practice/Posttest*** routines are designed to improve speed or accuracy.

- The ***Pretest*** identifies students' speed or accuracy needs.
- The ***Practice*** provides a variety of improvement drills.
- The ***Posttest*** (a repeat of the Pretest) measures improvement.

LESSON 146 DATABASE: REVIEW

OBJECTIVES:

- Improve keyboarding skill.
- Review database tables.
- Type 40/5'/5e.

A. WARMUP

Type each line 2 times.

Speed	These short, easy words help you when you build your speed.
Accuracy	Even Jacques may gaze up to find six crows in the blue sky.
Language Link	James and I grew up in Montana; we always go home in March.
Numbers	If we need 56 points, then 47, 29, 38, or 10 will not help.

| 1 | 2 | 3 | 4 | 5 | 6 | 7 | 8 | 9 | 10 | 11 | 12

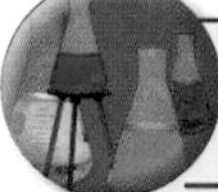

SCIENCE CONNECTIONS

The hermit crab must use the empty shell of another animal for its home. Each time the hermit crab grows too large for its "borrowed" home, it moves out and finds a larger shell in which to live. During this time, the hermit crab is vulnerable to attack by predators. Most other crabs grow a new shell when they get too large for the current one.

RESOURCES

Lesson Plan 146

Courseware Lesson 146

Student Data Disk

Student Manual

Supplementary Production Activities

Multicultural Activities

Grading and Evaluation

B. PRETEST

Take a 1-minute timing on the paragraph. Note your speed and errors.

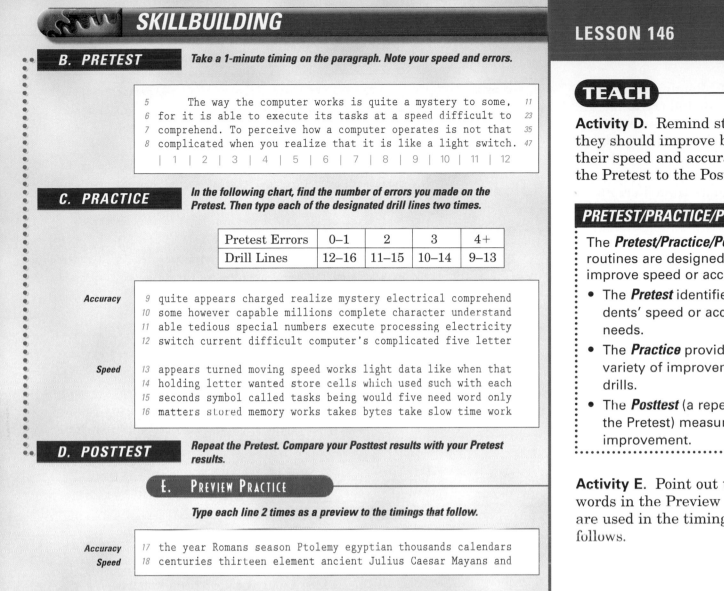

```
5      The way the computer works is quite a mystery to some,   11
6  for it is able to execute its tasks at a speed difficult to  23
7  comprehend. To perceive how a computer operates is not that  35
8  complicated when you realize that it is like a light switch. 47
   | 1 | 2 | 3 | 4 | 5 | 6 | 7 | 8 | 9 | 10 | 11 | 12
```

C. PRACTICE

In the following chart, find the number of errors you made on the Pretest. Then type each of the designated drill lines two times.

Pretest Errors	0–1	2	3	4+
Drill Lines	12–16	11–15	10–14	9–13

Accuracy

```
9  quite appears charged realize mystery electrical comprehend
10 some however capable millions complete character understand
11 able tedious special numbers execute processing electricity
12 switch current difficult computer's complicated five letter
```

Speed

```
13 appears turned moving speed works light data like when that
14 holding letter wanted store cells which used such with each
15 seconds symbol called tasks being would five need word only
16 matters stored memory works takes bytes take slow time work
```

D. POSTTEST

Repeat the Pretest. Compare your Posttest results with your Pretest results.

E. PREVIEW PRACTICE

Type each line 2 times as a preview to the timings that follow.

```
Accuracy  17 the year Romans season Ptolemy egyptian thousands calendars
Speed     18 centuries thirteen element ancient Julius Caesar Mayans and
```


TEACH

Activity D. Remind students they should improve both their speed and accuracy from the Pretest to the Posttest.

PRETEST/PRACTICE/POSTTEST

The ***Pretest/Practice/Posttest*** routines are designed to improve speed or accuracy.

- The ***Pretest*** identifies students' speed or accuracy needs.
- The ***Practice*** provides a variety of improvement drills.
- The ***Posttest*** (a repeat of the Pretest) measures improvement.

Activity E. Point out that words in the Preview Practice are used in the timing that follows.

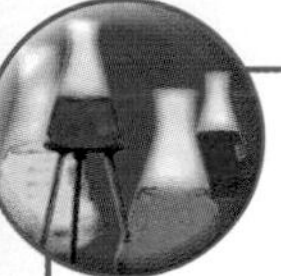

Science Connections

Have students form five groups. Assign each group one of the following topics about comets to research: Halley's comet and the history of comets; composition of comets; solar effects; periods and orbits; and comet groups. Each group is to write a short report.

interNET ACTIVITY

Have students find sites related to comets. Have them work in small groups to share information. A search of the Internet should yield interesting NASA and National Space Science Data Center (NSSDC) sites.

Activity F. Remind students that they should try to improve speed with each 5-minute timing. The goal for these timings is to type 40 words a minute for 5 minutes with no more than 5 errors.

F. 5-MINUTE TIMINGS

Take two 5-minute timings on the paragraphs. Note your speed and errors.

Goal: 40/5'/5e

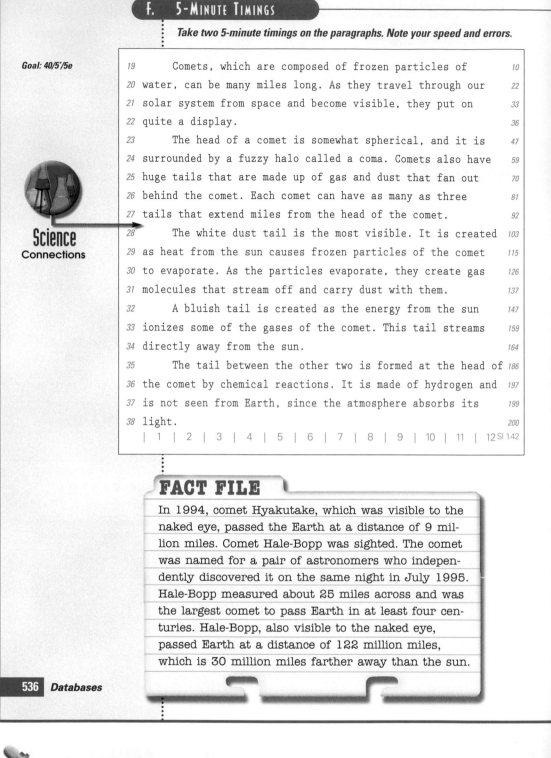

Science Connections

Comets, which are composed of frozen particles of 10
water, can be many miles long. As they travel through our 22
solar system from space and become visible, they put on 33
quite a display. 36

The head of a comet is somewhat spherical, and it is 47
surrounded by a fuzzy halo called a coma. Comets also have 59
huge tails that are made up of gas and dust that fan out 70
behind the comet. Each comet can have as many as three 81
tails that extend miles from the head of the comet. 92

The white dust tail is the most visible. It is created 103
as heat from the sun causes frozen particles of the comet 115
to evaporate. As the particles evaporate, they create gas 126
molecules that stream off and carry dust with them. 137

A bluish tail is created as the energy from the sun 147
ionizes some of the gases of the comet. This tail streams 159
directly away from the sun. 164

The tail between the other two is formed at the head of 186
the comet by chemical reactions. It is made of hydrogen and 197
is not seen from Earth, since the atmosphere absorbs its 199
light. 200

| 1 | 2 | 3 | 4 | 5 | 6 | 7 | 8 | 9 | 10 | 11 | 12 SI 1.42

FACT FILE

In 1994, comet Hyakutake, which was visible to the naked eye, passed the Earth at a distance of 9 million miles. Comet Hale-Bopp was sighted. The comet was named for a pair of astronomers who independently discovered it on the same night in July 1995. Hale-Bopp measured about 25 miles across and was the largest comet to pass Earth in at least four centuries. Hale-Bopp, also visible to the naked eye, passed Earth at a distance of 122 million miles, which is 30 million miles farther away than the sun.

JOURNAL ENTRY

Have students write about the most interesting observation of the night sky they ever had.

ACTIVITY 11

Database Table 3

Open the file DT3 and make the following changes:

1. Add a new field named *Highest Point;* specify it as a number field and format the field with commas.
2. Position the field *Highest Point* as the last field of the table.
3. Enter the elevations for the states as shown in the first illustration.
4. Add the records shown in the second illustration on the next page to Database Table 3.
5. Print the table.
6. Close the table window.

Alabama	2,407
Alaska	20,320
Arizona	12,633
Arkansas	2,753
California	14,494
Colorado	14,433
Connecticut	2,380
Delaware	442
Florida	345
Georgia	4,784
Hawaii	13,796
Idaho	12,662
Illinois	1,235
Indiana	1,257
Iowa	1,670

FACT FILE

The highest mountain in Africa is Mt. Kilimanjaro, which is 19,430 feet high.

TEACH

Activity 11. Make sure students open the correct file, DT3. This file will be used in Activities 12 through 26.

Out-of-Class Activity

Have students work in pairs or small groups to compile pictures of state birds. Assign states to each group. Have groups create a database of their research information. Use the database on page 543 as a model. Have student groups prepare an oral report that includes what resources were used.

Multiple Learning Styles

Have students think about an archetype of higher learning, such as Einstein. Have students think about something they are having trouble learning and have an imaginary conversation with the archetype to ask them to help in the learning process.

ASSESS

- Check to see if students show signs of improvement from the Pretest to the Posttest.
- Check to see if students are increasing their word a minute speeds as they complete each 5-minute timing.
- As students begin working with the database tables, walk around the room and provide assistance to individual students as needed.
- After students finish each activity, have them view their work on the screen to see if they made any errors. If errors were made, have students edit their work and make corrections.

CLOSE

If students do not finish the activities during the class period, make sure they save their work so that they can edit it the next time this class meets.

Remind students to clean up their workstation when they leave.

PORTFOLIO *Activity*

If students' portfolio goals include showcasing their best work, they may want to include a database table from this lesson. Encourage students to evaluate their work and include comments in their portfolio.

State	Capital	Date of Statehood	State Bird	Highest Point
Kansas	Topeka	1/29/1861	Western meadowlark	4,039
Kentucky	Frankfort	6/1/1792	Cardinal	4,145
Louisiana	Baton Rouge	4/30/1812	Eastern brown pelican	535
Maine	Augusta	3/15/1820	Chickadee	5,268
Maryland	Annapolis	4/28/1788	Baltimore oriole	3,360
Massachusetts	Boston	2/6/1788	Chickadee	3,491
Michigan	Lansing	1/26/1837	Robin	1,980
Minnesota	St. Paul	5/11/1858	Common loon	2,301
Mississippi	Jackson	12/10/1817	Mockingbird	806
Missouri	Jefferson City	8/10/1821	Bluebird	1,772
Montana	Helena	11/8/1889	Western meadowlark	12,799
Nebraska	Lincoln	3/1/1867	Western meadowlark	5,424
Nevada	Carson City	10/31/1864	Mountain bluebird	13,143
New Hampshire	Concord	6/21/1788	Purple finch	6,288
New Jersey	Trenton	12/18/1787	Eastern goldfinch	1,803
New Mexico	Santa Fe	1/6/1912	Chaparral bird	13,161
New York	Albany	7/26/1788	Bluebird	5,344
North Carolina	Raleigh	11/21/1789	Cardinal	6,684
North Dakota	Bismarck	11/2/1889	Western meadowlark	3,506
Ohio	Columbus	3/1/1803	Cardinal	1,550
Oklahoma	Oklahoma City	11/16/1907	Scissor-tailed flycatcher	4,973
Oregon	Salem	2/14/1859	Western meadowlark	11,233
Pennsylvania	Harrisburg	12/12/1787	Ruffed grouse	3,213
Rhode Island	Providence	5/29/1790	Rhode Island red	812
South Carolina	Columbia	5/23/1788	Carolina wren	3,560
South Dakota	Pierre	11/2/1889	Red-necked pheasant	7,242
Tennessee	Nashville	6/1/1796	Mockingbird	6,643
Texas	Austin	12/29/1845	Mockingbird	8,749
Utah	Salt Lake City	1/4/1896	Sea gull	13,528
Vermont	Montpelier	3/4/1791	Hermit thrush	4,393
Virginia	Richmond	6/25/1788	Cardinal	5,729
Washington	Olympia	11/11/1889	Willow goldfinch	14,410
West Virginia	Charleston	6/20/1863	Cardinal	4,863
Wisconsin	Madison	5/29/1848	Robin	1,952
Wyoming	Cheyenne	7/10/1890	Western meadowlark	13,804

Teacher Notes

LESSON 147 DATABASES: SORT AND QUERY

OBJECTIVES:

- Learn rules for hyphenating words.
- Improve keyboarding skill.
- Learn to sort database tables.
- Learn to query database tables.

A. WARMUP

Type each line 2 times.

Speed	1	The dog and cat went to eat their food from the round dish.
Accuracy	2	Liza gave Max and Becky a quaint photo of a jar of flowers.
Language Link	3	The 3 students tried to finish their project before Monday.
Numbers/Symbols	4	I concluded that 1/3 of $39 = $13, and that 20% of $10 = 2.

| 1 | 2 | 3 | 4 | 5 | 6 | 7 | 8 | 9 | 10 | 11 | 12

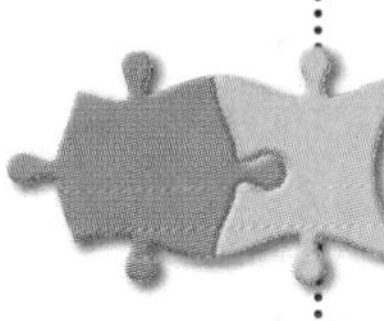

LANGUAGE LINK

B. HYPHENATED WORDS

Study the rule and examples that follow. Then edit lines 5–8 by inserting hyphens where necessary.

Rule 47: Hyphenate compound numbers (between *twenty-one* and *ninety-nine*) and fractions that are expressed in words.

Seventy-five of the members voted to repeal the law—this was nearly two-fifths of the membership.

Thirty-five letters were sent to Mr. Alexander to thank him for his excellent service.

RESOURCES

 Lesson Plan 147

 Courseware Lesson 147

Student Data Disk

Student Manual

Language Link Worksheets

Supplementary Production Activities

LESSON 147

FOCUS

- Apply the Language Link rule for hyphenation.
- Use 30-second timings to build speed.
- Learn database features: Sort Database Tables and Query Database Tables.
- Sort and query database tables.

BELLRINGER

As soon as students arrive at their workstations and log in, have them type the Warmup. Go over the purpose of each line as shown to the left of the copy.

TEACH

Activity B. Discuss the Language Link hyphenation rule with students.

Solutions: Two-thirds of the membership must be present to enact a rule.

We observed twenty-nine infractions during the investigation.

Bancroft Industries reduced their sales force by one-fourth.

After we add all the numbers, we must increase it by fifty-five.

TEACH

Activity C. Remind students that the goal for 30-second timings is improved speed with each timing.

Activity D. Have students turn to Lesson 147 in their Student Manual and read the explanation for the software they are using. Then have them complete the practice activities that follow.

STUDENT MANUAL

Be sure students turn to the correct lesson in their Student Manual.

5 Two thirds of the membership must be present to enact a rule.
6 We observed twenty nine infractions during the investigation.
7 Bancroft Industries reduced their sales force by one fourth.
8 After we add all the numbers, we must increase it by fifty five.

SKILLBUILDING

C. 30-Second Timings

Take two 30-second timings on lines 9–10. Then take two 30-second timings on lines 11–12. Try to increase your speed on each timing.

```
9       Presentation software will enable you to create some     11
10  colorful, animated, and visually exciting presentations.     22

11      You can include photos, clip art, sound, animation,      11
12  and a variety of colors, which will make a great impact.     22
    | 1 | 2 | 3 | 4 | 5 | 6 | 7 | 8 | 9 | 10 | 11 | 12
```

COMMUNICATION FOCUS

Write a short paragraph or two about your opinions on graphic presentations. Ask a teacher how he or she uses graphical presentations such as transparencies and PowerPoint® slides.

FORMATTING

D. Software Features

STUDENT MANUAL

Sort Database Tables   Query Database Tables

Study Lesson 147 in your student manual. Complete all the practice activities while at your computer. Then complete the jobs that follow.

TECHNOLOGY TIP

Adding photos, clip art, sound, or animation increases the size of a file. It may take longer to open or save a file containing these elements than it would to open or save a text-only file.

ACTIVITY 12
Database Table 3

Open the file DT3 and follow these steps:

1. Sort the table on the *State Bird* field in ascending order.
2. Print the table.
3. Do not save your changes.

ACTIVITY 13
Database Table 3

Using Database Table 3, perform the following sort:

1. Sort the table on the *Date of Statehood* field in ascending order.
2. Print the table.

ACTIVITY 14
Database Table 3

Using Database Table 3, perform the following sort:

1. Sort the table on the *Highest Point* field in descending order.
2. Print the table.

ACTIVITY 15
Database Table 3

Continue using Database Table 3 and perform the following sort:

1. Sort the table on the *State Bird* field in ascending order, and then sort the *State* field in descending order. Be sure the *State Bird* field is listed first.
2. Print the table and compare your results with Activity 12 results.

ACTIVITY 16
Database Table 3

Perform the following sort to return Database Table 3 to its original format:

1. Sort the table on the *State* field in ascending order.
2. Close the table window.

ACTIVITY 17
Database Table 3, Query 1

Create the following query on Database Table 3:

1. Select the *State* and *Date of Statehood* fields, and sort the data on the *Date of Statehood* field.
2. Print the results of the query table.
3. Close the query window(s).
4. Name the query Q1.

TEACH

Activity 12. Make sure students open the correct file, DT3. This file was last used for Activity 11. DT3 will be used for Activities 13–26.

Activity 13. Be sure students sort in the correct order.

Activity 14. As students work on Activity 14, walk around the room to make sure students understand the directions and are able to execute them.

Activity 15. Have students read the instructions once, then have them read the instructions again to be sure they understand what to do.

Activity 16. Have different students read aloud the steps for this activity. Stop after each step to make sure all students understand the directions.

Activity 17. Read the instructions aloud to students, stopping after each step to make sure students understand what they are to do.

Social Studies Connections

In the late 19th and early 20th century the U.S. government officially sanctioned land rushes, opening land to settlers for homesteading. Have students research to learn about your state's position on homesteading during this era.

interNET ACTIVITY

Have each student pick a different state and search the Internet for that state's official Website. Each student is to then prepare a short oral presentation about the Website including contents and appearance.

TEACH

Activity 18. Have students read the instructions once, then have them read the instructions again to be sure they know what to do.

Activity 19. Read the instructions aloud to students, stopping after each step to make sure students understand what they are to do.

Activity 20. Have different students read aloud the steps for this activity. Stop after each step to make sure all students understand the directions.

Activity 21. As students continue to work on this activity, walk around the room to make sure they understand the directions and are able to execute them. If you notice several students having trouble with the same step, go over this step again with the class.

Activity 22. Check to be sure students perform the sort correctly.

PORTFOLIO *Activity*

If students' portfolio goals include demonstration of progress, they may want to include one or more of the database tables from this lesson. Encourage students to evaluate their own work and include comments in their portfolio.

ACTIVITY 18

Database Table 3, Query 2

Create the following query on Database Table 3:

1. Select the *State* and *Date of Statehood* fields, and sort the data on the *Date of Statehood* field.
2. In the *Date of Statehood* field, specify selection of those states that acquired statehood in the 1700s.
3. Print the results of the query table.
4. Close the query window(s).
5. Name the query Q2.

ACTIVITY 19

Database Table 3, Query 3

Create the following query on Database Table 3:

1. Select the *State* and *Date of Statehood* fields, and sort the data on the *Date of Statehood* field.
2. In the *Date of Statehood* field, specify selection of those states that acquired statehood in the 1800s.
3. Print the results of the query table.
4. Close the query window(s).
5. Name the query Q3.

ACTIVITY 20

Database Table 3, Query 4

Create the following query on Database Table 3:

1. Select the *State* and *Date of Statehood* fields, and sort the data on the *Date of Statehood* field.
2. In the *Date of Statehood* field, specify selection of those states that acquired statehood in the 1900s.
3. Print the results of the query table.
4. Close the query window(s).
5. Name the query Q4.

ACTIVITY 21

Database Table 3, Query 5

Create the following query on Database Table 3:

1. Select the *State* and *Capital* fields, and sort the data on the *Capital* field.
2. Print the results of the query table.
3. Close the query window(s).
4. Name the query Q5.

ACTIVITY 22

Database Table 3, Query 6

Create the following query on Database Table 3:

1. Select the *State* and *Capital* fields, and sort the data on the *Capital* field.
2. In the *Capital* field, specify selection of those states with capitals that begin with the letter *C*.
3. Print the results of the query table.
4. Close the query window(s).
5. Name the query Q6.

JOURNAL ENTRY

Have students write about which season is their favorite and why. Then ask them to write a poem about this season. Read a few selections in class.

ACTIVITY 23

Database Table 3, Query 7

Create the following query on Database Table 3:

1. Select the *State* and *State Bird* fields, and sort the data on the *State Bird* field.
2. Print the results of the query table.
3. Close the query window(s).
4. Name the query Q7.

ACTIVITY 24

Database Table 3, Query 8

Create the following query on Database Table 3:

1. Select the *State* and *State Bird* fields, and sort the data on the *State Bird* field.
2. In the *State Bird* field, specify selection of those states with the cardinal, mockingbird, or robin as the state bird.
3. Print the results of the query table.
4. Name the query Q8.

ACTIVITY 25

Database Table 3, Query 9

Create the following query on Database Table 3:

1. Select the *State* and *State Bird* fields, and sort the data on the *State* field.
2. In the *State Bird* field, specify selection of those states with the cardinal, mockingbird, or robin as the state bird.
3. Print the results of the query table.
4. Close the query window(s).
5. Name the query Q9.

ACTIVITY 26

Database Table 3, Query 10

Create the following query on Database Table 3:

1. Select the *State* and *Highest Point* fields, and sort the data on the *Highest Point* field.
2. In the *Highest Point* field, specify selection of those states with elevations of 10,000 feet or higher.
3. Print the results of the query table.
4. Close the query window(s).
5. Name the query Q10.

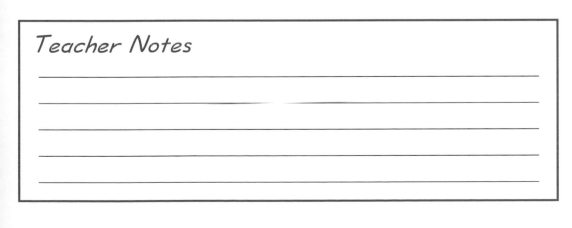

SOCIAL STUDIES CONNECTIONS

South Carolina was the first state to secede from the Union on December 20, 1860, so that it could become the first Confederate State. (It was readmitted to the Union on June 25, 1868.)

LESSON 147

TEACH

Activities 23–26. Have students read the instructions carefully. Walk around the room to make sure students understand the directions and are able to execute them. Provide help as needed.

ASSESS

- Check to see if students are increasing their speed as they complete each 30-second timing.
- Watch students as they complete Language Link activity to see if they are able to apply the hyphenation rule.
- Make sure students are able to sort and query database tables.
- As students begin working with the database activities, walk around the room and provide assistance as needed.
- After students finish each activity, have them view their work on the screen to see if they made any errors. If errors were made, have students edit their work and make corrections.

CLOSE

If students do not finish the databases during the class period, make sure they save their work so that they can complete it the next time this class meets.

Teacher Notes

LESSON 148

FOCUS

- Use 30-second OK timings to improve accuracy.
- Use 5-minute timings to build speed.
- Learn database features: Database Table Reports.
- Learn how to create database table reports.

BELLRINGER

As soon as students arrive at their workstations and log in, have them type the Warmup. Go over the purpose of each line as shown to the left of the copy.

TEACH

Activity B. Point out that 30-second OK timings are designed to encourage accuracy.

Activity C. Point out that words in the Preview Practice are used in the 5-minute timing that follows.

LESSON 148 DATABASES: REPORTS

OBJECTIVES:

- Improve keyboarding skill.
- Create reports based on database tables.
- Type 40/5'/5e.

A. WARMUP

Type each line 2 times.

Speed	1 The paper might run low before we can finish that next job.
Accuracy	2 Judi's dog jumps over major hurdles to beat Max for prizes.
Language Link	3 Lee attended a fast-paced meeting on January 23 at ten p.m.
Numbers/Symbols	4 On 10/14/98 Steven ran 38 laps; on 10/25/98 he ran 67 laps.
	| 1 | 2 | 3 | 4 | 5 | 6 | 7 | 8 | 9 | 10 | 11 | 12

SKILLBUILDING

B. 30-SECOND OK TIMINGS

Take two 30-second OK (error-free) timings on lines 5–6. Then take two 30-second OK timings on lines 7–8. Goal: no errors.

```
5      Hazel hurt an elbow when she bumped into the chair as     11
6  she was quickly running through the room to avoid the fire.  23

7      The six jet-black vans zipped quietly through the wet     11
8  grass, but they could not finish the entire course in time.  23
   | 1 | 2 | 3 | 4 | 5 | 6 | 7 | 8 | 9 | 10 | 11 | 12
```

C. PREVIEW PRACTICE

Type each line 2 times as a preview to the timings that follow.

Accuracy	9 events written calculate combination sixteenth chronologist
Speed	10 calendars tracking notable cycles errors unique epoch orbit

RESOURCES

Lesson Plan 148

Courseware Lesson 148

Student Data Disk

Student Manual

Supplementary Production Activities

Grading and Evaluation

D. 5-Minute Timings

Take two 5-minute timings on the paragraphs. Note your speed and errors.

Goal: 40/5'/5e

Social Studies
Connections

All calendars begin with an epoch, a span of time 10
marked by a notable event. From the start, the method of 22
tracking time was based on one of three major cycles. The 33
cycles included the orbit of the sun, orbit of the moon, and 45
a combination of both of their paths. 53

Due to the errors and omissions of the calendars of 63
the sixteenth century, a French chronologist named Joseph 75
Scaliger, proposed a new plan. He sought a time prior to 86
any event written in history. 92

Scaliger based his work on three unique cycles. One of 104
these was the twenty-eight-year cycle, the time after which 116
weekdays and days of the month repeat in the exact same 127
order. Another cycle was the nineteen-year Metonic orbit, 138
the time after which moon phases repeat on the same day of 150
the year. The third cycle was the fifteen-year indication, 162
which is also the Roman business and tax cycle. 172

He used these cycles to calculate a start date earlier 183
than all written events. His epoch was named the Julian 194
period after his father, Julius. 200

| 1 | 2 | 3 | 4 | 5 | 6 | 7 | 8 | 9 | 10 | 11 | 12 SI 1.46

TEACH

Activity D. Remind students that they should try to improve speed with each 5-minute timing. The goal for these timings is to type 40 words a minute for 5 minutes with no more than 5 errors.

Activity E. Have students turn to Lesson 148 in their Student Manual and read the explanation for the software they are using. Then have them complete the practice activities that follow.

STUDENT MANUAL

Be sure students turn to the correct lesson in their Student Manual.

FORMATTING

E. Software Features

STUDENT MANUAL

Database Table Reports

Study Lesson 148 in your student manual. Complete all the practice activities while at your computer. Then complete the jobs that follow.

CULTURAL CONNECTIONS

Have students research the history of the calendar and create a timeline on the computer of significant dates. Timelines should include the following calendars: Babylonian, Egyptian, Greek, Roman, Gregorian, and modern.

Social Studies Connections

Have students choose a calendar on the timelines they created in the Cultural Connections activity. Then, have them research the culture in which this calendar was created and write a short report. Post the reports and timelines around the room.

TEACH

Activity 27. Make sure students open the correct file, DT4. This file was created in Activity 8 in Lesson 145.

Activity 28. Make sure students open the correct file, DT2. This file was last used in Activity 5 in Lesson 143.

ASSESS

- Check to see if students complete each 30-second timing without errors.
- Check to see if students are reaching the goal on a 5-minute timing.
- Make sure students are able to create database table reports.
- As students begin working with the databases activities, walk around the room and provide assistance to individual students.
- After students finish each activity, have them view their work on the screen to see if they made any errors. If errors were made, have students edit their work and make corrections.

If students do not finish the activities during the class period, make sure they save their work so that they can edit it the next time this class meets.

CLOSE

DATABASE APPLICATIONS

ACTIVITY 27

Database Table 4, Report 1

Create a report using Database Table 4 and name it DR1. Complete the following steps to format the report. (The exact sequence of steps will vary according to the software program you are using.)

1. Select a column format for the report.
2. Select a format/style.
3. In the header, left-align the title *Salary Ranges*, and right-align your name.
4. Select a font size for the title and your name that is larger than the data text.
5. Preview/run the report.
6. Print the report.
7. Close the report.

ACTIVITY 28

Database Table 2, Report 2

Create a report using Database Table 2 and name it DR2. Complete the following steps to format the report. (The exact sequence of steps will vary according to the software program you are using.)

1. Select a tabular format for the report.
2. Select a format/style.
3. In the header, left-align the title *Olympic Tryouts*, and right-align your name.
4. Select a font size for the title and your name that is larger than the data text.
5. Preview/run the report.
6. Print the report.
7. Close the report.

PORTFOLIO *Activity*

Print one of the reports you just completed and place it in your portfolio. Then, write a short paragraph describing what you have learned about databases and what other uses you would have for setting up databases.

Teacher Notes

LESSON 149 DATABASES: FORMULAS

OBJECTIVES:

- Improve keyboarding skill.
- Learn about hyphenating compound adjectives.
- Create and use formulas in database tables.

A. WARMUP

Type each line 2 times.

Speed	1 We will try as hard as we can to start the car in the cold.
Accuracy	2 Two sax players in the jazz band gave a quick demo for Tom.
Language Link	3 Al cut the grass, trimmed the bushes, and pulled the weeds.
Numbers/Symbols	4 Our guess was 15% off. Abe had #66; Vi had #77--nobody won.
	| 1 | 2 | 3 | 4 | 5 | 6 | 7 | 8 | 9 | 10 | 11 | 12

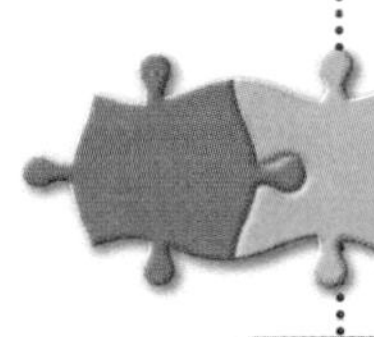

LANGUAGE LINK

B. HYPHENATED COMPOUND ADJECTIVES

Study the rule and examples below. Then edit lines 5–8 by inserting hyphens where needed.

Rule 48: Hyphenate compound adjectives that come before a noun (unless the first word is an adverb ending in *ly*).

We reviewed an up-to-date report on Wednesday.

We attended a highly rated session on multimedia software.

5 As stated in the above mentioned letter, she went to court.
6 You can order our products by calling our toll free number.
7 Their new, easy to operate recorder goes on sale next week.
8 She drove behind a slow moving vehicle for seventeen miles.

RESOURCES

 Lesson Plan 149

 Courseware Lesson 149

Student Data Disk

Student Manual

Language Link Worksheets

Supplementary Production Activities

LESSON 149

FOCUS

- Apply the Language Link rule for hyphenating compound adjectives.
- Use 12-second timings to build speed.
- Learn a database feature: Create Formulas in Database Tables.
- Create and use formulas in database tables.

BELLRINGER

As soon as students arrive at their workstations and log in, have them type the Warmup. Go over the purpose of each line as shown to the left of the copy.

TEACH

LANGUAGE LINK

Activity B. Go over the Language Link rule for hyphenating compound adjectives with students to make sure they all understand the rule. After students have completed typing, have them check each other's work for accuracy.

Solutions: As stated in the above-mentioned letter, she went to court.

You can order our products by calling our toll-free number.

Their new, easy-to-operate recorder goes on sale next week.

She drove behind a slow-moving vehicle for 17 miles.

TEACH

Activity C. Remind students that the goal for 12-second timings is improved speed with each timing.

Activity D. Have students turn to Lesson 149 in their Student Manual and read the explanation for the software they are using. Then have them complete the practice activities that follow.

STUDENT MANUAL
Be sure students turn to the correct lesson in their Student Manual.

Activity 29. Make sure students open the correct file, DT5. This file was last used in Activity 10 in Lesson 145. The file will be used again later in this lesson.

PORTFOLIO *Activity*

If students' portfolio goals include demonstrating progress, they may want to include a database table from this lesson. Encourage students to evaluate their work and include comments in their portfolio.

SKILLBUILDING

C. 12-Second Sprints

Take three 12-second timings on each line. Try to increase your speed on each timing.

```
9  Six men plan to take the boat trip to the side of the lake.
10 We must be ready when it is time for us to go to the shore.
11 This is what she said about it when she wanted to meet him.
12 Our real wish will come true many days from this very hour.
```

FORMATTING

D. Software Features

STUDENT MANUAL

Create Formulas in Database Reports

Study Lesson 149 in your student manual. Complete all the practice activities while at your computer. Then complete the jobs that follow.

DATABASE APPLICATIONS

ACTIVITY 29
Database Table 5

Open the file DT5 and make the following changes:

1. Add three new fields in this order at the end of the table: *Wholesale Price, Difference, Inventory Value.*
2. Enter the wholesale prices for the titles as shown in the illustration.
3. Close the table window.

548 ***Databases***

FACT FILE

Ask students: Where is the largest library in the world? (in the U.S.) What is it called? (The Library of Congress) Explain that the library houses more than 28 million books with collections that include works in 470 languages. Have students research more about the Library of Congress and then write a short report.

Title	Wholesale Price
Out of the Dust	$9.57
View From Saturday	$2.70
The Midwife's Apprentice	$6.57
Walk Two Moons	$2.97
Sarah, Plain and Tall	$8.97
The Bridge to Terabithia	$2.97
Roll of Thunder, Hear My Cry	$9.57
Mrs. Frisby and the Rats of NIMH	$10.20
Summer of the Swans	$2.97
Sounder	$8.97
Island of the Blue Dolphins	$3.30
Johnny Tremain	$12.00

ACTIVITY 30

Database Table 5, Report 3

Create a report using Database Table 5 (DT5), and name it DR3. Complete the following steps to format the report and perform the calculations. (The exact sequence of steps will vary according to the software program you are using.)

1. Change the print orientation to landscape.
2. Include only the *Code, Title, Quantity, Copies Available, Retail Price, Wholesale Price, Difference,* and *Inventory Value* fields in the report.
3. Select a tabular format.
4. Select a format/style.
5. In the header, left-align the title *Newbery Titles,* and right-align your name.
6. Select a font size for the title and your name that is larger than the data text.
7. Enter a formula in the *Difference* field that will calculate the difference between the retail and wholesale prices of each book.
8. Enter a formula in the *Inventory Value* field that will calculate the total value of the inventory for each book.
9. Preview/run the report.
10. Print the report.
11. Close the report.

Teacher Notes

TEACH

Activity 30. Have different students read aloud the steps for this activity. Stop after each step to make sure all students understand the directions.

ASSESS

- Watch students as they complete the Language Link activity to see if they are able to apply the hyphenation rule correctly.
- Check to see if students are increasing their speeds as they complete each 12-second timing.
- Make sure students are able to use formulas in a database table.
- As students begin working with the database activities, walk around the room and provide assistance as needed.
- After students finish each activity, have them view their work on the screen to see if they made any errors. If errors were made, have students edit their work and make corrections.

CLOSE

If students do not finish the databases during the class period, make sure they save their work so that they can complete it the next time this class meets.

Remind students to clean up their workstation when they leave.

LESSON 150

FOCUS

- Use 5-minute timings to build speed.
- Learn a database feature: Database Tables and Charts.
- Type a 2-page academic report, inserting a spreadsheet chart and database table.

BELLRINGER

As soon as students arrive at their workstations and log in, have them type the Warmup. Go over the purpose of each line as shown to the left of the copy.

TEACH

Activity B. Point out that words in the Preview Practice are used in the timing that follows.

LESSON 150

DATABASES: SIMULATION

OBJECTIVES:

- Improve keyboarding skill.
- Type 40/5'/5e.
- Insert database tables and charts.

A. WARMUP

Type each line 2 times.

Speed	1	Gloria has to read the pages of this book before she stops.
Accuracy	2	Paula rejoiced at the amazing reviews of six quality books.
Language Link	3	As you can see the man will not be able to finish the exam.
Numbers	4	I set tabs at 6, 15, 20, 35, 40, 60, 78, and 96 on the job.
		| 1 | 2 | 3 | 4 | 5 | 6 | 7 | 8 | 9 | 10 | 11 | 12

interNET CONNECTION

Connect to the Internet. Search the Internet for rules governing e-mail and Internet communications. These rules are often called netiquette. Look up this word in an Internet dictionary and note its meaning in your journal.

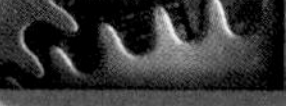

SKILLBUILDING

B. PREVIEW PRACTICE

Type each line 2 times as a preview to the timings that follow.

Accuracy	5	honest business etiquette particular appropriate punctuality
Speed	6	common things demand doing learn about vital other seem rule

RESOURCES

 Lesson Plan 150

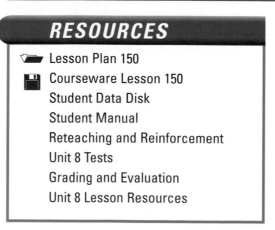

 Courseware Lesson 150

Student Data Disk

Student Manual

Reteaching and Reinforcement

Unit 8 Tests

Grading and Evaluation

Unit 8 Lesson Resources

C. 5-Minute Timings

Take two 5-minute timings on the paragraphs. Note your speed and errors.

Goal: 40/5'/5e

People with technical skills are in demand for many 11
kinds of jobs. Once on the job, however, you will need more 23
than technical skills to survive. You must be able to deal 34
with the unwritten company rules. 41
When you begin a new job, you will need to learn about 52
the rules of that particular workplace. Some rules will be 64
written, but others will not be. Observing these unwritten 76
rules can be vital to your success in business. 86
Every office has its own way of doing some things, yet 97
there are some basic rules of etiquette that are common in 109
all places of business. There are distinct behaviors that 120
seem to be required of each person who becomes an expert at 132
succeeding in business. For example, knowing the rules for 144
dressing appropriately and being well-groomed always helps. 156
In addition, if you are honest, courteous, well-mannered, 168
and punctual, you will probably be seen in a favorable way 179
by your peers. 182
Each employee should quickly become familiar with the 193
standard protocol of the company. 200

| 1 | 2 | 3 | 4 | 5 | 6 | 7 | 8 | 9 | 10 | 11 | 12 SI 1.48

TEACH

Activity C. Remind students that they should try to improve speed with each 5-minute timing. The goal for these timings is to type 40 words a minute for 5 minutes with no more than 5 errors.

Activity D. Have students turn to Lesson 150 in their Student Manual and read the explanation for the software they are using. Then have them complete the practice activities that follow.

STUDENT MANUAL

Be sure students turn to the correct lesson in their Student Manual.

FORMATTING

D. Software Features

STUDENT MANUAL

Inserting database tables and charts

Study Lesson 150 in your student manual. Complete all the practice activities while at your computer. Then complete the jobs that follow.

Unit 8 Lesson 150 **551**

JOURNAL ENTRY

Brainstorm with students about the rules of etiquette in your school and classroom. Write these on the board. Then have students write about how they feel about each rule and why. After writing, discuss the entries.

TEACH

Activity 31. Before students begin Activities 31, 32, and 33, have them read the information on Hurricanes on pages 553–554. Point out that the information in these activities will become part of this report.

Activity 32. Remind students to specify the size of the fields to accommodate the long entries.

DATABASE APPLICATIONS

ACTIVITY 31
Spreadsheet 49

Create a spreadsheet using the following data. Save the spreadsheet as SS49.

Decade	Number of Fatalities
1940s	216
1950s	877
1960s	587
1970s	217
1980s	118

1. Create a vertical bar chart.
2. Title the chart *U.S. Hurricane Fatalities.*
3. Title the *x*-axis *Decade.*
4. Title the *y*-axis *Number of Fatalities.*
5. Minimize the spreadsheet program.

ACTIVITY 32
Database Table 6

Follow these steps to create Database Table 6 and name it DT6:

1. Define the five fields as shown in the illustration. The only field that should be designated a number field is *Fatalities.*
2. Specify the size of each field as shown above the column.
3. Enter the records.
4. Close the table window.

Hurricane	Year	$ Damage	Fatalities	Initial Hit
Diane	1955	$4.2 billion	184	North Carolina
Betsy	1965	$6.5 billion	75	Bahamas and Florida
Camille	1969	$5.2 billion	259	Alabama, Mississippi, and Louisiana
Agnes	1972	$6.5 billion	129	Florida panhandle
Alicia	1983	$2.4 billion	18	Texas
Hugo	1989	$7.2 billion	56	South Carolina
Andrew	1992	$25.0 billion	26	South Florida

interNET ACTIVITY

Have students use the keyword hurricane to search the Internet, or provide them with the address for The Weather Channel (www.weather.com) or Accu-Weather (www.accuweather.com). Have them type a list of safety tips.

ACTIVITY 33
Report 72
2-Page Report

Format the following 2-page report in MLA style. Follow these steps to complete the report:

1. Insert the spreadsheet chart that you created in Activity 31 after the first paragraph of the report.
2. Horizontally center the chart.
3. Insert the database table you created in Activity 32 at the end of the report.
4. Horizontally center the table.
5. Insert a row at the beginning of the table. Center, bold, and type in all caps the table title, Hurricane Damage.
6. Where possible, modify the appearance of the database table to resemble the format of a word processing table.
7. Size the chart as necessary to keep the report to two pages.
8. Save the report as R72.
9. Print the report.

Science Connections

Hurricanes

A hurricane is the most powerful type of storm. Hurricanes are large, swirling, low-pressure systems that form over oceans and have a minimum wind speed of 75 miles per hour. These storms kill people and animals and cause extensive damage. The deadliest hurricane ever recorded is the Great Hurricane of October 1780, which killed over 22,000 people in the Caribbean. The 1950s claimed the most hurricane fatalities in the United States, as illustrated in the following chart.

Because of improved forecasting and technological advances, the number of injuries and deaths from hurricanes has decreased. A hurricane watch is issued when there is a threat of hurricane conditions within 24–36 hours. A hurricane warning is issued when hurricane conditions are expected in 24 hours or less. Careful and strategic planning can also reduce the risk of injury or death. Hurricane preparations should include knowing the safest evacuation route, locating the nearest shelter, maintaining disaster supplies, developing an emergency communication plan, and making arrangements for pets.

Naming hurricanes began in 1951 to avoid confusion when more than one storm was being followed. For two years, the names were taken from the international phonetic

Unit 8 Lesson 150 553

TEACH

Activity 33. Have students read the instructions once, then read them again to be sure they understand what to do.

Be sure students format the report correctly and insert the spreadsheet and the database in the correct position.

CULTURAL CONNECTIONS

Have students contact the local chapter of the Red Cross to have a speaker visit your class. Have students type a list of questions ahead of time. Ask the speaker to provide information on how students can get involved in the Red Cross and help your community.

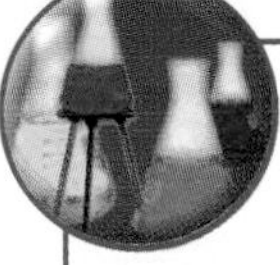

Science Connections

Invite a local weather reporter to speak to your class about weather patterns your region. Have students research the weather-related disaster that is most likely to strike your region, and list what to do.

ASSESS

- Check to see if students are increasing their word a minute speeds as they complete each 5-minute timing.
- Make sure students are able to insert database tables and charts into their documents.
- As students begin working on the activities, walk around the room and provide assistance to individual students as needed.
- After students finish each activity, have them view their work on the screen and make any corrections.

CLOSE

Remind students—for the last time—to clean up their workstation when they leave.

PORTFOLIO *Activity*

If students' portfolio goals include showcasing their best work, they may want to include the documents from this lesson. Encourage students to evaluate their work and include comments in their portfolio.

alphabet used at that time—Able, Baker, Charlie, etc. Beginning in 1953, female names were assigned to hurricanes; but since 1979 male and female names have been alternated.

Separate sets of hurricane names are used in the central Pacific, the eastern Pacific, and the Atlantic Basin. The first hurricane of the year in the Atlantic Basin and the eastern Pacific receives a name beginning with the letter *A*. The name of the central Pacific's first storm of the year continues from the list of names from the previous year.

The following table is a random list of hurricanes and the damage they left behind. In general, the table illustrates the decrease in the number of fatalities in recent decades.

*inter*NET CONNECTION

Connect to the Internet. Enter the following URLs to learn more about weather and hurricane names: *http://www.snobird.com/names98.htm* and *http://kids.mtpe.hq.nasa.gov/archive/hurricane/names.html.*

PORTFOLIO *Activity*

Make a list of the names of the most destructive hurricanes that have hit the U.S. in the last twenty years. Illustrate the information in a table or chart that you feel shows your information in a format that is easy to understand. Then, print a copy of your chart and a copy of the report in this lesson and add them to your portfolio.

Teacher Notes

DIAGNOSTIC PRACTICE: ALPHABET

The Diagnostic Practice: Alphabet routine is designed to diagnose and then correct your keystroking errors. You may use this program at any time throughout the course after you complete Lesson 18.

DIRECTIONS:

1. Type one set of the Pretest/Posttest lines 1 time. Identify your errors.
2. Note your results—the number of errors you made on each key and your total number of errors. For example, if you typed *rht* for *the,* that would count as 1 error on the letter *t.*
3. For any letter on which you made 2 or more errors, select the corresponding drill lines and type them 2 times. If you made only 1 error, type the drill 1 time.
4. If you made no errors on the Pretest/Posttest lines, turn to the practice on Troublesome Pairs on page SB3 and type each line 1 time. This section provides intensive practice on those pairs of keys commonly confused.
5. Finally, retype the same set of Pretest/Posttest lines, and compare your performance with your Pretest.

PRETEST/POSTTEST

Set 1

```
Buzz quickly designed five new projects for the wax museum.
John's wacky quip amazed but also vexed his new girlfriend.
Zed quickly jumped five huge barrels to warn Max and Teddy.
Orville quickly objected to Wes dumping five toxic hazards.
From the tower Dave saw six big jet planes quickly zoom by.
Beverly, has John kept that liquid oxygen frozen with care?
```

Set 2

```
Did Robert move that psychology quiz to next week for John?
Stanley, cover this oozy liquid wax before Jack mops again.
The six heavy guys jumped for eighty waltzing quarterbacks.
Skip was quite vexed by the seventeen jazzmen from Cologne.
The eight taxi drivers quickly zip by the jumble of wagons.
While having Joel wait, Ben quickly fixed the many zippers.
```

Set 3

```
Last week Jed McVey was quite busy fixing the frozen pipes.
Vic quickly mixed frozen strawberries into the grape juice.
Five big jet planes zoomed quickly by the six steel towers.
Jeff amazed the audience by quickly giving six new reports.
Sixty equals only five dozen, but we promised Jackie eight.
Joel quietly picked sixteen razors from the blue woven bag.
```

SKILLBUILDING *(continued)*

INDIVIDUAL REACHES

A Ada and Anna had an allowance and always had adequate cash.
B Barbara grabbed back the brown bag Bob bought at a bargain.
C Charles can accept and cash any checks the church collects.
D David drove down and deducted the dividends he had divided.
E Everyone here exerted extra effort each week we were there.

F Fred Ford offered to find fresh food for five fine fellows.
G Guy suggested getting eight guys to bring George's luggage.
H Hank hoped that she had withheld the cash they had to have.
I Iris insists their idea is simply idiotic in this instance.
J Jack and Jerry joined Joe just to enjoy a journey to Japan.

K Kathy asked Ken to take a blank checkbook back to her bank.
L Larry helped several little fellows learn to play baseball.
M Mr. Ammon made many mistakes in estimating minimum markets.
N Nan never knew when any businessman wanted an announcement.
O One or two of those older tool orders ought to go out soon.

P Please provide proper paper supplies for plenty of persons.
Q Quentin quietly inquired what sequences required questions.
R Run over for another order from the firm across the street.
S She says she sold us some shiny scissors sometime Saturday.
T Try to get the truth when they talk about better attitudes.

U Unless you pour out your mixture, you could hurt our stuff.
V Vivian raved over violets and even saved several varieties.
W William will work well whenever we know where we will work.
X X-rays exceed examinations except for external exploration.
Y Yes, any day they say you may be ready, you may try to fly.
Z Zenith Franz realizes that he idealized the zigzag friezes.

TROUBLESOME PAIRS

A/S	Sal said he asked Sara Ash for a sample of the raisins.
B/V	Vera very bravely was verbose with a bevy of beverages.
C/D	Candie decided the December calendar decal could decay.
E/W	Weni knew in weekday weather weak weeds grew elsewhere.
F/G	Goeff goofed by finding the gulf for the grateful frog.
H/J	Judith wore jodhpurs; she joshed with John and Johanna.
I/O	Iona totally foiled Olin's spoiled oily ointment plans.
K/L	Karl liked to walk seven kilometers quickly with Kelly.
M/N	Many have names of maidens among the main mason manors.
O/P	Opal and Polly phoned three opera pollsters in Phoenix.
Q/A	Quin quickly qualified this quality quart quartz quota.
R/T	Robert tried trading rations to three terrific skaters.
U/Y	If you are busy, buy your supply of yucca Yule in July.
X/C	Cal expected the excitement to exceed all expectations.
Z/A	The five sizable, lazy zebras zigzagged as Eliza gazed.

DIAGNOSTIC PRACTICE: NUMBERS

The Diagnostic Practice: Numbers routine is designed to diagnose and then correct your keystroking errors. You may use this program at any time throughout the course after you complete Lesson 26.

DIRECTIONS:

1. Type one set of the Pretest/Posttest lines 1 time. Identify your errors.
2. Note your results—the number of errors you made on each key and your total number of errors. For example, if you typed *24* for *25,* that would count as 1 error on the number *5.*
3. For any number on which you made 2 or more errors, select the corresponding drill lines and type them 2 times. If you made only 1 error, type the drill 1 time. If you made no errors on the Pretest/Posttest lines, type the drills that contain all numbers on page SB6 and type each line 1 time.
4. Finally, retype the Pretest/Posttest, and compare your performance with your Pretest.

PRETEST/POSTTEST

Set 1

```
ripe 4803, ire 843, wee 233, ore 943, pier 0834, wire 2843,
Silvio marked the chalkboard at 25, 30, and 45 centimeters.
Alice put markers at 10 km, 29 km, 38 km, 47 km, and 56 km.
Bob lost checks Nos. 234, 457, and 568. Mandy lost No. 901.
Please clean Rooms 340 and 380. Kerbey will clean Room 443.
Those five passengers are 25, 39, 42, 45, and 50 years old.
```

Set 2

```
wee 233, tie 583, toe 593, pure 0743, pour 0974, rout 4975,
Iva put 428 in group 1, 570 in group 2, and 396 in group 3.
The party governed during 1910, 1929, 1938, 1947, and 1956.
The total of 198, 384, 275, 470, and 672 is easy to figure.
They had 92 or 83. He has 10 or 74. We have 56 or maybe 57.
Check lockers 290, 471, 356, and 580 before school Tuesday.
```

Set 3

```
pie 083, rye 463, your 6974, tier 5834, eye 363, pipe 0803,
Read pages 100, 129, and 138; summarize Chapters 47 and 56.
By May 1, ship 29 seats, 38 stoves, 47 tents, and 56 coats.
The 29 females lived 180 days at 4387 South Parkview Court.
Janet read pages 105 through 120 and pages 387 through 469.
Marvin easily won the bulletins numbered 12,345 and 67,890.
```

INDIVIDUAL REACHES

aqa aq1a a1a 111 a1a 1/11 a1a 11.1 a1a aq1a 11.1 11,111 a1a
1 ant, 11 arms, 111 aunts, 101 apples, 131 animals, or 1.11
Henry read 111 pages in 1 hour and ate 1 apple in 1 minute.
Crystal wrote 1 story that was 1,111 pages long on 1 topic.

sws sw2s s2s 222 s2s 2/22 s2s 22.2 s2s sw2s 22.2 22,222 s2s
2 sips, 22 sets, 222 sites, 212 socks, 231 soldiers, or 2.2
She moved to Room 221 with 2,223 students for about 2 days.
Today 202 computer students were solving 322 math problems.

ded de3d d3d 333 d3d 3/33 d3d 33.3 d3d de3d 33.3 33,333 d3d
3 dots, 33 dogs, 333 drops, 323 dimes, 321 daisies, or 3.33
The 3 doctors and 3 nurses did the 3 surgeries in 33 hours.
Your 3 cats and 23 dogs liked to romp on the 330-acre farm.

frf fr4f f4f 444 f4f 4/44 f4f 44.4 f4f fr4f 44.4 44,444 f4f
4 figs, 44 fans, 444 farms, 434 finals, 431 friends, or 4.4
Meredith flew 444 miles to see 4 friends at 434 Oak Street.
Florence sold 41 fish dinners to the 44 customers at 4 p.m.

ftf ft5f f5f 555 f5f 5/55 f5f 55.5 f5f ft5f 55.5 55,555 f5f
5 foes, 55 facts, 555 foals, 545 fowls, 543 flights, or 5.5
Fred found 55 facts in 545 flights from 514 foreign places.
Theo found that flight 5253 leaves at 5 a.m. from gate 545.

jyj jy6j j6j 666 j6j 6/66 j6j 66.6 j6j jy6j 66.6 66,666 j6j
6 jaws, 66 jets, 666 jeeps, 656 jokes, 654 journals, or 6.6
She had 6 jobs to do in 66 hours. Julia worked 664 minutes.
Her 6 math tests had 165 problems to be done in 60 minutes.

juj ju7j j7j 777 j7j 7/77 j7j 77.7 j7j ju7j 77.7 77,777 j7j
7 jugs, 77 jars, 777 jumps, 767 joggers, 765 jewels, or 7.7
Joe saw 7 joggers run 177 miles across 7,777 acres of land.
The 7 suits were shipped to 7167 East 7th Avenue on July 7.

SB5

INDIVIDUAL REACHES

```
kik ki8k k8k 888 k8k 8/88 k8k 88.8 k8k ki8k 88.8 88,888 k8k
8 kegs, 88 kits, 888 kilns, 878 kickers, 876 knocks, or 8.8
The 8 keys fit 887 kits; Kim found 8,876 knots in the kits.
The 8 kind ladies got 882 kimonos for 188 kids in the play.

lol lo9l l9l 999 l9l 9/99 l9l 99.9 l9l lo9l 99.9 99,999 l9l
9 laps, 99 lots, 999 loops, 989 lilies, 987 lifters, or 9.9
Lillian said 9 times to leave 99 lilies for the 989 ladies.
My 9 lawyers had 19 leaky pens, 89 legal pads, and 9 limos.

;p; ;p0; ;0; 000 ;0; 0/00 ;0; 00.0 ;0; ;p0; 00.0 00,000 ;0;
10 pots, 20 pins, 300 parts, 400 plants, 500 parades or 0.0
The 10 party stores put 100 pots and 200 pans to pick from.
The 10 books had 23,000 pages in each; Paul read 500 pages.
```

All numbers

```
a1a s2s d3d f4f f5f j6j j7j k8k l9l ;0; Add 6 and 8 and 29.
That 534-page script called for 10 actors and 17 actresses.
After 1,374 miles in the car, she must then drive 185 more.
The 141 professors asked 4,690 sportscasters 230 questions.
```

All numbers

```
a1a s2s d3d f4f f5f j6j j7j k8k l9l ;0; Add 3 and 4 and 70.
They built 1,200 houses on 345 acres in just under 3 years.
Six boys arrived on May 26, 1994, and left on May 30, 1998.
Marlee bought 15 new books, 62 used books, and 47 new pens.
```

All numbers

```
a1a s2s d3d f4f f5f j6j j7j k8k l9l ;0; Add 5 and 7 and 68.
The 4 stores are open from 9:30 a.m. until 6:00 p.m. daily.
I gave away 2 pans, 4 plates, 8 glasses, and 25 containers.
She moved to 705 Garfield Street, not 507, on June 4, 2000.
```

PACED PRACTICE

The Paced Practice routine builds speed and accuracy in short, easy steps, using individualized goals and immediate feedback. You can use this routine any time after completing Lesson 18.

This section contains a series of 2-minute timings for speeds ranging from 14 wam to 60 wam. The first time you use these timings, take a 1-minute entry timing. Then, select a passage that is 2 wam higher than your current keyboarding speed. Use a two-stage practice pattern to achieve each speed goal—first concentrate on speed, and then work on accuracy.

SPEED GOAL: Take three 2-minute timings on the same passage until you can complete it in 2 minutes (do not worry about the number of errors).

When you have achieved your speed goal, work on accuracy.

ACCURACY GOAL: To type accurately, you need to slow down—just a little bit. To reach your accuracy goal, drop back 2 wam to the previous passage. Take three 2-minute timings on this passage until you can complete it in 2 minutes with no more than 2 errors.

For example, if you achieved a speed goal of 30 wam, you should work on an accuracy goal of 28 wam. When you have achieved the 28 wam goal for accuracy, you would then move up 4 wam (for example, to the 34 wam passage) and work for speed again.

ENTRY TIMING

```
     If your mailbox is full of mail that you do not want,   11
your name is on a mailing list. Firms buy mailing lists so   23
that they can send you their ads. Unless you write and ask   34
each company to take your name off its list, you will keep   46
getting junk mail.                                           50
```

14 wam

```
     Tourists like to meander through the Boston Gardens
during the summer. They stroll the shady paths and then
stop to ride on the swan boats.
```

16 wam

```
     Pleasure boats and large tankers pass through the
Cape Cod canal every day. The canal is spanned by two
high bridges for auto traffic and by a railroad bridge.
```


SB7

SKILLBUILDING *(continued)*

18 wam

Each year, many Americans suffer a stroke. It can cause serious problems. For some, it can become difficult to walk or to use an arm. For others, a stroke can affect their speech.

20 wam

Many people think angora is the wool of sheep but it comes from goats. The goats are sheared two times a year. The wool is washed through a special process. It can then be dyed and spun into strands.

20 wam

The old woman who walks in the park always has a huge smile on her face. She talks to the people who cross her path. When she makes new friends, she offers assistance in her quiet way and is excited.

22 wam

There is no substitute for the taste of ice cream on hot, humid days. Choices of all types are out to engage the eye, and the sharp clerks will fix just the mix and size to suit you best. A cup or a cone would be great.

24 wam

To see the artists' pain is a joy. To watch the zeal with which they work to have the exact color show up on the pad is exciting. As they glide the new brush quickly across the pad, the radiant hues take form and bring smiles to our faces.

26 wam

When you work with people every day, you get to know what it is that they like best. You also find out quickly what does make them frown. A bit of extra kind effort in a dozen little ways will make your office a pleasant place in which to complete all duties.

28 wam

When shopping in this country, we[1] generally accept the price tag on [2]merchandise for the final price the[3] store will consider. If we really [4]want an item, we pay the amount ask[5]ed. In other nations, prices might [6]vary each moment, depending on the [7]ability of the purchaser to bargain.[8]

30 wam

National parks are owned by the peo[1]ple of America, and they are preserves[2] for wildlife and timber. The parks a[3]re cared for by the government to be s[4]ure they remain protected and guarded[5] resources. The rangers help prevent f[6]orest fires, analyze weather conditio[7]ns, and keep watch on the wild animals.[8]

32 wam

You simply do not go rafting down the [1]quick river flowing through the Grand Ca[2]nyon without plenty of skill and help. T[3]he hazards can be just too severe. The b[4]eautiful canyon is rocky, thorny, and ho[5]t during summer months. At times, it is [6]so windy that sand sprays may hit you in[7] the face with a brisk and stinging jolt.[8]

34 wam

A batik is a dyed cloth that has hot wax[1] placed on it to form a design. First the a[2]rtist melts wax, tints it various colors, [3]paints a design, and then dyes the cloth. S[4]ome artists prefer to paint the cloth with[5] a clear wax. Then the batik is dyed again [6]and again with many colors. Only the port[7]ion not covered with the wax becomes colored.[8]

SB9

SKILLBUILDING *(continued)*

36 wam

An interesting and exciting hobby for you could be working with plants. You have missed a joy if you have never waited with expectation for a tiny sprig to sprout into a plant. Actually, plants make wonderful pets for apartment dwellers. They neither bark nor meow, and the neighbors don't grumble about being kept awake or about being annoyed by a noisy pet.

38 wam

Have you ever been on a fairly long trip by car only to find yourself bored because you didn't have much to do? You, the passenger, can engross yourself in a great book. This answer to the boredom can make time appear to pass more rapidly. You could purchase several paperbacks at a local bookstore; and as you read, you can capture numerous hours of entertainment and enjoyment.

40 wam

Today, a quick way to get from one destination to another is by plane. For your flight, you can choose from among many airlines. In addition, airlines throughout the nation offer daily service to many cities here and abroad. Passengers on domestic and international flights should allow enough time before departure to secure seats on board the plane and to check in baggage at the airport terminal.

42 wam

Every year when winter approaches, you might look up at the sky and see hundreds and maybe even thousands of birds flying toward warmer weather. Quite simply, they migrate south just to escape the severe days that come so soon. Some experts hypothesize that birds migrate because they physically cannot last in the harsh winters of the frigid north. Other experts think that birds migrate to locate better food sources.

44 wam

Most successful newspapers are large businesses with an extensive staff and several readers. Now, though, there is a growing number of smaller papers. Their aim is to focus on a community or one subject. A small paper that is well produced will concentrate on and promote a local public. In addition, for those who are in the business, operating it is challenging and rewarding. Moreover, papers provide everyone a vehicle for free speech.

46 wam

Results of a citizenship test taken by a selected group of high school students were surprising. The test was conducted to determine how much knowledge young people have about our system of government. Also, it questioned whether they know how to split their ballot when they vote. Only one-third of the students participating in the program knew that a voter could divide his or her party choice. The majority was ignorant of the political system altogether.

48 wam

Veterinarians are doctors who are trained to treat and to prevent disease in animals. Although they attend different medical schools than doctors trained to treat people, their program of study and training are similar. Vets can limit their practice to one kind of animal. If they choose to specialize in horses, they can be highly paid because the patients might be priceless race horses. Some vets, on the other hand, would rather work with or conduct research on wild animals.

50 wam

The Inca Indians lived hundreds of years ago near what is now called Peru. They were a great nation known for their many unique buildings. These buildings, in fact, are still visible in ruins deep in the jungle. The temples that remain can be scrutinized for clues about their religion, beliefs, culture, and way of life. Some knowledge already exists, for we have learned that they were a people of numerous skills. Perhaps in time we can uncover the answer to the secret of why the Incas vanished.

52 wam

The brain controls conscious behavior like walking and thinking. It also controls involuntary behavior like the heartbeat and breathing. In humans, it is known to be the site of emotions, memory, and thought. It functions by receiving information through nerve cells from every part of the body. When the brain receives an influx of data, it needs to evaluate the data and then zip off commands to an area of the body like a muscle. Or, the brain might simply store the data. Neurons can process a large amount of data.

54 wam

Working in a place where everyone gets along would be great. However, we all know that the chance of finding a job in a place like that really seldom happens. Each of us has a different personality. When we mix together all of those personalities, the results are quite varied. There will be those who get along with everyone and find no fault with anything. But, by and large, each of us can and will have a difference of opinion with someone at some point. We need to bring qualities like zeal and a good attitude to every job situation.

56 wam

Each June, July, or August, some firms put a closed sign at the front door. They let their employees have the entire month off. All of them like to zip out of town for a nice relaxing vacation. During this month, everyone can enjoy a little time in the sun, or in a boat. Some head for the mountains for a camping or hiking trip. In the summer, most of us usually do less indoors and spend quite a lot of time outside. Many winter resorts have summer activities. Their activities can be enjoyable and quite varied. They do a lot of business during the summer.

58 wam

It has been more than a hundred years since the phone first touched our lives. It has modified the way all of us around the world converse. There are more ways than just a phone to help us quickly stay in touch with others. A computer connected to a modem or fax machine or a pager can be used to carry messages from place to place. The use of these carriers can be quicker and more cost-efficient than the use of the telephone. Today, using more than one of these communication devices is a common practice. We can choose to stay in touch by phone, fax, e-mail, page, or letter.

SKILLBUILDING *(continued)*

60 wam Many standard dictionaries give brief essays on topics such as the history of English, what is good usage, and the different dialects of English. Usage refers to how words are used in speaking and writing. A regional way of pronouncing a word is considered dialect. Quite frequently, a dictionary will give instructions on how to use the word. The most obvious information appears first. It is correct syllable division and spelling. When you type a paper, you need to be razor sharp on the correct way to hyphenate a word. Do not be lax in your writing. Use a dictionary to help check every report.

SUPPLEMENTARY TIMINGS

TIMING 1

Raising dogs can be a combination of both fun and hard 11
work. Before you even start, you have to decide just which 23
breed can best adapt to your lifestyle. If you need a dog 35
to protect your house, a poodle will not give you enough 46
protection. If you are in your own apartment, a collie may 58
be too large. When you have chosen the dog for you, expect 70
to have to train it. This can be done quickly with a new 81
puppy that is willing to learn. 87

| 1 | 2 | 3 | 4 | 5 | 6 | 7 | 8 | 9 | 10 | 11 | 12 |

TIMING 2

For students who can speak a foreign language, there 11
is an amazing job market today. Many major companies in 22
other countries have been buying control of or investing 33
in American firms. Their demand for workers with foreign 45
language skills can be seen in the large number of help 56
wanted ads for experts with language skills. 65

The fact that so many Americans cannot speak, read, 76
or write another language is tragic because the countries 87
of the world today are closely linked. International trade 99
is now vital to business and government, and young people 111
cannot afford to be unequipped to meet the changes and 122
challenges of the future. 127

| 1 | 2 | 3 | 4 | 5 | 6 | 7 | 8 | 9 | 10 | 11 | 12 |

SKILLBUILDING *(continued)*

TIMING 3

Businesses and individuals can write letters to 10
officials in Washington. There are several persons to whom 22
you might send such a letter. These include the President, 33
senators, or representatives. The people who are elected 45
to go to Washington take along a staff who answers most 56
of the mail from their constituents. Using the mail is one 68
way legislators continually keep in touch with what is 79
going on in their individual congressional districts. 89

People send inquiries on many topics. They may want 100
to express a positive feeling or they may want to complain 112
about taxes, pollution, or foreign policy. Some letters do 124
influence how lawmakers make their decisions. 133

| 1 | 2 | 3 | 4 | 5 | 6 | 7 | 8 | 9 | 10 | 11 | 12 |

TIMING 4

Autumn in the "northlands" is very exciting. You 10
jump up in the early morning; walk out under a clear, blue 22
sky; and feel the strong chill in the air. The leaves have 34
lost their brilliant green. It appears that they have been 45
tinted by someone passing by. The truth is that during 56
the night hours, a frost has painted the green to hues of 68
brown, yellow, orange, and scarlet. It is a breathtaking 79
panorama in Technicolor. The leaves seem not to move in 91
the quiet breeze. Then, suddenly, a brisk puff lifts them 102
from the limbs and carries them gently like feathers to 113
the ground below. You watch as legions of leaves jump free 125
and float to the earth, covering it like a quilted blanket 137
that looks much like moss. When you walk on top of the 148
blanket, it cushions each step you take as though you were 160
walking on air. 163

| 1 | 2 | 3 | 4 | 5 | 6 | 7 | 8 | 9 | 10 | 11 | 12 |

TIMING 5

Have you ever felt rundown, tired, and fatigued? 10
The symptoms listed above are common to many of us today. 22
They affect our job performance; they limit the fun we 33
have with our family and friends; and they can even affect 44
our good health. Here are a few of the ways by which we 56
can quickly minimize the problem and become more active in 67
all the things we do daily. 73

It is essential that we get plenty of sleep so that 84
we are rested when we get up each morning. We must eat a 95
good breakfast so that we can build up energy for the day 107
that follows. Physical exercise is a necessity, and it 118
might be the one most important ingredient in building up 129
our energy reserves. We must engage in vigorous exercise 141
to make our hearts beat faster and cause our breathing 152
rate to appreciably increase. These are things that can 163
help us increase our energy and make us healthier people. 174

| 1 | 2 | 3 | 4 | 5 | 6 | 7 | 8 | 9 | 10 | 11 | 12 |

SB17

SKILLBUILDING *(continued)*

TIMING 6

Many people have wondered what might possibly be 10
the greatest structure on earth. The tallest buildings, 21
the longest bridges, and the mightiest dams might all be 33
examined in order to find the answer to this difficult 44
question. In the minds of many people, one of the greatest 55
structures ever built was the Great Wall of China. It is a 67
well-known fact that its features are so impressive that 79
astronauts can view the wall from their spaceships. 89

The structure was built primarily by mixing earth 99
and bricks. It is wide enough at the top to permit several 111
people to walk abreast on it. It winds for miles through a 123
large section of the country, over mountains and across 134
valleys. It was constructed to keep out unwelcome tribes. 146
It is believed that building the wall required the labor 157
of many thousands of persons for dozens of decades. The 168
first sections of the Great Wall were built in the Age of 180
Warring States. 183

| 1 | 2 | 3 | 4 | 5 | 6 | 7 | 8 | 9 | 10 | 11 | 12 |

TIMING 7

Did you ever look up at the sky during the night and 11
see a shooting star? Most likely what you saw was a meteor 23
racing across the sky. Sometimes meteor showers are visible 35
to the naked eye. At such times you do not need special 46
glasses or binoculars to view these space voyagers. Between 58
midnight and dawn is the best time to look for them. If you 70
are outdoors you will get a much better view. 79

Every year meteor showers are caused by the extra 89
scrap matter of comets. When the comets are quite close 100
to the sun, more debris accumulates and there are likely 112
to be more meteors. Each summer, from around the middle of 124
July through the middle of August, a meteor show may light 135
up the night sky. At peak times, you may be able to see as 147
many as a hundred meteors in a night. In the city, the 158
bright meteor show has to compete with the bright city 169
lights. From the ground, the meteors may look as though 180
they are coming from the constellation Perseus. 190

| 1 | 2 | 3 | 4 | 5 | 6 | 7 | 8 | 9 | 10 | 11 | 12 |

SKILLBUILDING *(continued)*

TIMING 8

Genealogy has become a fascinating science to some 10
people. You do not need to be a scientist to get involved 22
in genealogy. You do not even need a college degree to 33
trace your roots. There was a time when you might have 44
wanted to trace your family tree to prove that one or more 56
of your ancestors came over from Europe on the Mayflower. 67
But, today we trace our roots as expressions of personal 79
and cultural pride and identity, no matter how humble a 90
person's origins might be. 95

There are genealogical societies throughout the 105
country. It seems we all want to know where we came from 117
and how we arrived here. Genealogy can be a complex field. 128
It can encompass religion, demographics, geography, legal 140
history, ethnic and women's studies, photographic imaging 152
and library research. But, getting started at tracing your 163
roots does not have to be complicated. You simply start 175
with what you know and then move toward the unknown. The 186
library at your school or in your city can help you get 197
started with your research. 203

| 1 | 2 | 3 | 4 | 5 | 6 | 7 | 8 | 9 | 10 | 11 | 12 |

TIMING 9

One of the many unique features of a democracy is 10
that everyone of legal age has the right to vote. Voting 22
should be taken seriously because it is a responsibility. 33
It is obvious that a government will not be representative 45
if citizens do not take an active part in choosing the 56
people to represent them. It is easy to be critical of our 68
leaders, but some of the blame rests with those who do not 80
care enough about our country to vote. 87

Citizens can vote for many levels of government. 97
Federal, state, county, and city elections must be planned 109
for every year in which the terms of officials have ended. 121
Primaries are held to narrow the number of candidates. The 133
year in which a president is chosen can create a lot of 144
excitement, but citizens should be interested in and vote 156
for their choice in each election. 163

A good voter should pay careful attention to the 173
main issues and the candidates. Newspapers, public debates, 185
and interviews are good sources of information. Choose the 196
officials who share your views and are qualified to do 207
the job. 209

| 1 | 2 | 3 | 4 | 5 | 6 | 7 | 8 | 9 | 10 | 11 | 12 |

SKILLBUILDING *(continued)*

TIMING 10

If you are not a classical music fan and do not 10
often go to the theater, you probably think, as do most 21
concert goers, that music before Bach is a mystery. Many 32
music fans think of classical music as intensely lyrical, 44
with madrigals and dances that are accompanied by various 56
horns, bells, drums, violins, and other instruments. But, 67
music and opera have been performed and listened to for 78
almost five centuries. One way to approach this music is 90
to just relax and enjoy its strangeness. While you are 101
listening, make a mental note of what sounds are pleasing 112
to your ear and what sounds seem like irradiating noise. 124
You can train your ear to pick up the music of the violin, 136
cello, trumpet, clarinet, harp, piano, piccolo, xylophone, 147
tuba, and even the flute. Melodies played as intended by 159
the composer may sound quite odd to the untrained ears 170
of today's listeners. One reason for this might be that 181
the tuning of instruments has changed. Also, the listeners 193
of the fifteenth century most likely had their own ideas 204
of what constituted harmony and enjoyable music. 214

| 1 | 2 | 3 | 4 | 5 | 6 | 7 | 8 | 9 | 10 | 11 | 12 |

SB22

TIMING 11

If you love mystery, you will be intrigued by the 10
speculation over how plants and animals first arrived in 22
Hawaii. Most people's ideas of a Hawaiian paradise include 33
swaying palms, dense jungles, and luscious fruit ready to 45
be picked. For millions of years, the chain of Hawaiian 56
Islands were raw and barren places where there were no 67
plants or birds. These lush Pacific Ocean islands are a 78
geological mystery. They formed spontaneously more than 90
two thousand miles from any continental land. They were 101
isolated from the normal spread of plants and animals. 112
The flora and fauna that did reach them found a foreign 123
ecosystem. They had to adapt or perish. Many of the birds 135
and plants became so specialized that they were not only 146
limited to specific islands but also to single isolated 157
island valleys. It was fortunate that the soil was rich. 169
There were no other plants or animals with which to 179
compete. The climate was variable and nearly perfect for 190
most growing things. The evolution of the plants and 201
animals on these isolated islands appears to have evolved 213
very quickly. 215

| 1 | 2 | 3 | 4 | 5 | 6 | 7 | 8 | 9 | 10 | 11 | 12 |

SB23

SKILLBUILDING *(continued)*

TIMING 12

Productivity measurement techniques are often used 10
in word processing installations today to evaluate the 21
output that is produced. This technique allows management 33
to compare workloads in order to improve scheduling and 44
work dispersal. 47

Productivity measurement also can help a company 57
by recording, calculating, and tracking employee production 69
over a period of time. Supervisors are then able to create 81
performance standards designed for their organization. 92
This method of measurement can be used to assist managers 104
in making reliable decisions regarding salary increases 115
and promotion of word processing personnel. 124

A measure of production might also assist those 134
who are more capable in a variety of ways. For example, 145
when compared to their peers, their abilities and skills 156
will be highlighted. Using this particular technique, all 168
the employees can be evaluated on a parallel basis. Very 179
talented workers can be rewarded. Lastly, this measurement 191
technique can assist in removing the subjectivity that is 203
found in company measurement systems that are used for 214
employee evaluations. 218

| 1 | 2 | 3 | 4 | 5 | 6 | 7 | 8 | 9 | 10 | 11 | 12 |

TIMING 13

It is quite possible that Ellis Island is part of 10
your family history. For many years, Ellis Island was an 22
immigration station. In the early part of the twentieth 33
century, it served as the main gateway to our country. 44
Twelve million foreigners had passed through its doors by 55
the middle of the twentieth century, when it closed. Ships 67
unloaded their passengers at the docks in New York. Then, 79
passengers quickly transferred to boats and barges for the 91
the trip to Ellis Island in New York Harbor. It was the 102
first place many of our forebears saw when they arrived 113
in America. 115

This country is made up of immigrants, along with 126
native American Indians. An immigrant is someone who moves 137
from one country to another. The immigrant usually plans 149
to make the new country home. Millions of Americans can 160
trace their family history to one or more ancestors who 171
first arrived in the United States through Ellis Island. 183
Today, it is a museum. Millions of dollars were raised to 194
fix up the neglected building. The museum is located only 206
one mile from New York City and a few hundred yards from 217
the docks of New Jersey. 222

| 1 | 2 | 3 | 4 | 5 | 6 | 7 | 8 | 9 | 10 | 11 | 12 |

SB25

SKILLBUILDING *(continued)*

TIMING 14

The Hawaiian Islands have much to offer the tourist. 11
One attraction is the beautiful parks. The flora, fauna, 22
and buildings are protected by federal law. Hawaii's state 34
bird, the nene, is endangered. When visitors feed these 45
birds, they attract them to parking lots and roadsides. 56
This places the birds in danger from auto traffic that 67
might injure or kill them. Visitors should avoid feeding 79
the birds or animals found in state parks. 87

The volcanoes of the Hawaiian Islands add mystery 97
and exotic scenery. A wonderful way to observe the raw 108
power of a volcano is by taking a helicopter tour. The 119
helicopter is well-suited for the air maneuvers needed 130
to get a close view. The pilot usually flies over areas 142
with the most volcanic activity. They often dip low over 153
lava pools, skim still-glowing flows, and circle towering 165
steam clouds rising from where the lava enters the sea. 176
You might like to spend a full day at Kilauea enjoying 187
the sights. Atop Kilauea, you can quietly appreciate the 198
beauty of this impressive volcano. It is four thousand 209
feet above sea level and about ten degrees cooler than 220
the coast. 222

| 1 | 2 | 3 | 4 | 5 | 6 | 7 | 8 | 9 | 10 | 11 | 12 |

TIMING 15

Before the middle of the twentieth century, workers 11
were treated as just another element of the production 22
process. Men and women worked under dismal conditions. 33
Most of the time, they were required to work twelve to 44
sixteen hours a day and the work week was six days long. 55
Wages were low. Health and safety hazards were ignored by 67
employers. If the employer provided any fringe benefits, 78
they were meager. Even though workers were exploited, they 90
were grateful to have a job. Over time, working conditions 102
and the treatment of workers have improved. 110

Effective management is a focus in today's work world. 122
A scientific approach in the management of employees may 133
be used. The scientific management tool allows managers 144
to motivate workers by offering a pay incentive to improve 156
both the quality and quantity of the product workers 167
produced. For example, if a project generally took an 177
employee ten minutes to do, a wage incentive plan would 189
pay a bonus for work completed in less than ten minutes. 200
Management has learned that workers produce more and better 212
products when their working conditions are improved, and 223
wage incentives are provided. 229

| 1 | 2 | 3 | 4 | 5 | 6 | 7 | 8 | 9 | 10 | 11 | 12 |

SKILLBUILDING *(continued)*

TIMING 16

Although heavy campaigning for a number of months 10
now leads up to a national convention for both parties, 21
this was not practiced in the early days of elections in 33
our country. Originally, candidates were selected by the 44
members of their party congress. Selecting candidates in 56
this manner is called the caucus method. Caucusing was 67
later dropped, and nominations were made informally at 78
meetings by state officials. 83

When the national convention process started, it 93
brought more national participation into the selection 104
process. When the first television camera was used, the 116
exposure increased even more. More citizens began to get 127
actively involved in politics. The use of the camera made 139
it seem as though they were at the convention. It has been 150
judged that over seventy million people watched during 161
the early years when conventions were televised. Today, 173
most Americans have watched at least one convention. 183

The expense of a national convention is quite high. 194
Citizens who are delegates feel that their participation 205
is worth whatever it costs to go. The parties do not pay 217
for television time. Sponsors pay for the commercials, and 228
any difference is paid for by the media itself. 238

| 1 | 2 | 3 | 4 | 5 | 6 | 7 | 8 | 9 | 10 | 11 | 12 |

TIMING 17

Taking tests can be an ordeal. Even for students 10
who are fully prepared and aware of the teacher's goals, 21
testing can be stressful. They can become victim to test 33
anxiety. It is perfectly natural for people to feel some 44
anxiety when confronted with a test. Anxiety can work as 56
a positive motivational factor at times. It can improve 67
your concentration, encourage you to do well, and sharpen 78
your performance. However, if it does cause stress, try 90
to rid yourself of sweaty palms, the fear of failure, and 101
the knot in your stomach. 106

It might help to realize that most teachers want 116
their students to do well on tests. They might discuss a 128
test ahead of time. Pay attention to these discussions. 139
There are strategies you can use to help reduce anxiety 150
in a test situation. You might use relaxation techniques 162
before and during a test when you feel yourself becoming 173
anxious. You could visualize yourself as being successful 185
and keep a confident attitude during the test. You could 196
remind yourself that the test is not a life threatening 207
situation and you can survive it. You need to recognize 218
that the test is important, but you might ask yourself 229
just how much of an effect it will have on your life five 241
years from now. 244

| 1 | 2 | 3 | 4 | 5 | 6 | 7 | 8 | 9 | 10 | 11 | 12 |

SB29

SKILLBUILDING *(continued)*

TIMING 18

    Do you live beyond your means? Are your expenses more 11
than your income? Do you borrow money to pay off debts? 22
If you do, you are in the best of company. Our government 34
consistently operates on a deficit. In fact, it runs two 45
different deficits: one with its citizens, and the other 57
with the rest of the world. Some economists feel these 68
two deficits are related because if one of them were not 79
so large, the other would not be as large either. 89
    Is all debt bad? No, deficit spending, within reason, 100
is healthy. It fuels the economy. When you buy a new car 111
on credit, you support the autoworkers. A problem arises 123
when the government has to borrow money to spend beyond its 135
means. It borrows from its citizens—you and me. It also 146
borrows from foreigners. Foreign countries purchase our 157
treasury debt. These investors want to be properly 168
compensated for assuming the debt. The almost daily 178
borrowing that the government has to do often overwhelms 189
credit markets. This keeps interest rates high, which 200
creates an appealing investment. 207
    Government debt is a bit like individual debt. The 217
difference is that the government debt is much larger. 228
The moral of this story is that a little debt is okay, 239
but a lot of debt can get you into big trouble. 249

| 1 | 2 | 3 | 4 | 5 | 6 | 7 | 8 | 9 | 10 | 11 | 12 |

TIMING 19

Some specialists who work in memory training tell us 11
to think of memory as something we can control through the 23
use of strategies and organization. If you are trying to 34
remember a new name, spend a few seconds creating a mental 46
image to go along with the name. For example, to remember 57
the name Morehouse, you could make a mental image of a 68
person standing by a growing house. If you often misplace 80
your keys or your glasses, you could keep these objects in 92
one specific location. Then, make a conscious effort to 103
return them to the same spot each time you have finished 114
using them. 117

Anxiety is the number one cause of slips of memory. 127
There are several strategies that can help with recall. 139
You can reduce anxiety block by not drawing attention to 150
it. For example, if a word is at the tip of your tongue, 161
keep talking while the brain keeps searching for it. A 172
helpful way to remember numbers is by connecting them to 184
a phrase, such as the old adage about Columbus sailing 195
the ocean blue in fourteen hundred and ninety-two. You 206
can also try to remember numbers by connecting them with a 218
birthday or by making number patterns. Another approach to 229
improve memory could be aerobic exercising, which speeds 241
blood to the brain and sharpens memory performance. 251

| 1 | 2 | 3 | 4 | 5 | 6 | 7 | 8 | 9 | 10 | 11 | 12 |

GLOSSARY

A

Alignment The horizontal positioning (such as left, right, or center) of text.

Anchor A home-key position that helps bring each finger back to its home-key position. Also indicates what a text box is attached (anchored) to.

Ascending Sort A sort of data in alphabetical (A-Z) order or numerical (0-9) order.

AVERAGE A built-in spreadsheet formula that adds and divides numbers.

B

Bar Chart A graphic illustration of spreadsheet data.

Bibliography An alphabetical listing of all the books and articles consulted by the author of a report.

Bold A print enhancement used to make characters appear darker than other text to add emphasis.

Bullets and Numbering A word processing feature used to arrange items in a list with each item beginning with a bullet or a number.

Byline The name of the author of a report typed a double space below the title.

C

Cell The box formed at the intersection of a row and a column.

Center Justification An alignment feature that centers text between margins.

Center Page A software command that automatically centers copy vertically on a page.

Center Tab A type of tab used to horizontally center text at a particular position on a line.

Clip Art Graphic images that can be inserted into documents.

Close File A software command that enables you to exit the current document without exiting from the program.

Columns Information arranged vertically.

Constants Unchanging values that are used in formulas.

Cut/Copy/Paste A feature that enables you to move or copy text from one place to another.

D

Data File or Data Source The document that contains the variable information, such as name and address, used to personalize a form document.

Database A software program used to organize, find, and display information.

Date Insert A software feature that enables you to insert the current date into a document.

Decimal Tab A tab setting used to align a column of numbers at the decimal point.

Default Settings Settings that are preset by the software and that remain in effect until the user changes them.

Descending Sort A sort of data in descending alphabetical (Z-A) or numerical (9-0) order.

Desktop Publishing Special software or software features that enable you to design and create documents such as newsletters, flyers, and brochures.

Dot Leader Tab A tab setting that inserts leaders (a line of dots or other characters) between one column and another.

Drop Cap A large first letter that drops below the regular text.

F

Field A category of information in a database.

Field Name A name used to identify the contents of a field.

File A document or a collection of related records.

File Name A unique name given to a document so that it can be saved and retrieved.

Fill Shading or patterns used to fill an area. In a spreadsheet, to enter common or repetitive values into a group of cells.

Fill Handle The small box in the lower right corner of an active spreadsheet cell that can be dragged to create the desired fill.

Filtering The process of finding and selecting information from a database.

Find and Replace A software command that enables you to search for and replace specific text, formatting commands, or special attributes.

Flush Right Alignment of text at the right margin.

Font A set of type characters of a particular design and size.

Footers Repetitive information or text that is repeated at the bottom of a page throughout a section or a document.

Footnote Feature A software feature that automatically positions reference notations at the bottom of the page on which the footnote number appears.

Form File The main document or form letter to which variable information must be added.

Formula A mathematical expression that solves a problem (for example, adding, subtracting, multiplying, dividing, or averaging).

Full Justification An alignment feature that aligns text at the left and right margins by adding space between characters.

Function Keys Special keys located at the top of the keyboard (F1, F2, F3, etc.) that are used alone or with the Ctrl, Alt, and Shift keys to execute software commands.

G

Graphics Pictures, clip art, bar graphs, pie charts, or other images available on or created on a computer.

Gridlines The lines appearing around the cells in a table.

H

Hanging Indent A temporary left margin that indents all lines but the first line of the text.

Hard Page Break A manually inserted page break that does not change regardless of the changes made within the document.

Hard Return A code entered into a document by pressing the ENTER key that indicates the end of a paragraph or section.

Header Repetitive information or text that is repeated at the top of each page of a section or a document.

Help On-screen information about how to use a program and its features.

I

Indent A temporary left margin that is used to align text at a set position to the right of the margin.

Insert A software command that enables you to add text, page and column breaks, graphics, tables, charts, cells, rows, columns, formulas, dates, time, fields, and so on, to a document.

Insertion Mode An input mode in which the existing text moves to the right as new text is added.

Insertion Point A vertical blinking bar on the computer screen that indicates where an action will begin.

Italic A special font attribute used to highlight text.

L

Landscape Page orientation in which data prints across the wider portion of the page.

Leaders A row of characters that leads the reader's eye across a page.

Left Justification A feature that aligns text at the left margin.

Left Tab A tab setting that moves the insertion point to the left when the tab key is pressed.

Letterhead Stationery that has information such as the company name, address, and telephone number printed at the top.

Line Draw A software feature that enables you to draw a variety of lines in a document.

Line Spacing A software command that enables you to set the amount of space between lines of type.

M

Mail Merge A process of combining information from two documents to produce personalized documents.

Margins The blank space at the top, bottom, left, and right sides of a document.

Military Style Date A date typed in the following sequence: day, month, and year (12 March {year}).

Modem A device that enables computers to "talk" to one another.

N

Nonprinting Character A character or symbol that appears on the screen but does not print.

O

OCR Format A format for an envelope address in which all lines are typed in all capital letters with no punctuation.

Open A software command that enables you to retrieve a file that was previously created and saved.

Open Punctuation A punctuation style for letters in which there is no colon after the salutation and no comma after the complimentary close.

Orphan A single line of a paragraph that appears at the bottom of a page.

P

Page Numbering A software command that automatically numbers the pages of a document.

Page Orientation The direction in which you can print on a page.

Password A word or series of characters that are used to limit access to files or computer systems.

Pie Chart A graphic illustration of spreadsheet data that compares the sizes of pieces to a whole.

Point Size A reference to the size of type; 72 points equal one inch.

Portrait Page orientation in which the data prints across the narrower portion of a page.

Print Preview A software feature that enables you to view an entire document before it is printed.

Q

Query A database feature that enables you to locate records that meet certain criteria.

R

Range A group of spreadsheet cells.

Record A group of fields that contain the data that makes up a file.

Reveal Codes A software feature available in some programs that enables you to display formatting codes on screen.

Reverse Printing A method of printing type in white or another light color on a black or dark background.

Right Justification A software feature used to align copy at the right.

Right Tab A tab stop that aligns text at the right.

Row Height The distance between the top and bottom borders of a cell.

Ruler A graphic display that can show margin settings and tab stops.

S

Scrolling The activity of moving text up and down or left and right to reveal additional copy on your screen.

Search A software feature that enables you to to look for text or formats within a document.

Search and Replace A software feature that enables you to look for text or formats and replace them with other text or formats.

Shading A software feature used to add fill to cells or boxes to add visual interest.

Soft Page Break A page break that is automatically created by the software when text is too long to fit on a page.

Sort A software feature that enables you to rearrange data in a particular order.

Special Characters Unusual characters that are not available on the regular keyboard.

Spell Check A software feature that checks the spelling of words in a document.

Spreadsheet A software program that enables you to perform various calculations on the data.

Standard Punctuation Punctuation that consists of a colon after the salutation and a comma after the complimentary close.

Status Line A line displayed at the bottom of the screen that provides the page number, section number, vertical position in inches, and line number of a document as well as the horizontal position of the insertion point.

Subscript A character that is positioned a half line below the writing line.

SUM Function A built-in spreadsheet formula that adds a range of cells.

Superscript A character that is positioned a half line above the writing line.

T

Tab Stop A set position that enables you to quickly move the insertion point to that position.

Table A grid of rows and columns that intersect to form cells into which information can be typed.

Template A predefined document format.

Text Box A created box that can contain text or art.

Text/Word Art A word processing feature used to create special effects with text.

Thesaurus A software feature that you can use to find words that are similar to words you want to replace.

U

Undo A software command that reverses the last action taken.

V

Vertical Text Text that is arranged vertically on a page.

W

Widow The last line of a paragraph that is carried forward to the top of the next page.

Word Wrap The automatic wrapping of text from the end of one line to the beginning of the next line.

Worksheet A spreadsheet form that enables you to input data and formulas.

X-Axis A horizontal bar-chart scale that displays a range of values.

Y-Axis A vertical bar-chart scale that displays a range of values.

Z

Zoom A feature used to enlarge or reduce an image on the screen.

INDEX

M

N

O

P

Q

R

IN4

V

W

1-Minute Timings

2-Minute Timings

3-Minute Timings

5-Minute Timings

IN5

Photo Credits

1, Roger Tully/Tony Stone Images; **17,** NASA; **22,** Aaron Haupt; **29,** Uniphoto; **67,** Yomafa Toyohiro/FPG; **71,** Aaron Haupt; **75,** Aaron Haupt; **88,** Aaron Haupt; **98,** NASA/The Stock Market; **101,** Aaron Haupt; **109,** Aaron Haupt; **110,** Fotosmith; **113,** Kennan Ward/The Stock Market; **116,** Richard Harrington/FPG; **117,** Gail Shumway/FPG; **119,** Telegraph Colour Library/FPG; **122,** Library of Congress; **128,** Aaron Haupt; **131,** Aaron Haupt; **137,** Michael Krasowitz/FPG; **139,** Al Satterwhite/FPG; **152,** Michele Burgess/The Stock Market; **153,** SuperStock; **161,** Aaron Haupt; **164,** Doug Martin; **166,** Gabe Palmer/The Stock Market; **172,** Syme Thayer/FPG; **179,** Aaron Haupt; **180,** Michael Keller/The Stock Market; **194,** Telegraph Colour Library/FPG; **217,** David Tejada/Tony Stone Images; **223,** KS Studios; **236,** TRAVELPIX/FPG; **240,** Frank P Rossotto/The Stock Market; **243,** Telegraph Colour Library/FPG; **248,** Art Wolfe/Tony Stone Images; **256,** SuperStock; **275,** Jose L. Pelaez/The Stock Market; **277,** Robert S Semeniuk/The Stock Market ; **284,** Uniphoto; **287,** Lawrence Sawyer/The Picture Cube, Inc.; **293,** Ron Chapple/FPG; **299,** Telegraph Colour Library/FPG; **302,** Aaron Haupt; **314,** Matt Meadows; **339,** E Nagel/FPG; **342,** Roger Tully/Tony Stone Images; **352,** Robert S Semeniuk/The Stock Market; **367,** Palmer Kane/The Stock Market; **382,** Aaron Haupt; **391,** Norbert Wu/The Stock Market; **398,** Palmer Kane/The Stock Market; **405,** Josef Polleross/The Stock Market; **426,** Ron Chapple/FPG; **435,** Borland; **468,** Uniphoto; **471,** Joe Cornish/Tony Stone Images; **483,** SuperStock; **487,** Jim Rorabaugh; **509,** Anthony Edgeworth/The Stock Market; **510,** Ian Murphy/Tony Stone Images; **515,** PhotoDisc/Nick Koudis; **517,** Thomas Brakefield/The Stock Market; **521,** Reuters/Mike Blake/Archive Photos; **526,** Glencoe File; **534,** Norbert Wu/The Stock Market; **548,** SuperStock; **COVER,** Aaron Haupt.